Securing Client/Server
Computer Networks

Other Related Titles

BAKER • *Network Security: How to Plan for It and Achieve It*

BAKER • *Networking the Enterprise: How to Build Client/Server Systems That Work*

BATES • *Disaster Recovery Planning: Networks, Telecommunications, and Data Communications*

BATES • *Wireless Networked Communications: Concepts, Technology, and Implementation*

BERSON • *Client/Server Architecture*

BLACK • *Network Management Standards: SNMP, CMOT, and OSI, 2/e*

BLACK • *TCP/IP and Related Protocols, 2/e*

COOPER • *Computer and Communications Security*

DAVIS/MCGUFFIN • *Wireless Local Area Networks: Technology, Issues, and Strategies*

DAYTON • *Multi-Vendor Networks: Planning, Selecting, and Maintenance*

FEIT • *SNMP: A Guide to Network Management*

FEIT • *TCP/IP: Architecture, Protocols, and Implementation*

FORTIER • *Handbook of LAN Technology, 2/e*

GRAHAM • *The Networker's Practical Reference*

GRINBERG • *Computer/Telecom Integration: The SCAI Solution*

HEBRAWI • *OSI Upper Layer Standards and Practices*

KAPOOR • *SNA: Architecture, Protocols, and Implementation*

KESSLER/TRAIN • *Metropolitan Area Networks: Concepts, Standards, and Service*

KUMAR • *Broadband Communications: A Professional's Guide to ATM, Frame Relay, SMDS, SONET, and B-ISDN*

MCDYSON/SPOHN • *ATM: Theory and Applications*

MINOLI • *1st, 2nd, and Next Generation LANs*

MINOLI • *Imaging in Corporate Environments*

MINOLI/VITELLA • *ATM and Call Relay Service for Corporate Environments*

NAUGLE • *Network Protocol Handbook*

NEMZOW • *Enterprise Network Performance Optimization*

NEMZOW • *FDDI Networking: Planning, Installation, and Management*

NEMZOW • *The Token-Ring Management Guide*

PELTON • *Voice Processing*

PERLEY • *Migrating to Open Systems: Taming the Tiger*

PETERSON • *TCP/IP Networking: A Guide to the IBM Environment*

SACKETT • *IBM's Token-Ring Networking Handbook*

SIMON • *Workgroup Computing: Workflow, Groupware, and Messaging*

SIMONDS • *McGraw-Hill LAN Communications Handbook*

SPOHN • *Data Network Design*

TERPLAN • *Effective Management of Local Area Networks: Functions, Instruments, and People*

VAUGHN • *Client/Server System Design and Implementation*

In order to receive additional information on these or any other McGraw-Hill titles, in the United States please call 1-800-822-8158. In other countries, contact your local McGraw-Hill representative.

Securing Client/Server Computer Networks

Peter T. Davis, Editor

McGraw-Hill
New York San Francisco Washington, D.C. Auckland Bogotá
Caracas Lisbon London Madrid Mexico City Milan
Montreal New Delhi San Juan Singapore
Sydney Tokyo Toronto

McGraw-Hill

A Division of The McGraw-Hill Companies

Library of Congress Cataloging-in-Publication Data

Securing client/server computer networks / by Peter T. Davis, editor.
  p. cm.—(McGraw-Hill series on computer communications)
  Includes bibliographical references and index.
  ISBN 0-07-015841-X
  1. Client/server computing. 2. Computer security. 3. Computer
networks—Security measures. I. Davis, Peter T. II. Series.
QA76.9.C55S37   1996
005.8—dc20   96-107
                                                                      CIP

1 2 3 4 5 6 7 8 9 DOC/DOC 9 0 0 9 8 7 6

ISBN 0-07-015841-X

The editors of this book were Brad J. Schepp, acquiring editor, Michael Christopher, manuscript editor, David M. McCandless, associate managing editor, and Lori Flaherty, executive editor, and the production supervisor was Katherine G. Brown. This book was set in ITC Century Light. It was composed in Blue Ridge Summit, Pennsylvania.

Printed and bound by R. R. Donnelley & Sons Company, Crawfordsville, Indiana.

McGraw-Hill books are available at special quantity discounts to use as premiums and sales promotions, or for use in corporate training programs. For more information, please write to the Director of Special Sales, McGraw-Hill, 11 West 19th Street, New York, NY 10011. Or contact your local bookstore.

MH96
015841X

None but a mule denies his family.
ANONYMOUS

To the memories of Georgina Eddy Davis, Clement Beecher King, Margeurite Ostiguy King, and Estelle Ostiguy Nelson, for their generous gifts of love.

Contents

Part 2   The Tools

Part 3   The Client

Acknowledgments

A special thanks is given to the following people:

Brad Schepp for again helping with the book, Stacey Spurlock for administrative help, and everyone at McGraw-Hill who helped with the finished product, especially Joanne Slike, Michael Christopher, and David McCandless.

Of course, I would like to thank all the contributors to this book. I must also thank Earl Boebert, Ken Cutler, Stu Henderson, Scott McDermott, Jane Wilson, and Alex Woda for their help in finding contributors. Also, thank you to everyone who encouraged me to compile the book and to those who said they would buy it.

Ray Kaplan and Robert Clyde would like to acknowledge that their work is based on and includes previous work by Ray Kaplan, Robert Clyde, Rick Anderson, Joe Kovara, and others. Ray Kaplan would like to acknowledge Scott Scudamore, DEC Security Management; Leo Demers, VMS DEC Product Management; Bill Gossman, CyberSAFE NT Wizard; and Mark Ryland, Microsoft NT Evangelist.

I also would like to thank Janet for her encouragement and understanding.

Foreword

Spend a few minutes with me while I tell you why I think this book is important. The book is about the interaction of two ideas, "client/server" and "information security."

Client/server is an idea. It is a metaphor for thinking about how two processes relate to each other. It belongs on the same list as master/slave, host/guest, and peer/peer. It also is a metaphor for talking about how to use computers to do work. In this case, client/server goes on a list with such ideas as batch-oriented, terminal-oriented, and online transaction processing.

While we use client/server to talk about the use of workstation applications with relational database management systems, the idea is older and more important than that. The idea was used in operating systems before there were workstations. It is used at every level in the modern network. For example, a workstation might be a client of a minicomputer, the workstation operating system might be a client of a file server running on the minicomputer, and the workstation application might be a client of a database manager whose files are stored on the file server.

Client/server is an important idea because we can do things with it that we cannot do without it. Indeed, it is so powerful that it might be one of the most important ideas of the decade. It is powerful because it enables us to use relatively cheap computing power to exploit relatively expensive communications capacity. By using clients and servers that know about each other, talking in a language specific to the application, we can get the maximum amount of information or user functionality across a communications channel in the minimum number of bits.

To appreciate this, it might be useful to spend a little time talking about the ideas of C. E. Shannon, the father of modern information theory. Shannon defined the "bit" as the amount of information that reduces uncertainty by half. By that definition, all bits are not equal. The more important the uncertainty to reduce, the more important the bit. The more one knows about the intended significance of a bit, the more efficient it is.

As George Gilder reminds us, Shannon also told us that there are two equally effective methods of getting a message across a crowded room. The first is to shout the message once in a very loud voice. The second is to whisper the message over and over again, using feedback to know when the recipient has gotten the whole message. Until recently, we have relied almost exclusively upon the former method, because the latter required too much processing at the end points. However, as the cost of processing power falls, the efficiency of the latter strategy improves. Client/server configurations exploit cheap processors to enable this strategy.

Actually, I can think of a third way. The originator could whisper the message to each of the people near him. Each of them could then whisper it to each of the people near them, and so on. The message would follow a number of different paths. Each person, including the recipient, would get the message from several sources and could use this redundancy to compensate for any noise in the system, for errors in transmission, and for lost messages. While such a network of people tends to be slow and error-prone, such a network of computers is both fast and error-resistant.

Shannon also told us that the bandwidth of a communication medium tends to decrease as its length increases. Thus, while a pair of copper wires can carry millions of bits per second for a short distance, their capacity might fall to hundreds of bits per second for a distance of miles. Again, Shannon pointed out that, within limits, we could use repeaters, multiple paths, and sophisticated signaling to compensate. Because all of those things were expensive, we forgot Shannon's second message for a few generations. As the price of processors began to approach the price of sand, we thought about them again.

When I was young, the Bell system told us that the maximum capacity of a telephone line was 300 bits per second. Even for this speed, one had to have a "conditioned" line and a very expensive modem, leased only from them. When I heard them talk, I concluded that they meant both theoretically as well as practically. In fact, what they meant was that, given the wires, repeaters, paths, and signaling used in the telephone system at the time, this was the practical limit. Today, a modem forty-eight times as fast as that can be purchased mail-order for $50. Using a $200 modem, whose price will have fallen measurably while this book is in preparation, we routinely achieve 100K. The 300 bps modem cannot even be given away today because, among other reasons, it uses the expensive medium too inefficiently.

Client/server moves the maximum information per bit, and it also provides the maximum user functionality per bit. Users can mark, select, scroll, page, and otherwise exercise the maximum control over the data in client/ server. Experience and survey data demonstrate a significant positive impact on user performance and satisfaction.

There are still more advantages. One of the advantages that management expects from the use of client/server is rapid application development and deployment. While this is likely to be the result in the long run, it will not be true until the necessary management infrastructure is in place. Client/ server offers the opportunity for more granular security, audit, and control, but this advantage does not accrue automatically.

By the end of the decade, the use of client/server will be so ubiquitous, routine, and automatic that we will not notice or think about it. All computer and communications mechanisms and applications will employ it. It will have fallen, along with such technology as television, beneath our level of notice. Indeed, shortly thereafter, the idea of the computer might fall to the level of notice that we grant the electric motor. That is, it will be noticeable more for its absence than for its presence, more when it fails than when it works as expected.

Eventually we can expect that clients and servers will plug together in much the same way as we expect of components in our entertainment system. Like Lego blocks, they will present "standard interfaces." Until then we will have to give considerable thought about how we put them together. But in the short run, client/server can be expected to give us a little difficulty. We will have to decide upon standards and conventions for its use.

Client/server makes multiple processes in different places appear to the user as an integrated whole. In the process it conceals where things take place, where control is exercised, whether it is exercised, and who is exercising it.

We usually think in terms of one client to one server. In fact, one server usually has many clients. Therefore, in order to minimize the number of points of control, preference should be given to the server as the point of control. In practice, we are seeing controls focused in the client application. While it is possible to implement appropriate controls in this way, it is more difficult to operate them this way.

These problems are further complicated by the modern network connecting the clients to the servers. Unlike the more traditional hierarchical networks, the modern network is flat; messages flow from client workstation to client workstation as easily as they flow from client to server. The modern network is dynamic rather than stable. We cannot rely upon its configuration. Addresses are arbitrary rather than fixed. We cannot rely upon either the origin or destination addresses. We cannot rely upon the network to tell us where a message came from or to ensure that it goes only where it is addressed, as we have done in the more traditional circuit-switched, point-to-point net.

Any workstation can eavesdrop on the local network, using software readily obtained from the Internet. While others might not be able to see traffic on the other side of a router, they can eavesdrop on all the traffic that passes on the wire connected to their system. The fruits of this eavesdropping will usually include user identifiers and passwords. However, because many workstations can be easily salted with password grabbers, eavesdropping is not necessary. Because network addresses can be faked, servers that rely upon the address of the client can be spoofed. Client-based controls can be bypassed.

Some of these problems are related to client/server, some to the modern network. If either is to deliver the benefits that it promises, these problems must be addressed. Traditional access control is necessary but is not sufficient for dealing with the problems. We will require new tools, including one-time passwords and cryptography. We will need new ideas, including digital signatures and enterprise security architecture.

The problems are too serious to be ignored. They must be effectively addressed if we are to enjoy the benefits of the technology. The control of these problems and the use and application of these new tools and techniques comprise the subject of this book. I hope you will agree with me that this book is important.

William Hugh Murray
New Canaan, Connecticut

Introduction

Some books are to be tasted; others swallowed;
and some to be chewed and digested.
                                    FRANCIS BACON

My books are water; those of the great
geniuses are wine. Everybody drinks water.
                                    MARK TWAIN

The books that help you the most are those
which make you think the most.
                                    THEODORE PARKER

As a daily user of local area networks (LANs) and modern database and data communications technology, I know that client/server computing represents both the present and the future of business computing. Client/server computing is hot. All you have to do is look at the new products. In the want ads in major urban centers you will find companies searching for Powerbuilder, Visual Basic, or C++ developers, and the more generic "communications experts."

Security is also receiving a lot of attention these days, what with the Internet and its problems. However, security of client/server systems is not well-understood. This is partially due to the various platforms encompassing client/server computing. It is hard enough to find an expert in OpenVMS security. It is even harder to find one who also is an expert in UNIX and MVS/ESA security. Because it is hard to find an expert knowledgeable in all areas of client/server computing security, the need obviously exists for a practical, understandable book. I hope this book will fill that need.

Client/server computing has become the key delivery vehicle for many strategic applications. Security, database, communications, and contingency issues must all be considered when implementing a client/server application. Control concerns abound, because these client/server systems use data in more ways and more places than ever before. The risk in a client/server system is greater than the sum of the risks in its parts.

This book addresses security exposures with distributed databases, systems availability and performance, and application development and conversion issues. The microcomputer revolution that started with the introduction of the Osborne portable computer in 1981 has culminated in the client/server computing revolution of the 1990s. The proper use of client/server computing is therefore a key issue to a business, so that its vast investment in the technology can be fully realized.

Client/server computing also provides a business with a number of other challenges. It changes the way organizations share information and the control structures within those organizations. Cooperative software, such as client/server databases, workgroup software, and electronic mail systems, have leveraged the organization's investment in microcomputers but have also added to the concerns of management.

Business users need help to learn and use client/server computing in an efficient and effective manner. Proper training is a major requirement, but it must take a form that is itself very efficient and effective. Again, this book provides such a way to discover the main issues associated with different products.

Introducing and maintaining client/server applications in a business is not a trivial task. Unfortunately, few books today can help a system developer, a system administrator, a security professional, or an auditor even understand client/server computing, let alone secure it!

Securing Client/Server Computer Networks is the first book to steer administrators through complex client/server computing security concepts. Most other client/server computing books document the Open System Foundation standards for security, but none provide practical advice on what this means. This book is devoted to helping developers and administrators plan and implement security across various platforms, from the desktop to the mainframe.

Security in any environment calls for specialized expertise; therefore, experts in the appropriate fields wrote each chapter. For example, an expert in UNIX wrote the UNIX chapter, while a TCP/IP expert wrote the chapter on TCP/IP.

Reading the Book

We intended this book for individuals who are exploring client/server computing and security; that is, to fill the gap for individuals looking for straightforward help for securing their applications and networks. It does not matter whether you are a security administrator or a planner, a systems auditor, a user or a client, a designer of a new network, a manager of an old network, a network administrator, a system administrator, an owner of a network or an application, or a senior manager who wants to understand client/server computing. If you are interested in client/server computing, this book is for you.

We aimed this book at a wide audience because we believe in the need to proselytize systems professionals and their customers on the evolving client/server technology and its attendant risks. Everything needed for a basic understanding of the issues is included, so you need not be an expert to get the most from this book. For users of all levels, the book will provide a comprehensive, task-oriented compendium of useful information.

Organizing the Book

The book is organized to help the reader grasp the complexities of client/server computing and security. Rather than simply providing technical details on a number of software products, it guides the developer/user/administrator through an exploration of client/server computing, starting with simple concepts, at an easy-to-follow pace, and progressing through more complex issues and tasks.

The book accomplishes the above by first introducing key client/server and security concepts, then building on these concepts through the use of specific products or techniques. Such an approach will help build your understanding of security and client/server computing.

We encourage you to read the first chapters of the book in sequential order; they tend to build on each other, after which you might read any topic out of sequence and still understand the issues. However, by reading the entire book, you will truly appreciate how complex security is in a client/server system, especially one using different operating systems, different database management systems, different protocols, and different hardware.

In addition, the book breaks the client/server application into key components and control zones. It describes the major control concerns involved in each zone and includes detailed plans for investigating control concerns in a comprehensive manner. Among the components discussed are the application development tools, client, middleware, and server environments.

Part 1: The Concepts

In Part 1, we discuss the background issues to the book. We describe client/server computing, the applications, and security needs.

Chapter 1, *Introducing Client/Server Computing*, focuses on defining the terminology for the book. In this chapter you will learn about empowerment, the client/server building blocks (i.e., the client, the middleware, and the server), the different types of service (i.e., file, database, transaction processing, groupware, and object), the different types of middleware (i.e., general and service-specific), and the state of the client/server infrastructure. This chapter also dispels some client/server computing myths.

Chapter 2, *Introducing Client/Server Standards and Applications*, introduces you to the promise of open and distributed systems. In addition to defining open systems, this chapter provides the role of the open standards, particularly Distributed Computing Environment (DCE).

Chapter 3, *Introducing Client/Server Security Concepts*, starts with a look at the vulnerability of networks. This chapter also introduces you to operating system security, communication security, distributed security services, the National Computer Security Center's (NCSC's) evaluation model, Kerberos, secure single sign-on, and risk assessment.

Part 2: The Tools

In Part 2, we explore the framework for developing client/server applications.

Chapter 4, *Securing Rapid and Object-Oriented Development*, introduces you to rapid development, its characteristics iteration, small teams, joint user/systems responsibility, use of prototyping tools, warrooms and workshops, and timeboxing and its security and management issues. This chapter also introduces you to Object-Oriented Development or OOD, its characteristics (i.e., encapsulation, inheritance, and polymorphism) and its security and management issues.

Part 3: The Client

In Part 3, we turn our attention to the client (i.e., the personal computer or workstation) and a client database management system.

Chapter 5, *Securing the Desktop*, draws a parallel between the security considerations of the traditional mainframe environment and the desktop tier of client/server environments. The chapter highlights the relative risk of client/security from three perspectives: general, physical, and logical. Furthermore, the chapter addresses the control features available for the desktop, that mitigate the noted weaknesses. Finally, the chapter discusses some of the specific products available in the market to supplement client/server security.

Chapter 6, *Securing the Front End*, introduces you to procedures, functions, objects, and structured query language. The chapter introduces graphical user interfaces (GUIs) and object-oriented interfaces (OOUIs) and the risks associated with their use. Also, you will learn about network connections and their risks and database connections and their risks. The chapter also covers front-end application, development, distribution and management, and change management security.

Chapter 7, Securing DB2/2, introduces you to DB2/2, the concept of client/server database processing, and security requirements (i.e., isolation, integrity, and access control). You will learn about IBM's strategy to provide an infrastructure for client/server applications extending across platforms using DRDA.

Part 4: The Middleware

Because clients and servers need to communicate, they need an agent or middleman acting on their behalf. Part 4 looks at communication protocols, gateways, middleware, and system management systems.

Chapter 8, *Securing Client/Server TCP/IP*, provides, after a short history, basic TCP/IP terminology. Then the chapter delves into basic TCP/IP vulnerabilities (i.e., masquerading, disclosure, modification, and denial of service). No discussion of TCP/IP would be complete without looking at the Internet and its emerging security architecture, which includes establishing client/server requirements (i.e., gateway friendly transactions, reliable delivery, and cryptographic protection).

Chapter 9, *Securing APPC/APPN*, deals with one of the emerging enterprise protocols, SNA/APPC. In this chapter, you will learn about CPI-C, APPC, and APPN. This chapter also deals with their security options. In addition, the chapter deals with using APPC/APPN to authenticate systems, users, transactions, and logical units.

Chapter 10, *Securing VTAM*, provides a network overview and VTAM fundamentals. The securing VTAM section includes a discussion of identification and authentication, authorization, availability, and audit features.

Chapter 11, *Securing NetView™*, provides an overview of NetView for mainframes, NetView/6000, and NetView OS/2. In addition, the chapter covers NetView security and control features, including security definitions, functions and operator profiles, commands, and logs.

Part 5: The Server

Because clients are nothing without servers, in Part 5 we provide information on various services, such as file, database, transaction processing, and groupware.

Chapter 12, *Securing NetWare 4.x*, provides an overview of NetWare 4.x features, including user authentication, NetWare Directory Services (NDS), audit trails, the Windows-based user and administration tools, and time synchronization servers. In addition, the chapter covers several topics in detail, including identification and authentication, NetWare Directory Services (NDS), directory and file system security, audit trails, and security utilities.

Chapter 13, *Securing OS/2 LAN Server*, covers the basics of LAN Server security, such as logging on for MS-DOS and Windows clients and access control profiles. Items discussed in the chapter include the OS/2 client logon and the UPM logon shell. Advanced topics also get coverage, including

API and local security, remote execution, forwarded authentication, preferred logon validator, inheritance, and peer services on OS/2 Clients.

Chapter 14, *Securing UNIX*, is a comprehensive look at UNIX security. This chapter provides a brief introduction to UNIX as a basis for trustworthy, reliable infrastructures for educational, research, business, and military applications. Also, the chapter discusses UNIX from a security perspective. In addition, it offers a guided-tour, lay-of-the-land perspective rather than concentrating on any single, technical aspect of UNIX.

Chapter 15, *Securing OpenVMS Systems*, describes the issues around operating system and network implementation and controls, user account definition and password controls, and information access and protection. The chapter starts with a discussion of the basic OpenVMS control mechanisms: data protection and account privileges. It ends with a discussion of the basic OpenVMS security issues: system setup, installed privileged images, system logical names, batch and print queue protection, account setup, account privileges, password controls, volume, directory and file protection, access control lists, and finally, network setup.

Chapter 16, *Securing Microsoft Windows NT*, provides the definitive work on Microsoft Windows NT. To help you understand all the features of Windows NT, we show you how it compares to OpenVMS, DEC UNIX, POSIX, OSF, and other standards. You also will learn about the inherent security features of Windows NT.

Chapter 17, *Securing MVS*, describes how MVS operates and includes discussions of MVS hardware controls (i.e., dual-state system and privileged instructions, storage protection and software controls, input/output management and System Authorization Facility, and MVS control areas).

Chapter 18, *Using RACF to Control MVS-Based Servers*, describes the method for identifying the user, including defining user and group profiles. This chapter also explores controlling MVS subsystems, VTAM, IMS, CICS, DB2, APPC, and servers. In addition, the chapter discusses privileged authorities, RACF mandatory access control, and secured sign-on.

Chapter 19, *Securing ORACLE*, describes the process of database initialization, including starting an instance, mounting the database, and opening the database. The chapter also examines database security concepts, such as user profiles, privileges, and roles. In addition, you will learn about application and distributed database security concepts, such as user authentication, views, triggers, and data replication. Finally, this chapter covers database backup and recovery and database auditing.

Chapter 20, *Securing Client/Server Transaction Processing*, describes the requirements for client/server transaction processing software and defines the function and role of a TP monitor. In this chapter, you also will learn about the history and the services of CICS, such as peer-to-peer and Remote Procedure Call (RPC) communication facilities and Inter-System Communication (ISC) mechanisms—that is, Distributed Program Link (DPL),

Distributed Transaction Processing (DTP), Transaction Routing (TR), Function Shipping (FS), and Asynchronous Transaction Processing (ATP). Finally, you will learn about the authentication, transaction authorization, and resource authorization facilities of CICS.

Chapter 21, *Securing Lotus Notes*, looks at groupware in general and Lotus Notes in particular. You will learn about management issues with Lotus Notes, such as change management, security, and productivity. In addition, this chapter introduces you to Notes communications, databases, applications, and electronic mail. You will learn about protecting access to databases, user IDs and passwords, user ID certificates, user logoff, encryption, and dial-up.

Where applicable, we have included some other beneficial information to assist in your understanding of client/server computing, standards, security, and networking. Most chapters conclude with a *Select Bibliography* containing a comprehensive list of books, manuals, publications, periodicals, and articles supporting the chapter and a *Glossary* containing definitions of the major terms used in the chapter.

In addition, some contributors have provided information on security products, organizations, mailing lists, and Usenet Newsgroups that can serve as useful starting points for your review of the technology.

On behalf of all the contributors, I hope you learn as much from reading this book as we did in writing it. If you have any comments about the book or client/server computing itself, or ideas for additional chapters, please send electronic mail to Peter T. Davis at `pdavis@can.net`.

The Concepts

Ideas are the factors that lift civilization. They create revolutions. There is more dynamite in an idea than in many bombs.

JOHN H. VINCENT

The vitality of thought is in adventure. Ideas won't keep. Something must be done about them. When the idea is new, its custodians have fervor, live for it, and if need be, die for it.

ALFRED NORTH WHITEHEAD

1

Introducing Client/Server Computing

Peter T. Davis

*When you cannot make up your mind which
of two evenly balanced courses of action you
should take, choose the bolder.*　　W. J. SLIM

*In the advance of civilization, it is new
knowledge which paves the way, and the
pavement is eternal.*　　W. R. WHITNEY

What is *client/server*? Is it a technology? An architecture? A methodology?
A religion?

Reading the current literature doesn't help you answer the question, for
you will find the term used loosely to mean a technology, an architecture,
and a methodology too. Asking information professionals also doesn't help,
should you believe the survey shown in Table 1.1. The only thing of which
you can be certain is that client/server has become something of a mantra in
many organizations. The fervor in labeling technology as client/server is sur-
passed only by the hubbub surrounding the Internet.

There are those who say client/server is not really a technical creation,
but a state of mind. A religion, perhaps? But client/server emphasizes people, not technology. Maybe a Luddite cult? Client/server helps organizations
set priorities, starting with the basic relationships between clients and
servers. Client/server systems have grown up in the same atmosphere, and
respond to much the same kind of thinking, that created the modern organization's strong interest in both customer and service.

TABLE 1.1 What Does Client/Server Mean?

The splitting of application processing and application services between processors	33%
A paradigm in which clients and servers split aspects of presentation and business logic	30%
A decentralized strategy that allows distribution of information	27%
A system in which central processor meets requests from remote processors	27%
An architecture that allows applications to be segmented into tasks	17%
Distributing applications into a linked presentations piece and a services piece	12%
A few PCs and a lot of hype	11%
Network-centric computing	6%
Any software or hardware that sells	6%
A strategy that cuts and improves customer service	3%

NOTE: *Total exceeds 100 percent due to respondent's multiple answers.*
SOURCE: *Information Week*

Power to the People

Above all else, client/server is a human technology. It helps people do their jobs. The ultimate client is always a person. Client/server works with modern styles of management seeking to empower front-line employees by giving them more authority to make better decisions. Client/server technology supports that process by providing the information to make those decisions.

Gone are the host-centric days when one referred to consumers of service as end users. That term envisions the human client as sitting out at some remote point, removed from things that really are important. End user has become almost synonymous with necessary evil. In a client/server setting, the individual is at the center of things, not at arm's length. So, this book will focus on clients and not on end users.

Some personal computer enthusiasts have negatively criticized client/server and other forms of networking as returns to the past. They lament losing the freedom formerly associated with using their PCs. That might be happening, what with network management, centralized backup, and centralized system administration. However, a properly conceived client/server system really enhances the power of individuals. Instead of restricting employees, it offers access to resources that could not possibly have been available on an isolated stand-alone system.

The key phrase is *properly* conceived. It isn't enough to appreciate only the technical nuances of a client/server system. If you only focus on the technology, you run the risk of replacing a rigid old system with a rigid new system. Euphemistically, this is equivalent to paving over the old cow pasture, putting lipstick on a pig, or electronic varathane-glossing-over of the old technology. A client/server system must meet technical specifications, of course, but the technology only gains value when you use it to expand human potential. It cannot be technology for technology's sake, which is the trap we fell into in the early 80s.

Client/Server Computing Myths

Yes, yes, but what *is* client/server? Maybe you can get the answer to this question by looking at what it is not. There are many client/server computing myths. First, many people believe that client/server computing must involve a relational database management system (RDBMS). However, there are many uses of client/server, especially file, database, transaction, groupware, and distributed object services.

Second, everybody believes that client/server means downsizing and the elimination of the mainframe. But as you will see in Chapter 2, mainframes can be an integral part of your client/server system. In truth, client/server computing liberates or empowers the mainframe and lets it do what it does best . . . processing. For mainframes to succeed as servers, however, they will have to learn to meet PCs as equals on the network. In the client/server world, mainframe servers cannot continue to treat PCs as dumb terminals. They must support peer-to-peer protocols, interpret PC messages, service their PC clients' files in their native formats, and provide data and services to PCs in their most direct manner. However, client/server computing might be associated with downsizing, upsizing, or rightsizing (or is it capsizing?).

Third, many people entering client/server computing believe that it will reduce information technology costs, while in reality it increases information technology (IT) effectiveness. In truth, the literature doesn't necessarily support the notion that client/server reduces IT costs.

Fourth, some people think that client/server distributes applications, but it really defines IT environments. The IT environment comprises all the components, be they software, mainframe, PC, LAN, database, or transaction processing.

Fifth, everyone believes that client/server must split the application across different platforms. The idea of splitting an application along client/server lines has been used over the last ten years to create various forms of LAN software solutions. Notwithstanding which, there is no reason to assume, either, that client/server requires a particular division of labor between its major components. For example, many developers assume that they are supposed to provide a user interface and other elements of the presentation services at the client workstation. This belief ties in with the desire for a graphical or an object-oriented user interface. There also is a natural assumption that the task of managing the data warehouse is properly assigned to a server. However, the best reason to divide a client/server application in this way is that it's a good idea that suits your need. The worst reason is that you think it's required.

It really isn't the separation of powers that defines client/server or makes it valuable to its users. Just the opposite is true. You can identify a good client/server program by how well its elements cooperate, not by how effectively they are separated. You can place many elements of the application on either side, or both, and you can let process control pass between them.

Client/Server Building Blocks

Simplistically speaking, client/server computing comprises three building blocks: the client, the server, and the middleware (the slash that ties the client and server together). Client/server computing provides an open and flexible environment where mix and match is the rule. You mix and match using the (/) middleware. The client applications will run predominantly on PCs and other desktop machines at home on the LAN. The successful servers will also feel at home on LANs and know exactly how to communicate with their PC clients. Client/server, the great equalizer of the computer business, encourages openness and provides a level playing field in which a wide variety of client and server platforms might participate.

The open client/server environment also serves as a catalyst for commoditizing hardware and software. The PC is a good example of a computer commodity; it can be obtained from multiple suppliers and is sold in very price-competitive market situations, such as appliance and department stores. LAN adapters, protocol stacks, network routers, and bridges rapidly are becoming commodities. You can run down to your local mom and pop computer store and purchase these items. On the software side, workstation operating systems, SQL database management systems, and imaging software are approaching commodity status. The Distributed Computing Environment (DCE), described in Chapter 2, should make instant commodities out of remote procedures, network directory software, security services, and distributed system management. These emerging technologies mean you are facing an era of widespread client/server computing. Clients will be everywhere. They will come in all shapes and forms, including desktops, palmtops, pen tablets, and handheld communicators. These clients, wherever they are, can obtain the services of millions of servers.

Client/Server Characteristics

The above probably helps but it still doesn't define client/server for you. In that case, perhaps you should look at some of the characteristics of client/server systems, as follows:

Asymmetrical protocols

There is a one-to-many relationship between a server and its clients. Clients always initiate the dialogue by requesting a service, while servers passively wait on requests from the clients. This is antithetical to the host-centric systems that polled users for requests.

Encapsulation of services

The server is a *specialist*. A message tells a server what service is requested; it then is up to the server to determine how to get the job done. Again, this is different from host-centric systems, which performed many services, such as file and print. Because of the specialization, you can upgrade servers without affecting the clients as long as someone doesn't change the published message interface.

Integrity

The server code and server data is maintained centrally, resulting in cheaper maintenance and the guarding of shared data integrity. At the same time, the clients remain personal and independent.

Message-based exchanges

Clients and servers are loosely coupled systems interacting through the passing of messages. The message is the delivery mechanism for the service requests and replies.

Mix-and-match

The ideal client/server software is independent of hardware or operating system software. Ideally, you can mix and match client and server platforms.

Scalability

Client/server systems are horizontally and vertically scalable. Horizontal scaling means adding or removing client workstations with only a slight performance impact. Vertical scaling means growing by migrating to a larger or faster platform(s).

Service

Client/server primarily is a relationship between processes running on separate machines. The server process is a provider of services. The client is a consumer of services. In essence, client/server provides a clean separation of function based on this idea of service. In other words, it is the partitioning of the processing activity between a cooperating set of resources, a client, and one or more servers.

Shared resources

A server can service many clients at the same time and regulate (or throttle) their access to shared resources.

Transparency of location

The server is a process residing on the same machine as the client, or on a different machine across a network. Client/server software usually masks the location of the server from the clients by redirecting the service calls when needed.

Let's first look at one of the most important features from this list service. While database management is by far the most familiar form of client/server computing, there are other consumable services.

Consumable Services

Many systems with very different architectures have been called client/server. For instance, in Chapter 17, you will see that mainframes make good servers. System vendors often use client/server just as though they coined the term, and that it only can be applied to their specific packages. For example, file service vendors swear they first invented the term, and database service vendors are thought by many as the only client/server vendors. Database management, using Windows or another graphical display (such as MacOS or XWindows), is the fastest growing client/server subspecies. But, neither the database nor the interface is an essential client/server element. To add to the confusion, you can add distributed objects, TP Monitors, and groupware to the list of client/server technologies. So who is right? Which of these technologies is the real client/server? The answer is all of the above.

Typically, client/server solutions sell as shrink-wrapped software packages, and many are sold by more than one vendor. Each of these solutions, however, is distinguished by the nature of the service it provides to its clients.

File Service

With a file server, the client (typically a PC) passes requests for file records over a network to the file server (see Figure 1.1). While more sophisticated than its predecessor, disk service, file service still is a very primitive form of data service, necessitating many message exchanges over the network to find the requested data.

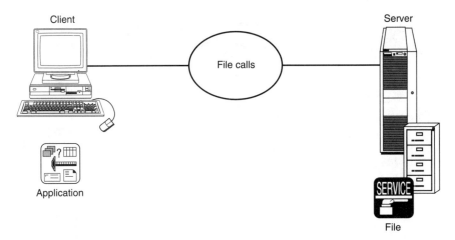

Client   Server

File calls

Application

SERVICE

File

Figure 1.1 File service

However, file servers are useful for sharing files across a network. They
are indispensable for creating shared repositories of documents, images,
drawings, and other large data objects; for example, binary large objects, or
BLOBs. In Chapters 12 and 13, we introduce you to file service and NetWare
and OS/2 LAN Server respectively.

Database Service

From the description so far, it should be obvious that client/server is more
than database management. However, in practice, a database usually is the
server part of the client/server dyad. Database management is not normally
a highly visible role. Front-end products with their objects, graphics, and
colors have the glamorous part of the job. Database management is a dirty
server job, attracting little notice until something goes wrong.

The typical database server is a faceless product that has no direct or visible contact with human clients. That makes it a little harder to describe
and understand a server than its highly visible front ends. One thing is certain, though; database servers, many running on PC-based front ends, have
developed to a point where they offer the performance and the reliability of
larger systems, at personal computer prices.

With a database server, the client passes requests, usually structured
query language (SQL) calls, as messages to the database server (see Figure
1.2). The server returns the results of each SQL command over the network. The code that processes the SQL requests and the data reside on the
same machine. The server uses its own processing power to find the requested data instead of passing all the records back to a client as was the
case for the file server. The result is a much more efficient use of distributed

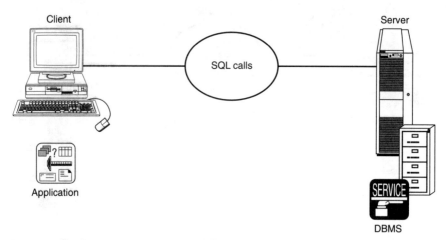

Figure 1.2 Database management system (DBMS) service

processing power. With this approach, the server code is shrink-wrapped by the vendor. But you often need to write code for the client application (or you can buy shrink-wrapped clients).

Database servers provide the foundation for decision-support systems requiring ad hoc queries and flexible reporting. Examples of client/server RDBMSs are Database 2/2, Informix Online, Interbase, NetWare SQL, Oracle Server 7.0, SQL*Base, and SQL Server. Chapters 7 and 19 introduce you to DB2/2 and ORACLE database management systems.

Transaction Service

With a transaction server, you create the client/server application by writing the code for both the client and server components. The client component usually includes a graphical user interface (GUI) or an object-oriented user interface (OOUI). The server component usually consists of SQL transactions against a database. The client invokes remote procedures residing on the server with an SQL database engine (Figure 1.3). These remote procedures on the server might execute a group of SQL statements. The network exchange consists of a single request/reply message (as opposed to the database server's approach of one request/reply message for each SQL statement in a transaction). The SQL statements all either succeed or fail as a unit. These grouped SQL statements are called transactions.

These network applications have a name: Online Transaction Processing, or OLTP. They frequently are mission-critical applications calling for a one-to three-second response one hundred percent of the time. OLTP applications also require tight controls over the security and integrity of the database. In Chapter 20, you will learn about CICS/6000.

Groupware Service

An emerging class of client/server systems addresses the management of semi-structured information, such as text, image, mail, bulletin boards, and the flow of work. Figure 1.4 shows how groupware works. These new client/server systems place people in direct contact with other people. Lotus Notes is the leading example of such a system, although a number of other applications, including document management, imaging, calendaring, and workflow, are addressing some of the same needs. Specialized groupware software can be built on top of a vendor's canned set of client/server application program interfaces (APIs). In most cases, a developer can create applications using a scripting language and form-based interfaces provided by the vendor. The communications middleware between the client and the server is vendor-specific.

Object Service

With an object server, the client/server application is written as a set of communicating objects (see Figure 1.5). Client objects communicate with server objects using an Object Request Broker (ORB). The client invokes a method supported by an object server class. The ORB locates an instance of that object server class, invokes the requested method, and returns the results to the client object. Server objects must provide support for concurrency and sharing. The ORB brings it all together. After years of development, some vendors have shipped commercial ORBs, such as DOE from Sun, DOMF from HP, DOMS from HyperDesk, and DSOM from IBM. Unfortunately, I

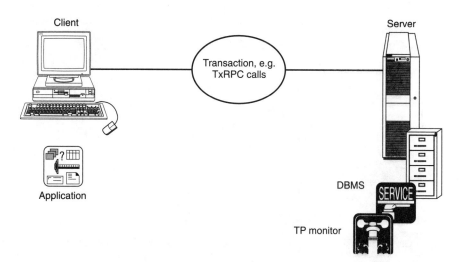

Figure 1.3 Transaction service

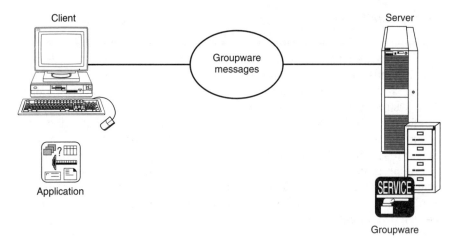

Figure 1.4 Groupware service

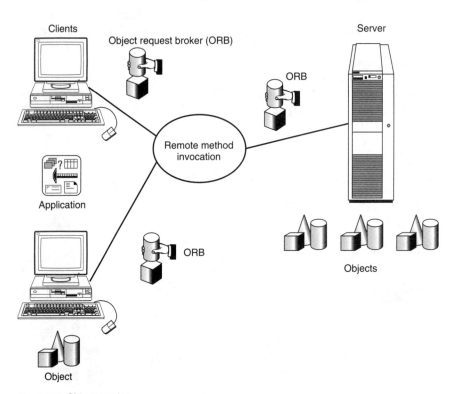

Figure 1.5 Object service

have not included any examples of object servers in this book. On a practical level I just don't see them yet.

Using the Network to Your Advantage

There is a secret to the high performance and success of all these services. Today's servers aren't limited by the computing power of the individual systems on which they run. They take advantage of all the computing power the network has to offer. The network establishes the division of labor between the client and server.

The computing power to do this has been available for quite a while. Like all else in networks and client/service computing, the key to success has been teamwork. It took client/server software technology to maximize the network's power and put it to useful and productive work. The earliest networks were either host-based, dumb-terminal systems or LANs put together to share files and printers. Client/server software maximized the hardware and made the network a system in its own right.

Client/server is based on software, not hardware. It is the software that took the local area network beyond file and printer sharing and turned it into an enterprise-wide computing resource.

Reasons to Convert

So why are some organizations converting to enterprise-wide client/server computing? A common reason to install a client/server system is to downsize from mainframes and minicomputers. Other enterprises are acting for just the opposite reason; that is, they are upsizing, from stand-alone PCs to networks, or from file-server LANs to enterprise-wide networks. Downsizers in particular are seeking lower cost. The cost of even a top-end LAN server is a fraction of that of a larger system of the same capacity.

However, the anticipated savings often are less than expected. One reason is the software for the client/server system. The hardware might be inexpensive, but the software is not. Then there is the cost of training and other personnel expenses. Again, these are big ticket items.

But we digress from our definition of client/server.

Client/Server Building Blocks

Everyone is familiar with the concept of architecture as applied to the construction of buildings. Architecture helps us identify structural elements that might be used as building blocks in the construction of ever more complex systems (or buildings). Traditionally you bought a home, not a plan, just as users in the computer industry bought solutions to business problems, not grand client/server architectures. But architecture determines the structure of the houses, high rises, office buildings, and cities in which you live and work.

In the computer analogy, architecture helps you determine the structure and shape of the client/server systems you can build to meet various needs. Increasingly, organizations are purchasing client/server systems at commodity prices. The horizontal diversification and commoditization of the computer industry might have come a tad too early for the client/server mass market. Nothing is better than horizontal competition within an established vertical infrastructure.

Unfortunately, the vertical infrastructure that will create the client/server playing field still needs to be deployed. Having recently purchased a new personal computer, I experienced similar problems myself. A large ad from a computer warehouse screamed at me about tremendous savings for the particular model I wanted. When I went to the computer warehouse, I could not find anybody who had the foggiest idea about the technology I wanted. In truth, I ended up teaching them about the product. Incredibly, neither the salesperson nor the cashier had any clue as to the contents of the published ad. Not only that, but the published ad was inaccurate, because it stated that the particular model came with an internal modem, which it did not. In the end, I told them that I wished I had spent the extra $200 and had gone to my usual computer dealer! This is an excellent example of a poor client/server relationship. But again, we digress. Let's look at the client/server relationship.

The Client/Server Relationship

Though a client/server system usually includes computers, networks, and dedicated hardware, strictly speaking, it doesn't need any of these things. Client/server is a software architecture that exists whenever two programs talk with each other in a client/server relationship.

This also is a peer-to-peer relationship. The server responds to the client, but neither is truly superior to the other. Peer-to-peer, like client/server, is another term whose definition depends on the circumstances. For example, a peer-to-peer LAN gets its name because it does not absolutely rely on a server. In mainframe parlance, peer-to-peer refers to ready communication with a host system. When discussing client/server architecture, peer-to-peer describes the cooperative relationship between the two major components.

In the enterprise network, the peer-to-peer definition distinguishes client/server from two other leading architectural styles:

1. The hierarchical architecture, in which one process, the parent, is said to own a subsidiary or child process.

2. The stand-alone or monolithic architecture, in which a single program controls all database processes from keyboard input through query processing and final output.

The hierarchical form of architecture is usually mainframe-centered. The parent and child processes might have some resemblance to modern client/server architecture, but they do not operate as equals. The child depends so greatly on the parent that, if the parent dies, the child usually perishes automatically. These systems have reputations as being slow, clumsy, and unresponsive to a user's needs. They are responsible in part for the phenomenal growth of PCs in the business environment.

On the other hand, the monolithic architecture is the most simple and straightforward. This group includes many mainframe programs. It also takes in many personal computer products, including those which follow the Dbase standard. Though this is the simplest form of database application, it can be the hardest to use effectively, particularly if performance is an issue. A stand-alone program must attend to all these functions:

- Read the data file format
- Record changes and new information
- Retrieve data, with as little delay as possible
- Know and observe its own internal processing logic
- Present a consistent, easy-to-use interface

A client/server application must do these things, too, but it splits them up. The server system's developer already should have taken on the job of managing the database. The application developer usually needs to worry about the front-end system, at the client end. The front-end system handles the screen display, accepts input, and sends queries to the database. When the requested information comes back, the client system takes care of displaying and printing it. A modern front end also can massage the information, interpret it, and import it to a PC application program.

The front end need not have anything to do with the server's processing logic, data format, or retrieval methods. The server should handle that, translating the client's instructions into its own internal language. The server already should have the means to do this when installed. Neither the application developer nor the user should have to worry about it.

While the stand-alone database program is a single application, by definition a client/server system has two. If it were not already in place, creating that second program would represent much extra work for application developers. Some application programmers might be tempted to write their own back-end programs to match their front ends. Usually, though, that is wasted and unnecessary effort.

The front-end developer's most important task is to create an application that can link the back end with the human component. This application should have only three major tasks:

1. Present an attractive and efficient interface to the user.
2. Send the appropriate data queries to the back-end.
3. Present the results of the query and manage the data locally.

The front-end application has fewer functions than a stand-alone database manager. What's more, many front-end products come in shrink-wrapped form for installation on client PCs.

Establishing Communication

There is another element to client/server computing—getting the client and the server to talk with each other. That also is the application developer's responsibility, with help from the server. Each server has a well-defined method of communicating with its clients. The client developer simply must choose the right method.

The usual communication method is the server's application program interface, or API. The API usually takes the form of object libraries. The client program makes calls to functions in those libraries. These object libraries function accordingly, then contact the database. Many PC database applications now have client/server built in. A good example of this is Microsoft's Excel spreadsheet software, which can generate SQL commands for downloading data.

The problem is not for want of such software, capable of helping us establish the client/server relationship, as you will learn in the next section on middleware.

Middleware

Middleware is a vague term covering all the distributed software needed to support interactions between clients and servers. Some people sarcastically refer to it as muddleware, because it helps the user "muddle through" the process of making the client and server talk. Think of it as the software that's in the middle of the client/server system. In this book, middleware is represented by the slash (/) in client/server. It's the glue that lets a client obtain service from a server.

Middleware starts with the API set on the client side used to invoke a service, and it covers the transmission of the request over the network and the resulting response. However, middleware does not include the software that provides the actual service. That's in the server's domain. Nor does it include the user interface or the application's logic, because that's in the client's domain.

It's hard enough to get diverse systems and applications to work together. If this chapter has shown you nothing else so far, it should be that the means for getting them together are equally diverse. There are many gaps to bridge. So, this new class of software has been invented to help build those bridges.

Middleware specifically is directed at the problems of linking the pieces of client/server systems. It is a layer of software that provides a common interface and translation between an application and the operating system. In that sense, middleware acts like an API. Middleware goes farther, however, adding a level of intelligence that helps an application find the information it needs.

You can divide middleware into two broad classes:

1. General middleware is the substrate for most client/server interactions. It includes communication stacks, distributed directories, authentication services, network time services, remote procedure calls, and queuing services. This category also includes the network operating system extensions, such as distributed file and print services. Products that fall into the general middleware category include Open Software Foundation's DCE (defined in Chapter 2), Novell's NetWare, Named Pipes, LAN Server, LAN Manager, Banyan's Vines, TCP/IP, APPC, and NetBIOS. In Chapters 8 and 9, you will learn about TCP/IP and APPC. We also include the Message-Oriented Middleware (also known as MOM) products from Covia, IBM, Message Express, Peerlogic, and System Strategies.

2. Service-specific middleware is needed to accomplish a particular client/server type of service. This includes:
   - Database-specific middleware, such as IBI's Enterprise Data Access/SQL (EDA/SQL), IBM's Distributed Relational Database Architecture (DRDA), Microsoft's Open Data Base Connectivity (ODBC), Oracle's Glue, SQL Access Group's SAG/CLI, and the Integrated Database Application Pro-gramming Interface (IDAPI).
   - OLTP-specific middleware, such as Tuxedo's ATMI and /WS, Encina's Transactional RPC, and X/Open's TxRPC and XATMI.
   - Groupware-specific middleware, such as the Messaging API (MAPI), Vendor Independent Messaging (VIM), Vendor Independent Calendaring (VIC), and Lotus Notes calls.
   - Object-specific middleware, such as the Open Management Group's ORB and Object Services and ODMG-93.
   - System Management-specific middleware, such as the Simple Network Management Protocol (SNMP), the Common Management Information Protocol (CMIP), and ORBs.

New and Existing Products

Middleware is an idea that is still under development, and it includes several types of products. Both new and older products have found homes under the middleware umbrella. The umbrella covers IBM's Systems Application Architecture (SAA), Digital's Network Application Services (NAS), as well as simple messaging programs. Middleware's common element is the ability to hide from the user the complexities and differences of network protocols and operating systems. Ideally, the application will have a single interface into the middleware environment. If that is so, you could move the application from one environment to another without changing it.

Message delivery systems are a fast-growing category. These use APIs to connect various e-mail front-end applications to server-based message processing systems. Other forms of middleware include systems that use remote procedure calls (RPCs) and structured query language (SQL). Systems using multiple platforms and protocols let applications retrieve, exchange, and store data without regard to their underlying networks. They also let you mix different front-end applications and back-end database managers.

In each case, middleware earns its name by fitting in between the network and the application. It shields users from complex network addresses by providing a software bridge between the application and the operating system. It is equally kind to application developers. They can spend more time writing good applications and less time worrying about network mechanics. Middleware also lets you take advantage of varied products; you are less likely to lock yourself into a short list of proprietary products.

Encapsulation

Middleware products disguise system resources through a process of encapsulation. Encapsulation, as you already learned, hides the details of individual system elements behind an interface common to all those elements. In application development, encapsulation gives programmers a generic interface they can use effectively to reach all the networks in the system. When the system changes, as it will, you need only adapt the encapsulating software. The applications' relation with this software will remain the same.

Middleware and the database

Middleware has become particularly important in managing client/server databases because, despite the trend toward downsizing, many key databases are on large systems and will continue to be. The mainframes offer processing power, enhanced security, and management control. They also represent very large investments. Because there are mainframe databases, it will be necessary to provide transparent, high-performance access from PCs and LAN servers.

Middleware also helps solve the problems of transparent access to distributed databases. It provides an intervening database manager that serves as a gateway to varied files and systems in other locations.

What is middleware?

Middleware generally has four basic components:

1. A client API that the application program uses.
2. A network gateway that manages the network linkage.
3. An ASQL translator that converts SQL commands from a client into the data management language of the server.
4. Host server software that provides access to data sources on large systems.

Not all systems have all four components. The API, for example, is generally limited to database management. Nevertheless, these do form a common pattern.

The Middleware API

Each middleware product has its own API, consisting of procedural calls that let the application program communicate with a DBMS. Using these API calls, a program can connect to a DBMS, retrieve data, and end the connection.

Beyond these basic functions, each API has a unique set of features. As in so many other components of enterprise networking, no two database managers have identical APIs. Each API also has its unique syntax. That means middleware itself, supposedly a solution to the problem of network diversity, can become part of the problem. Even front-end products that support middleware APIs probably will support only the most popular.

The Network Gateway

The network gateway component serves as a protocol converter and gateway concentrator. It transmits API messages over a network, using a designated LAN protocol. When you need to use a WAN protocol, the gateway function will handle the conversion. Here, too, a particular middleware product might handle only a popular selection of network protocols.

You can load the gateway on a client workstation or a server. On the server, it acts as a concentrator that supports application connections from multiple workstations.

The SQL Translator

In Chapter 2, you will read a little about standards. However, at this time, it is important to bring up SQL standards. While SQL supposedly is a standard product as defined in either ISO's SQL-89, SQL-92, or SQL3 standards, it isn't. Vendors add enhancements to provide their products with a competitive advantage. Your SQL version might use commands that are not understood correctly or at all by another SQL database management system.

Of course, this situation has spawned middleware gateways that will convert the SQL syntax and semantics and data types, as well as map the data dictionaries of the client and server.

Host Server Software

Host server products try to achieve fast performance while retrieving data from a remote database and returning it to the client applications. Vendors have included support for short and long run transactions and for remote procedure calls.

So you have an architecture and you want to apply it. The first step is to evaluate the current infrastructure, or your existing hardware and software components.

The State of the Client/Server Infrastructure

An infrastructure provides the components that make it easy to create, deliver, and manage client/server applications. The telephone and cable companies are renewing the physical infrastructure, laying high bandwidth transport media, and developing switching systems. The challenge for client/server is to add to this physical infrastructure the client/server technology that will meld it all together. The elements we need are:

- Transport protocols supporting networked exchanges and allowing information to be moved reliably. In Chapters 8 and 9 you will learn about the two predominant transport protocols.

- Network operating systems guaranteeing the confidentiality and integrity of data and servicing requests. Again, you will learn about two of the most popular network operating systems in Chapters 12 and 13 (NetWare and OS/2 LAN server respectively).

- Databases for storing, retrieving, organizing, and securing multimedia data. As mentioned, Chapters 7 and 19 provide information on DB2/2 and ORACLE.

- Information appliances allowing the exchange of data and organizing client activities. CICS/6000 (Chapter 20) and Lotus Notes (Chapter 21) are good examples of information appliances.

- Distributed network management systems monitoring and controlling the network. A popular network management system, IBM's NetView, is covered in Chapter 11.

Summary

I hope you now know the answer to the "What is client/server?" question. However, the harder questions are: How do you protect the client? How do you protect the server? How do you protect the middleware? What security measures go in the client and what measures go in the server? Can the client/server security architecture accommodate businesses of all sizes? How are the traveling laptop users safely brought into the client/server fold? Can LANs be secured? How do you control application and network changes? How do you assure the integrity of the data warehouses? What security features are available in different products? Can you adequately secure client/server computing systems? These all are good questions. By the end of this book, you should have the answer to at least these questions.

In the next chapter, you will explore further some client/server concepts.

Select Bibliography

Baker, Richard H. 1993. *Networking the Enterprise*. New York: Windcrest/ McGraw-Hill.

Hourt, Johnson M. and Barry Rosenburg. 1995. *Client/Server Computing for Technical Professionals: Concepts and Solutions*. Reading, MA: Addison-Wesley.

Orfali, Robert, Dan Harkey and Jeri Edwards. 1994. *Essential Client/Server Survival Guide*. New York: Van Nostrand Reinhold.

Introducing Client/Server Standards and Applications

Peter T. Davis

Business is like riding a bicycle; either you keep moving or you fall down.
ANONYMOUS

A man to carry on a successful business must have imagination. He must see things as in a vision, a dream of the whole thing.
CHARLES M. SCHWAB

As you saw in Chapter 1, there is a war going on out there about what is client/server, who has it, whether it costs or saves money, and what effect, if any, it has on people. Vendors assure you that their product certainly is client/server, but they do not talk about the effort it might take to implement securely and effectively your application in a client/server environment.

As discussed, client/server computing is the use of computer systems (i.e., a client and a server) with a clear and defined interface between them (the slash). Often client/server computing entails a client process that accomplishes part of the application, and calls on the server by communicating via a network to perform other parts of the application. Client/server and these networks are being driven by the promise of open systems.

The Promise of Open Systems

A big reason for the growing interest in open systems is their ability to support distributed computing, which is at the heart of enterprise networking and client/server computing.

The way you use computers now should differ from the way you expect to use them in the future. Should your organization be typical of those still considering enterprise networking and client/server computing, you might have a mix of software and hardware from different suppliers and manufacturers. Characteristically, different workgroups, many in different geographic regions and sharing little information and few resources, operate their own computing resources. Because most of the computer systems are proprietary, it is hard to exchange information among these different systems without major programming efforts. This is not how you see the future.

The Open Future

No doubt, in your view of the future you see all these problems solved. You wish to share processing and data across heterogeneous environments, and to use all resources available in your organization. You just might wish to gain access to data on another department's computer, or to have the use of a remote color laser printer. Or, you recognize that the desktop client/server computing revolution, ironically, has replaced one form of centralized computing with another. Instead of central control at the mainframe you have dispersed control to the departmental and workgroup levels. You'd like a system that is easier to manage. Still, you don't want to revert to the mainframe days, when data was managed so carefully it could hardly ever be used. You want a system that uses information to truly empower your employees, which is the indisputable promise of client/server computing.

As you know, this integrated future is a vast improvement over the situations facing most organizations now. The vision naturally makes you anxious to get there. You want to rid yourself of the unplanned hodgepodge left over at your organization and move to a system where everything works together, no matter what or where it is.

Open and Distributed Systems

That's why the movement to enterprise networking also is often a movement to open systems. Simply put, when a system is truly open it knows no geographical limits. Ideally, access to a computer in the next state or province should be no more difficult than access to a computer on the next desk. In short, the open system is capable of being a distributed open system, one sharing information and resources throughout your organization.

A truly distributed open system is a step beyond client/server computing. In client/server computing in its simplest form, one server meets the needs of several clients. In a distributed open system there are several servers, perhaps one in each department. Each serves a group of clients within its group, or members of other workgroups.

There is one real problem. Many organizations that have rushed to embrace open systems have run smack into brick walls. Businesses need distributed open systems now, to capitalize on business opportunities and to keep from being left behind. However, a continuing lack of tools and applications often restrains them.

This is because open systems tools and applications depend on standards; that is, on uniform specifications that all elements can meet to work together. From a business perspective, the people developing these standards are working at a frustrating, snail-like pace. The standards' bodies are interested in making sure they get it right (and properly so), but they sometimes seem oblivious to the immediate needs of their ultimate customers. They must work slowly when they want their standard to stand up to the test of time, like ISO's OSI standard which is over 25 years old. Within a few years, these bodies might complete the groundwork for products their business clients need now.

Frustrated by the delays and lack of genuine progress, many businesses and organizations have taken matters into their own hands. They have formed their own business-sponsored standards' groups and have set their own specifications without waiting for the standards' organizations. Others are patronizing vendors who can meet their needs now, though they do so with proprietary systems and run the risk of future incompatibility.

These practical responses will become either brilliant calculations or dangerous traps—the difference will lie in why you acted. You will not be trapped if your near-term response is a well-planned step which "respects" your architecture and includes an identified migration path toward your ultimate business goals. (In other words, your immediate response anticipated the next step.) So, before you make a decision, be sure you are making it for good reasons.

Defining Open Systems

Like many ideas in enterprise networking, the definition of open systems is a bit fluid and subject to interpretation. It has both technical and operational elements. The technical part of the definition includes network protocols and application program interfaces (APIs). On the business side, open systems mean timely and unimpeded access to applications and information.

Departmental users look at open systems in relation to the work they must do and the information they need to do it; i.e., through the business perspective. Vendors think of open systems in technical terms; i.e., in terms of the types of technology they are trying to sell. It's important to keep both elements in mind. Judge the technology by how well it can meet your organization's needs.

Open systems also must meet other needs and standards as well, including these:

- They must allow for innovation. The purpose of open systems is not to achieve a technology in which everything looks the same, but to establish an atmosphere in which all kinds of information technology work together.

- They must meet management's needs. The business view of open systems, including the need for secure systems, must receive at least as much respect and attention as the technical view. As previously mentioned, the main purpose of the technology is to serve the business client.

Base your decisions on how well the system can do the job, and how well it can adapt to your future needs. The real advantage of open systems is that they often can meet your needs. Open systems should include standards-based products and technology, an open development infrastructure, and a solid management directive. Why do you need standards-based products and technology?

The Role of Standards

Standards probably are the most familiar component of open systems. Of course, the standards are important. They form the basis of such useful working features as portability and interoperability. By themselves, however, they cannot establish open systems.

One source of confusion is that people tend to think of open systems and proprietary systems as directly opposed. By that logic, the use of generally published standards distinguishes the two. Of course, the real opposite of an open system is a closed system, because a closed system involves the risk that you someday cannot adapt or expand.

A proprietary system is not necessarily either open or closed. Even the most open system has some elements proprietary to individual vendors. A proprietary system does have some of the same risks as a closed system, but you can control and balance that risk. Often, proprietary systems offer better service and are more innovative than those conforming tightly to the accepted standards. A fully open system reduces the risk of being left with no future, but it also denies you access to an individual vendor's innovations in the present.

What's more, existing standards don't define everything. For example, in some areas there is more than one standard, and in others there are none at all.

Three Levels of Standardization

The standardization creating an open system takes place at three levels:

1. Standard hardware and software platforms. For example, most PCs use Intel chips and the MS-DOS operating system, often with Windows.

2. Standard applications. Standardization at this level does not always contribute to an open environment. When an organization standardizes on particular systems or software packages, it locks its employees into the chosen systems. They are unable to take advantage of competing applications.

3. Middleware. This is the layer of software that often lies between an application and the operating system or platform. Middleware is not part of either the application or the platform. Examples include databases, graphical interfaces, electronic mail, system management tools, and application development tools.

Middleware's Critical Role

Given the recent emphasis on open, standards-based technology, middleware is drawing more attention. It is becoming more platform-independent. Middleware uses standard protocols and interfaces where they are available and mature.

Also, many examples of middleware are not based on standards. It often is appropriate to use nonstandardized technology. If proprietary technology solves a business problem, and if there is no standards-based solution available, then you would be foolish to overlook a proprietary solution.

Standard middleware is the model adopted by users who decide to standardize on a particular component or set of components. Users wanting to find standardized middleware, such as a specific vendor's database, should make sure they are not trading off software portability for hardware portability. They could find themselves locked into a software architecture instead of their desired hardware line.

There are alternatives in the standardized middleware model that can minimize this potential pitfall. Standardization at the middleware level represents the most flexible open systems' model. It offers more choice and, if implemented in a disciplined way, does the best job of avoiding proprietary products.

Maintaining a Profile

To guard against being locked into a particular form of middleware, many businesses and standards-setting organizations have adopted a process called *profiling*. A profile is a suite of standards that specify the functions you need to meet the requirements for a given purpose.

Profiles pay off in many ways. They give you a way to capitalize on the use of standards within your own organization. In a business setting, profiling often takes the form of organizational guidelines, standards, or specifications. The companies often use these in the standards requirements sections of RFPs. For example, the U.S. government asks for POSIX-compliant software in their RFPs.

A profile can specify either a complete open systems environment (OSE) or an application-specific environment specified through Application Environment Profiles (AEPs). An AEP identifies the needs of the application area, cites the standards available that meet those needs, and notes any gaps existing between the needs and the standards. There might be nonstandardized technology available to fill these gaps.

The Standard-Setters

A model also can represent an OSE profile. Varying market conditions and customer needs can often produce differences among various organizations' profiles. Several standards organizations have produced OSE profiles, including:

- The Open Software Foundation's (OSF's) Application Environment Specification (AES). The AES originally specified many formal standards. Items added to the AES include the Motif Graphical User Interface and the Distributed Computing Environment (DCE).

- The National Institute of Standards and Technology's (NIST's) Application Portability Profile (APP). APP relies heavily on formal standards from the Institute for Electrical and Electronic Engineers (IEEE).

- UNIX International's (UI's) Atlas for Open Systems. Atlas is a framework for procurement similar to IBM's Systems Application Architecture. Atlas specifies UNIX System V, Open Systems Interconnect (OSI) networking standards, and the popular Motif and OpenLook GUIs. It also specifies such distributed computing technologies as OSF's DCE and Sun Microsystems' Open Network Computing (ONC).

- X/Open's Common Application Environment (CAE). X/Open's model is based on its X/Open Portability Guide (XPG). Version 3 of this profile (XPG3) is a widely accepted profile in the industry today.

Impatience with the Process

A most frustrating characteristic of these standards organizations is that they have been exceedingly slow in publishing their standards. That delays the products business customers would like to have right now. This frustration has spawned many new kinds of standards from new kinds of standard setters, often user-driven. The result has been that customers and vendors have tried to fill the voids, adopting standards of their own where none existed. Examples include the Standards for Open Systems (SOS) and the User Alliance for Open Systems. Both organizations are trying to ease the move to cost-effective open systems by putting forth their members' requirements.

Open Systems Choices

With all these emerging organizations and standards, how can you expect open systems to be open? Open systems supposedly are uniform. In fact, they might be a little less uniform now than they were a few years ago.

In the past, distributed systems were proprietary. Each major computer manufacturer, such as IBM and DEC, designed its hardware and software to provide interoperability among its systems. If you stayed with your chosen vendor, things could hardly be more uniform.

Modern desktop-centered computing can make uniformity or standardization seem like an impossible dream. Two industry-sponsored organizations, though, offer competing systems that easily could reduce the available choices. One choice comes from the Open Software Foundation and the other from UNIX International. Both aim to provide distributed platforms spanning multiple architectures, communications protocols, and operating systems.

OSF's product is the Distributed Computing Environment (DCE). UI calls its effort the Atlas distributed processing architecture. Both DCE and Atlas address distributed computing problems, but they do not compete directly. DCE provides basic distributed computing services, whereas Atlas extends those basic services. Because Atlas incorporates DCE services you should find applications portable and interoperable between them. Beyond the DCE functions, Atlas supports distributed transaction processing and fault-tolerant support services.

DCE and Atlas seem well on their way to becoming the recognized standards for distributed computing. DCE responds in particular to the needs of customers who are trying to create distributed environments on their own. Between them they represent most major vendors in the computer industry, more than 200 organizations.

Independence from UNIX

UI and OSF are known best for their competing versions of UNIX, but neither distributed environment depends on any particular operating system. DCE works as well on the MacOS as it does on UNIX. Atlas also provides interoperability with non-UNIX operating environments. UI and OSF are open systems organizations, wherein UNIX is only part of the broader open systems philosophy. Like distributed computing, this philosophy is based on interoperability, scalability, portability, and compatibility among heterogeneous architectures.

The two systems can work together as well. UI has incorporated OSF's DCE into Atlas' basic structure. This means UI will take advantage of OSF's interoperability features.

What Is at the Basis of DCE and Atlas?

Both systems rest on client/server foundations. A distributed computing environment includes two or more client/server combinations in a network. With more than one server, you can split, modularize, and spread the applications, services, and data across the servers. Servers then can pass information among themselves; thus, a server can be a client to another server.

A distributed environment consists of several important elements:

- A distributed file system. This component provides global file access, using, for example, OSF's DFS and Sun's Network File System (NFS).

- Communication. This is the backbone of distributed computing. Both DCE and Atlas support ISO's OSI networking protocols. They also support TCP/IP, X.25, and others.

- Remote procedure calls. RPCs manage communication among applications distributed across heterogeneous networks. Distributed systems also need name or directory services to manage and control location, changes of resources, applications, and even users. They also need time services to synchronize the activities of various computers in the distributed environment.

- Security. As with any kind of network, you need authentication and authorization mechanisms to control users.

- Transparency. Human clients can use all these features without having to worry about them, or even knowing that they exist.

The LAN Factor

Open systems also have important foundations in local area networks. LAN technology encompasses several methods, including RPCs, transport protocols, and network authentication and authorization systems, to help provide interoperability at the local network level. In this book you will learn about network authentication and authorization systems.

Alone, these developments are not enough to support an enterprise network. In combination, they also are often insufficient. What's more, they don't work readily together. It can be a daunting challenge to try to figure out what platforms, protocols, naming services, authorization systems, and other features work with other elements of the network. Expanding the scope from a LAN to an enterprise network increases the challenge. What's more, you soon won't be rid of the varied LANs and other divers systems that probably sprung up around your organization. As a practical matter, you'll probably find yourself integrating them into the system, not replacing them.

Atlas and DCE can help you overcome many of these problems. DCE incorporates various forms of technology into an integrated product. Atlas adds additional functions.

So . . . What Is DCE?

The Open Software Foundation designed the Distributed Computing Environment as a comprehensive enterprise-wide networking scheme. DCE should make commodities out of network directory software, remote procedures, network security services, and system management software. It has gained attention from many vendors, including some non-OSF members.

One big advantage of DCE is that it is a true distributed file system. This system is based upon the Andrew File System (AFS) developed at Carnegie Mellon University. AFS provides a common environment for a workstation on a network.

DCE also is strong in Remote Procedure Calls (RPCs). The DCE RPC lets a program on one system call a subroutine on another, even when the second system has a different processor and operating system. If the target system is different it can translate the information to its own format.

Network security also is a major DCE feature. It lets the target system authenticate each procedure call setup. This attempts to keep users from accidentally or intentionally writing programs that might cross a network, gain unauthorized access, or damage files. The authentication can have multiple levels with associated privileges. For example, an individual might be allowed to read data but not to change it. In the next chapter you will be introduced to client/server security issues and measures.

DCE Up Close and Personal

More than 100 vendors now support DCE, including IBM, DEC, Bull, HP, Siemens, and Hitachi, whose customers, in turn, include the world's largest companies and organizations. DCE will be incorporated, among others, into:

- Unicos from Cray
- ACE, OpenVMS, OSF/1, and Ultrix from DEC
- Domain, HP/UX, and OSF/1 from Hewlett-Packard
- AIX, MS-DOS, MVS, and OS/2 from IBM

- SINIX from Siemens
- Integrity and Guardian from Tandem

A key to this level of interest, from PCs to supercomputers, is OSF's multivendor, multitechnology approach. It is the result of OSF's Request for Technology process, which solicits technology from the computer industry at large. Interested companies submit their products; from those submissions, OSF chooses those it adjudges as the industry's best. OSF then includes these submissions in DCE. Sources of the chosen technology include start-ups such as Transarc, OSF members DEC and HP, and even UI member Sun. Specifically, DCE's technology includes:

- AFS distributed file system from Transarc
- Concert Multi-Threads Architecture (CMA) from DEC
- DECdns name service from DEC
- DECdts time service from DEC
- DIR-XX.500 directory service from Siemens
- Enhanced Network Computing System/RPC from HP and DEC
- Kerberos security service from MIT, with HP extensions
- LM/X PC integration technology from Microsoft
- PC-NFS from Sun

Basic Services

DCE's services, as shown in Figure 2.1, fall into two categories, fundamental distributed services and data sharing services.

The fundamental services group includes tools that software developers can use to build user services and applications. These services include:

- Remote procedure calls. As you read previously, an RPC lets you build applications that use individual procedures running on computers across a heterogeneous network. It includes two components that help in building client/server applications, an *RPC facility* that provides simplicity, performance, portability, and network independence, and a *compiler* that converts client and server interface descriptions (Interface Definition Language or IDL) into C source code. This lets RPCs behave like local procedure calls when compiled and linked into run-time libraries.

- Directory service. The directory service provides a single naming model for resources such as servers, files, and disks in a distributed environment.

- Time service. DCE maintains a distributed time reference to synchronize activity and events among the computers on a network. The time service

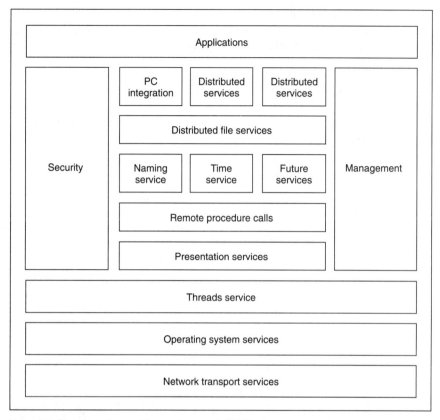

Figure 2.1 Distributed computing environment (DCE)

provides APIs for using timestamps and for obtaining universal time from public sources.

- Threads service. As you saw in Chapter 1, threads control program flow. They let an application process many commands simultaneously. Programmers can use this feature within local or distributed environments. Thread service also is useful in client/server control, because a server can initiate many threads to clients.

- Security service. This service authorizes, authenticates, and manages user access to individual hosts on the distributed network. It includes a secure RPC to protect the integrity of communication, Kerberos authentication to validate the identity of a user or service, authorization tools that control user access to resources, and a user registry to manage user account information. Again, in Chapter 3, you will learn about authentication and authorization services.

The data sharing services are based on the Fundamental Distributed Services standard. These provide extra functions without the need for extra programming. In DCE, these services include:

- A distributed file system. DFS is the key information-sharing component. It joins the files and directories of individual workstations and provides a consistent application interface. DFS provides a uniform namespace or single image file system for distributing across file servers, and file location transparency.

- Diskless support. The distributed file system supports diskless workstations and provides protocols for diskless support.

- Personal computer integration. PCI lets UNIX, MS-DOS, and OS/2 users share files, peripherals, and applications.

In summary, DCE is the epitome of middleware, for it provides an operating system-independent layer of glue, including distributed directory services, network security, remote procedure calls, threads, and distributed time.

Enough standards! The problem is not a dearth of standards but perhaps a plethora of them!

Open Development

However, you don't need just an open system. You also need an open development environment that ensures that your technology will be useful and long-lived. Open systems promise to support distributed applications that will significantly enhance productivity throughout your organization. If you are to keep your system open you must set it up in the most effective possible way for the largest possible number of users, now and in the future.

A true open system provides continuity. Your newly developed technology can take advantage of existing technology. Your design of new elements should take advantage of existing components so that future developments can take advantage of them. Standards help assure you that you can continue this process, continuously building on your previous work.

Application development in an open system also requires discipline. It's easy to take an open system and slam it shut by using closed applications. For example, you could buy a SQL database whose query language observes the established standard. However, as you just read, most SQL versions include proprietary extensions. If you rely on these vendor extensions you have effectively closed your system.

There is another common hazard in the incompatible networks that might be springing up throughout your organization. Often, these networks develop because their users have felt left out and ill-served by the corporate development process. These networks are sometimes invaluable, as they do often serve short-term needs, but they will be in place for years, standing in the way of your organization's progress.

Manage the Process

As you noted in Chapter 1, technology must serve the organization. Never should it be the other way around, though it often is. Without intervention or direction from management you will continue to have isolated islands of information through the organization. People will use information as a weapon, trying to over regulate its use when your organization's real objective is to share it.

You must make sure your technology reflects the needs of the entire organization, by establishing requirements that you include in requests for proposals, and by ensuring that all purchase decisions reflect those requirements. Make sure, too, that management directives reflect the needs and views of all involved groups. This consensus-building process becomes increasingly important as organizations decentralize their decision-making processes.

The Benefit of Open Systems

Open systems will bring a greater sense of control to your systems, from both technology and management perspectives. Because open environments are more predictable, management can allocate resources and manage change easily. Management will find they can plan and manage technology investments, and respond to changing needs and objectives, better. Management also will experience less emphasis on technology and more on business requirements.

Management's job is to run the business. Ideally, an open system will let managers do exactly that. The best thing technology can do for a manager is to make itself invisible. Then, management can concern itself with how to use the technology to improve the business. There will be less need to worry about how to make the technology work.

Systems, software, training, and development expenditures within open systems will come in manageable chunks. That means your planning can be more accurate. Management can plan investments smoothly and in natural increments, taking a long-term approach to the return on these investments. In Chapter 5 you will learn one way to manage these chunks.

Open systems also help create a flexible, transportable environment. As organizations change roles, or as they create new divisions to tap market opportunities, their applications, data, and systems can move with them. Also, they quickly can add new resources to serve new goals.

The object of client/server computing and an enterprise network is to give employees easier access to more information. Open systems can play a major role in meeting that goal.

In the past, many employees resisted computer technology in the workplace. Sometimes, the employees had emotional reasons to resist. More often, they found the computers simply too hard to learn and use, suggesting a failure to integrate seamlessly technology with the job. Technology should make an employee's work easier, not harder. With open systems, employees can gain new opportunities without having to learn and understand the technology. You get the gist of this when you think of the difference between using MS-DOS and MS-DOS with Windows.

To date, the best-rewarded employee often was the one who understood how to get information, by navigating the network, reaching the mainframe, and using the complex report writer (perhaps, SQL). The employee who can do these things is better prepared to gather and distribute information from the organization's databases. Open systems can help make information available to all employees easily and effortlessly, so they can put it to use productively and economically. Employees who learn how to retrieve this information, and to link it with business objectives, will reward themselves while rewarding their organizations.

Some Problems

All this describes an ideal application of open systems. As anyone knows who has looked into the subject, most open systems applications are far from ideal. One big area of conflict has been between two competing ideas of proper timing. Businesses want useful systems and applications yesterday. The bodies that set standards have taken a careful, even leisurely, pace. Vendors have been caught between their customers' demands and a lack of standard specifications for their products. This conundrum has plagued especially the development of security tools and techniques.

Client/Server Applications

It cannot be repeated often enough. Client/server has to do with the *application*, not the technology used to implement it. With the availability of reasonably priced units, personal computers became a big part of client/server computing in the mid-1980s. Once PCs and workstations became available on office workers' desks, interaction with humans could be handled more easily by the PC or workstation because of its attractive and colorful screen images and easy access, using mouse devices. With faster desktop units, sound cards, and enhanced graphics, it now is possible to enrich applications with moving images, still pictures, spoken instructions, and dynamic user interaction. This now creates a new type of threat as someone runs through your office yelling, "File, Close, No." However, by using the power in the client's workstation, the server can be relieved of the duties of interaction with humans and can be oriented toward processing large amounts of data or performing complex calculations. Successful implementations of client/server applications recognize whether the required processing belongs on a powerful PC, a midrange, or a mainframe.

Another development that came about in the mid to late 1980s was the availability of software that made development of applications much easier and much more user-friendly. Various application development packages have emerged that offer rapid prototyping and reuse of common code (that is, object-oriented programming). In Chapters 4, 5, and 6, you will learn about some of these techniques and tools. These packages run on the PC and have price tags commensurate with PC software. The investment in prototyping an application, or in some cases of building it and throwing it away, can be low.

Use of the PC development packages allows applications to be created faster. It is even possible to give the end user the capability of ad hoc creation of an application, or ad hoc combination of data from multiple databases. One of the benefits, when the application is so implemented, is that the employee (the client) becomes event driven rather than process driven.

Therefore, employees can react directly to changes in the business environment. However, such a capability is a management challenge. The employees (that is, clients) have to be encouraged to look at their jobs in a new way. The word empowerment has come into popular use because end users have to be rewarded for using the client/server applications, and for being creative and responsive.

Client/server technology is new, and user expectations are unmistakably high. Client/server teams are under the gun because the technology is new, user expectations are high, and obstacles line the way. While client/server computing has enormous momentum and promise, reader polls and consultants' studies reveal that a majority of such projects are overdue, over budget, and short of expectations.

One reason for late projects is poor planning. If you have not allocated at least forty percent of your development time for testing, unpleasant surprises probably await you. Thorough testing of all components of a client/server system is critical, more so when you consider how complicated it is to test applications that are based on a graphical user interface and prototyping. Test the system completely. Your development credibility and that of the project depend on it.

Productivity and Quality

Managers frequently must deal with decisions concerning the way information systems support their operations. The recent movements of business process reengineering and rightsizing provide you an opportunity to reexamine methods of effective deployment and management control of information systems.

Information technology must be viewed by managers as an instrument to improve productivity and quality of an organization's products and services. Productivity and quality come from people's thinking about their work (not their computers). The effect of such improvement must be understood, quantified, and realized as part of new technology investment and operations.

To determine what impact IT needs to have on a process you must first understand the detailed activities of the process itself. Detailed observations must be performed to evaluate exactly how much motion IT can extract from an activity. It is essential that you identify the exact amount of material, labor, and other resource requirements to be reduced by an IT application. For example, going from a hierarchical menu structure to a graphical user interface in a customer service department might save forty-five seconds per customer call. Or, the immediate availability of scheduling information in a shipping department might permit prepacking of fifty units per hour, thus increasing shipping capacity by eight percent.

Clearly, you can eliminate waste from processes by workflow changes or other improvements that only are tangential to IT. The result of such a productivity analysis can serve two purposes: You can discover new applications or determine whether an intended application is justifiable.

Management Control

Managers tend to have great difficulty in perceiving installed information technology in their areas or departments as variables of improvement. A considerable amount of education, persuasion, and leadership behavior is required on the part of a systems professional to convince colleagues that more can be done at a lower cost when proper analysis is performed first.

A good way to do this is to make performance integral to the enterprise model. In this way, performance standardization is done in cooperation with those responsible for results. Integral to this management philosophy is the notion of continuous improvement with respect to current performance levels. This is why every manager needs to understand the current performance standards for information technology, for without these standards, management decisions will be made on the basis of technical constraints and not performance improvement.

The distribution of computing resources and the increased education of department managers has shifted control and responsibility over their information resources away from systems professionals. Just as quality cannot be the responsibility of one staff person in the form of a quality manager, information management, such as security, cannot be a central responsibility on the lone shoulders of the systems professional. The need for cohesive planning, standardization, integration, and education remains.

The movement to rightsize information technology originates in the great price/performance differential between traditional mainframe technology and microcomputers. Reductions in hardware and software cost, while permitting proliferation, also lower the barriers to implementation.

Many rightsizing projects are forced into existence due to internal performance concerns. Operating system upgrade costs, expiring maintenance contracts, or obsolete storage or communications facilities usually are associated with large amounts of replacement or upgrade capital. Managers should view these events not as problems that must be hidden, but as opportunities to achieve cultural change in the way technology is utilized. Rightsizing represents such an opportunity and, if coupled with analytical techniques, should lead to a stronger correlation between expenditures and productivity and quality improvement.

The current tendency to downsize or rightsize is an opportunity to reverse this trend and impose traditional asset-management disciplines onto IT investments. This shift will incorporate technology into established productivity and quality management models.

Mainframe-, PC-, or Network-Centric

This is not to imply that mainframe computing will or should cease. Centralized processing and mainframe-level capacities are so intrinsic to the nature of many core business systems that no total replacement scenario is likely to be cost-effective or functionally capable.

You should not be worrying about whether your systems are mainframe-centric or PC-centric. What matters is whether your systems are network-centric. This architectural approach draws upon the entire spectrum of technologies, using each where it makes the most sense and allowing them all to work together.

Viewed from this perspective, the greatest immediate strengths of small systems are complementary ones. They offer capabilities and benefits beyond what our existing systems deliver. In fact, many companies use the new client/server technologies to breathe new life into their existing systems.

By applying client/server tools, you can break your core business systems out of the glass house and extend them into the workplace with application-specific interfaces that reduce training time and invite broader access.

The immediate value of small, networked tools lies in their ability to integrate information technology with the way people work. Systems should accept input from a variety of devices, thus allowing users to capture data where it is generated or request information through tools that are consistent with their skill sets and individual needs.

Likewise, system output should not be data but should be more pertinent, personalized, and timely information presented in a variety of forms, each appropriate to the information context and relevant to the frame of reference to maximize productivity. For example, executives might get information presented in the forms of graphs or charts, while analysts might get the same information in the form of tables.

Small system technologies allow us to approach these ideals. Compared with previous approaches, they enable you to provide more intuitive solutions and meet users on more human terms. The system interface activity becomes a seamless part of the work process, end-to-end, as opposed to a handoff or interruption in the workflow.

The enterprise network environment that embodies these attributes will typically involve multiple computing devices working together. It will be a world not just of multiple clients per server, but multiple servers per client.

As technology costs decline, another aspect of these innumerable network links will be multiple clients per user, which implies a diverse array of desktop and mobile devices tailored to both business and individual needs for universal access to system resources.

The servers will encompass processing platforms of every scale, as the needs of the specific business dictate. And business imperatives alone will dictate whether any given database is dispersed, distributed, or centralized.

In short, while client/server approaches are not the new model of enterprise computing, they will play an instrumental role in any information systems strategy that hopes to achieve maximum business advantage.

Why Were the Chapters Selected?

You should have figured out by now that it is impossible to write a book on all aspects of client/server computing security. There are too many variables. Just look at the different operating systems. Every operating system would by itself merit a book on security. For example, there are presently at least six titles dealing solely with UNIX security. Then you could write a security book on each of the DBMS, and you could add a book on TP monitors, such as CICS, and another on Lotus Notes. You get the picture. So, the products selected are widely used products that many organizations see as strategic. But how do they fit into a real example?

To answer that question, let's assume we are dealing with an insurance company. This fictitious company, based in New York, is responsible for processing accident claims. The company has 25,000 employees at more than 1300 branches and offices around the world. They service ten million people in the states and write 100,000 checks per week.

The company needs a system that would make the processing of claims more efficient, to save time for their employees and to better serve their customers. When the company's office receives a claim they generate a form that is filled in by an adjuster in an office. The claim sits on the office LAN until processed.

Records from the collision and repair shops, witnesses, the claimants, and the police can be scanned in at the workgroup computer (perhaps a UNIX box). The adjuster can retrieve these documents at any time and print them off, when required.

At specified intervals, the LAN server triggers an update of the division's information on the minicomputer system. Weekly statistics are sent to the corporate system residing on the mainframe. Now, when a field manager wants to analyze historical data his query might access the local area network's server, the minicomputer's server, and the mainframe.

In this simple example, you can see you might use an architecture such as that shown in Figure 2.2. While this one demonstrates the use of a DBMS (DB/2) and a transaction processor (CICS) proprietary to IBM, you could substitute other products from other vendors. As you move from chapter to chapter, keep this complex architecture in mind and try to figure out where the particular product fits in. Remember, client/server is application-oriented.

Summary

Client/server is not technology although new technology makes it possible; it is a distributed way of doing data processing.

Client/server is application-oriented. Sometimes you can buy a packaged client/server solution meeting your requirements, such as a LAN network operating system (for example, Banyan VINES, IBM OS/2 LAN Server, Microsoft NT Advanced Server, or Novell NetWare) or a distributed relational database (for example, Informix, Oracle, or Sybase). But often you will be building your client/server application to fit your business. This is where the art of programming will be exerted. All the traditional analyses of processing required versus power available, network load, data availability, integrity, and recoverability will come into play. It is possible that client/server also will require a change in corporate culture if it is to be effective where management wants it to be effective; namely, on the bottom line.

It is clear that the value of information technology needs to be seen not simply in terms of its relation to the state of technology but in terms of its beneficial or detrimental effect on the organization as a whole.

In the next chapter you will learn about some general client/server security issues, before starting in on specific security issues associated with a particular product. Security is an important client/server consideration when your net worth is on the network!

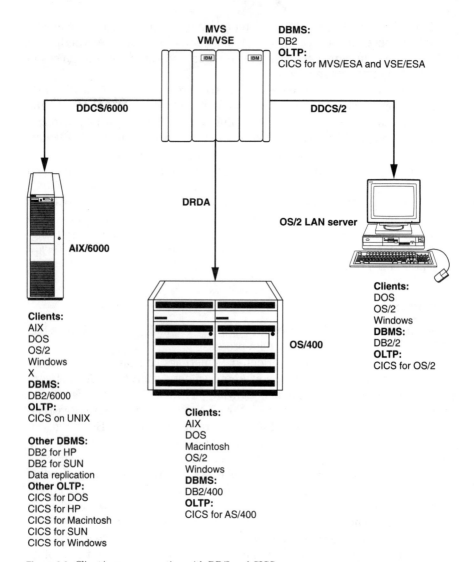

Figure 2.2 Client/server computing with DB/2 and CICS

3

Introducing Client/Server Security Concepts

Peter T. Davis

It is not the crook in modern business that we fear but the honest man who does not know what he is doing. OWEN D. YOUNG

He that will not apply new remedies must expect new evils. FRANCIS BACON

Network security is cited as one of the most critical concerns of business to-day. Ernst & Young's 1994 study of 1271 corporate managers proves this point. As you can see from Figure 3.1, clearly 85 percent of the respondents felt network security was a concern. With increased access through dial-in, and with the proliferation of PCs and global networks such as the Internet, it is becoming an increasingly important factor in network design. And networks and their designs are critical components of your client/server system.

Unfortunately, security often is not given the consideration it deserves in client/server systems, partly because the implementation of security represents a cost that does not reflect an immediate return and partly because purchasers of client/server technology are sometimes unaware of security issues and concepts. Sadly, in many cases it might take a serious breach of security to emphasize its importance.

Yet evidence of network insecurity is all around us. In recent years, security problems with networks have received much public attention. The media has carried stories of high-profile malicious cracker (a cracker is a

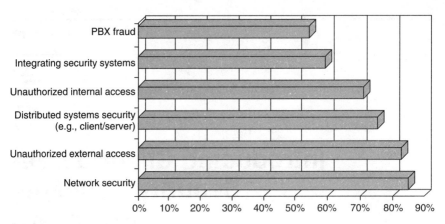

Figure 3.1 Technology issues

person who attacks and breaks into computer systems) attacks against government, business, and academic sites. It's fairly common to read about some cracker breaking into a networked computer system just for the fun of it, or just to see if it could be done. Upon reading such a news story, have you ever asked yourself how many other undetected attackers are breaking into computer systems with malicious intent? Seemingly, crackers roam networks with virtual impunity, hiding their tracks by moving from one unwitting and receptive system to another. Is this a problem of today's PC networks?

Are Networks More Vulnerable?

Conventional wisdom holds that PC networks lack many security features of larger minicomputer or mainframe systems. In the traditional computer network with dozens of dumb terminals connected, all the processing takes place on one machine, the minicomputer or the mainframe. All the screen handling, program logic, referential integrity checks, security checks, and similar functions are done on that minicomputer or mainframe. The terminal simply provides a view into that bigger machine.

As you saw in Chapter 1, many developments are combining to change that comfortable picture. Ease of use has become important, illustrated by the spread of graphical and object-oriented user interfaces. Databases that once lived on large systems are migrating to network servers. There's a movement in the opposite direction, too, as stand-alone PC databases migrate into client/server architecture. Generally, the data is moving away from the client as the program logic moves toward the client.

Often, though, confidentiality, integrity and availability tend to be forgotten, particularly in networked systems. One reason is a tendency to think of network resources as inexpensive and easy to replace. Another problem is that it is harder to protect a network than it is an isolated larger system.

Confidential information could be reasonably protected when it resided on a single large system with its multiple built-in protective mechanisms. You could put all your eggs in one basket and watch that basket real carefully. But confidential information is much harder to protect now that PCs and networks have entered the picture. MS-DOS, the prevailing PC operating system, has almost none of the technical checks and balances that large systems provide. It cannot protect even itself, a truth known by anyone who has had a virus. Another serious problem is that desktop workstations are physically more accessible than their larger counterparts. Walking around your office should convince you of this accessibility . . . and vulnerability.

This does not prove the case for mainframe security. It just means that networks often lack built-in security measures. System administrators must provide them. You cannot sit back and let a networked client/server system take care of its own security. You must actively provide it. But you can do that.

It's probably true that if you need ironclad protection for truly sensitive data, a LAN might not measure up to a well-protected mainframe or minicomputer. Still, it is possible to achieve a high degree of security, even in the open environment of an enterprise network. For example, you might have sensitive information on a network, that must be available to dial-in access from employees across the country. Borrowing from mainframe technology, you could implement a call-in system, where an inbound caller cannot immediately gain access to the full network. The system would accept the caller's login information, hang up, and redial a telephone number associated with that identification.

What's the Problem?

Client/server systems can deliver many advantages when compared to isolated computer systems. Unfortunately, robust security is not currently on the list of client/server advantages. Why? In short, a network is involved. And in most cases, the network connecting clients and servers is a less-than-secure vehicle that crackers can use to infringe upon computer systems and their various resources. For example, using publicly available utilities, a cracker can write a simple program that uses a network to connect to a host from a remote machine to discover user passwords. Other utilities and hardware let an attacker eavesdrop on a network, or "sniff" the network to read packets of information. The information contained in gathered packets can reveal useful information, or holes that a cracker can use to break into a computer system.

Protect Yourself

I hope that client/server vendors and integrators will not see me as disingenuous should I suggest that client/server computing security is difficult at best. Vendors and integrators are selling client/server products as the simple answer to all your informational needs. What they don't tell you is that client/server is very complex, in most instances much more complex than the technology it is replacing.

In theory, converting to client/server should be easy. Just plug in the right hardware, install the correct software, hand a development team a set of application building tools, and you're there. But in the ever-present real world you probably will run into some problems. You can solve most of these by adjusting your perspective. If you're coming from a large-system environment, you'll find that there are major differences between the applications you're familiar with and the client/server software and applications. If your background is in PCs, you'll encounter the complications of widespread networks and multiple users.

Unlike the PC and mainframe, software and data no longer are on a single system over which you could exercise tight control and management. Resources might be scattered around the building, around the city, around the country, or around the world. Response time might be slower than users expect, as data queries scour the network looking for pieces of information here and there. The usual security measures might not be in place. Information might be vulnerable to the accidental keystroke that erases everything. No matter how much you try to persuade hesitant beginners that they cannot do this, they can.

A client/server system requires that you manage your own security. That kind of active self-protection would be necessary with any kind of system. A network whose managers want to control dial-in access is in much the same position as a large system requiring the same controls. Physical protection is another common concern for systems of all sizes. Just as large systems are located in secure, dedicated rooms, a LAN also can be physically isolated. You can place power supplies and hubs in locked closets; file servers can go in secure rooms. The networked PC workstations, then, present little more security risk than dumb terminals connected to a mainframe. And, the workstations are becoming "dumb and dumber." Many organizations are installing workstations without floppy (dumb) or hard (dumber) disk drives.

Selective Security

The placement of your assets also can boost security. You might want to run application programs on desktop computers, but keep the data itself on a larger, better-protected system. In particular, large corporate databases are remaining on the mainframe computers, with access provided by gateways and similar communication links. This pattern might have only a little to do with security.

Some organizations, after installing an extensive network system, have left important records on the mainframe. The main reason is the mainframe's ability to handle the sheer volume of data. Security is a secondary benefit. Besides, it would take you well into the twenty-first century to off-load all your legacy systems from the mainframe to your client/server systems, with their network operating system security measures.

NOS Security

Network operating systems and allied utilities are increasingly providing security features the PC operating systems do not. These include programs to scan for viruses, and utilities that can restrict access to specified directories or files. Most network operating systems, including NetWare (Chapter 14) and OS/2 LAN Server (Chapter 15), include account control features that restrict users to particular workstations and particular times.

You can use these features to keep people from logging in from home or after hours. For example, you can use an account control feature to permit logins to the human resources department's network only during normal working hours. This helps keep unauthorized users, from inside or outside your organization, from looking at confidential employee information.

In addition, most network operating systems let administrators set up different levels of access to files and data. While users might need access to certain types of corporate data, for example, they won't need the ability to change or delete that data. Granting them read-only access to those files protects the data from both deliberate and accidental modification. Unlike MS-DOS, some computer system operating systems also have built-in security features. NetWare, OS/2 and UNIX control access and limit the permitted types of use of designated directories and files. OS/2 also can restrict the number of licensed application programs that operate on a network. This helps you prevent the use of pirated software.

Secure Client/Server Communication

Client/server computing is a distributed model of computing; that is, a network sits between different computers that cooperate to run an application. A user sits down in front of a client workstation to run a front-end application that communicates with the server across a network. As explained earlier, the network between clients and servers is vulnerable to eavesdropping crackers, and such vulnerability can lead to several different types of security problems.

- A cracker can sniff the network to obtain user IDs and their corresponding passwords, and then connect to the server as an impersonator to read or change data.

- A cracker can sniff the network to read confidential data that is sent between a client and a server.

- A cracker can sniff a network and modify information that is sent between a client and a server.

Encryption can solve all three of these problems (as well as others). Encryption is the transformation of readable data, called plaintext, into unreadable data, called ciphertext. Only those knowing the decryption key can make sense out of the encrypted data. Users of all types of computer systems probably have some exposure to the idea of data encryption at some level. For example, most operating systems one-way encrypt their passwords to the database. In addition, all UNIX systems support the crypt command, and many support the des command to encrypt data files on a disk.

Distributed Security Services

The client/server environment introduces new security threats beyond those found in traditional host-centric systems. In a client/server system, you cannot trust any of the operating systems on the network to protect the server's resources from unauthorized access. Assuming for a moment that you could totally secure client machines, as you just read, the network itself is highly accessible. Listening devices, such as sniffers, squawk boxes, and data line monitors, easily can read or record traffic between machines and introduce forgeries and Trojan horses into your system. A recent Internet incident involved the discovery of password sniffer programs on hundreds of systems throughout the net. This "incident" was really a series of incidents on host systems around the Internet, involving the exploitation of known vulnerabilities.

The password sniffer scenario is relatively simple. After obtaining privilege on a host system, the attacker installs a sniffer program to monitor the system's network interface port and to collect login information, including passwords. Monitoring a network port is not the problem, because authorized individuals need to do this for effective system management. The real problem was that most computer systems employ reusable passwords for authenticating users. There was no exposure for systems employing one-time passwords or other advanced methods (such as smart cards, tokens or dongles) for user authentication.

This is not an Internet vulnerability; Internet protocols do not require host systems to use passwords for user authentication. Also, you should note that encrypting network layer information would not have solved this specific problem, because the monitoring occurs at a point in the compromised systems where messages were unencrypted anyway. In summary, while there were known vulnerabilities exploited in this incident, which security experts previously hypothesized, they were vulnerabilities in the security mechanisms of host systems and not in the Internet itself. This means the servers must find new ways to protect themselves without creating a fortress mentality that upsets users. Client/server requirements further complicate security.

To maintain the single system illusion, every trusted user must be given transparent access to all resources. How is that done when every PC poses a potential threat to network security? Will system administrators be condemned to spend their working lives granting access-level rights to users, one at a time, for each individual application on each server across the enterprise? Let's find out what the network operating systems (NOSs) have to offer.

C2 Security on the Network?

As for most computer system elements, there are security standards for network security systems. A commonly accepted security standard is the National Computer Security Center's (NCSC's) evaluation model.

Developed by the U.S. Department of Defense, the NCSC evaluation model has been widely adopted by the commercial sector and most non-military government organizations to protect sensitive information. The security model is based on the overall concept of a trusted computing base (TCB), and follows four basic principles: identification and authorization, discretionary access control, audit, and object reuse.

The implementation of these four principles forms the system's TCB, a collection of security-related features and functions, which can be hardware, software, or a combination of both. A fundamental aspect of the TCB is the concept that, if you can trust all the security features, then the network itself can also be trusted.

There is an overall maxim supporting the TCB, one of "assurance" that the TCB must be self-protecting against tampering and malicious, inadvertent altering and attempts to circumvent it. All security features must be protected from unauthorized access, and all access must be controlled by these features.

To date, no NOS has yet achieved C2 level security (but Windows NT Server and DCE might be coming close). C2 is a defined level for operating systems requiring users and applications to be authenticated before gaining access to any operating system resource. To obtain C2 certification on a network, all clients must provide an authenticated userid, access control lists must protect all resources, audit trails must be provided, and access rights must not be passed to other users that reuse the same items. Let's go over the security mechanisms a modern NOS can provide to meet (and even beat) C2 level security on the network.

Authentication

Are you who you claim to be? The problem of authentication for network services is not specific to the client/server world. In fact, the issues of network authentication are so universal that network authentication systems have existed for quite some time, and several important distributed computing systems include built-in facilities for network authentication. In traditional systems, the OS uses passwords for authentication. NOSs have to do better than that. Any hacker with a PC and network sniffer knows how to capture a password and reuse it. OK, so let's encrypt the password. But, who is going to manage the secret keys? And, can't you just replay an encrypted password?

Luckily, NOSs have an answer: Kerberos. The Open Software Foundation's Distributed Computing Environment (OSF DCE) includes a version of the Kerberos authentication mechanism.

Kerberos, developed by MIT's project *Athena*, adopted the position that it is next to impossible to make sure each workstation on the network is secure. Instead, the project team took it as a given that some impersonation would take place on the LAN and decided to protect themselves against it. The result was a software fortress called Kerberos that delivers a higher level of security than traditional passwords and access control lists. Kerberos is a secret-key network authentication system that uses DES for encryption and authentication. It automatically authenticates every user for every application.

In essence, Kerberos acts as a trusted third party that allows two processes to prove to each other that they are who they claim to be. It's a bit like two spies meeting on a street corner and whispering the magical code words that establish the "trust" relationship. Both parties obtain the magic words separately from Kerberos. Kerberos determines who the users are and what functions they can perform, thereby controlling access to resources such as data and programs residing in files and directories.

The Kerberos protocol, especially with the add-ons introduced by the OSF DCE, fulfills the authentication requirement of C2. It allows servers to trust their clients (mostly PCs) and vice versa. You must remember that we could always put a Trojan horse on the server side, so the servers also need to prove their identity.

Several major database vendors have openly committed to supporting the OSF's DCE and will deliver products in the near future. The support of a network authentication system is a very attractive model to employ for network security, especially from an administration point of view. The reason is that security for all entities on the network, which might include thousands of clients and many servers, is centrally managed by a single secure system.

Authorization

Are you allowed to use this resource? Authorization means the capability to identify and authenticate users, including intruder detection and lock-out, before they access any information on the network. Once the NOS has authenticated the clients, the server applications are responsible for verifying what operations the clients are permitted to perform on the information they try to access (for example, a database server might control access to customer data on a per-individual basis).

In most networking environments, there are three basic user rights or attributes: directory, file, and trustee. The set of trustee rights and attribute assignments is frequently referred to as an Access Control List (ACL). Servers use Access Control Lists to control user access. ACLs can be associated with any computer resource. They contain the list of names (and group names) and the type of operations they are permitted to perform on each resource. NetWare's administration services, for example, make it easy for network managers to add new users to groups without having to specify access rights from scratch. NOSs can easily meet C2's ACL requirements. You will learn more about this subject and mandatory access control also.

Audit Trails

Where have you been? Audit services allow network managers to monitor user activities, including attempted logons and the servers or files used. The audit function usually provides a facility to monitor all users for system usage, and is achieved by monitoring all user workstations and recording transaction activity. Audit services are pieces of the arsenal needed by network managers to detect intruders in their own organizations. For example, they can monitor all the network activity associated with a suspect client workstation (or user). Knowing an audit trail exists usually discourages insiders from tampering with servers using their own user ID, but they can do it under somebody else's logon. Most NOSs support audit trails, and that should make the C2 accreditation people happy. In summary, it looks like C2 security on a network is well within the reach of a modern NOS, like OSF's DCE.

Is C2+ Security Possible on the Network?

Many experts believe you need C2+ security when traffic moves over unsecured wide area networks. How can you guarantee that vital messages are not tampered with? You don't want the data in an electronic fund transfer to be intercepted and rerouted from your account to somebody else's. Modern NOSs, like the OSF's DCE, provide at least two mechanisms for dealing with these types of situations.

1. Encryption allows two principals to hold a secure communication. Each principal must obtain a copy of a session key from a trusted third party (for example, see previous discussion on a Kerberos server). This session key can then be used for encoding and decoding messages. Another approach is to use a public key encryption technique, such as RSA. But encryption might be an overkill in some situations, because it introduces performance overheads and might be subject to government restrictions.

2. Message authentication codes (MAC) or cryptographic checksums, less extreme solutions, ensure that data is not modified while passing through the network. The sender calculates a checksum on the data, using a session key to encrypt it, and appends the result to the message. The receiver recalculates the checksum, decrypts the one received in the message using the session key, and then compares the two. If they don't match, the message is suspect. Without the session key, intruders will not be able to alter the data and update the checksum.

Most likely you will require encryption to provide a secure single sign-on.

Single Sign-On Makes It Easier for the User

Already users are complaining about having to do multiple sign-ons to different servers and resource managers. Modern NOSs provide the technology that allows a user to access any server resource from anywhere, including hotel rooms, offices, homes, and cellular phones, using a single sign-on. How is that done? With Kerberos-like security, of course. You simply log on once, get authenticated, and then obtain a set of security tickets (also called tokens) for each server with which you want to communicate. All this activity is conducted under-the-cover by the NOS's security agents. No password is stored in the login script on the client, and no telephone callbacks are required. It doesn't get any easier, as long as you can remember your password.

Password Security at the System Level

As previously mentioned, the first line of defense against illegal entry into a multiuser client/server system is user identification and authentication. Multiuser operating systems and network operating systems employ user names and passwords to identify and authenticate users when connecting to the system.

The most obvious way, therefore, that someone can break into a system is by obtaining a valid user's name and password. With this information, a cracker can connect to the computer as the user. The cracker then has access to the user's resources on the computer system, which might include access to important files, directories, and databases. The cracker also can exploit holes in the operating system to get other system resources, most notably the system's user password file. If the cracker can break the password file, then the cracker can connect to the system as other users who might have greater privileges.

The problem of password security is certainly not new, and it exists today in both isolated and networked computer systems. For example, a cracker might discover a user's password when:

- The user picks a short password or one that is easy to guess, such as a common word or a spouse's name.

- The user writes a password on a piece of paper next to the computer, where anyone might see it.

- The users trustingly share their passwords with another user.

The combination of a good security policy and strong password management facilities can minimize problems with system password security. A good security policy sets guidelines for minimum password lengths, types of passwords that users should and should not choose, how often users should change passwords, and so on. To back up a security policy, most multiuser operating systems and network operating systems supply password management utilities that the system uses to check for guessable passwords, to force minimum password lengths, and to require users to change regularly their passwords. There are even publicly available freeware programs (for example, Crack for most UNIX systems) that the administrator can use to test the strength of user passwords.

Password Security at the Application Level

Now that you understand the basic issues of password security at the system level, the next step is to understand password security at the application level. Because database systems form the basis of the majority of client/server applications, let's use them as examples. Similar to multiuser operating systems, multiuser database systems have independent identification and authentication mechanisms to protect against illegal entry into the database system itself. Therefore, the same issues of password security at the system level also exist at the database level.

In host-based database systems, a database user at a terminal starts a session on the host computer and then uses the session to start an application on the host, which connects to the database system. Many database systems, including DB/2, Informix, and Oracle, can authenticate database users without database passwords, by using information contained in the host's operating system authentication mechanism. This approach has several advantages. For example, database security administration is easier because it is centralized at the system level, and database security benefits from the password management facilities available at the operating system level. A disadvantage of external host-based database user authentication is that there is one less hurdle to prevent an illegal database entry. That is, once an attacker breaks into the host's operating system the attacker also can access any databases to which the operating system user has access.

In most cases, client/server database systems do not require a database user to start a host session on the database server when connecting across a network to a database. Therefore, operating system authentication is not feasible. Instead, the database server uses internal identification and authentication mechanisms to protect against illegal use of the database system. This could cause problems should you buy off-the-shelf, generic, client/server applications. The vendor generally will place the security in the application and designate the data as PUBLIC. This means that anyone who can use Microsoft's Visual Basic, Access, or Excel could access the data directly.

Unfortunately, most of today's client/server RDBMSs do not have adequate password management facilities similar to those found in operating systems and network operating systems. Consequently, there is no easy way for the database administrator to ensure that users will choose good database passwords and change them frequently. Furthermore, in the absence of a true database password management facility, most of today's relational database systems let users change their passwords by using simple, ad hoc SQL utilities. This is another serious exposure because, unlike operating system password utilities, the SQL utilities usually do not require the user to verify the database account's current password before letting the user change his (or her) password. Therefore, it's very easy to change another user's password.

For example, a manager, using an ad hoc SQL query tool that issues any type of SQL command, decides to get a cup of coffee and leaves the workstation unattended for just a few minutes. An attacker walks by, uses the connected workstation to issue a simple command that changes the password, and then escapes unnoticed. The manager returns and works for the rest of the day, unaware that the password has changed. Meanwhile, the attacker is in another office, connected to the database as the manager, looking at confidential database information such as customer lists and employee salaries!

The appearance of several third-party database password management vendors validates the need for such utilities. One example is BrainTree Technology Inc., which develops password management tools for client/server database systems.

Besides the standard ways of discovering database user passwords, client/server systems introduce an entirely new hole in database password security—the network. As mentioned, it's very easy for a cracker to sniff a network and trap login packets. When clients send user IDs and their accompanying passwords in the clear (not encrypted), it's like giving a cracker the combination to the safe.

These Things Can Help

The basic problem is not that smaller systems lack security and reliability. It is that security measures do not exist automatically as they do on larger systems. You must create them yourself.

The solutions to problems of LAN reliability are generally simple. Among them:

- Maintain a central help desk and provide full-time access.

- Obtain and use the best network management tools to diagnose network problems, before they become severe.

- Make sure all connections remain in good condition.

- Back up data frequently, particularly data on file servers. Keep at least one copy of the backup data offsite.

- Back up the system as well as the software.

- Provide alternate facilities and routes.

- Install uninterruptible power supplies, especially for network servers.

- Install fault-tolerant features; for example, mirrored servers or disk drives. Some network operating systems, such as NetWare, can detect the failure of one drive and automatically switch to its duplicate.

- Make use of available reliability and security features that are generally available in network-oriented hardware and software. For example, on the software side, MS-DOS and OS/2 database management systems are taking on tasks that once required a minicomputer or mainframe. LAN-based database servers offer many standard features of large-system DBMSs, such as rollback and two-stage commit.

However, not all your solutions will be technical ones. Some very effective solutions involve management policies aimed at your organization's most valuable resource . . . people.

A Protection Strategy

People think of crimes as being committed by mysterious strangers: shadowy muggers or scheming hackers. But whether in computers or other areas of life, most crimes are committed by somebody the victim knows and trusts. In business, that usually is an employee. The second most likely cause of data loss is the simple accident—the mispunched key at a critical moment or the cup of coffee spilled on a floppy disk.

Even so, when it comes to security, many organizations focus on protecting themselves from outsiders rather than from insiders. Organizations spend much money on expensive security systems, when they might better spend their time more productively by making sure passwords are properly used, educating their employees on the need for security, and ensuring that backups are performed regularly.

The $64,000 Question

How much security do you really need? That's the $64,000 question to ask when planning for network security. Its answer depends on the answer to another question: "What would the damage be if the most sensitive information on your system was compromised?"

If you answer, "Not much," then you might need only to warn your workers not to write their passwords on stick-on notes. If the damage would be severe, you must do more to make sure your network is secure. What and how much you must do depends on several things, such as security features in the network operating system and applications, physical protection of the server and communications media, and the kinds of threats facing your organization. Many users do not view all these items as a whole. In part, that's because vendors tend to offer piecemeal solutions. These products can respond to one security threat easily, but your system probably has holes somewhere else.

Rate Your Risks

Developing an effective protection strategy requires that you identify the specific risks you face. Classify your PCs and networks on how they are used. Their use usually is an index of the security threats they present. You then can develop a security plan that responds to those risks. This could range from locked rooms for a network carrying a payroll application to regular virus detection on a PC used chiefly for word processing. One company developed a three-level system for classifying PCs and networks:

1. Systems that handled highly confidential data, such as client records and information on corporate strategy.

2. Mid-level systems handling information whose disclosure would not be a serious threat, but whose loss would cause problems.

3. Systems that held only departmental files and personal work.

Once it established the security classification, the company instituted security measures to match. The top-category systems got a security package that included passwords, data encryption, and audit trails. These systems also were physically secure and isolated from other networks. For the mid-level systems, where loss of data is the greatest threat, the company required password access to sensitive files and limits transfers of files and programs. Regular backup also became a priority here. Bottom-level systems often reside on individual PCs, where the emphasis is on regular virus scanning. Some also might require password access.

What You Can Do

Whatever the system, security problems tend to fall into the same few broad categories. Many PC network security problems are the same as those of minicomputer and mainframe security. A few preventive measures will take care of most potential security problems. The major challenge is to make administrators and users aware of the potential problems and inform them of the tools available to solve them.

The two best steps an organization can take are to make regular backups and to set up a system of passwords. Take the time to make sure you have backups that are both available and safe. In particular, regular backups help with the small, everyday problems of lost files and data.

Instituting passwords is probably the most important security measure you can take on any system. But what makes a good password? Most important, it should be hard to guess. That creates an immediate source of conflict with users, because they want passwords that are easy to remember. It also should be changed frequently. Again, this conflicts with users who want to use their password for life, because they thought so hard to create a good one. Even so, enforcing good password choices and limiting their lifetimes is a high-payoff security measure.

There are programs that will run through a password file looking for the most-used ones. Hackers use these programs to find passwords they can use to break into your system. System administrators can use the same programs to identify easy-to-guess choices within their own systems, and get them changed.

Depends on People

Whatever the protection plan, it ultimately depends on your people, not technology. Client education always will be an important element of any security program. The most serious threat to your system comes from inside, not outside. That threat is much more likely to be accidental than deliberate. Typical problems involve acts such as accidentally erasing a file—things that are preventable with proper precautions. Proper training can teach and motivate employees to take precautions. For example, you cannot back up all the files on individual systems from a central location. The users must do that. Consider regular education on the personal aspects of computer security. Back them up with a regular newsletter, or with articles in other company publications.

Don't Overreact

The two most heavily publicized types of security problems, hackers and viruses, also are among the least serious threats to most systems. Security experts estimate that only a handful of hackers would cause deliberate damage to a system. The number of actual virus infections also does not match the perceived threat.

There is, however, the so-called "newspaper effect" that causes many system administrators to worry most about the most highly publicized external threats. The effect is worsened when their bosses ask them how they are dealing with such threats. This often means they give too little attention to the basic measures, such as backups and passwords, which can protect them from the more serious internal threats.

On a percentage basis, the threat from viruses is small. An estimated eighty percent of all damage is caused internally. Still, the threat is real. It can become more serious when a networking project progresses from LANs to WANs. Departmental LANs are closed systems, and many have no external gateways at all. Once you go through a gateway to an enterprise network you've multiplied the number of people who might gain access to your data.

Most hackers gain their access by discovering or guessing commonly used passwords. That means a well-managed password system that avoids common usages is the best defense. Carelessness and ignorance by honest employees make up the largest menace to information security. A survey by the Executive Information Network showed that fifty-five percent of all computer security losses could be attributed to errors or omissions. Dishonest and disgruntled employees accounted for twenty-five percent of losses. External threats, such as natural disasters, caused the remaining twenty percent. That leaves only five percent for all other causes, including invasions by outsiders.

Commonsense Protection

Viruses are a case in point. They exist, but only a minority of all PC users have been victims. One generally recommended protective measure is to get software only from reputable vendors, buy it shrink-wrapped, and avoid public domain software and shareware. If you must download bulletin-board programs, try to limit yourself to those whose source code is available. This lets the system administrator examine for suspicious code.

Because even commercial software has been known to conceal viruses, users should run virus-scanning software at least once a month—more often when users are adding software or sharing a PC. One word of caution, though; virus-scanning software works well and is constantly being improved, but it is not foolproof. Don't rely on this strategy alone.

The Human Factor

The real security challenge for a network administrator is how to manage the human factor. PC users constantly frustrate security professionals with their less-than-careful habits. These are people, for example, who use stick-on notes to post their passwords in plain sight. In particular, those who have come to regard PCs as truly personal tools might not understand that, in a networked environment, they might become responsible for corporate data that needs more protection.

For that reason, many security experts and PC managers say user education is a critical part of their security policies. Training is a high priority, concentrating on such subjects as how to recognize hazards and observe security procedures. Your security training program might, therefore, include sessions on managing change.

A new network is a major change in the way an organization does business. A system is most vulnerable at times of change. It's a time when errors are frequent. A new program disk might contain a virus. Access controls might not yet be in place or might not work properly. Good training should help managers monitor and educate their employees more closely during this period. Your users need to understand that even transferring a file from a floppy disk to a hard drive is a significant change in their system. You wouldn't let your mainframe application programmers install new software without insisting on adequate testing and control over the change.

That means there is a potential hazard they should be trained to recognize. This is one area where security professionals can continue to use their talents in a networked environment. They can maintain the confidentiality, integrity, and availability of the data. This lets the users go about their own jobs.

The Ease-of-Use Factor

This division of labor can help overcome another security problem. Maintaining a high degree of security in a networked environment can conflict with a major objective of downsizing: ease of use. Users often aren't receptive to mandated security procedures. And, more than personal preference is involved here. Often, obtrusive security measures can keep people from doing their jobs effectively. The security features that keep out the bad people can be just as effective—and frustrating—at keeping out the good people. Some information system security professionals don't like to concede that point, but they must.

One solution is to carry out as many security measures as possible at the network level, rather than at individual workstations. This can include the use of a secure operating system and keeping critical components within locked rooms.

Involve Everybody

These measures still won't work if they appear to the employees like edicts handed down from the mountain. Individual departments, and individual users, are intimately familiar with the dimensions of any conflict between security and ease of use. Contrary to some managers' cynical expectations, most employees want to do their jobs effectively. They will resent any security measures, imposed from above, which keep them from doing it.

Involve employees in these discussions. Solicit their ideas for striking the balance. Not only will you have the benefit of their knowledge and understanding, but you will have the enthusiastic participation that comes from a sense of ownership in the results.

Security is not entirely a matter for security officials or information systems professionals. Other people, such as building managers and electricians, also have roles in keeping your resources secure. Include them in your planning. They probably can give you some good ideas about things to do or to avoid to make your system more secure.

Another important measure is to involve the users. To resolve conflicts between security and ease of use, many organizations have set up a cooperative working arrangement in which users can discuss their needs and problems with security and systems professionals. This process can break down resistance and build cooperation by helping each side understand the other. It also gives the participants a sense of ownership in the rightsizing, downsizing, or upsizing project. There's no better way to build enthusiasm and support.

Summary

A client/server system gives users more access to corporate data, and more control over how they use it. This can cause experienced IS professionals to blanch. They worry, with good reason, that some users might lack the knowledge and sensitivity to protect their information adequately from theft and corruption. They also worry because they know that even well-intentioned and informed users might not have the necessary tools to protect their sensitive resources.

If the users' roles are changing, though, so are those of the professionals. Security professionals must shift their emphasis from implementing security measures to providing advice. This is the key to maintaining confidentiality, integrity, and availability while giving employees the vast advantages of greater access to information.

By now, I hope you have realized that some traditional controls, such as proper documentation, technical education, and management approval, are still relevant. However, some traditional controls are no longer relevant for today's communication networks. You should be looking at replacing your reusable passwords with one-time passwords or biometrics. Some old techniques are finding new meaning in network security. Bastions and firewalls provide just some of the ways you can apply old techniques to protect yourself from the outside world.

Implementing security measures should be evaluated using the same methodology you would use for any security decision; i.e., risk assessment. There are always trade-offs involved in the use of technology, especially one as potentially universal in your organization as the use of client/server systems. The challenge, of course, is to find the right balance of risks and costs versus the benefits.

In this chapter you learned about overall security issues. In the remainder of the book you will learn about security issues specific to particular client/server technologies. You begin in *Part 2: The Tools* by looking at development tools.

Select Bibliography

Davis, Peter T. 1994. *Complete LAN Security and Control*. New York: McGraw-Hill.

Ernst & Young. 1994. *2nd Annual Information Security Survey: Trends, Concerns, and Practices*. Cleveland, OH: E & Y.

Hafner, Katie and John Markoff. 1991. *Cyberpunk: Outlaws and Hackers on the Computer Frontier*. New York: Simon & Schuster.

Muffet, A. "Almost Everything You Ever Wanted to Know About Security." Available via gopher at gopher.ind.net as security.faq.txt.

Sterling, Bruce. 1992. *The Hacker Crackdown: Law and Disorder on the Electronic Frontier*. New York: Bantam Books.

Stoll, Clifford. 1989. *The Cuckoo's Egg*. New York: Doubleday & Company.

Additional Information Sources

alt.security (Security issues)
comp.admin.policy (Site administration)
comp.protocols.kerberos (Kerberos authentication server)
comp.security.announce (Security announcements)
comp.security.misc (Security issues of computers and networks)
comp.security.unix (UNIX security discussion)

comp.society.privacy (Effects of technology on privacy)
comp.unix.osf.misc (Open Systems Foundation products)
comp.virus (Computer viruses and security)
sci.crypt (Cryptology issues)

Part 2

The Tools

Every great man is always being helped by everybody, for his gift is to get good out of all things and all persons.

JOHN RUSKIN

Light is the task where many share the toil.

HOMER

4

Securing Rapid and Object-Oriented Development

Larry A. Simon

*He who chooses the beginning of a road
chooses the place it leads to. It is the means
that determines the end.*
HARRY EMERSON FOSDICK

Two new frameworks for speeding application systems development have come to the forefront in recent years. The first, Rapid Development, is a fresh approach to managing systems development projects. The second is Object-Oriented Development, a radically new way of organizing the internals of computer systems.

Rapid Development

Rapid Development[1] as we generally know it today is an outgrowth of a key idea developed within Dupont in the early 1980s. This idea, known as Time-boxing, was to turn traditional systems development project management "inside out" by recommending the inverse of accepted practice. Timeboxing firmly fixes the project schedule and makes the deliverable the variable component.

---

[1]Variations of iterative development are commonly known by names such as RAD (Rapid Application Development, a trademark of James Martin) and Accelerated Systems Development (a service mark of Ernst & Young).

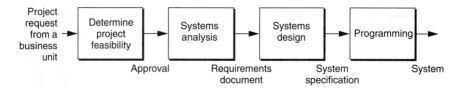

This diagram shows the so-called "Waterfall" model of systems development, which is falling out of favour. The output from each phase is shown as an arrow.

Figure 4.1   The traditional approach

To appreciate the power of this idea, we need first to take a look at traditional project management methodology, as shown in Figure 4.1. The previously accepted approach to constructing a new system was to do the development in a number of distinct phases.[2] The first of these was to undertake a cost-benefit analysis for the proposed system. The requirements for the system, at this point in the process, were rarely understood much more than superficially. Nevertheless, a project plan would be put together, setting out a timeline often more than a year in duration.

The objective of the second phase, Systems Analysis, was then to develop a requirements document, which set out an exhaustive list of all business requirements that the application would need to fulfill. The resulting tome would typically exceed one hundred pages of text and technical diagrams. The objective for the requirements document was in many ways an idealistic one, as only a fraction of the desirable features could be surfaced and captured in practice. People would run out of patience with a seemingly long, abstract documentation process with few tangible results other than pages of unintelligible jargon.

Once the scheduled time for the phase had elapsed, the requirements document would be handed by the systems staff to the sponsoring senior executive for approval. After reading a few pages into the document, and having not understood much of what he or she had seen, the executive would then move on to other business. Not seeing any real alternative, the sponsor would eventually sign off on the document, trusting success to the information technology specialists.

In the next phase, called System Design, the technical solution intended to meet the documented requirements would be planned out. The internal organization of the programs and databases would be designed in this phase. Although supposedly fully fleshed out in the previous phase, additional business requirements would continue to surface throughout the de-

---

[2]This philosophy of systems development project management is usually referred to as the "waterfall model." This is because the phases are like a river between waterfalls. Once you go over a waterfall, you can't return to the previous river section. There is really only one way to go: downstream.

sign phase. As various design alternatives were considered, contradictions and areas in which the requirements had not been sufficiently detailed would become apparent. Seeing rough-cut screen designs would often lead users to talk about details that had previously gone undiscussed, some of which would more often than not prove to have fundamental design consequences. Much rework ensued.

In some organizations, where systems design was considered a purely technical activity to be hidden from the sight of the business managers, the situation was even worse. Alternative design options would not be discussed outside of the information systems organization. The people for whom the system was being built would be largely unaware of the decisions taken until the system was ultimately delivered, at which point they would have no choice but to live with the consequences for years to come. In the worst cases, the specification would be "frozen" at some point in the analysis or design phase, meaning that desired changes after that point would not even be considered.

If the specification wasn't frozen, the schedule would almost always slip as this additional development work was uncovered. The deliverable then became a moving target. Wanting to produce a quality product and genuinely hoping to satisfy their customer, the systems staff would treat all such changes as equally high priorities. The user staff, having no sense for the time or cost impact of their requests, would do nothing to alter such a perception. The project manager would begin to talk about how the scope of the project had changed, but would also promise to make up the time slippage.

As a result, the agreed delivery date would come and the system wouldn't be ready. The project sponsor would then be told that the delay would be at least several weeks in duration.[3]

Now, consider the message that the project staff has sent in this situation. There is no reason for anyone in the sponsoring organization to believe that the new deadline will be any more reliable than the last. An even more uneasy feeling will develop as people begin to question whether the development team could deliver at all. And, they begin to refer to the project as Ishtar, Alberta Tar Sands or Hubble!

Study after study has shown that nine out of ten large application development projects fail to deliver a usable system. A staggering percentage of projects are terminated before completion. With the time frame of these conventional projects spanning years, it's no surprise. Business require-

---

[3]In the early 1980s, a researcher once tracked the actual percentage completion for a small number of systems projects versus the percentage completion claimed by the project manager. He discovered that, when the project manager claimed the project was ninety percent complete, it was actually about fifty percent done. Even more interesting is that the number climbs to ninety-nine percent at about eighty percent actual, drops back to ninety percent shortly thereafter, then climbs slowly back to one hundred at one hundred percent.

ments are sure to change significantly over these time spans, making such projects an attempt to hit a moving target. As the pace of business change increases daily, the problem is only becoming worse.

Rapid Development, as shown in Figure 4.2, has evolved as a response to this problem. Following are the six key differences, summarized in Table 4.1, between conventional development project management and Rapid Development.

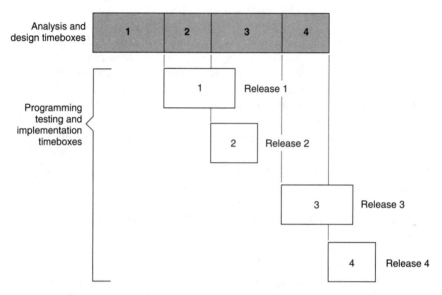

This diagram shows the Rapid Development approach. Deadlines, once established, are fixed. The output from each analysis and design timebox is one or more of (in order of preference): (a) a prototype which can be converted into a production version with minimal tuning, (b) a CASE-based design model, (c) a working prototype, (d) a mockup of the system, or (e) a specification for an implementable release.

Figure 4.2 Rapid development

TABLE 4.1 Differences Between the Conventional and the Rapid Development Approaches

Conventional approach	Rapid development
Distinct phases	Iterative
Linear schedule	Timeboxes
IS-driven	Partnership between users and IS
Specify then program	Prototype, then use while prototyping some more
One large project	Many small simultaneous projects
Hand-coding	Sophisticated tools

1. Iteration rather than phasing. Rapid Development's most fundamental distinction is the absence of the specific period of time in the project plan when the information systems professionals "go away" and write the system. There is never a "frozen" specification. Instead, the software is "grown" in an evolutionary fashion, adding function incrementally and in priority order.[4] This is what is referred to as "iteration." Rather than trying to develop the entire system in its entirety in a single pass, a solution which will solve the immediate problem is built first, then elaborated. Distinct parts of the system might be constructed simultaneously by multiple teams. As requirements are surfaced, they are immediately assigned priorities and implemented or deferred. The approach recognizes that design is incremental; people can't envision something as complex as an entire computer system in its final form, especially when starting with a blank slate. People are always better at improving a rough design than at beginning one. To capitalize on this fact, a throw-away prototype (which, in the classical approach, would not be created until late in the Design phase) is often built as one of the first activities of a Rapid Development project.

2. Small teams. What would have traditionally been managed as a single three-year, fifty-person, $30 million project becomes a portfolio of overlapping five-month, five-person, $400,000 projects. Rapid Development projects are no more than four to six months in duration, and are staffed with no more than six full-time team members. Small is beautiful when it comes to rapid systems development. The approach faces up to the past experience that large systems projects are inherently unmanageable, and so it insists that you avoid them altogether. Rather than attempting to schedule activities beyond about a year, the project team recognizes that the target will drift too much over that time period to allow meaningful advance timelining out that far.

3. Joint user/systems responsibility. Rapid Development projects depend on partnerships between business and systems personnel. One or more people from the sponsoring business unit will need to be on each team full-time. These jointly staffed teams report to an appropriately skilled project manager, who could be from either organization.

4. Use of prototyping tools. The project staff uses prototyping tools to do screen and report layouts as they gather requirements and design the user interface. Staff who will be hands-on users test design alternatives to see what will work in day-to-day use. Screens presenting essentially the same information might need to be designed differently for different

---

[4]"Priority order" includes the notion of precedence in addition to business importance. "New reporting" might be the number one priority of the board of directors, but can only come after the feeder systems that gather and reduce the data to be reported have been built.

audiences, and this is taken into consideration. Ideally, the prototyping tools used are powerful enough to allow the prototype to become the final production system, without requiring a separate coding step. CASE and fourth-generation language tools are often used to allow direct generation of the production system from the prototype.

5. Warrooms and workshops. As much information as possible is gathered through group workshop sessions rather than through interviews. JAD[5] sessions are used extensively. A "warroom" is permanently reserved for the exclusive use of a small number of related teams. Team members use this room as a meeting place to exchange ideas, display work in progress (prototypes, process and data models, timelines, mockups)[6] and to conduct the JAD sessions.

6. Timeboxing. A timebox is simply an agreement that a team will deliver a quality product, meeting previously agreed-to business objectives, on an agreed date. The analogy sometimes used is that of an evening news broadcast. Every night, at precisely six o'clock, your local television station delivers exactly the same number of minutes of news. Every activity that the news team undertakes through the day is focused on meeting that objective. Sometimes the news is more engaging than at other times, but a polished, professional product is always delivered at the appointed hour. With timeboxing, each project within the overall portfolio has a strict deadline. Each project delivers a usable, debugged, tested component of the system on the agreed date. If something has to give to meet the date, that "something" will be advanced system features or user interface cosmetics. The delivery date is sacrosanct.

Applied to systems development, the overall idea is to have many precisely timed minor releases rather than widely spaced, late, major ones. Each release must still be high quality. It must be usable, reliable, error-free, and must demonstrate reasonable performance. The focus of the first project of a series is on features that are necessary to handling core transactions. Subsequent releases build on each other, so that noncritical, but still desirable, features can be added if cost- justified. If other work proves to be

---

[5]Joint Application Design is a technique that was developed at IBM in the 1970s. Originally used to describe a session in which systems staff and users jointly fleshed out requirements, it has now come to mean just about any workshop session involving representatives of both groups.

[6]It is a useful technique when pictorial techniques such as data flow, entity or object diagramming are being used to have the models be taped up on the walls. It doesn't take very long before managers start dropping around to look at them, and are soon asking for copies for their offices. This is when momentum really starts to build. Comments like "This is the first time I've really understood how our business operates!" begin to come out. When an accounting manager sees the complexity of some of these models, he or she begins to appreciate the complexity of systems development, and expectations begin a process of self-management.

of higher priority, however, resources will be able to move to the new key areas rather than getting stuck focusing on relatively low-return activities that are difficult to abandon because the overall design depends on them.

Security and Management Issues

Along with advantages of the Rapid Development approach come a series of unique or heightened challenges.

- Securing the warroom. Depending on the nature of the project, there could be a need for warroom security measures. This would be contrary to the whole objective of the warroom concept, and is to be avoided if possible. Care should be taken to apply security measures only to the extent necessary for the protection of truly proprietary information.

- Lack of formal specifications. The absence of detailed requirements documents makes these kinds of systems somewhat more difficult to audit. When using the Rapid Development approach, quality is measured in terms of sponsor satisfaction rather than as conformance to written specifications. Given that traditional specification documents were typically incomplete and inaccurate in any case, conformance testing never did yield much assurance.

- Testing and performance. Automated testing is growing in popularity and becomes critical in Rapid Development. A long acceptance testing cycle would be contrary to the objective of reduced systems delivery time. Nevertheless, regression testing is critical, and throughput (or "stress") testing assumes an even more important role. When the programs are written in a fourth-generation language rather than a standard commercial third-generation programming language (for example, COBOL or C) performance can be a key issue.

- Scope creep. The tendency in systems development projects is to slowly expand the project scope as relationships with out-of-scope business areas become apparent. The argument in favor of the traditional approach is that it effectively controls scope creep by freezing the specification at some point. Rapid Development recognizes that this is an unacceptably simplistic solution. As a result, scope creep can be a serious issue and must be carefully managed. Continuous testing of costs and benefits of added work needs to take place.

- Burnout. This kind of work is intense. The rigid deadlines instill a new urgency in team members. It's an energetic environment, wherein both business and systems staffs must learn to work closely together, although used to radically different languages and focuses. Hours tend to be long. Vacation time should be scheduled well in advance. Yet, even with the rigors of participation, most team members will look back on their time on these projects as high points in their careers.

- Tool reliance. The tools used must be bugfree and must produce a stable production-grade system with acceptable performance. Tool problems can bring a project to a sudden and lasting standstill. Vendor tool support is key.

- Need for higher-skilled staff. Rapid Development projects require staff with higher skill levels than do conventional projects. Team members need to be able to work well together in a pressure situation. They all need to be comfortable with the development tools being used on the project, most of which have very steep learning curves. An ideal team would have the following characteristics, several of which could be represented in a single person.
  ~An innovative, conceptual thinker
  ~A detail-oriented thinker
  ~Someone with broad knowledge of the business
  ~Someone who intimately knows the business processes affected
  ~A facilitator
  ~A tool expert
  ~A systems analyst/modeler/architect
  ~Someone with project management skills

- Coordination between teams. The various teams involved in a large system will be working on separate but related components. One team, for example, might be working on the employee hiring subsystem. A second team could be working on the payroll component. There is a need for coordination to ensure that data generated by one subsystem will be compatible with the others. If the project teams are using formal modeling techniques (such as data or object modeling) the models need to be reconciled. This role is cross-team in scope.

- Infrastructure costs. The additional cost associated with sophisticated prototyping tools, reserved facilities, and full-time participation cannot be ignored. Some of these costs are infrastructural in nature, however, and should be allocated over several projects.

Object-Oriented Development

The second innovation we will explore in this chapter represents a true paradigm shift. Most working programmers today have been taught that systems consist of two independent components, data and process. Data are simple facts about the business and its environment; for example, a customer's name, an account balance, an employee salary. Process is the collection of computations that convert one or more pieces of data into others, such as the calculation of an employee bonus or of taxable income. Some systems development methodologies carry this notion so far as to recommend that requirements gathering for data and process be done by different people with different skill sets.

Just as timeboxing is almost the exact opposite of standard project management practice, Object-Oriented Development turns programming dogma on its ear. The object-oriented view is that computer systems should be software analogs of real-world systems. Why? Real-world systems have had the benefit of millions of years of evolution. Nature has tried almost every conceivable systems organization, natural selection weeding out all but the best ones.

Let's take a moment, then, to reflect on the systems of the living world. Nature consists of a vast number of discernible subsystems, highly dependent on each other. For example, a body consists of trillions of cells. The cells all have one or more specific life functions they carry out, like producing hormones or moving bones. The activities they perform to fulfill their functions are analogous to a systems developer's notion of process.

Cells are also each in some particular state (e.g., dormant, reproducing, growing). This is equivalent to saying they contain data.[7] They also need to coordinate their actions, so cells communicate with each other. They send chemically encoded messages back and forth to evoke specific behaviors in each other.

This way of describing nature works at other scales as well. An entire animal, for example, shows the same characteristics. It is a distinct unit in some (rather complex) state, can undertake processes which will change its state (for example, by eating), and has a mechanism for communicating with other animals.

The revolutionary idea behind Object-Oriented Development is this. If software is intended to record and process knowledge about the real world it ought to be structured in such a way that you can easily match up the software components to their real-world equivalents. Because nature has chosen to build things out of distinct units that communicate through messages, perhaps this is in some important way an optimal organization for systems in general.

The ultimate in computer systems analysis would be to find a way of structuring programs which would be so natural that no "translation" from real-world concepts to computer concepts would be needed. Regardless of ubiquitous "computer literacy" programs, most people still have little patience for computer jargon. Systems professionals deal in data structures,

---

[7]Systems (in the general sense of the word) are fully described by some set of variables. The values of those variables at any point in time constitute the system's state and are called **state variables.** As a result, it is equivalent to say that the variables have a specific set of values, and to say that the system is in a specific state.

clipping windows, and normalized entities, not in purchase orders, customers, and invoices.

The beauty of an object-oriented purchasing system is that one can indeed find software constructs called Purchase Order, Customer, and Invoice. These constructs are examples of what are called *classes* in the terminology of Object-Oriented Development. These classes are templates that define the data structure of individual purchase orders, customers, and invoices that the system records and processes. We would refer to the software analog of a specific purchase order as an object of class Purchase Order. You might be tempted to conclude that classes and objects are simply record layouts and individual records by a new name, but as we will see, there are some important differences.

Encapsulation

Classes also define which operations are valid for the type of object in question, and the logic involved in performing those operations. Figure 4.3 shows an example of a class definition.

To be really precise, a class is a categorization of similar things that we are interested in storing information about. A class isn't the collection of actual group members, though it is a template for a generic member; it defines

Class name: Customer	
Attributes	Methods
name	change credit limit
address	print customer information
birth date	generate form letter
credit limit	print transaction history
home phone number	archive
business phone number	change customer address
transaction history	change customer phone number
activity status	update transaction history
	deactivate

This diagram shows an example of a class definition. A class has a name, a list of attributes and a list of methods. The attributes can be simple data elements or complex objects in their own right. The methods are the set of valid operations one can perform on an object of this class.

Figure 4.3 A class

what kind of things we are interested in grouping, and describes what we need to know about each member of the group.

The items grouped don't need to be physical things, such as people or documents. They also can be conceptual in nature. An object-oriented system to assist computer auditors might be built using classes such as Account, Transaction Stream, Security Objective, and Control, all of which are abstractions.

Classes tend to fall into two major categories. In addition to the business-related kind (our examples so far), they also can be real or conceptual things in the realm of computers and operating systems. For example, Disk, Window, and Menu are classes you would likely find predefined in an object-oriented programming system such as Smalltalk. As a result, people sometimes speak of objects of the two types of classes as *business* and *technical* objects, respectively.

The description of a class is not complete until we have identified the operations that can be performed on objects of that class. This is what makes a class quite different than a simple record layout or data entity type. These operations are referred to by various names, depending on the methodology or object-oriented programming system being used. Some methodologies refer to the operations as *methods*. Others call them *services*. Regardless of what terminology is used, the key is that the only way to see or alter the information "inside" an object is through these operations. These ideas, that data and computation are bound together and that an object's data is protected by a layer of services code, are collectively referred to as *Encapsulation*. Encapsulation is the first of three characteristics a programming language or systems design discipline must employ in order to be fully object-oriented.

I will use the term *method* to refer to the program code that implements a particular operation. Although people often talk about the methods as if they were part of an object, they are actually stored as part of the object's class definition. Because all objects of a particular class will have exactly the same methods, there is no point in actually duplicating the code in each object. It is stored only once, as part of the class, where it is invoked when needed. We say that the set of methods for a class defines how an object of that class will behave when its various capabilities are called upon. As a result, the methods for a class are sometimes collectively referred to as the class's *behavior*. An object's behavior is invoked (that is, a method is executed) when some other object sends the first object a message, bearing the name of the method to be executed.[8]

---

[8]Usually, optional parameters can also be attached to a message. For example, the "change credit limit" message would also contain the new credit limit amount.

Inheritance

Code reuse has been the holy grail of systems development productivity since computers were invented. The concept of the subroutine was born almost simultaneously, as the first attempt to encourage reuse. Later, as assemblers and third-generation languages such as COBOL came on the scene, other ways of easing reuse were devised. Mechanisms were provided for automatically inserting standard, often used code fragments into the right place in programs. Even though most compilers provided these kinds of capabilities, many programmers still preferred to take a copy of an entire working program as a starting point for a new one, rather than use the compiler facilities to copy in just the common routines. Unfortunately, any undiscovered bugs in the duplicate program were then replicated in the new one. If such an error were eventually discovered and fixed in one of the these programs, it would likely remain uncorrected in the others, waiting to strike again.

Making reuse happen is, in fact, largely a management issue and not a technical one. Even with macro or "copy book" kinds of facilities, almost three-quarters of application code written in large companies duplicates already-existing program code. Various tools have come and gone, each billed as solving the reuse problem (e.g., data dictionaries, and repositories), and now some people are putting forward object-oriented technology as the solution. As you shall see, object-oriented programming systems, through the inheritance mechanism, provide a way of achieving a high level of reuse, but only when the discipline to use inheritance properly is present.

To understand inheritance, we must first look at the hierarchical nature of classes.[9] Let's say you were examining an object-oriented human resources system for a hospital. What classes would you find? It's a fair bet that you'd see a class called something like *Employee*.[10] You would expect that the data elements associated with employees would be identified as part of the definition of the Employee class. You also would expect, because of encapsulation, to find all the code associated with processing changes in employee status. Operations to handle the hiring, terminations, promotions, and salary adjustments of employees would be typical components of the Employee class definition.

Now how about employee subgroups? There would probably be additional information that would need to be recorded for doctors, for example. The hospital administration would no doubt be interested in the year each doc-

---

[9] Groupings are not necessarily hierarchical in nature. Many object-oriented programming languages, however, require that groupings be treated as a strict hierarchy.

[10] The convention being used here is the one employed in the Smalltalk programming language. Class names are capitalized, method names begin with a lowercase letter, and if the name of a class or method is longer than one word the words are strung together (for example, AdministrativeStaffMember, calculateDeductions).

tor was licensed to practice, among other things. The hiring rules for doctors would also be somewhat different than those for other staff. Specialized methods would be required to deal with those differences. So we would expect to see a subclass of Employee, called something like *Doctor*. Doctor is where the differences in data and methods between Doctor objects and other Employee objects would be specified.

Because Doctor would be identified in our human resources system as a subclass (i.e., a more specialized kind) of Employee, the object-oriented programming system that the application was written in would then interpret this to mean that all the data and rules associated with Employee also apply to Doctor. The exception would be wherever Employee's data and methods were explicitly overridden by new data items or methods in the Doctor subclass. This automatic mechanism is Inheritance: Doctor inherits the data and code of Employee. This is one of the key sources of power of the object-oriented approach. If a class behaves similarly to an already existing class, the programmer can make the new one a subclass. He or she then needs only to program the differences in behavior from the already existing class, not the entire behavior from scratch. Figure 4.4 provides an example of hospital class hierarchy structure.

One could then imagine a whole tree of such relationships.

Polymorphism

The third characteristic that distinguishes object-oriented languages is *Polymorphism*. Polymorphism means having the ability to send copies of a message to two or more objects of different classes and having them respond in different ways. Continuing with our hospital system, let's suppose that the

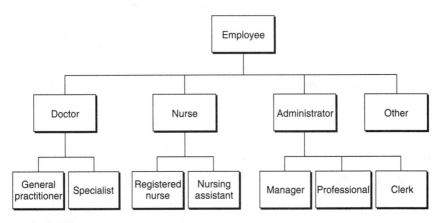

This diagram shows a possible class hierarchy structure for hospital employees. Note that this shows how employees are categorized, not what the reporting relationships are.

Figure 4.4 A class hierarchy example

hospital has a policy of announcing doctor promotions in a local trade publication. Let's say the promotions method is invoked by sending the message "promote." If we send this message to an object of class Doctor, let's suppose the system prints off a promotion notice to be mailed to *Hospital News*. If the object is of another class (but still a subclass of Employee, of course), perhaps only an internal notice is generated. So, Doctor objects behave differently than other objects when sent this message.

This is another very powerful facility for a programming language to have. Consider how this situation would be handled in a conventional programming language. Employees who are doctors would probably have a special code identifying them as such. The programs of the system would be littered with tests to see if the record being processed was one with that special code, so that the appropriate processing could take place. If the coding scheme changed, or if the processing needed to be altered, a programmer would have to go looking through the entire system to find all the places where variables holding the special code were compared to the "doctor" code. There could be dozens of such comparisons sprinkled through a million lines of program code, and they could be tough to spot.

But with an object-oriented system, there is no need to use such special codes to mark particular types of objects. When it comes time to promote a doctor, some other object sends the "promote" message to the object representing the doctor to be promoted, and the appropriate method for promoting a doctor is automatically invoked (because the object that received the message was of class Doctor). On the other hand, if we were promoting some other kind of employee than a doctor, a different method (whatever was appropriate to the class of the receiving object) would be invoked by the "promote" message. Whatever processing is associated with the "promote" method of an object's class is what gets invoked when the object is sent the "promote" message.

The beauty of this feature is that the programmers responsible for maintaining the system will know exactly where to look if the rules around promoting doctors change—at the "promote" method of the Doctor class.[11] The programming efficiencies that result are enormous, particularly once the system is out of development and into maintenance, where the programmer's knowledge of the overall system is often quite limited.

Security and Management Issues

Encapsulation as a security feature

Encapsulation provides a natural way of building security into a system. First of all, the fact that data in an object cannot be directly accessed pro-

---

[11]Or possibly the classes above it in the inheritance tree.

vides some security in and of itself. Any method that reveals data within an object can have security measures built into it. Most object-oriented languages provide a facility whereby a programmer can check the identity of an object making a request, and one could use that information to verify that it has the appropriate authority. What differentiates this from other approaches is that the programmer knows there is no other way that code anywhere in the system can get at that salary figure, except through the secured method.

Inherited security

It is possible to secure a large variety of types of objects by making use of the inheritance mechanism. By securing Employee in some manner, all of its subclasses should inherit the same security features. A loophole to keep in mind is that, as we have seen, a method can be overridden by re-specifying it in a subclass. If a different method with the same name is placed in a subclass, it takes precedence for that subclass and all its descendants in the inheritance tree.

Object generations versus formal releases

By structuring a system in object-sized packets rather than programs and databases, it becomes possible to add capabilities to a system in an object-by-object fashion, without necessarily requiring formal, staged releases. If the programming staff of our hypothetical hospital wished to introduce a new Doctor object, they could create a subclass of Doctor (say NewAnd ImprovedDoctor), which would inherit all of the capabilities of the existing Doctor class. The programmer could then add new methods to perform new functions, and override existing methods with updated ones. If created properly, objects of this new class will behave just like the old object (or in compatible ways) when sent messages by other objects. As other application objects were also upgraded over time, with code that calls on the newer methods of the NewAndImprovedDoctor objects, the new features would be brought into use as needed.

Using object-oriented programming systems is one way of meeting the prototyping tool requirements of Rapid Development.[12] The two techniques, when used together, form a particularly powerful combination, enabling significant improvements in systems quality and timeliness.

---

[12]In fact, the two approaches work so well together that some authors claim that iterative development is the only way one would ever build an application using object-oriented programming. The fact of the matter is that a development project using object-oriented techniques can be either iterative or phased, depending on the nature of the project.

Testing objects

Many of the traditional testing strategies for software work just as well with objects. Stress and regression testing, for example, can be done in the same way for object-oriented systems as for more conventional ones. Use of objects would appear to enable a more structured approach to testing, however. Each method appears as if it could be tested in turn, providing a high level of assurance that most of the "threads" through the code have been tested. One could imagine that we might soon see specialized object testing tools that automatically exercise each of the methods of a particular class of object in turn. Unfortunately, things are not quite as straightforward as they might appear at first glance. One difficulty is that the order in which the methods get called matters. For example, what happens when the "pregnancyLeave" method is called before the "setNewHireInfo" method is used to set the gender (let alone the name and address) data element inside Employee? Should Employee's developer simply assume that programmers working on other objects in the system will never make the mistake of attempting to call on pregnancyLeave before setNewHireInfo? Or if not, what should the pregnancyLeave method do in this case? These are design decisions that will need to be handled by the developer, and which will have implications for the testing approach.

But the problem is still more fundamental than this. The reason that the order in which the methods get called matters is that the state of the object at the time the method is invoked matters. This means that it isn't sufficient to simply test a class and its methods; actual representative objects of the class need to be tested. A representative sample of typical objects could be tested, but in general, no universal test of all possibilities can be created, as we would have to test all (or some large sample) data value combinations for each method. You might yet see specialized object testing tools, but much of what we already know about testing nonobject software is still applicable.

Library facilities

A growing list of tools now provide workgroup development features, managing code being worked on simultaneously by a number of programmers. These tools allow classes to be grouped together into applications. Application boundaries are less distinct, however, when systems are object-oriented. A class such as Employee can be part of what would traditionally be several applications. The way this is typically handled is that the application groupings are allowed to overlap. These tools are helpful in managing releases of applications and classes.

Reuse

As mentioned, it is often said that object-oriented languages promote reuse of code. Through reuse, the object-oriented approach achieves its productivity gains, reported in some cases to be as high as 5:1 over conventional languages. You've seen an example of this reuse already with our Employee and Doctor classes. Doctor effectively reused, where appropriate, the code already existing in Employee. The programmer needed only specify what differentiated a Doctor from an Employee in order to code the Doctor-related processing.

There is nothing in an object-oriented programming system, however, that forces a programmer to write truly object-oriented applications. Even in a highly Object-Oriented Development environment like Smalltalk, where the interface to the operating system goes through a purely object-oriented layer, it is possible for a programmer to write what is still essentially a data-and-procedure application. As a result, code which is billed as object-oriented need not be any more reusable, or make any more use of reusability features, than conventional code. Languages like C++, which are extensions of nonobject-oriented languages, are particularly likely to encourage lapses into a conventional style.

Good object-oriented programmers, in fact, spend much more time reading code than writing it. They go out of their way to look for opportunities to make use of previously existing code. In order to reuse code, they must first be able to find similar existing code. They then need to verify that it will handle the new situations being coded. The inheritance tree gives some good clues as to where to look. When they develop new classes, they attempt to make them general and flexible so they can be reused by others. This requires a substantial time investment, and undisciplined developers will not make the extra effort.

Reuse can actually be achieved in any programming language, with appropriate code librarian tools, when people are willing to trade off short-term for long-term productivity. The object-oriented approach simply makes reuse a little easier.

Object persistence and object-oriented databases

In most object-oriented programming systems, objects exist in main storage only. When an application is terminated, the objects are lost. Most object-oriented programs store data in a conventional relational database or in flat files, copying data back and forth between objects in memory and tables on a disk as necessary. Object-oriented databases are beginning to appear, which manage the process of moving data back and forth between disk and main storage in a more transparent fashion. Objects in an object-oriented database appear to an application to be like other objects, except they are persistent. That is, they survive shutdowns of the system. Many of the advanced features of relational databases are beginning to appear in their object-oriented counterparts. The object-oriented databases are, however, less mature technology and need to be managed as such.

Select Bibliography

Booch, Grady. 1991. *Object Oriented Design with Applications*. Redwood City, CA: The Benjamin/Cummings Publishing Company, Inc.

Connell, L. John and Linda Brice Shafer. 1989. *Structured Rapid Prototyping*. Englewood Cliffs, NJ: Prentice Hall, Inc.

COOT, Inc. 1991. *The Smalltalk Report*.

Digitalk Inc. 1993. *Smalltalk, Programming Reference*.

Martin, James and James J. Odell. 1992. *Object Oriented Analysis and Design*. Englewood Cliffs, NJ: Prentice Hall, Inc.

Merlyn, Vaughan and John Parkinson. 1994. *Development Effectiveness*. New York: John Wiley & Sons, Inc.

Parkinson, John. 1991. *Making CASE Work*. Manchester: NCC Blackwell Limited.

Shlaer, Sally and Stephen J. Mellor. 1992. *Object Lifecycles, Modeling the World in States*. Englewood Cliffs, NJ: Prentice-Hall, Inc.

The Client

Nothing is more satisfying than when timing and delivery occur in perfect sequence.   ANONYMOUS

If you want good service, serve yourself.   SPANISH PROVERB

5

Securing the Desktop

Cheri A. Jacoby and Denise A. Silon

*The reason the way of the transgressor is
hard is because it's so crowded.*
KIN HUBBARD

As the primary front-end device in either a two- or three-tier system architecture, the desktop component of a client/server system is typically the least mature with respect to security. To fully appreciate this lack of sophistication we need a definition of the desktop, complete with a historical understanding of its use over the past several years.

The client/server desktop typically consists of a personal computer which comprises both hardware and software. The desktop software typically includes two parts, the operating system that controls the internal processing of the PC and application software. In the client/server environment, application software is split among the various hardware components of the system overall, so that the desktop receives only a small portion of the programming logic necessary for the system to run as a whole. The desktop portion of the application software is known as the presentation logic, or graphical user interface (GUI). According to the MIS Training Institute & Entellus Technology Group, Inc. document entitled *Audit and Security of Client/Server Architecture: Client/Server Audit Program*, the GUI basically:

> contains the programming logic to control how and what a user sees on their computer screen. The GUI is developed by an application designer using a programming language like C++ or by using a front-end tool like Visual Basic,

Powerbuilder, SQL Windows, and etc. Each of these front ends allows the developer to set up a Common User Interface (CUI) usually under Microsoft Windows. This allows the user to view the application data in easy to use menus. These menus include such items as popup menus, check boxes, buttons and data windows. Each of these are combined on the CUI to allow a user to select what they want when they want.

A variety of desktops, described by the operating system employed, have emerged in the marketplace as companies adopt client/server architecture in increasing numbers. See Figure 5.1 for a projection of the number of desktop systems in use.

Desktop hardware and software contrast markedly with dumb terminals, which were used as the front-end, user devices in the traditional mainframe environment. The inherent attraction of the PC for client/server configurations is its internal processor, which allows the PC to handle processing tasks at a much cheaper cost than the mainframe.

However, the comparison between actual mainframe processing costs and expected client/server costs is somewhat misleading. Keep in mind that, while actual hardware and software costs dropped in price over the years during the mainframe's heyday, the overhead costs associated with developing and enforcing security policy and procedures within this environment diminished the benefit of these savings. And while client/server processing costs appear smaller than their predecessor's, this configuration's true costs are not entirely quantifiable because similar security-related policies and procedures are not yet developed (nor enforced) to

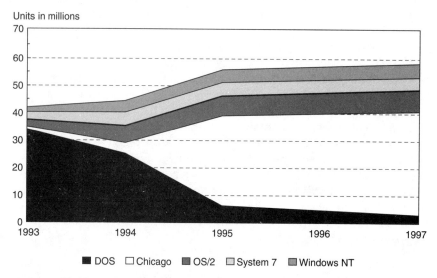

Figure 5.1 Worldwide new shipments and upgrades of desktop operating systems. *(Courtesy IDC, 1994)*

mirror the same high level of security control over this increasingly critical processing platform as exists over the mainframe.

Nevertheless, as corporate culture continues to place a significant amount of attention on at least the server hardware in client/server technology, security for the architecture in whole, including the desktop, must be administered with equal emphasis on all processing platforms of the respective configuration. Furthermore, while security administration is relatively simple for a single server or mainframe, the desktop gives new meaning to security administration when several clients (and possibly hundreds) are included within the security scope.

Whether a company adopts a two-tier or three-tier architecture for its client/server implementation, the security considerations of the desktop remain the same. Only the relative risk associated with the objects on the desktop will change and dictate the types of controls that should be implemented to mitigate this "client/security" risk.

As noted above, the mainframe environment enjoyed the benefits of steady growth for a period of more than twenty years. During that time, user demand for security controls over mainframe systems, and application programs, and data resulted in a market response to develop products to achieve those ends. However, client/server has gained wildly in popularity only since the early 1990s, and its hardware components, including the user-friendly PC, has not been subject to the same security considerations that the mainframe has.

As a result, client/server configurations have raised security concerns among the user group over a much shorter period of time, and the market has not yet had the opportunity to react adequately to this demand. At this point, users are only beginning to realize the need for security control at the PC level, much less demand security enforcement tools from the market. As a result, the security products available today typically address a single security weakness rather than serve as a comprehensive tool for client/security control. Once users are able to consistently articulate their client/security demands, the market will react accordingly. Meanwhile, the client/server user community must wrestle with the existing, single-purpose security products available and apply theory to fill in the gaps that these products leave.

Theoretically, security control objectives in the mainframe and client/ server environment are the same. The main difference between the two processing configurations lies in the sophistication and variety of control mechanisms available, as well as the domain of, and entity responsible for, policing the control.

The remainder of this section will draw a parallel between the security considerations of the traditional mainframe environment and the desktop tier of client/server environments. It will highlight the relative risk of client/ security from three perspectives: general, physical, and logical. Furthermore, it will address the control features available for the desktop to mitigate the noted weaknesses, and finally, it will discuss some of the specific products available in the market to supplement client/security.

Client/Server Productivity and Security Trade-Off

A preface is necessary for discussion on desktop security with respect to the emerging trend toward open systems. According to the *Price Waterhouse Technology Forecast: 1995*, management which has embraced client/server technology must "focus on the trade-off of balancing adequate information technology protection with end-user productivity and the expenses of administering and auditing security across a wide variety of computer systems. With the introduction of open systems and client/server computing, management needs to reexamine the business goals of information technology security in their organizations."

The immaturity of software products currently available, to administer and audit desktop security, necessitates a cost-benefit analysis by management to assess the theoretical, manually enforced measures it will employ to protect its resources at an adequate level. Taken a step further, management must clearly define what constitutes an adequate level of protection per data or application software category.

Notwithstanding the level of security desired, the related risks are significant regardless of the processing platform. From the *Price Waterhouse Technology Forecast: Version 4.0*, they include the "loss of confidentiality, loss of privacy, violations of proprietary and other rights, improper alteration or loss of data and systems, and malicious denials of service." The Technology Forecast continues to highlight the primary goals of information security which are threefold:

1. Confidentiality (i.e., protection against unauthorized or undesirable disclosure)

2. Integrity (i.e., protection against unauthorized or undesirable modification)

3. Nondenial of service (i.e., protection against undesired degradation of computing or transmission resources)

The strategic and tactical methods discussed in the remainder of this section will meet the security objectives noted in the above model.

General, Physical, and Logical Security Domains—A Definition

Computer security is defined by three, distinct domains that are mutually dependent as depicted in Figure 5.2; these domains are general, physical, and logical security.

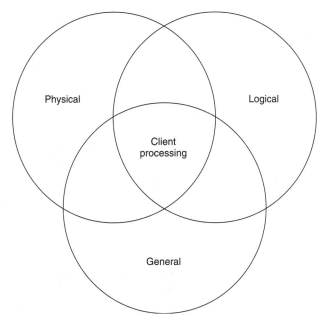

Figure 5.2 Interdependency of security domains.

The general security domain is best described as the overall control environment of a company. That is, it comprises management's attitude and policies about security controls to aid in the protection and distribution of its information assets. General security is the most pervasive of the three domains, but is the more difficult strategy to develop and tactically exercise.

The physical security domain is the strategy employed over the protection of tangible, desktop hardware and media. In the client/server environment, the physical security domain is not simply limited to the confines of a data center that traditionally housed the mission-critical mainframe processor, nor is it limited to this data center that might now, and ideally should, house the server hardware. Instead, the physical domain and related tactical security plan of client/server processing must include in its scope the multitude of desktops that are spread out over a large geographic area, making them administratively difficult to identify and track. A direct correlation exists between the physical proximity of client hardware to the administrator, and the effort required to track its movement and relationship to the system configuration. Furthermore, a direct correlation exists between the number of desktops and the effect that physical abuse, accidentally or intentionally afflicted by the user community, has on the performance of the client/server system. In contrast, the mainframe physical domain standard of control requires that the processor remain protected from casual user contact within the data center, substantially reducing the system risk although the number of users is equal.

The logical security domain incorporates the variety of security software features and controls that are available to promote confidentiality, integrity, and nondenial of service, such as user authentication via the entry of passwords. Of the three domains, the end user is perhaps the most familiar with the purpose but not the administration of logical security controls. Administration of passwords, computer user identification numbers, and user access was perhaps the responsibility of one or more data security officers in the traditional mainframe environment; the user community was rarely involved in the decision making aspects of this security domain. Again, however, client/security could involve the decentralization of logical security administration to best meet the needs of the client/server configuration and implementation.

These three domains, though distinct, are mutually dependent on each other and, when working together, provide an umbrella that can protect the desktop from the raindrops of the client/server processing monsoon. While each domain plays a critical role, no domain is adequate in and of itself; general security awareness and policies are ineffective without physical and logical tools to enforce the policy. Physical security controls are worthless within an otherwise careless user community. Logical controls over a PC, no matter how artfully deployed, are meaningless if passwords are handwritten on a note pasted to the CRT screen.

As alluded to earlier, it is important to recognize the increasingly important role that the general and physical security domain will play in client/server processing environments. Over many years, the mainframe, which contained all the processing logic and data of mission-critical applications, was secured via general and physical security policies that were developed, administered and enforced by the information technology department in a centralized locale, the data center. However, with the advent of open systems and the desktop processing inherent to client/server architecture, the general security attitude and physical protection of these many desktops, each of which could have an equal impact on the integrity of the system, must expand. Full, strategic implementation of the three security domains requires organizational or cultural change and the willingness of the user community to adopt the significant responsibility which goes hand in hand with the privilege of information empowerment.

No security architecture is completely foolproof, and client/server environments are no exceptions. Because the physical configuration of client/server systems divided into three separate tiers provides an opportunity for a security breach to occur on each of these different processing platforms, potentially affecting the integrity of the entire system of desktops and servers, the risk is high that these three security domains will not be adequately addressed by all processing platforms of the system.

While this section could address the three security domains for the entire client/server environment it will address the desktop only, for this platform in particular is now most susceptible to significant risk as its role in the processing of mission-critical applications increases.

General Risk

General security risk is the risk that the user community, under the leadership and vision of management, will harbor a reckless attitude toward its information resources. The general security domain serves as the foundation of a sound security architecture; the risks must be embraced by the support of management and awareness and commitment by the user group as a whole.

General information risk is relatively well-defined and addressed by mainframe security policies. However, the advent of client/server has identified a true need for the user group to expand its understanding and scope of general security risk to include information processed on the desktop as well. This widening of risk scope requires a significant cultural change for most companies. The desktop, once a stand-alone device for word and spreadsheet processing of noncritical information, is now the front-end device for exponentially more powerful information processing. To draw an analogy, the desktop should command the same general security respect as the front door of the office building, the payroll register or, at the very least, the petty cash box. And general security risk is reduced only when each employee understands the information privilege and empowerment given to them and accepts the obligation to protect that information as they would any tangible asset.

However, although general security awareness is increasing in the client/server community, the implementation of controls generally occurs only after a significant security violation occurs, affecting either the confidentiality, integrity, or availability of information. As is the case in disaster recoveries of other types, some companies don't recognize the need for better controls until an unfortunate episode makes their insufficiency painfully obvious.

General Controls

General controls are best provided when an organization designs a comprehensive set of clearly articulated, written policies and procedures describing the role of information systems within the organization as well as the responsibility of each user with access to these resources. Again according to the *Technology Forecast: 1995:*

> A successful general security program requires a balanced approach, with attention to organizational, cultural, technological and legal factors. Managers

understand the need to establish internal controls. Security is important to the success of an organization because it is fundamental to the accuracy and reliability of information technology systems that support their objectives of internal control reduction, rightsizing and customer service. Information technology security is the only way management can automatically enforce their policy decisions on computer systems for which they're responsible.

Of foremost importance when migrating to a client/server environment, companies should recognize the need to promote a general security awareness among the entire information systems user community, especially the users who work with desktop devices. This awareness should serve the dual purpose of ensuring that all users are on the same playing field and understand the rules of the game; further, the awareness program should deter the increasingly PC-literate types from independently troubleshooting performance and configuration problems of the one-time harmless desktops within their own departments. This awareness program can be enforced by holding employees accountable for their use and misuse of information resources.

Most companies venturing into the client/server environment are more technically sophisticated than other companies, and the chance is great that client/server desktop users are PC-literate. However, the bonus of relative computer literacy among the user community at large carries greater risk at the desktop component in the client/server environment, where the GUI and other key application processing resides. The phrase "a little knowledge is a dangerous thing" is no more evident than when increasingly computer-literate users attempt to troubleshoot performance problems on the PC. The chance that such users might directly access the relatively insecure operating system of the PC to manipulate programs, data, or configuration unintentionally against corporate standards certainly exists. The end result could be a denial of service, one of the situations the third primary security objective attempts to avoid.

This general security awareness program can be adopted by a company via the development of a comprehensive, clear, well-documented set of security policies and procedures that can be introduced in a security awareness campaign aimed at the user community when the client/server environment is introduced. However, awareness alone is not enough—each user of the system, including new hires of the company, should receive training in this policy and, upon completion of training or at least by the time the user is given access to the system, their understanding should be confirmed whereby they sign an agreement to that effect. An organization is better off to deny access to information resources altogether, absent the written agreement of the user to keep these resources confidential and protect their integrity and availability. Even when the implementation of such a control does nothing to deter a user from abusing their information resources privilege, management has legal retribution for breach of contract afterward.

The company must promote a general awareness among the entire user community of the relative security risks associated with the equipment each user will have contact with. In the mainframe processing environment, security policies and procedures more than likely have been defined. However, these policies and procedures might not address client/ server desktop PCs. The user community's previous exposure to PCs typically involves using it as a tool for spreadsheet or word processing analysis; very few mission-critical applications were processed on PCs in the past. With the advent of client/server, however, the user might continue to consider the PC a low-risk processing tool, because the GUI presents them with the same "look and feel" of a windows-based PC. Therefore, management should truly champion a general security awareness program in conjunction with the introduction of client/server, to heighten security awareness for desktop resources.

Physical Risk

Physical risk encompasses the physical security of the desktop. In a traditional mainframe environment, the hardware containing the operating system and application programming logic is contained within a single box, which is confined to a data center subject to years of heightened physical access restrictions. Although some physical risk is associated with dumb terminals connected to this protected mainframe, the relative risk with this device is considerably less than that required of a processing unit, such as the desktop.

Furthermore, physical risk involves not only the potential for accidental or intentional damage to key hardware, but also processing interruption due to human error, disasters, or intentional sabotage. In a simple client/server environment, a many-to-one relationship exists among the clients requiring physical security protection and the server that might receive the historical physical security protection once afforded the mainframe. In essence, the desktop magnifies physical risk to a great degree; the relative risk associated with each desktop unit is minor, but the geographical area under risk, which includes all desktops, is considerably larger. Depending upon the scope of the client/server implementation, the desktop tier might be defined as under twenty units to several hundred of the same. Physical security risk at a minimum involves the tracking of all this equipment inventory throughout the entire geographical area of the system configuration.

Physical Controls

Physical controls, while easily defined, are considerably more difficult to enforce in the client/server environment. Again, an organization must balance the cost benefit of implementing the multitude of sound physical controls available for desktops against the cost of policing the same.

Without question, all desktops should be located in a secure area, under the access protection of locks, gates, guards or human supervision. In addition to this minimum amount of physical control, management should take a physical inventory of all desktops by serial number and geographic location, and should update this list as necessary for movement or upgrades. This list should be supplemented by a network configuration that depicts the same information. Obviously, regular maintenance of the two control lists should occur in tandem.

Two techniques exist to maintain the integrity of the physical inventory listing: *full* and *false inclusion testing*. Full inclusion testing involves the periodic sampling of desktops out in the field, and tracing key information such as location and serial number to the master physical inventory listing. This technique can help information technology management identify departments who have perhaps improperly obtained permission to acquire hardware and pirate software to access information resources. Ideally, a general security policy will discourage such actions, but full inclusion testing will uncover noncompliance with policy.

False inclusion testing involves the sampling of desktops from the master inventory list, and tracing the location and serial number of each item to the physical device in the field. Again, management can easily identify circumstances in which equipment has been moved or is missing against a general policy that requires all physical movement of desktops to be subject to the direct control of the information technology department.

Nonetheless, to the extent possible, a centralized group, ideally the information technology department, should administer physical control over the desktop in conjunction with those in the user community who are responsible for complying with this policy. A physical inventory of all desktops is absolutely necessary to ensure that all units are accounted for and receive the required maintenance during system upgrades.

It has been not at all uncommon for organizations to be completely unaware of the total number and location of all desktops units; local-area-networks of PCs have historically "appeared" in departments, while their users have touted the efficiency of the processing platform. However, these departments lack the sophistication and resources to adequately track all devices and manage the physical security risks of their desktops. Again, the physical protection afforded in the desktop paradigm must shift to resemble traditional mainframe physical controls as much as is feasible.

In addition to physical inventories by serial number and location, management can tag equipment to deter, not prevent, theft. Many fixed-asset application systems that track owned and leased property provide tags to identify the assets; such systems can easily and ideally be used for physical desktop management.

In addition, many products are currently available on the market to physically lock or bolt equipment into place and prevent movement altogether.

Or, the equipment can be simply anchored to a desk using a cable slipped around the table leg. The latter device is not particularly aesthetically pleasing and neither technique promotes the portability of the desktop, which is inherently one of its advantages. Again, management must weigh the cost-benefit(s) of such physical controls.

Physical security also entails environmental controls. As is the case with nearly any computer device, desktops should be neatly organized on a desk, table, or credenza that provides for proper ventilation of the equipment and conceals the system wires and cables, thereby reducing the risk that someone might overturn or unplug the equipment and interrupt the availability of the resource. The company also should discourage eating or drinking around the unit to prevent damage to the processing efficiency or availability of the unit.

One desktop risk often overlooked with regard to physical security is the protection of media, especially with the availability of a floppy drive and diskettes to access the contents of the desktop hard drive. While companies take great heed to anchor desktops to prevent theft, historically no measures are taken to protect backup and other diskettes that contain application programs, GUI, or data. Although a guard might question the removal of a desktop from the premises because its large size would make the theft difficult to accomplish without being noticed, a guard more than likely will never identify the theft of an easily concealed diskette containing proprietary information.

A company can deter such theft by removing the floppy drive of a desktop; however, this means of control will more than likely lessen the productivity of the user and limit the advantages of using a PC as the front-end hardware in the client/server environment. Nonetheless, general security policy should address the protection of not only the equipment and online information of computer resources, but also the physical media upon which it is carried, such as diskettes and hardcopy reports. Ideally, the general security policy should address the backup of critical data, which should not be stored on the desktop where it can be copied to diskette. The three-tier client/server architecture specifically identifies a server as the data storage device so that greater, centralized control can be maintained over this mission-critical data.

Logical Risk

Because of the usage history of the PC, logical security products for the desktop are relatively new and unsophisticated, leaving logical security risk at a high level. Accordingly, the employment of a proper balance of controls within the three domains of general, physical, and logical is critical in the client/server environment. Moreover, as is the case with physical security administration, the effort required in desktop, logical security administration increases.

While a many-to-one relationship existed among terminals and the main-frame, logical security administration was primarily centralized around the mainframe, as depicted in Figure 5.3.

In the client/server environment, security administration is necessary for all processing components of the configuration. Whereas the mainframe was typically the only true processor requiring supplementary security soft-ware, the many desktops connected to the one or more servers in a client/server configuration require security administration as well, as depicted in Figure 5.4.

This task is more cumbersome and complex, given the use of remote and dial-in PCs in the configuration as well.

According to the *Technology Forecast: Version 4.0*, "the proliferation of personal computer and workstation networking is creating increased secu-rity problems in three primary areas: disclosure of data (including pro-grams), alteration of data or programs and damage to equipment." Logical risk involves the potential for unauthorized users to gain access to sensitive information resources, as well as the risk that authorized users can be de-nied access to the system resources.

Logical security risk also encompasses the risk that users will pirate desk-top software in violation of licensing agreements and place it on other desk-tops within the client/server environment, with unknown effects to the

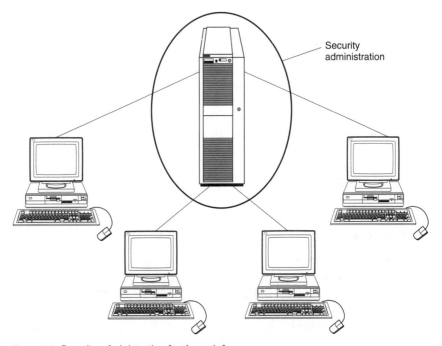

Security administration

Figure 5.3 Security administration for the mainframe.

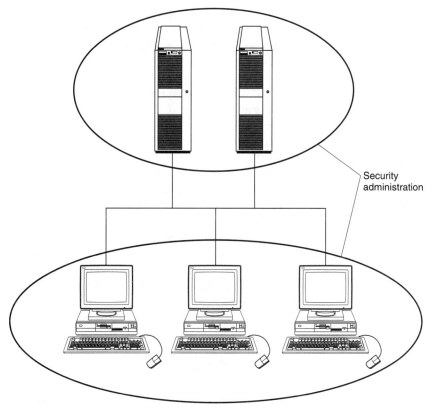

Figure 5.4 Security administration for desktops.

system (possibly including the introduction of a virus). Software pirating can entail the illegal copying of desktop software between devices within the organization, or the introduction of outside personal software or games on organizational desktops.

Naturally, logical security risk increases as the GUI handles increasingly critical functions and processing. With a desktop operating system, the ability to manipulate the programs resident on the device is great. Finally, logical security risk can be defined as the ability for increasingly computer-literate users to tinker with an individual desktop configuration, to the detriment of the client/server system as a whole.

Logical Controls

As noted above, PC users historically have not made strong demands for security-related features within desktop software and the operating system in particular; therefore, the typical desktop operating system is not particularly security-oriented. And although client/server applications might contain relatively sophisticated logical security controls, the integrity of these controls can be violated through the desktop operating system.

One of the greatest risks with desktops is that the operating system is easily and directly accessible to the casual end user, exposing the overall system to a wide variety of risks. Again, while the client/server application might contain a sound security architecture, that architecture might not be enough to counteract the damage of viruses that attack at the operating system level, potentially corrupting the data that is passed to other tiers of the client/server architecture.

However, with the wildly growing popularity of client/server architecture, the market will demand that desktop operating systems contain logical security controls, such as user authentication. Operating system vendors have been relatively slow in providing these features; according to the *Technology Forecast: 1995*, "the goal of system software vendors is to provide a robust platform for the common desktop machine, broadly supported by independent software vendors and widely accepted by end users." This effort is hampered, however, by a general ignorance in the user community regarding the need for logical security controls at the desktop tier, let alone their ability to completely and consistently describe the security features desired.

Logical security is typically defined as the protection of information resources via user authentication, or the use of a password and user profile that permits access to a specific subset of data files and programs. However, logical security controls are much more comprehensive than the scope of user authentication.

However, the desktop virus problem has become widespread. According to the *Technology Forecast: Volume 4.0*, "numerous would-be anti-viral tools have emerged, but all are somewhat limited by their inability to detect and remove hitherto undiagnosed viruses. They are themselves subject to causing further viruses with possibilities for embedded Trojan horses and other unanticipated effects" on the client/server system.

A variety of logical security controls can be employed to combat the risks highlighted in the previous section. A security administrator should be appointed to manage the desktop operating system. This administrator should assign a unique identification account (ID) to each user on the operating system. To the extent possible, users could be identified to the operating system of only a single, physical desktop as an added security measure; however, the cost-benefit of this practice must be weighed because, again, it reduces the practicality of using desktops as the client/server front end.

The security administrator also might use the operating system, or a third party security product, to restrict the number of concurrent sessions per user to one, which would streamline the access audit trail and provide a measure of accountability for access, because user ID sharing will be discouraged. Access to the system might be restricted by time of day or day of the week as well. Tools are available to automatically log a user off the desktop after a predetermined period of nonuse, which is practical for the department in question. In Windows-based operating systems, password-protected screen savers also might serve as logical security controls; note however, that screen saver software is activated only after the initial log-on session is performed.

Once user IDs are established for the system, auditing of user access activity is essential in conjunction with timely resolution of questionable activity. One of the most significant, yet common, logical security weaknesses in organizations today is not the absence of adequate security features but the presence and nonuse of these features. For example, crackers are completely familiar with the security weaknesses of any given operating system. Naturally, their penetration efforts will be spent exploiting these known weaknesses. Should these efforts fail to provide the cracker with a quick hit, he then will move on to the known security features of the operating system or third party security product, which is not used at all or not used properly.

Desktops are extremely vulnerable to cracker activity. To emphasize the importance of controls within the three security domains, casual, physical access to the floppy drive makes it possible for an unauthorized user to load keystroke capturing software onto the hard drive of the machine in an undetected fashion. This type of software runs at the operating system level and does not disrupt application processing. Passwords, which normally are encrypted within the system and masked from view when typed during log-on, can be captured in plain text with ease. The cracker can then return the next day and download the captured data onto a diskette; at which point he can then access the mission-critical client/server software by posing as an authorized user. To mitigate this risk, controls can be employed to restrict a user's access to the hard drive. Such controls would force the presentation of a menu upon successful user authentication, or to at least detect changes made to key operating system files.

Moreover, with respect to the three-pronged security domain discussion earlier in this section, logical security administration can be enhanced by limiting the software that is resident on the PC and making it a corporate policy that only the IS department is responsible for software maintenance, upgrading, and configuration. This policy will deter users from placing unapproved personal or pirated software on a desktop. Such software can affect the processing efficiency of the equipment for business purposes. It might also violate licensing agreements and cause other unknown results, because a single workstation is now working with a version of software that could be out of sync with the client/server system corporate standards.

Ideally, the desktop software should be limited to a minimum of the following: the operating system, virus detection software, desktop application software as is practical and appropriate (for example, WordPerfect and/or

Word), and finally, the client/server-configured GUI designed to place the maximum number of system processing functions on the desktop that are feasible from a processing efficiency perspective.

Nonetheless, different types of operating systems are popular on the market today including MS-DOS, Windows, IBM's OS/2, and Microsoft's Windows NT. Although Windows is the overwhelming market favorite today, it is seriously deficient with regard to security features. Organizations must address these weaknesses with the use of third-party, logical security software as is appropriate, keeping in mind that these products typically address only a single security threat rather than serve as a comprehensive access-protection and violation-detection tool.

However as noted in the *Technology Forecast: 1995*:

> IBM's OS/2 and Microsoft NT both provide a solid basis for access control security. Both use microprocessor hardware memory-protection features to isolate each logical task's address space from other tasks. This type of memory protection is a fundamental integrity and confidentiality mechanism, similar to features available in mainframes for decades. Microsoft Windows NT provides a significant number of security features including password-based user authentication and access controls on objects in the file system. IBM OS/2 operating system implements memory protection; it requires optional security products to add access authentication and auditing, but provides a solid base for development. Both [products] are responding to market demands for better security in multiusers, server and desktop operating systems.

Summary

As users become more comfortable with client/server technology, they will quickly place a high priority on their security concerns with regard to this inherently unsecured configuration. Until vendors are able to provide comprehensive logical security controls over the desktop operating system, the user community must address its security objectives by assessing the risk over the three domains of general, physical, and logical security.

Select Bibliography

MIS Training Institute & Entellus Technology Group, Inc. 1995. *Audit and Security of Client/Server Architecture.*

Price Waterhouse. 1995. *Technology Forecast: 1995.* "Desktop Operating Systems, Level 3.1; Open Systems, Level 4.1; Security Level 4.3; and Client-Server and Distributed Computing, Level 4.5." Menlo Park, CA: Price Waterhouse.

Price Waterhouse. 1993. *Technology Forecast: Version 4.0.* "Architectures: Security," Chapter 4.5. Menlo Park, CA: Price Waterhouse.

6

Securing the Front End

Frank Lyons

We have met the enemy and they is us.
POGO

Every corporation seems to be moving towards a client/server processing environment. The obvious reasons are to reduce the CPU costs and to empower the user. But the real question is, what is client/server computing and what are the exposures that need to be mitigated?

Starting with the first part of the question, one needs to look at the practical definition of client/server. Basically, the client/server environment is structured to split an application's processing across multiple processors, to gain the maximum benefit at the least cost while minimizing the network traffic between machines. The key phrase is "to split the application processing."

In a client/server mode, each processor works independently but in cooperation with other processors. Each relies on the other to perform an independent activity to complete the application process. A good example of this would be the Mid-Range computer, normally called a file server, which is responsible for holding the customer master file while the client, normally the personal computer, is responsible for requesting an update to a specific customer. Once the client is authenticated, the file server is notified that the client needs Mr. Smith's record for an update. The file server is then responsible for obtaining Mr. Smith's record and passing it to the client for the actual modification. The client performs the changes and then passes the changed record back to the file server which in turn updates the master file.

In this scenario, each processor has a distinct and independent responsibility to complete the update process. The key is to perform this cooperative task while minimizing the dialog or traffic between the machines over the network. Networks have a limited capacity to carry data and, if they become overloaded, the application's response time would increase. To reduce traffic, static processes such as edits and menus are usually designed to reside on the client. Update and reporting processes usually are designed to reside on the file server. In this way, the network traffic to complete the transaction process is minimized. In addition, this design minimizes the processing cost, because the personal computer usually is the least expensive processor. The file server is the mid-price component and the mainframe is the most expensive.

Statistics reveal that most corporations are only using ten percent of the personal computer processing power that they have installed. If this is true, then most organizations could continue to exploit the power of the personal computer without investing in new computer equipment. Future client/server applications might further rely on the personal computer by upgrading its memory to 64 Megabytes, 132 Megabytes, or even 500 Megabytes of random access memory (RAM). In addition, if the speed of the personal computer continues to increase, from that of a 486, 33 MHz CPU running at 20 MIPS to that of a P6 chip running at 200 MIPS (and possibly, to one running at 1000 MIPS by the end of the century), you will be looking at a desktop fifty times faster than the desktop of today. If this becomes the standard configuration, many of the application processes, such as sophisticated graphics and virtual reality, will in the future reside on the personal computer. Coupled with the increases in the network's capacity, especially with the implementation of Asynchronous Transfer Mode (ATM), the acceptance of Object Database Management Systems (ODBMS), and incorporating some hybrid of the Relational Database Management System (RDBMS), the client/server architecture will become a predominant implementation strategy to delivery services.

There are many client/server models. First, one could install all the application's object programs on the personal computer. Second, one could install the static object program routines, such as edits and menus, on the personal computer and the business logic object programs on the file server. Third, one could install all the object programs on the file server. As another option, one could install all the object programs on the mainframe. Which model you choose depends on your application design, the speed of your networks, the location of your user base, and the legacy systems you already have installed.

Not only must you worry about the programs and their installation, but you must also decide where to place the data files themselves. Today you will hear about the three-tier architectural model. This means that multiple personal computers talk to a file server, which in turn talks to the mainframe to obtain legacy data to complete the transaction process. This accessing and exchanging of data must be completed within a one- to two-second response time, or less, to meet the service level goals of the application. Within this complex, multiple operating systems, database management systems, and platforms environment, the auditor and security professional must identify the exposures and recommend effective controls to mitigate the risks. In this chapter, we will explore the exposures for the front end of the client/server application.

The front end is called the desktop, which includes the user's workstation or personal computer. The front end is a computer with hardware and software components. Each front end has an operating system to control the activity of the application software. The application software that runs on the front end is called the Graphical User Interface (GUI), or an Object-Oriented User Interface (OOUI).

The GUI contains the programming logic to control how and what a user sees on the computer screen. The GUI is developed by an application designer using a programming language like C++, or by using a front-end tool such as Visual Basic, Powerbuilder, SQL Windows, or Smalltalk. Each of these front ends allows the developer to set up a Common User Interface (CUI), usually under an environment similar to that of Microsoft Windows.

All of this allows the user to view the application data in easy-to-use menus. These menus include such items as popup menus, check boxes, buttons, and data windows. Each of these are combined on the CUI to allow a user to select what they want when they want it. These front-end tools also allow for the interchange of data between popular PC products, such as Excel and the user's application GUI. This interchange is completed by using either Microsoft's Dynamic Data Exchange (DDE), Dynamic Link Library (DLL), or Object Linking and Embedding (OLE). By using this type of interface, the application's GUI can use additional PC products and tools to further enhance the user's ability to obtain pertinent data for a transaction process.

Therefore, one could look at client/server as the vertical integration of data from the old mainframe world, and end-user computing as the horizontal integration of the data on the workstation. This is not an absolute and perfect definition, but from a conceptual point of view it allows us to define the two terms and explain their level of integration.

Each GUI is made up of several screens. The main screen is designed to present a consistent "feel" to the application. The main menu calls submenus, depending on the user's selection or transaction activity. The menus themselves have the ability to attach a programmed routine behind each of the buttons, check boxes, or data windows. These programmed routines are usually written in a script language provided by the GUI tool itself. Scripts are noncompiled versions of a program that are dynamically interpreted to perform a routine. These scripts usually depend on the GUI product being used, along with embedded Structure Query Language (SQL). Within the script one of three activities can be performed: procedures, functions, and objects.

Procedures

Procedures are programmed routines that use some type of programming language, along with a Database Management Language (DML) called Structure Query Language (SQL). These procedures are called from the front-end GUI but are usually stored on the back end on the file server within the Database Management System (DBMS). A user must be authorized within the DBMS to run the procedure. This authorization check is completed in the back end by the DBMS.

Functions

Functions are programmed routines that are very much like procedures, except that they are configured to perform a routine that returns only a specific value to the front-end user. Functions also are stored usually in the back end within the DBMS. Again, the user must be authorized by the DBMS to call the function.

Objects

Objects are programmed (i.e., compiled object code) routines that simplify a process for a front-end application or user. Microsoft's Visual Basic has many of these object types that are called VBXs. You can purchase an object from a vendor to help build applications. These objects remove some of the difficulty of developing client/server applications by providing common routines that are easy to use and incorporate within an application.

Structured Query Language

Structure Query Language is used within procedures, functions, and scripts, but it can also be used directly by the end user to query the DBMS to obtain specific application data. These types of requests are called *dynamic queries*. Dynamic queries can be activated by products such as Microsoft's Access, or in many cases, right from the front end with products such as Powerbuilder. Dynamic queries can be very processing-power intensive, and if not used properly by educated users they can and will increase a client/server application's response time. For this reason, many designers prefer not to allow dynamic queries by end users, but rather to compile procedures and functions to perform limited *static* query retrievals.

What Is a Graphic User Interface?

The Graphic User Interface (GUI) is a front-end presentation display that allows the user to work with a friendly and more robust application interface. The major players that have a significant base in the industry are: Microsoft's Windows, IBM's Presentation Manager (OS/2), OSF's Motif and OPEN LOOK (using X-Windows under UNIX), and Macintosh from Apple Corporation.

GUI features

Here are the general features of the GUI.

- Primary window. The primary window builds the Common User Interface (CUI) for the application or the corporation. This includes the Window's border, window title, menu bar, scroll bar, small icons, and information area.

- Pushbuttons. Pushbuttons allow you to make a selection, such as OK or CANCEL.

- Check boxes. Check boxes are smaller boxes than pushbuttons. They allow you to select certain items within a group, such as a listing of directories or files. Each item has a box for selection.

- List boxes. A list box is a box that lists many entries and allows you to move the cursor down the list and click on an entry, to pick that item.

- Data fields or entry fields. These boxes allow for entering and editing of data. Items such as the customer's name, address, and telephone number can be used within them.

- Text box. A text box is usually used in a word processor to edit the actual text of the document. A good example is a grammar checker within a word processor.

- Menu bars and pulldown menus. These are among the major parts of the window. You can pull down a menu selection and perform some type of activity. For example, the FILE menu might allow you to open, close, or save a file.

- Radio buttons. These are round selection boxes that allow the user to select one of the entries. Each of these items is mutually exclusive, so choosing one button automatically deselects any other button that was already selected.

- Icons. These are picture representations of an item, such as an application, or a table.

- Popup windows. Help screens typically use popup windows to present the help comments.

- Message and dialog boxes. Messages and dialog boxes allow for the display of messages to the end user's interface. These include information messages, warning messages, and action messages.

The GUI interface to the end user is a key component of the client/server application. Because the user will be using the GUI interface for most of his interaction with the application, it is imperative that the GUI be properly designed. Development methodologies and standards need to be written and followed, to help ensure the reliability and usability of the application system.

GUI/OOUI Risks

There are several risks in using the graphical user interface itself, such as Trojan horses, wrong versions, or poor design.

Trojan horse

The GUI (or OOUI) is written in a source code form and compiled into a runtime version. The runtime version is stored on the personal computer, or on the file server, and is downloaded to the personal computer after a user signs onto the network. Because this runtime version can be simulated by an educated perpetrator by using their own GUI tool, a Trojan horse version of the GUI could be installed on the workstation to execute when the user turns on the computer. This spoof version could make the interface look exactly like the network and application front end. But with this spoof program the perpetrator could then capture the real user's ID and password.

Wrong version

Because the runtime version of the GUI resides on either the file server or on the personal computer, the amount of copies of this runtime version *could* be one copy for each end user. With this number of copies out in the field, there is the possibility that some end users might be running the wrong version. Controls should be in place to ensure that, once a GUI is updated, all end users automatically obtain the new version.

Poor design

The design of the GUI is important to the overall effectiveness of the application process. Design methodologies and user usability testing are important, to ensure that the GUI interface does not adversely affect the reliability, security, and control of the system.

Controls

All is not doom and gloom, as following are some controls for you to use:

- Load GUI from the server
- Use a management distribution software product
- Use version control software
- Perform usability testing
- Prototyping

The GUI's Extended Attributes

Of all the error conditions that can occur, the errors and omissions threat still accounts for about sixty-three percent of the total possible threats. Certain features within each GUI tool allow the designer to elaborate on the edits, controls, and security characteristics of the application. These attributes are listed as *potential* controls and will be discussed in detail in the application security section.

Controls

The following are some useful controls:

- Headers
- Initial values
- Validation rules
- Display formats
- Comments

Workstation Risks

As you learned in Chapter 5, a standard personal computer is not very secure without the addition of third party security products. This is because most of the personal computer's password mechanisms can be defeated by a knowledgeable person without much effort. In addition, the personal computer's operating system thinks that the person who turns on the computer owns all the files on the computer itself, and therefore allows the user to access all configuration files and data files without restriction. This might all change with the improved operating systems coming out, to allow for multitasking and multiuser environments under a tighter security system. Until then, application data should not be stored on this platform unless a separate security product is installed.

In the client/server environment the personal computer should only be used to work on select application records for a brief period of time. These records should not be stored on the hard disk of the personal computer. If you do allow the user to store data on the personal computer, then you must perform a data sensitivity or risk analysis to determine the level of exposure in order to install the proper third party security product. Many of these products are on the market. The best ones would not only authenticate the user's activity but would also encrypt sensitive data to the hard disk and to the network.

Unfortunately, the workstation is a cracker's dream. There are products in the world today that either capture the password as it is sent from the workstation or as it is keyed on the workstation. Two of these products that are offered on the public domain are THEFT and GETIT. Both of these products can capture the userid and password from the workstation as a user signs onto the network. These products can be controlled by ensuring that the AUTOEXEC.BAT and CONFIG.SYS files of the disk operating system on the workstation have not been modified to execute these programs during startup. This control can be automated by allowing the file server to interrogate the AUTOEXEC.BAT file during sign-on.

Other exposures are present in front-end products like the Windows Operating System. Windows has a recorder function that would allow someone who has access to the personal computer the ability to turn this function on and record activity including the userid and password. This facility should be removed from the operating environment or a sweep program should be written to automatically clear the storage of the recording function.

Workstation risks—startup files

Startup Files within this environment should be properly protected from unauthorized modifications. This could be accomplished in several ways. One is to download the configuration files from the server when they do not conform to company standards. Secondly, a security software product could be installed on the personal computer to protect the configuration. Files that need protection are the following:

- AUTOEXEC.BAT (DOS environment)
- CONFIG.SYS (DOS environment)
- Startup folders (OS/2 environment)
- Startup files (OS/2 environment)

Workstation risks—the unattended workstation

An unattended workstation could allow an unauthorized user to submit activity as the signed-on, authorized user. The actual application data could be changed or the personal computer's configuration could be changed to spoof the real user. Controls could include PC security software or Time Out software.

Workstation risks—special front-end functions

As previously mentioned, some operating systems have special features built-in that can pose a risk to your workstation, such as recorder functions, trace-type functions within the operating system, and DDE , DDL, or OLE. The best defense is to remove such facilities as Recorder and Trace.

Workstation risks—configuration/inventory management

Nonstandard PC configuration and nonapproved PC software (such as Bindview and Frye utilities) also pose a risk to your workstation, as does inventory control software such as Brightworks.

Network Connection Risks

Usually, within a client/server environment the processors sharing the work must communicate their intentions to each other over a network. To effectively communicate, they must observe a set of rules called a *protocol*. There are too many protocols by various vendors to explain them in detail within this section. You will learn about two such protocols in Chapters 8 and 9.

However, it is worth noting that the communication process actually sends the data across the network in the form of packets that are constructed according to the protocol rules. This means that all the data for any activity that is going across the network is available to read with the use of the proper equipment. Data such as userids and passwords, memos, and files can be obtained and read.

Recently an audit team reviewed nine different authentication processes to see whether the userid and password could be caught in clear text as a user signed-on to the file server or to the mainframe computer. In seven of the cases, the userid and password were obtained in clear text, using a network diagnostic tool called LANalyzer from Novell, Inc. In the last two cases, one being a Novell 3.11 file server and the other the LAN Support product from IBM, the userid and password were encrypted as they went across the wire.

Any product that emulates a 3270- or 5250-type terminal is a one-sided solution that does not normally encrypt the userid or password over the network. Any x-type product, in most cases, also does not encrypt the userid or password. The only way to ensure that your sensitive data is protected is to use an effective encryption solution. You could encrypt just the userid and password, but in this case the actual data that travels over the network can still be captured and read. In this case, the information obtained could be replayed later onto the network to have the file server decrypt it. Or, it could be used to obtain the real password by using a Crack program.

Operating systems such as Novell's new 4.x release (see Chapter 13) are now employing a challenge-and-response system that authenticates the user without sending the password in any form across the network. This implementation is similar to the Kerberos product from MIT. Kerberos works well within the UNIX environment, by only passing the userid to the file server, which computes an authentication key based on the userid and the encrypted password that the file server has stored in its database. The key is passed back to the user's personal computer and the user is required to enter his correct password at the terminal to break the key that, in turn, sends an encrypted response back to the file server. Anyone trying to capture the sign-on process would never capture the real password.

Another one-time password key that cannot be compromised is the S/KEY from Bellcore Morristown, New Jersey. Bellcore has been using this technique for over three years. It is available by anonymous ftp on the Internet.

Client/server environments, along with user mobility, have created an expansion of dial-up services to access application data remotely. For proper controls and as a matter of policy, no user should connect to the network with a remote communication package without approval. All dial-up connections should be userid and password protected. An authentication system, such as LeeMah's TraqNet, should be used to ensure that only authorized users can sign-on remotely.

Oracle will be providing a Secure Network Services, network security for the client/server database environment. Secure Network Services is an add-on package to Oracle's SQL*Net connectivity software. Secure Network Services is based on data encryption technology from RSA Data Security Inc.

Call back or smart cards also should be considered to protect the authentication process. Remember that if a cracker can dial-up to your network, he or she does not need file server access but only network component access (routers, hubs, and bridges) to obtain userids and passwords. All he or she has to do is connect to one of your network components and capture all the messages as they pass through the unit where the hacker has control.

Products like PC Anywhere should be inventoried and evaluated as to their ability to protect themselves from unauthorized use. When and where possible, all these products should be eliminated so a single point of entry can be established to the network. This single point of entry could validate all user and vendor requests to access services.

A communication gateway could be established to define an access control list (ACL) to authenticate all users before any access to the network itself. These gateways, purchasable from companies like Cisco, have filters that can be programmed to verify incoming users before allowing them into the network. Many people call this type of implementation a *firewall*. Many good options are available, but they usually require some level of investment and administration.

Another control implementation would be to implement a stand-alone hardware and software system such as Network Encryption System NES from Motorola, Inc. This solution, and others like it, also would encrypt all the data moving across the network and would eliminate the danger that someone could read the userid/password and data. Freeware products such as Pretty Good Privacy (PGP) also are very popular in encrypting sensitive data across networks.

Network risks—network interface

In order for your workstation to communicate with the file server, the information must be formatted into a packet and sent across the network. The formatting is completed by the use of software drivers. These drivers need to be properly protected to ensure that they perform only the stated task.

An example would be a set of drivers that are very popular is Novell's Open Data-Link Interface (ODI) drivers. These drivers allow for multiple protocols to reside on the workstation and communicate with different file server environments. This driver set implementation allows you to communicate without rebooting your workstation. The NET.CFG file is used to configure the LAN drivers for the different hardware configurations. Another file that allows the workstation to talk with the file servers is LSL.COM. LSL.COM is the Link Support Layer file which enables the workstation to communicate using several protocols. NE2000.COM and TOKEN.COM communicate directly with the LAN (NIC card) boards. Drivers also are called MLIDs (Multiple Link Interface Drivers).

Protocol stacks files such as IPXODI.COM and TCPIP.EXE manage communications among network stations.

Controls

Following are some controls to protect your software drivers:

- PC Security software. This can protect all driver configuration files.
- NIC's ID and PC's ID. Tie the network interface card's ID (NIC) to the physical ID of the workstation. This will ensure that the activity is coming from the proper location.

Database Connection Risks

Client/server computing is based largely on the database management software that supports the applications. From a risk point of view, you need to identify the Systems Manager (System Administrator or Database Administrator) for the database management software (that is, System or Sys for Oracle, sa for Sybase, or Sysadm for DB2).

You also need to verify that the tables holding the application data are properly protected through program procedures or views. This is an important point within the database management software, because it controls who has what access and rights to the application data.

In addition, you need to inventory all program procedures that access the application data, and to review those users with execute authority to be sure they need this level of authority. A program procedure is a compiled program process that allows a user to execute the procedure.

Additionally, you need to review a user's direct view rights to see if his access authority pertains to his job responsibilities. A view is a definition created in the database management system, which allows a user to use a special program product, such as a query report writer, to directly access the data. A view allows the database to restrict the data field and what access rights a user has while using the report writer.

The combination of client libraries and server listeners makes up the database middleware. Each database has its own Application Program Interface (API), and the middleware products allow for the front-end GUI to communicate to the back-end database management system. Microsoft's Open Database Connectivity (ODBC) is by far the most popular API standard at this time. Other popular solution sets are Distributed Relational Database Architecture (DRDA) from IBM, and Information Builder Inc.'s Enterprise Data Access (EDA)/SQL. As the client/server applications grow in their criticality, size, and complexity, the need for transaction processors will become evident. Products such as IBM's CICS or Novell's Tuxedo are transaction monitors that will help in securing the end-to-end communications within a client/server environment.

Database Front-End Risks—GUI

There are risks with initialization files and preferences files.

- ODBC.INI file. The Open Database Connect file allows you to connect to ODBC databases, such as ORACLE, and to manipulate them from within a GUI front end. The GUI interface for ODBC allows the transfer of data between the front-end application and the Oracle database management system. The ODBC interface defines:
  ~A library of ODBC function calls to connect to the back-end DBMS, execute SQL statements, and retrieve result sets.

~A standard way to log on to a back-end DBMS
~A set of SQL syntax
~Standard data type representations
~A standard set of error codes

- PB.INI File (as an example of a Powerbuilder front-end GUI). When Powerbuilder connects to a database, it uses the values set in the Preferences to identify the back-end DBMS and the database by name. The entries in this file can be changed through Powerbuilder, or directly by using a text editor. All the entries in this file are necessary to allow for the proper connection to the DBMS. This file could contain the password of the user trying to connect.

- Other files. Other initialization files are used to connect the application's front end to the DBMS's back end, such as DB.INI or APPL.INI. These files need protection due to the sensitivity nature of the parameters:
  ~ Database name
  ~Password
  ~Database variables
  ~Controls
  ~PC security software

Front-End Application Security

Following are the steps to ensure front-end application security.

1. Determine which GUI product or language the application is using to connect the user to the application system. Using the definitions of the front-end GUI obtain the following:
   - The application name
   - The objects associated with the application
   - Procedures
   - Scripts
   - Functions
   - User or system objects
   - The menus associated with the application, along with the:
     ~Edits
     ~Rules
     ~Conditional Variables
   - The database(s) associated with the application and where the data is stored. The storage of information could be on a PC database, such as Watcom, or a back-end database such as Sybase or Oracle on the file server.
2. Obtain all the table definitions along with all the columns for the application. Also, list any default values for the columns, rules, and triggers that are associated with the columns or rows.

3. Determine what is stored on the front end and in what format (source or object). For the best control of the GUI it would be wise to store the GUI on the file server and download the executable or runtime version. This would prevent anyone from replacing the GUI on the personal computer and perhaps spoofing the end user.

4. Obtain a listing of all menu screens and events for each screen. These events would be in the form of check boxes, popup menus, icons, or similar events. Each one would have an associated script that would execute when the event was activated. Activation occurs when a user moves the mouse around and makes a selection.

5. The scripts would have the name of the remote procedures that is being called along with any functions or embedded SQL. By reviewing the script you will be able to determine what action the front end is expecting from the back end.

6. Determine:
   * Who can modify the front end
   * Who has access to the source
   * Where the source is stored
   * Whether the GUI source is backed up regularly or every time a change to the source is completed
   * Who has access to the program generator that can create the runtime versions of the GUI

7. Determine how any modifications are completed. Do they use Version control? Are they downloaded from the back end (file server)? Check-in/Check-out features of a product such as PVCS, from Inversolv, or HPS from Peer, Inc.

8. Obtain the application object by name.

9. Determine the application behavior, such as which libraries contain the objects that are used in the application and what processing should occur when the application begins and ends (open event and closed event scripts).

10. Review the Comments box to see whether an appropriate level of documentation is completed for the application. The Comments box is optional but is available for all object types.

11. To display the application's Structure, determine what menus call other menus.
    * Open the application painter and select the application object.
    * Click on the application icon to show all the global objects that are referenced in a script for the application object.
    * An asterisk following an object name indicates that the object is a descendant of another object.

- To see the inheritance hierarchy for a descendant object, select Object Hierarchy from the popup menu.
- The following types of references are listed when an object is expanded:
  ~Menus
  ~Data windows
  ~Custom user objects
- Objects that are directly referenced in scripts also should be displayed. Objects that are referenced only through instance variables or attributes should be displayed. And, objects that are referenced dynamically through string variables should be displayed.

12. Obtain a listing of the scripts. Scripts typically include the following:
    - References to objects and controls. Objects such as windows, Data-Window objects, Menus and user objects, and controls such as CommandButtons and RadioButtons.
    - DataWindow objects have Display formats, Edit styles, and Validation rules. Review the formats, edits and validation routines for each field and determine whether adequate security and control is being maintained.

13. Determine that all variables are properly defined to maintain their integrity within the application front end. Variables are defined to hold values in the scripts. Each variable has a scope, which specifies where in the application the variable can be used. Global variables are accessible anywhere in the application. Local variables are accessible only in the script where they are declared. Instance variables are associated with one instance of an object, such as a window. Shared variables are associated with a type of object.

14. For built-in functions, determine that all functions are properly defined to maintain the appropriate level of security and control. Global functions are available anywhere within an application. These are called *public* functions. Object-Level functions are associated with particular types of objects and controls. These functions can be restricted as follows:
    - Public. In any script in the application.
    - Private. Only in scripts for events in the object where the function is defined. You cannot call the function from the descendants of the object.
    - Protected. Only in scripts for the object where the function is defined and its descendants.
    - For user-defined functions, review all user defined functions to ensure that their purpose and scope do not affect the overall integrity of the application's front end. User-defined functions are written to perform processing unique to the application.

15. Obtain a listing of all windows and menus. This will probably be in a library like Powerbuilder's PBL files. Review:

- Icons and their functionality.
- Popup menus for completeness and consistency.
- Event lists.
- Parent and child menu relationships.

16. Review the Database Management Interface. This provides the ability to work with a particular database management system, such as Oracle, from the front-end GUI tool. The opportunities to use these features would be restricted by the DBMS itself. For example, in most cases only the database administrator would have the opportunity to create production tables. To make this determination you would have to look at the data dictionary tables of the database management system.

   The capabilities from the front end are listed here, but the real authority must be provided in the DBMS itself. Review display formats, edit styles and validation rules. You also must review the:
- Database painter
  ~Create, alter, and drop tables.
  ~Drop views.
  ~Create and drop indices.
  ~Create, alter, and drop keys.
  ~Define and modify extended column attributes.
- Data Manipulation painter
  ~Retrieve rows.
  ~Insert rows.
  ~Update rows.
  ~Delete rows.
  ~Save data.
- View painter
  ~Create views.
- Data Administration painter
  ~Define security: grants and revokes.
  ~Execute SQL.

17. Determine where the executable modules are stored. Consider library and version control.

18. Determine whether a System Development Methodology is available and being utilized.

Development Security

The development of client/server applications entails several risks. The first risk is the skill level of the client/server development team. In dealing with new products, the network, and a new operating environment, the client/server development team might not be fully experienced.

To compensate for this risk, a management policy must be written that requires a peer review of all new client/server application designs. This review would be performed by an internal or external expert as a matter of policy. From the review procedure, a better overall design could be accomplished and a cross-training of experience could be transferred.

The second risk is the design methodology. In the client/server world, the application development process takes on a rapid development approach (see Chapter 4). With this approach, the application development is designed for quick deployment. There also might be a tendency not to use a formalized, structured development methodology. This rapid approach might serve as a quick solution but might not lead the application toward the openness and interoperability necessary to quickly modify the application to take advantage of new hardware, software, or corporate goals.

To offset this risk without restricting the application development process, it would be wise to establish a data classification methodology that would help to define organizational data into four classes. The highest class would be corporate data. The next class would be divisional data; then departmental; and finally, user or local data. Using this classification, an organization could employ a quick risk assessment for any application that used corporate, divisional, or departmental data. The level of risk would be mapped into the number of steps required to meet the minimum methodology standard. The higher the risk the more steps required. In addition, this classification methodology could be used to store application objects in a repository or dictionary at each level. This would allow for their reuse for other application development processes. Finally, the classification methodology could be used to tag the data and track its movement throughout the network. With this approach, corporate standards, procedures, and documentation requirements all become part of the application development process.

The third risk is library control over objects for the client/server application. These objects are represented in both source and object form. They include menus, programs, scripts, and windows. Only the object versions of these objects should be stored within the user environment. Using a version control or check-out/check-in system over the updating of objects will maintain integrity and control over the application's execution. The original source code should be placed on a protected library and, of course, stored offsite for additional protection. Besides version control, the system also could be set up to verify the integrity of critical objects by using a check sum total on these objects when the workstation signs on to the file server.

The trouble is that, in today's fast developing client/server world, it appears that management might have gone crazy. Management seems to be sending a strong message that essentially says to the design team, "Implement the system as fast as you can." Along with this message, management seems to be saying, "Don't worry about documentation, integrated testing, separation of duties, tuning, or change control. But do worry about making the user happy as fast as you can." The developers hear this message and are responding by eliminating the one key ingredient that makes sense out of the entire process, and that is a development methodology. Because six out of ten client/server applications do not initially work, we still need a development methodology.

Development methodologies have been around for many years now. These methodologies have provided a structured approach to the process of building a large, complex computer system. In today's client/server world, some of the developers that I talk with will say that the client/server development process is too intuitive for these old methodologies, and it is like, well, "surfing." That is, you have to feel your way with the development process. As a person who prefers methodologies, I interviewed one of these successful developers to help nail down a client/server methodology that we could all use to help guide us during the application development process. Mind you, it was difficult at first because the developer said that a methodology would not work and did not exist. Yet this designer had developed four major client/server applications successfully over the last five years. So, to elicit this information from him I interviewed him in detail about how he developed the client/server applications. The result of the interview follows.

The Client/Server Application Development Methodology

The client/server development process involves seven steps. It is important to note that this methodology assumes that you have done your up-front analysis and have collected the business rules from the user.

1. Establish the client/server model

The process of rightsizing an existing application or designing a new one begins with choosing a suitable client/server architecture. No single approach can meet all your needs, so when choosing a model or base configuration you want to design for:
- Scalability and flexibility to meet increasing end user needs
- Maximizing performance without changes in physical configuration
- Minimizing system maintenance costs
- Establishing effective security and control

Based on these criteria you would choose of the following models.
- Model 1—database server model

This model is a two-tier model with clients on workstations (tier one) connected to a server (tier two). In this architecture, all application logic and user interfaces execute on the client, and the data-access functions execute on the server, which is typically a relational Database Management System (DBMS) accessed via Structured Query Language (SQL). The database server model is suited to building applications such as systems for decisions support, executive information, and small-scale data entry and retrieval applications. However, due to its architectural limitations it lacks the ability to support production applications that involve high transaction volume.

- Model 2—transaction server model

This model is a two-tier model that divides the application between clients and servers, allowing developers the chance to build more sophisticated applications. A transaction is a logical unit of work that the client requests the server to perform. It can range from a simple SQL statement to something as complex as massive calculation routines, nested stored procedures, and data manipulation.

In the database server model, the client retrieves and manipulates the data via SQL statements. The transaction server model permits a message to be sent to the server that accomplishes both data access and data manipulation, with only the necessary results being passed back to the client. This model is far more effective at balancing the processing load between client and server. It also takes advantage of the power of the stored procedure, and lets it do the work on the server while the user-intensive tasks can be done on the client.

- Model 3—three-tier transaction server model

This is a three-tier model that divides the application between clients and servers and allows for real-time interfaces to existing mainframe systems. This model will balance the processing between client and server and, additionally, will embrace the host or mainframe systems(s) to allow for the real-time data feed to and from existing legacy systems. This model will account for the negotiation of mainframe data, as well as local and remote server data in its processing.

2. Ensure that the current network infrastructure supports the model

In the client/server development process, it is imperative to design your systems to minimize network traffic while trying to complete a transaction process. The network designers need to be notified of your new client/server application, so they can ensure that the network has the capacity to properly handle the new application. Certain criteria need to be presented to the network designers to ensure that the application will work in a stressful environment. This criteria or information includes the following:
- Geographic access required
- Network traffic counts

- Bandwidth (existing and projected)
- Transmission speeds
- Packet size
- Number of users
- Anticipated growth rate
- Number of connections
- Physical lines
- Number of file servers
- Anticipated response time

3. Design initial database structures

The Database Administration (DBA) Group must identify and create databases, tables, rules, triggers, and default values. Ideally, the Logical Data Model in some fashion should now be in place for the DBA to draw from and extract these objects, and their relationships to one another. These relationships correlate as follows:

Subject Areas (Logical Collection of Entities): Databases
Entities: Tables
Attributes: Columns
Domain values: Rules, defaults
Relationships: Triggers

4. Design presentation layer templates

This step requires that, for each application or for all the corporation's systems, you design the Common User Interface (CUI). This step would help complete the presentation side of the application, or what is commonly referred to as the Graphical User Interface (GUI). This would include the following:

- Determine the navigation of the system, that is:
  ~Number of items on menu selections; on the submenu?
  ~Menu bar common across the application?
  ~DBMS disconnect process?
- Determine the look and feel of the system; that is:
  ~Common object attributes, such as color, tab order, 3-D look, border, or pointer?
  ~Icons?
  ~Point-and-click versus drag-and-drop?
  ~Types of objects (dropdown list boxes, list box, radio button)?
- Create window templates that will be inherited or copied.
- Determine window application interfaces (DDE Dynamic Data Exchange) of the system.
  ~Establish the Client interfaces such as Word Perfect, Lotus, etc.
- Determine sign-on security requirements
  ~A common security process at login time?
  ~Authentication process on the file server or database server?

- Determine Help/Error message handling
  ~Micro help facility?
  ~Focus sensitive help?
  ~Interface with Windows helps?

After establishing all of the above, the GUI team can begin to build Template window structure. These structures are to be "Blessed by the user" for they will establish the building blocks from which all future windows will be built.

5. Develop the legacy access/integration model

During this step, the link to the mainframe or other cross platforms is designed. This design effort would include the following:
- Determine mainframe navigation paths.
- Development of traffic-cop mainframe programs responsible for feeding and being fed by existing mainframe applications.
- Establish all input/output parameters for the traffic-cop programs.
- Develop common cross-platform error-handling routines.
- Develop audit process(es) to keep track of information transmitted across platforms.

6. Develop the full presentation layer

During this step, common coding techniques/standards are established as follows:
- Determine naming standards for the application.
  ~Variables
  ~Structures
  ~Functions
  ~User objects
- Establish data query standards.
  ~Dynamic SQL
  ~Embedded SQL
  ~Common data return codes
- Create global structures and object level structures.
- Create user-defined functions and associated parameters.
- Establish and create data presentation styles.
- Tabular, freeform, label, graph etc.
- Create interface to database objects (stored procedures).
- Input parameters, output parameters, return codes, cross reference of available stored procedures and user functions to increase reusability.
  ~Management of GUI source and object libraries
  ~Check-in, check-out procedures
  ~Copying, moving, deleting library entries

7. Develop the Full Database Object

The Database Administration Group can now begin to identify and create the required stored procedures. Stored procedures are really program processes that are stored within the DBMS and are callable, if you have the proper level of authority.

In actuality, the coding of the stored procedures can be done by any developer who is knowledgeable in SQL (with some review process by the DBA Group for final approval). During this final phase the following would be completed:

- Establish SQL standards, workload per procedure.
- Code interface with GUI scripts that fires off the stored Procedure, input parameters, and output parameters.
- Establish methods for handling remote procedure calls (RPCs).
- Code the RPCs.
- Establish database commit and rollback logic.

Roll-Your-Own Applications

With the introduction of new client/server tools, the end users of the world are beginning to create "roll-your-own" application systems within corporate America. These users are getting smarter about what they want and how to use client/server and PC tools to obtain what they need. With this advance, the audit, security, system administration, and network professionals within the organization are having sleepless nights worrying about the implications of these end-user applications. The major risk is that this new organizational data, which might be used to make critical decisions, might not be properly defined or protected.

As the personal computer changes its characteristics from a machine that processes at twenty to ninety million instructions per second (MIPS) to a machine that processes at five hundred MIPS, the amount of end-user development should correspondingly increase.

As computer science graduates find obtaining a job with the IS department difficult, they will be forced to take jobs with end-user organizations. These graduates will naturally rely on their level of experience and will bring with them a set of skills on how to use client/server and personal computer tools.

Let's look at the problem. First a user decides that he or she can write their own application using one of the new tools "Roll-Your-Own." The data that is created could originate with the application or it could be derived from other corporate data to which the user has access. More than likely the user will store this data on his own personal computer. Any application data used in a critical business decision, or sensitive data that could adversely affect the company, should have its integrity tested and certified. The problem is that the user might not know—or might not care—about the certification process. More important, he might not even know how to identify sensitive and critical application data to determine whether certification is really even necessary.

A second problem, and a potentially greater integrity risk to the organization, is the lack of data identification and definition. This risk results directly from the fact that the personal computer is just that . . . a personal computer. Thus, if the data on the computer is not integrated into the corporate data architecture, then no one, except who the users deem worthy, will ever know that this data is available for consumption.

This could lead to a lack of access to corporate decision information. It is my fear that, should we not set up certain standards and procedures today, the users will rightfully establish dynamic data on their personal computers that is not registered in the corporate data architecture. This could lead to having a major percentage of our corporate data in parochial databases, which for all intents and purposes would then be unreachable by core systems.

To prevent these problems we need a new approach to the way we handle roll-your-own systems. There are three available approaches.

Data sheet approach

The data sheet approach uses a dynamic capture routine that is stored on the second tier of the application architecture, or the file server. Each time a user logs into the file server (or each week, month, or whenever) the dynamic program routines scans the personal computer's hard disk to identify any new programs or executables that would indicate the user might be developing a roll-your-own application. Once identified, the user is notified politely that any new application should have a data sheet completed. The user can elect to fill it out immediately or wait until the dynamic routine ages the request for a period of time. When the user does fill out the data sheet it would ask some very simple but important questions such as:

- Is this new application a parochial application for your own use? A departmental system? A divisional system? A corporate system?

- Does the application have any sensitive or critical corporate data?

- Does the application use any sensitive or critical corporate data as input?

- How many users will the application support?

- Does the output produced feed any other corporate systems?

- Is the output used to make tactical or strategic decisions by management at the department or higher levels within the organization?

- Are you aware of integrity procedures to verify the accuracy of your application?

Online help would assist the user in understanding each of these questions in greater detail. The data sheet would be completed and stored on the file server in a special area that would be available for review by a designated person or group, such as the corporate information officer (CIO). Armed with this information, the CIO can make a decision either to have a more in-depth risk analysis performed on the application or to have the application ported to a more secure environment.

This porting should be designed to be completed automatically by the dynamic routine. Of course the user would be notified of the porting, and would approve it before any action would be taken. Also, the porting process would be done without requiring any additional effort by the user. That is to say, the system should be ported and automatically documented by identifying the development tools being used by the user, to flowchart and understand as much of the system as possible. Any data definitions would be captured when possible, or otherwise completed by using an online documentation facility. By using this technique and working with our creative users we should be able to control the definition, location, and access of our most precious commodity, corporate data.

Enterprise-Wide Repository

Another approach to the problem is to create an enterprise-wide repository. In this approach a computer-aided system engineering (CASE) tool could be used. Many of these tools exist, but in today's client/server environment a tool like HPS from Seer, or IEF from Texas Instruments, would allow an end user to use a rapid application development (RAD) approach without losing sight of the fact that all corporate data should be properly defined and referenced by corporate administration. Although this second approach requires an up-front investment for the initial software architecture, it should save money in the long run.

Vendor Solution to the Rescue

The third approach would be to work with a vendor that has developed an integrated software solution to capture all of your fragmented data and place it into a repository. You need to spend the time and effort to convert and properly define the vast amounts of fragmented data that are building up in your organization today.

In all of these approaches, the main point is to ensure that data as a corporate resource is properly protected and presented. As new information is created and as new reports are generated, by various end users using many state-of-the-art tools, the possibility of errors and omissions rises. To protect the decision maker, a new standard needs to be established. This standard is called the integrity check. Any report, no matter where it was generated from, should have an integrity check completed when important decisions are to be based on the report. This integrity check standard would list the integrity standards and would allow the user to perform his own check. If management is ready to make a decision based on an end user-generated report (or, for that matter, any generated report), they can ask if an integrity check has been completed and by whom. If management is making a critical decision, they could even ask for a second opinion on the integrity check by performing an additional check. In this way management can have a quantifiable way to verify that the information they are using to make decisions has at least been independently verified.

Management Issues

Data definition and classification are at the core of our business today. The better understanding you have of your data the better you can maintain integrity and control. With the explosion of end-user applications, the potential for data errors and omissions is at its greatest point in history. By taking some preliminary measure now, your corporate reports today and in the future might actually reflect an accurate assessment of your corporate database.

This methodology would also relate to application development in that these applications would be analyzed to determine the level of participation by different organizations. For example:

- Parochial application system. These systems would be developed without the requirement that they be reviewed by any other individual or organization.

- Departmental system. These systems would be evaluated by the department manager, and the manager might solicit an analysis from I/S or other departments for input or assistance in development.

- Divisional system. These systems would require a mandatory review by all departments within the division to ensure that the proper priority, responsibility for development, and data definition and classification are maintained.

- Corporate system. These are core systems and require significant resources and approval from all affected parties.

Distribution and Management Security

System management is much more complex in the client/server environment. The integration of applications, computers, and networks makes these three separate but logical parts of the systems difficult to manage under one umbrella.

The multivendor diversity in the client/server environment makes the ability to manage the complete system solution under one management product almost impossible. This is because each of the parts have their own unique characteristics.

To alleviate the problems associated with heterogeneous systems, certain key players in the industry began to employ three different approaches. First is the management of the components from a network management system. Companies such as IBM with their NetView product (see Chapter 12), Novell with their NetWare Management System (NMS), Cabletron's Spectrum, HP's OpenView, and Sun Microsystem's SunNet Manager have products that allow for the management of the various component parts of the client/server environment.

Second is the use of intelligent agents that reside out in the environment and feed back specific information based on event tracking. One of the most popular today is the Simple Network Management Protocol (SNMP). These agents reside on other network components, such as bridges, routers, and hubs, and allow the system manager to establish alarm thresholds as well as event tracking categories. Armed with this information, the system manager can quickly determine the health of the client/server environment.

Third is the use of independent network probes that allow the system manager to distribute intelligent network probes with the sole purpose of tracking and feeding back critical information on the health of the client/server environment. These probes, from companies such as RMON Systems and AXON, are highly intelligent and dedicated to the task of watching client/server activity. With these probes you can write your own application routines to perform additional checks and balances, such as audit trails and violation logs.

But the major problem in the client/server world is the distribution of software. Several products allow for this distribution to occur in an orderly fashion. These are listed in the following section.

Change Management

Change control within the client/server environment still is a key control component to help to ensure the integrity and control of the system. Change control in today's downscale environment is a challenge, due to the limited staff and lack of established procedures within the client/server environment. It is as though the client/server environment is always changing. Some changes are tested right in the production environment because of the inability to create an adequate test environment. With this in mind, new, inventive controls are necessary to maintain the integrity from one change to the next.

A change library system is necessary to track the source and object code for both test and production. A change tracking system that allows us to track changes to the front end and the back end is also needed. Finally, we need a simulated testing environment within the complex web of the network.

The change library system that most companies are using today is Intersolv's Personal Version Control System (PVCS) and Legent Corporation's ENDEAVOR.

Intersolv has also teamed with Novadigm Inc. to develop an interface between PVCS and Novadigm's application deployment platform (EDM). The EDM/PVCS interface lets application development administrators use EDM's policy-based configuration manager to distribute applications to authorized client desktops whenever a production version change is promoted through PVCS. Intersolv also acquired The Software Edge Inc. The Software Edge develops the Defect Control System (DCS), a problem tracking tool for software developers.

These products should provide for the storage of the current version along with all changes that can be rolled back to previous versions if necessary.

Runtime distribution of modules can be accomplished by using DCAF within the OS/2 environment. Products like SYNCHRONY from Telepartner International also store modules within a distributed environment with a central repository.

Finally, you need to design a test environment or design an integrated testing server within your corporate network web. This test server would have dummy information on it that would simulate the production environment, but it would also allow us to run all the production queries against a production system and the test system at the same time.

Summary

Client/server environment is an exciting architecture that is helping to redefine the end user's role in application systems. It also is presenting management the opportunity to save on processing dollars in the long run. But moving quickly to capitalize on these benefits also has increased the risks. These risks need to be properly addressed.

One future solution is the implementation of security and audit probes within the network environment. These probes, from companies such as AXON's distributed LANServant, allow an administrator to measure and control the movement of data within the client/server environment. As an example, a user might have read authority of the customer master file but should not be transferring the complete customer master file to his personal computer. The existing security system on the file server would not only allow read but also a complete read or copy of the master file. With the probe in line, the request could be evaluated and rejected even before it was received by the file server.

These probes are SNMP-compliant and can be implemented anywhere within the network environment, then set up to communicate with only the designated administrator. Trends could be established and samples obtained to identify suspicious activity.

This really approaches the re-engineering of the audit and security world, which is another topic for another book. These and other tools will continue to make this an exciting time for all involved.

Related Security Products

AM:PM
Tangram
Raleigh, NC 27606

Cisco packet filters and routers
Cisco, Inc.
1702 Townhurst Drive
Houston, TX 77043

DB2
NetView DISTRIBUTION MANAGER & OS/2 CID
IBM Corporation
Kingston, NY 12401

ENDEAVOR
Legent Corporation
Vienna, VA 22070

HERMES
Microsoft Corporation
Redmond, WA 98052

LANalyzer
Novell, Inc.
1610 Berryessa Road
San Jose, CA 95133

LANServant
AXON Networks, Inc.
199 Wells Avenue
Newton, MA 02159

NetWare NAVIGATOR
Novell Inc.
Provo, UT 84606

Network Encryption System NES
Motorola Inc.
1500 Gateway Blvd.
Boyton Beach, FL 33426

Norton Administrator for Networks
Symantec Corporation
Cupertino, CA 95014

ORACLE
Oracle Corporation
500 Oracle Parkway
Redwood Shores, CA 94065

Personal Version Control System (PVCS)
Intersolv
Beaverton, OR 97006

SUDS
Frye Computer Systems, Inc.
Boston, MA 02111

Sybase
Sybase, Inc.
6475 Christie Ave.
Emeryville, CA 94608

SYNCHRONY
Telepartner International
Framington, CT 06032

TraqNet
LeeMah DataCom Security Corporation
3948 Trust Way
Hayward, CA 94545

7

Securing DB2/2

Darren M. Jones

The Gods see the future
Mere mortals but the present,
While the wise man knows things just
about to occur.   PHILOSTRATOS
      in *Life of Appolonios of Tyana*

Philostratos' cynicism towards prognosticators could find some justification in the way the advent of client/server computing has been handled by computer security professionals. In a number of ways, it caught the computer security profession off-guard.

A quick glance at computer security conference brochures and proceedings from the past few years shows just how recent a development client/server security is. None of the conference brochures I've archived, for example, highlight detailed sessions on client/server security until 1993. This lack of attention existed even though data communications journals were focusing on client/server security as long ago as 1988.

Much of the trade press did not provide a great deal of guidance for security practitioners either, treating the control implications as anecdotal asides to their uncritical enthusiasm for the new technology. This lack of guidance has brought a clear challenge to security professionals, to quickly get caught up in understanding client/server security risks and to deal with the exposures even more quickly. The challenge is to provide adequate advice on identification, authentication, and authorization in order to develop secure applications.

This challenge is heightened by the fact that our understanding of controls in the systems we secure has necessarily been broadened by the systems' increased complexity. One of the benefits is that we must be more vigilant in providing a framework of control within and around client/server systems. We must also anticipate changes in systems architecture and design appropriate controls. Failing that, at the very least we must be aware of the changes taking place and must respond to them quickly. A valuable lesson in securing client/server systems is that no two application systems have the same control requirements, or, by extension, the same profile of risks and exposures.

Introduction to DB2/2 and Client/Server Database Processing

In this chapter, I will focus on the use of IBM's Database 2 for OS/2 (DB2/2) to manage data in client/server systems. IBM also markets Database 2 for MVS (DB2/MVS), Database 2 for AS/400 (DB2/400), and Database 2 for RS/6000 (DB2/6000). DB2/2 acts as both a data manager and a client enabler for DB2/400, DB2/6000 and DB2/MVS. To security practitioners already responsible for controlling the MVS version of DB2, the security concepts applied in DB2 on these other platforms will be quite familiar. This familiarity will be needed, as organizations that invested in the mainframe-based DB2 in the mid-eighties are currently the major users of DB2 on these other platforms. Given the predominance of the various DB2s among corporate users of IBM's enterprise systems, the security practitioner will find more and more client/server systems to secure which make use of DB2's multiplatform infrastructure.

Relational database management systems, such as DB2/2, are a prevalent technology in client/server applications. A control exposure in the implementation of DB2/2 will place at risk any client/server system that uses that software for data management or data presentation. In relational database systems, data is represented by a number of columns and rows which are contained in tables. Using Structured Query Language (SQL), rows and columns within the tables can be manipulated and modified, allowing databases to be flexible and easy to manage.

In a client/server system, programs running on the client machine contain SQL statements that send requests for data across the network to an RDBMS running on a server machine. The query searches the database, finds the data, and sends it back over the network to the client. Depending on whether the client machine itself has a robust database manager, the data can be moved from the server to the client machine, where additional SQL commands can be run against the data subset. The key is that data can be dispersed to locations where it is most economical to store. For example, some data can be moved to a LAN file server (which acts as the "client" to the mainframe's "server"), from where various end-user workstations can access it (the workstations acting as "clients" to the LAN file server's "server"). By economically dispersing data across platforms, the client SQL can be run against either mainframe DB2, DB2/2 or DB2/6000. On OS/2 machines, the client enabler software allows OS/2 Database Manager to submit SQL queries against DB2 databases, no matter where they exist.

A security exposure in one component of a client/server system can place at risk the entire system. As a result, a greater burden is placed on security professionals, because the security professional must understand the security requirements of each software component, each application system, and of the collective architecture. In a system that distributes DB2 data across platforms, security in each of the DB2 implementations in the system must be a high priority.

Linking Databases Together with DRDA

Some RDBMS strategies (such as IBM's Distributed Relational Database Architecture or DRDA) provide an infrastructure for communications in client/server applications extending across platforms. The existence of DB2 databases on several platforms, and a DRDA infrastructure that links them, means client/server applications can distribute mainframe and midframe-based databases. This linking can be done through Token Ring networks, for example, and the user can perform on-the-spot queries directly from windows on a remote machine.

Under DRDA, a single client/server transaction can update multiple databases, with the RDBMS automatically coordinating the update process. DB2 databases on the various platforms also can respond to requests from DRDA-enabled clients, which include the full suite of DB2 products, Oracle, and Informix. At present, DB2/2 only can be used as a client (to, say, a MVS DB2 database) in the DRDA client/server configuration. However, it is possible to use DB2/2 on a LAN file server as a client to a mainframe DB2 database (thus gaining the benefits of DRDA), and distribute data to the client DB2/2 database. Then, the LAN users could use DB2/2 to access this LAN-based DB2/2 database, acting as clients to the LAN DB2/2's server. In short, DB2/2 can either be a client or server, or both. In Figure 7.1, a client/server system using DB2/2 and DB2 on the mainframe under such an approach is presented.

DRDA is the mechanism that provides workstations with near-seamless access to DB2 databases across all platforms. The key to DRDA's operations is that OS/2's Database Manager SQL transactions can be delivered to and processed by DB2 without any database or network protocol translation. IBM is augmenting DRDA's client/server infrastructure with an enhanced product called DB2 Client/Server version 2.[1]

---

[1]For a particularly detailed introduction to DB2 Client/Server, refer to the article "DB2 Client/Server Version 2: A Technical Overview" by Michael Cotignola, Steven J. Liszewski and Douglas J. Stacey, (p30–43), *IDUG Solutions Journal*, (October 1994).

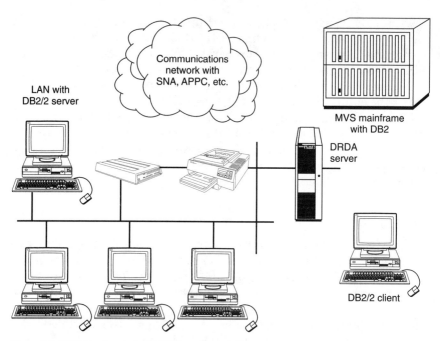

Figure 7.1 DB2/2 connected with DB2 on the mainframe

One exciting prospect arising from the development of this software is that DB2/2 will no longer be restricted by DRDA as a client—DB2/2 databases will be server-enabled. That is, it would be possible to have MVS DB2 databases act as clients to DB2/2 server databases.

Security Requirements in a DB2/2 Client/Server System

Databases are usually placed on the server component of the client/server configuration, and perform functions such as managing database calls, optimizing performance, executing queries, providing security, controlling data integrity, and coordinating recovery. Because the application server is responsible for managing the database resources, its security requirements dictate which security features are required of the application clients. Security professionals must have some approach to managing the security features required by all servers in a client/server system. Specifically, the approach must apply these features in a consistent, controlled manner, to reduce the chance that data might be compromised by weak security in one of the system's components.

As you might expect, certain basic control principles can be universally applied to all client/server database implementations. Specifically, this chapter will apply these principles to DB2/2.

- Identify all users of the DB2/2 system.
- Limit SQL access to key application tables.
- Ensure that each application plan accesses only the required, approved objects.
- Segregate access within the DB2/2 tables with database views.
- Use table checks to enforce data integrity and business data rules.
- Protect the DB2/2 system catalog.
- Manage and control all system-wide and database-specific attributes.
- Secure intersystem database communications.

This chapter will describe these controls in detail, and provide concrete examples of these critical concepts.

Identifying all users of the DB2/2 system

Under all circumstances, the user connecting to a DB2/2 database must be identified and authenticated. This is particularly the case in client/server systems, wherein there is a greater possibility of remote access.

Database software systems identify the end users who connect with and perform operations on the various database resources. The identifier used to connect to DB2/2 is known as the authorization ID or "authid." To ensure that this authid specifically identifies the user as an individual, it should be assigned to one specific person. To make sure this association happens, the DB2/2 authid is generally assigned to the OS/2 LAN Server user ID. In addition, DB2/2 can build a list of additional authids which can be related to LAN Server Group IDs. These authids can be used to group individual authids with similar access requirements, and manage access to DB2/2 information. When DB2/2 performs security checking against a resource, the individual and group authids are checked to see if at least one of them permits the user to access the object.

As alluded to above, DB2/2 user identification can be linked with the local area network operating system—in this example, an OS/2 LAN Server. This linkage is implemented using Communications Manager/2 and OS/2's User Profile Management (UPM). A natural question would be to ask why DRDA does not manage user identification. However, DRDA is a database communications architecture, concerned primarily with facilitating speedy inter-database and cross-platform communications and operations. DRDA does not provide its own security, but instead relies on the components it manages to achieve the desired level of control. This makes it all the more critical for the security practitioner to ensure that all the client/server system components have effective user logon controls. Because logon typically takes place at the client workstation or at a LAN file server, this means placing effective controls in LAN Server and UPM.

An individual OS/2 client workstation can access DB2/2 in a variety of ways. The authentication manager, UPM, recognizes the following three types of workstation logons:

1. Local, where the user ID and password are authenticated at the individual workstation by UPM.

2. Node, where the user ID and password are authenticated at the individual workstation by UPM, and the logon information is stored by UPM and used when a client process attempts to access a remote server. When an attempt is made to connect to the remote server, the user ID and password are passed on to the server and re-authenticated.

3. Domain, where user ID and password are received by UPM and passed on to IBM LAN Server for authentication at the LAN Server domain.

There are three types of UPM user ID authorities: user, local administrator, and administrator. User is the authority with no special privileges; it simply permits the user to connect with UPM and UPM-controlled OS/2 services (such as LAN services or DB2/2 services). The local administrator has full control over any databases locally resident on that machine. Administrator authority has full control over any databases locally resident on that machine, and can maintain the UPM definitions as well.

Where local UPM authentications occur, each client workstation must have an administrator ID set up in UPM for client/server processing to occur in DB2/2. This raises an interesting problem, as the client/server system now must be concerned with connections received from UPM administrator IDs on the client workstations.

UPM's default (that is, installation) ID has administrator authorities and is called USERID. The default password is the not-so-clever PASSWORD. In a peer-to-peer OS/2 configuration, a person could conceivably access another person's machine by logging in to that Local Workstation as USERID with the default password. This person would then have full, unauthorized control over the machine's UPM definitions as well as full control over all UPM-protected services (such as DB2/2). This exposure underscores the need to changes USERID's password on every client workstation on the client/server system, and to remove USERID from the DB2/2 system's list of authorized authids. A further step in improving control would be to disable USERID on the server machine's UPM configuration to prevent it from logging on to the server machine at all.

Limiting SQL Access to Key Application Tables

Users access data from relational tables with SQL, a data access language that is based on accessing rows and columns of data. There are three types of SQL: Data Definition Language (DDL, which is used to define database objects), Data Control Language (DCL, which is used to manage the structure of database objects), and Data Manipulation Language (DML, which is used to manage the information in the database objects). The most basic command structure in DML is SELECT <rows> FROM <table> WHERE <column=some value>, and this chapter will give several examples of SQL queries using the SELECT FROM WHERE format. Other SQL commands include ALTER (to add or remove columns to or from the table), DELETE (to remove rows from a table), INSERT (to insert rows into a table), and UP DATE (to change specific data elements in a table).

Control over which SQL commands a user is permitted to run against a database is the very basis of all DB2/2 security. All SQL falls into two categories, dynamic and static. Static SQL uses query statements that are packaged into application program routines (called *plans* in DB2/2). Dynamic SQL uses statements that are built by the user and submitted interactively against the DB2/2 table. In DB2/2 terms, the SQL is dynamically "bound" to the database. Users must have the SQL command privileges required to execute a dynamic SQL statement.

For example, FLYONS cannot issue the dynamic SQL SELECT PROJECT ID FROM DJONES.PROJECTS unless DJONES has granted him SELECT access to DJONES.AUDITS. Likewise, INSERT, UPDATE, DELETE and AL TER commands are accepted or rejected on the same basis.

In this chapter, I will refer to an example database, called DJONES.PROJECTS. Table 7.1 gives a partial listing of rows and columns contained in this table, which I use in DB2/2 to manage the online documents and diagrams I have prepared for my various writing and research projects. Keep in mind

TABLE 7.1 A Partial Layout of DJONES.PROJECTS

RECNO	SPONSOR	TITLE	DUE_DATE	WORD_LENGTH
1	PDAVIS	Securingf DB2/2	Nov. 30	6000
2	UWATERLOO	Rights to Non-Discrimination	Jan. 4	500
3	UWATERLOO	Politics and Liberty	Feb. 14	500
4	UWATERLOO	Liberty & Robert Nozick	Mar. 14	1000
5	NONE	Review: Order & History (Voegelin)	Open	3000
6	JFRASER	Auditing DB2/2 Client/Server	Open	5000
7	MONTPELERIN	The Legacy of F. A. Hayek	Mar. 31	5000

that the shaded column, called "RECNO" in the figure, does not really exist in DB2/2. In my client/server DB2/2 system, I would want to give the project SPONSOR (Peter Davis) access to information regarding the project he is sponsoring. In this case, PDAVIS is Peter's user ID on my OS/2 system. I would also want to give access to other writers on the project (e.g., Cheri Jacoby and Frank Lyons), so they could offer comments on my section. As a result I will create OS/2 user IDs for them as well.

Because DJONES created the table, he has full authority over DJONES. PROJECTS, and can GRANT or REVOKE access as he sees fit. When someone creates a table in DB2/2, the authid that person was using is assigned as the first qualifier in the table name. Every table created by DJONES will be prefixed DJONES. Hence, DJONES will have full authority over every table prefixed with DJONES, meaning that he can add, change or delete rows or columns, and can even drop the entire database itself.

A primitive way of managing DB2/2 security would be for DJONES to explicitly GRANT each user every privilege required. In our example, DJONES would GRANT SELECT access to every individual who needs access, such as PDAVIS, FLYONS, and CJACOBY. However, managing access this way is an onerous task in a DB2/2 client/server system, because of the number of database objects likely to be on the system.

A more efficient approach is to group users that have similar access requirements, and grant access to the group authids. In our example, PDAVIS, FLYONS, CJACOBY and the rest of the contributors to this book would be assigned secondary identifiers of AUTHORS. Therefore, when DJONES GRANTs access to his tables, rather than issuing one GRANT statement for every person in AUTHORS, he would instead simply GRANT SELECT TO AU THORS; that is, to the secondary identifier or Group ID. Everyone who has this secondary identifier could then access DJONES.PROJECTS.

It is also a good idea to make sure that all database tables are owned by, and that all explicit privileges are granted to, authids that are linked to group IDs. This method divorces DB2/2 objects and privileges from individual users, and helps to maintain a functional approach of managing objects. When ownership is assigned to authids linked with individual user IDs, and employees change jobs or leave the company, the authid would have to be reassigned to another employee. This would have to be done to prevent the "cascading REVOKE" phenomenon, in which database objects are dropped because the object owner authid no longer exists on the system.

For example, if the authid DJONES is removed from the system, then all database objects owned by DJONES will also be removed from the system—for example, the DJONES.PROJECTS table. One effect is that everyone in AUTHORS will no longer be able to access DJONES.PROJECTS, because the table no longer exists. More significantly, when database objects are removed in this manner, any application program or procedure that requires access to the deleted object will fail. For client/server applications, this can be especially disastrous. A key control point in the design of a client/ server application is to ensure that no DB2/2 objects are owned by authids connected with individual user IDs. Rather, all DB2/2 objects should be owned by an application identifier.

Each individual DB2/2 database can have access segregated among users by function. ALTER gives the user the ability to add columns to a table. DELETE enables the user to delete rows from the table. INDEX allows the user to create an index on the table. INSERT permits the user to add rows into a table. REFERENCES is the privilege the user has for creating referential constraints on the table. As mentioned, UPDATE lets the user change information in a table.

In the course of planning the security of your client/server system, you will have to determine which authids actually have the ability to UPDATE or INSERT information into specific tables and databases. Table authorization information is kept in the DB2/2 system catalog table, called SYSIBM.SYS-TABAUTH. Table definition information is kept in the system catalog table SYSIBM.SYSTABLES. By linking information together between these tables, a good picture of security over this table emerges. For instance, to determine who can access information in the tables (that is, the GRANTEE) owned by DJONES, the following SQL gives a listing of all authids (both related to user IDs and Group IDs) that have access:

```
SELECT DISTINCT S1.DBNAME, S1.NAME, S2.GRANTEE, S2.UPDATEAUTH,
S2.INSERTAUTH, S2.SELECTAUTH
FROM SYSIBM.SYSTABLES S1, SYSIBM.SYSTABAUTH S2,
WHERE S2.TTNAME LIKE 'DMJ*' AND S1.NAME = S2.TTNAME AND (S2.UPDATEAUTH
= 'Y' OR S2.INSERTAUTH = 'Y' OR SELECTAUTH = 'Y');
```

As the results in Table 7.2 show, users who can submit SQL as the authid AUTHORS can read information in the DMJ@CLSERVER table. Because AUTHORS is a group ID, it will be defined in UPM. The next step would be to assess which user IDs in UPM can connect with the AUTHORS Group ID.

Ensuring that Each Application Plan Accesses Only Required, Approved Objects

Dynamic SQL is not the only method available for accessing DB2/2 databases. In fact, most application systems are actually defined to DB2/2 as a collection of SQL statements embedded in program code (this is called a plan). When an application user manipulates a database, the plan which contains the SQL statements is used by the application program. The SQL

TABLE 7.2 Listing of Authids with Access to Tables Prefixed with DMJ

DBNAME	NAME	GRANTEE	UPDATEAUTH	INSERTAUTH	SELECTAUTH
DJONES.PROJECTS	DMJ@CLSERVER	AUTHORS			Y

is, in effect, submitted by the plan, under the access authorities of the plan. There is a requirement, then, to ensure security over the methods used to access the data. In some ways, using plans to access data can simplify security management (because well-controlled plans still protect the application table) and get away from defining rows in the SYSIBM.SYSTABAUTH table to identify all authorized users.

These static SQL statements and objects are specified to DB2/2 at the time the application is implemented. The person creating the plan must have the authority to execute each of the static SQL statements contained in the plan. When users are granted authority to execute, they automatically receive authority to execute each of the static SQL statements the plan contains. No explicit table privileges are required; rather, access controls are placed over the plan itself. If you can execute the plan you have access to the table; if you can't, you don't.

If someone uses a plan to DB2/2 access information, there is no way the person can get the plan to operate outside of the way it has been coded. That person would need to change the plan and re-implement it. This is called *re-binding* the plan in DB2/2, and it can only be done by authids that have BIND authorities over the plan in question. For example, if DJONES had a plan called DMJREAD which reads the DJONES.PROJECTS database, there is no way a user of DMJREAD can get it to do anything except READ information from the PROJECTS database.

In client/server systems, there are benefits to defining methods of access as plans, rather than granting explicit authid access to raw database tables. These benefits derive from improved simplicity. For example, if there are only two defined plans that access DJONES.PROJECTS (call them DMJREAD and DMJWRITE) and there are no other ways to access this database, the burden on the security practitioner is greatly reduced. The security responsibility becomes a straightforward matter of connecting users to DMJREAD or DMJWRITE. In analyzing client/server systems, the security practitioner also must understand what each of the plans does and ensure that the operations performed are commensurate with the application's control objectives.

In some organizations, the practice of granting PUBLIC access to plans is followed. This approach places the onus on the application developers to control access to the programs that execute against the plan. The security practitioner should investigate the appropriate system catalog tables (for example, SYSIBM.SYSPLANAUTH) for a full list of PUBLIC plans and their definitions. Then, these plans can be investigated and the appropriateness of granting PUBLIC access can be assessed.

A related issue is the assignment of ownership of plans. Again, if ownership is assigned to user identifiers (e.g., DJONES), plans might be dropped without warning if the plan owner's privileges on the database tables are removed. This is a variation of the cascading REVOKE phenomenon described before, and developers should be vigilant in ensuring that it either never occurs or that its occurrence does not adversely affect the client/server system.

Now, in reviewing the security of DJONES' client/server system, there are plans in addition to authids that have the ability to access the tables. To determine who can access information in the tables owned by DJONES, the same SQL will give a listing of all authids and DB2/2 plans that have access:

```
SELECT DISTINCT S1.DBNAME, S1.NAME, S2.GRANTEE, S2.UPDATEAUTH,
S2.INSERTAUTH, S2.SELECTAUTH
FROM SYSIBM.SYSTABLES S1, SYSIBM.SYSTABAUTH S2,
WHERE S2.TTNAME LIKE 'DMJ*' AND S1.NAME = S2.TTNAME AND (S2.UPDATEAUTH
= 'Y' OR S2.INSERTAUTH = 'Y' OR SELECTAUTH = 'Y');
```

As the results in Table 7.3 show, users who can submit SQL as the authid AUTHORS, or who can execute the plans called DMJREAD and DMJ-WRITE, can access information in the DMJ@CLSERVER table. The next step is to determine which authids have the ability to EXECUTE the plans that have the ability to access the tables. Additionally, the security practitioner can confirm the identity of those users able to BIND (i.e., change) the plans. The following SQL gives a listing of all authids that have access to the plan DMJREAD, the results of which are displayed in Table 7.4:

```
SELECT DISTINCT NAME, GRANTEE, CONTROLAUTH, BINDAUTH, EXECUTEAUTH
FROM SYSIBM.SYSPLANAUTH
WHERE NAME = 'DMJREAD' AND (CONTROLAUTH = 'Y' OR BINDAUTH = 'Y' OR
EXECUTEAUTH = 'Y');
```

In some DB2/2 client/server implementations, the Remote Procedure Call (RPC) approach is used to link program objects on remote client machines to DB2/2 plans. These RPCs provide the client machines with uniform methods for accessing the same plans, and by extension, the same data. The RPC is initiated at a requester machine, executes static SQL in the

TABLE 7.3 Listing of Authids with Access to Listing of Plans DMJREAD and DMJWRITE

DBNAME	NAME	GRANTEE	UPDATEAUTH	INSERTAUTH	SELECTAUTH
DJONES.PROJECTS	DMJ@CLSERVER	AUTHORS			Y
DJONES.PROJECTS	DMJ@CLSERVER	DMJREAD			Y
DJONES.PROJECTS	DMJ@CLSERVER	DMJWRITE	Y		Y

TABLE 7.4 Listing of Authids with Access to Plan DMJREAD

NAME	GRANTEE	CONTROLAUTH	BINDAUTH	EXECUTEAUTH
DMJREAD	AUTHORS			Y
DMJREAD	DJONES	Y	Y	Y
DMJWRITE	PDAVIS			Y
DMJWRITE	DJONES	Y	Y	Y

DB2/2 plan, and performs the defined operation on the server database. These RPCs specify which data is to be used by which function, in which way, via which screens, and thus provides controls over access to DB2/2 data, and over how that data is presented.

The task for security practitioners is the same, to assess what each RPC gains access to in the client/server system, and determine the appropriateness of access that the RPC users have.

Segregating Access within DB2/2 Tables with Database Views

SQL queries can also be on virtual database tables, called *views*, which consist of specific rows and columns from one or more base tables. Views can also display virtual fields, which consist of calculations or conversions based on column values in the table. A table might store investment fund values in U.S. dollars, but the view might display it in Canadian dollars for fund valuation reports. This presentation technique will be prevalent in companies (such as The Mutual Group) which have foreign subsidiaries. In this age of simplifying the presentation of data to the user, the desired effect of views is to hide the calculations underlying the system from the end user.

Views can also be used to restrict access to particular parts of a table, so that end users may not access rows and columns they do not need to access. The following is an example of a view statement:

```
CREATE VIEW VPDAVIS
AS SELECT *
FROM DJONES.PROJECTS
WHERE SPONSOR = 'PDAVIS';
```

Suppose a control objective in DJONES client/server system is to limit PDAVIS access to only the projects where he is the sponsor. The view VP-DAVIS would fulfill that objective, as PDAVIS would have his access limited by this view. This concept has significant implications for securing client/server systems, particularly where the clients require access to similar functional information but only need to see the data related to their geographical location. For example, a RPC could initiate the DB2/2 plan DMJ WRITE, but because the RPC came from PDAVIS' client workstation, the VPDAVIS would be accessed, not the base table.

Table 7.5 shows the results of a query to determine which GRANTEEs have access to tables prefixed with "DMJ."

Now, users who can send SQL via the view called VPDAVIS can access the DMJ@CLSERVER table, but only in the limited ways that VPDAVIS can operate. Because DB2/2 considers a view to be a type of plan, SYSIBM.SYS PLANAUTH will depict the list of authids able to use VPDAVIS.

TABLE 7.5 Listing of Authids with Access to Tables Prefixed with DMJ

DBNAME	NAME	GRANTEE	UPDATEAUTH	INSERTAUTH	SELECTAUTH
DJONES.PROJECTS	DMJ@CLSERVER	AUTHORS			Y
DJONES.PROJECTS	DMJ@CLSERVER	VPDAVIS	Y		Y
DJONES.PROJECTS	DMJ@CLSERVER	DMJREAD			Y
DJONES.PROJECTS	DMJ@CLSERVER	DMJWRITE	Y		Y

Using Table Checks to Enforce Data Integrity and Business Data Rules

Database views provide the ability to configure access to a database according to the way users want to see the database. In addition to limiting and simplifying database access, views can be used to enforce business rules and improve data integrity. DB2/2 has a WITH CHECK OPTION that can be specified when a view is created. This feature causes DB2/2 to apply business rules, by checking the WHERE clause in any subsequent UPDATE or INSERT statements which take place through the view. If the UPDATE attempts to make a change that runs against the rule, it will fail.

For instance, suppose VPDAVIS was created with the SQL command:

```
CREATE VIEW VPDAVIS AS SELECT * FROM DJONES.PROJECT
WHERE SPONSOR = 'PDAVIS' WITH CHECK OPTION
```

If a user of VPDAVIS tried to INSERT a record to DMJ@CLSERVER with SPONSOR = 'FLYONS', the attempt will fail. For this reason, table checking through view definitions is often used in client/server applications to enforce data integrity rules.

The security practitioner can quickly determine whether the WITH CHECK OPTION was used to CREATE an existing view. The VPDAVIS view can be investigated with the following SQL, to give information on the creation of the view:

```
SELECT DISTINCT S1.NAME, S2.VCAUTHID, S1.CHECK, S1.TEXT
FROM SYSIBM.SYSVIEWDEP S2, SYSIBM.SYSVIEWS S1
WHERE S1.NAME = 'VPDAVIS' AND S1.NAME = S2.DNAME ;
```

Table 7.6 depicts the results of the above query, which shows who created the view, whether the view has any CHECK constraints, and the SQL used to CREATE the view.

Other integrity features exist in the form of *triggers* and *event alerts*. Triggers allow for the system to instruct DB2/2 to automatically enforce business policies whenever a given database event occurs. Such activities can cause a trigger to execute, which in turn causes a user-defined function to occur. This could involve consulting data in other tables or updating other tables.

TABLE 7.6 View VPDAVIS CREATE Information

NAME	VCAUTHID	CHECK	TEXT
VPDAVIS	DJONES	Y	CREATE VIEW VPDAVIS AS SELECT * FROM DJONES.PROJECTS WHERE SPONSOR = 'PDAVIS' WITH CHECK OPTION

The trigger mechanism can also function as an alerter, enabling a database event to cause a non-DBMS activity to occur. This could be generating an e-mail message when someone makes a change to a specified table. For example, an attempt to UPDATE a column to change SPONSOR to 'FLYONS' through the VPDAVIS view could generate an alert to the Netview/2 network incident tracking system.

Protecting the DB2/2 System Catalog

I have made several mentions of the DB2/2 system catalog in this chapter. The system catalog defines structures for database tables, plans, and views, and also defines access authorities of specified authids to particular objects. As one might expect in a DBMS, the system catalog is really a collection of relational tables which defines all the application tables, objects, and users in the system. For example, when you grant an authid access to a table you INSERT a record with the authid's authorities into SYSIBM.SYSTABAUTH. As several of our examples have noted, the DB2/2 system catalog can be queried to give you, among other things, an accurate understanding of how well-controlled the database objects truly are.

In DB2/2, the system catalog is kept in tables prefixed with SYSIBM. User permissions are maintained in the following tables:

SYSIBM.SYSDBAUTH contains database privileges.

SYSIBM.SYSINDEXAUTH contains privileges granted on indexes.

SYSIBM.SYSPLANAUTH contains privileges granted on plans.

SYSIBM.SYSTABAUTH contains table authorization privileges.

Layouts for these catalog tables are depicted in Table 7.7. When an authid is granted an authority, it is recorded in the related system catalog authorization table by entering a 'Y' in the appropriate column. For example, if authid CJACOBY is granted SELECT authorities against the DMJ@CL SERVER table, there would be a 'Y' recorded in SYSIBM.SYSTABAUTH's SELECTAUTH column where TTNAME = 'DMJ@CLSERVER' and GRANTEE = 'CJACOBY'.

In addition to using information from these tables to better plan the security for DB2/2 application systems, the security practitioner also must ensure that the system catalog tables themselves are protected from corruption.

This required protection implies strong security controls, so that only authorized users, such as database administrators, can make updates. Table 7.8 depicts the other catalog tables that have been mentioned in this chapter. Note that although these particular catalog tables are not used to manage access to information DB2/2, it is nonetheless advisable to protect them from unauthorized changes.

TABLE 7.7 The System Catalog Authorization Tables

SYSDBAUTH	SYSINDEXAUTH	SYSPLANAUTH	SYSTABAUTH
GRANTOR	GRANTOR	GRANTOR	GRANTOR
GRANTEE	GRANTEE	GRANTEE	GRANTEE
DBADMAUTH	NAME	NAME	TCREATOR
CREATETABAUTH	CREATOR	CREATOR	TTNAME
BINDADDAUTH	CONTROLAUTH	CONTROLAUTH	TABAUTH
CONNECTAUTH		BINDAUTH	CONTROLAUTH
		EXECUTEAUTH	ALTERAUTH
			DELETEAUTH
			INDEXAUTH
			INSERTAUTH
			SELECTAUTH
			UPDATEAUTH
			REFAUTH

TABLE 7.8 Other System Catalog Tables Mentioned inThis Chapter

SYSCOLUMNS	SYSTABLES	SYSVIEWDEP	SYSVIEWS
NAME	NAME	BNAME	NAME
TBNAME	CREATOR	BCREATOR	CREATOR
TBCREATOR	TYPE	BTYPE	SEQNO
REMARKS	CTIME	DNAME	CHECK
COLTYPE	REMARKS	DCREATOR	TEXT
NULLS	PACKED_DESC	VCAUTHID	
CODEPAGE	VIEW_DESC		
DBCSCODEPG	COLCOUNT		
LENTH	FID		
SCALE	TID		
COLNO	CARD		
COLCARD	NPAGES		
HIGH2KEY	FPAGES		
LOW2KEY	OVERFLOW		
AVGCOLLEN	PARENTS		
KEYSEQ	CHILDREN		
	SELFREFS		
	KEYCOLUMNS		
	KEYOBID		
	REL_DESC		

Managing and Controlling System-Wide and Database-Specific Attributes

A familiar concept to security practitioners is the management and control of powerful privileges in the system. DB2/2 is no different from other operating environments, as the DB2/2 implementation has powerful authorities that must be controlled. These authorities are used to manage the database software, by performing such activities as managing security and fine tuning operating parameters. Control of these authorities is a necessary step in securing any client/server system that uses DB2/2.

In DB2/2, administrative authorities are used to control both the DB2/2 operating environment and the databases contained in it. These SYSADM authids can create or drop any database, catalog remote databases, access and modify data stored in any table, give any authid access to any resource, and execute any program. Authids with SYSADM authorities are typically used to solve critical problems, or to install and maintain DB2/2 software. These authorities extend across the entire DB2/2 system, and poor control over these privileges places at risk all data in the system. SYSADM authorities can be granted to other authids (through use of the GRANT SQL command), but in DB2/2 only a user with SYSADM authorities can grant SYSADM to anyone else.

In addition to providing system-wide privileges, DB2/2 can allow privileges to be segregated to specific databases. Controlling the activity of DB2/2 databases requires the use of powerful commands to perform such activities as reorganization, recovery, and repairing of databases. The DBADM privilege confers these capabilities, and DBADM users can also run database utilities, issue database commands, and access any data in the databases.

Other authorities that are in effect for specific databases include CREATE TAB, CONTROL, BINDADD and CONNECT. CREATETAB is the privilege for creating tables, and its use should be restricted as the creator of a table automatically has CONTROL authority over it. BINDADD allows the user to create new plans to run against the database. As with the creator of tables, the creator of a package has CONTROL authority over that package. CONNECT enables the user to access the database, by issuing the DB2/2 CONNECT TO statement. Authorities over databases are specified in the SYSIBM. SYSDBAUTH system catalog table.

When a database is created, DB2/2 automatically assigns default privileges to that database. The creator of the database is granted DBADM authority. In addition, CONNECT, CREATETAB, BINDADD and SELECT privileges are automatically granted to PUBLIC. To provide for better security over databases, the security practitioner should ensure that the default PUBLIC access authorities are removed.

Where the client/server application involves distributed databases, the security practitioner should insist that consistent standards of control be applied to each database. If a DB2/6000 table that has only two DBADMs is mirrored to a DB2/2 table that has several dozen users with DBADM privileges, the security practitioner should insist that the DB2/6000's security standards be applied in DB2/2.

Securing Intersystem Database Communications

DB2/2 provides a complex and flexible security structure for distributed and nondistributed operations. Where databases are distributed, as in a client/server application, the first consideration is to ensure that there is a comprehensive and controlled method for determining who will be allowed to connect to the database. Security professionals need to be able to control which client workstations are allowed to connect to which database servers. Having allowed a client/user ID combination to connect to a server, the next step is to control the authorities and privileges that are granted to these users.

If user IDs and passwords are defined locally to the workstation in UPM, the user ID is used by DB2/2's precompile and bind processing for SQL access to databases. Communications Manager/2 uses the client-supplied UPM user ID and password for server validations within DRDA. Where OS/2 LAN Server is used for user authentication, the LAN Server user ID is used in DB2/2 processing.

Because OS/2 is not a multiuser operating system, the client workstation might not require user IDs and passwords to power up the machine. Therefore, UPM will not have any information to pass on to DRDA, as it will not have been invoked. In this case, DB2/2 at the server machine will prompt the user for a user ID and password to satisfy server security requirements. It is the security practitioner's responsibility to make sure this validation takes place before any connection to server machines takes place.

User validation in DRDA-connected systems can be complicated, as it generally depends on the communications protocol in use. For example, in a NetBIOS protocol, the user logs in to the client workstation under UPM (or IBM LAN Server) and invokes Distributed Database Connection Service (DDCS/2) router services to initiate client/server communications with a mainframe DB2 database. When the DDCS/2 router requests that a server session be allocated, this information user ID and password information is passed on to the DRDA server, where security measures are applied. As before, it is the security practitioner's responsibility to make sure this validation takes place before any connection to server machines takes place.

The complications inherent in this intersystem processing are demonstrated in Figure 7.2. Essentially, the security practitioner must work with networking professionals to activate the network system options necessary to provide a secure client/server infrastructure. To get a better understanding of

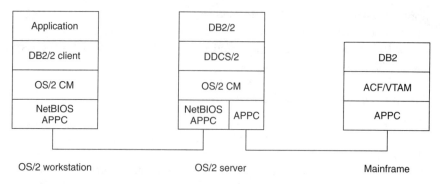

Figure 7.2 Intersystem database communications under DRDA

the various communications and database software components that can affect a client /server transaction, it's helpful to get a networking systems professional to chart all of the network operating systems and communications protocols which pass the client/server SQL request from client to server.

Fortunately, security methods within DB2 across platforms are very similar, so it should be a relatively simple matter for consistent security standards to be applied in all client/server DB2 databases. Determining what happens to SQL requests and user IDs and passwords within the data communications network is a much more complicated matter. The level of complication can vary, depending on the software and protocols used, and I recommend that you closely read some of the other chapters in this book to gain a better appreciation of the security measures that can be applied.

Summary

In this chapter, you have been presented with some basic methods to control client/server systems that use DB2/2. As no two client/server applications are the same, so no two client/server applications have the same profile of risks.

Through understanding the particular system's control objectives, and by investigating the controls described in this chapter, you can tailor your approach to security and apply tests to each client/server application encountered. Rigorous, ongoing management of risk should be a mainstay of the security strategy for client/server systems, so that the risk profile for each client/server application can be updated to reflect changes in the software, the data communications configuration, or the business objectives. By anticipating the effects of such changes, security professionals can provide critical insight into controlling the client/server architecture. The security professional can demonstrate the wisdom and foresight that would impress even Philostratos.

Recommended Journals/Publications

- *Client/Server Today*
- *International DB2 Users Group (IDUG) Solutions Journal*
- *Platinum Database Edge Journal*
- *Select Bibliography of IBM Publications*
- *Client/Server Computing: The Design and Coding of a Business Application (GG24–3899)*
- *Client/Server Computing: Application Design Guidelines: A Distributed Relational Data Perspective (GG24–3727)*
- *Distributed Relational Database Architecture Reference (SC26–4651)*
- *DRDA Connectivity Guide (SC26–4783)*
- *IBM DATABASE 2 OS/2 Guide (S62G–3663)*
- *IBM DATABASE 2 OS/2 Information and Planning Guide (S62G–3662)*

The Middleware

No one can whistle a symphony. It takes an orchestra to play it.
HALFORD E. LUCCOCK

The power of the waterfall is nothing but a lot of drips working together.
ANONYMOUS

8

Securing Client/Server TCP/IP

Dr. Richard E. Smith

It is a good thing to learn caution from the misfortunes of others. PUBLILIUS SYRUS

The probability that we may fail in the struggle ought not to deter us from the support of a cause we believe to be just. ABRAHAM LINCOLN

TCP/IP (Transmission Control Protocol/Internet Protocol) is arguably the most widely used family of networking protocols in the world. A host using TCP/IP can send data directly to more hosts of different kinds spread across a larger area than he can do via any other networking protocol. This is because TCP/IP is the language of the Internet, that ubiquitous consortium of interconnected networks. In fact, the word Internet is a contraction formed of "interconnect" and "network" to reflect how the protocol makes the interconnected boundaries disappear between networks.

Until recently, a knowledgeable developer could easily implement a network service using TCP/IP. The developer simply implemented the service using a TCP connection between client and server, and published the service's address. Clients across the room or across the ocean could use the service directly with acceptable reliability, performance, and security. Initially, Internet connections were costly, and hosts handling Internet traffic were managed by professionals with rare and well-paid skills.

Times have changed. The Internet is no longer the proverbial small town wherein homes and businesses leave their doors unlocked. Today, the mere act of connecting a computer to the Internet invites a variety of probes by the curious and sometimes by the malicious. Modern computer software is complicated and security weaknesses can go undetected for years. Generic weaknesses in TCP/IP protocols likewise go for years without being exploited. But attacks on Internet hosts grow more sophisticated every year. Several organizations now track and report on computer security vulnerabilities. The Computer Emergency Response Team (CERT) at Carnegie Mellon University is perhaps the best known public source of such reports.

Network services designed for a simpler era no longer protect information and computing assets without extra measures. The growing threats have prevented some organizations from connecting to the Internet at all. Many organizations communicate with the Internet through special gateway connections that apply various security measures: filtering routers, firewalls, guards, and gateways of various types. These devices all reduce Internet security threats by restricting the flow of data through the connection. These restrictions occasionally prevent older Internet services from functioning normally.

Practical TCP/IP services must be able to work in today's Internet environment, threats and all. The service must avoid the models of the oldest and least secure Internet services. Modern TCP/IP services must follow a modern, transaction-oriented service model that allows them to interact cleanly with security gateways. Modern services also should provide their own mechanisms for retransmission and duplicate detection, because they might be relayed above those services provided by TCP/IP. Finally, modern services must make provisions for integrity seals and cryptographic services, to support higher levels of security.

Existing TCP/IP application protocols meet many of these requirements in one way or another. Transaction-oriented protocols have a long history, and relays for e-mail have been a fixture in TCP/IP networks for well over a decade. Some security features are available as options with existing applications protocols; they operate with some degree of compatibility with existing network software. For example, cryptographic services might be added to e-mail via special client software; these clients embed an encrypted message within a standard e-mail message body and use the standard e-mail queuing and delivery software. The e-mail recipient then uses a special client to decrypt and read the message. Similar approaches have been proposed and developed for improving the security of other application level protocols.

TCP/IP Essentials

The TCP/IP acronym represents the central pair of protocols in the Internet protocol suite, a comprehensive set of computer communications protocols. Like all modern protocol families, the TCP/IP family is organized into

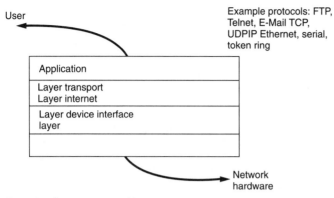

User

Example protocols: FTP, Telnet, E-Mail TCP, UDPIP Ethernet, serial, token ring

Application

Layer transport
Layer internet

Layer device interface
layer

Network
hardware

Figure 8.1 Internet protocol layers

layers (see Figure 8.1). Layering allows substitution of different network protocols in order to provide different types of network services. Different types of networking hardware (e.g., serial lines, Ethernet, and token rings) use different versions of the Network Interface layer. Different applications (e.g., file service and e-mail) use different versions of the Application layer. The Transport layer uses TCP to provide a reliable data stream between two hosts, or it uses the User Datagram Protocol (UDP) if a more efficient but less reliable transport protocol is adequate. Every mixture of protocol services uses IP in the Internet layer.

TCP/IP emerged from the development of packet-switched networking, funded primarily by the Advanced Research Projects Agency (ARPA) of the U.S. Department of Defense in the late 1970s. By then, the growth of computer networks had spawned numerous techniques to interconnect computers, and few managed to interoperate effectively. The Internet Protocol (IP) was developed to solve this problem. IP provided the simplest packet networking service possible, a service that practically all networking techniques could provide. This service was combined with a procedure for automatically forwarding packets between networks when a packet's destination address was not on the current network.

As shown in Figure 8.2, a host sends data to a host on a different network via a boundary host, sometimes called a *routing host* or *router*. The routing host looks at the packet and determines which network the packet should be sent to, and the host address on that network. This process occurs several times if the data must traverse several networks to reach its destination. Host computers on early packet networks used IP and the rest of the TCP/IP family to connect their local networks to national and international long haul networks, leading to the modern Internet.

A host computer often runs several different TCP/IP services and protocols simultaneously. Data follows different paths through the protocol

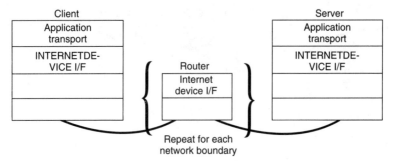

Figure 8.2 Packets are routed between networks at the Internet layer.

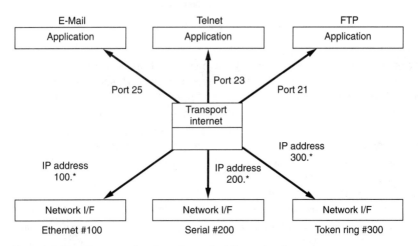

Figure 8.3 IP addresses and port numbers select the protocols used.

stack, according to addresses in the data packet (see Figure 8.3). A packet arriving at a network interface will travel "upwards" until it arrives at the Internet layer. Then its path depends on the port number in the packet's protocol header. Many port numbers belong to particular application layer protocols; for example, a port number of 25 appears in e-mail packets. The Internet layer uses the port number to invoke the application software associated with that packet.

Application layer software provides TCP/IP client/server functions. The protocols use preassigned port numbers to identify server software. When client software on a host seeks service from another host, it opens a connection to the host. The client receives an arbitrarily assigned port number and uses the server's preassigned port number. Packets going from client to server use the server host's address and the server's port number as the destination. Packets returning from the server to the client use the client host's address and the client's port number as the destination.

Data produced by the application layer moves "downwards" through the protocol stack until it arrives at the Internet layer. Then the packet is treated like any Internet packet and routed according to its IP address. The routing process chooses which version of the Network Interface layer to use. Each host contains a separate version for each of its networks.

Internetwork routing relies on the format of IP addresses. A complete IP address contains two parts: a network address and a host address. The network address identifies a specific network among all those on the Internet. The host address identifies an individual host on a specific network. Each Internet layer has a routing table that associates IP addresses with network destinations reachable from that host. Data travels from the Internet layer to a particular Network Interface layer according to the following situations:

- If the network address in a packet matches one of the host's Network Interface layers, then the packet goes to that layer. The Network Interface layer translates the host address into a physical network address and transmits the data to the destination host.

- If the network address in a packet does not identify a network connected to the host, the routing table provides the IP address of another host that will route the packet. The network address of this other host determines which Network Interface layer receives the packet, and the host address to which the packet is sent.

Each host that receives an IP packet repeats the routing process until the packet arrives at the destination. Originally, the Internet contained numerous timesharing hosts that resided on two or more TCP/IP networks and routed traffic between them. Today, many intermediate hosts performing this task might simply be routers, hosts whose only purpose is to connect two or more TCP/IP networks together.

The path a packet follows through the Internet usually depends on the current connections and load being carried by Internet hosts and routers. There are several routing protocols that automatically reroute traffic when a particular router or communications trunk is too busy. TCP/IP applications cannot normally tell what route the data took when it is received.

Basic TCP/IP Vulnerabilities

This discussion will focus on four general threats to information traveling on a computer network.

- Masquerade
- Disclosure
- Modification
- Denial of service

Masquerade refers to messages containing bogus identification information. At the TCP/IP level, often this refers to bogus IP addresses, which are
attempts by one host to generate traffic appearing to be from a different
host. The "IP Spoofing" attacks reported by CERT in early 1995 are classic
examples of host masquerade. The attacks used a clever sequence of forged
packets to masquerade as a trusted host and penetrate the targeted host.
An attacker also could use bogus port numbers to simulate a different
server or client. Because individual application layer protocols have distinctive methods for identifying specific individuals, some masquerades involve application layer data alone. It is simple to forge an Internet e-mail
message that masquerades as a message from a different person.

Disclosure refers to undesired revelation of the data contents of messages. For many years this was not a problem in the TCP/IP community, because most applications were for academic or governmental purposes
where confidentiality was not important. But many routers and routing
hosts now have been deployed as part of the Internet's explosive growth.
Packets travel through numerous systems and organizations. Every router
and routing host can spy on the contents of every packet it handles.
Improper disclosure has sometimes led to masquerade attacks because several protocols use secret passwords for authentication. Confidentiality depends on effective security and good behavior in numerous independent
organizations; sites have reported subversion by both outsiders and insiders. CERT has reported several disclosure attacks targeting password traffic; one in early 1994 led to nationwide broadcast and news reports warning
Internet users to change their passwords. Early applications of electronic
commerce on the Internet have met some resistance, because credit card
numbers in messages are vulnerable to disclosure.

Modification refers to the undesired changes to the data contents of a
message. These attacks have been rare, because a masquerade attack is often easier and equally effective. The "IP Hijack" attacks reported in early
1995 provide a good example. The attacker modified software in a host so
that he could hijack an authenticated connection that a different user had
established to a different host. Thus, the message traffic produced by the
authorized user was replaced by the attacker's traffic.

Denial of service refers to actions that prevent network services from
being used when they should be available. This might include activities that
crash hosts or routers, or activities that block or shut down a service. A typical attack is the flooding attack wherein a host or network is overwhelmed
with traffic. The basic countermeasure is to shut down the traffic source;
properly implemented flow control should prevent such attacks from actually damaging the target. Other attacks occasionally target specific services,
hosts, or individuals.

To some extent, random behavior of network components could cause
any of these to occur. Dropped bits or crossed wires could cause the wrong

data to go to the wrong destination. Software errors could modify packets being routed. Confidential messages or passwords could be dumped accidentally on a console screen. The Internet protocols are generally designed to identify and detect random, unintended data changes or unexpectedly heavy traffic flows. The distinguishing feature of a true attack is usually that it bypasses the integrity and control measures provided by TCP/IP software.

The Emerging Internet Security Architecture

The original Internet protocols are incredibly successful from a connectivity standpoint. Before the Internet protocols were established, a connection spanning multiple networks would be constructed laboriously by hand. The Internet protocols allow a host in an organizational network on one continent to automatically open a real-time connection with another host on another continent, using standard application level protocols. Despite exponential growth in Internet connectivity since the early 1980s, the Internet protocol family continues to work effectively. No comparable communications system has grown so fast, so effectively, with so little central control.

Unfortunately, TCP/IP's security properties have not been comparably robust in the face of evolving Internet security threats. Originally, Internet hosts were expensive devices, residing in locked machine rooms and managed by a small community of skilled professionals. Internet security was similar to telephone system security, because Internet hosts and the people responsible tended to take such matters seriously. Unlike telephone central offices, however, Internet sites were not communications service providers, and for many years legal constraints on behavior were weak or nonexistent.

Personal computers and workstations violated the original assumptions underlying TCP/IP security. Before personal computers, the only people who could easily generate arbitrary packets on the Internet were highly trusted individuals: service technicians or systems programmers assigned to Internet hosts. Then low-cost personal computers allowed anyone to create an Internet site for a relatively low cost. These low-end hosts could produce whatever traffic they wanted as long as it did not interfere with their service provider or produce serious complaints. These changes also made it possible for a routing host to be sitting on some individual's desk. The Internet's vast extent then made it probable that some of these routing hosts would be subverted, either by the owner or by others.

The first approach to the growing problem was to improve host security. Many site security problems could clearly be blamed on poor host security: subtle configuration flaws, buggy software, absence of security patches, and so on. Solving the security problem at the hosts would clearly have the least impact on the original Internet architectural concept and on existing services. The objective was to solve the Internet security problem by securing all hosts at each site.

In practice, however, this approach could not keep up with network growth. There were never enough trained administrators or security analysts to check every host, nor did administrators always have the authority to close the holes they found. And securing a site's hosts would never prevent attacks on the site's traffic as it crossed the Internet. Host-based security measures have been doomed by the technical, economic, and political realities of Internet growth.

Site security and firewalls used

Given this situation, network service groups in organizations have turned to firewalls to control the Internet security threat. Firewalls allow the network service group to install defenses against Internet attacks without administering the uncounted individual host computers being installed by separate departments. Individual departments retain responsibility for buying and installing hosts while the central group manages security primarily with firewalls. This is much more realistic from an organizational perspective. The organization focuses its Internet security efforts at the Internet access points instead of distributing responsibility (and risk of failure) over a much larger population. The result is more reliable and cost-effective security.

Firewalls provide a perimeter defense employed at every point where the site's internal networks connect to the external Internet. Figure 8.4 provides an example of a firewall. The defense employs one or more of the following techniques: a packet gateway (also called filtering routers), a circuit gateway, and an application gateway.

Packet gateways operate at the Internet protocol layer, and many commercial routers can perform packet filtering. They examine individual Internet packets and discard packets that violate the site's expectations. For example, some sites do not accept incoming Internet connections for Telnet, the remote terminal emulation protocol. The packet gateways at such sites simply discard all incoming packets attempting to reach port 23, the well-known port for the Telnet server. The benefits to this approach are low cost, minimal effects on communications performance, and minimal effects on supported applications.

However, packet gateways are difficult to configure correctly. General guidelines are widely available, but the specifics must be tailored precisely to the network and gateway configuration. Minor errors can open very easy-to-exploit holes. For example, IP spoofing attacks could easily penetrate sites that failed to block the "impossible case" of external packets containing a source address of an internal host.

Another problem with packet gateways is the assumption that they can always distinguish "good" and "bad" traffic on the basis of predetermined information in IP packets. Typical filtering rules rely heavily on port numbers, yet these numbers do not appear in packets representing additional

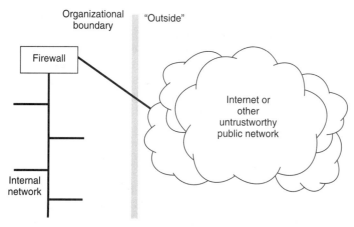

Figure 8.4 Firewalls protect internal networks by controlling message flow.

"fragments" of another packet. Such packets often represent a "don't know" case for the gateway, and they must often be forwarded to prevent "breaking" a legal connection. The Internet's File Transfer Protocol (FTP) does not use predefined ports for its data connection; an effective packet filter needs a good deal of looseness to allow such connections to be made. Even a highly restrictive packet filter must let in large amounts of traffic if it is to support basic IP services such as e-mail and file transfer.

Circuit gateways eliminate many packet filter shortcomings by handling data at the Transport Protocol layer. The circuit gateway can control access based on the network originating the traffic, the host address, and the port number (that is, type of service). Data traverses the gateway using a form of proxy service that forwards data on a connection between the actual server and client. To provide a service to internal clients, a proxy service will present server style incoming connections on the inside network, and will generate client style connections to servers on the outside network.

Because the circuit gateway operates at a higher protocol level, it eliminates many packet level security problems, including many variants of IP spoofing and the "don't know" cases noted above. A major shortcoming of circuit gateways is that they often require customized client software that knows how to reach its circuit gateway. Another shortcoming is that individual user identities are never visible at the circuit level in Internet protocols; the form and meaning of user identities are usually application-specific.

Application gateways apply security filtering at the application protocol layer. They provide the most capable security service of any gateway approach, though generally at the most cost. Unlike circuit gateways, application gateways generally contain several proxy services, one per application. These proxy services on application gateways are tailored to the specific applications, allowing access control to be applied according to application-specific data formats. This allows the gateway to control access based on user identities, which are invisible to lower protocol layers.

Furthermore, cryptographic services are applied most reliably at the application level. Several application-specific cryptographic services have been proposed and implemented. E-mail has used application level gateways for over a decade to provide simplified e-mail addressing for large sites; this has provided solid groundwork for providing relatively safe e-mail connectivity.

Establishing Client/Server Requirements

TCP/IP protocols can provide relatively secure and reliable service despite their weak security tradition. The challenge is to use existing protocol services as much as possible, and to augment their behavior when additional service and security assurances are needed. This approach takes advantage of existing work to reduce technical risk and development effort. The technical approach taken must address the following three issues, though their implementation can be phased in to respond to evolving threats.

- Gateway friendly transactions
- Reliable delivery
- Cryptographic protection

When designing for security, the safest approach is to identify the worst case from a security standpoint, and a strategy for sensibly scaling back according to the perceived threat and the costs of countermeasures. The worst might not happen, but it is prudent to have a strategy if it does. Because application level gateways promise the greatest degree of security we will focus on client/server solutions that can operate successfully even when such gateways are in place. Compatibility with application level gateways requires a few simple steps that will not significantly affect the development of a client/server system.

The following sections examine TCP/IP security in the context of an example client/server application: a customer order entry system using TCP/IP messages. The customer uses client software to send a message that identifies the customer and the list of items being ordered. The server software accepts the order for the vendor. The vendor then processes the order by delivering the ordered items to the customer, along with a list of unavailable items. The focus of the example shall be in providing the customer with a way to tell the vendor what items are needed. The resulting system is very similar to Internet e-mail and, in fact could be implemented atop existing e-mail software.

We begin by deciding what the system must do, and how this behavior is affected by threats against the system. This is primarily a requirements-analysis exercise that relates design alternatives to system and security threats. Once we have developed requirements and design alternatives, we can sensibly trade off between threats and the costs of countering them. The first step is to be specific about the system's objectives:

Objective 1 The system shall process every order a customer sends.

Objective 2 The system shall only process orders a customer sends.

It probably is true that no system can unconditionally achieve either objective. A variety of threats from malicious agents to unreliable delivery services prevents such reliability. Ordering messages might get lost before the server receives them. An individual masquerading as a customer might post an order, or perhaps a legitimate order might be received twice through a technical error. We address these issues through requirements definition.

Our next step is to define precise technical requirements that set technically practical objectives. This yields a short list of requirements that, taken together, convincingly achieve the system's objectives and address the security threats. These requirements should be rated according to their importance. The most likely threats, or those threatening the organization with the most damage, should carry the most weight. Less likely or less damaging threats carry less weight.

For example, a vendor of heavy machinery cannot afford to ship two cranes to a customer when only one was required. The vendor's order entry system would place heavy weight on requirements that reduce the risk of processing the same order twice. A vendor who processes numerous relatively small orders, on the other hand, might place less weight on such requirements, or might place a limit on the size of the order handled without additional assurances.

The prioritized list of requirements drives the technical aspects of the system. While the highest priority requirements carry the most weight, all requirements must be planned into the software, protocols, and processes. Threats will always evolve over time along with increases in the system's use and in the attackers' capabilities. The system must be planned to allow upgrades that address the evolving threats.

The remainder of this chapter will examine specific protocol mechanisms associated with the three issues noted above: transactions, reliability, and cryptography. For each mechanism we will review how it works, compare it with mechanisms in existing TCP/IP protocols, and then relate it to required capabilities and to potential threats. These mechanisms might be fundamental aspects of an existing TCP/IP service or an optional service like e-mail cryptography.

Gateway Friendly Transactions

The first step in developing the order entry system is to ensure architectural compatibility with application layer gateways. We achieve this through two objectives. First, the client/server protocol should be relatively state-less. This is true of Internet e-mail messages and of requests generated by Sun's Network File Service (NFS) protocol. Second, the service must pro-vide the complete, unambiguous address of a message's destination within the application's message. This is different from most Internet protocols (such as FTP and Telnet) in which the destination host address is estab-lished at the transport level and never directly represented in the applica-tion level protocol data stream.

Stateless Protocol

The key element of a stateless protocol is that it incorporates all informa-tion associated with a transaction in a single message. For example, a single order message could identify the customer, vendor, and the list of items be-ing ordered. The message also could include any necessary security valida-tion or authentication data. The client would generate and transmit an order with a single network connection, delivering the order directly to the vendor or to a relay on the route to the vendor. The vendor would receive this single message, validate it, and send back a single acknowledgement if necessary.

Several Internet protocols implement variants of this stateless property. The earliest such protocol was e-mail, because the delivery of the message contents embodied the entire objective of the protocol. Sun's Network File Service (NFS) is probably the first protocol to make its stateless nature a philosophical statement regarding protocol design. Each Usenet news arti-cle represents a stateless "deliver me" command like e-mail messages. The World Wide Web protocol family produces essentially stateless request and response pairs.

The principal motivation for statelessness is that it is the most efficient way of sending information through relays and security gateways. If the client breaks an order up into independently delivered messages, then we increase the cost of application proxy servers at security gateways. If indi-vidual messages in a transaction need to be separately processed by the server, then the proxy server needs to check the messages individually. Security checks also are more feasibly applied to a complete set of informa-tion than they are to piecemeal elements of a transaction. This also allows a site to apply security checks to orders it sends or receives at the security gateway if desired. It is more efficient to apply digital signature checking, or other cryptographic protections, to a single, complete order message. Digital signature checking is very time-consuming and should not be per-formed any more often than is absolutely necessary. When performed across an entire, atomic transaction, the digital signature can efficiently val-idate both the message's source and the integrity of its contents. Digital sig-nature checking could even be performed at security gateways.

Compare this with using a stateful protocol such as Telnet as the implementation model. For example, the order entry system might be an interactive program executed on the server system, using a remote login. Telnet uses a single TCP connection between server and client. Most data transmitted on a Telnet connection is treated as a sequence of possibly unrelated data bytes. There are no assumptions made about the format or meaning of the data bytes, other than that they belong in a particular sequence and travel in a particular direction. This makes the protocol fairly easy to implement and extremely difficult to secure. There is no way to associate contents of the data stream with its security properties because there is no particular structure to the Telnet data stream. Because all of the ordering and integrity protections on Telnet data are provided by TCP, any TCP vulnerability can be used to disrupt or subvert a Telnet connection. There is no way of efficiently applying digital signatures to an arbitrary Telnet data stream.

The requirement statement leading to a stateful protocol in the order entry application would be as follows:

Requirement 1 Each order submitted by a customer shall consist of a single, atomic message.

Requirement 2 Each order shall uniquely identify the customer.

Requirement 3 Each order shall uniquely identify the vendor.

Requirement 4 Each order shall contain a list of all items being ordered.

Requirement 5 Any order response sent by the vendor shall consist of a single, atomic message.

As noted earlier, the customer order system could be implemented entirely with Internet e-mail. Some readers might note that the Simple Mail Transfer Protocol (SMTP) that delivers e-mail between systems is not really a stateless protocol itself. This points up the distinction between the stateful transfer protocol and the stateless message protocol. RFC 822 is the official standard for e-mail message contents and format, and it is clearly a stateless protocol. An RFC 822 e-mail message is either received entirely and correctly, and then delivered, or it is not correctly received and is discarded. Partial messages are never delivered. This, in essence, is the stateless protocol.

Application Level Address Data

By providing application level address data, the destination of every message is always completely identified within the application data being sent. This allows application gateways to extract such information and forward a message correctly. The alternative is old-style destination addressing in which the destination is specified at the transport level and never explicitly included in the application level data stream. Application gateways handle such addresses very poorly, and such addresses cannot be passed from one gateway to another.

Originally, all TCP/IP services used direct host-to-host connections. To send e-mail from one host to another, the sending host would open a direct connection to the receiving host and transfer the e-mail directly. As networking evolved, people found it useful to share e-mail among a variety of networks, not all of which were TCP/IP compatible. An early example was CSNet, a consortium of university computer science departments that wanted a low cost e-mail facility. The system consisted of an e-mail gateway that forwarded e-mail to some campuses via low cost dial-up telephone connections, and to others via higher performance (and more expensive) packet switching networks, including Telenet and the ARPA Network.

This technique worked because the e-mail messages themselves each contained the destination addressee for the message. The sending computer did not need to connect directly to the receiving computer in order to successfully transfer e-mail. As long as the e-mail reached a relay system that knew how to examine the address field and forward it correctly, the e-mail would eventually arrive at its destination.

Compare this with FTP and Telnet, the earliest Internet protocols. In both cases the client software must identify a destination host with which it desires to interact. In both cases, the client software must establish a direct connection with the destination host and has no other way to specify the destination host's identity. This works poorly when there are one or more security gateways between client and server. Because the destination address is provided at the network level and not at the application level, an application gateway proxy cannot pass the client's request along to another server or gateway. The destination address is not provided through the application level protocol, so the gateway proxy cannot see it.

Internet e-mail is not the only protocol to provide application level address data. Network news messages provide a source address for each article, and the address can often be used to transmit an e-mail message to the article's author. The Universal Resource Locator (URL) format established for the World Wide Web protocols is also application level address data. These gateway-friendly protocols provide the destination address as part of the protocol instead of hiding the information in a lower-level protocol transaction.

The order entry application could provide application level addresses by specifying the network address of the vendor's server and the customer's client in application level protocol messages. If many vendors use this protocol, or if it is based on some existing protocol like SMTP e-mail, security gateways can implement proxies that will forward authorized requests and responses across their protected boundaries. The requirement statements for application level address data in the order entry application are as follows:

Requirement 6 Each order submitted by a customer and each response sent by the vendor shall contain a complete, unambiguous network address indicating both the message sender and recipient.

This requirement requires further refinement for specific cases. The developer must decide whether the client and server addresses need a form of individual identity (similar to e-mail messages) or whether a host address is sufficient. If host addresses are sufficient, the requirement should specify the form they must take. An implementation using e-mail could specify e-mail addresses as unique identifiers.

Requirement 7 Each vendor shall be uniquely identified by an Internet e-mail address.

Requirement 8 Each client shall be uniquely identified by an Internet e-mail address.

Reliable Delivery

The next issue in client/server security is reliable message delivery. Gateway-friendly transactions place the emphasis on individual messages; we must now decide how to handle unreliable delivery. In practice, the sources of unreliability are largely eliminated by using TCP to transfer messages between hosts. E-mail messages are very rarely lost, damaged, or duplicated despite the risks present at e-mail gateways. However, mishandling is even more likely when messages traverse security gateways. Some gateways might discard messages without warning when the message somehow violates the access rules. Perhaps reliability services are not needed immediately, but the general design should incorporate reliability requirements.

In some circles, reliability is not a security issue. Our initial discussion of threats identified denial of service as an important threat, though there are never enough countermeasures to thoroughly address that threat. And because our objective is to have a protocol that works effectively through security gateways, it is important to address unreliability potentially caused by such gateways.

Data Integrity

The first part of reliable message delivery is a method of recognizing when a message arrives intact. No further processing is worthwhile if a message has been damaged, or if there is no way to tell if a message was damaged. The traditional, effective approach is to define a valid message in such a way that accidental changes will invalidate it. This usually involves checksums.

Data integrity mechanisms are implemented both TCP and UDP. Application layer protocols have traditionally relied on the Transport layer protocols to validate the integrity of data sent across the network. In practice, messages are rarely damaged at relay and gateway sites. The network news protocol probably relays the most information of any Internet protocol, and users rarely encounter damaged news articles despite its lack of integrity checks.

We shall still define an integrity requirement although it might acquire a relatively low priority:

Requirement 9 Every order and acknowledgement shall contain checksums to validate the integrity of critical information in the message.

Positive Acknowledgment

The positive acknowledgement protocol is the second basic tool for reliable message delivery. The classic elements are periodic retransmission and acknowledgement upon receipt. The host sending the message will send the message repeatedly. The recipient of a message will send an acknowledgment to a message's sender as soon as a message is received. The sender stops sending copies of the message once its acknowledgement is received.

This mechanism is implemented in TCP, and Internet protocols have traditionally expected TCP to provide reliable delivery services when needed. More recent application protocols built upon UDP also use a positive acknowledgement protocol. NFS uses one built atop Remote Procedure Call (RPC). Some observers note the absence of retransmission in SMTP as a rationale for calling it a "Simple" protocol.

A key point to efficient acknowledgement is to accurately estimate reasonable delivery times. To avoid unnecessary retransmission, the retransmission time must be longer than the expected round-trip delivery time for messages. Unnecessary retransmission wastes host and network bandwidth. But timely message delivery requires prompt retransmission to reduce delays for lost messages.

Here is the retransmission requirement for the order entry system:

Requirement 10 The order entry client shall transmit an order repeatedly until it receives a confirmation message from the vendor.

Note how this relates to Objective 1 to process every order a customer sends. It does not quite meet the objective because orders will not be received or processed if a network failure prevents the order's delivery. However, the retransmission guarantees that the message will either be delivered to the server or that the client will have a clear indication that the order was not received. Positive acknowledgements do not necessarily require complicated software. For example, an e-mail implementation of the order entry system could rely on manual acknowledgements and retransmission. The vendor could manually generate acknowledgements and customers could manually retransmit orders when they failed to receive a timely acknowledgement.

Duplicate Detection

The important side effect of a positive acknowledgement protocol is that it might generate duplicate messages. Therefore, the acknowledgement protocol must be extended to handle potential duplicates. The protocol requires some method to distinguish unique messages from one another. In the order entry example we could require an order identifier consisting of the customer's identity combined with a unique, customer-generated order number. The server would examine incoming orders and discard any whose identifying data was identical to an earlier order.

This leads to an important semantic issue. Every unique order identifier must be associated with a separate message, and not with the objective of spending particular amounts of money at particular times, or acquiring particular items. The system works predictably as long as two or more order messages sent with the same unique identifier also contain identical contents. Otherwise, the client has no way of knowing which order with a given identifier is, in fact, being processed by the vendor. The client cannot assume that an order was lost simply because no acknowledgement was received; the acknowledgement might have been lost or delayed. If the client sends a different version of the same order, the first might be processed anyway because it arrived first.

TCP provides duplicate detection along with retransmission. As described previously, older TCP/IP applications rely entirely on TCP to provide duplicate detection. The stateless NFS protocol does not actually perform duplicate detection; requests are simply repeated if received an extra time. The network news protocol is one of the few application protocols that actually detects duplicates. As news articles propagate through the system, adjacent news sites will try to send articles from one to the other. If the recipient already has received a particular article, it discards the second copy based on the unique identifier carried in each article.

Here are the duplicate detection requirements for the order entry system:

Requirement 11 Each order shall contain a unique identifier for that order, assigned by that customer.

Requirement 12 All orders containing the same customer identifier and order identifier shall be identical in contents.

Requirement 13 When the order entry server receives an order, it shall send an acknowledgement back to the client containing the client's identifier and the unique order number.

Requirement 14 Additional orders received with the same customer and order identifiers shall be acknowledged and discarded.

Note that these requirements can be met by a manual system operating on orders transmitted via e-mail. These requirements are somewhat risky to

implement manually, because it might be tempting for an operator to modify a retransmitted order.

Cryptographic Services

Evolving Internet services are leading to broader use of cryptography. Even
relatively weak cryptographic techniques can secure important traffic against
most Internet attackers. Cryptographic services generally provide two
mechanisms: *confidentiality* and *nonrepudiation*. Confidentiality is the
typical use of cryptography: encrypting data to hide its contents from disclosure. Nonrepudiation is a strong form of authentication that ties the
sender's identity to information in a message.

Effective use of cryptography is a broad and complex subject. We minimize our risk of error by relying on existing cryptographic systems. These
systems will provide us with protocols to use encryption for confidentiality,
and digital signatures for nonrepudiation. The systems also generally provide procedures for handling cryptographic keys, a risky problem area. In
all cases, it is important to take the time to study the cryptographic services
being used, and how they work. Pay close attention to identified weaknesses and how they could affect the system in actual use.

There are two approaches to cryptography in today's Internet environment. First, there is network encryption. This usually provides encryption
on leased communications lines between two separate sites belonging to
the same organization. This secures those lines against disclosure. A few
more expensive systems exist that will encrypt IP packets before transmission across the Internet, to a matching decryption box at the destination.
Network encryption protects traffic against disclosure. It does not provide
nonrepudiation, nor does it provide reliable integrity protection. While
some encryption facilities claim to detect breaches of traffic integrity, it is
difficult to do so reliably. The second approach to cryptography uses it with
the application protocol layer. This approach has been successfully applied
to e-mail and work is proceeding on other applications, notably World Wide
Web. Application layer cryptography provides either nonrepudiation, confidentiality, or both.

Three well-known cryptographic systems have been developed for e-
mail: the Message Security Protocol (MSP), Privacy Enhanced Mail (PEM),
and Pretty Good Privacy (PGP). MSP was developed for the U.S. Government under the Secure Data Network System (SDNS) program. PEM is a
variant of MSP that has become something of an Internet standard. PGP is
a simplified system intended to provide similar capabilities to the other two.
PEM and PGP both rely heavily on public key cryptography. These systems
provide the following facilities.

Identification certificates. These are data structures that associate
user identities with cryptographic keys, usually based on public key algo-

rithms. A user might have one or more certificates, each containing identification data such as a personal name and title, some keying material, and a cryptographic integrity checksum to validate the certificate's contents. Certificate formats usually conform to the X.509 standard accepted by the International Standards Organization (ISO). Certificates are publicly distributed so that others might use them to receive e-mail or validate digital signatures authored by the certificate's owner.

Message encapsulation formats. These are data structures that place the text of a message, markings regarding its handling, encryption key identification, and digital signature data in well-defined locations.

Digital signature procedure. This is a procedure that uniquely marks a message in a manner that is only possible by the holder of a particular signature certificate. The signature algorithm will detect any attempt to change the message so as to modify its contents or the identity of the author. The recipient can always validate the author and the integrity of a message by checking its digital signature using the author's certificate.

Encryption and decryption procedures. This is a procedure that disguises the information contents of a message so that it might only be decoded by the desired recipient. The author uses public key techniques to produce an encryption key that can only be recovered by the message's recipient. That key is used to encrypt the message. The recipient uses a decryption procedure to recover the encryption key and decode the message.

This brief description of cryptographic services should be sufficient to direct your requirements-definition task. The practical application of cryptographic services requires procedures to create, update, and distribute certificates for authorized users, as well as the procedures for applying the algorithms to application-specific data messages. We shall assume that the key and certificate-management procedures established by a chosen privacy protocol might be effectively adapted to use with the order entry system.

Nonrepudiation

Nonrepudiation requires a strong identification and authentication facility, with a strong checksum covering the contents of a message. The digital signature provides this capability. The digital signature procedure computes a message's hash value (essentially a large checksum) over the message contents and combines it with the author's public keying material. A special validation procedure allows recipients to recompute the digital signature, using information in the author's publicly distributed certificate. The procedure detects modifications to the protected contents of the message, or to the author's identification data.

One-way passwords are another popular approach to authentication on the Internet. They are often used with Telnet sessions to authenticate the user when a connection is initially received by a server. This approach is effective only as long as the associated connection retains its integrity. It is vulnerable to attacks such as the IP Hijack attack described earlier. The fundamental limitation is that one-way passwords identify who initiated the connection but are unaffected by breaches in the connection's integrity. Thus, nothing strongly binds the authentication with the data carried by the connection. Digital signatures overcome this limitation by being associated with the integrity of a single, complete message.

The nonrepudiation requirement is as follows:

Requirement 15 Each message shall be digitally signed by the message's originator, either the client on the customer's behalf or the server on the vendor's behalf.

This is the only requirement that strongly supports Objective 2. The requirements that place the author's name and source identification data provide identification. They do not provide authentication because they are easy to forge. The digital signature is the only strong authentication mechanism appropriate for this application.

Confidentiality

Confidentiality on the Internet can only be achieved through encryption. As described earlier, there are several ways to do this, including variations of link and packet encryption. However, link and packet encryption interact poorly with application gateways, because they hide the contents of application messages on which access control decisions might be based.

The confidentiality requirement is stated as follows:

Requirement 16 Each message shall be encrypted by the message's originator, either the client on the customer's behalf or the server on the vendor's behalf.

Design Trade-Offs

We shall now review the requirements in the context of two specific design solutions directed at two different situations. In both cases we shall rate the significance of the individual requirements and indicate how they shall be addressed in the design.

E-mail-based manual system

This implementation is for a relatively low volume system where review by sales personnel is an important part of the order entry process. This might be true when handling particularly expensive orders, because sales personnel would want to resolve problems or ambiguities directly, if they occur.

- **Requirement 1** Atomic order messages.
  Priority High.
  Implementation Use the body of e-mail messages to contain the list of items being ordered.

- **Requirement 2** Unique customer identification.
  Priority High.
  Implementation Use the customer's e-mail address as a unique identifier.

- **Requirement 3** Unique vendor identification.
  Priority High.
  Implementation The vendor shall establish an e-mail address to which orders shall be sent. This address shall be the vendor's unique identifier.

- **Requirement 4** Complete list of items.
  Priority High.
  Implementation Place the list of items in the body of the e-mail message.

- **Requirement 5** Atomic order responses.
  Priority High
  Implementation E-mail sent to the vendor's ordering address shall be answered by sales personnel. The sales person shall immediately send a reply as soon as an order is received at the ordering address.

- **Requirement 6** Application level addresses.
  Priority High
  Implementation The e-mail messages containing orders and acknowledgements always contain the complete e-mail sender and recipient addresses.

- **Requirement 7** Unique server e-mail address.
  Priority High.
  Implementation As indicated in Requirement 2.

- **Requirement 8** Unique client e-mail address.
  Priority High.
  Implementation As indicated in Requirement 3.

- **Requirement 9** Checksum on critical information.
  Priority Low.
  Implementation Customer shall specify the total cost in the order. If the total cost fails to match the cost of individual items, the order will be returned to the customer for correction.

- **Requirement 10** Retransmit until acknowledgement.
  Priority Medium.

Implementation The vendor's objective shall be to respond to all orders within two hours of submission. If no acknowledgement is received by then, the customer shall retransmit the order.

- **Requirement 11** Unique order identifier.
Priority Medium.
Implementation The customer shall be instructed to assign a unique number to each order submitted to the vendor.

- **Requirement 12** All orders match identifiers.
Priority Medium.
Implementation The customer shall be instructed to retain a copy of every order submitted, at least until the order has been acknowledged by the vendor. If the customer needs to retransmit an order, the customer must retransmit it exactly without changes.

- **Requirement 13** Order identifier in acknowledgement.
Priority Medium.
Implementation When the vendor acknowledges an order, the acknowledgement will include the customer's order number.

- **Requirement 14** Duplicates acknowledged and discarded.
Priority Medium
Implementation If an order is received with a duplicate order number, the vendor shall send an acknowledgement to the customer with that order number and then discard the duplicate order.

- **Requirement 15** Digital signatures on messages.
Priority Low.
Implementation If required by evolving security threats, the vendor shall acquire PEM or PGP e-mail server software and provide client software to all customers. The mail package's digital signature service will then be used to validate messages and their source.

- **Requirement 16** Encrypted messages.
Priority Low.
Implementation If required by evolving security threats, the vendor shall acquire PEM or PGP e-mail server software and provide client software to all customers. The mail package's encryption service will then be used to protect message contents from disclosure.

Automated system similar to e-mail

A higher volume order entry system will require more automation in order to operate reliably. Priorities are modified somewhat to reflect the larger volume and the greater likelihood of random errors or fraud. This implementation substitutes custom servers and clients; the client software at least enforces a structure on orders sent to the server. Both server and client incorporate digital signatures using mechanisms from PEM or PGP.

- **Requirement 1** Atomic order messages.
  Priority High.
  Implementation Use the body of the e-mail messages to contain the list of items being ordered, so that existing mail relays might be used to transmit orders.

- **Requirement 2** Unique customer identification.
  Priority High.
  Implementation Customers shall be identified by identity strings in their public key certificates. These strings shall appear in orders from the customer.

- **Requirement 3** Unique vendor identification.
  Priority High.
  Implementation Vendors shall be identified by identity strings in their public key certificates. These strings shall appear in order acknowledgements from the vendor.

- **Requirement 4** Complete list of items.
  Priority High.
  Implementation Place the list of items in the body of the e-mail message. The list of items shall follow a precisely defined format that is enforced by the client software.

- **Requirement 5** Atomic order responses.
  Priority High.
  Implementation When the server receives an order message, it validates the message format and sends an acknowledgement.

- **Requirement 6** Application level addresses.
  Priority High.
  Implementation The e-mail messages containing orders and acknowledgements always contain the complete e-mail sender and recipient addresses.

- **Requirement 7** Unique server e-mail address.
  Priority High.
  Implementation Each vendor server shall have a unique e-mail address.

- **Requirement 8** Unique client e-mail address.
  Priority High.
  Implementation Each customer client shall have a unique e-mail address.

- **Requirement 9** Checksum on critical information.
  Priority High.
  Implementation Both server and client software provide digital signatures across the data stored in orders and acknowledgements.

- **Requirement 10** Retransmit until acknowledgement.
  Priority High.
  Implementation The server software shall send an acknowledgement as soon as an order has been received and its format validated. This should take a small amount of time (to be determined). The client shall continuously retransmit the order if the acknowledgement has not returned within twice the expected round-trip transit time.

- **Requirement 11** Unique order identifier.
  Priority High.
  Implementation The client software shall insert a unique identifier in each order it generates. This shall be unique even if multiple clients are being used by a single customer; that is, it might be generated using the client's host address as well as a serial number for orders from that client.

- **Requirement 12** All orders match identifiers.
  Priority High.
  Implementation The client shall only create a single order with a particular unique identifier.

- **Requirement 13** Order identifier in acknowledgement.
  Priority High.
  Implementation When the vendor acknowledges an order, the acknowledgement will include the customer's order number.

- **Requirement 14** Duplicates acknowledged and discarded.
  Priority High.
  Implementation If an order is received with a duplicate order number, the server shall send an acknowledgement containing that order number to the originating client, and then shall discard the duplicate order.

- **Requirement 15** Digital signatures on messages.
  Priority High.
  Implementation Digital signatures shall be used to validate messages and their sources.

- **Requirement 16** Encrypted messages.
  Priority Low.
  Implementation If required by evolving security threats, the vendor shall acquire PEM or PGP e-mail server software and shall provide client software to all customers. The mail package's encryption service will then be used to protect message contents from disclosure.

Summary

It is not enough to secure one's traffic while it crosses the Internet; all security measures must operate effectively together. Client/server systems must be constructed so that they interact reliably and effectively with security firewalls. And future network services must be able to support increasingly stronger security countermeasures as the threat continues to evolve.

Security must start with an evaluation of system requirements and must follow the necessary trade-offs between the real threats and costs of countermeasures. The network environment is no different from any other environment: there is no such thing as absolute security. There must always be a trade-off between risk and reward.

Select Bibliography

Cheswick, William R. and Steven M. Bellovin. 1994. *Firewalls and Internet Security: Repelling the Wily Hacker*. Reading, MA: Addison-Wesley.

Comer, Douglas. 1991. *Internetworking with TCP/IP, Volume 1: Principles, Protocols, and Architecture*. Englewood Cliffs: NJ: Prentice-Hall, Inc.

Schneier, Bruce. 1994. *Applied Cryptography: Protocols, Algorithms, and Source Code in C*. New York: John Wiley & Sons.

Security Products: Application Gateway Firewalls

Border Network Technologies: JANUS products
1 Yonge St., Suite 1400
Toronto, Ontario, Canada, M5E 1J9
(416) 368-7157

Checkpoint Software: Firewall-1 products
CheckPoint Software Technologies Ltd.
One Militia Dr.
Lexington, MA 02173
(800) 429-4391

Secure Computing Corporation: Sidewinder products
2675 Long Lake Rd.
Roseville, MN 55113
(612) 628-2700

Trusted Information Systems: Gauntlet products
3060 Washington Rd.
Glenwood, MD 21738
(301) 854-6889

Security Products: Cryptographic Software

CIS: Certificate issuing system for PEM users
RSA Data Security, Inc.
(415) 595-8782

COST-PEM: PEM for personal computers and workstations
COST Computer Security Technologies AB
Sweden
+46-8-739-1839
Internet e-mail: sead@dsv.su.se

FJPEM v1.1: PEM implementations for 10 platforms
Fujitsu Labs
Japan
Internet access: sh.wide.ad.jp:/WIDE/free-ware/fjpem

RIPEM: Example source code for a PEM implementation
Mark Riordan
Michigan State University
Internet access: ripem.msu.edu

RSAREF: Cryptographic software for PEM implementations.
TIPEM: Software toolkit for PEM messaging applications.
RSA Data Security, Inc.
Internet access: rsa.com

SecuDE PEM: PEM based security toolkit for UNIX systems.
Gesellschaft für Mathematik und Datenverarbeitung
Germany
Internet e-mail: Schneider@darmstadt.gmd.de

TechMail-PEM-a7: Macintosh implementation of PEM.
Massachusetts Institute of Technology
Cambridge, MA
Internet access: net-dist.mit.edu:/pub/TechMail-PEM

TIS/PEM: source code for PEM development

Trusted Information Systems
3060 Washington Rd.
Glenwood, MD 21738
(301) 854-6889
Internet access: FTP.TIS.com

TMAIL: PEM implementation of UNIX e-mail software.

9

Securing APPC/APPN
Richard Daugherty

Progress always involves risk; you can't steal
second base and keep your foot on first.
FREDRICK WILCOX

CPI-C (Common Programming Interface-Communications), APPC (Advanced Program-to-Program Communications) and APPN (Advanced Peer-to-Peer Networking) are three integrated, yet independent parts of an overall communications system. CPI-C provides a system, language, and protocol-independent interface for both APPC and OSI-TP (Open Systems Interconnect-Transaction Programs). APPC provides the conversational protocols for applications. It can use both APPN and subarea SNA for routing and data transport. In addition, the use of MultiProtocol Transport Network (MPTN) technology allows APPC to use other transports like TCP/IP and NetBIOS. APPN provides the network routing and transport functions. APPN in turn uses APPC protocols for its control functions.

This chapter briefly introduces all three components. It identifies the security services available to APPC users and needed by clients and servers. Next it covers specific product implementations of authentication, access control and confidentiality. It also describes the general direction of future APPC and APPN security. The chapter concludes with suggested sources of additional information and assistance on CPI-C, APPC, and APPN.

What Are CPI-C, APPC, and APPN?

The conversational model for distributed system provides the ability for two programs to exchange messages, using a conversation. The conversation can be as simple as one program sending a single record to the other. Or, it might be as complex as multiple records being sent in both directions, with two-phase commit protocols used to ensure consistency of the final program results.

Figure 9.1 shows two transaction programs, or TPs. Let us call one the client and the other the server. In this case, the client TP is the application program that requests an action from the server program. The client TP uses a conversation as its communication path to the server TP. Clients and servers use the CPI-C interface to create and destroy the conversations. The TPs use CPI-C calls to send data, receive data, and otherwise control the conversation.

CPI-C is a thin interface for APPC (See Fig. 9-2.) The underlying APPC implementation constructs the conservation. When the client requests the creation of a conversation to the server, the APPC function [1] on its system first creates a session to the LU where the server resides. APPC can use either APPN or subarea routing to determine the path the session will use through the network. APPN provides the data transport services used to move the data to the destination system. The High Performance Routing (HPR) extension to APPN adds support for nondisruptive rerouting around network failures, and enables better throughput on high bandwidth networks.

APPC with CPI-C provides many services to application TPs. The TPs might exchange data, using either full or half duplex flow control. Full duplex allows both programs to send data at the same time. With half duplex the two programs take turns sending, and only one will have send permission at any time. APPC guarantees reliable, in-order delivery of all data sent. APPC also provides a rich set of program synchronization functions, ranging from a simple "did you get it" to two-phase commit protocols.

CPI-C and APPC support many options for developing multiuser servers; these include the ability to accept multiple conversation and nonblocking

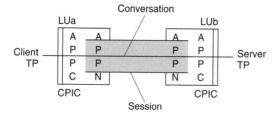

Figure 9.1 Conversations and transaction programs.

---

[1]APPC is referred to as Logical Unit (LU) type 6.2 or LU 6.2. It is documented in [TPRM] and [PEER].

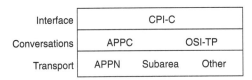

Figure 9.2 Relationship of CPI-C, APPC, and APPN.

operations. APPC also can apply end-to-end data compression, transparently, to the application programs.

APPN provides the network discovery and routing functions for APPC. APPN networks consist of two types of nodes: end nodes and network nodes. End nodes are nodes that support LUs (logical units) with clients and servers and sit, logically, at the periphery of the network. Network nodes provide network topology, routing, and transport services to end nodes. Every node has a special APPC LU, called a *control point* (CP). The network node control points manage the network topology and perform route set-up.

Figure 9.3 shows a small APPN network. It consists of a local area network (LAN) connected to a wide area network (WAN). The LAN has three end nodes connected to it. End node EN2 has two LUs (LUb and LUc) active on it. Network node NN1 is also on the LAN. The WAN backbone consists of four additional network nodes. When an LU on the LAN needs to establish a session with another LU, (e.g., LUf) it asks network node NN1 to determine the route. If NN1 does not know where the destination LU is, it will send a LOCATE request to the other network nodes. In this case, NN1 will find out that LUf is on EN5 and connected to NN4. A likely route will be EN1-NN1-NN2-NN5-NN4-EN5.

A Sample Program

First let us look at a simple CPI-C client/server example. The client TP sends a query to the server. The server sends back an answer to the query and the client receives the response. A CPI-C pseudo-code representation of the two programs is in Figure 9.4.

First the client program issues Initialize_Conversation. This creates a local handle for the conversation and initializes starting characteristics. For this example, the CPI-C Side Information entry, called "Server," contains the destination information. The side information contains the names of the server's LU and TP. It also contains a mode name that describes the characteristics of the session the conversation will use. Between steps 1 and 2 is where the client program could make calls to change the conversation's characteristics. For example, an application might issue a Set_Conversation_Security_Type call to request the usage of DISTRIBUTED security. When the client issues the Allocate call in step 2,

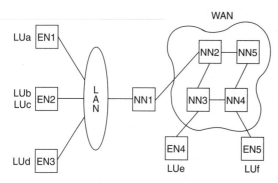

Figure 9.3 Sample APPC/APPN network.

Client TP   Server TP

1. Initialize_Conversation("Server")
2. Allocate()

                                               3. server start by system
                                               4. Accept_Conversation()
5. Send_Data(Query)

                                               6. Receive(Query)
                                               7. determine answer
                                               8. Send_Data(Query_Answer)
                                               9. Deallocate()
10. Receive (Query_Answer)
11. Process answer

Figure 9.4 Simple Client/Server written with CPI-C.

the local LU builds the conversation startup request to send to the partner system. The local LU establishes the session that the conversation will use. Also, the LU determines the security information to send with the startup request. Normally, the conversation startup request is not sent at this time. However, for our example, it is sent immediately.

When the server's LU receives the conversation start-up request, the LU uses the security information in the startup request to validate the user and determine the user's authority to this Server TP. If the user is authorized to the server, the server is automatically started in step 3. It is possible that the server was already running, in which case the LU would not have to start it. In step 4, the server TP accepts the inbound conversation. At this time both TPs are active with a conversation using a session.

Meanwhile the client issues a Send_Data call. For this example, the data transmitted contains a query. The data is sent over the conversation.

The server issues a Receive for the data in step 6. The server then processes the request in step 7. This processing can cause the server to access many resources, including resources subject to access control checks. In steps 8 and 9, the server sends the answer back to the client and then ends the conversation using a Deallocate.

The client then receives the data and the conversation-ending indication in step 10.

With this example in mind, what areas require security? The application used a side information entry called "Server" to set the addressing for the server. If an attacker could change the side information values they could substitute a rogue server. In most cases, this could only be used in a denial of service attack. But, if the client is using the information from the server to make an important decision, like an ATM determining how much money to dispense, then being able to change the server destination could lead to security problems.

The next place that has security concerns is step 2. When the session to the destination is established, how does the client system know that it has reached the destination? How does the server system know which client system has really initiated this session? APPC's session-level LU-LU verification, described later, provides this LU identity verification. This verification is very important if the LUs make decisions based on the other identity. One common LU-identity-based decision is what type of security information the server will accept from the client. Step 2 is when the client's authentication information is determined.

When the conversation start-up request is received, the server's LU must determine whether the client is valid and has permission to request the services of this server. It also must determine whether an already running program is allowed to act as the server for this request.

Finally, in steps 5-6, and 8-10 the data transmitted on the session between the client and server must be protected.

CPI-C, APPC, and APPN Security Options

APPC supports a wide range of security services and policies. User authentication is supported with user IDs and several options for performing the authentication. APPC also can authenticate LUs to each other. Access control to transaction programs is provided. Encryption is used to ensure the confidentiality of data in transit.

Table 9.1 lists the APPC options related to security. Each option has a unique option set number and an option set name. The table contains the set number and the name. It also indicates what options are strongly recommended for client and server systems. The rest of this section discusses the options, giving a description of the function provided by each of them. From the table you can see that there are about 20 options. Why are there so many options? APPC is used by a very wide range of devices and systems. It has been implemented in everything from printers to multiuser mainframe systems. Many options are not needed in all environments or markets. Also, new security functions are added as additional options—this helps guarantee that yesterday's implementations will continue to interconnect with newer implementations.

TABLE 9.1 APPC/APPN Security Related Options

Set number	Set name	Client	Server
211	Session-level LU-LU verification (also called Partner LU Verification and BIND Security)	Yes	Yes
212	User ID verification	Yes	Yes
213	Program-supplied user ID and password	Yes	
214	User ID authorization		Yes
215	Profile verification and authorization		
216	Origin LU authorization		
217	Profile pass-through		
218	Program-supplied profile		
219	Send persistent verification	Yes	
220	Receive persistent verification	Yes	
221	Send Sign-On/Change-Password (also called PEM— Password Expiration Management)		Yes
222	Received Sign-On/Change-Password (also called PEM or Password Expiration Management)		Yes
223	Password Substitution	Yes	Yes
224	Security Program Strong	Yes	
230	Distributed Authentication	Yes	Yes
611	Session-level mandatory cryptography	Yes	Yes
617	Session-level selective cryptography		
1070	(APPN) Session Cryptography	Yes	Yes
1102	(APPN) End Node Authorization		

What is needed on both the client and server systems?

Every system needs session-level LU-LU verification (#211) and user ID verification (#212). Also, to provide confidentiality, session-level mandatory cryptography (#611) option is needed. In an APPN network, the APPN session cryptography (#1070) option is required to support session cryptography.

New options that are useful for both client and server systems are password substitution (#223) and distributed authentication (#230). Password substitution protects user passwords while they are in transit through the network. Distributed authentication integrates third-party authentication services, like Kerberos, into APPC.

The session-level LU-LU verification (#211) option is at the base of all the APPC/APPN security options. LU-LU verification allows the two systems to be certain that they are communicating with each other. It addresses the problem of an attacker attaching a new system to the network and masquerading as another system.

APPC has two algorithms for LU-LU verification, the original, basic algorithm and a later, stronger, enhanced algorithm. Both algorithms require the LUs to share a password. Additional data is exchanged during session startup to prove that each LU knows the same password value. The enhanced algorithm is fully described in [EBINDSEC].

Figure 9.5 illustrates the enhanced algorithm's flows. In step 1, the origin node places a challenge (challenge1) into the session BIND[2] request being sent to LUb. Step 2, has LUb placing a different challenge (challenge2) and a reply (reply1) to the received challenge into the session BIND response. The reply is a DES MAC (Message Authentication Code) computed over the string "challenge1, challenge2, (LUb XOR challenge1)", using the shared password as the MAC key. In step 3, LUa verifies LUb's answer by independently performing the computations. If the result matches, LUa builds a reply (reply2) to the new challenge (challenge2) by computing a DES MAC over just the two challenges, challenge1 and challenge2. LUa sends this reply to LUb. As the final step, LUb performs the same computation to validate LUa's identity.

User ID Verification

The user ID verification (#212) option easily could have been split into separate client and server side options. For the server side, this option allows the receipt and verification of user IDs using passwords. It also allows the server system to identify client systems that are trusted to perform authentication, and therefore to send user IDs with an "already verified" indicator. Already verified is useful when the client system is a trusted multiuser system. Examples of trustworthy multiuser systems include MVS/ESA, VM/ESA, and centralized UNIX systems. Already verified also is useful when establishing communications between servers; for example, a workgroup database server contacting a corporate database server.

User ID verification (#212) allows the client application to ask the client LU to send security information to the server. This specification is called SECURITY(SAME). If the server system trusts the client system, then the client's user ID and the already verified indicator will be sent. Otherwise, the client's LU might attempt to locate a password for the user, and if one is found, to send it with the user ID. If a password cannot be located, then the request is downgraded to an anonymous request.

If the underlying transport network does not provide adequate data confidentiality, then the client and server systems need the session-level man-

Figure 9.5 Enhanced LU-LU verification.

---

[2]BIND is the request that is sent between systems to request the creation of a new session.

datory cryptography (#611) option. Session cryptography is not needed if the links are either physically secure or have confidentiality by using encrypting devices. Session cryptography consists of two phases. The first phase is the negotiation of a session key to be used for a session. The second phase uses the session key to encrypt and decrypt the data sent over the session. The process of encrypting and decrypting is the same for both Subarea and APPN networks. However, the protocol used to perform the first phase of negotiating the session key is different in an APPN network. The APPN session cryptography (#1070) option provides that support for these changed network flows.

Figure 9.6 gives an overview of session key negotiation in an APPN network. In this figure, LUa shares a key-encrypting-key (KeyA) with its network node (NN1). Likewise LUb shares one (KeyB) with its network node (NN3). The two network nodes, NN1 and NN3, share KeyNet. The middle network node (NN2) does not have access to any of the encryption keys. When the APPN locate for LUb arrives at LUb's network node, NN3 creates the temporary session key that will be used to encrypt the session data. NN3 places two copies of this key into the APPN Locate response message. The first copy, KeyNet(SK), is encrypted using the KeK that is shared with network node NN1. The second copy, KeyB(SK), is encrypted using the KeK for LUb.

LUa's network node (NN1) translates the first copy from KeyNet(SK) to KeyA(SK). This allows LUa to import the session key into its cryptographic facility. LUa forwards LUb's copy of the session key, KeyB(SK), to LUb in

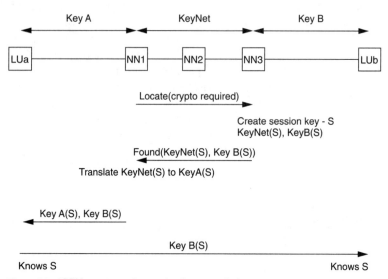

Figure 9.6 APPN cryptography session key negotiation.

the session start-up request. Upon receipt, LUb imports its copy of the session key. Then, both LUa and LUb have access to the session key (SK) and can securely transmit data.

In the above example, a system compromise at NN1 or NN3 might allow an attacker access to the session key. However, a compromise at NN2 will not expose the key, because NN2 cannot decipher the session key. The APPN cryptography option allows many choices on how key-encrypting-keys are shared between nodes. If the owners of LUa and LUb were concerned about the security of the network nodes NN1 and NN3, they could share a KeK between LUa and LUb. In that case LUb would generate the session key and the network nodes would not have access to it. This gives a network administrator significant flexibility, between managing a large number of keys versus the number of keys that can be exposed by a single system.

Password substitution (#223) changes the way passwords are transmitted and verified. When password substitution is active (that is, supported by both systems), then all passwords transmitted between the two LUs are transformed. This transformation creates a substitute that is only usable once and is tied to the specific session that the password will be sent over. The substitution algorithm is a one-way transformation. The effort to start with a substitute and work backwards to the password is the same effort as that required to break the DES encryption algorithm. The full algorithm is documented in [PWSUBS].

Distributed authentication (#230) is the most recent enhancement to the APPC security architecture. At this time, no products have announced support or availability. The distributed security support will allow the replacement of the current user ID and password authentication with the usage of third-party authentication services. The OSF Distributed Computing Environment (DCE) security service is the first choice for usage by APPC. Other possible choices include Kerberos and KryptoKnight. OSF DCE provides the most function with its support for delegation, allowing the server to make requests under the client's identity and authorization data transporting the group memberships that are essential to reasonable security administration. The integration of OSF DCE's security services into APPC will allow for a single-sign-on environment across conversations and remote procedure call applications. Also, the DCE User Registry can be leveraged to greatly reduce the management overhead associated with multiple user IDs and passwords.

Every system should support session-level LU-LU verification (#211) and user ID verification (#212). If data confidentiality is required, then session-level mandatory cryptography (#611) and APPN session cryptography (#1070) are needed. Finally, products supporting password substitution (#223) and distributed authentication (#230) are starting to be available and offer significant security advantages for both clients and servers.

What is needed only on the server system?

Along with the options needed on every system, a server should support user ID authorization (#214). Receive persistent verification (#220) and receive sign-on/change-password (#222) also provide additional value in many cases, and should be considered for any server platform.

The user ID authorization (#214) option adds the ability for the server LU to enforce access-control decisions to transaction programs. If the server LU does not provide access control, it will often have to be built into the application code.

Persistent verification is split into server (receive #220) and client (send #219) support options. Persistent verification modifies the normal user authentication processing so a password is provided only on the first conversation start-up request between two systems for a user. The first conversation startup request includes a request to sign-on the user. Subsequent requests are then sent with the user ID and an already signed-on indicator. Persistent verification reduces the concerns associated with APPC passwords flowing in the clear, by reducing the number of times they flow. With persistent verification, the clear password exposure is comparable to that associated with 3270 terminal logins. This only reduces, but does not eliminate, the risk associated with clear-text passwords. Two solutions to remove this risk completely are as follows:

- Use session-level encryption to encrypt all data on the session, including passwords.

- Use password substitution to ensure that the passwords are not exposed in the clear.

In the future, the use of distributed authentication will eliminate the use of clear-text passwords.

An early issue with APPC was the need to use a regular terminal logon to change the user's password once a month. The Sign-on/Change-Password TP was created to eliminate this requirement for terminal emulation. This service transaction program has two usages. The first is as a straightforward front end for the security subsystem's change-password processing. The second usage is as a predictable first request when persistent verification is being used. In this case, by using the Sign-on/Change-Password TP to perform the initial sign-on, the user can be assured that future requests will process without security failures.

In summary, server systems should require session level LU-LU verification (#211), user ID verification (#212), and user ID authorization (#214) options. For data confidentiality, session-level mandatory cryptography (#611) and APPN session cryptography (#1070) are needed. Additional options worth having include password substitution (#223), distributed authentication (#230), receive persistent verification (#220), and receive sign-on/change-password (#222).

What is needed only on the client system?

A client-only system also should include the program-supplied user ID and password (#213) option, and the security program strong (#224) option. In addition, the client needs to send persistent verification (#219) and send sign-on/change-password (#221) to take advantage of the companion server support.

Program-supplied user ID and password (#213) allows the application program to directly supply the user ID and password that will be sent to the server system. It is needed when the server does not accept already-verified user IDs from the client, and the client's LU cannot determine the correct user ID and password for the specific destination.

Security program strong (#224) is a variant on program-supplied user ID and password. With SECURITY (PROGRAM_STRONG), the local LU will fail the conversation startup when the partner LU does not support password substitution. This ensures that the program-supplied password is not exposed on the network.

Send persistent verification (#219) performs the client-side half of the overall persistent verification flows. With it, the first conversation startup request made using SECURITY (SAME) for a user contains the user ID, password, and a sign-on indicator. The LU remembers that the password was sent. On the second, and later SECURITY (SAME) requests for the same user and destination, the LU sends just the user ID and a signed-on indicator to the server system. This support requires that the local LU can determine the user ID and password that should be sent in the conversation first startup request. Over time it is expected that the use of distributed security will replace this option.

If the server platform has the sign-on/change-password TP, then send sign-on/change-password (#221) is a useful option to have on the client. The change-password function can, in some cases, eliminate the need for a user to directly login to some systems. The change-password function will allow the user to change his password at a destination system using an APPC transaction.

A client platform should have session level LU-LU verification (#211), user ID verification (#212), and program-supplied user ID and password (213). Additionally, password substitution (#223), distributed authentication (#230), send persistent verification (#219), send sign-on/change-password (221), and security program strong (#224) are all desirable. Finally, for data confidentiality, session-level mandatory cryptography (#611) and APPN session cryptography (#1070) are required.

What does my APPN network node need?

Even though APPN network nodes provide critical network functions, their security requirements are quite modest. Network nodes need to support session-level LU-LU verification (#211) and end node authorization (#1102). Network nodes might also require support for session-level mandatory cryptography (#611) and APPN session cryptography (#1070).

Session-level LU-LU verification (#211) can be used to control the nodes that are allowed to connect to the network. LU-LU verification can also be used to prevent the attachment of rogue systems to backbone nodes. End node authorization (#1102) enables a network node to pre-configure the LUs that reside at a given end node. This also allows the network administration to control the attachment of rogue systems. End Node Authorization also allows the network node to override the end node's specification of session mode and class of service. This override can be used to enforce encryption policy, by re-placing modes that do not require cryptography with modes that do.

Session-level mandatory cryptography (#611) and APPN session cryptography (#1070) can be used for two separate functions. First, they are needed in network nodes that support end nodes that use session cryptography. The second usage is between network nodes, to provide data confidentiality for network topology information.

Also, when the network node provides its administration facility through APPC conversations, then the network node is acting as a server. The administration function needs the same security services as any server.

What is needed only in special cases?

So far we have covered most of the common APPC security options. The remaining options are not widely implemented.

Three options are related to profiles. The profile field is an additional value that can be used to further restrict the resources that a user can access. The options dealing with the profile field are profile verification and authorization (#215), profile pass-through (#217), and program-supplied profile (#218). Currently the profile field is only used by APPC/MVS. APPC/MVS passes it to the security subsystem as the initial logon group.

Origin LU authorization (#216) adds the ability for the server LU to make access-control decisions based on the name of the client's LU. To date, the only implementation of this option is by APPC/MVS.

Session-level selective cryptography (#617) adds the ability for the application program to identify the pieces of application data that require confidentiality. For some applications, this allows increased throughput by reducing the amount of data that is encrypted. This advantage occurs when the portion of the application data that requires confidentiality protection is small.

Using the Option Sets

Up to this point we have been trying to describe the architecture in the abstract. We will now begin to discuss specific security policies and how they can be implemented with existing products. Most of these examples will be based on APPC/MVS, Communications Manager/2, CICS, and VTAM. Some examples will include methods that complement current architecture.

Authenticating systems

When a session is started, the two LUs can use session-level LU-LU verification to perform mutual verification.

In VTAM, the VERIFY parameter on the APPL statement specifies the requirement for LU-LU verification. When NONE is coded, LU-LU verification will not be used. A value of REQUIRED means that LU-LU verification is required and sessions will not be established with systems that cannot be verified. A value of OPTIONAL allows the installed security subsystem to control the usage. In all cases, VTAM does not store the verification password. The LU-LU passwords are always stored by the security subsystem.

When the security system is RACF,[3] the passwords are stored in the KEY field of an APPCLU resource profile. The resource profile name is formed from the local and remote LU names. VTAM also allows the installation to force the usage of the Enhanced LU-LU verification algorithm. This is done by specifying SECLVL=LEVEL2 on the APPL statement. VTAM performs the LU-LU verification for most MVS and VM based APPC implementations. This includes APPC/MVS, APPC/VM, DB2, and others.

CICS/ESA does not use VTAM's support for LU-LU verification. However, like VTAM, CICS uses the security product to hold the verification passwords.

Communications Manager/2 also supports LU-LU verification. The administrator defines the LU to LU passwords in the SNA features section of Communications Manager/2 SETUP utility. Or, they can be supplied using the DEFINE_LU_LU_PASSWORD verb in the node definition file (.NDF file). However, until OS/2 provides file system security this means the passwords can be accessed by anyone with physical access to the system.

Other systems that implement LU-LU verification include OS/400, AIX/SNA Services, and the 6611 Router.

Authenticating users

The APPC architecture allows user IDs and passwords to be from one to ten characters long. The vast majority of systems limit this length to eight characters. OS/400 does support full ten-character user IDs and passwords.

---

[3]Please note that any security product that has the appropriate level of function can be used, not just RACF.

Specifying what's acceptable on inbound conversations

The first action needed on the server system is to define what type of authentication information the client system is allowed to send. This information is sent to the client system when a session is created between the client and server systems. How this is defined at the server system is different for each platform.

Communications Manager/2 (CM/2) uses a parameter on the DEFINE_ PARTNER_LU verb. Setting the CONV_SECURITY_VERIFICATION parameter to YES allows the partner to send already verified user IDs in addition to user IDs with passwords. Setting it to NO prevents the partner from sending the already verified indicator. Omitting the parameter uses the default value of NO. If the partner LU definition is omitted, then definition is taken for the DEFINE_DEFAULTS verb.

User IDs and passwords can be defined to Communications Manager/2 by the DEFINE_USER_ID_PASSWORD NDF verb, or Communications Manager/ 2 can use the User Profile Manager (UPM). When Communications Manager/2 receives a conversation start-up request with a user ID and password, it checks to see if DEFINE_USER_ID_PASSWORD was done for the user ID, and whether the password matches. If the define was not done, then Communications Manager/2 will pass the user ID and password to the UPM for validation.

APPC/MVS specifies what is acceptable from the client LU by using the APPCLU resource class. Besides being the storage location for LU-LU verification passwords, the CONVSEC field in the profile specifies the security types acceptable from the remote system. It can have the following values:

NONE	no security tokens
CONV	user IDs with passwords
PERSISTV	user IDs with passwords or persistent verification flows
ALREADYV	user ID with either passwords or the already verified indicator
AVPV	user IDs with any of passwords, persistent verification, or already verified

When APPC/MVS receives a user ID (with or without a password), it calls the installed security subsystem to do the authentication. This means that, even if the client system already verified the user ID, the user must be defined at the APPC/MVS system. For requests that arrive without a user ID, the TP executes under a security environment that does not have a valid RACF user ID. This restricts anonymous requests to accessing only resources that are defined as allowing everybody access.

CICS/ESA does not use the APPCLU resource class to determine the security values acceptable from the client system. CICS/ESA instead requires that the acceptable security be specified with the ATTACHSEC parameter on the CONNECTION definition.

Getting the correct information sent

The client application has multiple choices for the type of security information that will be sent with the conversation start-up request. These choices are SECURITY(NONE), an anonymous request with no security; SECURITY (PROGRAM), the program supplies the user ID and password; SECURITY (PROGRAM_STRONG), a program supplied user ID and password that must not be exposed in clear-text form on the network; SECURITY(SAME), a request that the underlying system determine the information to send; SECU RITY(DISTRIBUTED), a request to use third-party authentication; SECU RITY(MUTUAL), a request to use third-party authentication and to perform a mutual authentication before any data is sent. Because products have not yet implemented SECURITY(DISTRIBUTED) or SECURITY(MUTUAL), they are not further described in this section.

SECURITY(NONE) is straightforward and the start-up request is sent without a user ID or a password. SECURITY(PROGRAM) will cause the client's LU to place the program-supplied user ID and password in the conversation start-up request, if the server accepts user IDs and passwords from the client system. Otherwise, the conversation start-up request is sent without the user ID and password. SECURITY(PROGRAM_STRONG) is similar to SECURITY(PROGRAM), except that a password substitute will be sent. If password substitutes are not accepted by the partner, the conversation start-up request is failed at the client system.

The action taken for a SECURITY(SAME) request is system-dependent. The meaning of a SECURITY(SAME) request is for the local system to determine the security information that will allow the destination system to re-create the client's security environment. APPC/MVS extracts the user's ID and primary group from the current security environment (for example, RACF ACEE) and sends them with the already verified indicator. If the partner does not trust the MVS system to send the already verified indicator, then the request is sent anonymously by not including the user ID and profile.

Communications Manager/2 provides additional options under SECU RITY(SAME). It will call the OS/2 User Profile Manager (UPM) to get the user ID and password of the currently "signed-on" user. If a user is signed-on, for example, and he did a LAN Server Logon, then that user's ID and password are used as the security information sent to the destination system. It also is possible to define specific user ID and password combinations for different destination LUs via UPM. This supports the cases where the user ID or password for separate systems must be different. One caveat with this support is that it, in general, forces the user's LAN user ID and password to be the same as their user ID and password at the destination. While this is acceptable in many cases, it does mean that the passwords will have to be synchronized. The sign-on change-password TP can be used to assist in this synchronization.

Access Control for Transaction Programs

APPC/MVS provides user ID authorization (#214) by using the installed security subsystem. Every conversation startup request is subject to an access control check. The check determines if the user ID (and optional profile) is authorized to execute the requested server TP. This check is done using the APPCTP resource class. APPC/MVS then will start the server TP as the received user ID. This causes further access control checks to use the received identity. The user would still need access to the other resources required by the TP; for example, executable code and data sets.

APPC/MVS also supports a model where the TP is started under a separate user ID and is switched to the user's ID when it accepts the conversation. These TPs are called multitrans TPs. A multitrans TP allows a server to be written where the server has access to resources beyond those of the end user. In this case, the TP can open data sets during its initialization leg to which the user does not have access rights. This enables the creation of servers that filter data for the user.

Another important model that APPC/MVS supports is called the *Server Facility*. With the server facility, a running program registers itself to APPC/MVS as the server for some set of TP names. As the server registers, APPC/MVS will check the APPCSERV class to see if the server is allowed to service that TP name. When the server accepts a conversation, APPC/MVS does not switch its security environment. Instead it creates a new security environment with the user's ID, and makes that available to the server. If the server has the appropriate authorization,[4] the server can switch to the user's identity. A normal server will not be able to directly use the new security environment. For this reason, many server facility servers implement their own access control.

Communications Manager/2 provides minimal support for user authorization. A TP can be defined to either require security or to not require security. If the TP requires security, then Communication Manager/2 will fail any conversation start-up requests that do contain an authentic user ID. But, any further access control must currently be implemented in the TP. The TP can extract the received user ID using the CPI-C `Extract_Security_User_ID` call.

Ability to Access an LU

The main method for controlling access to an LU is by using LU-LU verification. LU-LU verification can be used to prevent any user from a given LU access to any TP at another LU. It enforces this by preventing any sessions between the two LUs.

---

[4]Specifically, APF authorized, Supervisor State or Key 1.

APPC/MVS has two additional ways to control access. They provide additional granularity and control. First, APPC/MVS can make an access control check to determine whether the received user ID is authorized to the destination LU. This is done by checking for access to the APPL resource with the same name as the LU's name. This can be used to selectively authorize people to access certain LUs; for example, to separate test and production systems. APPC/MVS also can make a check to determine whether the user is allowed to "come from" a given source LU. This is the origin LU authorization (#216) option. This check is made against the APPCPORT class. It is most useful in conjunction with RACF conditional access control lists, where a user can be authorized to certain resources, but only when they "come from" a certain port of entry; for example, to ensure that the customer master file can only be accessed by people who are sitting in high security rooms.

Confidentiality

APPC does data confidentiality at the session layer. The application program selects cryptography by specifying the name of a mode that is configured for session-level cryptography. The modes #INTERSC and #BATCHSC are often defined either to provide confidentiality or to ensure that all data flows over installation controlled and protected links.

VTAM implements the session cryptography option for MVS and VM APPC products. VTAM added APPN session cryptography in Version 4, Release 1. To support cryptography, VTAM requires that a cryptographic product be installed. Two choices are the IBM Programmed Cryptographic Facility (PCF) and the IBM Integrated Cryptographic Service Facility/MVS (ISCF/MVS). VTAM uses the cryptographic product to perform the encryption and decryption operations and to store the encryption keys.

Configuration of cryptography with VTAM consists of defining the cryptographic requirements of the local LUs, remote LUs, and modes. A VTAM application's (local LU) cryptography requirement is defined using the ENCR parameter on the VTAM APPL statement. This parameter can have one of the following values:

COND	Cryptography is supported and will be used with partners that also support cryptography
NONE	Cryptography is not supported
OPT	Cryptography is supported if the system has a cryptographic facility
REQD	Cryptography is required for all sessions and all data
SEL	Cryptography support is required for every session, but encrypting of the data is controlled by the VTAM application

For a nonhost LU, the ENCR parameter is on the LU statement. Its values can be:

NONE	Cryptography is not supported
OPT	Cryptography is supported, but not required
REQD	Cryptography is required for all sessions and data
SEL	The same as OPT

To define a mode's encryption requirement, use the ENCR parameter on the MODEENT statement. A mode can require any or no encrypting, mandatory for all data, or selective.

Cryptographic facility-specific procedures are used to generate and control the encryption keys. VTAM uses the LUname as the key label for either a local or remote LU's shared key-encrypting-key. When VTAM is acting as the network node for the two LUs, LUa and LUb, it will request the cryptographic facility to generate the session key. VTAM then will request copies of the session key encrypted under the key-encrypting-keys named LUA and LUB.

What's Coming?

The largest change facing APPC security is the coming usage of third-party authentication services. This usage will force a change from today's short user IDs to significantly longer names. The integration will lead to the shifting of security processing out of the communications protocols and into separate security services. The widespread availability of security servers that support the GSS-API[5] is anticipated. This will lead to a natural decoupling of changes in security functions from the rest of the APPC implementation and protocols.

Where to Go for More Information

For additional information, I recommend the following sources: *CPI-C Programming in C*, by John Q. Walker and Peter Schwaller; *CPI-C 2.0 Reference SC26-4399*; *APPN Architecture and Product Implementations Tutorial, GG24-3669*; and *The Best of APPC, APPN, and CPI-C CD-ROM, SK2T-2013*. *The Best of CD* contains many documents, samples, and other helpful files.

Two sources for getting questions answered are the APPC Information Technology Exchange forum on CompuServe (GO APPC) and the bit.list-

---

[5]GSS-API is the Generic Security Services Application Programming Interface. It is an Internet Engineering Task Force standard, and is documented in RFC 1508 and 1509.

serv.appc-l USENET newsgroup. IBM's APPC Market Enablement team actively monitors the APPC areas on CompuServe. The anonymous ftp site, ftp.raleigh.ibm.com contains many useful files in the directory pub/protocols/APPC_APPN. In addition, the URL http://www.raleigh.ibm.com/acc/ acchome.htm is an excellent starting page for timely CPI-C, APPC, and APPN information.

Acronyms

- **APPC** Advanced Program-to-Program Communications
- **APPN** Advanced Peer-to-Peer Networking

Select Bibliography

IBM. *APPN Architecture and Product Implementations Tutorial.* GG24-3669.

IBM. *CICS Inter-Product Communication.* SC33-0824.

IBM. *Communications Manager/2 System Management Programming Reference.* SC31-6173.

IBM. *CPI Communications: CPI-C Reference Version 2.0.* SC26-4399.

IBM. *CPI Communications: CPI-C 2.0 Specification.* SC31-6180.

IBM. *MVS/ESA SP V4 Writing Servers for APPC/MVS.* GC28-1070.

IBM. *MVS/ESA SP V4 Writing TPs for APPC/MVS.* GC28-1121.

IBM. *MVS/ESA V4 Planning: APPC Management.* GC28-1110.

IBM. *SNA Advanced Peer-to-Peer Networking: Architecture Reference.* SC30-3422 [APPN].

IBM. *SNA LU 6.2 Reference: Peer Protocols.* SC31-6808 [Peer].

IBM. *SNA Transaction Programmer's Reference Manual for LU Type 6.2.* GC30-3084 [TPRM].

IBM. *The Best of APPC, APPN, and CPI-C CD-ROM.* SK2T-2013.

IBM. *VTAM Network Implementation Guide.* SC31-6419.

IBM. *VTAM Resource Definition Reference.* SC31-6427.

Walker, John Q. II and Peter J. Schwaller. 1994. *CPI-C Programming in C: An Application Developer's Guide to APPC.* New York: McGraw-Hill, Inc.

Enhanced Bind Security [EBindSec] available via anonymous ftp: ftp://networking.raleigh.ibm.com/pub/standards/ciw/sig/sec/ebinds ec.ps.

Password Substitution [PWSUBS]-available via anonymous ftp: ftp://networking.raleigh.ibm.com/pub/standards/ciw/sig/sec/pwsubs .ps.

Related Security Products

- ACF/VTAM Version 4 for MVS/ESA
- APPC Networking Services for Windows

- CICS/ESA
- Communications Manager/2
- MVS/ESA SP: JES2
- MVS/ESA SP: JES3
- OS/400
- RACF

10

Securing VTAM

Barry D. Lewis

*Half the work that is done in this world is to
make things appear what they are not.*
ELIAS ROOT BEADLE

We follow the path of your application to the mainframe where it encounters
VTAM. What is this acronym and how does it affect our application? What
are the inherent exposures, and how will we help ensure that our application remains protected from unauthorized access? What are the areas we
need to manage to properly secure VTAM? In this chapter we provide an understanding of the product, the exposures you might find, and the solutions
to the problem of ensuring adequate security and control.

This is a highly technical area of the operating system and, as such, is often "worked over easy." On the other hand, once involved, it is very easy to
get carried away into the more esoteric realms and lose track of your primary objective—ensuring security. It is not expected that you become a network systems programmer. You should have the necessary knowledge level
to know when to ask the network programming staff to explain those areas
where you need additional detail, and when to rely on your own objectives
and experience.

We begin with an overview of what hardware and software components a
network typically consists of, and where VTAM fits into the picture. Later,
we will explore the security infrastructure within VTAM and how you can
best ensure an adequate level of control.

Network Overview

In a typical IBM mainframe environment, VTAM is but one component. Where does it fit? What action does it perform? How does it relate to the rest of the mainframe? We need to answer each of these questions to ensure that our application remains secure and cannot be adversely affected through VTAM. Note that, although we use the IBM corporation as our model, the discussion and facts contained in this chapter are equally applicable to equivalent products that support the IBM System 370/390 Architectures and the SNA protocol (refer to the previous chapter).

VTAM poses some major concerns for our application. First, it is a single point of failure. If VTAM is unavailable, no work will get done. Your operating system might still continue to run and applications might continue to process, but unless our users can sign onto the system and access these applications, all is moot. So VTAM is critical from an availability point of view. In addition, with no controls in place, your organization might be subject to unauthorized use. For example, someone could create a service bureau using your computing facilities, and this could go unnoticed for some time. Further, there are operational control issues to resolve. Will we allow operators to override certain options upon starting the system, and can system programmers perform VTAM changes dynamically? As we progress through this chapter we will address these questions.

For our purposes, we will assume a host computer using a more recent model line—the IBM ES/9000-type processor supporting the MVS/ESA operating system. Older machines consist of the 3080 and 3090 series. On these processors we run the operating system MVS/ESA, and the subsystems such as TSO, CICS, or IMS, and the Session Managers such as TPX, CA-VMAN, and NetView Access Services. The operating system and subsystems typically occupy our attention and resources when considering security measures. Organizations use access control software such as RACF, CA-Top Secret, or CA-ACF2 to implement security measures over the data, files, and programs being run and, to some extent, the operating system parameters themselves.

So what is VTAM? We have used this acronym seven times already, and by now you must be wondering if we will ever define it! The acronym stands for Virtual Telecommunications Access Method. This is the software that manages the elements of hardware that we take for granted, such as the terminals or workstations we use in our day-to-day jobs. These terminals must be identified not only physically, by being attached to a controller and eventually to the mainframe, but by some sort of software that tells the mainframe what the device consists of and how the mainframe should communicate with it.

Ever wonder what happens when you press a key on your workstation and the mainframe responds? There are the more obvious physical connections; that is, your workstation is somehow connected to the mainframe. And there are software connections, something that must translate all the different pieces into some semblance of order and understanding.

The hardware you see and use will typically consist of a microcomputer or a nonintelligent (dumb) terminal, such as a 3278. Most organizations today are moving toward the multitasking capabilities of microcomputers to help enhance your day-to-day work; however there are still some who retain the older style, nonintelligent terminals. Regardless, as an end user you sit in front of a terminal and access the mainframe. When you send a command by typing on your keyboard, the terminal sends that command through some type of emulator board to a line (probably coax or twisted pair) connected to a terminal control unit. The terminal control unit is normally a 3274 device. The 3274 devices handle the traffic for a multitude of workstations, whether they consist of microcomputers using 3270 emulation or 3278s. It is the TCU that also connects such hardware devices as ethernet interface couplers (EIC) or token ring interface couplers (TIC), which help connect workstations found in local area networks to the mainframe.

The TCU sends your keystroke down another line (that is typically either a leased or dial-up line) to a telecommunications control unit or front-end processor, which is connected to the mainframe. This device normally consists of a 3745 communications controller. The front-end processor contains a number of communications ports to which are attached, directly and indirectly, the terminal control units (TCUs). The 3745 then forwards your command on to the mainframe through its physical connection, and the requested action occurs. These pieces of hardware help get the message from your workstation to the mainframe and back.

But software must be involved to do all the translating between these various devices, and that's where VTAM comes into play. Your workstation runs a myriad of software, such as Windows or OS/2, and user applications such as WordPerfect and Lotus. To communicate with the mainframe, however, you need another piece of software that will let you use the hardware we identified earlier. This might consist of a product like DCA's Attachmate. Within the terminal control unit is microcode and other software, which then sends the request to the communications controller. IBM's Network Control Program (NCP) resides here in the 3745 and forwards the request to the host, where it finally arrives and talks to VTAM. Without VTAM the mainframe would not recognize any of these pieces of hardware, including your workstation, and will not know how to send or receive information from you. This simplistic overview attempts to give you a general idea of how all the pieces of a network fit together, and the role that VTAM plays.

In addition to the overall concept above, the Network can be further defined. You might come across terms such as *Domain* and *Subarea* during your review. Domain is used to define a particular set of network components. You might think of a domain as a group of network components.

Many large organizations have more than one domain, and each group might interact with each other. You need to be aware of what this means as you attempt to define the security over your network. A network domain typically consists of items such as:

- A systems services control point (SSCP), normally related to the host processor

- A 3745 with its network control program (NCP), often called a front-end processor (FEP) subarea

- The terminal control units (TCUs)

- The terminals or workstations themselves

- System network interconnect (SNI) links, which are special links designed to allow each domain to talk with others.

Within a domain might be a number of subareas. The 37x5 is used to control (eventually) a number of terminals and workstations. These are often in remote locations. For example, you might have a data center in the suburbs of a large city and a number of offices and terminals in a small town nearby. For network efficiency, you might place a 3745 in the smaller town. All the components, from the 3745 to the actual user's workstations, collectively become known as a subarea. Typically, as soon as a second 37x5 is attached to the system, your technical support staff will speak in terms of subareas and your control objectives will have to take this into consideration, for reasons which will become apparent later.

The picture in Figure 10.1 outlines how the general hardware and software you will find within a typical Network interact and what might constitute a domain and a subarea.

From the picture you can see that a number of physical devices need to talk to each other, and to the mainframe, for your connection to work. The picture shows a rather simplistic view that is useful for our purposes; it is not our intention to become network specialists; we merely need to have a general understanding so we know what we are attempting to control.

So now that we have a general understanding of the network, where does VTAM enter the picture, what does it do, and what security controls do we need to understand and implement?

VTAM Fundamentals

First, although you will typically see and hear the word VTAM, you should be aware that the more complete name of the product is ACF/VTAM which stands for Advanced Communications Facility/Virtual Telecommunications Access Method. As you saw in the earlier picture, VTAM runs as a subsystem of the MVS operating system. So what does this mean? We use VTAM

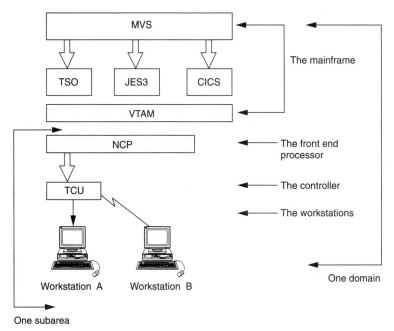

Figure 10.1 A network overview.

to define our Network independently of the hardware in use and provide the capability for information transfer between workstations and other MVS subsystems (VTAM applications). In other words it "owns" all the resources and allows us to talk to the system and receive responses.

The other program that works closely with VTAM is the Network Control Program (NCP). This is software that resides within each 37x5 communications controller and supports IBM's Systems Network Architecture (SNA) architecture. In addition to SNA support, the NCP provides support for connecting an organization's Local Area Networks to the mainframe. Together these software products help support and position the organization for communication via terminals, workstations and networks.

Within the NCP generation file, which is the source of information loaded into the communications controller, you will find the actual definitions of all the lines, whether dial-up or leased line, for example. As you can see from Figure 10.1, the 37x5 controller and the associated NCP program, help protect the mainframe from line failures and other general line problems, ensuring that major problems with lines or terminals don't adversely affect the mainframe. You can occasionally see this at work when your workstation isn't working and you are unable to communicate with your mainframe yet you know that the machine and your application are still running. This level of protection is essential as the size of your network grows. Today's organizations have thousands of telecommunications lines and end-user work-stations and cannot afford to have one area impact the rest due to equipment failures.

Securing VTAM

Now that we have a basic understanding of how all the network components interact and where VTAM fits within the scheme of things, we need to review and understand the security and control components. We also need to address the five basic components of security: Identification, Authentication, Authorization, Availability, and Audit. By addressing these basic precepts we help ensure that our exposures are minimized and appropriately managed.

To quickly review, *Identification* involves ensuring that we know who the user is, whether it is a person or a process (e.g., an application such as payroll). This is typically accomplished using an Account name. The industry also recognizes vendor-software-specific words such as Userid, Logonid, and Acid as meaning the identifier. We will use the term *Account* in our descriptions.

Although we have identified you through the Account you might be using, we do not know if you are the person behind the Account without some other piece of data, and this is *Authentication*. The other piece of data most often used of course, is a password. So when you sign on to the system using your Account and enter a valid password, you have been Identified and Authenticated. Note that many organizations recognize the weakness inherent in most passwords and are beginning to employ more complex Authenticators, such as challenge response units and voice analysis.

So now you have been Identified and Authenticated as a valid user. Next you need to be *Authorized* to perform certain functions, such as access the Accounting data or input the latest sales information. Rules need to be written within your organization's access control software to allow you the necessary level of authority to that data. Then you are Authorized.

For most individuals and processes, this is the level of security they require. However, the organization needs to be assured that the system, files, programs, and network are *Available* when they need to be. In part, this is accomplished through the judicious use of appropriate access controls. Are the necessary controls in place to prevent someone from accidentally or intentionally affecting the system? Are adequate backups and recovery processes in place?

Finally, how can we assure ourselves that everyone is performing the functions he should and is not attempting access to things he does not need or should not have? This is the job of *Audit*. A very complex field; suffice it to say that, in our example, can we prove who has performed certain critical functions and are all users only performing those actions that they should?

These five aspects of security must be applied to VTAM. We must ensure that we can demonstrate that controls over our network and VTAM are adequate. Adequate control over VTAM will help ensure that your systems are not compromised through the use of approaches that cannot be controlled by your third-party, access-control software. While controls are important and necessary, you also need sound, effective audit trails to help ensure that potential problems are quickly discovered and rectified. Finally, with all systems, an underlying yet often neglected component is availability. Delete a file or remove a parameter and your network can come crashing down, resulting in business units with no access to the critical day-to-day data they need.

Managing risk and applying information security principles differs from industry to industry. What might be effective for a manufacturer of paper products, such as envelopes, might be not nearly secure enough for a high-tech aerospace manufacturer. In this chapter we will review the available controls. Deciding what features to implement, and how detailed those controls will be, requires a solid understanding of your organization and its particular needs.

Identification and Authentication

No specific Identification controls exist within VTAM. In Chapter 13, you will learn of identification controls specific to Netview, a package that eases administration of VTAM. To access VTAM however, you use the controls provided by the access control package used in your organization. This means that within CA-ACF2, CA-TSS or RACF an Account has been set up and provided to you. Normal identification and authentication controls are used. With the Account, you will have a password that is only known to you and together, these control your access to the system.

To ensure that this area of control is managed appropriately you will have to review the access control software. You should look for appropriate naming standards over accounts. Are accounts easily identified by the name they are given? For example, is there a standard governing the accounts given to people that is different from the accounts given to processes? Are passwords required for all accounts that are assigned to individuals? Are the password controls in place appropriate? For example, is the minimum password length at least five characters? Is a history kept of previous passwords, and are controls in place to prevent their reuse?

You should ensure that old or unused accounts are removed in a timely fashion and are not left on the system. Verify that administrators do not create new accounts in advance of their needs, by assigning them a standard default password. This quickly becomes known, rendering the new accounts vulnerable to misuse by unauthorized persons.

Authorization

Once you have ensured that staff members are properly identified and authenticated, you need to verify that all access is properly managed and authorized. There are a number of libraries and files that need to be managed to ensure the security and control of VTAM. Some of these relate directly to VTAM, while others are operating system-related libraries that can impact VTAM.

To ensure that proper controls are in place we need to review what libraries are being used to define and control the network. We must know what change control mechanisms are used to manage the updating of information in these libraries, and we must determine who has update access. This area requires the most attention during a review of VTAM security. Identifying and locating the proper files is a first step that needs to be followed by an in-depth review of access levels. This needs to be followed by a thorough review of the pertinent data to be found inside the files.

To determine the libraries used for network activation and definition, you need to know how MVS approaches the task. Put simply, the network is started like any other task within MVS. A started task is begun that specifies where the libraries and files the network uses can be found. A started task can be simply defined as a job that can be started from an operating system console, or as part of the operating system's Initial Program Load (IPL). VTAM is typically always started during the normal IPL stage. This job sets out where the libraries are and starts the actual network program. In addition to these libraries, there are a number of system libraries that are needed.

When you start up your system, several things occur. The one item of concern to us here is the execution of the network start-up command. You need to find the command to know what started task procedure is being used. MVS looks in the COMMNDxx member of SYS1.PARMLIB to find out what it should use as a start command. There might be many things started during an IPL but you need to look in this library and find the command used at your organization. Most of the time this command will look similar to the following: S NET, LIST=xx.

This begins the process by specifying which procedure to use. In this example, MVS will look for a started task called NET. MVS will typically look for this in the SYS1.PROCLIB library (where such tasks are usually placed) and this is the next place you need to review. The NET procedure is used to initiate the network program and specify all the associated libraries, for both VTAM and the NCP. If you see the LIST=xx parameter attached to the start command, it is specifying that the network should run using specific network options.

These options are found within the SYS1.VTAMLST library in the member called ATCSTRxx. In the LIST command, the two characters specified indicate the actual member to be used. For example, LIST=00 means look for `SYS1.VTAMLST(ATCSTR00)`. This dictates the next place you need to look as you continue your path through the network review.

In the above examples, there are a number of items you need to assess. Who can modify data within SYS1.PARMLIB and SYS1.VTAMLST? Is the list restricted to only those systems programmers assigned the task of maintaining the Network and Operating System? Is an appropriate change control process used to verify that changes only occur when authorized? And is an audit trail kept to ensure that management can assign accountability for any change that occurs?

In addition to the start-up parameters mentioned above, the SYS1 .VTAMLST library contains two more important pieces of information. All three pieces need to be reviewed. The member names you need to look for include:

ATCSTRxx	the Start-up parameters.
ATCCONxx	the Configuration lists.
APPx	the Application definitions.

The start-up parameter member takes you even further into the system. This member specifies where you will find the network's configuration parameters and includes the option of specifying whether your console operators can override the settings when they bring up the system. They can do this by specifying a different ATCCONxx member for MVS to use. While operational realities might deter your organization from instituting such strict controls, we believe that operators should not be allowed to override the start-up parameters. Regardless, you should institute a process to verify whether anything was changed during the system IPL such as by reviewing the system log files.

TABLE 10.1 Listing of ATCSTR00

MAXSUBA=7,	maximum subarea's assigned and active
ITLIM=32,	maximum concurrent sessions
CONFIG=00,	ATCCONxx field
MAXAPPL=100,	maximum VTAM applications
CSALIMIT=1000,	maximum CSA used by VTAM
NOPROMPT,	Do not prompt for operator override
TNSTAT,CNSL,	tuning stats
SUPP=NOSUPP,	console message suppression
...	

Within the ATCSTRxx member (refer to Table 10.1) are two parameters which control these options. The first parameter tells the system where to find the configuration lists that should be used, and the second parameter controls whether operators can override setting during the IPL. The parameters are:

CONFIG=XX   This specifies the ATCCONxx data set name.
Prompt/No Prompt This allows operators to override.

The two characters shown in the CONFIG= statement, identify the ATCCONxx member in use. In our example this means the configuration lists will be found in the ATCCON00 member (refer to Table 10.2) of SYS1 .VTAMLST. So what will we see within a configuration list and how does this concern us?

The file provides a list of additional members that are used to further configure your organization's network. The primary items we are concerned with include:

APPL	Application Programs (such as IMS and TSO)
LOCx	SNA Terminals that are locally attached
USSTAB	The Unformatted System Services Table

In Table 10.3 you will find applications defined, such as CICSAPPL. This points to a member within SYS1.VTAMLST, typically called APPx where each application is defined. Within this member, look for the parameter called ACBname to tell you which applications have been defined within your organization.

TABLE 10.2 Listing of ATCCON00

LOGOAPPL,	x
LOCALSNA,	x
SNIPATH,	x
JES3TSO,	x
CICSAPPL	

```
**********************************
*/*  THIS MEMBER SPECIFIES LOCAL SYSTEM TERMINALS (LOCALSNA)
*/*  SYSTEM APPLICATIONS (xxxAPPL)
**********************************
```

TABLE 10.3 Listing of CICSAPPL

CICSAPPL VBUILD TYPE=APPL	APPLICATION MAJOR NODE	
CICSPROD	APPL EAS=1,	
	ACBNAME=CICSPROD,	
	AUTH=(ACQ,BLOCK,PASS)	
CICSTEST	APPL EAS=3,	
	ACBNAME=CICSTEST,	
	AUTH=(ACQ,BLOCK,PASS)	
CICSP1 APPL	EAS=1	ESTIMATED CONCURRENT SESSIONS
	ACBNAME=CICSP1,	APPLID FOR ACB
AUTH=(ACQ,BLOCK,PASS)		

Additionally, you should verify whether encryption is being used by any of the applications. Use of encryption will mean you need to add a whole new section to your review, which we will not get into in this chapter. For example, managing encryption techniques means there is a need for key management and, as such, you will need to verify how keys are controlled, who controls them, and how and when they are changed. You can discover whether an application is using encryption by reviewing each ENCR option in the application definition. Generally, you will find this option set to None as encryption is not widely used. The following chart shows an example of these options:

ACBname = CICSPROD
the name of the subsystem (VTAM APPLID) ENCR equals NONE

can be set to REQD/SEL/OPT/,NONE, to identify the session level encryption in use

---

Apart from the review items already mentioned, you want to identify all currently defined VTAM applications and ensure that access to them is controlled by external logical access control software, such as CA-ACF2.

Next, the LOCx member contains those terminals that are attached locally to your mainframe. They do not include terminals attached to a separate mainframe, or those attached to T1 lines. The primary security control to consider is whether any of these local terminals are automatically attached to an application. Look in the LOCx member and find the following parameter to identify such terminals:

LOGAPPL=CICSTEST This terminal is automatically signed on to the CICSTEST application.

List all the terminals that permit such an event and determine what each terminal is used for and under what circumstances. For example, ensure that access from these terminals is limited to read access only, such as one used by multiple staff in a customer service department.

Finally, the Unformatted System Services Table (USSTAB) option within SYS1.VTAMLST must be reviewed. Again, more than one member can exist and you need to view the USSTAB option within the configuration list to determine which member is in use. Why should we be concerned about this obscure-sounding table? Because it is used to create the first screen users see when powering up their terminals. From a security perspective, it can be used to provide users with a custom menu or to customize logon commands. For example, use CICSP for CICSPROD or TSOB for TSO.

Another thing we might look for when reviewing this area is whether a message is being shown on the initial logon screen, indicating that this is a private system and unauthorized access is prohibited. Some organizations still issue a Welcome message. Today it is considered better to remove any messages that welcome a user, because they have been used successfully in court to get unauthorized users acquitted. Additionally, this is an area in which you can begin to comply with some sort of standard sign-on screen for your users. Make the VTAM logon screen look similar to others already in use (or planned), such as that which users might see when accessing the system through a Local Area Network. Any step taken to make access more straightforward and simple for the user saves your organization valuable time and effort.

Finally, the Session Management Exits within VTAM allow a programmer to add additional functionality. An exit can be defined simply as a place where VTAM will look for additional instructions before continuing processing. These are sometimes referred to as *exit points*, and as such they are potential points of entry for unauthorized access or misuse of resources. As with any exit, you need to discover whether they are in use, find out what they are being used for, and review whether the security and controls governing them are adequate. VTAM has two primary exits that we should be concerned with:

Session Management module IXTEXCAA
Session Authorization module ISTAUCAT

For the most part you will rarely find these exits in use. The session management exit can be used to restrict access to particular terminals, or to provide access controls over dial-up access. The session authorization exit can also be used to restrict the use of a terminal. For example, you could specify that this terminal can only access your e-mail system.

No simple way exists for you to determine whether these exits are in use. You will need to search authorized program libraries for the module names mentioned above, and talk to your network programming staff. If you discover exits are in use, verify that appropriate change controls are used, that the function of the exit is well-documented, and that proper management sign-offs are in place.

A review of VTAM would not be complete without mention of its primary companion, the Network Control Program (NCP). This runs inside the 37x5 Communications Controller and manages the controller activities. A review of the SYS1.PROCLIB member called NET (from our earlier discussion) will provide us with the names of the libraries where we will find the NCP definitions in use. As usual, you must review the system generation Job Control Listing (JCL) to detect what load library was used to initially load the NCP, thus verifying which NCP definition is actually in use.

If you have been involved in data processing for some years, you will remember that the 3705 was one of the earlier controllers. This early machine was phased out and replaced around the beginning of the 1980s with the 3725. Around the end of the 80s, these began to be replaced with the more modern 3745. This controller has the capacity to run in a dual mode, requiring two NCP programs, and therefore you will need to ensure that the necessary controls are in place for both programs.

As with VTAM, you need to focus on the level of access control in place over all the NCP Libraries. Again, as with VTAM libraries, only those staff who maintain the network require access, and consideration can be given to restricting this access to read-only on the production libraries until a change is required, and is authorized via your change control process. In this manner, network changes cannot be made unless properly authorized and appropriately scheduled. You should review the controls in place over the NCP generation and load process to ensure that the proper versions are loaded, especially where the 3745 supports multiple processors.

As well, you should manage the size of the dump datasets in use on your system. Should these files become full, the network will become unavailable. Put a process in place to constantly monitor the size of the dump datasets and their present status to ensure that you will not be caught with such a failure.

Finally you should understand a couple of the key internal components of the NCP. Include a review of these specific technical items as you gain more understanding to complete the overall security and control of the NCP.

Referring to Table 10.4, you will find these particular fields buried within the NCP source library. The BUILD statement is used to indicate the beginning of the NCP macro instructions. Specifically, the Loadlib statement tells you where the NCP generation file is located, and the model indicates the type of communications controller. Look for appropriate access controls over this library and use the model statement to indicate whether you need to be concerned about dual-processing controllers.

TABLE 10.4
NCP Parameters

- BUILD
  Loadlib = (member name)
  Model = 3745
- PCCU
  Dumpds = ddname
  Autodmp = yes|NO
- GROUP
  Dial = yes|NO

The Programmed Communication Control Unit (PCCU) macro instruction is used here to identify the name of the dump dataset to be used
(DUMPDS), and to indicate whether the NCP should automatically generate a dump when encountering an error (AUTODMP). This is where you
will find the actual dataset names of the dump files for you to review. In general, most organizations do not allow automatic dumps and have them created when necessary, so the AUTODMP parameter is typically set to NO.

Finally, the GROUP parameter might be used to cluster lines with similar
attributes; for example all dial-up lines. Within each group is a parameter
called DIAL, which specifies whether dial-up access is permitted. Lines
with a dial-up function need to be additionally protected to ensure that no
unauthorized access is permitted. For example, you might set up parameters within your access control software to require additional identification
such as an additional password or a challenge response unit, when using
these lines.

Availability

This is an often overlooked area of security and control. In VTAM, however,
it is essential to manage the integrity and control issues because any errors
that occur and make VTAM unavailable affect the entire user community.
As we have gone through each of the earlier sections, an underlying aspect
concerned the availability of the system. More specifically, are dynamic
VTAM changes allowed and under what circumstances are they allowed?
What authorities are needed to perform these changes? VTAM availability
can easily be compromised through the incorrect use of certain commands.
If these are to be used, they should be restricted to senior technical staff
and perhaps only authorized during noncritical business periods.

In part, control over Availability is also accomplished through the judicious use of appropriate access controls. Are the necessary controls in
place to prevent someone from accidentally or intentionally having a negative impact on the system through the manipulation of a necessary file? If a

system outage does occur, are there adequate backups and is there an effective, efficient recovery process in place to help ensure that the impact is minimized?

Are the procedures and steps necessary to recover VTAM fully documented and understood by your organization's staff? While it is important to attempt to prevent any system outage, it is equally important to ensure that you can recover as quickly as possible to minimize the impact of any outage.

Finally, consider reviewing any network trouble-reporting procedures and see if they are fully manual or whether aspects have been automated. An automated process helps ensure that shift changes, fatigue, or other priorities do not interfere with the effectiveness of the existing trouble-reporting process. Determine whether adequate escalation procedures are in place for resolving serious problems and see whether they are followed.

Audit

Finally, you need to assure yourself that everyone is performing functions they are authorized to perform and are not attempting to access things they do not need or should not have. The use of VTAM commands is tracked in a number of places, including the System Management Facility (SMF) and system console logs. Create a process that ensures the integrity and safety of these logs. For example, in general, no one should have write access to the SMF data files and the console logs. These logs provide important data concerning commands that were run, and start-up options that were used, during the IPL of the system. Gather this data on a regular basis and review it for inconsistencies.

In addition, your access control software provides extensive audit reporting over data access and other day-to-day activities. These reports must be reviewed to ensure that any file updates are done by authorized staff, and that attempts to read or update these files are documented and reported to management in a consistent and simple manner. Far too many organizations attempt to log every access, resulting in massive reports that are never reviewed due to their size. Keep reporting simple, put it in business terms, provide it on a regular basis, and expect appropriate follow-up. By following these basic steps you will enhance the control over your network.

Summary

Although VTAM is a complex and highly technical area, a number of possible exposures warrant our attention. By following the general process endemic to security and control, we show that it is possible to understand the issues in a way that remains familiar to us. We have reviewed the specific needs of Identification, Authentication, Authorization, Availability, and Audit in VTAM, and have discussed some of the areas we should consider when attempting to verify that security and control issues are properly managed.

Use this guide to begin your understanding of security within VTAM and gradually supplement that understanding with additional reading and discussions with your network staff.

Select Bibliography

Cooper, Arlin J. 1989. *Computer and Communications Security*. New York: McGraw-Hill.

Federal Information Processing Standards Publication 83. September 1980.

Guidelines on User Authentication Techniques for Computer Network Access Control. National Bureau of Standards.

IBM. *ACF/VTAM Planning, Installation and Customization*. Publication number SC31-6002.

IBM. *Planning and Reference for Netview, NCP and VTAM*. Publication number SC31-6811.

Lewis, Barry D. 1994. *Audit and Review of VTAM & Netview*. Auerbach Publications.

National Research Council. 1991. *Computers at Risk*. National Academy Press.

11

Securing NetView™
John G. Tannahill

*He is most free from danger, who, even when
safe, is on his guard.* PUBLILIUS SYRUS

This chapter discusses the security and control issues relating to the
NetView family of products, specifically including NetView 2.3 in the IBM
mainframe environment (note that NetView 2.4 is now generally available).
An overview of NetView/6000, NetView/OS2 and the related security and
control issues will be provided.

The chapter also will provide an overview of the primary functions of
NetView network management tools in general, and the functions of the
above products in particular. The main subjects covered are a set of security
and control objectives, and an overview of the main features of NetView in
relation to security and audit implications.

Our discussion begins with an overview of the NetView family of products in relation to the IBM SystemView strategy, which says, "SystemView
is a system management strategy for planning, coordinating and operating
heterogeneous, enterprise-wide information systems." It now is essential
that network management products should support multivendor protocol
networks. Within this strategy, the main key concept that applies to
NetView includes:

- A Manager, which is the system component that is used to both control
  and administer network resources.

- An Agent, which is the network resource controlled by the Manager.

- A Domain, which is the combination of the Manager and the Agents which it controls.

This concept should be borne in mind as we follow through our discussion of security and control issues.

Security Review Objectives

The main objectives to consider when conducting a security review of mainframe NetView applications are to ensure that:

- Proper identification and authentication is established for NetView users.
- Only authorized persons are permitted access to the network management functions.
- There is proper segregation of duties, and that functions are provided based on job responsibilities.
- Appropriate audit trails are maintained and used.
- NetView software libraries are properly protected by an access control mechanism, such as RACF.

Overview of NetView

In a typical information systems environment, the network is likely to include the use of a combination of the following communication protocols:

- SDLC (SNA)
- TCP/IP
- IPX/SPX (Novell)
- NETBIOS/NetBEUI (OS/2)

The network devices that communicate with each other in the network, using the above protocols, need to be managed and controlled. This is the primary function of the NetView application system. We shall shortly discuss the specific application functions that are provided. The host-based version replaces and consolidates a number of previously used network management tools such as NCCF and NPDA.

Current versions of the NetView application used in the IBM mainframe MVS environment include Versions 2.2, 2.3, and the newly released version 2.4. NetView generally is used as a host-based product, but the NetView family of products now can be integrated with one another. For example, NetView/6000 can send network management information to the mainframe-based NetView for further action and processing. It is used primarily as a network management tool for both SNA and non-SNA Networks.

In addition to network management, NetView can be used for automation purposes, such as operator console automation. For example, NetView can be used to intercept certain console messages and run CLISTs based on the console message content. Such an example, which is of interest for security and control purposes, is the automated dump of System Management Facility (SMF) datasets when a console message is received that a specific dataset is full and SMF is switching to the next dataset.

In a typical SNA network environment, there are likely to be a number of NetView applications in use, for both automated operations and network management functions. Normally, you will find one NetView application being used for network management for each MVS region available. NetView systems can be central, distributed, or stand-alone, and can be considered as either *Focal Point* or *Entry Point* systems. A focal point NetView is one that receives network management information. Contrast this to an entry point NetView, whose function is to collect network management information and send it to the focal point NetView.

It also should be noted that multiple focal point NetViews can exist in a single environment. The main differences between them relate to the type of network management information that they receive. To identify and understand how many and in what manner NetView applications are being used in your environment, it is essential to obtain both physical and logical network configurations, and to review the MVS and NetView parameters discussed below.

NetView 2.3 is a VTAM application (see Chapter 10). In identifying the network management components of NetView used in a specific MVS environment, the following Partitioned Dataset (PDS) members should be reviewed:

- **SYS1.PARMLIB(IEFSSNxx)**
  This will identify the NetView subsystems defined in the Subsystem Name Table

- **SYS1.PARMLIB(COMMNDxx)**
  This will identify the NetView-started tasks for the NetView address spaces, which at a minimum will comprise the primary NetView address space and the NetView Subsystem Interface address space (SSI), which is used for message capture from other subsystems.

The JCL for the NetView-started procedures themselves should be reviewed. This will be located in the SYS1.PROCLIB dataset or in one of its concatenations.

An abbreviated version of the start-up procedure is shown in Table 11.1. The procedure in Table 11.1 will identify all key datasets and related members used in the NetView definition. The first step in a security review is to determine that the libraries associated with the NetView product are prop-

TABLE 11.1 Partial Listing of NetView Start-Up Procedure

```
//NETVIEW PROC

//* ***************************************************

//*  NetView Started Task

//* ***************************************************

//NETVIEW EXEC PGM=BNJLINTX

//DSIPARM DD DSN=SYS1.NETVIEW.DSIPARM.DISP=SHR

//DSIPRF  DD DSN=SYS1.NETVIEW.DSIPROF.DISP=SHR

//DSILOGP DD DSN=SYS1.NETVIEW.DSILOGS.DISP=SHR

. . . .

/*
```

erly protected by the external security manager used in the environment (An example is RACF 1.9.2 or RACF 2.1). Update access to the libraries should be restricted and controlled through a combination of change control and access control procedures. In certain circumstances, depending on the NetView parameters set in relation to operator identification and authentication, that is, where NetView passwords are used rather than RACF authentication, read access to the DSIPARM dataset (discussed below) also must be restricted.

A summary of the library definitions is as follows:

- The DSIPARM dataset contains key information concerning the security environment in which NetView will operate. In particular, the DSIDMN, DSIOPF and DSICMD members of this dataset will be discussed in detail.
- The DSIPRF dataset contains specific NetView operator profiles and also will be discussed later.
- The DSILOGP dataset specifies the dataset location of NetView logs and audit trails.
- The SYS1.CNMSAMP dataset contains the IBM default entries and sample members for each key NetView dataset. A point to note is that PDS members in this dataset have a different naming convention than that used for the actual NetView members. For example, the DSIOPF default member can be found in SYS1.CNMSAMP (CNMS1012).

NetView Security and Control Features

The primary control features within NetView can be summarized as follows:

Identification and authentication

This can be provided by NetView internally, or by an external security manager such as RACF, CA-ACF2 or CA-Top Secret. It should be noted that the CA-ACF2 interface is not supported in NetView versions prior to 2.3.

Function security

NetView has security mechanisms to restrict the network management functions available within the product. These include the capability to restrict specific functions (scope of commands) to specific operators or classes of operators and to restrict the network resources which an operator can control (SPAN controls).

In reviewing NetView security, you must determine what security parameters are in place. It should be understood that all functional security is currently provided by the NetView product itself, and not by an external security manager, such as RACF. However, RACF 2.1 has introduced the following new resource classes specifically for the NetView product:

- **NETCMDS** Control of NetView commands
- **NETSPAN** SPAN Controls
- **RODMMGR** Resource Object Data Manager

If your installation has now installed this level of RACF, this is the preferred route for security implementation. We shall now identify and discuss specific areas of the product that should be looked at when performing a detailed security review.

NetView Security Definitions

The screen in Figure 11.1 shows the initial NetView application sign-on. This is the best place to start the description of NetView security mechanisms. This screen would normally be accessed from a VTAM logon screen or a VTAM session manager such as TPX or NetView Access Services. Let's discuss the content.

The NetView VTAM applied is normally identified by the first three characters of CNMxxxx.

The components of the logon screen in which we are interested are:

- **DOMAIN** This identifies the NetView application which is being accessed.
- **OPERATOR-ID** This is the NetView Operator (user ID).
- **PASSWORD** This is the RACF or NetView Internal password.

```
NN    NN                      VV          VV
NNN   NN  EEEEEE  TTTTTTTT  VV      VV  II  EEEEEE  WW          WW  TM
NNNN  NN  EE         TT     VV      VV  II  EE      WW    W     WW
NN NN NN  EEEE       TT      VV    VV   II  EEEE    WW   WWW   WW
NN  NNNN  EE         TT       VV  VV    II  EE      WWWW WWWW
NN   NNN  EEEEEE     TT        VVV      II  EEEEEE   WW   WW
NN    NN             V
```

(C) COPYRIGHT IBM CORP. 1992 - ALL RIGHTS RESERVED
US GOVERNMENT USERS RESTRICTED RIGHTS - USE, DUPLICATION OR DISCLOSURE
RESTRICTED BY GSA ADP SCHEDULE CONTRACT WITH IBM CORPORATION
LICENSED MATERIAL - PROPERTY OF IBM
DOMAIN =xxxxxx

OPERATOR ID ==>   (OR LOGOFF)
PASSWORD ==>   (LEAVE BLANK TO CHANGE PASSWORD)
PROFILE ==>   (PROFILE NAME, BLANK=DEFAULT)
HARDCOPY LOG ==>   (DEVICE NAME, BLANK=DEFAULT, OR NO)
RUN INITIAL COMMAND ==> (YES OR NO, DEFAULT=YES)

ENTER LOGON INFORMATION OR PF3 TO LOGOFF

Figure 11.1 NetView main menu

TABLE 11.2 DSIDMN Identification and Authentication Parameters

MINIMAL	operator ID only (i.e., no authentication)
NORMAL	operator ID and password (NetView internal)
MAXIMUM	authenticate by external security manager (e.g., RACF)

- **PROFILE** This identifies the operator profile (if other than the default which has been assigned for the particular operator).
- **INITIAL COMMAND** This identifies a command or CLIST to be executed when sign-on is complete (optional).

To understand how the above information is used by NetView for security purposes, you need to review the DSIPARM(DSIDMN) member.

First, The option statement in this member specifies:

verify=MINIMAL; NORMAL or MAXIMUM.

The setting determines the level of identification and authentication control performed by NetView. Table 11.2 sets out each parameter and describes the basic function it performs.

The NORMAL setting is the default. Where this setting is used, the MAX LOGON parameter that also is contained in this dataset member is relevant and specifies the maximum number of invalid logon attempts allowed before the session is terminated. This parameter has no meaning for the other settings.

The preferred setting is MAXIMUM, because this is the only option that provides the level of password management and control available in RACF which is normally required in an IBM mainframe environment.

Another area covered in this member is Remote Resource Definition (RRD). This indicates other domains in which a user in the current NetView domain can establish a session. The identification and authentication mechanism used is dependent on the OPTION statement for the specific domain to which the operator is trying to establish a session with. An example statement is:

```
CNM01 RRD
CNM02 RRD
```

This means that the current NetView application can establish cross-domain sessions with the CNM01 and CNM02 NetView application systems. It also should be noted that DSIDMN contains the statements indicating the type of NetView. For example, NETVTYPE DISTRIBUTED.

Another security feature relating to this area is the RMTCMD command processor. This determines the security checking done when a remote user attempts to perform an automated logon. The options are to perform no security checking, provide access based on an internal security table in DSI PARM, or to call RACF based on general resource class checking.

NetView functions and operator profiles

To understand and review how NetView functions are restricted, it is necessary to understand the dataset members used by NetView and their interrelationship. The members can be summarized as follows:

- DSIPARM(DSIOPF). This dataset member specifies the NetView user IDs (operators) and the operator profiles to which the specific operator is associated.

- DSIPRF. This dataset contains a member for each operator profile.

- DSIPARM(DSICMD). This dataset member specifies commands that can be issued through NetView. Understanding the contents of these members is key to implementing appropriate security.

- **NetView operator definitions**. As noted above, these are specified within the DSIPARM(DSIOPF) member.

This member contains a set of statements relating to each NetView operator. Table 11.3 provides a simple example which was excerpted from the IBM default member. This example will be used to demonstrate how the datasets, members and related statements link together to provide an overall security picture.

TABLE 11.3 DSIOPF Sample

OPER1	OPERATOR	PASSWORD=OPER1
	PROFILEN	DSIPROFA

The statement in Table 11.3 shows the definition of a NetView operator, OPER1 who has a password OPER1 and is associated with the NetView profile, DSIPROFA. This profile is defined as a member in the DSIPRF dataset. Some points to note that are of a significance to the security of the environment are:

- A NetView operator can be associated with more than one profile. This would be specified in the PROFILEN statement, separated from the first profile by a comma.

- The use of internal NetView security for authentication purposes (VER IFY=NORMAL) represents a serious security exposure because READ access to the DSIPARM dataset will allow anyone access to all of the NetView operator passwords. Use of an external security manager eliminates the use of the clear text password (although it is still defined in this dataset member). When you are using internal security, ensure that READ access is restricted to the minimum number of people and clearly understand that, if more than one person has READ access, then you have lost individual accountability for use of the operator IDs.

- In addition, where the VERIFY=NORMAL setting is used, review the DSIOPF member and ensure that initial passwords for the default NetView user IDs (IBM-supplied defaults) have been changed. A complete list of these default user IDs and their associated passwords (that is, in this application, the password equals the user ID) can be found in member SYS1.CNMSAMP(CNMS1059).

Examples include:

```
OPER1      password=OPER1
OPER2      password=OPER2
NETOP1     password=NETOP1
REMOPER    password=REMOPER
```

The next area of security concern is identifying the personnel within the organization with access to the NetView application. Each operator ID defined in the DSIOPF member should be associated with a specific individual, and that individual should perform a job function that requires access to NetView's network management or operations functions. (It should be noted that NetView does contain and use a number of "automation" operator IDs, such as AUTO1, that have no association with specific users).

The normal functional groups which you would expect to be defined to the NetView application are:

- Operations (both Host and Network Groups)
- User Help Desk
- Technical Services (Network Group)

Any other functional areas defined should be investigated and specifically authorized by data center management.

The next area of discussion is the NetView functions and the related security definitions. Figure 11.2 is the second screen an operator will see after the initial logon is complete. In this figure, you can see the main functions of NetView.

A brief description of each main function is as follows:

- **BROWSE**. This function allows an operator to review online various datasets containing network definitions and information, including VTAM network definitions, NetView logs, and NetView datasets.
- **NCCF (Network Communication Control Facility)**. This function is the primary command and network log facility and allows an operator to execute VTAM, NetView Clists, and commands from any NetView panel.

```
CNM1NETV                    NETVIEW™ MAIN MENU

OPERATOR ID = JOHN1         APPLICATION = CNMxxx

Enter a command (shown highlighted or in white) and press enter.

Browse Facility            BROWSE Command
Command Facility           NCCF command
Help Desk Facility         HELPDESK Command

Hardware Monitor           NPDA command
Hardware Monitor for 4700  TARA command (MVS only)
Session Monitor            NLDM command
Status Monitor             STATMON command

News                       NEWS command
PF Key Settings            DISPFK command

To Exit NetView™           LOGOFF command


        PF1    Help for Using NetView™

CMD     browse

PF1 = Help     PF2 = End      PF3 = Return   PF4 = Top      PF5 = Bottom
PF6 = Roll     PF7 = Backward PF8 = Forward  PF11 = Entry Point
```

Figure 11.2 NetView main functions

- **HELPDESK (Network Management Productivity Facility)**. This function provides a help desk function and allows an operator to record information.

- **NPDA (Network Problem Determination)**. This function provides the Hardware Monitor capabilities and relates to physical network resources.

- **NLDM (Network Logical Data Manager)**. This function provides the Session Monitor capabilities and relates to logical network resources.

- **STATMON (Status Monitor)**. This function is used to collect, store, and view information about the status of network resources, such as application major nodes and CDRMs in a single domain.

It also should be noted from the function screen that NetView has a command line interface that will allow operators to execute either NetView commands and CLISTs or normal MVS console commands such as MVS, JES2, and VTAM.

Other NetView 2.3 components worth mentioning are:

- **NetView Graphic Monitor Facility**. This facility provides graphical views of SNA network resources, which change as the status of the resource changes; for example, from active to inactive.

- **Resource Object Data Manager (RODM)**. This facility provides for collection of configuration information, such as hardware and communication lines relating to non-SNA network resources, which are part of the network.

- **NetView Graphic Monitor Facility Host Subsystem (GMFHS)**. This provides the capability for graphical views of non-SNA network resources, and communicates with RODM.

It should be understood that RODM is a powerful tool and provides the basis for automated network management applications.

The next section of this chapter discusses the security facilities within NetView to provide the appropriate functional security restrictions. This will include operator profiles and their relationship to commands and tasks available within NetView.

NetView Operator Profiles

Operator profiles allow you to control the operator classes that a user can access, by specifying the relationship of the operator to the profiles in DSI PARM(DSIOPF). In addition, each NetView function, task, or command can be assigned to an operator class. This is specified in DSIPARM(DSICMD). The relationship of operator classes to operator profiles is specified in the individual members of DSIPRF. In terms of functional security, if your operator profile has access to an operator class that is assigned to, for example JES2 commands, you can then execute those commands.

As stated above, operator profiles are specified as members of the dataset DSIPRF. Each member should be associated with a NetView profile defined in the PROFILEN Operator Definitions. For example, in Table 11.3, we identified that OPER1 was associated with the profile DSIPROFA, so a dataset member called DSIPROFA should exist in DSIPRF. Each dataset member which specifies an operator profile consists of the statements in Table 11.4, which is an example of the DSIPROFA member.

The two main items to note from Table 11.4 are that Operator Command Classes 1 and 2 are associated with this profile, and that the SPAN control statement exists to provide restriction of network resources which this operator can control. The <spanname> identifies a SPANLIST entry that will be contained in the DSIPARM(DSISPN) dataset member. This dataset member associates SPANLISTs to VTAM major nodes (the definition of network resources). It should be noted that the DSIPROFA member could also have contained an ISPAN statement which would have indicated the Initial SPAN of control for the operator at initial logon. To change the SPAN of control to that defined in the SPAN statement, the operator is required to use a:

```
START SPAN=<spanname>
```

Moving our discussion back to the security facilities available to restrict commands, the next area to review is the definition of NetView commands.

NetView Commands

As discussed above, each command can be related to a specific class. A list of all the commands and their classes is contained in the DSIPARM (DSICMD) member. For example, the following statements could be defined:

```
VARY        CMDCLASS 1
```

In the above simple example, the VTAM VARY command is associated with CMDCLASS 1 and is therefore available to execute to any operator who

---

TABLE 11.4 DSIPROFA Member of DSIPRF

DSIPROFA	PROFILE	IC=xxxx
	AUTH	MSGRECVR=NO,CTL=GLOBAL
	OPCLASS	1,2
	SPAN	<spanname>

has an operator profile with the OPCLASS 1. Also, it should be noted that MVS and JES2 commands can be issued from NetView consoles. This is normally done by prefixing the command with the MVS verb. For example:

MVS $p (JES2 purge command)

It also should be noted that command keywords can be used in the DSICMD member to provide further restrictions on subfunctions available with specific commands. The KEYCLASS parameter is used for this purpose.

From a security perspective, great care should be taken in reviewing this area of NetView. You should review, at a minimum, all the sensitive VTAM, MVS, and JES commands to determine what CMDCLASS they have been assigned (if any!). It also is important to associate the command classes available to each operator profile, and the relationship between profiles and NetView operator IDs. A simple way to do this is to develop an access matrix, as shown in Table 11.5.

The focus of the security review will be related to the operator IDs that have been assigned to operator profiles that have access to sensitive commands.

In summary, the security review steps should include:

- Ensuring that access to all sensitive MVS, JES2, VTAM, and NCCF commands through NetView is controlled.

- Developing a matrix of users who can use commands through NETVIEW, and determining what commands are authorized for use. This information is obtained from the DSICMD dataset.

- Identifying the sensitive commands and, on a sample basis, assessing the appropriateness of assignment of these privileges (that is, based on job related need).

The last area of discussion relating to NetView 2.3 is the security procedures relating to NetView Logs.

TABLE 11.5 Operator/Class Access Matrix

Operator	Operator Profiles			
	OPCLASS 1,2	OPCLASS 2	OPCLASS 3	OPCLASS 4
OPER1	DSIPROFA			
OPER9			DSIPROFE	

NetView Logs

The main consideration is to determine how the NetView logging facility is used for security, control, and monitoring purposes. This would include an assessment of the adequacy of the audit trail and the retention period for log datasets.

Before leaving the NetView mainframe application, it is worthwhile summarizing some of the new features available within NetView 2.4 with security and control significance. These include:

- Increased functionality in the area of APPN networks.

- Dynamic configuration changes. For example, definition of NetView operators.

Other Products in the NetView Family

To discuss the security and control features of products such as NetView/6000 and NetView OS/2, it is necessary to provide a brief overview of SNMP (Simple Network Management Protocol) and the related functions. SNMP is currently the de facto standard for integrated network management in multivendor environments. SNMP was originally developed in the late 1980s, to manage TCP/IP-based networks. Looking back at the SystemView concepts above, these are consistent with the primary components of SNMP. Essentially, the three major components of SNMP are:

- SNMP Manager

- SNMP Agent

- Management Information Base (MIB)

In simple terms, the SNMP Manager manages SNMP Agents within a network segment. The SNMP agent can be any network device, such as a workstation, host computer, bridge, or router. Shortly, we will discuss the NetView SNMP Managers. The Managers contain a description of the Management Information Base for each Agent. The Agent maintains a specific Management Information Base relating to its network resources. The MIB description held by the Manager is used to poll the Agent devices. The Management Information Base is the definition of objects that are stored in the Agent for the Manager to access. The MIB objects can include values that describe the status and the operating parameters of the device. You define MIB objects in accordance with the Structure of Management Information (SMI). The tree structure of the MIB database is normally in three parts: a root, a subtree, and a leaf which represents a single MIB object.

SNMP currently has two versions: SNMPv1 and SNMPv2. SNMP has five basic functions which are used between the Manager and the Agent to send information and make requests. These functions are summarized as follows:

- GET   This request is issued by the Manager to the Agent to request information about a specific object in the MIB.

- GETNEXT   This request is issued by the Manager to the Agent to request information about the next object in the MIB.

- GETRESPONSE   This command is issued by the Agent to the Manager in response to a GET command.

- SET   This command can be used by the Manager to store values in the Agent MIB.

- TRAP   This command is issued by the Agent to the Manager to report significant network events, such as the Agent device is initializing itself or that there has been an authentication failure (to be discussed shortly).

The main general security concerns brought up by the use of SNMPv1 relate to the lack of authentication of the source of a Manager request, and the capability to capture and view the network management information as it passes across the network. As a result of these weaknesses, many installations restrict the use of SNMP Managers to the use of read-only functions. That is, the GET function is normally disabled.

SNMPv2 provides a number of additional security mechanisms to try to address these issues. The main features of these mechanisms are as follows:

- Secret Key Authentication between a Manager and an Agent

- DES encryption of network traffic between a Manager and an Agent

- Access control to the Agent MIB by the Manager

The discussion of this area is limited, because both NetView/6000 and NetView OS/2 currently use SNMPv1. The primary security mechanism used by both of these products is the concept of "community strings." Essentially, community strings are associated with each SNMP request or command. The community string determines who may have read-only or read/write access to an MIB object. SNMP defines a community as a relationship between an Agent and a Manager.

There can be multiple Managers. Community strings are normally set at either PUBLIC or PRIVATE and are included in the SNMP request. These strings are known to the Agent and have a value associated with them of read-only or read/write. When the Agent receives a request, it will check the validity of the request from the specific Manager and the type of request. A Trap (or alert) is available to send information to the SNMP manager if invalid requests are received. This function is limited as a security mechanism because it is based on the source address of the Manager sending the request, which can be spoofed.

Our discussion will now move to two specific IBM network management products available. It should be clearly understood that we are only discussing two of the many network management products available from IBM in this area. This will provide an indication of the functionality and security capabilities that are currently in use.

NetView/6000

NetView/6000 is a multivendor, multiprotocol network and systems management product. It currently is available as two levels of product, NetView for AIX and NetView Entry for AIX. Both levels are currently at Version 3. The product normally is used to manage IP-addressable devices in the network.

The primary difference between the two levels is that the NetView Entry product is restricted to thirty-two managed nodes, and also does not have relational database support, which is available with the expanded version. The relational database support includes the capability to use databases such as DB2/600, Oracle, and SYBASE to store network information.

The product has an extensive number of features including:

- Graphical User Interface to display network information
- A Manager Takeover function
- Support for Trouble Ticket/6000
- AIX System Management Interface Tool (SMIT)
- MIB Loader and MIB processing
- MIB Browser and MIB Data Collector
- MIB Application Builder
- Optional cooperative management between NetView AIX and a host NetView

The primary security information relates to the product's use of the following applications that can be used of the AIX operating system, as either manager or agent applications. The Manager application is "snmpinfo", which supports all SNMP functions and the SNMP Agent application is "snmpd".

A number of files have security significance, and AIX permissions should be reviewed to ensure that access is appropriately restricted. These files include:

- etc/mibs/*: MIB information
- etc/community: definition of community strings

- etc/smpd.conf: relationship of community strings to SNMP permissions; traps

In addition, the content of the configuration file should be reviewed to ensure that SNMP Managers and Agents have the proper read-only or read/write permissions. A final word in this area is that the security of the NetView /6000 application also is dependent on the general AIX security implementation, and this should be looked at as a matter of course.

Our discussion now moves to the latest network management product offering from IBM. The NetView OS/2 product Version 2 will be generally available in March 1995.

NetView/OS2

This product provides a full suite of SNMP management capabilities. It uses SNMPv1. The SNMP Manager runs on an OS/2 workstation running OS/2 version 2.0 or higher. The SNMP Agents supported include OS/2, MS-DOS, Windows, Macintosh, and Novell NetWare. It should be clearly noted that this product also has the capability to support a remote command line interface, which means that any operating system command or function for the Agent operating system can be executed from the Manager workstation—not only SNMP commands.

In terms of security, NetView OS/2 has no identification or authentication mechanisms and is reliant on both restriction of physical access to the Manager workstation and the standard OS/2 security features of boot passwords and keyboard lock facilities. In terms of SNMP security, the issues relating to SNMPv1 discussed above are applicable. NetView OS/2 does use community strings, and the SNMP GET command can be disabled.

Summary

We have seen that the trend in network management products is moving in the direction of end-to-end control and management of multiprotocol, multivendor network environments. The rich functionality of the NetView network management products requires careful understanding and review in terms of the security issues, most of which have been identified and addressed in this chapter.

Acronyms

CDRM   Cross Domain Resource Manager

JCL   Job Control Language

MIB   Management Information Base

MVS/ESA	IBM Multiple Virtual Storage/ Enterprise Systems Architecture
RACF	IBM Resource Access Control Facility
RODM	Resource Object Data Manager
SDLC	Synchronous Data Link Control
SNA	Systems Network Architecture
SNMP	Simple Network Management Protocol
TCP/IP	Transmission Control Protocol / Internet Protocol
VTAM	Virtual Telecommunications Access Method

Select Bibliography

CompuServe. *IBM NetView Forum*
IBM. September 1994. *IBM NetView for AIX; IBM NetView Entry for AIX.*
IBM. *IBM NetView for OS/2.*
IBM. *IBM Networking Solutions*, Volume 2, Edition 2 (3014-9021-4).
IBM. April 1994. *IBM Open Blueprint Introduction*, First Edition.
IBM. *NetNews—IBM's Quarterly Networking Magazine.*
Netview Installation and Administration Guide (MVS) Version 2 Release 3 (SC31-6125-01)
IBM. September 1994. *NetView Version 2 for Network and System Management.*
Planning and Reference: NetView; Network Control Program; VTAM (SC31-6191)

The Server

A good servant is a real godsend; but truly 'tis a rare bird in the land.
MARTIN LUTHER

In this world it is not what we take up, but what we give up, that makes us rich.
HENRY WARD BEECHER

12

Securing NetWare 4.x

John G. Tannahill

*All business proceeds on beliefs, or
judgments of probabilities, and not on
certainties.*   CHARLES ELIOT

This chapter discusses the security and control issues associated with Novell
NetWare 4.x. The main areas of discussion focus on the specific security features of the product, and security and control issues common in the local and
wide area network environments in which the product is used. The current
version of NetWare 4.x is 4.1; however, many environments are still using
version 4.02. It also should be noted that the other main Novell NetWare versions in business use today are the 3.x versions, such as version 3.12. There
are major security and control differences between 3.x and 4.x versions, and
these will be highlighted as you progress through the discussion.

The major conceptual difference between the two versions is that NetWare
3.x operating systems are based on a single server concept. For example, a
user is required to logon to each server in a NetWare 3.x LAN on an individual basis, whereas NetWare 4.x is based on the concept of a global enterprise
network that only requires a user to have a single user ID and password to access global network resources, regardless of where those resources reside.

This chapter assumes that the reader has a basic familiarity with NetWare
3.x security concepts and terminology.

The beginning of any discussion in the area of local area network security involves the control objectives and security functions that are required to perform a security review. These areas can be considered as follows:

- **Identification and authentication** This area relates to ensuring that all users and processes are properly identified and authenticated prior to allowing access to network resources. NetWare 4.1 has two levels of authentication: initial and background authentication.

- **Resource access control** This security area relates to ensuring that users are appropriately restricted to the network resources that they are authorized to access. Two areas of NetWare 4.1 that will be discussed here are NetWare Directory Services (NDS) object security and the standard directory and file system security that was available in previous releases of NetWare versions, such as NetWare 3.12. The point at which these two levels of security meet is the VOLUME object which has security implications and will be discussed in detail later.

- **Audit trails** NetWare has significantly enhanced accountability and audit trail information in the 4.x version. Our discussion in this area will focus on the AUDITCON utility.

Other security and control issues will focus on areas such as encryption of information during network transmission. The initial steps in undertaking a security review of a NetWare 4.x environment should include:

- Obtaining physical and logical network configuration diagrams.

- Obtaining security policies, standards, and procedures, with particular emphasis on local area network security administration procedures.

- Developing an understanding of the design of the NetWare Directory Services tree. For example, is the design based on organizational structure, geographic locations, or organization functions? Is a single NDS tree used for the organization or are multiple NDS trees used (as might be the case in service bureau organizations)?

- Identifying the security administration groups and their related job functions.

- Identifying the communication protocol stacks used in the local and wide area network environments. For example, either IPX/SPX, TCP/IP, or SDLC.

- Identifying network operating systems used, such as NetWare 4.x; NetWare 3.x, OS/2 LAN Server; UNIX variants, etc. In particular, we need to develop an understanding of how the NetWare 3.x and 4.x versions are being used. For example, 3.x versions are used in stand-alone environments or are being accessible from 4.x environment, using "Bindery Emulation."

- Identifying mission critical application systems operating in the environment. In this area, it also is important to identify the location of presentation, application, and data management functions spread across multiple platforms.
- Identifying different time zones involved in the wide area network.

The purpose of obtaining this information is to understand the network environment and to define the scope of the security review.

NetWare 4.x Overview

The purpose of this section is to provide a brief overview of the main security features of NetWare 4.x, and to highlight the main areas of significant enhancement or change over NetWare 3.x versions. These new features include user authentication, NetWare Directory Services (NDS), audit trail facilities, Windows-based user and administration tools, and time synchronization servers.

User Authentication

Users are no longer required to login to individual NetWare servers. The network operating system manages network resources on a global network basis, and access to these resources is based on authentication of a message request by an object (such as a user) to access the resource. The means of user authentication is now based on RSA encryption techniques, using public and private encryption keys. A user password is no longer transmitted across the network.

A summary of the initial authentication process (user login) is as follows. A user requests login from a client workstation. This request is received by "authentication services" on the server, which returns an encrypted private key to the client workstation. The client uses the user password to decrypt the private key and uses the private key to build an encrypted "authenticator" that is then sent to the server. The server decrypts the authenticator with a public key. This authenticator is used in the background each time a user requests access to network resources during a session.

NetWare Directory Services (NDS)

NetWare Directory Services (NDS) is a logical database of network objects. These objects are either "container" objects or "leaf" objects, and are structured in a hierarchical tree format. Container objects consist primarily of Organization (O) and Organizational Unit (OU) objects, whereas Leaf Objects consist of, for example, users, server, volumes, and print queues.

Container objects are either parents of leaf objects or act as a container for other Container Objects. Leaf Objects represent network resources which can be used. Each object in the NDS tree has associated properties. The properties of the object are associated with values. This will be discussed in more detail later.

It clearly should be understood that the NDS tree objects are separate from the NetWare Directory and File system that uses the same concepts as NetWare 3.x.

Audit Trail Facilities

The main new feature in this area is the AUDITCON utility, which provides a number of significant audit trail capabilities. These capabilities will be discussed later in the chapter.

Windows-Based User and Administration Tools

The main NDS and security administration tool is called NWADMIN (Windows version), which is the conceptual equivalent of SYSCON in NetWare 3.x environments. In addition, a number of utilities from the 3.x environments have been removed, replaced, or enhanced. For example, the SECURITY utility no longer exists.

Time Synchronization Servers

The other main new feature of 4.x is the introduction of time synchronization servers, which are required to ensure that the distributed network servers are kept in synchronization by use of a universal network time, as opposed to a local time zone. Time Servers are classified as a Reference Time Server that gets its time from an external source such as an atomic clock; a Primary Time Server that gets the correct time from the Reference Server; and Secondary Time Servers, which are informed of the correct time by the Primary Time Server. The deployment and use of time servers will depend on the size of the network.

Our discussion will now focus on specific areas of NetWare 4.x that are of significance from a security perspective.

Identification and Authentication

Novell has introduced a number of important security changes for identification and authentication. The primary focus is on the requirement for a user to sign on only to the network once, and the fact that the password only is used in the initial authentication process. As discussed above, all ac-

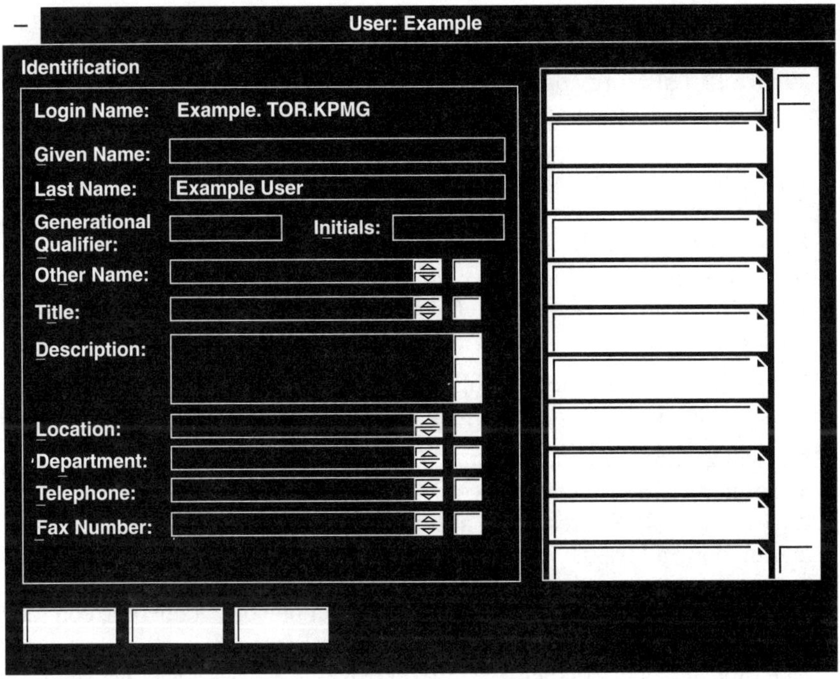

Figure 12.1   User set-up using NWADMIN utility

cess to network resources after initial authentication of the user are based on an authenticator.

Figure 12.1 provides an example of how a user is setup using the NWADMIN utility. This also illustrates the concept of user as an object and the properties associated with the object, such as Login Name, Last Name, Title, and Description. "Example User" is an example of a value of the Last Name property.

Another new important concept is that of "Context," which identifies the location of an object within a container object in the NDS tree. Within an NDS tree, each leaf object has a Common Name (CN). When using objects, a context must be specified. For example, name contexts for a user are set up in the NET.CFG workstation file. An example of a context for user John in the Security group of the Consulting division of ABC company might be:

CN=JOHN.OU=SECURITY.OU=CONSULTING.O=ABC, or
JOHN.SECURITY.CONSULTING.ABC.

When a user is using objects in the same container as the user object, the object (for example, VOLUME) can be referred to by its common name, as opposed to the requirement to use the full name if the object were located in a different container. CX is a utility that a user can use to display objects in a container, or to change the context in which they are currently operating.

Figure 12.1 also provides examples of the main security issues associated with user identification and authentication. These include:

- **Login restrictions** Does the user account have an expiry date (for example, belongs to a consultant or temporary employee)?

- **Password restrictions** Does the user require a password? Are unique passwords required (default = No)? Minimum Length of the password (default = 5 characters)? Length between password changes (default = 40 days)? Is the user allowed to change the password (default = Yes)?

- **Login time restrictions** This relates to the capability to restrict the days and hours of the day in which a user can login.

- **Network address restrictions** This relates to the capability to restrict a user login to a specific physical workstation, based on the MAC (Media-Access Control) Address that, in turn, is based on the network and workstation node address.

In addition, it is possible to restrict the number of concurrent connections (sessions) a user can have active at the same time.

The above security controls are consistent with those available in NetWare 3.x versions.

An important change from NetWare 3.x is the difference between SUPERVISOR and ADMIN user IDs. In NetWare 3.x, the SUPERVISOR user was an all-powerful user ID, which operated above the privilege hierarchy associated with Directory and File Trustee Rights relating to each Novell server. This user ID, and user IDs that were supervisor-equivalent, were normally provided to local area network administrators.

This user ID does not exist in NetWare 4.x. When NetWare 4.x is installed, a user ID (object) called ADMIN is automatically created, with rights to create and maintain objects. These rights are provided at the root level of the NDS tree. It should be noted that the ADMIN user can be deleted or renamed when other user objects have been created and given Object Rights of Supervisor. Great care must be taken in the use or removal of the ADMIN user ID. This concept means that the provision of security and administration rights over objects are key to NetWare 4.x security, because these rights can be distributed over a large number of users in a large enterprise network.

Another important security facility is the Intruder Detection Lockout. This facility can be set for a container such as an organizational unit, using the NWADMIN utility, and would apply to all user objects within that container. The main settings include:

- The limits for the incorrect number of logins; for example, three.

- How long is the retention of the bad login count; for example, 24 hours.

- Should the account be locked after detection.
- How long should the account be locked after intruder detection.
  The key security review issues in this area are:
  ~Does the ADMIN user object exist? If so, what are the password, login, and network address restrictions associated with the user ID? Who has the password for this user ID, and is it restricted to a single user to ensure individual accountability for its use?
  ~Obtain an overview of the logical security design for network administration; that is, how has the security administration structure been set up in relation to NDS Object and Property Rights and the Directory and File System Rights? This will be discussed further in the sections of the chapter relating to these issues.
  ~Does the actual set-up of user objects in terms of password, login, and network address restrictions conform to company standards? For example, concurrent connections should be restricted to one. This should be tested periodically on a sample basis.
  ~How are login scripts used in the environment? (Note that a number of different types of login scripts are available in NetWare 4.x; that is, system, profile, and user login scripts.)
  ~Are NCP Packet Signatures used in the network environment? This should be considered as a method of preventing the spoofing of client workstations. (This capability was provided by the HACK.EXE program for NetWare 3.x environments. The program originated in the Netherlands and is freely available on the Internet.)

Our next area of discussion includes the concepts and security issues relating to the NDS tree.

NetWare Directory Services (NDS)

NetWare Directory Services is the key component of NetWare 4.x based on X.500 addressing to allow for a single logical database (NetWare Directory Database) of network resources. Directory services replace the server-based bindery objects of NetWare 3.x versions. It should be noted that the NDS tree can be located on a single file server, or can be partitioned across several file servers. NDS is a tree structure with a root and two types of objects—container objects and leaf objects. These objects have been briefly described above. Figure 12.2 provides a simple example of a possible design of an NDS tree for an organization.

It is worth providing a brief explanation of the main components of an NDS tree. The Root object represents the highest reference point in the NDS tree and is used as an access point to Country or Organization container objects. This should not be confused with the root directory of a volume.

Objects in the NDS tree consist of either container or leaf objects. Each object contains an Access Control List (ACL), which specifies the list of objects that have rights to this object. Objects do not contain lists of what objects they have rights to, which is important to understand in a security review. Object and property rights are discussed below.

There are three types of container objects: Country (C); Organization (O); and Organizational Unit (OU). The only required container object is the Organization container. Use of container objects is dependent on the design of the NDS tree.

Leaf objects are at the end of the branches of an NDS tree; that is, they don't contain other objects and they represent the network resources that can be used. The main leaf objects are: Alias; Bindery; Directory Map; Group; NetWare Server; Organizational Role; Print Queue; Print Server; Printer; Profile; User; and Volume.

Our discussion will now focus on Object and Property Rights. Object rights relate to NDS objects and work in a flow-down concept, in that trustee assignments to objects flow down the NDS tree until blocked by an Inherited Rights Filter (IRF), or by another set of trustee assignments at a lower level of the tree. The object rights which can be assigned to a trustee are summarized in Figure 12.3.

Property rights relate to the properties of an NDS object. An example of certain of the properties of the user object are shown Figure 12.1. The property rights which can be assigned to a trustee are summarized in Figure 12.4. It should be noted that property rights can relate either to All Property rights (that relate to all properties of an object) or to specific properties of an object.

Object and property rights are assigned to trustees using the NWADMIN or RIGHTS utilities. A trustee must have Supervisor object or property rights; or Write or Add Self property rights to grant trustee object or property rights to others.

As discussed above, rights flow down the NDS tree until blocked by an Inherited Rights Filter (this is similar in concept to the Inherited Rights Mask (IRM) used in the NetWare 3.x directory and file system security). The IRF is a list of rights for a specific object, which can block the flow down of rights from container objects. The IRF cannot be used to grant

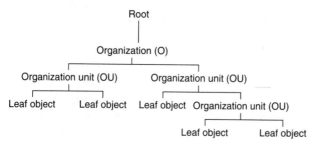

Figure 12.2 Simple netware directory services (NDS) tree structure.

Right	Description
SUPERVISOR	All privileges, including access to all properties
BROWSE	Ability to see object in NDS tree
CREATE	Ability to create object below this object in NDS tree
DELETE	Ability to delete object from NDS tree
RENAME	Ability to change name of the object

Figure 12.3 Object rights

Right	Description
SUPERVISOR	All rights to the property
COMPARE	Right to compare any value with the value of the property
READ	Right to read value of the property
WRITE	Right to add, change or delete value of the property
ADD SELF	Right to add itself as value of the property
	e.g. to Group

Figure 12.4 Property rights

rights. At a minimum, the write property right to the Access Control (ACL) property of an object is required to set or change the IRF for the object. Another important point to note is that the IRF can be used to block Supervisor rights to objects and properties; however, you should do this with caution.

The main area of interest in a security review are the Effective Rights to objects and properties. Determination of effective rights is based on a combination of trustee assignments and the IRF for an object. This can be a complex administration area as a result of the number of places in the NDS tree in which a user object can be granted trustee assignments; for instance, explicit trustee assignments to the object, inherited trustee rights from the trustee's container, inherited trustee rights from the object's container, and inherited trustee rights from the trustee's and objects container. It is fortunate that a number of NetWare utilities allow a person performing a security review to view directly the Effective Rights for an object (this can be done using NWADMIN). A simple example of effective rights is as follows, for user object John who has trustee assignments to Volume APP1:

- John's Trustee Assignments to OUAPP1 (Container in which APP1 resides) are [BCD]

- Inherited Rights Filter for APP1 is [CR]
- Effective Rights to APP1 would be Create i.e. [C]

This simple example illustrates that the IRF can only take away rights. The trustees assignment did not contain the READ right and although this is provided in the IRF, it will not be taken into account in determining effective rights.

The key security review issues in this area are:

- Identification of critical network resources.

- Ensuring that Supervisor Rights for objects and properties that relate to the above network resources are restricted to authorized security administrators, and that there is appropriate segregation of functional responsibilities.

- Ensuring that Effective Rights to objects and properties are appropriate for user responsibilities and job functions. (It should be stressed that these rights are applicable to management of the NDS tree and not the directory and file system, which will be discussed below, although Volume objects should be the subject of special consideration in a security review.)

- Identification of Bindery Emulation objects that allow access to NetWare 3.x servers in a NetWare 4.x environment. (It should be noted that once this object is accessed, it is then necessary to login to the NetWare 3.x server. This will provide access to NetWare 3.x directories and files as if the user had logged into the server directly.)

An important point to consider is that Leaf objects can be moved from one part of an NDS tree to another. This will change the object and property rights for an object as a result of being in a different container. It is important that appropriate procedures be in place to assess the security implications of moving leaf objects, and that appropriate audit trails are in place to identify when this occurs.

Directory and File System Security

This area is consistent with previous versions of NetWare, such as NetWare 3.x. The main consideration from a NetWare 4.x-specific perspective is that the Volume object represents the root directory of a directory and file system, and therefore as an example a user who has Supervisor rights to the Volume object has full supervisor rights to the root directory and all subdirectories and files. A brief summary of the main security components follows.

Trustee assignment rights are similar in concept to that described for objects and properties above. The rights which can be assigned to trustees, for directories and files, are summarized in Figure 12.5. It should be clearly un-

Right	Description
SUPERVISOR	All rights to directory, subdirectories and files:
	(This right cannot be blocked by an IRF)
READ	Right to open directories, read files and execute programs
WRITE	Right to open directories and modify files in directories
CREATE	Right to create new subdirectories and files
ERASE	Right to delete directory, subdirectories and files
MODIFY	Right to change directory/file names and attributes
FILE SCAN	Right to 'see' directories and files with DIR or NDIR
ACCESS CONTROL	Right to change trustee assignments or IRF

Figure 12.5 Directory rights

Right	Description
SUPERVISOR	All rights to files:
	(This right cannot be blocked by an IRF)
READ	Right to read file and/or execute program
WRITE	Right to modify file
CREATE	Right to create new file
ERASE	Right to delete file
MODIFY	Right to change file name and attributes
FILE SCAN	Right to 'see' directories and files with DIR or NDIR
ACCESS CONTROL	Right to change trustee assignments or IRF

Figure 12.6 File rights

derstood that directory and file trustee assignments are not given through the NDS objects. However, users can be given directory rights based on rights granted to the Volume object, as discussed above and as illustrated in Figure 12.6.

It should be noted that a similar set of rights exists for individual files. Specific File Rights override Directory Rights. These rights are summarized in Figure 12.7.

The Inherited Rights Filter (IRF) for directories and files works in a similar manner to that described for NDS objects. The major difference is that the Supervisor rights to directories and files cannot be blocked by the IRF.

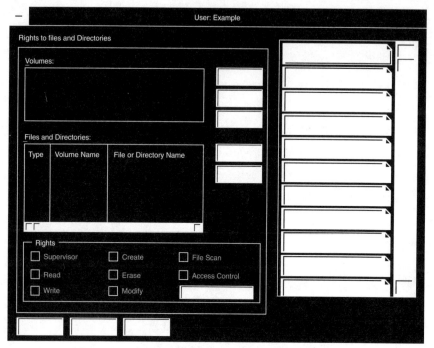

Figure 12.7 Rights to files and directories.

Effective Rights are similar in concept to that described for NDS objects; that is, effective rights are based on the combination of trustee assignments and Inherited Rights Filter (formerly Inherited Rights Mask (IRM) in NetWare 3.x).

As with NetWare 3.x, the use of directory and file Attributes is also available in NetWare 4.x. These attributes are similar in nature to MS-DOS file attributes and include Hidden (H); Execute Only (X); Archive Needed (A); and System (SY) as examples.

The key security review issues in this area are:

- Identification of critical applications and the volumes where they reside.

- Identification of all users and groups with Supervisor Rights to directories and files (note user objects with security equivalencies).

- Determination that effective rights to critical application and data directories and files are appropriate.

- Determination that Volume Object and Property rights are appropriate and do not introduce unintentional security exposures.

- Determination that SYSTEM directories are appropriately protected.

The main criterion is to ensure that the implementation of logical access control is appropriate for the application systems and the NetWare environments in which they operate.

Our next area of discussion is the new audit trail facilities within NetWare 4.x.

Audit Trail Facilities

NetWare 4.x introduces the concept of Auditor, which is separate from network administration and supervisor rights. The Auditor does not have a specific user account but is based on the use of a lockword (a password without a related user ID). The password and the audit trail information are based primarily at the volume level. The audit trail information is stored as a special system file on the volume to which it relates. Figure 12.8 shows the main menu for the AUDITCON utility. Audit Trails are based on settings within the AUDITCON facility. This facility is controlled via the auditor password.

The main events, considered as either NDS or Volume events that can be audited, include:

- Accesses and modifications to NDS tree objects
- Modifications to trustee assignments
- User logins
- Changes to user restrictions
- Creation, change, or deletion of directories
- Access to files

The capability exists within AUDITCON to view or print audit reports. Audit reports can be produced by using a number of different criteria, such as by date and time and by event.

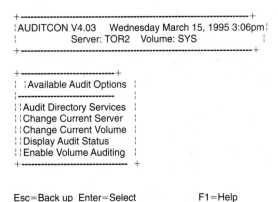

```
+-------------------------------------------------------------------+
| AUDITCON V4.03    Wednesday March 15, 1995 3:06pm |
|           Server: TOR2   Volume: SYS                |
+-------------------------------------------------------------------+


+----------------------------+
|  | Available Audit Options  |
|----------------------------
| | Audit Directory Services  |
| | Change Current Server     |
| | Change Current Volume     |
| | Display Audit Status      |
| | Enable Volume Auditing    |
+----------------------------- +


Esc=Back up  Enter=Select          F1=Help
```

Figure 12.8 Main menu of AUDITCON utility.

The key security review issues and questions in relation to audit trails are:

- Who controls and who has access to the Auditor passwords?
- What events are audited?
- How are the audit reports produced and to whom are they distributed?
- What procedures exist for review and follow-up action?
- How long are audit trails retained?

These issues should be addressed by and included in security administration standards and procedures.

Security Review Utilities

This area will discuss the utility programs within NetWare 4.x that are useful in the performance of a security review. The main differences between Version 3.x and 4.x utilities also will be explained.

As discussed above, the SYSCON utility in NetWare 3.x has been replaced by the NWADMIN utility in NetWare 4.x. The MS-DOS version of this utility is NETADMIN. The SESSION utility has been replaced by NWTOOLS (the MS-DOS version is NETUSER).

The NLIST utility displays information about objects and properties within specific name contexts. The following NetWare 4.x utilities also are useful in a security review:

RIGHTS	replaces RIGHTS; TLIST; ALLOW and others
FLAG	replaces FLAG; FLAGDIR, etc.
NDIR	replaces NDIR; LISTDIR; CHKVOL, etc.
NLIST	replaces USERLIST, SLIST
WHOAMI	replaces WHOAMI, NVER

In addition to the use of these utilities for performance of a security review, particular attention should be paid to sensitive utility functions existing in the NetWare 4.x environment, and how these are controlled. Examples include the RCONSOLE (remote console facility), SERVMAN (server console command utility), and PARTMGR (NDS partition manager).

Other Issues

A number of areas are important from a security perspective but have not been addressed in this chapter so far. These issues should be considered in conjunction with a logical security review of NetWare 4.x. They include:

- **Workstation security** Are physical and logical access control measures in place for workstations?

- **Physical and logical security of network hardware** Is there appropriate protection for various network hardware devices, including unused connection points, network hubs, routers, and sniffers (protocol analyzers)?

- **Partitioning and replication of the NDS tree** The security issues associated with this area should be considered at the network design stage. Because this involves the use of several NetWare servers to hold the NetWare Directory Database, there are a number of physical security, logical security and back-up and recovery issues.

- **TCP/IP services exposures** (for example, NFS.NLM facilities) NetWare is capable of hosting TCP/IP services such as the Network File System (NFS). Care should be taken to understand the services provided and to ensure that there are no security weaknesses in the design and implementation of the service. In addition, appropriate security measures, such as firewall policy and design, should be considered where internal corporate networks are connected to external networks, using the TCP/IP protocol suite.

- **Remote access** Appropriate security measures, such as end-user authentication/one-time passwords and the internal security features of the remote access software products, should be considered when remote dial-up access is available to the environment.

- **Transmission of clear text data across the network** This issue presents an exposure that is becoming increasingly well known and understood, in that data is transferred across Ethernet or Token Ring networks in an unencrypted format. The risks associated with this exposure are increasing due to the availability in the public domain of MS-DOS-based packet analyzer software, such as Gobbler and Beholder, that can be used to capture large amounts of data as it flows across the network.

- **Application development, maintenance and change control** This area is outside of the scope of this chapter but has been included here because it is important to view security issues from an application-system perspective, to identify the computer platforms involved and to ensure that there is appropriate placement of security features.

- **Back-up and recovery procedures and business continuance or resumption planning** These areas are critical from a security perspective as a result of the distributed nature of a NetWare 4.x environment.

A final thought. Appropriate security is dependent on an understanding of the host and network environments used in the organization. Before undertaking a NetWare 4.x security review, it is important to obtain an understanding of other operating system hosts (such as UNIX or MVS) and communications protocols (such as TCP/IP or SDLC) and the nature of their interconnectivity. This will ensure that the appropriate scope of the security review is both defined and understood.

Summary

This chapter provided an overview of the NetWare 4.x operating system functions and main security features. It is important to understand the concept of NetWare Directory Services and its applicability to enterprise networks, as opposed to the single-server network environment focus of NetWare 3.x. Many security issues have changed between these versions, including the approach to security administration, and these should be the focus of a security review of this area. Other areas which should be the focus of security review are the upgrade and migration activities associated with the change from NetWare 3.x to NetWare 4.x environments. It is more efficient and effective to perform the security design for the environment at this stage, as opposed to retrofitting security requirements when the NetWare 4.x environment is fully operational.

Acronyms

- **IPX/SPX** Internet Packet Exchange/Sequenced Packet Exchange
- **IRF** Inherited Rights Filter
- **LAN** Local Area Network
- **MAC** Media Access Control
- **NCP** NetWare Core Protocol
- **NDS** NetWare Directory Services
- **RSA** Rivest, Shamir, and Adelman encryption algorithm
- **TCP/IP** Transmission Control Protocol/Internet Protocol

Select Bibliography

Davis, Peter T. and Craig R. McGuffin. 1994. *Teach Yourself NetWare in 14 Days*. Indianapolis, IN: SAMS Publishing.

Dyson, Peter. 1994. *Novell's Dictionary of Networking*. San Jose, CA: SYBEX Inc. and Novell Press.

Herbon, Gamal B. 1994. *Designing NetWare Directory Services*. New York: M&T Books.

Nowshadi, Farshad. 1994. *Managing NetWare, Data Communications and Networks Series*. Reading, MA: Addison-Wesley Publishing Company.

Sheldon, Tom. 1993. *Novell NetWare 4: The Complete Reference*. Berkeley, CA: Osborne McGraw-Hill.

Online Novell References

- http//:www.novell.com (Novell's world wide web server)
- Novell NetWare 4.x CompuServe Message Forum
- comp.sys.novell and other various Internet newsgroups

Chapter

13

Securing OS/2 LAN Server
Gary Hunt

*A sense of the value of time—that is, of the best
way to divide one's time into one's various
activities—is an essential preliminary to
efficient work; it is the only method of
avoiding hurry.*   ARNOLD BENNETT

LAN Server is primarily an application that runs on the OS/2 operating system and enables OS/2 to share its resources with other machines connected to the network. Because LAN Server gives OS/2 this new capability, a key design goal of the LAN Server product is to provide a strong level of security protection for this added function.

In this chapter, we will take a careful look at the security mechanisms in LAN Server, focusing on what is protected and what is not. The goal of the first section will be to demonstrate that the security protection supplied by LAN Server is strong. This examination will be a detailed examination of LAN Server security, focusing on key protocol flows at the lowest levels of the LAN Server security technology. The second section will be to give the user perspective into the technology described in the first section. Finally, the third section will discuss general advanced topics.

However, before examining some of the low level details of LAN Server security, it will be helpful to first define some of the terms that will be used later with some common, everyday examples.

If you are thinking about security, you probably have something of value to protect. Because there is no such thing as a foolproof, totally secure security system, one key aspect of considering security is to match the investment you make in security with the value of the objects being protected.

In analyzing a security system, you can start by looking at whether the system is capable of keeping out anyone and everyone. If a facility is hard to access in the first place, the question then becomes, how do you give privileges to the people you do want to allow access? There are two parts to classical access control: identity validation and privilege granting. If identity can be established, privileges are best thought of as access rules associated with a protected resource where the rules can contain different privilege levels for different users.

One good illustration of a security system is an Automatic Teller Machine. The object being protected in this case is ultimately the money in the machine. When you insert your bank card, the ATM reads your account number and associates it with your name. This identity is the identity you want to be used for the transaction you are about to request, like withdrawing money from your checking account. However, an ATM (and your bank) does not believe it is sufficient for someone to possess a bank card to authorize transactions to your account (something you should be happy about), because bank cards can be stolen. So, before the ATM will process a transaction on your behalf it will ask you for your Personal Identification Number (PIN). Your PIN represents a shared secret between you and your bank that the ATM is designed to use to verify your identity. If you enter the correct PIN, the ATM on behalf of your bank is then satisfied that you truly are who your card says you are and then you are allowed (authorized) to make transactions against your account. One last important point is that you will be allowed to access your own account only.

The key to this whole process was implemented in two phases: first an identity verification phase and then a privilege granting phase.

This section will examine the security facilities in the LAN Server product, using the same model. This chapter will first consider whether LAN Server is capable of being configured to restrict any access to all data on server machines. Next, the chapter will discuss how and when LAN Server defines users and validates their identity before a user makes a request. Finally, it will look at the form access rules take, which are used to determine if an identified user has the privilege to perform the function he is requesting.

One other consideration for a security subsystem is the conflict between usability and security. During the examination of security on LAN Server, you will learn about design points where some amount of security has been sacrificed on behalf of usability.

The Basics of LAN Server Security

To examine how well LAN Server keeps users from accessing server resources, let's consider the case in which a new server is being added to an existing LAN Server installation.

The first topic to consider is general data security on the server machine. A critical aspect of a LAN Server is that the server code runs on OS/2 with all its capabilities still intact. With the exception of the local security feature of LAN Server, which we will discuss in the advanced topics section, LAN Server does not add any security to data on a server machine from the standpoint of access at the server keyboard/console. OS/2 does not have any concept of users, and all data is readily accessible from the OS/2 user interfaces. If data that needs to be protected (regardless of LAN Server) is stored on an OS/2 machine, the only facility available today is to provide physical security access to the PC hardware. In other words, place the OS/2 machine in a secure room. This fact is generally true of MS-DOS and Windows as well.

Because a LAN Server server is still an OS/2 machine, the above rule applies. If the server contains data that needs to be protected the machine should be placed in a secure location. The difference between a plain OS/2 machine and a LAN Server server machine, of course, is that LAN Server allows users other than the user at the local OS/2 keyboard to access data on the server. The design goal of security in LAN Server is to provide this remote data access capability in a secure fashion.

A good place to start in considering the LAN Server remote access security facilities is to consider a scenario in which a brand new LAN Server server is being added to an existing LAN Server installation.

When a LAN Server server is first installed and brought up, there are no access rules on anything other than data in the LAN Server Domain Controller Database (DCDB). (Another exception is printers, serial devices, and pipes. There are default root level profiles for these types of resources that will be discussed when root level profiles are defined.) The first rule regarding LAN Server security is that, should an access control profile (access control rules) not exist for a resource, the resource cannot be accessed remotely. So, even when there are existing LAN Server users connected to the same network, they will not be able to access any data on the new server remotely. In fact, a new server probably doesn't have any interesting data on it yet, but until the administrator creates access rules everyone can rest assured that remote access is not possible during the process of putting data on the server.

Security on LAN Server is very much like the security discussed above with ATM machines. LAN Server first determines if a user is really who he says he is, and then determines the privileges that user has by looking in a database of access control rules. Another way of saying the same thing is that LAN Server uses a user level security model to implement access control of its resources. LAN Server has a database of user definitions where users have IDs and associated passwords. The passwords are used like the PIN numbers for an ATM, to make sure a user is really who he says he is.

LAN Server also has a database of access control rules referred to in LAN Server as access control profiles (ACPs). There will be an access control profile for each resource that can be accessed remotely. Each of these ACPs will contain a list of users or groups, and the privilege that each of these users or groups should be granted for that resource. A complete list of the possible levels of privilege will be discussed below, but for example, one user might be given read and write privilege to a subdirectory on a server in an ACP. Other users might be given only read privilege, whereas other users might be allowed to read, write, create, and delete.

Returning to our scenario regarding a new server, as we said, no access rules exist after installation. The key to beginning the process of granting access to data on the server is that there is a predefined, default user ID with administrator privilege that seeds the process. This ID is the same on all servers when they are first installed, and it should be used to create a new administrator ID that will be the master administrator ID for future server administration. It is strongly recommended that, after this first administrator ID is created, the default user ID (USERID) be disabled or deleted and the master administrator ID be stored in a safe place, so there is at least one administrator ID that you can return to if all other administrator IDs are lost, deleted, or forgotten.

A key attribute of administrator IDs in LAN Server is that administrators can perform any management function, such as adding users and modifying access control rules. They also are not subject to any of the access control rules on any resource. You should be careful when giving a user administrator privilege.

After the new administrator ID is created, you should use it to create the initial set of user definitions for the server. Once these IDs are created, you can then create access rules for the server resources to be accessed remotely, and then you can give the users you have created the appropriate authority.

How Is Identity Checked with LAN Server?

Any user who wants to contact a LAN Server server must first have a session (in a transport protocol sense) with the server he wants to talk to. As a result, the protocol LAN Server uses to establish this session requires that a user validate his identity by sending his user ID and their Password to the server he wishes to contact. In LAN Server terms that will be used in this section, there is a "session setup" protocol flow between a client and a server that is required to establish a session.

The server will take the User Id and Password and decide if a session will be allowed with the user requesting validation.

Several aspects of this protocol flow are of interest. The first aspect is the process used to transmit a password from a client to a server. Most users are concerned that the client they are using might transmit their passwords in the clear. Although LAN Server does support a session setup protocol that specifies that passwords be transmitted in the clear (mostly because of old clients from many releases ago), the default session setup protocol that LAN Server uses involves a very strong encryption process referred to as a *challenge protocol*.

The goal of the challenge protocol is to make it close to impossible to determine the "in the clear" password from a user validation protocol flow. The first step of the challenge protocol is for the server to send a random number to the client. This number represents a challenge the server gives to the client, to produce a result using this number based on the password the server has as the valid password for the user.

The client receives this number, encrypts it using an encrypted version of the password the user entered at the logon screen as the encryption key (in comparison to encrypting the password using the random number as the encryption key), and transmits this result back to the server.

The server generates its version of the valid response by taking the password stored in its copy of the user definition database (that is stored encrypted in the same way as the client encrypted the password before using it) as the key to encrypt the random number, and performs the same encryption that was performed at the client. If the result returned from the client matches the result calculated at the server, the user is declared validated and a session is allowed. In the advanced section of this chapter we will discuss other special cases, but generally speaking, LAN Server will not allow the user to have a session if the result of this challenge is not correct.

One key attribute of this protocol is that the value transmitted from the client to the server for a particular user is different for each session setup (either to the same server or to different servers) because of the random number sent from the server to initiate the process. In other words, as long as the random number is different, the result generated by using the same encrypted password as the encryption key will result in a different value's being transmitted on the wire. This attribute of the challenge protocol is important if someone is monitoring the traffic between a client and a server. If an encrypted password were transmitted between the client and server, it would be the same value each time and, even though it was encrypted, this value would be sufficient for that person to use it to get a validated session to a server. In other words, if a server would accept an encrypted password as the credential necessary to validate a user, the person monitoring the logon protocol flow could use this same value to get a validated session for himself even though he didn't obtain the "in the clear" password. (In fact, if the server only accepted an encrypted version of a password the "in the clear" version would not be necessary.)

In summary, LAN Server uses a validation protocol that is stronger than either transmitting an "in the clear" or an encrypted version of the user password.

Once the server validates the identity of a user, it corresponds requests coming in on that session with the user associated with the session. For example, once a user connects to a server, he might then ask to read data from a file. With LAN Server, a request to open a file precedes any actual reads or writes. Part of that open request is an attribute that says whether the user is going to read only, or read and write. In this case, the attribute would be set to read only. The server would get the user associated with the session the request came in on, and would then look in the appropriate access control rules for that resource and determine if the user has the privilege to read the data in the requested file. If so, the server would allow the open to proceed. If not, it would return "access denied." If no rules existed that were applicable, the server would deny access as if the rule existed and specified that the user should not have access.

In summary, LAN Server uses a user level security model to implement access control of resources against requests that come in from remote clients. The first phase of user validation is performed when a client requests a connection with a server via a session setup protocol flow. The user validation flow is a strong validation that does not require the user password to flow in the clear or even encrypted. Once a user is validated, the user is given a session with the server. Requests coming into the server from that session are associated with the validated user and are controlled by the access rules associated with the resource to which access is being attempted.

The User Perspective

Many of the mechanisms described above do not have a direct correlation with actions performed by the user. The closest action a user can do to request a session with a server is to request to be connected to a shared resource, usually with a NET USE command. If the resource connection is with a server that the user is not currently connected to, a new session will be requested automatically using the protocol flow described above.

In theory, every time LAN Server requests a session with a server, the code could insist that the user re-enter his password by popping up a logon screen. However, most users would be willing to give up a small amount of security to reduce the number of times they have to logon.

LAN Server provides a logon capability designed to address this usability requirement. LAN Server clients are designed to store a user's password after an initial user logon process in the memory on the client, so the client software can respond to the server challenge anytime the user requests a session to a new server without having to go back to the user to obtain a password. If a user has the same user ID and password on all of the servers he accesses, he will have to enter his password only once.

LAN Server also has a facility for making sure a user has the same password on a set of servers automatically. This facility is called a *domain*. A domain is a group of servers that cooperate with each other to present a single system image to a user in several different ways. The attribute of interest to security is passwords. The effect of a domain on passwords is that a user can assume that they have the same password on all servers participating in a domain.

There are two techniques that can be used to produce this effect for the user. One technique would be to have all servers in a domain go to a central repository of user identities. This technique would have the advantage that changes to the user identity would have an immediate effect but a problem would be that, should the central repository became unavailable, the remaining servers in the domain could not validate user identities and would probably have to discontinue sharing resources until the repository came back on line.

A second technique is to keep a copy of the user database at each server so the servers can access it locally whenever they need to validate a user (local data is almost always available), but to declare one copy on one server as the master copy, allow changes to be made only to the master copy, then replicate changes made to the master copy with the copies, which are declared as slave copies, on the other servers in the domain. This technique has the advantage of being fault-tolerant, because there is no single point of failure that can affect the ability of any one server to validate users. But it has the disadvantage that changes made to the master copy will take time to propagate to the other servers in the domain. In the advanced section, we will discuss a feature called *forwarded authentication*, which helps alleviate this problem.

LAN Server is implemented using the second technique, which means that every LAN Server server has a copy of the User Database (a file called NET.ACC) and one server in a domain is declared the master (the Domain Controller), and the other servers are slaves that are synchronized with the master copy.

A key point to remember is that the session setup protocol above was a server-centric protocol that had no regard to domains. Adding domains does not change this protocol.

Within a domain, the servers still insist that a user validate his identity with the challenge protocol before allowing a session. The advantage a user gains is that, as long as replication is proceeding successfully between servers in the domain, the password supplied at domain logon time will be valid to all servers.

Another key point is that it can be used to make a connection to any server in an entire enterprise, regardless of domain. The session setup protocol is specifically designed to work in multiserver environments in which each server is totally independant. Adding domains does not change this capability. Domains simply reduce the number of user IDs that you will have to maintain, from the number of servers you need to access to the number of domains you need to access.

For example, if you had a need to access ten different servers, without domains, you would have to maintain an ID on each of the ten servers. If those ten servers where placed in two domains of five servers each, then the number of IDs you would have to manage would be reduced from ten to two.

Given this capability of domains, it is important to look for user access patterns when assigning servers to domains. The pattern that will yield the most benefit emerges when you can find a group of users that most often access a certain group of servers. If you can match groups of users to groups of servers such that, for the majority of the time the users are accessing servers within their domain, you will maximize this benefit of domains.

Returning to the topic of logon, the main purpose of logon with LAN Server is to give an ID and a password to the LAN Server client code that will be valid to the majority of servers you will attempt to access during your logon session. If you have a set of servers you access the most (and there are other users like you), ideally, the administrator who set up your LAN will have grouped these servers into a domain and you will want to enter the ID and password that is valid for this domain.

OS/2 Client Logon

Because servers will not give you a session unless you have a valid password for your user ID, a critical function of logon is to verify for yourself that you have entered your password correctly. With LAN Server's OS/2 client, you have three password validation options:

- Domain validated (default)
- Local validated
- Nonvalidated

When you use domain validated logon, the LAN Server client code takes your ID and password, discovers the server acting as the domain controller for your domain, and uses the challenge protocol in a session setup to make sure your password is valid. When we discuss nonvalidated logon below you will see that this domain validation is more for the purpose of usability than security, because the logon validation process itself does not connect you to any resources and that server will still insist on your successfully passing the session setup challenge.

You should note that there are two phases to LAN Server logon. The first phase is the password validation phase and the second phase is the logon services phase. Part of the logon services is to connect you to the resources either you or the administrator has configured you to connect to automatically at logon time. So, in fact, LAN Server logon can connect you to resources but not because of the first, password validation phase. The second phase, logon services, is provided for domain validated logons only.

Also, domain logon does not necessarily result in a session remaining after the logon completes. In fact, there will be no session remaining to any server if no logon assignments are made. This fact is important when considering how many users can be "logged on" at the same time. There is currently a 1000 session limit per server with LAN Server. However, because logon does not necessarily result in a session's remaining with the server performing the validation, there is no real limit to the number of users that can be logged on at the same time.

The second type of LAN Server logon from an OS/2 client is local validated logon. In certain cases, you might have a user database local to your client machine. The most common case would occur if you were running LAN Server Peer Services in user level security mode. In this case, you probably would create an ID on your local machine that you would use to administer the local peer function. You probably also would make the ID and password the same as the one you use to access domain resources. In this case, LAN Server would give you the capability to validate your password (for usability purposes) against your user identity in the local user database. Because this is the same ID and password that is stored on all the servers in your domain, this logon would then be valid for domain resources you request.

The final type of logon from an OS/2 client is no validation. On the surface, this type of logon appears to be a security hole. However, remember that you must have a session with a server before you can make any resource requests, and remember that the server will challenge you to produce a result with your password that it considers to be valid. If you were to enter a random or silly ID and password, such as BOGUS/DOODAH, you would be able to get this combination stored in the memory in the client but this fact alone wouldn't allow you to access any resources. If you then attempted to access a server, the server would ask you for your ID and password at session setup time, and if it didn't like your identity you would not get a session. In fact, there probably wouldn't be any server in your network that would allow BOGUS/DOODAH to access resources (with the possible exception of GUEST privileges).

An important attribute of LAN Server security is protection from access to server resources regardless of the behavior of the clients in the network. LAN Server security would not be as strong should it rely on clients to only allow domain validated logons. LAN Server security is stronger because it assumes that there are clients on the network with all kinds of logon rules. This fact drives our servers to insist on user validation before sessions are allowed, and only to allow requests from clients that have validated sessions. As you can tell, there is an important distinction between logon and sessions with LAN Server security.

The UPM Logon Shell

One other important user aspect of LAN Server logon from OS/2 clients is the UPM Logon Shell. Above, you saw that the LAN Server client software stores the user's logon password in the memory at the client so that it can be used as the default password for subsequent server connection requests. On an OS/2 client, the user password is stored a second place—in the UPM Logon Shell. The reason the password is stored in this second place is to provide a simulated single logon capability between different subsystems that utilize the UPM Logon Shell for logon services. The two most notable subsystems that utilize this shell are OS/2 Communications Manager/2 and OS/2 Database Manager 2/2 (DB2/2), from IBM (refer to Chapter 7 for information on DB2/2).

The UPM Logon Shell is a service provided by the UPM subsystem that eliminates the need for other subsystems to have their own Presentation Manager logon screen. When the LAN Server OS/2 client determines that a logon is needed because a LAN Server operation has been executed, LAN Server will request UPM to present a logon panel on its behalf. For example, if you open an OS/2 Window and type NET USE before you logon, LAN Server will determine that no one is logged on and will invoke a UPM logon panel automatically. Of course, the UPM Logon function is also available from a Workplace Shell icon and an OS/2 command line logon command.

There are three types of UPM logon, corresponding to the three subsystems that utilize the UPM logon facility. They are Domain, Local, and Node. Domain logon is a LAN Server logon. Local logon is utilized by DB2/2 to validate users for access to local databases. Node logon is used by Communications Manager to obtain a user ID and Password for communications manager protocol sessions, most commonly APPC/APPN. Node logon also is used by DB2/2 when the user is accessing remote databases, because DB2/2 uses Communications Manager as its transport mechanism.

Because each of these subsystems uses the same UPM logon facility and shell, the user gets the benefit of the fact that UPM can give information from a logon on one subsystem to another subsystem that requests a new logon. For example, as we saw above, the LAN Server NET USE command will automatically invoke a UPM logon if no one is currently logged on. When a user does a local logon to access a local DB2/2 database, the user ID and Password from this logon will be stored by the UPM logon shell as a local logon (no domain logon will exist at this point). In this state, if the user then types a NET USE command, LAN Server will still request UPM to present a domain logon panel. However, instead of presenting the panel, UPM will inform LAN Server that another logon is in effect and will give LAN Server the user ID and Password from the local logon. LAN Server will take this information and execute the LAN Server logon process we discussed above (either domain validated, local validated, or no validation; all three of these types being considered to be domain logons from a UPM perspective because they are associated with LAN Server). If the logon was successful, then LAN Server will execute the NET USE function requested without the user's being prompted to re-enter his user ID and Password, thus emulating single logon across multiple subsystems utilizing capabilities at the client.

If a user understands this facility, he can assure that he will always get this single logon emulation if he makes sure his user ID and Password are the same on all the subsystems he accesses. Later, in the advanced topics section, you will learn about Network Sign-on Coordinator, which is a facility (included with LAN Server 4.0) that helps a user maintain this synchronization.

Of course, the information sharing discussed above also is true when you logon to any of the subsystems first and subsequently attempt a function from one of the other subsystems. The key is that, because all these subsystems utilize the UPM logon shell, the user ID and Password entered will be stored by UPM so it can be used by any of the other subsystems.

UPM also includes a Presentation Manager User interface for managing user definitions. Because LAN Server also provides the facilities that allow the APIs that this user interface uses to be executed remotely on a LAN Server server, the combination of UPM and a LAN Server OS/2 client enables UPM to manage user definitions remotely, either to a domain or to a LAN Server Peer Services machine running user level security.

One distinction important to clarify is the difference between local logon from a UPM perspective and local validated domain logon from a LAN Server perspective. If you perform a UPM local logon you are doing a logon with the purpose of accessing a local DB2/2 database. In this case, your user ID and Password would be kept by the UPM logon shell but would not be given to the LAN Server client software. One similarity is that in both cases, the user ID and Password would be validated against the local user database.

If you perform a local validated domain logon, your user ID and Password will be checked against the local user database, it will be stored by the UPM logon shell, and additionally it will be given to the LAN Server client software to be used in subsequent server connection requests.

One last fact is that you should not worry if you do a UPM local logon instead of a LAN Server locally validated domain logon. When LAN Server determines that you need to logon, LAN Server will get the user ID and Password from the UPM local logon automatically without displaying a logon panel.

Logon from MS-DOS and Windows Clients

LAN Server includes client software that supports either MS-DOS or Windows, including Windows for Workgroups. This client function is referred to as DOS LAN Services (DLS) in LAN Server 4.0. Many of the important aspects of logon are the same as described above for the OS/2 client. However, there also are some differences.

First, the session setup protocol described above, which is used to obtain a validated session with a server, is the same on the DLS client. Also, this protocol is used when a user logs on to a DLS client. The result of logon at a DLS client also is the same, where the user ID and password are stored in the client memory to be used later when resource connections are requested.

One significant difference is there is no UPM facility included with the DLS client. The logon facility that is included in the DLS client includes both a logon command and a logon panel that has the same basic functionality as UPM on OS/2.

In addition, DLS includes a facility to enhance its support of multiple, independent, user level servers and share level servers, especially the DLS peer and Windows for Workgroups. This facility is based on a password repository stored at the client. Each user logging on to a DLS client will have a password file created for him automatically, if password caching is configured. The first time a user logs on to a DLS client, he will be prompted for the password for the password file that is about to be created. After the initial logon, the password the user supplies at logon time is actually the password for the local password file, even if a domain logon is requested.

It is best to keep in mind the purpose of each parameter on a DLS NET LOGON command. The user ID will be used to determine the proper local password file to use. The password will be used to unlock the user's local password file. Finally, the domain parameter will be used to find the proper password in the password file to send to the domain for validation and subsequent storage in the client memory as the default user ID and password, to use if no other user ID and password have been specified at resource connection time.

Once the password file is created, the DLS logon process will add any domain that the user logs on to and the password will be used. With this facility, a user can have different passwords on different domains that the logon facility at the DLS client will track. The user then will have to remember only one password, which is the password to the local password file. This facility is very similar to a key to the key's cabinet security model.

Passwords for independent and user level servers can also be stored in this password file. The user can add these passwords by using the NET PASSWORD command's servername parameter. The DLS command that will utilize this information is the NET USE command, which the user will use to connect to the independent server. When the user enters the NET USE command, the NET USE code will take the server name the user specified and will look to see if that server has a password associated with it. If it does, the password from the password file will be used during session setup. If it does not, the default logon password will be used.

Passwords for share level resources can also be stored in the password file. When a user attempts to connect to a resource that is shared on a share level server with a corresponding password, initially, the user will be required to enter the proper password at the end of the NET USE command. The NET USE command will take this password and automatically store it in the password file, associating it with the servername and netname for the resource. Subsequently, if the user attempts to connect to this same resource, he will not be required to enter the password because the NET USE command can then look in the password file and obtain the proper password automatically.

Access Control Profiles

In the discussion above, you saw that, once a user is validated it's a simple matter of looking at the appropriate access control rules to determine if a user is authorized to perform the function they are requesting. In this section you will look at the details regarding how rules are formatted and scanned, the Access Control Profile, and what is the process for finding the appropriate Profile to use.

First, an Access Control Profile is simply a list of user IDs and Group IDs that have a list of permissions associated with them. For example:

```
C:\DIR USER1:N USER2:R USER3:RWCDA USER4:XRWCDAP GROUP1:
R GROUP2:RWCDA
```

In this example, the resource these rules correspond to is the C:\DIR subdirectory on the server. As you can see from the example, letters are used in a profile to represent different privileges.

In LAN Server there are 8 privileges:

- **N**: None
- **X**: Execute
- **R**: Read
- **W**: Write
- **C**: Create
- **D**: Delete
- **A**: Attributes
- **P**: Permissions

With the exception of None, these permissions can be used in any combination (129 different combinations, considering None by itself and all combinations of the other seven). Note that privilege combinations can be associated with both user IDs and group IDs.

All these privileges are fairly obvious except two: Attributes and Permissions. Attributes allow a user to read and write attributes on a file or directory. Permissions is the privilege to modify the privileges stored in an

ACP. If you give a user Permissions privilege, they will be able to manage access control for the resource corresponding to the ACP.

Some privilege combinations might not be useful to some resources. Attributes is not useful for serial devices. Write without Read might not make sense, except in cases where students are taking a test and their answers are being written into a common area that you don't want other students looking at.

The first rule about the contents of an ACP is that, if a user is specifically called out in the profile (by user ID), the privileges associated with this entry are the privileges given to the user regardless of any other group memberships. This behavior is particularly useful if you want to give everyone in a group access to a resource except one user. In this case, you can associate the desired privileges with a group ID and also associate None with the user ID you want to deny.

If a user is not specifically called out, LAN Server looks at all the other groups in the profile when determining privilege level. If a user is a member of one of the groups that has privilege, the user gets those privileges. However, if a user is a member of more than one group with privileges, the user gets the privileges of the group with the most privilege. For example, if a user is a member of GROUP1 and GROUP2, GROUP1 having Read access and GROUP2 having Read and Write access, the user will get Read and Write access.

In fact, the privileges are united together to produce the resulting privilege. In the above example, if GROUP2 had only Write privilege, the user would still get Read and Write privilege, Read from membership in GROUP1 and Write from membership in GROUP2.

If a user is not specifically called out and is not a member of any of the groups in the profile, the user gets no access just as if his user ID was in the profile with None access specified. The key difference between not being in the profile and being in the profile with None access specified is that, if you are not there, a group might be added later that might give you access. If an administrator specifies that a user should not have access, by assigning None privilege to his user ID in a profile, no changes other than removing that entry will allow the user to access the resource.

Which Profile Is Used?

There is a specific ordering that LAN Server uses to determine which profile to use when a resource is being accessed.

In the case of files, LAN Server looks first for a profile on the file itself and, if it exists, it is used. For example, the following profile would be used to determine authorization for access to the file C:\DIR\FILENAME.EXT:

```
C:\DIR\FILENAME.EXT GROUP:R
```

This profile would be used even if there were a profile on the parent directory, C:\DIR.

If no profile exists for the individual file, LAN Server then looks for a profile on the directory that contains the file. In the example above, LAN Server would use the profile for C:\DIR to determine access to FILENAME.EXT if no profile existed for C:\DIR\FILENAME.EXT. This behavior applies to files and named pipes-type resources. Because printers and serial devices do not have directory structure, there will not be a profile on the parent directory and, in effect, this check is skipped.

Finally, if no profile exists for the individual file or directory containing the file, LAN Server looks for a root level profile, in this case on the drive. Root profiles on drives have specific formats; they include the drive letter followed by a colon but they do not have a backslash (that is, C:).

A profile that has a backslash after the colon (i.e., C:\) is a profile on the contents of the root directory only and applies only to the files that are contained in the root directory of a drive. A root level profile on a drive contains the access rules used by LAN Server for any file or directory that doesn't have specific rules associated with it.

Root level profiles are also used for printers, serial devices, and named pipes. The format for the root profile on printers is \PRINT, the format for the root profile on serial devices is \COM, and the root profile on named pipes is \PIPE.

Given this behavior, a root level profile is very useful in cases in which all the data on a particular drive can have the same permissions. In this case you can greatly reduce the access control management effort required for a drive, because you only have one profile to manage for all the data on the drive.

On the other hand, you should be careful with root level profiles because of the power of the facility. In the discussion above, we saw that LAN Server will not give access to a resource unless it has an access control profile. Because of root level profiles, it is not sufficient to look for a profile on a directory, or the files in a directory, to see if a resource can be accessed; you also must look to see if there is a root level profile. This capability is a good example of a trade-off between security control and usability in the form of cost of administration.

LAN Server provides one other facility for creating common access control for all data on a drive, or below a point in the directory tree, called apply (in the LAN Server 4.0 Administration Interface, apply is referred to as propagate). Apply is a function that you can invoke on any profile that exists on a directory. Apply is a function performed at profile creation time rather than at resource access and protection time. Apply is the ability to copy the rules in one profile over other profiles on directories below the selected point in the directory tree. The Apply command will replace any rules that might have existed with the new rules (except on profiles on individual files) and will create a new profile on directories that did not have one. The effect is that all subdirectories below the starting point will end up with profiles that match the parent profile. Apply is a good function to use if you have a subdirectory structure that you want to have the same rules for all the data in the directory structure.

There is one more important attribute about ACPs. LAN Server provides an ACP validation process that periodically checks to see if a resource really exists that corresponds to a profile. Generally speaking, it would be a problem if a profile existed on a subdirectory and the subdirectory and its contents were deleted and then replaced with a new subdirectory with the same name that had data that required new privileges.

When LAN Server determines that a subdirectory that has an ACP has been deleted, LAN Server will automatically delete the ACP. In the case of the Advanced server and the HPFS partitions it serves, ACPs will always be deleted when the subdirectory is deleted, because the ACPs are stored in the FNODE of the directory (when a directory is deleted, so is its FNODE).

In the case of the Entry server or FAT partitions on an Advanced server, the server must discover on its own that a subdirectory has been deleted (most likely because someone has asked for a listing of ACPs), so ACPs might exist for some short amount of time until LAN Server cleans them up.

A notable case to consider is sharing removable media like CD-ROMs. Many people share CD-ROMs on LAN Server by creating a profile on the root directory and then using apply to create the same profile on all subdirectories. This approach works fine until the CD-ROM is replaced and LAN Server discovers that none of the previous subdirectories exist anymore. In fact, even if LAN Server didn't delete them, the ACPs for one CD-ROM will not apply to another CD-ROM, so some sort of administrator action will be required in any case. What is recommended for CD-ROMs is that a root level profile be used instead of the apply function, in cases in which the same access rules are called for on all data for any CD-ROM that might be inserted.

If you use a root level ACP, it will not be deleted and it will be used regardless of the CD-ROM that is inserted.

LAN Server creates three default root level profiles at install, one for printers, one for serial devices, and one for named pipes. Make sure you look at these profiles when considering access privileges users have to these kinds of resources.

Advanced Topics

LAN Server has several advanced security topics, such as API security, local security, remote execution, granting access after a denial, logon changes with Peer Services on OS/2 clients, Access Control Profile(ACP) inheritance, forwarded authentication, preferred logon validator, guest sessions, and Network SignON Coordinator/2.

API security

LAN Server has a rich set of Application Programmer Interfaces (APIs) that can be called from various programming languages. These APIs access all the functions associated with LAN Server, and are used by the LAN Server user interfaces to present LAN Server administration functions to a user. These functions include:

- Defining user IDs
- Managing access control
- Defining resources, and other LAN Server specific functions

All these APIs also are remote enabled. In other words, not only can these functions be performed by a program running on a server, but they can be called from a program running on any client or server in the network and executed against any remote server.

When an API function is received from another machine, the process LAN Server uses to validate authorization is pretty much the same as when authorization is checked for resources access requests.

The key to this authorization check is that, because LAN Server knows what session an API function comes in on and knows the user associated with that session, it is an easy process to check whether that user has the privilege necessary to perform the function. For example, when an API call is received to add a new user ID, LAN Server checks to see whether the user making the request is either an administrator or an accounts operator. If so, the function is processed. If not, the function is rejected as access denied.

The authorization required to perform API functions is documented in the LAN Server Application Programmers Reference, included in soft copy form with the LAN Server 4.0 product.

However, an important fact to keep in mind when considering LAN Server security is that APIs called by programs running locally at a server are not checked for authorization by default.

Above, we saw that LAN Server does not change the behavior of OS/2 at the server machine so that resources that are shared with the network are still accessible via OS/2 user facilities at the server machine.

From a program security standpoint, there is no OS/2 facility to designate a process as a privileged process, one that has more privilege than any other process running in the machine. There isn't any way to associate a user ID with a process, either.

The server function has OS/2 processes running in the server that have to have as much privilege as any user that might make a request remotely, and as a result must be running with administrator privilege (which is the highest LAN Server privilege).

Because there is no way in OS/2 to make a privilege distinction between the privilege of the server processes and the privilege of any other process, all OS/2 processes have LAN Server administrator privilege.

This attribute of LAN Server APIs is another reason why you should keep your LAN Server server in a physically secure area when security is important. To address cases that servers placed in areas of general access, LAN Server Advanced provides a functional add-on in the form of the secure shell that makes a distinction between a privileged and nonprivileged process running on OS/2, and associates the locally logged-on user's privilege with processes spawned by programs run by that user.

Even though access control is not checked at a server against programs running locally, the user at the server keyboard still will be restricted by his level of privilege. When using the LAN Server user interfaces, the LAN Server user interfaces check a user's privilege before making an API call, and will reject functions that a user is not privileged to perform. As a result, this concern is limited to programs not included as part of the LAN Server product.

In summary, there are two important security aspects of LAN Server associated with the physical security of the server hardware. Unless you are using the LAN Server Advanced local security feature, anyone can access any data or execute a program that calls LAN Server APIs, including administrator APIs from the keyboard of the server machine.

Local security

The advanced version of LAN Server includes a function that enables security protection for data access against data on HPFS partitions from the local server keyboard. This function is referred to as Local Security. Described simply, Local Security enforces HPFS data access rules that you define for a server locally, at the server's keyboard. For example, if you have installed Local Security on a server, you will be required to logon at the server's keyboard before you will be allowed to access data on that server. Once you logon, the access rules that will be used are the same access rules that would be used if you attempted to access data on the server from a remote client. If you could not access data from a remote client, you would not be able to access the same data from the server keyboard. This capability is very important when you need to place a server that has security sensitive data stored on it in an open access area.

Local security is implemented by adding a secure shell to the OS/2 boot process. All OS/2 shells are added by modifying the OS/2 CONFIG.SYS file. As long as the CONFIG.SYS file is properly protected by an access control profile, local security will be effective. However, because the configuration of OS/2 contained in the CONFIG.SYS file is critical to the Local Security protection function, you should be careful whom you allow to access the OS/2 CONFIG.SYS file.

As long as the Local Security secure shell is executed during OS/2 start-up, the Local Security function will be very effective in protecting HPFS data from access from local keyboards. Local Security also protects API functions called by programs running at the server machine. Local Security does not protect printers, serial devices, or data on FAT partitions.

Remote execution

LAN Server has a function called *remote execution* that allows an OS/2 program to take its input from "standard in" and outputs to "standard out" (for example, command line commands like DIR, XCOPY, and NET SHARE) to be executed remotely on any server in the network. If you are an administrator, this function is available to you via the NET ADMIN command.

From a security standpoint, you must be an administrator on the target server, and access control is enforced in the same manner as described above for all other remote requests.

If you are a user, this function is available via the NET RUN command. Access control on the NET RUN facility is configured by putting the programs available to selected users in an isolated directory on the server and then setting the RUNPATH parameter equal to the local path to that directory. Then, the administrator sets the access control profile for this directory to control those users with access to the programs. If a user cannot access the program, they will not be able to NET RUN to a server.

Because LAN Server supports access control profiles on individual files, you can have different access rules for each program you place in the directory.

Care should be taken as to what programs are placed in the NET RUN directory. If you place the LAN Server NET.EXE program there, then any user that can access the NET.EXE program can perform any NET command on that server. A good rule of thumb is to not place any programs in the NET RUN directory that you don't want users to execute while they are at the server keyboard.

Alternatively, there can be advantages to the unlimited access rights of programs run using NET RUN. A good example of a program to run using NET RUN is a compile of a large program. Program compiles might be slower across a network because of the large size of the compiler executable and the large size of the source being compiled. If a compile script were created and placed in the NET RUN directory, a user could invoke a compile function remotely and the compile could proceed even though the user does not have access to the compiler executable, the source being compiled, or the resultant object code.

Granting access after a denial

Granting a user access after he has been denied is a very easy process. Simply modify a user's access rights in the appropriate Access Control Profile and the user will then be able to access without logging off or taking any other actions. (However, the user might have to exit and then re-enter the application he is using to access the data, if the application recorded the fact that some type of access had been denied and changed its own behavior accordingly.)

Another case that is very similar but takes more action, by either the administrator or the user, occurs when a user is denied access because he didn't have a user ID on the server he attempted to access. If the server did not allow a session (because the server was configured to deny guest sessions), the user will have been denied access at resource connection time (for example, when a NET USE command was issued). In this case, after the administrator has added the appropriate user ID (and it has replicated to the target server), all the user will need to do will be to retry the resource connection operation. In some cases, an application might have attempted to make a connection on behalf of the user. In such cases the user should retry the application function that failed previously.

In the event that a server allows guest sessions, a different set of actions will be required. In this case, it would not be sufficient for the user to simply retry the operation after the appropriate User Id had been added, because the user would then have a guest session to the server. In this case, the old session would have to be deleted and a new one created that will be associated with the new, appropriate user ID instead of the Guest account.

The administrator can perform this action by using the NET SESSION command to delete the session, and the LAN Server client software will automatically reconnect with the appropriate new credentials. The user can also delete the session by deleting all resource connections with the target server, using the NET USE command.

One final point regarding sessions. Be careful with dynamic shares when disconnecting resources or sessions from a client to a server. Dynamic shares are Aliases of type "As Required by User," and also non-Aliased home directories. LAN Server maintains a "use" count to these types of resources and will un-share them by default when the use count goes to zero. Disconnecting resources or deleting sessions might make use counts on dynamic resources go to zero, and if these resources are un-shared, LAN Server's auto-reconnect function will not be able to reconnect successfully.

To avoid this problem, change the CLEANUP parameter in IBMLAN.INI to No, which disables the un-share at zero use count. Changing the parameter might require you to also increase the MAXSHARES parameter, but generally speaking, having more active shares at a server should not be a concern.

(Shares do not take much server resources. The dynamic shares function is designed to help conserve server resources when they are extremely tight.)

Logon changes with Peer Services on OS/2 clients

When you install Peer Services on an OS/2 client, your client will be configured for local validation instead of domain validation. Keep in mind that an OS/2 client running Peer Services in user level security mode has a user database local to the client machine that is different and not synchronized with any domain. In such a case, your user ID and Password might be different in the local user database than on the domain you normally access.

This default logon configuration was chosen for OS/2 clients running Peer Services to address cases in which no domains exist or are not currently active. In these cases you would want users to be able to logon and share and access data on other peer machines, which this type of logon supports.

If you prefer domain logon, simply change the appropriate parameter in IBMLAN.INI on the clients you want to change. In LAN Server 4.0, this parameter is a WRKHEURISTIC that is documented with all the other WRKHEURISTICs right in the INI file. In LAN Server 3.0, there was a section called LSCLIENT and a parameter called LOGONVALIDATION that you will need to change from LOCAL to DOMAIN. Of course, you can also use the /V parameter as well, if you don't want to change your configuration but you want a different type of logon every so often.

One other factor to consider about local validated logon is that you will not get any logon assignments or applications if you use local validated logon. New users will not be expecting this anyway, so they will not be concerned. But if you add Peer Services to an existing OS/2 client, you might get questions about the fact that the logon process has changed and does not perform the same functions as before.

Access Control Profile Inheritance

Generally speaking, LAN Server will cause a newly created subdirectory to inherit the ACP from its parent if it exists. LAN Server is able to provide this function consistently when subdirectories are created remotely from a client. However, in some cases, ACPs are not inherited when they are created at the server machine's keyboard.

LAN Server can provide inheritance in remote cases because the LAN Server code is in the code path that performs this function. Because LAN Server Entry uses the standard OS/2 file systems to do file system work for it, no LAN Server code is executed when you create a new subdirectory at the server keyboard on an Entry server. As a result, no ACP inheritance occurs if you create a subdirectory at the keyboard of an Entry Server.

In the case of LAN Server Advanced, the server uses a special LAN Server version of the HPFS file system, called HPFS386. Because this file system is part of the LAN Server subsystem, ACP inheritance can be performed by the LAN Server code even when subdirectories are created at the server keyboard. However, like the Entry server, the Advanced server uses the standard OS/2 FAT file system for FAT partitions. As a result, if you create a subdirectory on an Advanced server for a FAT partition from the server's keyboard, it will not inherit the ACP from its parent.

Forwarded authentication

In our examination of the technology chosen for common user definitions among multiple servers, we saw that a replication method was chosen to eliminate a single point of failure for the function of user validation. The problem discussed at that point was the latency time required to propagate changes to the slave copies of the database.

LAN Server has a function called *Forwarded Authentication* designed to address this problem. Forwarded Authentication is an additional capability of the additional servers in a domain that allows them to authenticate a user to the database on the domain control (the master copy) when a user fails to authenticate to the copy local to the additional server.

There is a password expiration scenario that illustrates this feature best. If a domain has a policy that passwords expire every 45 days (for example), users will be required to change their passwords when this time elapses. LAN Server provides a password change facility as part of logon that allows users to change their passwords when they try to logon with an expired password. If a user has logon assignments to an additional server in a domain, and if they change their password (changing from an old expired one to a new valid one) at logon time, the change will be made first at the domain controller but will take a little time to reach the additional servers. At logon time, logon assignments are made almost immediately after the password change occurs, so the attempt by the user (done by the logon code on behalf of the user) to connect to an additional server will fail, because the client code will use the new password in the challenge protocol to a server that still has the old password in its local user database.

Forwarded authentication solves this problem by changing the additional server from immediately rejecting the session to checking the password with the domain controller, if a password is invalid in the local user database, before rejecting the session request. In this case, the new password being used by the client will be valid at the domain controller, and the additional server will validate the user and allow a session based on the validation of the password by the domain controller.

Preferred logon validator

Domain logon validation can be configured with three different preferences. Logon validation preference is stored with each user definition, so it can be different for each user.

Domain logon validation preference is controlled by the "preferred logon server" user attribute. You can specify that you want to be validated by the Domain Controller or by another specific backup domain controller. You can also specify that it would be all right if any server providing domain logon validation services validated your logon. This attribute is particularly useful in balancing domain logon load within a domain.

If you want to be validated by the domain controller, set this attribute to null (the default value). If you want to be validated by a particular server, set the parameter equal to the name of the server you want to be validated by. If you want to be validated by any server (the first one to respond), set this attribute to \ \ *.

You can configure any server in a domain to help with domain validated logons. Simply change the role of the user database on the server from "Member" to "Backup" and it will respond to domain validated logon requests. To make this server a full backup domain controller, configure the server to be an importer for the DCDBREPL service.

Guest sessions

All the discussion above assumed that a user definition existed for the user requesting a session in the session setup protocol. Another case that needs to be considered is one in which the user does not exist in the user database, and as a result there is no password to validate against. LAN Server handles this case with the concept of a GUEST user.

LAN Server can be configured to allow sessions to unknown users. When a session is allowed to this type of user, the requests that are made on this session are associated with the common GUEST account instead of the user who requested the session. When LAN Server looks in the access control profile, it will look for the privilege associated with the GUEST ID. The procedures used at this point are the same as those for any other user ID; if privilege for the GUEST ID is not specified, LAN Server will look to see if any of the groups the GUEST ID belongs to has privileges.

The GUEST ID is a default ID and by default does not belong to any groups. However, you can add the GUEST ID to any of the groups you use to manage access control, just as with any other user ID. If the GUEST ID is not in the ACP and the GUEST ID does not belong to any of the groups that have privileges, the request from the unknown user will be denied.

LAN Server can be configured to not allow any sessions from unknown users, by setting the GUESTACCT parameter in IBMLAN.INI to null.

Network SignON Coordinator/2

Network SignOn Coordinator/2 (NSC) is a facility that allows you to handle logons and password change functions in heterogeneous environments. NSC allows a user to create password change scripts that create a single user function that will change passwords on multiple, different subsystems. NSC also allows a user to create logon scripts, wherein a user can execute a single logon command that will logon to a set of different subsystems similar to the password change facility.

NSC can support a wide range of subsystems, including LAN Server, Novell NetWare, AS/400, MVS, and VM. In fact, NSC can support almost any subsystem that has a command line logon and password change commands.

In the case of LAN Server, NSC can be used to create a password change script that will change a user's password multiple domains with one user command. This capability makes it much easier for users to manage their passwords if they have the requirement to access multiple domains. An important point to remember is that, if the user ID and password supplied during LAN Server logon is valid for all the domains a user needs to access, the single LAN Server logon performed will be sufficient for any subsequent resource access attempt into any of those domains. NSC can be used by users to make sure their passwords are the same in all the domains they access.

NSC was created as a product separate from LAN Server but was shipped as one of the productivity aids in LAN Server 4.0, both in Entry and Advanced.

Summary

The main objective of the security model implemented in OS/2 LAN Server is to control the access of server resources from the network. The security model used is a user level security model. Classic user model access control consists of two phases, identification and then authorization.

Security in LAN Server is enforced when the server grants connections to clients. Clients request connections for any type of access with a "Session Setup" SMB request. For the server to grant a valid session, the client must first send the credentials of the user to the server. If the server validates the user credentials, the server associates the validated user identity with the session between the client and the server. After that point, any transaction that comes in on that particular session will be associated with the user identity.

Because the identity of the user making requests can be resolved, LAN Server then uses rules contained in access control lists associated with resources. One key attribute of this style of security is that all the responsibility for access control is held in the server. This attribute is critical to having a high level of security, since a truly secure system cannot rely on the behavior or implementation of other machines in a system or on a network.

Given that security on a LAN Server server is the responsibility of the server, the key design goal of having security functions implemented at the client can focus on usability instead of security. Keeping in mind that user credentials are sent to the server every time a connection is made with a server (at the insistance of the server), the client could pass this requirement on to the user and ask for a password any time a server connection is requested. With LAN Server, one way of asking for a session with a server is with the NET USE command. So, if usability were not an issues or design point, LAN Server be implemented to ask for a password each time a NET USE command is issued.

Because users prefer to be asked for their passwords only once, the LAN Server client is implemented to retain the initial password entered and to use that password (in association with the user ID) at subsequent session requests. LAN Server provides a Logon function in which the user supplies the user ID and Password that is retained by the LAN Server client code.

Chapter

14

Securing UNIX

Ray Kaplan and Robert Clyde

*To keep your secret is wisdom; but to expect
others to keep it is folly.*   SAMUEL JOHNSON

UNIX security has a reputation for complexity and difficulty of use. The good news is that it is not difficult. The bad news is that it is complex. As an operating system, UNIX is a lot like the city of Paris. Colorful, romantic, exciting, and most certainly foreign to those who do not live there. If offers an almost infinite number of places to explore and things to do, but it is easy to get very lost, very quickly.

At the same time, this era is characterized by many other complex, multiplatform computing environments, and vast conglomerates of integrated computer networks. The real issue for most organizations is how much and what kind of security satisfies the requirements of their particular environment. Finding the answer to this question is far from a trivial matter. It begins with deciding what you need to secure and how much you can spend to protect it. It ends with the enforcement of a security policy that guides the specification, implementation, management, and reporting of technical specifics. These specifics include technical, organizational, and personnel details.

Join us now for a guided tour of what is perhaps THE most interesting and varied operating system security landscape. We will focus on ensuring that top management can rely on a UNIX-based infrastructure to protect their organization's information assets. While we have tried to make this discussion UNIX-specific, securing a UNIX-based system is fundamentally the same as securing any other system or network component.

UNIX systems seldom stand alone in an infrastructure. In the few exceptions, such as single-use systems for real-time control and specific military applications, the focus of security can usually be narrowed to physical and personnel issues. However, UNIX systems usually are just one part of a larger computing infrastructure that includes other operating systems and network components. No single system or network component can be considered in isolation—as said by Robert Morris, Sr., "to a first approximation everything is connected to everything else."

Security Policy and Its Role with UNIX Systems

A security policy establishes who is authorized to access what information, and points to standards and guidelines describing necessary security measures that implement, audit, report, and enforce. Procedures implement standards and guidelines to carry out the established policy, under the guidance of a security architecture that supports the security policy.

There is an important reason to start with these basics. Any effort that does not start with well-formed, attainable goals will usually fail to meet its objective. UNIX security is no exception. Perhaps the best example of this is the recent explosion of interconnectivity over global networks such as the Internet. These efforts have focused on building firewalls to protect private networks from incursions. But experience shows that the problem is more basic. The real problem is the assumption that a firewall can compensate for a lack of adequate individual host security. The cultures of many organizations simply permit lax security for their individual hosts and network components. Firewalls are an important security technology, but we also believe:

- The security of individual hosts and network components in an infrastructure is the keystone of a plan to protect organizational information assets.

- Sophisticated, cryptography-based security technology is required to properly secure hosts and networks.

UNIX Security Will Default if You Let It

Every organization has an information security policy of some kind. In some organizations the policy is not explicitly written, but has been established by tradition and the general execution of business. Unfortunately, such a policy is risky because it can be interpreted differently by individual employees. It also can be difficult to enact disciplinary measures in response to the violation of an unwritten policy. A written policy gives a basis for uniform understanding and enforcement, and provides the security staff with a specific charter to carry out their duties. While the discussion of actually writing a security policy is outside the scope of this chapter, a few details may be helpful.

An information security policy should not be written in a vacuum. It should relate directly to the business needs of your organization, regardless of the system specifics that it will support. For example, the concerns addressed in a policy for a defense contractor performing top secret work are different from those required by a video store. However, both will have one goal: protecting the information assets of the organization.

Unfortunately, there is no such thing as a general security policy that is perfect for every organization. Otherwise, you could just buy it. Security tool vendors are very anxious to fill your needs. You can rest assured that they would love to sell shrink-wrapped, do-it-yourself kits if they could!

Your security policy should require little change after completion, and it should accommodate the procedures that will implement it. The key is to have the policy point to associated documents that contain UNIX-specific standards, guidelines, and procedures (see Figure 14.1). These associated documents contain specific information relating to computing platforms such as UNIX, technology, applications, user responsibilities, and organization structure. This fabric should support the specification and implementation of standards, guidelines and procedures that are UNIX-specific (see Figure 14.2).

The policy's statements cover at least the three basic goals of security:

- **Confidentiality**, which means assuring that sensitive data is read only by authorized individuals and is not disclosed to unauthorized individuals or to the public.

- **Integrity**, which means protecting data or software from improper modification (for example, a virus infecting a program or someone fraudulently changing accounts payable).

- **Availability**, which means ensuring that systems, networks, applications, and data are on-line and accessible when authorized users need them.

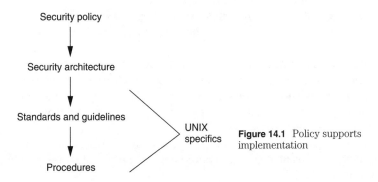

Figure 14.1 Policy supports implementation

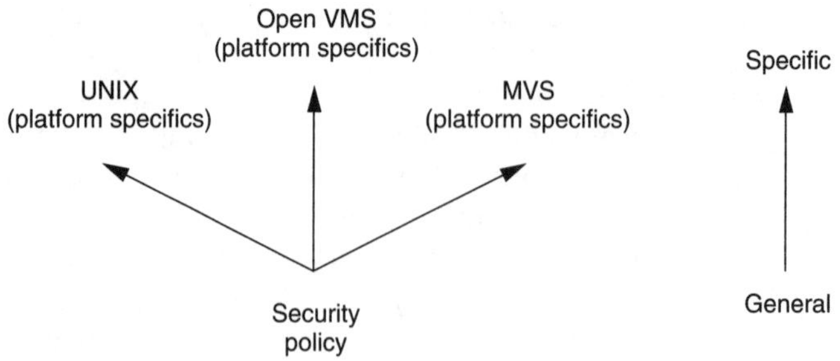

Figure 14.2 Platform specifics

For different types of applications, the required level of confidentiality, integrity, and availability changes. For example, a nuclear weapons research system requires a high level of confidentiality but might be able to withstand down periods of several hours. An information system reporting public stock trading values has a very low requirement for confidentiality but a high integrity requirement. A telephone switching system has a requirement for a very high level of availability so calls are not interrupted or unable to be placed.

In addition, to assure that the above goals are being met, the policy should include statements to cover:

- **Accountability**, which means the ability to tell who did what so there is a means for verifying that security goals are being met.

- **Resource control**, which means protecting computer equipment from accidental, natural, and deliberate harm, and restricting equipment access to authorized individuals only.

- **Separation of duties**, which is a concept fundamental to information security. Power should not be too concentrated in one individual. By separating responsibilities you can have checks and balances. For instance, the following types of duties should be separated:

  ~**Resources from data**, which means that the person responsible for inventory (for example) should not also be the person maintaining the inventory.

  ~**Origination from approval**, which means (for example) that the employee who signs checks should not be the person who creates them.

  ~**Creation from maintenance**, which means (for example) that the employee who creates new accounts should not be the same person who enters debits and credits.

  ~**Procedures from data**, which means (for example) that programmers writing accounting programs should not also enter data into those applications.

In large organizations, classifying data with labels that reflect its importance is sometimes worthwhile. This way you can have policy statements that refer to certain types of data. This also means that individuals must be cleared to access data with a particular classification. For example, company trade secrets might be classified as confidential. The policy should indicate a procedure for classifying data and clearing people requesting access. Many commercial organizations not oriented towards data classification may find it useful to label data by function instead (for example, payroll data).

Finally, the problem of how to implement technology that actually enforces a data classification scheme and makes the data's classification labels available to systems and applications is a hard, expensive one to solve. This classic idea of separation of duties may include the difficult task of separating the job of security administration from that of system administration.

But once a security policy has been established, it should be implemented with a tightly knit fabric of technology and procedures that rests on a solid security architecture. A security architecture is a high-level design that funnels the security policy into standards and guidelines. These standards and guidelines will govern which technology is selected and how it is implemented. Finally, the choice to implement the sophisticated thinking of data classification and separation of duties requires both trust assumptions and risk.

Trust Assumptions and Risk

As previously stated, securing a UNIX-based system is the same as securing any other operating system; all should be treated equally under the security policy. However, because no two are exactly alike, their differences must be accommodated. The differences between securing a UNIX and securing other operating systems involve the specifics of the operating systems themselves, such as capabilities and known deficiencies. The similarities involve the organizational basics of any infrastructure's security management.

CyberSAFE's Dr. Daniel Webb sums it up when he asserts that the security of an infrastructure depends on the trust assumptions that an organization makes. An organization's security policy and risk management strategy form the foundation for these trust assumptions. Where there is high risk, the security policy and the technology and procedures that implement it must be complete and strong. Where risk is low, they can be less so. However, even where risk is low, the amount of trust that can be placed in the infrastructure is important.

In a so-called "trusted" UNIX system, a trustworthy testing body offers "assurance" that a particular operating system implementation can be trusted within its design parameters. The cheap, off-the-shelf operating system implementations that many organizations buy do not offer any "assurance." Most organizations choose to use this cheap technology because they don't know any better. We'll explore "assurance" in the Trusted UNIX Systems section of this chapter.

Risk Management and Threats for UNIX

Author Robert Charette (see bibliography at the end of this chapter) presents a complete treatment of dealing with risk. Once the risks that an infrastructure faces are determined, they can be valued. Defining a security policy for UNIX requires knowing the threats and risks to your UNIX, and the countermeasures that can be used to balance them. Threats are the sources of potential security problems. Risks are the likelihood and costs of a particular event's occurring. Threats include human, natural, and technological adversaries such as accidents, acts of nature, and technical flaws.

On the human side, both accidental and deliberate damage are possible. Some human threats come from society, such as terrorism and war, and others come from inside users or outsiders, such as hackers. Recent studies show that inside users are a more common threat than outsiders, as Figure 14.3 demonstrates. This makes sense because inside users enjoy greater system access, and privileged users such as system and network administrators have the power to set aside security controls.

Assessing risk is an interesting science. Actuaries have been assessing risk for insurance companies for hundreds of years. Unfortunately, you may need to assign costs for events without the benefit of actuarial data. Costs should include more than just an estimate of the actual money that could be lost. For example, value also must be placed on loss of a critical UNIX-based network service or application, loss of life, injuries, lost privacy, legal liability, unwanted media exposure, and clean-up costs.

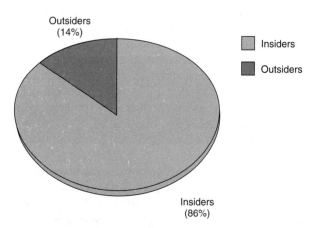

Figure 14.3 Insiders and outsider threats. *(Courtesy of Wall Street Journal, August 15, 1990)*

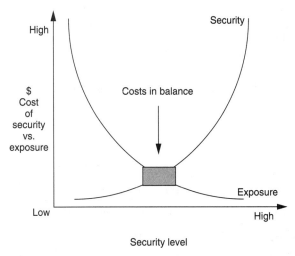

Figure 14.4 Balancing costs

Risk management is the process of balancing the cost of protecting against risk versus the cost of exposure. Figure 14.4 shows the basic theory. When the cost of protecting and the cost of exposure are at almost the same point, as illustrated by the shaded area, your security measures are properly balanced and prudent. Otherwise, you may be spending more on security than it is worth. Or, even more likely, you are spending too little and imprudently exposing your business to risk.

You can choose between three basic choices with regard to each risk:

1. **Accept** Security consultant Robert Courtney says, "Never spend more avoiding a risk than tolerating it will cost you." If the exposure is small and the protection cost is high, your best policy might be to accept the risk.

2. **Assign** In some cases it costs less to assign the risk to someone else than to directly protect against it. For example, most companies purchase fire insurance rather than build fireproof buildings. Of course, to obtain a reasonable insurance cost you will be required to take some precautions.

3. **Avoid** This involves putting the necessary measures into place to prevent a security-related event. You can also ensure that a security-related event becomes much less likely or less costly.

While risk management is a basic precept in security management, many organizations implement UNIX computing solutions without it. Because balancing risks is expensive and complicated, such organizations usually fail in their efforts to protect the information assets that their UNIX systems hold.

The Responsibility for UNIX Security

The security policy must indicate who is responsible for security. In the simplest sense, "everyone" is responsible. After all, users are both the primary safeguard of and the greatest threat to security. The policy should require all users to sign a contract that spells out their security responsibilities and acknowledges who owns the system and the data. The following points should be covered in the contract:

- The organization owns the systems and the data.
- Users agree not to make unauthorized copies of data or software.
- Users agree not to import or run any unauthorized programs or data.
- Users agree to choose passwords wisely and to keep them secret.
- Users agree to access the system and data only in authorized fashion.
- Users acknowledge right of organization to monitor system use for security purposes.

The policy must be published and made available to all users. Adherence to the security policy should be considered in each employee's performance review.

Certain individuals within the organization will be directly charged with security responsibility. The policy should refer to these people by function and title, not by name. In general, duties should be separated:

1. Security administrators should be responsible for managing and overseeing security.

2. System managers and IS directors should assist in implementing security. Ideally, the security administrator should be a different person, reporting to corporate security and not the IS function.

Finally, the qualifications and experience of those charged with responsibility for the security of UNIX must be considered. Securing UNIX is a difficult task requiring a high degree of UNIX-specific skill, knowledge, and experience.

Implementing a Security Policy to Support UNIX Security

For a UNIX-based infrastructure to be trusted, the security policy should be reflected in the details of its implementation. High-level policy statements ultimately will be distilled into many UNIX-specific details that will direct an organization's technical security management efforts. For instance, file protections must be specified. These specifics must be supported by procedures that monitor them.

Finally, the security policy must be enforced. At best, this is a difficult task. All information systems security controls must be enforceable prior to being adopted as part of standard operating procedure. The problem of distilling high-level requirements into enforceable, detailed, technical specifications is difficult. If nothing else, these efforts usually specify an overwhelming number of things to track.

Because the task of manually dealing with this huge amount of detail is onerous, effective tools and a high degree of security management automation are needed for the job. In a seamless implementation of a security policy, such tools provide a running view of the whole infrastructure, not just its UNIX systems. Such tools simplify detecting and reporting security policy violations. Some tools actually dynamically fix deviations from the security policy when they are discovered. Tools for UNIX security management are discussed in the security tools part of the security management section of this chapter.

The Role of Audit and Assessment in UNIX Security

The EDP audit function should periodically review the security of the information systems, to provide management with the assurance that the policy is really being followed. Outside security specialists should periodically review the information systems to provide technical management with assurance that the policy can be followed in the face of inevitable infrastructure volatility. Finally, technical management should periodically assure itself that the policy is being followed, by regularly assessing the implementation of the policy.

Trusting UNIX

In the end, trusting an infrastructure requires trusting its individual parts. This certainly includes any of its UNIX systems. Basic trust assumptions will determine the strength and completeness of the architecture, standards, guidelines, and procedures that support the security policy. This absolutely includes selecting a UNIX system that has the capability to support the security policy.

The amount of trust an organization can put in its infrastructure depends on:

- The strength of the security policy that protects it.
- The strength of the technology and procedures that implement the security policy.
- How completely the security policy is implemented, audited, assessed, and enforced.

UNIX?

UNIX has a colorful past that includes the contributions and involvement of its community. As a group of individual contributors, the so-called UNIX community has made UNIX what it is today. With more than twenty-five years of this evolution under its belt, UNIX almost has a life of its own.

Most people recognize that UNIX is an operating system. However, most do not recognize that the operating system they call UNIX is likely to be derived from UNIX and is not UNIX itself. UNIX IS the name of an operating system, but, which one?

UNIX—An Operating System in Transition

At this time, UNIX is a registered trademark of the X/Open Company, Ltd. It was purchased from Novell in 1994, after Novell bought it from AT&T's subsidiary, UNIX System Labs, in 1993. (Note: A complete and detailed history of UNIX can be found in Ed Dunphy's *The UNIX Industry and Open Systems in Transition*—see bibliography at the end of this chapter.)

For legal reasons having to do with trademark protection, AT&T required that the name UNIX not be used as a noun. It could only be used as an adjective. And, an operating system could be called UNIX only if it were licensed from AT&T. Hence, the use of the term UNIX as an adjective has become common, to describe everything from so-called "open" systems to a myriad of products and services that support UNIX and the other operating systems that were derived from it. As the current holder of the UNIX trademark, X/Open has recently changed the rules of the global UNIX game again. If a vendor's UNIX-based system passes the tests of X/Open's test suite, that vendor can call their operating system UNIX.

UNIX itself dates to the original, the work of Ken Thompson and Dennis Richie on a DEC PDP-7 minicomputer at Bell Labs, in 1969. UNIX also has roots that can be traced as far back as 1965. They include work at Bell Labs, General Electric, Bell Telephone, MIT's project MAC, and on Honeywell's MULTICS.

Today, most security problems with UNIX fall into several categories:

- Inattention to the need for a solid security policy as detailed above.
- Failure to identify security requirements and map them into the capabilities of the technology. Even UNIX systems that are not rich in security features can be securely managed by surrounding them with skilled, knowledgeable people and good security tools.
- Artifacts of the lack of concentration on security in the early stages of UNIX-based system evolution. Often these artifacts are only discovered after they surface amid ill-conceived rushes to embrace so-called open

systems. Everyone wants to immediately enjoy the obvious benefits of using widely accepted technology that is cheap and easy to apply.

Perhaps the best summary of this idea is found in a statement by Bill Cheswick of Bell Labs, from Cliff Stoll's critical comments on the information highway: "UNIX was designed as a power tool for the professional user. It's more like a locomotive or an aircraft than a car. It's a bear to set up and a nightmare to administer. It wasn't meant for granny."

Will the Real UNIX Please Stand Up?

The last time we looked there were more than eighty different UNIX derivatives, all claiming to be UNIX. All these UNIX systems are largely the result of contributions by individuals (users, administrators, programmers, researchers,) vendors, and governments. As a rule, manufacturers that move UNIX to their own hardware freely add, subtract, and modify features at will. However, the real UNIX actually recently has stood up (finally!) X/Open is attempting to align the UNIX industry by propagating several open standards. Because X/Open is the current owner of the UNIX trademark, this is standard UNIX, by definition.

Certainly, all this culture, history, and volatility has security-related ramifications. For instance, a vendor that moves UNIX onto his hardware may simply use part of the significant body of code that already exists rather than rewriting everything from scratch. As you might imagine, such code might behave poorly from a security point of view. A security-related bug could lay undiscovered in that code for many years. Worse, poor security-related behavior might not be discovered until the code was run in an environment in which security was critical.

Because some vendors do no security engineering, security practitioners are well advised to note that the onus for UNIX security is on them. Many UNIX vendors take extraordinary measures to ensure that their systems can be operated securely, but many do not. The common belief that an operating system vendor is paying attention to security is often fallacious.

Securing your particular UNIX-based environment requires an understanding of:

- Your security needs.
- The security features of your particular flavor of UNIX and how they map into your security needs.
- How well your UNIX vendor ensures that their product can be operated securely.
- The heritage of your particular flavor of UNIX and what its vendor has done to it.

Prevalent Derivatives

Several main threads of UNIX-related development are represented in commercially available operating system products:

- **AT&T System V** This includes Microsoft's XENIX, SCO UNIX, Sun's Solaris, and IBM's AIX.
- **Berkeley Software Distribution (BSD)** This derivatives stream includes BSDI, Sun OS, DEC's Ultrix, and HP's HP/UX.
- **Open Software Foundation (OSF)** This includes DEC's Digital UNIX (formerly DEC OSF/1).
- **Other UNIX derivatives** These include Linux.

You can spend a lot of money on UNIX derivatives that run on special hardware and offer more security than a commercial or educational institution is likely to need. Still, these derivatives are dirt cheap when you consider the technology they embody. You also can spend from $0 to $50 on Linux. It is a nifty UNIX derivative that has evolved to become what is probably the cheapest, most fun, fully functional OS currently available.

Each thread of UNIX system development has spawned many derivatives. Each derivative is implemented as its implementer sees fit. In the past, these efforts seldom included any concentration on security. Despite that, security always has been important to some organizations. Experienced members of the community still hack-in modifications to their UNIX system's kernel to make it robust enough to use as a firewall.

Known Security Problem Areas

The history of UNIX is interesting in and of itself. However, there is a more fundamental reason to study it. You can gain insight into the security of your particular flavor of UNIX by studying how it evolved. Developing an understanding of the security problems that your system's branch of the UNIX family tree has experienced can give you an idea of what you might have to deal with. Finding out how specific UNIX-based system families were compromised in the past can offer clues about how hard it might be to secure its successors. Such experience can usually pinpoint suspicious areas to explore.

If nothing else, such an exercise helps you map your security requirements into your system's capabilities. However, discovering a central theme in the historical security vulnerabilities that you find may be difficult. While there are several works in progress that will trace and document these vulnerabilities, we know of none that currently are available. Until such works become available, the UNIX community at large is the best source of this information.

New Directions in UNIX Security

Many vendors of commercial UNIX systems are aggressively developing and deploying systems with improved security. Vendors are interested in it at last because they now have evidence that some commercial organizations will actually spend money on it. However, many organizations are just now recognizing the importance of security and are just starting to do something about it. To this point, most commercial enterprises have not been willing to pay the freight for secure systems.

All this is a profound shift in the evolutionary track of UNIX development. It also has produced a lot of marketing noise that tends to obscure real security issues. You can't assume that your UNIX system vendor's sales representatives know what security is all about. He may not even know that it is important. Just because a vendor has a backroom full of security-wise developers doing the right thing with system's security features does not mean that his sales force will know about it. Often, if you seek security information by visiting a UNIX system vendor's booth at a trade show, you will be frustrated.

UNIX Security Standards

Some of the major efforts to standardize the UNIX universe now underway include:

- The suite of tests that X/Open offers to UNIX-based system vendors. If a vendor's UNIX-based system passes the tests, X/Open brands it as compliant with its Common UNIX Specification. This branding allows that vendor to use the UNIX trademark in the name of their UNIX derivative. It also assures the vendor that their offering is in step with the other branded vendors. Because X/Open is the current holder of the UNIX trademark, this is a major step in the evolution of UNIX. Accordingly, vendors attach some importance to this process.

- The emergence of client/server and distributed computing as commercial requirements is requiring vendors to implement new security models in their UNIX offerings. UNIX system vendors are aggressively adopting the relatively new standards in this area. UNIX systems that have security features aligned with many of the existing security specifications are emerging. These standards include IEEE's POSIX, the OSF's Distributed Computing Environment (DCE), and System V release 4.

- Security interface standards. The Internet community's General Security Services Applications Programmer Interface (GSSAPI) is becoming prevalent as the security services interface of preference. The GSSAPI is addressed in the Application Security section of this chapter.

Organizational Security Standards

In an ideal world, an organization would merely:

- Distill its security policy into a security architecture.
- Distill its security architecture into standards.
- Issue Requests For Quotation (RFQ) for solutions based on these standards.
- Pick the best offerings from the huge number of responses.
- Implement them.
- Live happily ever after.

You're right. This is a fairy tale for most organizations. Ironically, the technology and products that could make it a reality exist. However, it remains a fantasy for all but the most serious nongovernment organizations, because so few nongovernment organizations have a security policy complete or detailed enough to support such a reality. Moreover, most organizations do not have the top management commitment to security required to fund the effort.

The organizations that can make this a reality are generally users of so-called "trusted systems" in environments in which security is often a deadly serious business. In this arena, the specifications of security standards are tight and detailed enough that only a handful of vendors can successfully vie to supply a complete security solution. Top management knows that security is a priority and comes prepared to support it.

Before you give up on UNIX and hang your hat on the hope that Microsoft and NT will become a viable and complete solution, there is a way out. Try our prescription for aligning your security standards with industry standards and implementing a plan:

- Study the fabric of available UNIX security standards and select those matching your organization's needs.

- Where no standards exist or existing standards don't fit your needs, study the product offerings from UNIX system vendor's supplemental security tools (most have them), security product vendors, and security freeware. Often, you'll find that these sources have adopted de facto standards that you can adopt. Include de facto standards in your security standards as de facto standards awaiting formalization.

- Buy products and obtain freeware that implement the security technology you need to implement your plan.

- To some, betting your security on freeware is a bad joke because it usually can't be trusted. If your organization's policy prevents the use of freeware, use the ideas that it has as part of the specifications for a development effort. The whole idea is to gather up what you need to meet your organization's needs.

Operating UNIX Securely

This section discusses the operational aspects of security for UNIX. It offers perspectives on vulnerabilities, security management and security tools.

As stated, many UNIX systems were simply not designed with security in mind. This is the way that the first UNIX systems were originally shipped. Oddly enough, this sometimes means that systems are shipped with known security-related bugs, and administrative and management deficiencies that make them difficult to secure. To exacerbate this problem, many of the contemporary UNIX that have significant security features are shipped with little or no security enabled by default.

In many other cases, vendors are shipping their UNIX systems with increasing levels of security turned on. If we had our way, vendors would ship systems that came out of the box virtually unusable. That is, the system installer would have to knowingly, painstakingly (and painfully) reduce the level of the system's security taking careful note of the exposures that each incremental addition of usability and flexibility introduced. (Some UNIX system vendors are actually preparing to implement such a scheme, and others have already done it.)

Future UNIX systems are likely to allow absolutely no access by any means unless that access is specifically authorized, strictly controlled, and carefully audited. Many available UNIX systems already do this today. But, until this behavior becomes a de facto standard, security practitioners dealing with UNIX still have their hands full.

UNIX Security Problems

Security practitioners will have a difficult time gathering information on vulnerabilities in their UNIX—especially known bugs. As with other operating systems, vendors of UNIX generally don't tell you about all the security-related problems in their UNIX, unless they have already been fixed or there are patches available. In some cases, they are simply not paying attention. In other cases, they fear the public relations damage that could result. On the other hand, some vendors are quite open about making information available. The result is that security practitioners must aggressively seek out information about security deficiencies and their corrections.

Legitimate sources for this information include vendors, user groups, and the Defense Advanced Research Projects Agency's (DARPA) Computer Emergency Response Team (CERT) at Carnegie Mellon University. CERT is the Internet's security incident response capability. CERT distributes bulletins covering vulnerabilities reported by both vendors and other members of the computer community such as users and system administrators. An archive of these reports is available along with information on how to subscribe to the advisory service.[1]

Organizations from all over the world that maintain security incident response capabilities have allied themselves in an organization called the Forum of Incident Response and Security Teams [FIRST]. Because system vendors, researchers, and the security incident response teams from large organizations share information about critical problems, its membership is carefully restricted to those recognized by FIRST. Unfortunately, most of the UNIX-based system community is not represented in FIRST.

Due to the politics of security, vulnerability information usually is not even shared between vendors, except through the formal interaction of their incident response capabilities. Ironically, prototypes of system and network security-related incident tracking and vulnerability reporting databases are known to have been funded by the government and have been shown in public. But the ones that saw public exposure were stopped whenever the funding agency involved wanted to classify the effort that was making the information publicly accessible.

Thus, there is no publicly available system and network security-related incident tracking and vulnerability reporting database. Such a database might be a relational combination of reported vulnerabilities and incidents, which could answer queries such as "Show me recorded instances of compromise for version xxx of operating system yyy on zzz hardware." Or, "Show me a list of known vulnerabilities of the login sequence for version xxx of operating system yyy on zzz hardware." Or, "Show me a list of reported compromises of version aaa of third party product bbb running under version xxx of operating system yyy on zzz hardware." And, it would be nice for security practitioners to ask, "Show me known instances of password guessing attacks on version xxx of operating system yyy on zzz hardware at banks."

Of course, the inherent problem with the establishment of a widely available incident tracking and vulnerability reporting database is the question of making it available to anyone who wants access to it. Because this would necessarily include those that are not members of the "legitimate security community" there is considerable emotion involved. Even though such information is readily available now, it takes a lot of time and energy to find it.

---

[1]CERT Coordination Center, Software Engineering Institute, Carnegie Mellon University, Pittsburgh, PA 15213-3890, (412) 268-7090, FAX (412) 268-6989, cert@cert.org. FTP site and two mailing lists:

cert-advisory-request@cert.org
cert-tools-request@cert.org

CERT also conducts regular meetings with the Internet community in the form of Birds of a feather (BOF) sessions at USENIX conferences. Contact office@usenix.org

A properly designed and implemented incident tracking and vulnerability reporting database would make incident and vulnerability information available to anyone who wanted it, including the "bad guys."

There are those that say the mere availability of an incident tracking and vulnerability reporting database will cause more incidents. The counter argument asserts that, while this may be true, at least system and network managers would have a reference for information where they currently have none. One attempt at humor suggests that the implementation of a publicly available incident tracking and vulnerability reporting database might lead to vendors' shipping a document that describes the known vulnerabilities of their systems to their customers. The suggestion is that such a document might be like the warning from the surgeon general's warning on alcohol and tobacco products in the United States (i.e., "This product may be hazardous to your security").

FIRST is known to have been working on the problems associated with the design and implementation of an incident tracking and vulnerability reporting database. However, their discussions are carefully restricted to their membership, and the topic has apparently been under discussion for quite a long time with no movement. In addition, most members of the UNIX community are not members of FIRST, so they couldn't contribute to the discussions even if they wanted to do so.

It is widely known that the flow of complete, detailed, security-related information about the most serious bugs is carefully controlled, and that such information is not readily or widely available to those who need it to protect their systems and networks. Its availability seems limited to the computer underground. While this apparently serves those who know and control this information, it does little to help those who are trying to protect their systems and networks. Security by obscurity is certainly a flawed concept.

What the UNIX-based system community is left with is an odd situation wherein the best collections of vulnerability information are found only on the clandestine sources in the world's underground computer community. Sources of this information include the computer underground's many clandestine mailing lists, BBS, and hacker conferences. By and large, this information is viewed as illegitimate.

Even worse, most of this information is distributed through electronic mail and network file transfers. So, those who are not connected to a network connected to the Internet have a difficult time staying abreast. Many systems and private networks simply are not even tapped into the significant flow of security-related information that does exist.

Currently, CERT is reporting many incidents per day for UNIX. However, the general community of users and system administrators hear very little about the exact nature of these problems, how they can be used against their systems, or their fixes. One good source of this information is the

BUGTRAQ mailing list.[2] It is maintained by those who don't care about the politics of distributing vulnerability information.

Being a good citizen in the UNIX-based system community requires being plugged into CERT and taking advantage of the other sources of vulnerability information that are available. This usually means that someone from an organization must take the time to get on appropriate Internet mailing lists, read appropriate Network News groups, participate in vendor user groups, and generally keep their eyes and ears open. This is a security management commitment that can't be taken lightly.

Native Behavior

The following part of this section contains our sole concession to allowing this chapter to degrade into technical detail (see the selected bibliography at the end of this chapter for pointers to volumes of technical details). We have included examples of:

UNIX-based system command types by a user
```
The output from this command
More output from this command
```

Highly technical system practitioners may recoil at the simplistic examples that we have chosen. However, these examples only seek to illustrate one simple point; i.e., the native behavior of some UNIX systems is flawed from a security perspective. The references at the end of this chapter contains pointers to considerable additional detail.

To illustrate some common problems with the native behavior of some UNIX, we're going to take a quick look at one form of the use and abuse of privileges. These problems do not apply to all UNIX systems. This discussion is intended to give the security practitioner some feel for how the native behavior of UNIX systems can be a security concern.

A common problem in operating system design is how to do privileged operations on behalf of a user without actually giving the user the privileges that are required to do that particular privileged job. For instance, in some UNIX systems, when a user wants to change his password, he activates the passwd program. Because privileges are required to access the password file (where the user's encrypted password is stored), the passwd program acts

---

[2]This is the inventive, no-holds-barred mailing list for the discussion of security bugs that Scott Chasin maintains in the face of considerable criticism. It is available on the Internet. Apply for membership by sending mail, and telling them why you want to subscribe. bugtraq@crimelab.com is the list's reflector address, and information about subscriptions is available at bugtraq-request@crimelab.com.

in a privileged manner on behalf of its user, to change his password for him. This is done rather than granting the user direct access to the password file, whereby he might change the passwords of other users. If this "delegation of authority" is not carefully controlled, a user who is normally unprivileged could end up with unauthorized privileges and, therefore, the ability to disrupt the status quo of the system and the network. The reasons for this important consideration span the entire range of security-related concerns: the maintenance of confidentiality, integrity, and availability for data and user operations on the system and in the network. Generally speaking, an operating system carefully controls privileged operations in order to make sure that it can protect itself from users and users from each other.

In most UNIX that are not so-called "trusted systems," this delegation of privileges by the operating system is handled by giving a program the ability to "act as if" it were the owner of the program, or to "act as if" it were a member of the file owner's user group. When a program has been given the ability to act as if it were the file's owner, it is said to be either a SUID (set user ID) or SGID (set group ID) program, respectively. The delegation of this authority is accomplished by using the chmod command to change the permission or file protection bits of the program, such that the operating system will allow the program to "act as if" it were the file's owner when it is executed. The SUID or SGID program is allowed this permission by the operating system based on the setting of its SUID or SGID bits when the program is executed.

Commonly, the UNIX-based system command ls -l lists the permission or file protection bits of a file as groups of characters that reflect the files access controls, as well as the SUID or SGID capability when it has been set. These characters are:

r   read access
w   write access
x   execute access

Further, there are three file access categories:

owner   access control for the owner of the file
group   access control for the file owner's group
other   access for all others on the system

For instance, an ls -l command might show that a program is readable, writeable, and executable by its owner, but only executable by members of its owner's user group and others on the system. That is, we interpret the file protection as:

```
File    Owner    Group    Other
type    access   access   access
---     RWX      --X      --X
```

Using the `ls -lF` command, you would see something such as:

```
% ls -lF
total 19
-rwx--x--x   1 owner    501    Jul  7 12:01 test
-rws------   1 root     801    Jul 10 13:00 test1
-rwx--s---   1 owner    601    Jul 10 13:40 test2
```

In this example, the filename *test* is shown to have the aforementioned protections. When the `ls -l` command finds that the program has the SUID or SGID bit set, it changes the x (executable) notation to an s. In the above example, filename *test1* is shown to be a SUID program owned by user root (the UNIX superuser), and filename *test2* is shown to be a SGID program owned by user.

Many abuses of both SUID and SGID programs are possible. One of the many classic attacks on the security of a UNIX system using the SUID mechanism is for someone to "steal" a copy of an interesting, normally unprivileged program, change its mode to that of SUID, and use it against the system. The shell (command line interpreter) is an excellent choice for this sort of attack. As Garfinkel and Spafford[3] point out, if you were to leave your terminal unattended, a knowledgeable passerby might issue the following commands:

```
% cp /bn/sh /tmp/break-tmp
% chmod 4755 /tmp/break-tmp
```

The first command makes a copy of the shell into a file called break-tmp in the /tmp directory. Usually, files in the /tmp directory are both readable and writeable by everyone on the system. The second command changes the mode of the file such that it is SUID (the 4), read/write/execute by the owner (the 7), and read/execute by group and other categories (the 55). Given the success of these commands, the new copy of the shell is now SUID and, therefore, allows the attacker to act as if they were you. That is, this copy of the shell has access to all of your files, because when it runs it "assumes your identity" having been delegated that authority by the operating system due to its being both SUID and owned by you.

Imagine what would happen if a superuser walked away from his or her desktop computer or terminal and someone came by to make a copy of a program they had written to specifically attack the system SUID root. Surely, a major disaster could befall such an unaware, sloppy UNIX system administrator! Walking away from a terminal that is currently logged in, especially one that is logged in as superuser, is a sure invitation to disaster.

---

[3]Garfinkel, Simson and Gene Spafford. 1991. *Practical UNIX Security*. Sebastapol, CA: O'Reilly and Associates, Inc.

Most SUID and SGID programs are very carefully written such that they can only perform one or two narrow functions that require privileged access. In other classic abuses of the UNIX SUID and SGID capability, program bugs are exploited to allow attackers privileged access. Consider an editor (such as vi) that is SUID root. Such an editor program normally only allows its users to edit their own files and purposely does not allow any other access. In its past, the vi editor had a serious problem. You could put a shell command line in as the first line of a file that was being edited. When the editor was invoked on a file with such a first line, it would read the command line, execute it, and then continue to edit the file. Such imbedded command lines were typically used to change editor settings, such that the editing session could be specific to the current document. The problem came as a result of a programming error that allowed a user to escape to the shell as root, and to execute any command as the superuser. This bug was memorialized by the University of Toronto's Norman Wilson in a commemorative lapel button that saw wide distribution at USENIX and DECUS conferences during the 1980s. The button carried a particularly devious and destructive line that could be included in the first line of a file that was to be edited by the vi editor:

```
ei:!rm -rf /usr/ucb:
```

This line tells the editor to feed the command:

```
rm -rf /usr/ucb
```

to the shell and execute it. The result? All of the files in the /usr/ucb directory get deleted. Loosely translated, this spells disaster. All of the files in that directory were deleted.

Another example of this sort of bug can be found in older versions of the popular UNIX sendmail utility. A shell escape was built into this mail handling program. This was presumably a convenience to allow users to cause the mailers on other machines to do things for them besides simply accept mail. The escape was activated by including a | character as the first character of the shell command that was to be executed, and then sending this string as the addressee portion of the mail message. The mailer (which was SUID root) would dutifully recognize the | and would continue to feed the shell command that followed to the shell to execute as root. One of the many ways that this old bug could be used to attack a system was to get an easily accessible copy of an important file (such as the password file) into a public area (such as /tmp) where it could then be picked up and carried to another system for password cracking. In the most sophisticated versions of this attack that have been seen recently, the command transferred control to the contents of the mail message where it was the address line. The mail message contained an inventive script that ran as root. The script compiled, linked, and ran a program that set up a process to execute the commands of the attacker that came in over the network (as root), and then sent the output of these commands back to the attacker over the network. In essence, the attacker became a remote, root user on the target system.

As defensive measures, the security-conscious UNIX-based system administrator will want to monitor carefully the use of SUID and SGID programs on their systems. They should also keep themselves up to date on the latest information about serious security-related bugs that are found in such programs. Again, as Gene Spafford and Simson Garfinkel[4] point out, the find command can locate SUID and SGID programs.

For non-NFS file systems:

```
# find / -perm -002000 -o -perm -004000 -type f print
```

For NFS file systems

```
find / \( -fstype 4.2 -o -prune \)
-perm -002000 -o -perm -004000
-type f -print
```

Make sure that you only run the NFS-style find command on your NFS server, or you'll bury yourself in network traffic. Additionally, you may want to use the xdev option for the find command to prevent the search from crossing file system boundaries. Use these commands as superuser or you will miss files that are hidden in protected directories.

Both of these commands start at the root directory (/) and look for files that are SUID (protection bits of 004000) and SGID (protection bits of 002000).

The ncheck command will print the names of all SUID files on a file system by file system basis:

```
# ncheck -s /dev/rsd0g
```

Last but certainly not least, consider that remotely mounted file systems and locally mounted removable media can have SUID and SGID files on them as well. You do not usually want SUID and SGID files from remotely mounted file systems on your machine for obvious reasons—someone might nail you from afar (over the network) or from the floppy disk that they asked you to mount for them! Consider following Gene Spafford and Simson Garfinkel's advice to mount remote file systems and local removable media with the nosuid switch.

Now, for an interesting twist on this theme. Consider that the device /dev/mem that is accessible in most UNIX systems is actually the system's physical memory. Given that a user on his own UNIX-based system can

---

[4]Ibid

change this device to be owned by himself, consider what would happen if he then put it in a file system that was to be mounted on your system. Can you guess why common practice suggests that you use a -nodev with the -nosuid as suggested above? In case the answer escapes you, consider that, given access to physical memory, all bets are off. One with such access can observe and manipulate the system completely and at will.

While constant vigilance is certainly no guarantee that there will not be any problems with SUID or SGID programs, it is important to keep a close eye on both SUID and SGID programs on your system.

Misapplication

Many security problems with UNIX accrue to its misapplication. Any operating system that is misapplied is vulnerable to this problem, not just UNIX-based operating systems.

A simple example is the capability of some UNIX to allow individual users to authorize access to their accounts over the network. In systems that permit this, users edit a text file called rhosts in their directory, to insert lines that authorize this access. The security problem of allowing users to have this capability is that it allows users to specify the access policy for their systems, not the procedures that implement the security policy. Preventing users from taking advantage of this capability of a system that allows it includes putting an rhosts file in their directory that they can't modify, and the modification of the utilities (such as rlogin) that use the rhosts mechanism to remove that capability. Both of these solutions are not complete, cleanly implemented or easily managed. Using a system that permits users to change the system's access controls where a security policy's procedures state otherwise is a misapplication of that system.

Another good example can be found in an organization's desire to implement data classification for its electronic information resources. Once data has been valued and classified, it is labeled to identify its classification. Finally, everything that touches the data must honor its labels. That is a problem for most UNIX systems. Consider the difficulty of ensuring that users and applications, especially those with privileges, do not gain unauthorized access. In essence, the operating system must do two things:

- It must honor the labels for files that contain labeled data.
- It must assign and enforce access clearances to those users and programs that are authorized to access that data.

These jobs are considerably beyond the simple security controls that most UNIX systems offer. Only the so-called "trusted systems" that have built-in capabilities to deal with labels can do this job. The simple file permissions that most UNIX systems use cannot do this job. Attempts to use a system that can't enforce labels to enforce data classifications is a misapplication, because it can't do this job.

As continually stated in this chapter, an organization must match its security requirements with the capabilities of the security technology that it plans to use to implement the security policy.

Security Management

There are many aspects to managing the security of a UNIX system. Many, such as the need for skilled, knowledgeable staff, have already been mentioned. In addition, good security management is part of good system and network management; the technology does not take care of itself. It is extremely difficult to secure a system that is poorly managed—the best system and network security features and tools can be defeated or rendered useless as a result of sloppy management. People must have a franchise to do the security job, the time required for professional work, and a budget for training, books, and the tools.

Next, the security management problem must be understood. Because network security is generally dependent on individual host security, so host security is dependent on how well all the pieces fit together. A global view is necessary, which must include hardware, operating systems, utility programs, applications, and the network. For instance, a secure system is virtually impossible if users are allowed to have SUID programs under their control, or when vulnerable network protocols (such as X Windows) are allowed to reach hosts from uncontrolled parts of the network.

In today's networks, the security of your system is also very likely dependent on how well your counterparts in other parts of the organization are securing their systems. People must have top management's support to cut through organizational politics to solve organization-wide problems. In the end, the ability to run a secure shop will depend on both organizational cooperation and such mundane and seemingly unrelated things as fully functional and regularly tested backup procedures that provide the ability to recover from a security incident.

Simply stated, the job of security management is to manage the procedures that implement the security policy. In a small shop, this may even include writing and implementing a security policy. In a large shop, it may be broken into many, small tasks that are in each system manager's description, which are supervised by a central security organization.

Security, System, and Network Management

The security of an infrastructure begins with good system and network management. Well-organized system and network management is required as a foundation of security. It is problematic to try to secure an environment whose system and network management is not well-organized. In fact, it can be argued that an infrastructure that is not organized well simply cannot be secured.

System, security, and network management need to be recognized as trades that are key to the *trustability* and *usability* of an infrastructure. The elements of good system and network management need to be codified in standards. Then they can be implemented, periodically assessed, reported, and enforced.

This standard needs to be translated into guidelines and practices that guide personnel in managing their systems. Specifics for each type of platform need to continue to be developed from these overall standards, and they need to be codified in ways that are auditable and assessable. They need to be regularly audited, assessed, and reported so that individual system managers can be held accountable for them. These platform-specific standards, guidelines, and practices need to be part of the job responsibilities of each system manager. And their performance appraisals need to reflect how well such matters are attended to.

A good example is the security-related topic of intrusion detection. Consider that if a system or network's management is not well-organized it is quite likely that an intruder will never even be noticed as he traipses around, even by the most sophisticated intrusion-detection system. An appropriate analogy is someone's office. If the office is organized, with everything in its place, it is likely that an intrusion will be noticed because the intruder will probably disturb the office's order. If the place is an absolute mess it is certainly possible that the intruder's presence will not even be noticed.

UNIX Security Tools

We know of few systems that come with everything needed for adequate system or security management. This certainly includes UNIX. Certain tools are necessary to manage the security of most UNIX systems.

Tools and automation

You can save staff time and improve your security management with tools and widespread automation. The steps toward automation are straightforward. First, you must identify where tools are needed and any implementation problems that might confront your efforts.

- Security policy must establish criteria and help identify the problems to be solved.

- Tool selection will by guided by the standards derived from the security architecture.

- The fabric of security management (security management tools, their implementation, and their automation) must be trustworthy.

All the tools you need are not commercially available. However, a complete security tool box includes a mix of:

- Commercial hardware and software from UNIX system vendors.
- Commercial hardware and software from UNIX security tool vendors.
- Public domain UNIX security software.
- In-house development efforts.

An organization's technical management needs to learn enough about UNIX system security to direct tool acquisition efforts. And finally, an automated security management fabric should include tools for security management, assessment, and reporting.

Tool sources

You can get UNIX tools in several places: trade shows, conferences, membership organizations, product directories, periodicals, books, Internet resources, and User Groups.

Trade shows, conferences, and membership organizations. There are several major security conferences and trade shows. Talking to all of the vendors on the exhibit floor at a typical show is difficult. However, conferences such as the Computer Security Institute (CSI) and the MIS Training Institute, and various trade shows such as Interop/NetWorld, are full of low-cost training opportunities and excellent resources.

Product directories. A visit to a well-equipped public or university library will reveal specialized product reference services that are devoted to security. For example, both Auerbach and DataPro publish security reference services that list security-related products. Security organizations such as CSI, and trade shows such as Interop/NetWorld, often publish buyer's guides and have security vendor advertisements in their conference materials.

Periodicals, books, Internet resources, and user groups. A visit to your local technical book store will reveal quite an array of UNIX-specific books and periodicals that can be resources for tools. Besides suggesting solutions and offering printed source code, some publications actually come with security software that is ready to run on disks. Security-specific magazines such as Information Security News are also good sources of security tool information.

If your organization tolerates public domain security software, Internet resources for UNIX abound. CERT and COAST are two pointers that will get you going in this online world.

User groups such as DECUS and USENIX are gold mines. However, they are not profit-making organizations and their events are often run by volunteers. Therefore, you have to aggressively seek them out.

Selecting specific tools

The standards that are derived from the security architecture that supports the security policy can be distilled into specific, technical requirements. These requirements can then be mapped into specific, security tools, procedures, and practices. But one harsh reality awaits those who take this job seriously. The complexity of a solution tends to change as the problem that is "driving" it becomes better understood. The saving grace is that a better understanding of the problem results in a refinement in the range of acceptable solutions.

Our experience indicates that it is not possible to list all of the tools that can be used to increase UNIX system security. The number is huge. Besides, the problem is usually not a lack of tools. Unless there is a security policy to guide your efforts, the best you can do is adopt commonly accepted security practices. However, this may not meet your needs. Of course, any security tool vendor will tell you that its own offering is the best choice. The problem is obtaining the tools that meet your specific requirements. It's a straightforward exercise.

First, build a list of requirements and give those responsible for them a clear franchise to explore available tool offerings. This includes time and budget. The literature and manuals that come from various tool vendors can be used to make a list of what is important as a start. Excellent material that is available from UNIX security tool vendors provides their perspectives.

Studying the security manuals for the UNIX systems in question will allow you to make lists of the important things. Studying their security training materials will give you the perspective of your UNIX system vendor.

The result of these efforts will be a list of vendor offerings, public domain software, and third-party tools. Finally, those who are responsible for implementing and managing these security tools will have ideas about what tools are needed and how to automate them.

Tool types

Passive tools simply measure and report. Most tools fall into this category. While such programs usually need to run as root to make their measurements, they typically are not a danger to the system or network, though obviously, their results should be carefully protected. Such programs usually measure items such as password strength, user account integrity, operating system vulnerabilities, file system security, user environment security, and the security of the system's network configuration. Other examples of passive tools include so-called system integrity checkers and virus checkers. These programs typically maintain a database of file characteristics, such as strong checksums, to detect when a program has been changed.

Active tools interact with the running system and may dynamically change the running system's configuration. Here, the line between a security tool and a part of the operating system starts to blur. Examples include tools that change file protections that do not match a template; network traffic filtering daemons that accept and reject network connections based on site-specific criteria; and screen locking programs that lock the keyboard and blank the screen of an inactive workstation.

Last but certainly not least, intrusion detection systems are being developed that dynamically monitor a system and detect when the system is under attack. These intrusion detection systems also may dynamically change the system's configuration to defend against an attack.

The Role of Security Tools

Much of this chapter has discussed issues that may seem peripheral to selecting and using tools to better manage security. However, experience shows that even the best tools can be blunted by a lack of attention to any of the issues that other parts of this chapter address. The usefulness of a tool depends on both the context in which the tool is used and the intended purpose of the tool.

Security tool categories

We organize security tools into several categories:

- **Native tools**   Tools that come with the operating system's distribution.
- **Vendor add-ons**   Additional tools that UNIX-based system vendors can provide.
- **Tools from security tool vendors**   Additional tools that the vendors of security tools provide.
- **Freeware tools**   Additional tools that come from the vast collections of the UNIX community, especially Internet archives.
- **Custom tools**   Additional tools produced as a result of development efforts focused on solving specific problems.
- **Personal development efforts by individuals**   Additional tools that come from the midnight hacks of staff members.

The challenge is to provide the right mix of tools to fulfill your requirements. No one source can solve all the problems that you will identify in security policy implementation efforts.

Native tools. Although often not considered security tools, the standard system utilities are a major part of the security tool kit. Much security problem solving is done by writing scripts that invoke standard programs, which then filter, store, and report the output. However, you must understand how to use the native tools and their limitations. For example, the `find` command can be used to locate all of the SUID programs in your file system. However, as previously stated, using find on an NFS-mounted file system over the network may bring the network to its knees. Moreover, `find` cannot locate programs that exploit known security bugs.

As we pointed out, the UNIX culture suggests that, if you can't find something that does the job, then you modify something else or build it yourself. The task may be something as basic as formatting reports based on the output of existing programs, or as complex as crafting a fix for a bug. Making your own fixes for bugs is usually a nontrivial undertaking, because typically you require operating system source code and system programming skills. Finally, quick hacks aimed at closing one hole may open other holes and may create other problems that are not security-related.

Vendor add-ons. The first stop on your search for a tools supplier should be your UNIX system vendor. Most have supplemental security software available for their operating systems. Even if a purchase is not in order, contacting them can give you perspective on what additional tools they think you need.

Tools from commercial security tool vendors. In response to the relatively recent outcry over UNIX system security, commercial UNIX security tools have been appearing for several years. The obvious things to scrutinize in commercial security tool offerings are:

- Tool capabilities.
- How well they fit your needs.
- The tool vendor's reputation and standing in the security community.
- The tool vendor's ability to support you when you need help.

Paying money for a security tool that is commercially offered is no guarantee that it does not have Trojan horses, logic bombs, trap doors, or other bugs. What you get when you purchase software is legal recourse. However, it is likely that you'll have trouble holding the vendor responsible for any incidental damage resulting from the use of his software. Because commercial security tools tend to be more complete than in-house development efforts they are generally more expensive.

Freeware. Many tools are widely available on the Internet from a variety of sources, including user groups and individual programmers. Although these tools can provide excellent solutions, the buyer must beware. Good examples are found in two of the more famous freeware security assessment tools, COPS and SATAN.

COPS uses standard UNIX utilities to do most of its work, including the program rdist (remote file distribution). The rdist program is used by COPS to distribute itself across the network, and then to collect assessment results back to a central machine. For some time, rdist had a bug that allowed COPS to be compromised, a fact known to the underground but apparently unknown to many system managers.

SATAN uses the popular Mosaic World Wide Web viewer as its user interface. The version of Mosaic that was used for the initial version of SATAN had a serious security problem. While SATAN was running on your system, anyone on the network could gain root access to your system without your knowing it, so many system managers were lulled into a false belief that their systems were secure.

Despite the excellent reputation of their author, the accessibility and widespread use of freeware tools such as COPS and SATAN suggests that there will always be questions about the presence of Trojan horses, logic bombs, or trap doors. The best plan is to put such tools into the hands of competent system and network programmers who can ensure that they work properly before using them. If you can't tolerate the risk of running public domain software you are ill-advised to do so, especially if you don't have competent system and network programmers at your disposal.

Custom tools.   Some of the specific requirements for tools may not be met by any source. In this case, a development effort may be required. Such efforts can be initiated in-house or contracted out. One significant downside of the latter approach is that outsourced code will most likely end up being maintained by in-house staff after the employees or contractors who develop it leave. Tight control over the development process, including standards (coding standards, documentation, code reviews, etc.) and periodic review, is in order.

Care should be taken in contracting for security work, because this represents yet another opportunity for security problems. Ironclad contracts and source code audits by skilled, disinterested third parties are in order. Custom solutions may actually be a reasonable choice. If nothing else, a good way to make friends in the UNIX community is to contribute the tools you develop to its existing treasure chest.

Personal tool development efforts by individuals.   Don't overlook the gleam in the eyes of in-house staff, due to pride in their own midnight hacks. Staff that hacks together an elegant solution to a critical problem should be rewarded, even if their contribution does not end up being used in production. The long history of UNIX development proves that there is no substitute for the bright ideas and creative coding of traditional midnight hacks.

Trusted UNIX

To understand this branch of the UNIX family tree, a brief look at its connection to the larger body of trusted systems from which it derives is needed. Exactly how does one come to trust his UNIX-based system?

Answering this question will lead you on a merry chase that will include every aspect of system and network security currently known. It also will include many topics that will be new to most who consider themselves to be UNIX security-wise already. The pursuit of an answer will challenge most everything that many UNIX-based system and security practitioners know about how to secure UNIX. Our treatment of this important subject is brief, but the reader can use the reference list at the end of the chapter to gain a more complete understanding of this important area.

Trusting computers

To trust your UNIX system you must ensure that its security results from serious efforts to design, implement, test, deploy, and manage it so it is trustworthy by design. We define serious security as that which can be trusted within the parameters of its design and implementation, not that which is perfect. All things built by human beings have flaws, and computer systems are no exceptions. The goal is to gain some measure of trust in the technology.

Affordable, usable UNIX systems with serious security, which are suitable for commercial applications, are available. To keep this section focused on those systems we'll briefly concentrate on only one set of accepted standards for building so-called "trusted systems"—the Trusted Computer System Evaluation Criteria (TCSEC) of the U.S. Government. This is how the U.S. Government defines a small portion of the goals of the TCSEC:

- **Provide some assurance** Someone must ensure that a computer system's security features and architecture accurately mediate and enforce the security policy. Most contemporary computer systems embody native behavior and both systemic and endemic bugs that can compromise their security. Assurance provides the design, implementation, and testing that counters these threats.

- Specify particular, higher-level security features such as:
  ~**Mandatory Access Controls (MAC)** A means for restricting access to a system's resources based on their sensitivity. Most contemporary computer systems provide Discretionary Controls (DAC). Under this design, users may change the rules under which they own various resources (such as files), at will. In a Mandatory Control (MAC) scheme, a computer system strictly imposes the rules of a security policy on how its resources can be accessed, regardless of what the owner of those re-

sources tried to do with them. This scheme prevents users from changing file permissions, sharing resources with other users by copying files, and cutting and pasting freely between workstation windows. However, in practice, MAC usually is implemented over and above DAC to make the security system flexible.

~**Limitations on covert channels** Strict control of communication channels that can allow two cooperating processes to transfer information between them in a manner that might violate the system's security policy. Most contemporary computer systems allow processes to move data among themselves at will. The need to protect against this somewhat obscure vulnerability is hotly debated outside of communities (such as the Department of Defense) where even the leakage of a few bits (such as a short key to a cryptographic system) might compromise a secret.

However, this is not where this complexity ends. In practice, there are many other aspects of trusting computers that are equally important, complex, and cumbersome. The standards by which they are built is only the first line of defense in the battle to provide trust. Consider the problem of properly deploying a system that is otherwise trusted. Rules that enforce the security policy must ensure that a thief can't simply walk off with the system's disks (and hence, all of the system's programs and data) in hand.

With apologies to the American defense establishment, we offer this short history of the development of the TCSEC to serve as a basis for the brief discussion of the so-called "trusted" UNIX systems that are available. We admit that our version is histrionic.

- Traditionally, researchers and government agencies ponder questions such as how one comes to trust a computer system. Governments fund research and development, and some vendors actually build real operating systems, like MULTICS, that can be trusted.

- In the early 1980s, the U.S. Department of Defense makes an effort to codify the notion of trust in computer systems in the TCSEC. The resulting book is referred to as Orange Book because of its orange cover. The idea is that everyone could use this standard to build systems that could be trusted. The Orange Book offers an evaluation criteria for systems that are to be trusted.

  Corporate America scratches its collective head and decries the effort as much too "defense-oriented" for their needs.

- Vendors, other government agencies, and those who are trying to have trust in their systems try to figure out the Orange Book and apply it. Nearly everyone fails in the effort except:

  ~The very few commercial enterprises that are very serious about security.

~Government agencies (for example, the U.S. Department of Defense and the Department of Energy) that are required to implement it.

~The few system vendors with sufficient defense dollar funding to enable them to supply those government agency's needs.

~The few vendors who back their belief in the need for this technology in commercial systems with development resources.

- Most vendors of commercial security products realize that a sure way to bankruptcy is to foot the bill required to get on the sparse Evaluated Products List [EPL] that catalogues successful evaluations under the criteria.

- The defense establishments of other countries look at the U.S. DOD's efforts and choke. The politics of accepting an American solution is no small matter. They start inventing their own criteria.

- In the early 1990s the U.S. government admits defeat in its efforts to promote what had become a bookshelf of documents that supported the Orange Book. This collection is affectionately called "the rainbow series" due to their covers' varied colors. An effort, which included representatives from all areas of the industry, is begun to rewrite the U.S. evaluation criteria.

Several of the non-U.S. efforts to create an evaluation criteria succeeded in Canada and the U.K., others failed, and still others got married under common themes.

Commercial enterprises all over the world discover the value of such "trusted systems" when their bottom lines are eroded by attacks that sack their infrastructures right under their noses. Because these attacks are due to the lack of trust that they can place in their information systems, such commercial enterprises actually recognize security as a priority. They start to spend money on it, and start to give their own governments static about the "defense-oriented" flavor of the standards for these so-called "trusted systems."

Admitting that even it can't afford to implement its own requirements, the U.S. government relents. It funds the development of a more reasonable evaluation criteria for something called the Compartmented Mode Work Station (CMW). Because they need secure systems to implement seemingly mundane things such as office automation in the Air National Guard, the government makes sure that system vendors built lots of these systems. One CMW implementation is prototyped using Apple's UNIX derivative A/UX. All current CMW implementations that we know of are based on UNIX.

Commercial enterprises began to notice that tax dollars have actually made so-called "trusted systems" that they can use available in the marketplace. Many show interest, but few are yet serious enough about their security needs to pursue this technology. CMW vendors still anxiously await the awakening of corporate America.

The political and technical details of this chronology curl the hair of even the most dedicated security professional. UNIX has been well-represented throughout this drama. Frankly, everyone has always known how to secure a computer system:

- Lock it in a room that prevents anything from getting out (including stray electromagnetic radiation).
- Classify all data and strictly restrict the system to processing only one classification of data.
- Put a guard with a gun at the door.
- Strictly control everything and everyone that goes in or out of the room.
- If there is a network between two of these systems, carefully encrypt all of the traffic in an end-to-end manner with strong, secret encryption algorithms that can only be broken by a spy who steals the keys.

All of this is a simple proposition until you consider several important points:

- No one, including the government, can buy enough systems or networks to dedicate each of them to processing only one classification of data. Simple economics requires that any given system and network be capable of processing many different classifications of data (which must be kept separated) at the same time.
- The models that implement an evaluation criterion for trusted systems must be applicable to a wide range of needs, including those of corporate America and the defense establishment.
- The models that implement an evaluation criterion for trusted systems must allow some real work to be done. All available computing cannot be devoted to enforcing the security policy.
- The models that implement an evaluation criterion for trusted systems must be easy and cheap enough for system vendors to use so they can produce affordable products.

As a final result of all this, the development of so-called "trusted systems" has been focused on supporting many concurrent processes. In this Multi-level System (MLS) model, each process can be operating in a different classification or security compartment. In a commercial application, it is useful to think of a research engineer accessing R&D data (which might have a data classification of Trade Secret) and an administrative user in the human relations department accessing payroll data (which might be classified as Company Confidential).

As a summary, we present the classic Reference Monitor Model that is used to describe how security in a trusted system works in Figure 14.5.

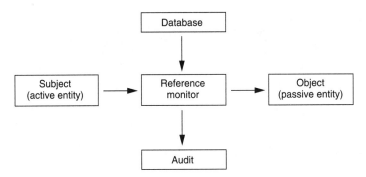

Figure 14.5 The reference monitor model

Basically, the Reference Monitor Model puts a mediator between the active entities and passive entities in a system. The parts of the model are:

- **Subjects** These are the active entities on the system that are accessing resources (processes, chron jobs, etc.). Think of them acting on behalf of users.

- **The Reference Monitor** This is a small, easily verified part of the operating system that enforces the security policy. It does so by applying rules from its database to the access requests that subjects make for system resources. It produces an audit trail.

- **Objects** These are the passive entities in the scheme—the system resources (such as files, devices, etc.) that subjects want to use.

Finally, we present a view of how X Windows can become trustworthy (see Figure 14.6). We use this example to illustrate the many differences between standard systems and those that are built to be trusted. In essence, everything that must be trusted is scrutinized under an evaluation criterion to ensure that it can enforce the security policy. Applications might merely be Commercial Off The Shelf (COTS) versions that rely on the trusted system to protect them. COTS usually doesn't include trusted versions, so vendors usually supply a suite of trusted network applications, such as telnet, the Berkeley "r" utilities (e.g., `rlogin`), and ftp. These trusted applications and the trusted X Windows software use the mechanisms that the trusted operating system provides to enforce the security policy by honoring the object labels (files, network connections, windows, etc.).

Real Trusted UNIX

As a result of this evolution, real, affordable, usable, trusted UNIX are available for commercial use today. At this point in the evolution of UNIX, all is coming together to allow commercial enterprises to buy these so-called "trusted systems"—especially CMWs—and to use them effectively.

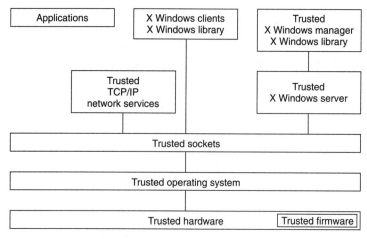

Figure 14.6 Trusted X Windows

Sun, HP, and DEC have all energetically joined the fray. With the recent defense budget cuts, many of the vendors that have been supplying so-called "trusted systems" to the government are looking for new customers. Many of them are aggressively courting corporate America's business with their considerable prowess in serious security for UNIX. At a recent trade show, we observed one such vendor's representative aggressively recruiting partners from the community of general, commercial software product suppliers. The surprise was that this vendor was actually willing to foot the significant bill for its new, commercial software product-supplier partners to have their products evaluated under the TCSEC. Obviously, their plan was to offer so-called "trusted systems" to the commercial community, complete with the software needed for commercial applications. We are truly witnessing the maturation of yet another branch of the UNIX family tree, one holding the promise for serious security that is affordable.

Our advice is to contact your UNIX-based system vendor and ask them about so called "trusted systems" and their CMW. If they don't have one, put a big black mark near their name and ask when they will have one. If they don't know about the technology of so-called "trusted systems" or have no plans to offer one, consider deleting them from your list of approved UNIX-based system vendors.

Networks

A detailed discussion of networks and distributed computing is outside the scope of this chapter. However, we would be remiss if we did not mention them.

Networking and the reference monitor

Figure 14.7 shows how the reference monitor that we mentioned earlier operates across a network. Note that the true identities of the remote system's reference monitors connected by the network are virtual. Unless these network connections employ strong authentication, the true identity of the remote reference monitors cannot be known. They are shielded from view by the network connection that may allow another system to falsify its identity. Network addresses are commonly used to identify the originators of network connections. Authentication is required because these addresses can generally be spoofed.

It is uncommon to find an enterprise-wide network in a modern enterprise that has a small number of network connections that all run the same protocol. Usually, many network connections handle traffic consisting of many protocols. Moreover, these protocols are usually from different protocol stacks. Figure 14.8 illustrates a simple case in which one system has many connections.

The proper way to secure this external connectivity is with an isolation mechanism specific to each connection and each protocol. Exploring the literature for clues on how to build an isolation mechanism will help you understand the problem.[5, 6] However, it is a complex task. Building these isolation mechanisms is considered an art.

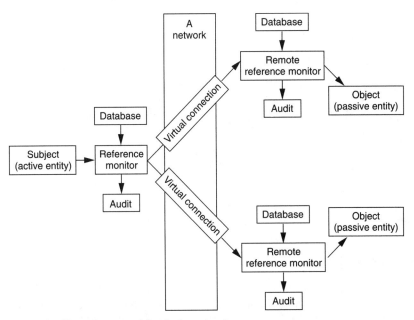

Figure 14.7 The reference monitor in the network

[5]Cheswick, William and Steven Bellovin. 1994. *Firewalls and Internet Security—Repelling the Wily Hacker.* Reading, MA: Addison Wesley.

[6]Chapman, D. Brent, and Elizabeth P. Zwicky. *Building Internet Firewalls*. Sebastapol, CA: O'Reilly & Associates.

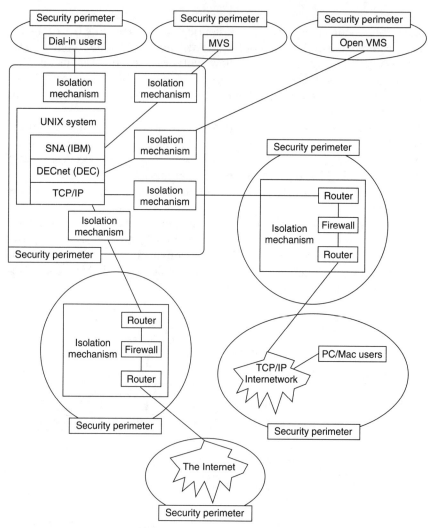

Figure 14.8 Security perimeters

Distributed Systems

Distributed computing in the UNIX system arena has traditionally been quite easy. A combination of capabilities, such as the Network File System (NFS) for file sharing and Sun's Remote Procedure Call (RPC) to take advantage of resources on other, remote UNIX systems, have been available for some time. In fact, other operating system vendors (such as DEC and its OpenVMS) even know how to play the NFS/RPC game. But the problem with the success of enterprise-wide, distributed computing efforts (such as the client/server paradigm) has been a lack of security features. And where they have been available they have lacked proper design, implementation, deployment, and management.

While improvements to NFS and RPC security have come in recent years, these improvements have largely paled in comparison to most organization's security requirements. The big news in distributed computing in recent years is the ability to do distributed computing securely. Yet another branch in the UNIX family tree is showing considerable promise for serious security. Many security technologies have matured and are now ready for commercial use.[7, 8]

First, let's briefly explore the cryptographic security technology that is needed for secure distributed computing.

Cryptography

Cryptography is the art of secret writing. It is the only way we know how to keep secrets. Here are the basics of how this important technology can be used.

Secret key cryptography. One category of cryptography is called *secret key cryptography*. Secret key algorithms use the same key to encrypt and decrypt messages. Because of this, these algorithms are also called symmetric cryptography. Figure 14.9 illustrates how such algorithms work.

Each party that is exchanging messages must share the secret key required to encrypt and decrypt messages. This secret is generated and distributed by a trusted third party. Typically, this trusted third party is a key distribution center.

These algorithms are popular because they are fast. Their downside is that key management is complex and does not scale well. Consider a network in which there are 10,000 nodes that want to interact, based on a symmetric key cryptographic scheme. Each of those 10,000 nodes needs to be given the key in a manner which does not reveal it.

Common secret key algorithms in use today include the Data Encryption Standard (DES), RC2, RC4, and IDEA.

Public key cryptography. Another category of cryptography is called *public key cryptography*. Public key algorithms use a pair of keys. Messages that are encrypted with one of the keys can be decrypted with the other. To make these schemes useful, one of the keys is a closely held secret and the

[7]Stallings, William. 1995. *Network and Internetwork Security—Principles and Practices.* New York: Prentice Hall.

[8]Kaufman, Charlie, Radia Pearlman, and Mike Speciner. 1995. *Network Security—Private Communication in a Public World.* New York: Prentice Hall.

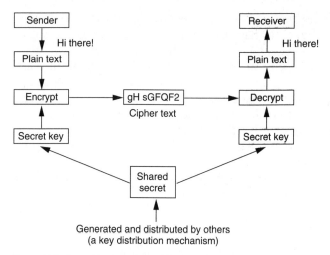

Figure 14.9 Secret key cryptography

other is widely and publicly distributed. These algorithms are called *asymmetric cryptography*.

The keys are generated as a pair—one that is made publicly available (the public key) and one that is a closely held secret (the private key.) A message encrypted with one key can be decrypted with the other. Now, all cryptography requires some form of mediation. Public key algorithms do not require a shared secret between communicating entities and a trusted third party. However, for them to be useful to us, this trusted third party is needed to vouch for the validity of public keys. In the case of public key cryptography, the trusted third party is called a *certification authority*.

Public keys can be distributed by a trusted, central authority, such as a directory or naming service. This greatly simplifies the key management problem that plagues secret key cryptography, and is a major reason why these algorithms are popular. The sender of a message encrypts a message with his private key and the recipient of that message uses the sender's public key to decrypt it. The downside of these algorithms is that they are slow. Figure 14.10 illustrates how these algorithms work.

The dominant public key algorithm in use today is RSA, which is distributed by RSA Data Security [RSA]. They offer a framework called Public Key Cryptography Standards (PKCS) that allows RSA to be used in building applications and systems. The Generic Security Service Application Programs Interface (GSSAPI) also accommodates public key cryptography.

Many vendors have used public key technology to build secure applications and systems. Public key cryptography is an important technology that is being incorporated into many distributed computing environments including Kerberos.

Kerberos

Our treatment of Kerberos is the most detailed, because Kerberos is an open, public standard that has been used in production by academic and commercial organizations for many years. Kerberos also is used as the primary security mechanisms of DCE, and is a major player in the development of the GSSAPI (see Chapter 2 for DCE security services).

Several common misconceptions about Kerberos deserve comment:

- Kerberos is an authentication protocol, not an encryption algorithm. It has been extended to offer privacy and integrity of network messages. It does not offer protection against traffic analysis or availability services. However, because it does offer authentication services it can serve as a platform upon which to build access control and nonrepudiation.

- Kerberos and public key cryptography are not mutually exclusive. OSF recently announced compliance with a developing standard for interoperability between public key-based systems and their Kerberos-based DCE. Other vendors will quickly follow suit.

- While adding any security to a system or network has a performance impact, Kerberos itself is not a performance problem. The network traffic that Kerberos generates is minimal. Its credentials and their exchange have been carefully minimized and optimized.

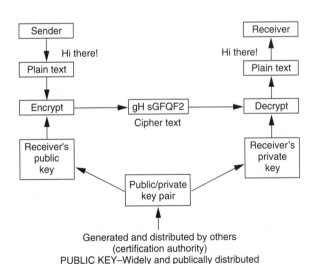

Figure 14.10 Public key cryptography

There are two major players in the Kerberos authentication scheme:

- Principals, which include clients that want to consume remote services and application servers that offer remote services.
- The Kerberos Key Distribution Center (KDC). The choice of this name was unfortunate. In the parlance of cryptography, a KDC distributes cryptographic keys. The Kerberos KDC has three parts: a database of encrypted passwords, an authentication server, and a ticket granting service.

The best way to think about Kerberos is as a suite of security services. Kerberos offers three of the services that can secure a network communications channel: authentication, integrity, and privacy services for network messages. Two of its primary uses are to prevent passwords from crossing a network in plain text and to authenticate the originators of network connections.

Principals that want to use Kerberos services must make explicit calls in order to obtain those services. Client and server applications that use Kerberos are said to be "Kerberized." This is done by inserting calls to a library of Kerberos services into each such client and server application.

Besides the basic capability to authenticate client applications to their servers, Kerberos allows them to have fully encrypted sessions. Paranoid clients also can request that the servers they connect with authenticate themselves as well. Kerberos even offers services for the truly paranoid. The protocol is sophisticated enough to permit a client and its server to painlessly negotiate a new encryption key for each and every transaction should they so desire.

Kerberos at work

A typical scenario finds a user sitting at his workstation, wanting to use a remote application requiring that he (the user) first authenticate himself. The user must authenticate himself to the application using Kerberos before the application will talk to him.

There are two major steps:

1. The user (or a program acting on his behalf) authenticates him(it)self to the Kerberos Authentication Server.
2. The user runs a program (for example, telnet or a database query tool). Then:
   - That program (for example, a telnet daemon or a database) retrieves the credentials necessary to use the remote service from the Kerberos Ticket Granting Service. These credentials are called *service tickets*.
   - Finally, the program that the user ran (for example, telnet or the database query tool) presents its service tickets to the remote service.

Figure 14.11 presents an overview of how a principal authenticates himself to Kerberos; gets; and then uses Kerberos credentials.

First, the user (or a program operating on his behalf) runs a Kerberos utility on his workstation (called kinit), which obtains the principal's

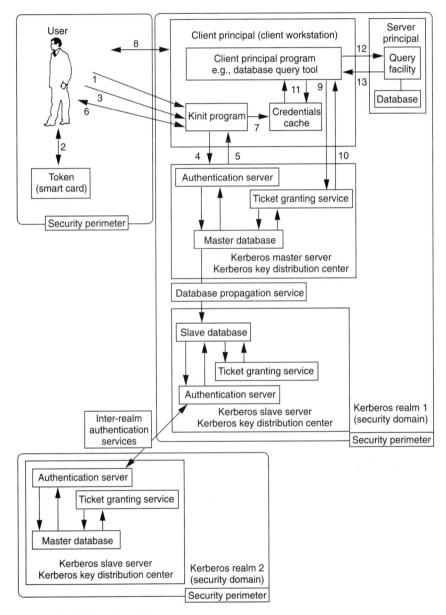

Figure 14.11 Kerberos in action

Kerberos credentials from the Kerberos Authentication Server (AS) and caches them on the user's workstation. The user's credentials are now available for any application which demands them. Referring to Figure 14.11, here is an overview of the details:

1. The client workstation user initializes Kerberos environment by running a program called kinit. A program operating on the workstation's behalf (such as the workstation's login program) could do this as well.

2. If a smart card is required, the user will interact with the card and will obtain a number from the card. This optional requirement is imposed on the user by the Kerberos administrator when the user's Kerberos profile is established. In a typical case, the card will offer a random number that changes periodically. Kerberos supports a variety of other tokens, including those that are challenge/response-based.

3. The user enters the number from the card.

4. The kinit program asserts its identity to the Kerberos Authentication Server by sending the client principal name to the Authentication Server.

5. The credentials that come back from the Authentication Server contain the name of the client, a time stamp, and a session key that will be used by both the principal and the KDC for subsequent communications. This is encrypted by the Authentication Server before it is sent back to the kinit program. It is called a *Ticket Granting Ticket* (TGT).

6. The kinit program prompts the user for his password.

7. If kinit can decrypt the TGT using this password, the TGT is saved in the principal's credentials cache.

The second step is for the client principal to request credentials to use a remote service, and then to authenticate himself to the service. This is done with service tickets obtained from the Kerberos Ticket Granting Service on behalf of the user. These transactions are based on the TGT that was obtained when kinit was run. Again referring to Figure 14.11, here is an overview of the details:

8. The user runs a Kerberized client application, such as a database query tool.

9. The Kerberized client application takes the client principal's TGT from the credentials cache.

10. The Kerberized client application sends the client principal's TGT and its request for a specific applications service ticket to the Kerberos Ticket Granting Service (TGS).

11. The TGS sends the application service ticket for the requested ticket back to the client principal program. The client principal program stores the application service ticket in the client's credentials cache with other service tickets that the client principal acquires from time to time.

12. The client principal program authenticates itself to the application server by presenting the application service ticket.

13. Optionally, the client principal program may require the server to authenticate itself.

It is important to note that an application server does not need to communicate with the **Authentication Server** during these exchanges. When the security manager of an application server wants to add it to the Kerberos fabric of a realm, an entry for it is put in the KDC's database. From that point on, no communication between the application and the KDC is needed because the service ticket contains the credentials that it needs to authenticate its users.

Security domains in Kerberos are known as *realms*. Typically, realms are defined using geographic, political, or administrative constraints. Each realm may have as many slave KDCs as needed to ensure availability. The performance issues of scale are not a factor for Kerberos, because its network traffic is low. Inter-realm authentication and automatic KDC database propagation services are provided. The inter-realm service keeps track of which realms Kerberos credentials have traversed. This information can be used to reject credentials that have passed through untrustworthy realms.

Kerberos is currently seeing application in authentication, secure communications (for example, encrypted communications), single sign-on, internetwork firewalls, and electronic commerce.

Enterprise-Wide Solutions

Many organizations are moving to enterprise-wide computing with distributed systems, based on UNIX that embrace standards such as The Open Software Foundation's (OSF) Distributed Computing Environment (DCE) and The Secure European System for Applications in a Multivendor Environment (SESAME). However, it is not clear how long these standards will take to become prevalent, if they ever will.

There are many other players in this volatile area, including Computer Associates' UNICenter and IBM's NetSP. Of course, every vendor claims to have the solution.

By most estimates, it will be a long time before these requirements and the intermingled themes of the architectures that are available for secure, distributed computing sort themselves out. In general, you'll be waiting on your UNIX system vendor to implement one or more of these schemes. Many vendors are moving aggressively to help your distributed computing efforts. Some solutions offer compatibility with only one or more of the major secured, distributed computing architectures. For example, IBM's AIX currently provides the capability to use its ACLs in DCE's access control environment. However, it is clear that any complete solution for enterprise-wide computing security must include the following functional requirements:

- Enterprise-wide security management
- User administration
- Access control
- Identification and authentication
- Monitoring and intrusion detection
- Secure messaging
- Data availability

Finally, there are some fundamental, required capabilities for enterprise-wide computing security solutions:

- Cross-platform, network-wide operation.
- Management from a single workstation.
- Easy to use without OS-specific expertise.
- Scalable to large networks.
- Allowing integration with existing management frameworks (for example, OpenView, NetView, Tivoli).

Some ideas of how security fits into an overall business architecture can be found in ICL's OPENframework distributed computing architecture.[9] At this writing, there are a number of viable enterprise-wide solutions emerging, as well as several that are available.[10] Of these, we'll briefly cover DCE and SESAME because they are the oldest of the lot. Finally, we'll touch on an important subset of enterprise-wide solutions, single sign-on.

OSF DCE

DCE is an environment for distributed computing that includes security services. It is a monumental, collaborative effort by most major computer

---

[9]Fairthorne, Belinda. 1993. *OPENframework Security*. New York: Prentice Hall.

[10]Johnson, Johna Till. March 1995. "Enterprise Security—Better Safe Than Sorry." *Data Communications Magazine*, McGraw Hill.

system vendors to agree on and implement standards for enterprise-wide computing.

Because its specifications include threads, RPCs, local and global directory services, a Distributed File System (DFS), and Distributed Time Services (DTS), it is much more than just security. Security is at its core and includes authentication (integrity and privacy) privileges, Access Control Lists (ACLs), and administration. DCE security is based on Kerberos. At this writing, DCE has just incorporated public key cryptography. Figure 14.12 shows how these pieces fit together.

Vendor commitment to DCE is thought to be high, and many major system vendors have already begun to ship DCE-compliant capabilities with their systems. However, DCE compatibility is popular enough among those who will use it that many vendors merely include the words in their marketing literature without any real commitment to it. While the security department may decide to use a security system like Kerberos, the decision to adopt DCE requires a significant, higher level management commitment. Adopting DCE as a computing strategy is a strategic, expensive, and long-term commitment. Many organizations are making this jump, but most have adopted a wait-and-see attitude.

An example shows how DCE security uses Kerberos. To communicate securely with an application server, a client must obtain a Privilege Attribute Certificate (PAC) from the DCE security server. To do this, the client obtains a Kerberos Ticket for the Privilege Service. Figure 14.13 shows how this works.

In the DCE model, an integrated set of independent, distributed services are provided across multiple systems. In DCE, the distributed computing

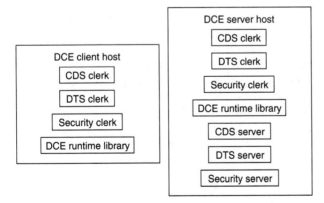

Figure 14.12 DCE architecture

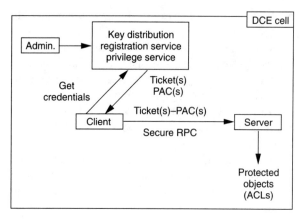

Figure 14.13 A DCE cell

environment can be divided up into domains called cells. The directory service is used to locate services and it has two components:

- A Cell Directory Service (CDS) for a local cell.
- A Global Directory Service (GDS) for all of the cells in a DCE environment.

Figure 14.14 shows how DCE cells interact within a global framework. Like most contemporary distributed computing models, DCE uses a client/server model. (The details of how DCE security works are left to the reader to explore, through books such as Harold Lockhart's *OSF DCE—Guide to Developing Distributed Applications.*)[11]

SESAME

The Secure European System for Applications in a Multivendor Environment (SESAME) is a specification for secure, distributed computing based on standards from the European Computer Manufacturer's Association (ECMA). ECMA TR/46 and ECMA 138 document ECMA's wide-ranging, vendor-independent distributed computing architecture. Three European computer companies (ICL, Bull, and Siemens Nixdorf Information systems [SNI]) cooperated to implement ECMA's design. ICL has designed a distributed computing architecture, called OPENframework, whose security follows SESAME. Like DCE, SESAME is a client/server architecture with a commercial bias.

This interesting model provides:

---

[11]Lockhart, Harold. 1994. *OSF DCE—Guide to Developing Distributed Applications.* New York: McGraw-Hill.

- Different security contexts for users, called roles.
- Security services for identification, authorization, audit, accounting, access control, and nonrepudiation.
- Delegation of roles for applications such as transaction processing.
- User security context which is kept in tokens.
- User state information that is dynamically available.

Figure 14.15 shows SESAME's architecture. SESAME supports an array of programming interfaces. SESAME implementations such as ICL's Access Manager include interfaces for the GSSAPI, RPC, DCE interoperability, and a scripting capability to deal with legacy systems that can't be modified to include security services. Its security services include interfaces to Kerberos, DCE, and legacy systems.

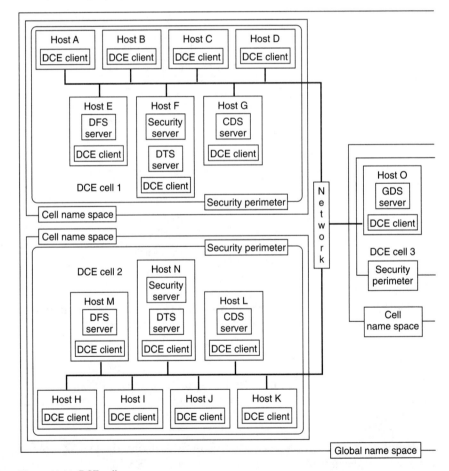

Figure 14.14 DCE cells

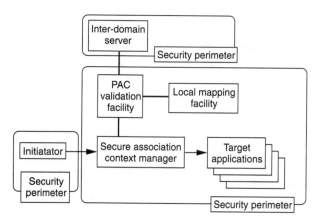

Figure 14.15 SESAME architecture

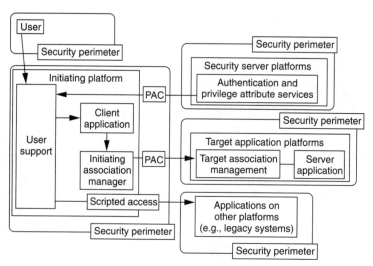

Figure 14.16 SESAME

Like DCE, SESAME uses Privilege Attribute Certificates that a client obtains from a security server. Figure 14.16 shows how this works.

Single sign-on

Those who actually have to implement enterprise-wide solutions face significant problems. The problem of deploying standards like DCE or SESAME, on the myriad of different systems that populate most contemporary infrastructures, is daunting if not simply insurmountable.

Moving an infrastructure to DCE or SESAME is a formidable task. This is especially true when an organization is moving to DCE while trying to solve the sticky problems that the new paradigms of distributed and client/server computing have wrought. These problems certainly include the burden of administering user logons and the security of the ever-increasing number of systems. Worse, users are caught in the middle of the paradigm shift as well.

Despite the prevalence and popularity of UNIX for the desktop, there is little homogeneity among the many applications that users typically need to access for their work. It is not uncommon for the user of a large commercial organization's information systems to have a dozen or more passwords to deal with. Much of this has to do with the legacy of mainframe system-based applications that require a separate logon with a different username and password for each application. However, even homogeneous environments of UNIX systems can overwhelm users and administrators alike with similar problems.

Organizations are clamoring for solutions to the nightmare of security administration until they can adopt standards like DCE or SESAME. As a result of this market demand, the landscape of the security industry is currently littered with much talk about how to effect a single, network-wide sign-on until DCE or SESAME arrives. Most of these so-called single sign-on solutions are not secure, and few offer compatibility with DCE or SESAME.

The availability of commercial Kerberos products compatible with DCE and SESAME is likely to follow closely. Using such technology, an organization could experiment with DCE and SESAME while solving some of their security administration nightmares and moving their applications toward the new distributed computing paradigm.

Because this chapter is focused on UNIX system security, we've left the exploration of the details to the reader. However, an example is in order because most UNIX system security does not exist in isolation. Our example is based on Kerberos because it is secure, readily available, and runs on many systems, including UNIX.

While many of the requirements for single sign-on problem are recognized, there is no definitive discussion of these issues available yet. Until such works become available, here are some of the criteria that have been documented by groups such as the New York Chapter of the Information Systems Security Association and a Consumer's Gas Cooperative:

- Provides subset of an enterprise security architecture that does user administration

- Uses central user administration from a central point.

- Accommodates both central and local (distributed) administration of user passwords.

- Uses no plain text passwords on the network.

- Does not store passwords locally on workstations.

- Complies with standards.

- Preserves existing mechanisms.

- Accommodates sophisticated authentication.

- Provides interoperability with other single sign-on environments.

- Allows users to use resources anywhere in the network no matter where they are. User profile knows what applications are authorized and where they are to be found.

- With a single sign-on user ID and Password, allows a user to login to the enterprise network and access all network services and applications needed to perform their jobs.

- Eliminates the need for users to have many different usernames and passwords.

This is a tall order, but available security technology is up to the job.

Kerberos single sign-on

A common, contemporary UNIX system security issue is that users and administrators have to deal with multiple passwords that end up being sent in the clear over the network. This design can allow a user sitting at any system that has a Kerberos client (for example, Windows NT or UNIX) to logon to any systems participating in the single sign-on fabric. Using this design, the administration of user identification and authentication can be centralized, because only one Kerberos Master Database is used. In addition, the fabric of Kerberos security services is available to all users, systems and applications in the single sign-on fabric.

In essence, the login programs of each platform that will participate in the single sign-on fabric are modified to authenticate a user to the platforms they will be using, and to obtain their Kerberos credentials. Because many vendors provide interfaces that allow additional authentication mechanisms to be plugged in, this is quite straightforward.

Another common, contemporary UNIX system security issue is securing a UNIX-based workstation user interface to an IBM mainframe and all the mainframe applications. The only problems with incorporating a mainframe into a single sign-on fabric occur because of idiomatic differences between system security environments. For instance, a complete solution must accommodate the difference between user identification and authentication between UNIX and IBM MVS mainframe environments. In a typical UNIX environment, a password file is used for user identification and authentication. In a typical MVS environment, an access control package (such as RACF, CA-ACF/2 or CA-Top Secret) is used for user identification, user authentication, and system resource access control.

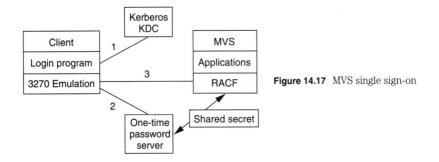

Figure 14.17 MVS single sign-on

One design allows MVS user's to login using a one-time password. This one-time password replaces the RACF password during the login sequence. Figure 14.17 shows how this works. The steps follow the Kerberos protocol that we discussed earlier in this section:

1. The user authenticates himself to Kerberos.

2. The Kerberos credentials are used to obtain a one-time password.

3. The one-time password is used to connect with RACF on the MVS system

Security for UNIX Applications

No discussion of an operating system's security would be complete without some mention of its application's security.

Application security problems

We discussed some of the security problems with UNIX system applications earlier in this chapter. We presented examples of security problems with vi, sendmail, SATAN, and COPS that all point to poor software engineering practices. We can be this harsh on the authors of these programs because experience shows that a good many security problems with applications turn out to be associated with flaws in privileged code.

Typically, a bug in code that runs as root allows some direct, unintended access to this privileged context. The bugs that allow shell escapes to end up with root are classic examples. However, this is far from the only kind of security bug that an application can have. Until a definitive dissertation on UNIX application security bugs shows up, consider concentrating on:

- Policy, architecture, standards, and guidelines.
- Competent programmers who understand security.
- Good software development tools.
- Good software development practice.

- Rigorous testing.
- Controlled deployment.
- Careful management and operation.

Security engineering must follow the well-known tenets of software engineering and produce bug-free code. Rigorous tests should be designed and run to reveal such problems. Finally, careful note should be made of the fact that bugs WILL exist. The name of the game is carefully containing their impact. Believe it or not, when you get right down to the basics of this problem, you'll be reading about the risk analysis that we mentioned early on in this chapter. Because this is not a dissertation on security engineering, the only thing we can do is point the reader to the considerable body of research, practice, experience, and tools now available. Robert Charette's book[12] is a good place to start.

The GSSAPI

The Generic Security Services Application Programmer's Interface (GSSAPI) is designed to allow programmers to write applications that need security services. Originally developed by DEC's Secure Systems Group as part of DEC's Distributed System Security Architecture, the GSSAPI has gone on to become a standard in the Internet community. The Internet's Request For Comment (RFC) 1508 specifies this interface, RFC 1509 specifies C++ bindings for it.

The GSSAPI is especially well-suited for isolating programmers from direct calls to the libraries that implement Kerberos. Some vendors even supply GSSAPI interfaces to their Kerberos libraries. However, the GSSAPI was designed to allow application programmers to code security into their applications without hard coding any particular security mechanism. The GSSAPI can accommodate most any security mechanism that someone wants it to support. The GSSAPI itself is a series of high-level calls to routines that do the dirty work of actually invoking specific security services. For instance, the GSSAPI's basic functions include:

- Acquiring credentials
- Freeing credentials
- Initiating a security context (for the client side)
- Accepting a security context (for the server side)

This nifty interface even includes calls to add integrity checks (digital signature) and privacy (for example, encrypt the contents of a message).

---

[12]Charette, Robert N. 1990. *Applications Strategies for Risk Analysis*. New York: McGraw-Hill.

Despite the fact that the GSSAPI is not well known, it still represents some of the biggest news in the history of UNIX security.

This is a perfect place for us to end our exploration of UNIX security. UNIX development continues, as it always has. The big news is that now this development includes serious security capabilities.

Summary

UNIX can be successfully used as the basis for a computing infrastructure that can be trusted to fulfill its role in protecting organization assets. Keeping in mind that vendors already provide everything you need to make this happen, perhaps the best summary of this chapter is the title of a contemporary country/western song: We're old enough to know better but still too young to care.

As security consultant William H. Murray is fond of saying, "Y'all be careful out there."

For Further Information . . .

Resources from your UNIX-based system vendor

We recommend that you seek out and explore:

- The security-specific sections of your UNIX-based system's manual set.
- Supplemental literature that deals with the security of your UNIX-based system.
- The system management, network management, and security-specific training and education that should be available.
- The security-specific threads in your UNIX system supplier's user group.

If any of these are not provided by your UNIX system vendor, consider deleting them from your list of approved UNIX system suppliers. Alternatively, you could plan to hire and support a team of extremely knowledgeable, experienced, old time, UNIX gunslingers to beat your UNIX systems into submission.

The larger body of UNIX-specific, security-related information

This resource list also stands alongside the huge, and well-understood body of UNIX-specific, security-related knowledge and experience that exists. You can explore this wellspring by:

- Seeking out and reading the security-related information available from UNIX-based system vendors and the vendors that supply add-on security products for UNIX.

- Ensuring that the people responsible for the security of your UNIX have secure, high-speed access to the Internet, the time to use it, and the empowerment to put it to use in your infrastructure.

- Getting involved with UNIX-specific professional societies and user groups.

- Seeking out and attending specialized UNIX-specific training in the form of seminars and conferences dedicated to the topic.

- Seeking out and attending the UNIX-specific sessions that have come to be a mainstay in many UNIX-related conferences.

The larger body of general, security-related information

This resource list also stands alongside the huge and well understood body of security-related knowledge and experience that exists. Your security-related efforts to deploy and maintain a trustworthy UNIX-based environment must include it. You can explore this wellspring by:

- Seeking out and reading security-specific books, periodicals and literature.

- Seeking out and joining general, security-specific organizations and attending their conferences.

Select Bibliography

A more complete annotated bibliography is available from:

Ray Kaplan
P.O. Box 23210
Richfield, MN 55423
(612) 861-7198
(612) 861-3736 (F)
Ray@rayk.com
www.rayk.com/rayk

UNIX security books

Arnold, N. Derek. 1993. *UNIX Security—A practical Tutorial*. New York: McGraw-Hill.

Braun, Christopher. 1994. *UNIX System Security Essentials*. Reading, MA: Addison Wesley.

Curry, David. 1992. *UNIX System Security: A Guide for Users and System Administrators*. New York: Addison Wesley.

Farrow, Rik. 1991. *UNIX System Security, How to Protect Your Data and Prevent Intruders*. Reading, MA: Addison Wesley.

Ferbrache, David and Gavin Shearer. 1993. *UNIX—Installation, Security & Integrity*. New York: Prentice Hall.

Wood, Patrick H. and Stephen G. Kochan. 1985. *UNIX System Security*. Hayden Books UNIX System Library.

UNIX books containing security information

Bloomer, John. 1992. *Power Programming with RPC*. Sebastapol, CA: O'Reilly & Associates.

Montgomery, John. 1995. *The Underground Guide to UNIX—Slightly Askew Advice from a UNIX Guru*. Reading, MA: Addison Wesley.

Rieken, Bill and Lyle Weiman. *Adventures in UNIX Network Applications Programming*. New York: Wiley.

Stevens, W. Richard. 1992. *Advanced Programming in the UNIX Environment*. New York: Prentice Hall.

Stevens, W. Richard. 1990. *UNIX Network Programming*. New York: Prentice Hall.

Security books

Caelli, William, Dessins Longley, and Michael Shain. 1991. *Information Security Handbook*. New York: Stockton Press.

DeMaio, Harry. *Every Manager's Guide to Keeping Vital Computer Data Safe and Sound*. New York: AMACOM.

Icove, David, Karl Seger and William Von Storch. 1995. *Computer Crime—A Crimefighter's Handbook*. Sebastapol, CA: O'Reilly & Associates.

Information Systems Security Association. *Guide for Information Valuation*. 401 North Michigan Avenue, Chicago, IL 60611.

Jackson, K.M. and J. Hruska. 1992. *Computer Security Reference Book*. London: Butterworth-Heinemann. U.S. Representative: CRC Press, 2000 Corporate Blvd. NW, Boca Raton, FL 33431 (800) 272-7737. (This book is a 950-page compendium of articles on security from a technical perspective, including significant discussions of policy, management and legal topics.)

Peltier, Thomas. *Policies and Procedures for Data Security—A Complete Manual for Computer Systems and Networks*, #722. Computer Security Bookshelf., P. O. Box 7339, San Francisco, CA 94120.

Russell, Deborah, and G.T. Gangemi. 1991. *Computer Security Basics*. Sebastapol, CA: O'Reilly & Associates.

Ruthberg, Zella and Harold Tipton. 1993. *The Handbook of Information Security Management*. Boston, MA: Auerbach Publications.

Schneirer, Bruce. 1994. *Applied Cryptography Protocols, Algorithms, and Source Code in C*. New York: John Wiley.

Wood, Charles Cresson. *Information Security Policies Made Easy—A Comprehensive Set of Information Security Policies*. This 100-plus page, 8.5" × 11" tome is a reference book on information system security policy development. It contains 525 example specific policies coupled with a detailed introduction to the subject of security policy formation, an extensive list of security standards, and a complete bibliography. This manual comes with machine readable copy for IBM PC and Macintosh on a 3½" disk. Baseline Software, P.O. Box 1219, Sausalito, CA 94966, (800) 829-9955.

UNIX conferences

USENIX Security Symposium
22672 Lambert St., #613
Lake Forest, CA 92630
(714) 588-8649
e-mail: conference@usenix.org

UNIX user groups

USENIX Association
2560 Ninth St., Site 215
P. O. Box 2299
Berkeley, CA 94710
e-mail—office@usenix.org

UNIFORM
2901 Tasman Drive, Suite 201
Santa Clara, CA 95054

Internet news groups

alt.2600
alt.security
comp.security.announce
comp.security.misc
comp.security.unix

General UNIX information

There is so much information out there, you can easily find most anything you are looking for in a good technical book store. For example, the Ed Dunphy book, *The UNIX Industry and Open Standards in Transition— A Guidebook for Managing Change* has a 29-page final chapter entitled "Getting Connected." This is a comprehensive list of UNIX resources and ideas on how to get connected to the larger UNIX community.

Unigram is a weekly, worldwide UNIX publication. It is available on paper and online, and at www.globalnews.com/UNI, though you'll only get a back issue at the WWW page because it is a subscription newsletter. It has no ads and sports 100,000 readers. Its news comes out of London, New

York, Tokyo (Kanji version), Moscow, and Sydney. Unigram is over 10 years old and is owned by APT, in London. It costs $495 a year in the US. Free trials are available.

The US franchise is:

G2 Computer Intelligence
3 Maple Place
Glen Head, NY 11545
516-759-7025

APT's US subsidiary:

APT Data America Inc.
27 East 21st St., 3rd Floor
New York, NY 10010 USA
ph: +1 212 677 0409
fax: +1 212 677 0463

APT London has other publications in the US, including a daily, *Computergram International*.

15

Securing OpenVMS Systems
Geoff Cooke

*He who trusts secrets to a servant makes him
his master.*   JOHN DRYDEN

If you are concerned with the nature and extent of your organization's dependence upon its corporate computer systems, or if you are becoming increasingly aware that the information they process and store is in many ways the lifeblood of your organization, perhaps you are considering steps to improve the integrity and security of your corporate OpenVMS systems.

Adequately securing corporate computer systems requires developing a sound security policy supported by pragmatic guidelines and practical procedures, having these procedures consistently implemented, and verifying their implementation on a regular basis.

The challenge is to develop procedures that ensure that information assets are adequately protected without impeding the day-to-day operations of your organization. The procedures developed need to address the overall impact of a number of issues, which include:

- Operating system and network implementation and controls.
- User account definition and password controls.
- Information access and protection.

Implementing these security procedures is usually the responsibility of individuals already overburdened with other conflicting tasks. While these individuals might have OpenVMS security management expertise, they are required to maintain security in an environment in which security is frequently not understood, nor is its potential impact fully appreciated.

Considering the growing number of users and the increasingly critical nature of corporate data, organizations must attempt to manage and optimize the complex interactions of all of the security features built into OpenVMS. In this complex task, undesirable compromises are frequently accepted simply because there is insufficient time and inadequate tools to evaluate the current situation and the alternatives available. Accomplishing more without strong management support ranges from merely formidable to well-nigh impossible.

Scope of This Chapter

This chapter provides an overview of OpenVMS security mechanisms. It explains how they work and how they can affect the integrity and security of the system and the information it processes and stores.

This chapter is not a complete and comprehensive coverage of all the facilities, abilities and loopholes of OpenVMS. OpenVMS is a large and complex operating system that has evolved over the past twenty years. The source for the basic operating system is many million lines of code—enough to fill a CD-ROM. Its basic documentation requires thirty-two three-inch binders, and the additional volumes required for its various supplemental languages, tools and facilities can increase this to well over fifty binders.

OpenVMS, unlike other general purpose operating systems on the market today, was actually designed with security as an intrinsic and inseparable part of the operating system. All systems running OpenVMS have the same set of comprehensive privilege and protection mechanisms.

These can be used to limit user access, provide auditing and accountability logs for all users and their actions, and provide a complete record of security-related actions throughout the system. All that is required is selecting and implementing the appropriate subset of these facilities to meet the security and integrity requirements of each system.

First we will discuss the basic mechanisms that control data access from the inside out, including data protection mechanisms and account privileges. Then we will discuss potential ways that these mechanisms can be either enhanced or overridden, depending on how other components of OpenVMS are implemented.

Data Protection Mechanisms

OpenVMS accounts are created in groups with the assumption that it is possible to group users that require access to the same information.

Account UICs

Each OpenVMS account is assigned a User Identification Code (UIC) consisting of a number for the Group the account is in, and a number for which Member of the Group the account is.

All activities, jobs, or tasks on OpenVMS systems are performed by processes that are assigned the UIC of the account that created them. For example, when a user logs in to an OpenVMS system, a process is created for him with his account's UIC. Owner and Protection Fields, Files, directories, disks and all other objects on OpenVMS systems have both an Owner field (the UICs of their owners) and a Protection field, which specify access for each of:

- The System (processes in the System Group, or with SYSPRV).
- The Owner (processes with the same UIC).
- The Group (processes in the same UIC group).
- The World (any process).

For example, a file that allowed:

- The System to have unlimited access
- The Owner to have unlimited access
- The Group to have Read & Execute access only
- The World to have no access

would have a protection field that showed: (S:RWED,O:RWED,G:RE,W).

Access control lists

For cases in which UIC-based protection lacks sufficient flexibility, Open VMS allows the establishment of Access Control Lists (ACLs) for objects. ACLs consist of one or more Access Control Entries (ACEs) that refer either to a UIC, a UIC Group, or to an IDENTIFIER that is created and granted to various accounts to form an arbitrary category. Each ACE also specifies what sort of access is to be allowed. An example of an ACE to grant Write access to holders of the Identifier eFINANCEi would be:

(IDENTIFIER=FINANCE,ACCESS=WRITE)

The reference monitor

All accesses between processes and objects are mediated by the OpenVMS Reference Monitor. Every time a process tries to access a file the Reference Monitor compares the UIC of the process with the Owner and Protection fields of the disk, directory, and file to determine if the access will be granted.

If an ACL exists, the Reference Monitor checks the accesses it allows first. If the ACL does not explicitly confirm or deny the requested access by the process to the object, then the Reference Monitor evaluates UIC-based protection.

Information Access and Protection

The data that forms one of the most valuable corporate assets is stored in various files, contained within directories on disks. Protecting this information involves implementing appropriate protection for the disks, directories, and files. Each disk, directory, and file has settings for both OWNER & PROTECTION, and the interactions between these settings are complex. In addition, each disk, directory, and file can have an Access Control List (ACL) established to further refine access.

Disk protection

The most common way to set up the ownership and protection of disk volumes is to have them owned by the system and to allow all users unlimited access. Additional protection is then established at the directory and/or file level.

However, substantially increased security can be implemented by having a disk device owned by an account, account GROUP, or IDENTIFIER. This can limit access to only those users that need access to the information and applications the disk contains.

Directory protection

Directories are the second line of defense for files stored within them, and should be protected to ensure that only authorized users can access, modify, replace, or delete files within the directory or the directories themselves. The various READ, WRITE, EXECUTE and DELETE (RWED) protections that can be applied to directories and their meanings are:

D   Can delete the entire directory (if it is empty).
W   Can update the directory (i.e., it can replace a file).
R   Can look up files with wildcards (i.e., DIRECTORY *.*).
E   Can access a known file by name in the directory.

Any directory with world write or delete access is open to drastic alteration by a large group of users, and the contents of that directory are at extreme risk. Directories with world read are nominally protected at best, and the information stored in those directories is accessible to all users on the system.

File protection

The protection settings of individual files is the last line of defense against casual attacks on the information stored in the file, and the only complete protection. The various (RWED) protections that can be applied to a file, and their meanings are:

D   Can delete the file.

W   Can update the file's contents (that is, replace, modify or delete contents of the file).

R   Can read the entire contents of the file (that is, COPY or TYPE the file).

E   Can execute the file if it is an executable file or command procedure

Do not assume that a file is protected because its directory is protected. OpenVMS programmers can access a file directly, bypassing all directory protection checking. All files with world WRITE or DELETE access are at risk. Files with world READ might have their contents more widely accessible than intended. All files should be protected as tightly as possible.

OpenVMS Security Issues

Some of the issues addressed in the rest of this section are straightforward: a potential for a security breach exists if the hole is not closed. Other issues, such as the length of passwords, will vary with the organization's requirements. Still other issues are procedural in nature, such as the need to monitor the current system for changes that can affect security.

It is important to understand the implication of each in overall system security, and to define procedures in your policy that are appropriate to your organization.

System setup

The integrity of the operating system itself is the intrinsic limit to the integrity and security of the system as a whole. If the operating system can be modified, either accidentally or otherwise, the entire system is at risk. To ensure a stable operating environment, the following issues must be addressed:

- What version of the operating system is being used?
- Are the operating system files protected against modification?
- Are important system parameters set appropriately?
- Is access to privileged images restricted?
- Is access to various devices controlled?
- Is access to and control of important queues limited?

If any of these are inappropriately set, the system will perform inadequately and the applications it supports will be open to disclosure or corruption.

Installed privileged images

The execution of an installed privileged image grants privileges to users executing the program for the duration of the program's execution. Substantial improvements in overall system security and integrity can be affected by:

- Understanding what programs users run.
- Understanding the privileges these programs require.
- Installing these programs with the required privileges.
- Ensuring that only authorized users can access the program.

Dramatic reductions in system security and integrity can result from:

- Changes in Directory & File Protection, allowing wrong users to run a privileged image.
- Changes in Directory & File Protection, preventing important users from running them.
- Images losing privileges, causing the program to halt.
- Images gaining privileges, granting catastrophic abilities to users.
- Additional images being installed with privileges, giving catastrophic abilities to users.
- New versions of a privileged image is installed, and this version is a Trojan horse.

A recent series of network-oriented attacks on OpenVMS systems was based on replacing the privileged image SYSMAN. The new version of this image records usernames and passwords for privileged accounts, and makes this information available to the attackers. With this information, the attackers gained complete control over the system. It is recommended that all installed privileged images be reviewed regularly to verify the requirement for each and every privilege. In addition, access to installed privileged images should be limited as much as possible.

Consider one of the following:

- Putting an ACL on each installed privileged image to limit access to desired users.
- Building custom DCLTABLES for each user group with only the commands required.

You can also install more critical images with the ACCOUNTING attribute, to provide a log of which users run each program and when. Monitor the installed images on a frequent basis to ensure that:

- There are no changes in Directory or File Protection.
- There are no changes in privileges any image is installed with.
- There are no additional images installed with privileges.
- The ACCOUNTING attribute is not removed for critical programs.
- There are no changes in version numbers of privileged images.
- There are no patches made to a privileged image.

System logical names

OpenVMS uses LOGICAL NAMES to define where operating system directories and files are located. All major application packages supported on OpenVMS systems also use Logical Names to define where information important to the application is stored.

The use of Logical Names allows great flexibility in setting up and modifying both OpenVMS and the applications, because important directories and files can be relocated to other disks as required for performance or growth of the system. System Logical Names used by OpenVMS include the SYSUAF RIGHTSLIST and NETPROXY logicals that point to the critical authorization databases. Redefining these Logical Names can result in:

- Denial of Access to all users.
- Granting of access to undesirable users.
- Granting undesirable attributes (privileges and others) to existing users.
- Granting undesirable access to and from other nodes in the network.
- Complete loss of control over the system.

The effect of changes to the Logical Names defined by an application will vary depending upon the application but can include:

- Complete failure of the Application.
- Data loss and corruption.
- Granting of inappropriate access to undesirable accounts.
- Uncontrolled system crashes.

It is recommended that all System Logical Names be defined as appropriate for the particular system. In particular, the logicals:

SYSUAF
RIGHTSLIST

NETPROXY
SYS$SYLOGIN
SYS$ANNOUNCE
SYS$WELCOME

which refer to files used during every login process.

All Application Logical Names should be defined as appropriate for the particular system. All System and Application Logical Names should be monitored frequently to ensure they are not changed.

Batch and print queue protection

The Digital Equipment Corporation standards for the ownership and protection of EXECUTION & BATCH queues allow any account to SUBMIT a job to any queue, but only accounts with special privileges can alter a queue or any job in a queue once it has been submitted.

Any variation from the standards might:

- Allow any account to start, stop, delete, modify or otherwise control the queue.

- Allow any account to start, stop, delete, modify or otherwise control jobs in the queue.

This could prevent critical tasks and jobs from running, or allow undesirable access to important information, printed forms, executing jobs and important devices. For example:

- Poorly protected check-printing queues allow uncontrolled printing of checks.

- Poorly protected payroll job queues allow uncontrolled access to salary and compensation information.

- Poorly protected execution queue allows submission of jobs with elevated privileges and priorities.

It is recommended that queues with special purposes have and maintain the appropriate protection. Ensure that queues for:

- Important applications have limited access.

- Production and printing of financial documents have all access rigorously controlled.

Account setup

Accounts are the mechanisms by which users gain access to the system; they are the "windows" into the system. In general, the fewer the accounts on a system the better the security. (The most secure system has no accounts, but accomplishes nothing.) In order to mitigate the exposure presented by each account, it should:

- Be uniquely identified.
- Have minimal privileges.
- Have minimal access rights.
- Have a secure password.
- Have limited access to applications.

Additional steps should be taken to ensure that:

- Accounts that are no longer required are disabled or removed.
- Accounts with infrequent usage are disabled until needed.
- Account passwords are carefully selected, regularly changed, and never written down.
- No account setting or attribute is changed without careful review.

Account privileges

OpenVMS accounts can be granted up to thirty-five Privileges. Some of these Privileges directly override the normal results of the Reference Monitor and might force the Reference Monitor to allow the access requested to the Object. The rest of these Privileges merely require more creative use before the user can override the Reference Monitor.

When a process has or gains sufficient Privileges, however temporarily, the process can:

- Alter the protection settings of the operating system, its parameters, files, and processes.
- Override protections applied to files, queues, jobs, and devices.
- Modify existing accounts and define new accounts, including new privileged accounts.
- Stop and destroy the recording of security events and accounting information.
- Halt the system immediately or at some later time.

Any Privileges above a minimal level (usually defined as TMPMBX) should be limited to system managers, security administrators, and other individuals who are entirely trustworthy and knowledgeable of the implications of any action they might take. These people should also need to have complete control of the entire system.

Great effort in reducing Privileges, or reducing the time Privileges are enabled, for all accounts is fully justified.

Password Controls

The password is half of the USERNAME and PASSWORD combination that should be required to access the system. In most organizations the USERNAME part is easy to determine (for example, last name, first name, employee number), which means that only the password is really protecting the account. When the password for an account is easy to guess, then little is protecting the account from abuse.

This chapter includes information on various aspects of passwords, such as password lengths and lifetimes, the appropriateness of passwords selected and, where applicable, use of OpenVMS password protection facilities. Each topic includes an overview of the issue, a review of the security risks, the audit criteria, the audit results, including references to any appendices. Applicable recommendations are also presented.

Accounts without passwords

While OpenVMS encourages the establishment and maintenance of passwords for every account, it is possible to set up an account such that a password is not required. If an account has no password, using the account to enter the system only requires knowing the account's USERNAME. Therefore, all accounts must have passwords.

Minimum password lengths

OpenVMS allows the establishment of a minimum password length for each user. When the user changes his password, choices shorter than the minimum length are not allowed.

The shorter the password, the easier and more likely it is to be guessed. For instance, a three-character password can be "guessed" by a password cracking program in less than four minutes; a four-character password would take less than twenty minutes; and a six-character password would take less than ten days. Many of the major break-ins that have occurred in the past have been successful because of poor password controls.

For any accounts with access to important information, or that can alter the system in any way, eight characters should be considered a minimum.

Maximum password lifetime

There is no restriction in OpenVMS on how many times you can change your password in a given period of time, but there is a maximum period of time that you can retain the same password. The OpenVMS operating system provides for automatic expiration through a date that is retained in the User Authorization File. Warning messages are displayed for several days in advance of the expiration date. When the password expires, the user is forced to change the password in order to log into the system.

The potential exposure caused by any particular password is reduced when passwords are changed frequently. If it takes fifty days to guess a password but it is changed every thirty days, then an active password is unlikely ever to be guessed. Change password lifetime for all accounts to thirty days. Change password lifetime for all accounts to ninety days.

Passwords checked against a dictionary

Starting with version 5.4, OpenVMS can prevent users from choosing any password in a dictionary of over 40,000 of words provided with the operating system. This dictionary can be supplemented or replaced and is simply an indexed file. When a user changes his password, the new password is checked and, if it appears in this dictionary, the user must select another password.

The dictionary checking facility might be disabled for some accounts, allowing users to choose passwords which might be guessable. All accounts should be enabled to check against the system dictionary.

Passwords checked for re-use

Starting with version 5.4, OpenVMS contains a facility to prevent users from re-using passwords within a one-year period. A record of a user's passwords is retained in a history file, and when the user changes the password the new choice is checked against the history file. Choices appearing in the history file are not allowed.

The history-checking facility might be disabled for some accounts, allowing users to re-use previous passwords. This could allow the user to toggle between two favorite passwords, each of which might be guessable. All new passwords should be checked against the account's password history. Remove the account authorization flag, DISPWDHIS, from all accounts.

Inappropriate passwords

Passwords may consist of letters, numerals, certain nonalphanumeric characters, or a combination. All passwords are stored in a one-way encrypted form. This ensures that no one, including the security administrator, can determine the actual password. However, users often choose easily guessable words for their passwords so they can more easily remember them.

A guessable password is an invitation to enter the system. A guessable password could be no password at all, the user's name or another pertinent item of information about the account, a birth date, or even a word that can be found in a list of commonly chosen passwords, such as the list of common North American place names.

All accounts must have passwords. Username (spelled forwards or backwards) may not be used as a password. Account Name (spelled forwards or backwards) may not be used as a password. Owner Name or any part of Owner Name (spelled forwards or backwards) may not be used as a password.

Inappropriate passwords should be changed immediately. These accounts represent a serious risk to the system. Suggest to users a password format that incorporates nonalphanumeric characters, random numbers, or other mechanisms which make a password more difficult to guess.

Generated passwords

Accounts of particular risk can be setup so that the user cannot select his own password. Instead, the system provides a list of generated passwords and the user selects a password from the list. This GENERATED PASS-WORD is particularly safe from password-guessing attacks, and therefore accounts with this kind of protection enabled have good passwords.

It is recommended that all users be forced to use sound and secure password criteria. There is a loophole in OpenVMS that allows users with system privileges to set and change passwords, either for themselves or for other users, effectively ignoring all password controls. Ensure that all passwords are changed, using the SET PASSWORD, command, not the AUTHORIZE command.

Data Volume Protection

Disk devices that are owned by the ACCOUNTS or ACCOUNT GROUPS that need access to the data stored on them can substantially increase security. It is important that each case be carefully documented and monitored to ensure that changes to these settings do not reduce data security or application availability.

It is recommended that ALL disk devices should be investigated to confirm that their ownership and protection settings are appropriate. Use GROUP, PRIVATE, or IDENTIFIER ownership where this would improve information security.

Directory Protection

Directories are the first line of defense for the files stored within them, and should be protected to ensure that only authorized users can access, modify, replace, or delete the directory or files within the directory. The various

(RWED) protections that can be applied to directories and their meanings are:

D   Can delete the entire directory.
W   Can update the directory contents (that is, replace a file).
R   Can look up files with wildcards (that is, DIRECTORY *.*).
E   Can access a known file by name in the directory.

Any directory with world WRITE or DELETE access is open to drastic alteration by a large group of users, and the contents of that directory are at risk. Even directories with world READ are nominally protected at best, and the information stored in those directories might be more widely accessible than intended. It is recommended that all directories with world access be carefully investigated, and all world access removed where operational considerations permit.

File Protection

The protection applied to the individual file is the last line of defense against casual attacks on the information stored in the file, and the only complete protection. The various (RWED) protections that can be applied to a file, and their meanings are:

D   Can delete the file.
W   Can update the file's contents (that is, can replace, modify or delete contents of the file).
R   Can read the entire contents of the file (that is, COPY or TYPE the file).
E   Can execute the file if it is an executable file (that is, @file or RUN file).

Users might think that, since the directory is protected, all files within that directory are similarly protected. This is not the case. Experienced OpenVMS programmers can access a file directly, bypassing the normal directory protection checks. It is therefore vitally important that the individual file's protection be evaluated.

Any file with world WRITE or DELETE access is open to drastic alteration by a large group of users, and the contents of that file are at risk. Even files with world READ are nominally protected at best, and the information stored in them might be more widely accessible than intended.

It is recommended that all files with world access be carefully investigated, and all world access removed where operational considerations permit.

Access control lists

Access Control Lists (ACLs) define additional rules for access to directories and files. Each Access Control List is made up of one or more Access

Control Entries (ACE) that are evaluated in order by OpenVMS when determining file and directory access. This is a sophisticated capability and the rules can become quite complex.

When the number of ACLs is extreme, it might be difficult to keep track of what access is actually being granted and/or denied. In addition, unless ACLs are constructed properly, they can result in different protection than that intended.

When ACLs are used, it is recommended that it be ensured there is no simpler way to protect the directories and files. When UIC-based protection is insufficient, try having the directories and files OWNED by an IDENTIFIER, and GRANTING this identifier to accounts that are to access the files.

Disk scavenging

OpenVMS allows a disk volume to be set up such that data is not actually erased when a file is DELETED. OpenVMS merely notes that the areas on disk that were used by the file are available for other uses.

This can create an opportunity for "disk scavenging" to obtain information. In order to eliminate this opportunity, disks should be set up either /HIGHWATER to cause OpenVMS to write a pattern on all disk space newly allocated to a file, or /ERASE_ON_DELETE to cause OpenVMS to write a pattern to all disk space occupied by a deleted file. The performance impact of using these facilities on system disks could be substantial. These options are not recommended for system disks except under the most severe security risk situations. On nonsystem disks, the use of one of these facilities is recommended.

Undefined owners

Files and directories might be owned by accounts that have been deleted from the system. Also, accounts that existed on the system on which the file was originally created, but which no longer exist on this system, are defined as files with Undefined Owners.

When a file is owned by an Undefined Owner, the owner is actually the UIC of the absent account. Since OpenVMS allows that UIC to be re-used, when a new account is created with it, the files belonging to the previous owner are automatically owned by the new account.

It is recommended that any files owned by Undefined Owners be investigated. Change ownership where possible, to the owner of the file's directory. Other files, or entire directories of files, that are unowned should be moved out of harm's way and put into a safe location until their disposal can be effected.

Misowned and misprotected files

Directories usually are used to group files containing similar information with similar access requirements. This would imply that all files in a given directory would have similar ownership and protection. The existence of files not owned by the parent directory might indicate a deeper problem, such as the fact that a copy command was executed incorrectly. This situation might force the owner of the parent directory to use unnecessarily open protection for the entire directory, just to have access to that file.

It is recommended that these files have their OWNER changed to better reflect their current use.

Network Setup

OpenVMS can support a variety of network and communications protocols, including TCP/IP, NETWARE, and others by adding software or hardware options. These networking options will not be discussed in this section.

The usual communications protocol used in a OpenVMS environment is DECnet, which is available in two versions called *Phase IV* and *Phase V*. This section will discuss DECnet Phase IV, because it is the most prevalent in North America.

The methods by which remote systems can access information and resources on a system, via DECnet, are controlled by various DECnet and AC-COUNT parameters. The DECnet parameters are set by NCP, the Network Control Program, and the ACCOUNT parameters are set by AUTHORIZE.

This section will review the most important of these parameters, and show how they can be used to limit access to a system via DECnet.

DECnet LINE

In order for two DECnet systems to communicate, a connection between them must be established. This connection is referred to as a LINE. Examples of LINEs are Ethernet lines, Synchronous and Asynchronous lines with modems, or eCIi (Computer Interconnect) connections between two VAX systems.

DECnet CIRCUIT

Once a LINE exists between two systems, DECnet establishes a CIRCUIT over which DECnet communicates between the systems. Because a single LINE (for example, Ethernet) can communicate between more than two systems, a CIRCUIT can be considered the logical connection between two systems.

DECnet LINKS and OBJECTS

Once a CIRCUIT is established, a PROCESS on one system can request a logical LINK to an OBJECT on another system. A single CIRCUIT between two systems can have multiple LINKS active at any one time, each LINK carrying information between a PROCESS on one system and an OBJECT on the other system.

It is the creation of LINKS to OBJECTS on other systems that can represent a security exposure. The DECnet parameters affecting the establishment of these LINKS can be divided into two classes:

- Those that control requests from processes on other systems for LINKS to OBJECTS on this system.

- Those that control requests from processes on this system for LINKS to OBJECTS on other systems.

Incoming link controls

The rules that control how or if a LINK can be established to an OBJECT on your system are controlled by various parameters set by the NCP and AUTHORIZE programs. These parameters are used when DECnet is initially started (from the PERMANENT DATABASE), or they might have been modified since (in the VOLATILE DATABASE).

Once a CIRCUIT has been established between a remote system and your system, and a LINK is requested from a PROCESS on the remote system to an OBJECT on your system, the following series of tests is made. The first successful test grants network access.

- When the request is an explicit request for an OBJECT on your system that is an executing process, it will be granted. The OBJECT on your system is responsible for any subsequent identification or authorization checks. (Limit these links by reducing the number of objects that are running processes.)

- When the request uses an explicit USERNAME and PASSWORD (ACCESS CONTROL STRING), and these correspond to a valid account authorized for network access on your system, the link will be granted. (Limit these links by removing NETWORK access for accounts with no need for it, and define proxies for accounts that require network access.)

- If the requested OBJECTSis PROXY INCOMING on your system is enabled, and a PROXY is defined from the account on the remote system to a valid account with network access on your system, the link will be granted. (These links are the easiest to control and document. They present a problem only if the PROXY is to a PRIVILEGED account, or to an account that can access critical information.)

- If the requested OBJECTSis DEFAULT USERNAME and PASSWORD are defined on your system, and these are for a valid account with network access on this system, the link will be granted. (Limit these links by setting the OBJECT USERNAME to a nonexistent or disabled account.)
- If the EXECUTOR DEFAULT NONPRIVILEGED USERNAME and PASSWORD on this system are defined, and these are for a valid account with network access on your system, the link will be granted. (Limit these links by setting the EXECUTOR DEFAULT NONPRIVILEGED USERNAME to a nonexistent or disabled account.)
- When none of the above is true, the link is denied.

Outgoing link controls

When a CIRCUIT has been established between your system and a remote system, and a LINK is requested from a process on your system to an object on the remote system, the following series of tests is made:

- If an explicit USERNAME and PASSWORD is used in the request (an ACCESS CONTROL STRING), then this information is sent to the remote system when requesting the LINK. (This method should be discouraged because it leads users to include valid USERNAMES and PASSWORDS in command files. Instead arrange to have a PROXY defined for users with valid access requirements on remote systems.)
- If the process on your system has no PRIVILEGES, and the NODE NONPRIVILEGED ACCOUNT / USER / PASSWORD is defined for the remote system, then this information is sent to the remote system when requesting the LINK. (Limit these links by setting these values so they refer to an invalid or disabled account on each system.)
- If the process on your system has PRIVILEGES defined, and the NODE PRIVILEGED ACCOUNT / USER / PASSWORD is defined for the remote system, then this information is sent to the remote system when requesting the LINK. (Limit these links by setting these values so they refer to an invalid or disabled account on each system.)
- If your system has NODE ACCESS OUTGOING enabled to the remote system, and your system has OBJECT PROXIES OUTGOING enabled for the object, then the username of the process on your system is sent to the remote system when requesting the LINK. (Limit these links by setting NODE ACCESS to NONE or INCOMING for systems where outgoing access to them is not desired.)
- If the process on your system has the OPER privilege and your system has OBJECT PROXIES OUTGOING enabled for the object, then the username of the process on your system is sent to the remote system when re-

questing the LINK. (Limit these links by limiting accounts with the OPER privilege.)

If none of the above is true, no user information is sent to the remote system when requesting the LINK.

16

Securing Microsoft Windows NT

Ray Kaplan (with Robert Clyde)

*Three may keep a secret if two of them are
dead.*   BENJAMIN FRANKLIN

There is a new kid in the distributed computing neighborhood, Microsoft's
Windows NT (referred to here as NT). However, merely assuming that this
young newcomer is a lightweight that can't compete might be a serious mistake. By some measures, NT is a fierce, skilled competitor—a new chal-
lenger that might actually dominate the fierce client/server war. Its
security-related capabilities are certainly nothing to be discounted.

The good news is that Microsoft's Windows NT has a chance to become
the de facto standard for part of our contemporary distributed infrastructures. Because of the sheer weight of its market presence, it will be seriously
considered by any organization that cares about the success of its distributed computing strategy. NT is everywhere—simply and unarguably ubiquitous. If nothing else, the relative ease of replacing an existing, non-Microsoft
infrastructure with a new one based on Microsoft's Windows NT makes NT
a clear winner by some standards. In addition, Windows NT's position has
been fortified with a base of training, support, applications, and applicable
user experience that at least matches—if not far exceeds—that of any other
operating system's history to date.

The bad news is found in its name. NT stands for New Technology. This
youngster is just what its name says it is—brand NEW. This is important because Windows NT must learn to walk and fight against considerable, well-
established competition—formidable adversaries who have long since learned

to win fights and stay ahead. As an operating system, Windows NT is full of new tricks, exciting possibilities, and new challenges. However, it is inexperienced, naive, and incompletely equipped compared to some of its older adversaries.

Join me now for a brief tour of what is a most interesting challenge in today's operating system security landscape.

A Tour of Windows NT Security

First, a note on terminology. For the sake of brevity and clarity, we often refer to Windows NT as, simply, *NT*. When we want to reference the Windows environment that is currently familiar to most people (for example, Windows 3.1 and its predecessors), we'll refer to it as the traditional Windows environment. Windows 95 is unambiguous.

Also, please note that we discuss NT from a security perspective only. And, we offer you a guided tour-style, lay-of-the-land perspective on NT security rather than concentrating on any single, technical aspect of this new operating system. This chapter contains few technical bits and bytes, because securing any operating system is much more than mastering the technical details.

Security Policy and Its Role for NT Systems

My own experience shows that security problems can always be traced to failures in one of the security policy implementation steps outlined in Chapter 14—policy, architecture, design, implementation, deployment, management, operations, and periodic assessment and evaluation. The biggest security failings in most client/server efforts are related to inadequate or nonexistent security policy. Most client/server efforts generally de-emphasize security until it's too late.

There are several steps to securing anything, including NT:

- Ensure that the security policy adequately expresses top management's wishes. If this doesn't work, the reason may be simpler than you think. Thirty-year industry veteran William H. Murray says he has never seen top management fail to sign off on a properly articulated security policy.
- Ensure that the security policy is implemented throughout each of the security policy implementation steps. These include:

  1. **Architecture** Design a strategy to support the policy by deciding what security services must be offered. For instance, you'll almost certainly need a key distribution authority for any authentication scheme that is chosen. How will the NT environment support this strategy and the organization's business needs?

2. **Design** Distill the architectural specifications into a design that can implement the security policy. For example, NT may have to fit into a larger, enterprise-wide security fabric. Connecting NT to a larger authentication framework may require an interface. How will the NT environment plug into the larger security infrastructure? The dicey part is dealing with details, such as the fact that version 3.5 of NT has no native support for the secure Remote Procedure Call (RPC) mechanism that an existing Open Software Foundation (OSF) Distributed Computing Environment (DCE) uses for its security. Third party products may be required. Are they available?

3. **Implementation** Make the design work. This is where detailed design work meets the real world. While it would be pleasant to discover that DEC and CyberSAFE Corporation both supply products that can interface version 3.5 of NT to a DCE environment, it might be expensive to discover that the wrong one was purchased.

4. **Deployment** Move the finished product through testing, a formal pilot program, and into production. Often, design issues such as scalability show up here. Does the solution really meet the needs of users in a real production environment?

5. **Management and operations** Ensure that the security solution can be managed and operated within the constraints of the security policy.

6. **Periodic assessment and evaluation** Ensure that your NT fabric's security is periodically assessed, evaluated, and reported. Simply setting security up during installation will not ensure that those initial setups are maintained, or that a security-related bug might not actually nullify everything. Capable third party assessment tools that can offer an enterprise-wide view of how the NT environment's security stacks up against the balance of the infrastructure may be needed. Native NT tools will never do this job.

   This process requires talent that is technically and organizationally qualified for each step. Insiders (such as the members of an implementation committee) generally need to be brought up to speed on the latest technology and technical issues. Outsiders (such as consultants) generally need to be brought up to speed on organizational issues. Every step is important. Providing the best possible security technology does no good unless it can be properly managed and operated. A general rule is that the expertise that will actually perform each step should be represented in the planning for every other step. Cross-pollination between steps is as important as ensuring that each is accomplished as a separate project.

- Ensure that the security policy implementation process is franchised by top management—they must make security a priority. Otherwise the whole issue will simply get lost among the other important items competing for attention.

- Ensure that the security policy implementation process is properly funded, managed, and monitored. Few experts work free, and even fewer vendors give viable products away. Projects don't manage themselves and goals don't attain themselves. Plan to devote resources to the NT security project: time, money, and personnel.

This work is not a complete dissertation on the implementation and deployment of security policy. Accordingly, let us look at a few common security policy implementation failures in the Windows environment as pointers for how to proceed with your own efforts.

The security-related problems of new, stand-alone client/server deployments can usually be traced to the fact that security was ignored until after the hardware was deployed. The security-related failures of new client/server systems that are deployed to front-end old-guard back offices can usually be traced to the failure to map the existing security of the back office across its security perimeter, into its new distributed front end.

In other cases, serious security design is compromised by allowing an ad hoc solution to be glued in place quickly. In still other cases, security is recognized as a hard problem and simply deferred until later—get this client/server stuff handled and then go back and fix the security. Sadly, in most of these cases, someone has to go back and redesign or reimplement after the fact . . . when it may be too late to build security properly, from the ground up.

In most cases where client/server security has failed, designers have usually pointed out the need for security, only to have the project's management push it aside. Serious security is expensive and might end up delaying the whole project, especially if it is single-mindedly focused on getting the implementation done in spite of the time needed to solve any hard problems.

Few understand the intrusive nature of robust security and even fewer plan for it. Just because NT was designed and implemented with security as a basic design goal by no means ensures that connections into the NT environment will fit the NT model. Further, even though NT has some sophisticated security features, they do not automatically adjust themselves to your requirements. If all this means expanding the project or delaying its completion to accommodate security, don't give up your security policy. Instead, give up the headlong rush into production.

NT Security Will Default if You Let It

Vendors always have to mold the basic capabilities of an operating system's security system into an operational model that they believe will do a good job of balancing ease of use, control of system resources, and protection of user resources. Ease of installation, management, and operation is also considered. Once this is done, vendors make assumptions about the best way to configure their operational model in the form of a default configuration.

As a result, while a system's security capabilities may be sophisticated and avant-garde, the vendor's choice of an operational model and the default configuration for it may not meet your needs. Sometimes these choices end up creating serious problems. Operational models for the interaction of user groups, permissions, rights, and default user accounts are classic examples. Security administrators only can hope that the vendor made reasonable choices.

A good argument can be made that vendors should ship software—especially operating system security—with a default configuration that initially allows no use of the system or the network. In such a scheme, a system administrator would be required to carefully and painfully open up each and every access path to every system resource, one painful step at a time. Ideally, this would be done under the control of the procedures that implement a security policy. This approach would make the system initially unusable and more difficult to install, configure, and manage, so everyone's job would be more difficult. Accordingly, vendors have traditionally opted for the path of least resistance: maximize ease of use and minimize the amount of work required to install, operate, and use the system. Only the test of time and experience will tell whether the vendor got it all right!

Like other vendors, Microsoft has molded NT into a model they believe is a good basis for secure, flexible operation. It's easy to see that Microsoft intends NT to be immediately and easily usable. They apparently intend that you will use their ideas as starting points for your own customization efforts. Unfortunately, their ideas might not meet your needs.

NT's Guest account is an example of how Microsoft has applied the model they designed for you in the form of the default configuration. Microsoft apparently wants to make your NT easy to use for casual, one-time or occasional use, either locally or from across the network. The existence of a controlled Guest account may meet your expectations and your security policy. However, it is insufficient to stop there. The devil is in the details. Let's look at some NT terminology, and then consider the Guest account as an example of the potential problems that you'll face when you deploy NT.

As with most other operating systems, each user has an account that can be password-protected. Access permissions specify the rules by which system objects (such as files) are accessed. Rights are authorizations for users to perform specific actions. Rights can override permissions.

NT systems are classified either as NT Workstations or NT Servers. A domain has at least one NT Server, usually among several NT Workstations. Accounts are defined either locally or on a domain level. You only can use local accounts on the system on which they are defined. Domain accounts can be used on any system in a domain.

Groups are collections of resource access permissions and system rights that can be assigned to all the members of the group at once. Groups can be defined as either Local or Global.

Local groups have two levels: Workstation Local Groups and Domain Local groups.

1. **Workstation Local Groups** These are called the Local level; they
   - Function on the local workstation.
   - Can contain accounts local to a workstation.
   - Can contain member accounts that do not have to be part of a domain.
   - Can contain user accounts or global groups from their own domain, or other trusted domains.
   - Do not have access to resources on other machines
   - Cannot be used on another workstation or NT Server

2. **Domain Local Groups** These are called the NT Server level; they
   - Function in one domain on an NT Server.
   - Can use resources on the NT Server.
   - Can't use resources on NT Workstations.
   - Can contain user accounts from the local domain or any trusted domain.

Global groups are groups of user accounts that can operate at the domain level. Only user accounts may be members of Global groups. A Global group can be placed into a local group. Global groups can access resources on their workstations, in a local domain, or in a domain that this domain trusts. A Global group cannot contain other Local or Global groups. When an account is created, it automatically becomes a member of the built-in domain users group. Members of the domain users group can access resources wherever the domain users group has permissions.

Finally, let's look at how the default security settings may bite you. On the NT Advanced Server, the Guest account is disabled by default. However, on the NT Workstation, it is enabled by default. Both are preconfigured as a member of the local Guest user group. Guest accounts can be configured to allow local access, network access, access for both, or access for neither. This can be done for workstations or domains. The guest account's profile cannot be changed from the default user profile, and the Guest account cannot be deleted—it can only be disabled or renamed. Now, here are the gotchas. The *Windows NT 3.5 Guidelines for Security, Audit, and Control*[1] point out several problems with having a guest account:

- When the account is enabled, it has no password.

---

[1]*Windows NT 3.5—Guidelines for Security, Audit, and Control*, Microsoft Press, Redmond Washington, 1994.

- The Guest account is a member of the default Everyone user group that contains all users with authorized access. When any user on the system grants access to their resources (for example, files) to members of the default Everyone user group, the Guest account and its Guest user group get that access by virtue of their membership in the default Everyone group. This is compounded by the fact that, by default, the Everyone group has Full Control rights to shared directories. If the Guest account were made a member of the domain users group, users from an untrusted domain could have access to it.

- The default configuration of NT's security may not be appropriate. All aspects of NT's security should be managed to meet your organization's needs as they are defined in your security policy.

Trust Assumptions and Risk

Curiously for some, most of the available information discusses security by starting with a discussion of business goals and basics, such as physical security. For those unpracticed in protecting systems and networks, the realization that they have to carefully sequester their new NT Servers behind locked doors will come as a shock. Even the prospect of using NT's security capabilities to form a common, interoperable, robust, and easily managed security infrastructure may not be a powerful enough incentive for converting to NT. However, the need for autonomy and independence, based on sound risk analysis and the simple need to feel protected from their adversaries, will justifiably keep many organizational units isolated and away from NT.

Even though NT is rich in security features, it is not likely that it can simply be installed to replace even some of the smallest departmental systems. A typical example can be found in many human resources departments. Due to the sensitivity of the applications and data with which HR departments deal, many have invested heavily in add-on security and networking products that carefully protect them from the incursions they fear most— those from other parts of the company over the company's own network. Even if NT comes to include sophisticated capabilities for the complexities of key management and encryption that many of these organizational units require, some units are still likely to stay with their own add-on security products even if they do move to an NT-based environment. If nothing else, the mere fact that they have something different from and incompatible with the rest of the company is reassuring enough for them to shy away from anything that might compromise their independence from the corporate network. People in some organizations simply don't allow their peers on their own corporate network.

Complete solutions to all security problems depend on matching the operating trust assumptions and the results of a risk analysis with the capabilities of the technology. If an NT deployment effort has not included this traditional exercise, it may find itself lost from the start. To a long-time security practitioner, it's painful to note that most LAN environments are out of control because of the apparent pressure to move NT into them. It's not that NT will fall short in most cases. It's more a matter of fear over the possibility that NT's sophisticated solution could abrogate the tenuous peace that now exists between most LANs and their supporting back offices. NT's sophisticated security capabilities certainly have the potential to make things better in a hurry. However, most infrastructures have clearly demonstrated that they are ill-equipped to deal with the security of their LAN mess. Frankly, I've met very few that I'm happy with. As a result, there is justifiable fear that getting a sophisticated tool like NT will be like giving a loaded pistol to a child.

There are some hair-raising possibilities for security disasters when you consider the flexibility and power of NT systems to become rogues, or merely to open gaping holes in the infrastructure by accident. The most serious security problems still happen at the hands of trusted insiders, be they accidental or malicious, and management of a herd of powerful, NT-based domains could be a nightmare. I've seen much less capable technology blow gaping holes in infrastructures.

Finally, there is the question of really, seriously, and completely matching the needs that trust assumptions and risk analysis reveal. In the UNIX chapter, we explored the nature of the problems associated with building and operating a system that can guarantee that different security environments can be kept separate. It's a hard problem that requires special operating system technology. As we will discover momentarily, NT is built to conform to the U.S. Government's class C2 security level. In this discretionary protection model, users are responsible for maintaining the protections on their resources. If they are going to be connected to a corporate network that may bring attackers to their doorstep, some organizational units will require the capability of a system based on the mandatory access control scheme found at the B and A levels of the government's evaluation criteria. In such a model, users are forced to adhere to a security policy by controls that strictly enforce it.

Because the organization of this discussion of NT closely parallels that of the UNIX chapter, we chose to suggest that you read the balance of this section there rather than repeat it here. NT has the potential to become more widespread than UNIX, and it's more capable than the MS-DOS and Windows that it will initially replace. The inevitable result is a requirement that security management become sophisticated enough—quickly enough— to deal with the coming tidal wave of NT. The main thing to stress is the genuine need to cling to the traditional risk assessment and security improvement techniques that have proven successful.

Windows NT Security

NT's security architecture is sophisticated and incorporates the industry's experience. Because the worlds of MS-DOS and the traditional Windows environment have little or no security, they are not useful models. But because NT is a new operating system that was designed with security in mind, a good comparison can be found in older, more established operating systems that are already rich in security features, both by initial design and constant improvement by their vendors. The fact that such old-guard systems bear the scars of their experience helps: the only way you can trust technology is observing its record in the field after you've examined its design and implementation. Other works in progress will compare NT security features to those of the other players in the battle for enterprise-wide computing, such as OS/2 and Novell's NetWare. In the interim, we believe that our choice of OpenVMS and Digital UNIX as comparisons for NT will serve you well. OpenVMS and Digital UNIX are rich in security features. Moreover, the security features of OpenVMS and Digital UNIX are products of considerable evolution.

Every vendor wants to own the largest piece of real estate in the enterprise-wide computing arena. You can't help wondering what effect NT's formidable market presence is having on them. DEC and Microsoft have recently entered into a partnership dubbed "NT Affinity for OpenVMS." Current trends indicate that the maturity and capabilities of OpenVMS will be used to leverage the strengths of NT.

Our choice of OpenVMS and Digital UNIX as comparisons for NT will be of particular interest to anyone using or planning to use Digital's AXP systems, because this hardware runs all three operating systems. Windows 95 is only mentioned in the initial parts of the comparison. It drops out of the discussion naturally, because it was not designed to meet the stronger security requirements that surround the designs of OpenVMS, Digital UNIX, and NT.

OpenVMS

Digital Equipment Corporation released VAX/VMS (Virtual Address eXtension/Virtual Memory System) in 1977. Its best features included compatibility with DEC's RSX operating system that was supported by a PDP-11 instruction set built into the VAX hardware on which it first ran. The VAX was the first 32-bit, virtual memory system to find widespread acceptance.

In 1984, DEC shipped version 4 of VMS, which included a significant enhancement to its security, asymmetric multiprocessing, and a distributed file system in the form of VAXclusters. This era saw strong support for a series of microcomputers: DEC's MicroVAX family. In the late 1980s, security continued to be enhanced as VMS came to support symmetric multiprocessing and saw VAXcluster technology come to use Ethernet as its connectivity. In the early 1990s, still more security was added as VMS came to support several new families of DEC processors, including DEC's 9000 series mainframe and a nearly seamless port to systems based on DEC's new 64-bit AXP Reduced Instruction Set Computer (RISC) processor. DEC's AXP processor family retains the lead as the fastest RISC processor that supports a variety of operating systems, including UNIX and Windows NT.

As these changes were happening, VMS became one of the few commercial operating systems to be evaluated at both the B and C levels of the U.S. Department of Defense's Trusted Computer Security Evaluation Criteria (TCSEC). In 1993, DEC changed the name of VMS to "OpenVMS" to emphasize its POSIX compatibility.

OpenVMS currently has two flavors that offer nearly identical features: a 32-bit version for DEC's VAX architecture and a 64-bit version for its RISC processor family, AXP. OpenVMS has a long-standing reputation for spanning the range of desktop-to-data-center as the glue that holds large-scale, enterprise-wide computing efforts together.

Digital UNIX

Since UNIX was first implemented on a DEC PDP-7 system in 1969, DEC systems have traditionally been key players throughout the evolution of UNIX. DEC's commercial UNIX implementations have included:

- AT&T System V
- Berkeley Software Distribution (BSD)
- Open Systems Foundation (OSF)

DEC's trusted UNIX system implementations include their MLS+ Compartmented Mode Workstation.

Most UNIX derivatives incorporate features from many different UNIX implementations, and Digital UNIX is no exception. Digital UNIX is a proprietary system that grew out of UNIX's own evolution. It is based on OSF's specifications and code for the implementation of a distributed, enterprise-wide computing environment. Consequently, many of its security features are generic to UNIX-based systems in general, as is its own rich set of security features. Like OpenVMS, Digital's UNIX offerings have similar long-standing reputations for spanning the range from desktop-to-data-center.

Windows NT and Windows 95

Windows NT is a new 32-bit operating system designed for operation on multiple platforms. Microsoft released the first version in 1993 and shipped version 3.5.1 in June of 1995. Windows 95 is a new 16/32 bit hybrid derived from MS-DOS and the traditional Windows environment, in an effort that began in 1991 and was shipped in the summer of 1995. NT and Windows 95 can both deliver services to the network because they are designed around a client/server model. Between these two systems, Microsoft now offers solutions that can move the current, traditional Windows environment into enterprise-wide computing.

Windows NT

NT attacks the enterprise-wide computing problem from the top down. NT accommodates the newest breed of Reduced Instruction Set Computer (RISC) processors (e.g., those from MIPS and DEC) with a design that can take advantage of many of their capabilities. NT also runs on traditional Intel-based architectures and has two flavors. Windows NT Workstation is for the desktop, and Windows NT Advanced Server (NT Server) is for the large-scale delivery of network services. Our comparison uses versions 3.5 and 3.5.1 of Windows NT. True to form for a new operating system, Microsoft is introducing new NT features quickly. At this writing, Microsoft is working on the next release of NT (code named *Cairo*), which is believed to be the long-awaited major enhancement that will position Microsoft as a major competitor in the war for client/server dominance.

Windows 95

Windows 95 (code named *Chicago*) was designed to help bridge the gap between existing, traditional, Intel-based (e.g., 386 and 486) Microsoft desktop environments and the world of enterprise-wide computing. Windows 95 attacks the enterprise-wide computing problem from the bottom up. We won't discuss Windows 95 in any detail, except to make sure you don't overlook it. Because Microsoft has just spent an estimated $100 million on advertising to introduce Windows 95 (expecting a profit in excess of $1 billion), there is very little chance that you could ignore it even if you wanted to.

A Note about Security Features

Like other operating system vendors, DEC and Microsoft ship their software with built-in capabilities that are supported. However, this is far from the whole story.

In general, these operating systems all support the following feature categories.

- **Native capabilities** Features that the vendor has built into the operating system as supported capabilities and utilities.

- **Optional, additional vendor products** Features that the vendor makes available as optional, supported products that can be licensed.

- **Custom products** Features that the vendor makes available as optional, supported, custom products that can be licensed. This category is usually licensed in conjunction with the consulting services necessary for support, outside the usual operating system and network support systems.

- **Unsupported products** Features that the vendor makes available as optional, unsupported software that can be licensed.

- **Unsupported freeware** Features that the vendor makes available as optional, unsupported freeware that does not need to be licensed.

- **Third party products** Features that third party providers supply to fill the gaps that the operating system vendors leave in their offerings.

- **User group freeware** Features that the vendor's user group makes available as unsupported software that can be purchased.

- **Unsupported user group freeware** Features that the vendor's user group makes available as unsupported products that are free.

- **General freeware and shareware** Features that operating system users have made available.

- **Custom made software** Given access to operating system source code and a commitment of resources, a good system programmer can add most any feature to an operating system.

Due to of this diversity of sources, the features that are available for a given operating system are virtually limitless. Merely keeping track of the freeware, shareware, and consulting services for a given operating system is a formidable task. The security tools section of Chapter 14 discusses this in some detail. This is important, because it is rare to find a serious computing effort that does not have to supplement an operating system's native capabilities. Security features are certainly no exception to this rule.

OpenVMS, DIGITAL UNIX, and NT are surrounded with a plethora of capabilities from all the above sources. Because DEC has been in the business of client/server, distributed, and enterprise-wide computing for a long time, both OpenVMS and Digital UNIX currently have the broadest selection of security feature implementations. Given the widespread deployment of NT, I might guess that Microsoft will soon have the broadest selection of security feature implementations, though this remains to be seen.

I will only discuss the native, built-in security capabilities of these operating systems in this chapter. However, I'd be remiss if I did not point you to some of the sources for non-native security feature implementations. I've discussed some of these in the resources section.

OpenVMS, Digital UNIX, Windows NT, and Windows 95

As you can see, all these operating systems share a number of similarities. Their differences are both subtle and striking. For example:

- All are designed to run on multiple hardware platforms. OpenVMS runs on DEC's VAX and AXP hardware. One primary design goal for Digital UNIX and NT was platform independence. Windows NT runs on Intel, AXP, MIPS, and others. Digital UNIX currently only runs on DEC's AXP, but may end up running on others as well.

- All have unique cultures. Each one comes equipped with a lengthy heritage that has fostered the development of its own idioms, styles, critics, and fanatic supporters. Given the constraints of their stylistic differences, all are complete computing cultures that can be applied in most any infrastructure.

- All are proprietary. From an interoperability standpoint, published interface standards and compliance with various industry standards make each of these systems "open" to varying degrees.

Hardware abstraction

All three also rely on a Hardware Abstraction Layer (HAL) that makes all processors look the same to the operating system code. The exception to this is DEC's VMS, which is wed to the DEC's older, 32-bit VAX hardware. OpenVMS, Digital UNIX, and NT rely on such code that DEC provides for them in order to run on DEC's AXP RISC processor. Other RISC chip manufacturers provide their own HAL for NT (and other operating systems) that is specific to their processors and the operating system's needs.

Open Systems

Interoperability is only one definition of open. To some degree, OpenVMS, Digital UNIX, and NT can all be classified as "open" by this definition. But those who try to turn the interoperability claims of vendors into the reality of a seamless infrastructure of heterogeneous systems, networks, and applications quickly find that they are naive. There is vast agreement among vendors, standards organizations, and third-party implementers. However, this agreement is far from universally realized and may never reach the interoperability utopia that all of us want and need. Politics, economics, individual implementer choices, substantive technical differences, and overall industry dynamics make interoperability problematic. At this writing, illustrative cases in point are the Microsoft approaches to:

- Authenticated Remote Procedure Calls (RPCs). Their NT mechanisms for these important services are generalized to allow most any security service provider to provide authentication and directory services. However, the NT services are the only ones that are currently supported. Here is what Microsoft says about this: ". . . Microsoft's view is that security service connectivity to DCE and other environments is mandated to minimize cost and truly enable distributed computing services."[2]

- X.500 directory service. More details reveal themselves in Microsoft's Future Products announcements:

    . . . . Cairo will also include a state-of-the-art directory service that is a superset of the X.500 model. Microsoft will provide the technology for this directory service to interoperate with X.500-compliant implementations such as the DCE Global Directory Service.[3]

You can believe that the vendors are going in the right direction. However, those who want to use security and directory service providers, such as Kerberos and X.500, will have to rely on third-party products that provide this interoperability for the short term. A detailed discussion of these individual issues is beyond the scope of this chapter, so I'll restrict my discussion to security services except for a few short comments.

TCP/IP world's most prevalent name service is the Domain Name Service (DNS). It is not extensible and its standards bearers have steadfastly refused to expand its capabilities so it could become a directory service. Their diligence has been rewarded by DNS's position as the lean, mean name service that keeps the majority of TCP/IP-based networks (including the Internet) glued together. In addition, DNS is one of the best examples of a client/server, distributed application. It is based on a highly distributed and redundant database.

But, because DNS has been slow to expand its capabilities, many name and directory-related network service demands have gone wanting as the larger and vastly more complicated efforts of the X.500 directory service evolved. X.500 is an important standard because it is being used as the basis for some of the work undertaken to solve the sticky problem of key and certificate distribution for the developing, public-key-based cryptography infrastructure. The Open Software Foundation's (OSF) directory services use an X.500 compatible Application Programmer Interface (API).

Because Microsoft is birthing NT as a serious contender amid all of this turmoil, they have seized the opportunity to up the ante. The Windows Internet Naming Service (WINS) is their name and directory service entry. It is designed to be compatible with NT, DCE, and DNS. Because Microsoft seems to be shedding their previous reputation for shipping software that does not work to customers who help them make it work, WINS may be-

---

[2]Microsoft www pages on *DCE*. Found at http://www.microsoft.com/.

[3]Microsoft www pages on *Full DCE Clients*. Found at http://www.microsoft.com/.

come the much needed bridge between the current disparate name and directory service idioms.

The non-Microsoft portions of the industry must also be considered carefully. Industry coalitions, such as X/Open, Common Desktop Environment (CDE), and Common Open Software Environment (COSE), are not merely waiting for NT to dominate.

Feature Creep

Perhaps the toughest part of developing a security policy and implementing it is discovering that some version of some software or hardware in your infrastructure can't support it, even with the addition of a third-party solution. Such cases are usually foreseen by complete work in the design phase, exemplified by additional security capabilities that show up (for example, new security features in the operating system), or rectified by customized solutions.

Vendors that wish to stay competitive add features as quickly as they can. Until recently, there has not been much of a market for security features outside of the military. Now that a good many commercial organizations are actually starting to pay for security, the battle for dominance in security features is a fierce one. Accordingly, the facts as I know them today will change by the time you read this, especially the relative positions of these operating systems in relationship to each other in specific areas. Therefore, the details of exactly how a specific feature of the current version of one system compares to those of another are left for future works, and for you to explore using your security policy as guidance. Where appropriate, version numbers are mentioned.

A General Comparison

Table 16.1 shows a basic comparison of the operating system features. All are clearly robust operating systems. Windows 95 is included for color. One difference is that Windows NT Workstations are designed for use by one local, interactive user at a time. The NT Advanced Server allows multiple users to access a Windows NT server at the same time. All the operating systems, including Windows 95, are true multitasking systems (able to have more than one process executing on one processor at the same time). However, Windows 95 does not support multiprocessing (the ability for a process to use more than one processor at the same time) and the others do.

As you can see, precisely enumerating differences is problematic. Accordingly, from here on we'll take a higher level perspective to finish introducing you to NT and its security. All three operating systems have an executive that does memory management, process management, and I/O. However, each has its own ways to do things.

TABLE 16.1 A General Comparison

Feature	OpenVMS	Digital UNIX	Windows NT	Windows 95
Protected memory	X	X	X	X[1]
Multi-user	X	X	X[2]	X[2]
Multi-tasking	X	X	X	X
Multi-processing	X	X	X	
Distributed architecture	X	X	X	X
Command shell	DCL[3]	sh,csh,ksh[4]	Win32[5]	
GUI	Motif	Motif	Windows 95[6]	Windows 95[6]
POSIX	X	X	X	
X/Open	X	X		
On-line documentation	Bookreader[7]	UNIX Man	Doc On-Line	
C2 security	X	X	X[8]	
B1 security	X[9]	X[10]		
B2 security			X[11]	
CMW		X[10]		
OSF DCE[12]	X	X	X	
Standard objects[13]	X	X	X	X

[1]Windows 95 does its best to protect memory, but since MS-DOS and previous Windows versions can freely write to physical memory, this is a difficult problem.

[2]NT Workstations and Windows 95 support one user. However, both systems can serve as network service providers.

[3]The Digital Command Language (DCL) is a fully featured, general-purpose, command-line interpreter. It is a programming language that is routinely used by users and system administrators alike. Applications can use it as their command-line interface. Compared to a UNIX shell, DCL is generally classified as overweight.

[4]Shells, of which there are many, are fully featured, general-purpose command-line interpreters—each with its own unique philosophy and capabilities. Most of them are routinely used as a programming language by users and system administrators alike. Applications can use it as their command-line interface. Compared to DCL, a shell is usually lean and mean (not classified as user-friendly, by design).

[5]The NT command prompt comes from NT's Win32 subsystem since Win32 handles all of NT's keyboard and mouse I/O. When you issue the Run command, Win32 establishes an appropriate Virtual DOS Machine (VDM) for the program that was invoked. Currently, NT supports MS-DOS, Win16 (traditional Windows), OS/2, POSIX, and Win32 VDMs.

[6]For want of a better way to be accurate in the midst of Windows and NT, suffice it to say that Windows 95 and NT will apparently come to look more or less the same to their users.

[7]Online documentation for OpenVMS can include applications and source code. It can all be made available networkwide.

[8]NT is known to be completing its evaluation under the C2 level of the NCSC's TCSEC.

[9]The security-enhanced variant of OpenVMS is called SE OpenVMS and has been evaluated at the B1 level of the NCSC's TCSEC.

[10]The MLS+ variant of Digital UNIX is being evaluated at the B1 and CMW levels of the NCSC's TCSEC.

[11]Microsoft has indicated that NT is being evaluated at the B2 level of the NCSC's TCSEC in the form of a variant from a third party.

[12]All offer some compatibility with the Open Software Foundation's Distributed Computing Environment.

[13]Everyone is on the object bandwagon these days and all of these operating systems offer some compatibility with the developing standards in this area. Microsoft and DEC have teamed up to provide DEC's Object Broker for NT and Microsoft is making sure that its Object Linking and Embedding (OLE) stays out in front of the feature wars. The DEC/Microsoft partnership is important since DEC's Object Manager is built on top of DEC's DCE architecture—including security.

File Systems

For want of an orientation for the forthcoming comparison of security features, I've picked file systems for discussion here. Because discussing file protections seems to be one of the easiest ways to discuss access controls at the same time, this will serve as a good introduction. Equally valuable comparisons are possible using any number of other operating system features.

A quick look at the file systems of these three operating systems reveals that Columbus was right. The world is really flat. Files are just blocks of data that are accessed by pointers. In general, the capabilities of all three operating systems allow the actual data to be located almost anywhere. The two most common locations of data are:

- On the disk of the local system or a remote system.
- In the memory of the local system or a remote system.

Directories are imposed by data structures and pointers that offer the illusion of a two-dimensional space. The depth of these two dimensions is limited by each file system's design. Network connectivity adds another level of abstraction by giving the illusion of a third dimension, whose depth is determined by the number of remote files systems that are available and their structures. Figure 16.1 shows a general construct to illustrate the concept.

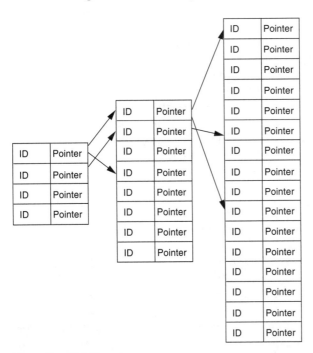

Figure 16.1 Flat file systems

In general, directories are just data structures that have pointers to the files they contain. Directories can generally contain other directories. Data structures of IDs and pointers are used to locate exactly where the data is actually located.

Typically, the dimensions of this model are constrained only by the limits of the technology used to implement them. These limits include processor speed, disk limitations (e.g., capacity, transfer access, and rates), operating system design, network propagation delays, management issues, economics, and the politics of inter- and intra-organizational connectivity. Given that the required trade-offs in the constraints are made correctly, the theoretical limits and available products already far exceed even the wildest imagination. However, the practical aspects of interfacing large distributed file systems to one another, and their management, tend to be the dominant limiting factors. All by itself, the interconnection between heterogeneous file systems across their security perimeters is a significant stumbling block.

Through some level of abstraction, all remote file access can be considered an implementation of a client/server model by file access standards. Only OpenVMS has a completely distributed file system.

VMSclusters

VMSclusters are interconnected, closely cooperating systems that can directly share resources, such as a common file system. In a VMScluster, each system's view of shared resources (such as the common file system) is carefully and dynamically synchronized between all of them. In addition, each system can have its own local storage that is not available as a shared resource. By comparison, most other remote file access schemes access remote files by "attaching" to the remote file system through a client/server-based scheme. This includes the ones that are currently used by Novell, Digital UNIX, NT, and most others. In contrast, the VMScluster design allows systems to share and run the same copy of the operating system across all of its systems, although they don't have to do this. This capability includes booting from the network.

File systems compared

Figure 16.2 illustrates the differences between these three operating systems' file systems.

In the OpenVMS world, the root of the file system is at the level of a disk volume, and all files fall under it. In UNIX derivatives, such as DIGITAL UNIX, the root of the file system is the focal point for all devices on the system that can be treated as a file. In most UNIX systems, most everything (including devices and memory) is treated like a file under a common root directory.

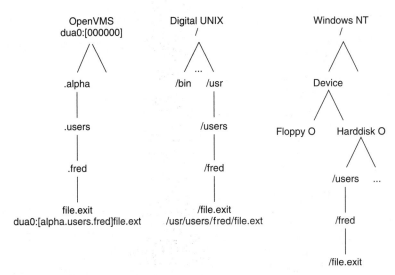

Figure 16.2 File system comparisons

Besides DEC's distribution of OpenVMS's native Files-11 file system with VMScluster technology, DEC and third parties make it available across many networks, such as DECnet. Digital UNIX supports its native file system (Virtual File System) and many others, including DEC's Advanced File System, the traditional UNIX file system, and extensive CD-ROM support. NT supports its native NT File System, the MS-DOS FAT file system, and OS/2's High Performance File System. Because Network File System (NFS) rides on top of an operating system's file system, all three operating systems support it and a variety of others, using either peer-to-peer or client/server network access idioms. Only OpenVMS and Digital UNIX support in-memory file systems.

The UNIX change root. A unique feature of UNIX derivatives is the `chroot` command. After a `chroot`, a user cannot access any file outside the target directory. Common practice is to make copies or links within the restricted directories to those files that `chrooted` users need. A danger is that files inside the chroot environment will be mapped to sensitive devices (e.g., disks) or programs that are insecure (e.g., Xmenu). Figure 16.3 shows how the user's view of their directory structure changes as a result of a chroot.

OpenVMS offers a similar capability as part of its ability to make users captive in a predefined environment that can include a portion of the file system. NT only supports the specification of a default file system when the user is authorized. In all cases, a clever user can get around these restrictions. However, these restricted file system environments make this more difficult because access controls still govern access. To violate these controls, a user must find a part of the file system that they can access.

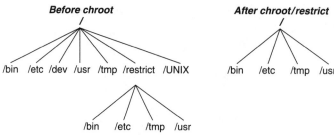

Figure 16.3 Users' views of chroot

Security Feature Comparison

While each of these systems lacks compatibility with all or part of various standards (de facto or otherwise) that may be desirable, their vendors know that they don't stand alone in the world of interoperability. The shopping list of security-specific standards that are important is lengthy, as are the broader contexts of operating system, interoperability, hardware, and software standards activities. This comparison is based on categories of security capabilities.

Comparison criteria

The security capabilities model used for this comparison includes Identification and Authentication, Access Controls, Object Reuse, Network Controls, and Audit Trails. These comprise the basic set of capabilities required by the three dominant standards bearers for the evaluation of trust in computer systems:

- U.S.: National Computer Security Center's (NCSC) Trusted Computing Security Evaluation Criteria (TCSEC).

- Canada: Canadian System Security Center's Canadian Trusted Computer Product Evaluation Criteria (CTCPEC).

- Europe: Information Technology Security Evaluation Criteria (ITSEC).

I picked out the TCSEC (or "Orange Book," as it is called) because it is the best-known one. Each publication in the NCSC's evaluation criteria documentation is nicknamed according to the color of its cover, which is usually bright and distinctive. Figure 16.4 offers a capsule view of the TCSEC's divisions.

Among other measures, trusted system evaluation criteria include a measure of the confidence that can be placed in a system's ability to enforce a security policy. This is called assurance. A good way to think about this is its economics. Figure 16.5 shows how the cost of this increases as more stringent security is added in higher levels of the TCSEC. It is not a linear progression.

As explained in the UNIX chapter, a Compartmented Mode Workstation (CMW) represents an attempt to overcome the problems associated with implementing trusted system technology in a widespread and inexpensive manner. As such, it is a mix of security features. While the CMW has fallen into disfavor of late, it's still interesting to see how all the TCSEC's divisions stack up against one another. Table 16.2 shows a comparison between the CMW and other divisions of the TCSEC.

Most operating systems include security features from evaluation levels higher than their evaluation level, because they are generally trying to keep up with their competition and offer good solutions to their customers. An example is found in Access Control Lists (ACLs). While not required at the C2 level of the TCSEC, most vendors provide them in their C2 systems. Finally, the C2 level is not magic. By some standards, it is inadequate. For instance, it is permissible to have a 1-character password under C2.

Another example is found in the concept of Least Privilege. A typical UNIX-based system implements an "all or nothing at all" philosophy for the control of system privileges with the Super User. Most system administrators will tell you that this does not afford the granularity necessary to properly control a system. Minimizing the number and power of privileges that each user has, including the system administrator, allows the role of security administrator to be defined and enforced. This is not required until the B2 level of the TCSEC. Accordingly, some C2 level UNIX systems incorporate Least Privilege by dividing up root permission into specific categories

D-Insecure-no security
C-Discretionary protection
      C1 Discretionary security protection
      C2 Discretionary access protection
B-Mandatory (nondiscretionary protection)
      B1-Labeled security protection
      B2-Structured protection
      B3-Security domains   **Figure 16.4**   TCSEC divisions
A-Verified protection
      A1-Verified design

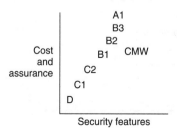

Figure 16.5 Nonlinear cost curve of increase security

TABLE 16.2   Selected TCSEC Division Features Compared

CMW vs Orange Book (DoD 5200.28-STD)
Using DEC's MLS

TCSEC divisions and classes	CMW features	Features missing from CMW
B1	Audit Object reuse Design/test documentation Identification-authentication System architecture Design specification verification Security testing	
B2	Mac labels Configuration management	Covert channel analysis Modular OS Formal model
B3	Trusted path Trusted facilities Management (TFM) Trusted recovery Trusted facilities manual Security features user's guide DAC (ACLs)	Covert channel analysis Formal model Separate domains Audit
A1	Trusted distribution	Security testing Design/verification documentation Configuration management Formal model Security analysis Formal covert channel analysis
Additional CMW features		
	Terminal IDs Dail-up Physical Annual accreditation Communications Access authentication	System security plan Protection Labels Personnel TEMPEST

of privileges and authorizations. While OSF includes Least Privilege as a C2 capability, the C2 levels of OpenVMS and NT do not include it.

DEC has succeeded in getting OpenVMS evaluated under both the C2 and more stringent B1 levels of the TCSEC. DEC is known to be pursuing that course with DIGITAL UNIX with its MLS+ variant. MLS+ is also being evaluated under the CMW level of the TCSEC. This is possible because Digital UNIX is based on the OSF microkernel architecture, which was designed to be evaluated under the B3 level of the TCSEC. As a differentiation, as the most common System V UNIX derivative, SVR4 cannot be evaluated at the B3 level because its kernel is not small and compact enough. However, B-level features are provided for SV UNIX in the form of enhancements to SV Release 3.2 (which is not compatible with SVR4). B level evaluation of SVR4 awaits a substantial redesign of its kernel.

Microsoft indicates:

- Both flavors of NT are now in the final stages of evaluation under the C2 level of the TCSEC and the Trusted Network Interpretation (TNI) or "Red Book."
- NT is being evaluated under what is likely to become Europe's common trusted system security evaluation criteria: the ITSEC.
- Third parties are working on NT enhancements for the B2 level of the TC-SEC.

The UNIX chapter provides a view of trusting computer systems that you can use to get your feet on the ground. The book *Computer Security Basics* (see bibliography at the end of this chapter) provides a good overview of the structure and requirements of the TCSEC and what they mean. Because current evaluation criteria are strict treatments of security issues in a military context, the problem for a commercial organization is to decide how to apply it to their needs. There is no dispute over the fact that evaluation criteria are necessary. The dispute is over what features are needed and how those features are applied. Contrary to popular belief, the TCSEC is applicable to commercial organizations. A further view of this is provided by *Trusted Systems: Applying The Theory in a Commercial Environment* (see bibliography).

As a result of everyone's experience with trying to apply evaluation criteria for over a decade, it's important to note that the TCSEC is under revision and is being renamed *The Federal Criteria for Information Technology* (or, *Federal Criteria* for short). Copies of current work on the Federal Criteria can be obtained from the National Institute of Standards and Technology (NIST). Suffice it to say that serious security requires rigor and experience. Some organizations are experienced with it because they are mandated to use specific technology in particular situations. These organizations include government organizations (such as the military) and com-

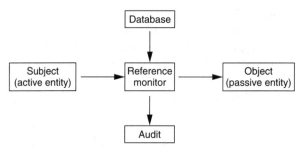

Figure 16.6 The reference monitor model

mercial organizations (such as those who value their information highly). Each organization has to sort this puzzle out for itself.

The Reference Monitor Model

Actually implementing security is an interesting challenge, especially for an operating system designer. One of the only ways that the industry has learned to build computer systems that can be trusted is based on a simple concept: carefully control every attempt to access data. For clarification, the security reference monitor model that was presented in the UNIX chapter is repeated in Figure 16.6. The reference monitor model is how most systems that can be trusted implement these concepts.

The reference monitor is a small, easily verified module of operating system code that mediates every access attempt of active entity to access passive entities in the system. The reference monitor is implemented as a small, well-structured set of code and provides a tamper-proof audit trail.

The active entities are called subjects and include system constructs that represent actual human users, such as process contexts. Passive entities are called *objects* and include system resources, such as files on disk. The rules which govern these access attempts are known as the *reference monitor database*. The set of hardware, firmware, and software that implements this mediation is called a *Trusted Computing Base* (TCB).

Reference monitors compared

The reference monitor's database is not really a true database. Moreover, the access rules for each type of access that the reference monitor controls are associated with the entity that is being accessed. Accordingly, the access rules for each of type of entity are stored in an appropriate place for each entity. For instance, it should be obvious that efficiency dictates that the access rules for a data structure that is in a system's memory needs to be stored right along with the data structure in that system's memory, even when it also is held in permanent storage on disk in a file. Therefore, it's easy to see that each operating system's reference monitor is stored in a variety of different locations specific to that operating system's design and the nature of the entities involved. These locations typically include:

- **User authorization files** Examples include NT's Security Accounts Manager (SAM) database.

- **The file system itself** For example, the file protections and Access Control Lists (ACLs) for NT's NT File System (NTFS) are stored in each file's security descriptor block as part of each file's Master File Table (MFT) on disk.

- **A portion of each process's memory allocation** For example, the access rights that an active NT's process has is stored in a subtree of NT's Registry. The Registry is one of the many innovations that Windows 95 and NT have in common.

Table 16.3 shows some of the items that make up the reference monitor database for each of the operating systems we are considering. As you can imagine, a complete treatment of these significant details is available in the technical documentation of each operating system. NT's specifics can be found in the technical references listed in the resources section of this chapter.

As you can guess, the reference monitor itself is not easy to implement. In fact, it is so difficult to do that most systems don't really have one set of

TABLE 16.3 Selected Reference Monitor Database Elements

OpenVMS	OSF/1	Windows NT
User authorization files	passwd and group files	SAM database
UIC-based[1] object protection	UID/GID[2] based protection	Owner can change ACLs
Access control lists (ACLs)	Multiple group ids (GIDs)	ACLs
Privileges and rights identifiers	root UID (superuser)	Rights
Installed images (programs) and Protected Subsystems[4]	SUID and SGID[3] file properties and Protected Subsystems[4]	Protected subsystems[4]

[1]UIC stands for User Identification Code, a two-part number used by OpenVMS to uniquely identify a user. The first number is the group number, separated by a comma from the second number which represents a unique member within a group.

[2]UID stands for User ID and GID stands for Group ID. The UID uniquely represents a particular user and controls the access that that particular user will have. Each user may have one or more GIDs representing the groups to which a user belongs.

[3]SUID and GID stand for the Set UID and Set GID properties, which can be set on a file. As will be explained later, these properties can be used to set up prvileged programs without assigning privileges to users.

[4]Another terminology conflict. "Protected Subsystems" are not the same thing in OpenVMS as they are in Digital UNIX and NT. However, for the sake of this comparison, all of them are represented to their respective reference monitors by their access control information.

code that implements it. Parts of the reference monitor itself are often scattered throughout the operating system and its components. Of course, there are reference monitor implementations that have done the work to meet more rigorous criteria. Multics and some B level UNIX derivatives meet the requirements of the B level of the TCSEC. This is where we start to see a security policy being imposed on the user, to strictly confine them to a specific, carefully controlled compartment. Starting at the B level of the TCSEC, users can't change the protections on resources they own beyond what the security policy allows. Constraints in this class are called *mandatory access controls* because the system forces the user to adhere to the security policy codified in the reference monitor's database. The access controls that are found at the C2 level of the TCSEC are called discretionary access controls.

Security-related architecture features

An in-depth discussion of each operating system's security architecture is underway. In the meantime, it's sufficient to say that the security-related architecture of OpenVMS, Digital UNIX, and NT are similar. Each of their reference monitor model implementations exert control over the securable objects that it manages. While they are not considered to be object-based systems like the NeXTSTEP UNIX derivative, all three use an object-based model to represent protectable system resources (such as files, processes, and memory). The difference between them is how central security is to their basic designs.

OpenVMS

OpenVMS does not implement the reference monitor as a security-related subset or secure kernel; it mirrors the basic concept. OpenVMS groups its protected objects into subclasses of object classes. Each object class groups objects that behave in a particular way and have a common set of attributes. Current OpenVMS protected object classes include:

- **Capabilities** System controlled access (i.e., a vector processor).
- **Common event flag clusters** Inter- and intra-process notification posting flag data structures.
- **Devices** Processor-connected data communication peripherals.
- **Files** Native, Files-11-based files, and directories.
- **Group and system global sections** Sharable memory sections.
- **Logical name tables** Resource alias names.
- **Queues** Batch, terminal, server, or print spooler job queues.

- **Resource domains** Lock Manager resource access synchronization name spaces.

- **Security class** Security class elements and control routines.

- **Volumes** Files-11 formatted, mass storage media mounted on devices.

OpenVMS collects most security-related, object manipulation commands under the SET SECURITY command language command.

Digital UNIX

Following OSF, Digital UNIX is based on the Carnegie Mellon University Mach kernel. Accordingly, its security is modular and compiled into the kernel, depending on a particular version's requirements. For instance, variants that meet the TCSEC's C and B levels require different modules to be compiled when the operating system is built. However, Digital UNIX does not currently implement some common features in its C2 offering, although it certainly could by its design. For instance, ACLs are likely to show up in version 4.

NT

All system resources in NT are treated according to its object-based design. Objects are run-time instances of an object type that is manipulated by a process. Each object has an object type, a list of operations that can be performed on it, and a set of object attributes. Objects can have subjects. Objects and subjects are manipulated by functions, and NT's Object Manager provides objects with retention, naming, and security.

Each object has data structures that contain information about the object, including its access controls. When an NT process wants an object, it acquires the object's handle (which points to the object) and instantiates the object. An object handle includes access control information and a pointer to the object. For instance, the handle for the Access Token object type contains:

- The object type designation
- Body attributes
  ~Security ID (SID)
  ~Group ID(s)
  ~Privileges
  ~Owner SID
  ~Primary group SID
  ~Default ACL
  ~Source
  ~Primary/impersonator designator

~Current impersonation levels
~Other information

- Object services
  ~Adjust token groups
  ~Adjust token privileges
  ~Get token information
  ~Open process token
  ~Open thread token
  ~Set token information[4, 5]

Objects are catalogued in an object namespace that is organized in domains of directories. NT object types include directories, object type, symbolic link, semaphore, and event, process and thread, section and segment, port, and file. New objects can also be added to NT as needed.

Securable objects are objects that have a security descriptor. They include both named and unnamed objects. There is considerable detail to be explored in NT's object-based design. So we don't get mired in it, here are the major groups of NT's current securable objects with a few comments on each:

- **Files** Only NT File System (NTFS) files and directories are securable objects.

- **Inter process mechanisms** NT provides six Interprocess Communication Mechanisms (IPCs): named pipes, mailslots, NetBIOS, Windows sockets, report procedure calls (RPCs), and Network Dynamic Data Exchange (NetDDE.) Mailslots and pipes are securable objects. Mailslots are file system-based IPCs that NT includes for LAN Manager compatibility. Named pipes are file system-based IPC based on OS/2 APIs.[6]

- **Kernel objects** As you would expect, NT's securable objects include processes. They also include threads (executable objects), access tokens, and file mapping objects.

- **Window management objects** NT splits the Windows environment into four objects: window stations (screen, keyboard and mouse), desktops (top-level window for a workstation), windows (subject of a desktop), and menus (desktop subjects).

- **Registry objects** NT's configuration database. Applications can use the registry as well. For instance, Microsoft Word version 6 puts configuration and user option information in the registry.

---

[4]*Windows NT 3.5—Guidelines*.

[5]Helen Custer, *Inside Windows NT*, Microsoft Press, Redmond Washington, 1993.

[6]Robert Cowart, *Windows NT Unleashed*, Second edition, Sams Publishing, Indianapolis, 1995

- **Service objects**   NT's Service Control Manager objects.

- **Synchronization objects**   These objects contain dispatchers that synchronize kernel activities. Synchronization objects include object Semaphores, events, mutexes, and critical sections. The user-visible objects that support synchronization include processes, threads, events, event pairs, and timers.

- **Private objects**   Objects created by applications.

Functions that manipulate the security descriptors of NT securable objects currently include groupings for:

- Files

- User (or window management) Objects

- Kernel Objects

- Registry Objects

- Private Objects

As you can imagine, each securable object has functions that are appropriate. These functions are named according to the object type that they manipulate and the function that they perform. For instance, file objects have GetFileSecurity and SetFileSecurity functions and Kernel objects have four functions that include Get and Set ObjectSecurity routines for both user and kernel objects.

Each securable object's security attributes are described by a security descriptor. Its attributes can include:

- Owner

- Primary group

- Access Control Lists

- Discretionary ACL

- System ACL

Security descriptors store this information in the form of Security Identifiers (SIDs) and ACLs. Security descriptors are manipulated by their associated Win32 object functions. For instance, Window object functions include a SetSecurityDescriptorSacl call to set system ACL information.

Security descriptors come in two flavors: absolute and self-relative. An absolute format descriptor contains pointers to its information. Self-relative descriptors contain information in one, contiguous block of memory. Absolute descriptors are used when default settings are required because an application can simply initialize a descriptor structure that points to pre-existing components.

Protected Subsystems

According to classic security terminology, protected subsystems are application programs that carry out functions for groups of users, maintain common data, and protect the data from access outside of that group. Unfortunately, each of these operating systems has a slightly different idea about them. However, the OpenVMS definition applies to all three:

> A protected subsystem is a gatekeeper to the objects belonging to the subsystem. Users have no access to the subsystem's objects unless they execute the application that serves as the gatekeeper. While a user is executing the gatekeeper, their context gains access rights to the subsystem's resources. When the user exits the gatekeeper, their context gives up those access rights.

In all cases, the idea is to have a program access protected resources on behalf of a user, without directly granting the user the same access that the program is using. Typically, programs need this access only in well-defined cases and periods of time. Providing controlled access to protected resources is a significant programming challenge. To ensure that its user can't accidentally access the protected resource in ways that were not intended, a program usually simply enables and disables privileges as they are needed. This is usually a tricky programming problem. Many times, a bug will accidentally allow the user more access than he is supposed to have, or will allow the user to retain access past the point beyond which it is actually needed. To prevent this breach of security policy, protected subsystems are used to carefully control how a user's context is granted access to protected resources.

OpenVMS

In OpenVMS, protected subsystems are established by the security manager by:

- Establishing protected subsystem manager access rights.
- Creating rights identifiers for subsystem managers (with SUBSYSTEM and RESOURCE control attributes).
- Granting those identifiers to the subsystem's managers (with SUBSYSTEM and RESOURCE control attributes).
- Protecting subsystem resources (including their directories, programs, and data files).
- Identifying the subsystem's resources with Access Control Lists (ACLs) that contain the subsystem's SUBSYSTEM rights identifier in their Access Control Entries (ACEs).
- Creating Access Control Lists (ACLs) that allow appropriate access for subsystem users by including their rights identifiers in the ACEs of the subsystem resource's ACLs.

The security administrator must identify each Files-11 volume as trusted with the /SUBSYSTEM switch on the MOUNT command before protected subsystems can be used on that volume. By default, the ability to use protected subsystems is enabled only on the system disk. When an authorized user executes a protected subsystem program, the protected subsystem's rights are added to the user's process rights list, but only for the execution of that program. Abnormal termination also causes the protected subsystem's rights to be removed from the user's process rights list.

Digital UNIX

In Digital UNIX, a protected subsystem is a more fundamental part of the TCB. Digital UNIX protected subsystems are groupings of controls by function. Table 16.4 lists these groups, their database names, and the controls that they catalogue.

These resources are protected with the group ID of the group that has access rights to access the groups programs and data. A protected subsystem's data can't be accessed directly—it must be accessed with the appropriate program. For instance, a user can't simply use the more utility to list the contents of /etc/auth/system/ttys. Programs that access protected subsystem data are SGID on execution to the subsystem's group.

NT

In NT, protected subsystems take two forms: Environmental and Integral. Both are user mode server processes that communicate by passing messages under the control of NT's Local Procedure Call (LPC) facility. They are created at boot time and run in user mode. LPC calls isolate protected subsystems from the executive. By using this client/server model, the NT executive's parts can run in many different, separate process contexts. In contrast, many traditional operating systems run in only one special process context. While OpenVMS and Digital UNIX offer a mix of these philosophies, NT's basic design is centered on a client/server model.

Environmental subsystems. NT was designed to provide a seamless graphical interface to applications written for other operating systems. An environmental subsystem is a user-mode server that provides an API to one of those operating environments. Environmental subsystems are emulators of these operating systems. They include:

- **Win32** All environmental subsystems are optional except Win32. The Win32 subsystem is preeminent because it handles mouse, keyboard, and screen I/O for all subsystems.

- **POISIX** Implements the IEEE 1003 standard and provides a C-based API.

TABLE 16.4 Digital UNIX Protected Subsystems

Group	Database name	Controls
Users	/tcb/files/auth/<a-z>/username	Username and ID
		Encrypted pwd
		Audit char
		Pwd gen param
		Successful login times and terminals
		Unsuccessful login times and terminals
Defaults	/etc/auth/system/default	Default pwd gen params
		Default # of unsuccessful logins / user allowed
		Default # of unsuccessful login attempts / terminal
		Default device assignment parameters
Terminals	/etc/auth/system/ttys	Device name
		User ID and time stamp of last unsuccessful login
		User ID and time stamp of last successful login
		Delay between login attempts
		# of unsuccessful attempts allowed before locking
Files	/etc/auth/system/files	Protection attributes for system files
		Pathname, owner / group, mode, and type
Devices	/etc/auth/system/devassign	Type
		Pathname

- **OS/2** Supports traditional x86-based, character cell applications on non-RISC processors.

- **MS-DOS—Virtual DOS Machines (VDM)** Supports Win32 and OS/2 real-mode applications by establishing Virtual DOS Machines (VDMs) that emulate a traditional Intel 80386 environment.

- **Win16** Supports a single, multithreaded VDM for traditional, 16-bit Windows applications.

Integral subsystems. Integral subsystems are servers that perform important NT functions such as:

- **Logon Process**   Controls all access to NT by dispatching local and network logons requests to NT's Security Subsystem for mandatory identification.

- **Security Subsystem**   Identifies and optionally authenticates NT's users and outfits their contexts with security and quota limit information from the appropriate policy database.

Figure 16.7 offers a model of NT's overall architecture in the form of the security perimeters of a typical environment.

The book, *Inside Windows NT* (see bibliography) presents many excellent graphics and summarizes what NT's pieces are and how they fit together.

Extendibility

An important note is that a system must be operated in accordance with rules that support the level at which the system was evaluated. In general, connecting an evaluated system to a network or adding a security feature enhancement to it extends its TCB. Accordingly, you may have compromised its ability to meet its evaluation criteria. The only ways that a collection of components (hardware, operating system, extensions to the security system, and network) can function at a specific level of an evaluation criterion is for each component (individually) or the whole pile (as a unit) itself to be evaluated.

Even then, making a trusted whole out of the pieces is problematic. Despite this, most organizations proceed to connect evaluated systems to unevaluated networks, and to add unevaluated security feature extensions as needed. As a result, they are accepting the risk that such unevaluated extensions will break the system's ability to enforce a security policy. Because most organizations worry about fulfilling their business needs before they worry about security, this is common practice. In fact, the market has come to demand documented, supported interfaces for extending security features from system vendors. Accordingly, OpenVMS, Digital UNIX, and NT

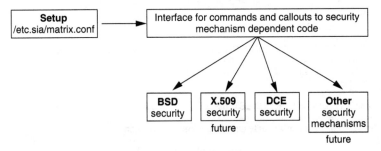

Figure 16.7 Digital UNIX security integration architecture

all allow their security features to be extended. It's not trivial to extend an operating system's security features, because there are a myriad of technical and policy-related questions to answer.

OpenVMS offers documented, supported interfaces for a number of security features, including identification, authentication, and password controls.

Figure 16.8 presents how Digital UNIX accommodates extensions of its security mechanisms.

SIA provides an interface for its reference monitor and modifies security-related commands, such as `login`, `passwd`, `su`, `chfn`, `chsh`, `ftp`, `xdm`, `lock`, `dxsession`, `telnet`, `rtools`, and `dtools`.

The logon sequence is an example of how NTs can be extended. Winlogon is the executable that provides NT's default logon capability. Its functions are implemented in two parts. Nonuser interface and authentication policy-independent functions and replaceable Dynamically Linked Libraries (DLLs) handle all identification, authentication, user interactions, and network provider interactions. The Winlogon DLL that handles NT's default interactive logons is called the Graphical Identification and Authentication DLL (GINA). Most any identification, authentication, or user interface can replace or supplement GINA.

DEC provides almost everything needed to add almost any kind of security feature, including source code. NT apparently lacks this flexibility.

Security Policy Implementation

The sections of the UNIX chapter (Chapter 14) that deal with security policy describe the implementation of a security policy as a process. This process includes configuring the security of each part of an infrastructure to adhere to the security policy. In essence, an operating system's design and implementation determines what security policies the operating sys-

```
root:2LqDt6lcMX9Q:0:1:Sytem PRIVILEGED Account:/:/bin/csh
service:PASSWORD HERE:0:1:Field Service PRIVILEGED Account:/usr/field:/bin/csh
nobody:PASSWORD HERE: -2:-2:anonymous NFS user:/:/bin/date
operator:PASSWORD HERE:0:28:Operator PRIVILEGED Account:/opr/opr/opser
daemon:*:1:1:Mr Background:/:
sys:PASSWORD HERE:2:3:Mr Kernel:/use/sys:
bin:PASSWORD:3:4:Mr Binary:/bin:
uucp:PASSWORD HERE:4:1:UNIX-to-UNIX Copy:/usr/spool/uucppublic:/usr/lib/uucp/uucico
uucpa:PASSSWORD HERE:4:1:uucp administrative account:/usr/lib/uucp:
news:PASSWORD HERE:8:8:USENET News System:/usr/spool/netnews:
sccs:PASSWORD HERE:9:10:Source Code Control:/:
ingres:PASSWORD HERE:267:74:& Group:/usr/ingres:/bin/csh
guest:1yt7jw.7yq3G.:268:15:DECNET GUEST:/users/guest:/bin/csh
sam::268:99:test user:/sam:/bin/csh
sso:3Wd8mJ5cR3zkg:6:7:System Security Officer:/usr/security:/bin/csh
```

Figure 16.8 Example of the digital UNIX password file

tem can support. This certainly includes its reference monitor. However, a security policy is actually implemented by configuring a system so that it can be operated in a way that meets the policy's requirements.

Typically, the security policy's implementation requires manipulation of the operating system's executive, file system, user authorizations, a separate audit subsystem, and the network. In OpenVMS and Digital UNIX, the choices for configuring a system to meet the requirements of a security policy's specifications are made using many different utility programs that actually manage the details. However, OpenVMS makes an effort to focus these activities in the SET SECURITY command, and DEC's Security Integration Architecture provides a focal point for most of this work for Digital UNIX. DEC may add an SIA-like capability to OpenVMS in the future.

Because security was a preeminent design goal for NT, the basic elements of an overall security policy are implemented in one place, under the User Manager utility's Policies menu. NT makes an attempt to steer you toward the correct implementation of your security policy by concentrating all the relevant, system-wide settings in one place.

Whenever security has to be customized beyond what the standard utilities can do, OpenVMS and Digital UNIX provide APIs for many of their security features, and source code where an API is inadequate. While Microsoft has given NT their Win32 API it is not clear that this interface will be adequate—only time will tell.

Identification, Authentication, Authorization, and Access Control

Using commonly accepted security terminology, we can add some definitions that will help keep us from getting mired down in trusted systems and evaluation criteria. Identification can be defined as *a system's ability to recognize an entity such as a user*. Authentication can be defined as *the verification of that identity*. Authorization is *the process of granting access rights*, and Access Control is *the process of limiting access by applying those rights*. Identification and authentication are accomplished by identifier and authentication schemes. User IDs and passwords are common examples. Authorization and authentication are the basis for authorization and access control.

None of this is trivial, and its implementation in enterprise-wide computing solutions is fraught with problems. Examples include:

- The potential of available interconnectivity manifesting itself in organizational network connections to suppliers, customers, and the global village at large. This makes unique identifiers and strong authentication critical. Neither is sufficient and both are necessary.

- The problem of mapping identification, authentication, authorization, and access control schemes across the boundaries of their security perimeters into others can be acute. Sophisticated schemes can be rendered vulnerable by inadequate interfaces and their inability to be compartmentalized. This is why the mandatory access controls of evaluation criteria's higher levels are important. A system which was evaluated at a lower level (for example, the C and D levels) must not be allowed to violate the security policy of any system to which it is connected. For instance, the capabilities of the B level of the TCSEC (and above) are required to contain the threat of an interconnected MS-DOS system (which has no security to speak of). A good example is found in the control of malware such as viruses. A mandatory access controls scheme is required to ensure that a user does not accidentally import untrusted software into his environment. This is accomplished by access controls that prevent a user from importing software from an untrusted environment(s). Solving this problem rigorously is important, yet most commercial organizations have yet to face it.

In the end, the completeness, reliability, and strength of any of these schemes is dependent on the strength and completeness of the authentication mechanisms that support them, and how completely and correctly they are mapped together. Common strategies for dealing with these problems include the use of contemporary standards, such as the X.500 directory service and its accompanying X.509-based certification for identification and authentication. Authorization and access control is the parlance of enterprise-wide computing solutions, such as DCE, SESAME, and others that extend complete identification and authentication schemes to authorization and access control.

Windows 95 Drops Out

Here is where Windows 95 starts to fade from our discussion. Windows 95 has security features, but they pale compared to those of the other three operating systems, by design. All three other operating systems have the necessary functionality for a C2 rating in each category.

Because Windows 95 is a brand new operating system, it would be incorrect to classify it as merely an extension of the existing MS-DOS and existing Windows worlds. In fact, Windows 95 appears to be quite avant-garde and able to provide a nice bridge between the current Windows environment and the new world of NT. Windows 95 appears to be slick, new, and capable. However, its capabilities stop quite short of the more complete security of NT and other operating systems that were designed to be secure. As an example, consider the security Application Programmer's Interface (API) for security services. Microsoft's strategic API is called Win32. In his book, *Inside Windows 95* (see bibliography), Adrian King points out that Windows 95 does not implement Win32's Security API calls because it can't support them. Accordingly, we restrict our comparison to OpenVMS, Digital UNIX, and NT from here.

Identification and Authentication

The first time a system can exert any control over a user comes at the user login. For all three operating systems, this process begins long before a user sees the login program's prompt for a username and password. However, there is much more to the story, starting with the information that each operating system uses for identification.

User identification, authorization, and access control information

OpenVMS, Digital UNIX, and NT all use schemes that include user identifiers. As you might imagine, these IDs figure prominently in how access to resources is controlled in each. In NT, each user and each group of users is assigned a Security Identifier (SID) that is unique across time and space. SIDs are used to create the Access Tokens that we'll discuss in the Access Control section. An important NT innovation is that no two users will ever have the same SID, and once a user account is removed from the system the SID is permanently removed. This is handy because it effectively prevents the transfer of anything from an old account to a new one, even if the usernames of the two accounts match.

Some notable differences between the access control schemes of these three operating systems include:

- The OpenVMS User/Group-based protection code scheme allows each user to be assigned to only one group, although each user can be granted multiple site-definable rights identifiers.

- Windows NT calls privileges, "rights," while on OpenVMS, "rights" are the identifiers that are used to specify access through ACLs. In Windows NT, user IDs and Group IDs are used to specify access within ACLs.

- OpenVMS has both ACLs and a User/Group-based protection code scheme. The OpenVMS User/Group-based protection code scheme pairs user IDs and Group IDs to identify users.

- Digital UNIX has access control lists in version 4. It has user IDs and Group IDs that are used to control access to system resources. These IDs are not paired to identify users as they are in OpenVMS, but users can be grouped.

- Windows NT has no paired, User/Group-based protection code scheme, but it does allow users to be grouped.

It should be noted that NT ACLs are sufficient for handling all object protection, so two different schemes are not necessary as they are in

OpenVMS. OpenVMS will probably always have two different resource protection code schemes, for backward compatibility and historical reasons.

In addition to customer-specified groups, Windows NT has built-in groups such as Administrators, Power Users, Users, Guests, Backup Operators, etc. While OpenVMS and Digital UNIX come with default groups, their group characteristics can be changed. Windows NT also has special groups such as Interactive, Network, System, etc. These are assigned to a user based on the type of login. Some NT groups are shipped preconfigured and can't be changed.

OpenVMS has similar built-in rights identifiers that are similar to NT's rights. However, OpenVMS rights are limited to access control amid a plethora of privileges. NT's rights implement most functions of OpenVMS privileges and access rights.

On OpenVMS, the AUTHORIZE utility is used to manipulate the authorization files, while on Digital UNIX the standard editor-based and adduser/ addgroup tools are used. Both can be supplemented with GUI-based tools. Under Windows NT, security is administered through the following menus: User Manager, File Manager, Printer Manager, and Server Manager.

Table 16.5 shows a comparison of the basic types of user authorization information that can be specified. OpenVMS has the most robust and flexible set of authorizations.

NT SIDs

An NT SID is a unique value of variable length that is used to identify a user or a group. During the login process, SIDs become part of their access token. SIDs identify owners and groups in security descriptor and Access Control Entries (ACEs) in ACLs. An SID contains a 48-bit issuing authority identifier, a revision level, and a variable number of sub-authority identifiers. The identifier authority consists of two values: the agency that issued the SID and a Relative Identifier (RID) to uniquely identify the user or group in that agency. Some SID authorities, such as SECURITY_NT_AUTHORITY, are predefined, and some RID values are used with it to create well-known SIDs. For instance, the group constant SECURITY_DIALUP_RID identifies users who use dial-up modems. Some RIDs are relative to each network domain. For instance, DO-MAIN_USER_RID_ADMIN is the administrative account in a domain. An alias is a group that can contain users or groups from other domains. For instance, DOMAIN_ALIAS_RID_ADMINS is a local group that is used for administration of the domain. Finally, SIDs are manipulated by Win32 functions such as AllocateAndInitializeSid and LookupAccountName.

Authorization Databases

OpenVMS, Digital UNIX, and NT all maintain user authorization information in databases. A glimpse of them is provided here to give you a sense of how they compare.

TABLE 16.5 **Basic Authorization Information**

Authorization information	OpenVMS	Digital UNIX	NT
User name	X	X	X
User ID	X	X	X
Encrypted password	X	X	X
Full name/comments	X	X	X
Groups, identifiers	X	X	X
Home directory	X	X	X
Login shell[1]	X	X	X
Login source	X	X	X
Password controls	X	X	Partial
Restricted work-times	X	X	X
Privileges	Many	Superuser	Many
Disable capability	X	X	X
Other attributes	X	X	X

As we get more detailed, the effort to compare and contrast continues to get more complicated. Accordingly, this figure lacks differentiating details. OpenVMS, Digital UNIX, and NT can all support most any authorization criteria and user controls that an organization cares to add—the sophistication and granularity of the built-in controls is what differs. By comparison, NT's capabilities are limited, but only by its immaturity. NT has no inherent limitations on providing such controls. Such facilities have simply not yet been provided by either Microsoft, third parties, or freeware—herein the subtlety.

[1]As mentioned earlier, OpenVMS and Digital UNIX offer considerable flexibility here.

[2]OpenVMS imposes control on logins according to the type as well as source. NT's controls are source-based.

[3]Thus far, OpenVMS offers the most sophisticated native controls over passwords—it comes with password history and password-criteria enforcement capabilities. In addition, some of NT's password controls are set on a system-wide basis.

- **OpenVMS** The OpenVMS user authorization database is spread over several files that include:

  ~SYSUAF.DAT: Primary user authorization file. This is known as the User Authorization File (UAF).

  ~RIGHTSLIST.DAT: List of rights identifiers. This is known as the rightslist and contains rights identifiers, their numeric translations, and their attributes.

  ~NETPROXY.DAT and NET$PROXY.DAT: Network proxy log-in list. This is known as the proxy database for Phase IV and Phase V (OSI-compliant) versions of DECnet.

~SYSALF.DAT: Automatic log-in facility (optional). This provides the capability for automating a users login sequence.

~VMS$OBJECTS.DAT: Security profile. This file stores configuration information (UICs, protection codes, and Access Control Lists (ACLs)) for protectable objects.

~VMS$AUDIT.DAT: Audit configuration. This file configures the system to audit and report events.

~ALTUAF.DAT: Alternate UAF (optional). This alternate SYSUAF can be used for maintenance or in emergencies.

- Among others, the OpenVMS User Authorization Record contains the following fields:

~Log-in Classes
-Local
-Dial-up
-Remote
-Network
-Batch
~Various flags
-Captive account
-use Captive accounts for tape operators for example
-Captive = chroot or rsh for UNIX
-Restricted account
-Pre-expired account
-Pre-expired password
-Disabled account
~User name
~Account name
~Encrypted password
~User Identification code
~Rights Identifiers
~Privileges
~Restricted work times by log-in class

Following is a sample OpenVMS authorization record that looks to an administrator using the Authorize utility.

```
Username: JONES     Owner: Michael Jones
Account:            UIC: [50,777] ([JONES])
CLI: DCL            Tables: DCLTABLES
Default:      CS$USER:[JONES]
LGICMD:
Login Flags:        Disctly Defcli Captive
Primary days:       Mon Tue Wed Thu Fri
```

```
Secondary days:        Sat Sun
Primary     000000000011111111112222        Secondary
000000000011111111112222
Day Hours 012345678901234567890123 Day Hours
012345678901234567890123
Network:   ---------#########------      ----- No access  ------
Batch:  #########-----##########      ##### Full access ######
Local:  ##### Full access ######      ----- No access  ------
Dialup: ----- No access    ------      ----- No access  ------
Remote:  ---------#########-------      ----- No access  ------
Expiration: 31-DEC-1990 00:00 Pwdminimum: 6 Login Fails:    0
Pwdlifetime: 30 00:00  Pwdchange: 17-MAY-1990 20:51
Last Login: 17-MAY-1990 21:00 (interactive),
(none) (non-interactive)
Maxjobs:  0 Fillm: 40 Bytlm: 8192
Maxacctjobs:  0    Shrfillm: 0        Pbytlm:  0
Maxdetach:  0    BIOlm:  18    JTquota:    1024
Prclm:     4    DIOlm:  18    WSdef:    1024
Prio:      4    ASTlm:  22    WSquo:    2048
Queprio:   4    TQElm:  10    WSextent:   4096
CPU: (none)    Enqlm:  75    Pgflquo:   10000
Authorized Privileges:
    TMPMBX NETMBX
Default Privileges:
    TMPMBX NETMBX
Identifier     Value        Attributes
   SUPPORT      %X80010010   NORESOURCE  NODYNAMIC
   ADMINISTRATION        %X8001000B  NORESOURCE   NODYNAMIC
```

Digital UNIX

The Digital UNIX user authorization database is spread over several files that can include:

- /etc/passwd: the standard UNIX password file. This file is readable to all users. It is supplemented by a shadow password file that is not readable to all users when the enhanced security option is employed.

- /etc/group: additional users assigned to groups. Users can belong to multiple groups. This file lists the groups to which users belong.

- rhosts: trusted remote users. This file in each user's directory contains system IDs of remote systems that are trusted (allowed to login to this account using Berkeley r services rlogin and rsh). This file contains the IDs of remote users who are allowed to access an account with the Berkeley r services (rlogin and rsh).

- /etc/hosts.equiv: trusted hosts. This file contains system IDs of remote systems that are trusted (allowed to login using rlogin or rsh).

- /etc/dnet_proxy—DECnet proxy. This file maps remote DECnet users to local user IDs.

.rhosts files are an extension of the UNIX philosophy. The fact that they allow individual users to override the security policy in some cases is considered to be an oddity by many. However, .rhosts are merely an ultimate form of discretionary access controls.

The contents of the Digital UNIX passwd file match that of the standard UNIX passwd file, and they are both simply text files that can be edited directly with a text editor. The fields include:

- User name

- Encrypted password

- User id (UID)

- Group id (GID)

- Comment field

- Default log-in directory

- Default shell

Unlike OpenVMS user IDs, Digital UNIX user IDs do not need a GID added to make them unique. Following is a typical UNIX password file as it would be displayed with an editor or a text display utility such as cat.

```
root:2LqDt61cMX9Qs:0:1:System PRIVILEGED  Account:/:/bin/csh
service:PASSWORD  HERE:0:1:Field  Service  PRIVILEGED
Account:/usr/field:/bin/csh
nobody:PASSWORD  HERE:-2:-2:anonymous  NFS user:/:/bin/date
operator:PASSWORD  HERE:0:28:Operator  PRIVILEGED  Account:/opr:/opr/opser
daemon:*:1:1:Mr Background:/:
sys:PASSWORD HERE:2:3:Mr Kernel:/usr/sys:
bin:PASSWORD HERE:3:4:Mr Binary:/bin:
uucp:PASSWORD HERE:4:1:UNIX-to-UNIX
Copy:/usr/spool/uucppublic:/usr/lib/uucp/uucico
uucpa:PASSWORD HERE:4:1:uucp administrative account: /usr/lib/uucp:
news:PASSWORD HERE:8:8:USENET News System: /usr/spool/netnews:
sccs:PASSWORD HERE:9:10:Source Code Control:/:
ingres:PASSWORD HERE:267:74:& Group: /usr/ingres:/bin/csh
guest:1yt7jw.7yq3G.:268:15:DECNET GUEST: /users/guest:/bin/csh
sam:268:99:test user:/sam:/bin/csh
sso:3Wd8mJ5cR3zkg:6:7:System Security Officer: /usr/security:/bin/csh
```

Following is a typical UNIX group file as it would be displayed with an editor or a text display utility such as cat.

```
system:*:0:root
daemon:*:1:daemon
uucp:*:2:uucp
rsrv3:*:3:root
bin:*:4:bin
tty:*:5:root
kmem:*:6:root
authread:*:7:root
news:*:8:uucp
rsrv9:*:9:root
staff:*:10:root
ris:*:11:ris
users:*:15:
guest:*:31:root
operator:*:28:root
ingres:*:74:ingres
users:*:99:sam,bill,ted
```

Windows NT

As discussed in the Reference Monitor Section, NT stores user authorization information in its Registry. For example, the access rights that an active NT process has are stored in a subtree of NT's Registry. The Registry is a secure, unified database that stores configuration data for user contexts and the system itself. Each body of this discrete information resides in a cellular structure called a *hive*. For example, this information includes the profiles of each user that is currently active on the system at the time. Each hive is backed by two disk files, a single data file for the information in that hive and a log file that tracks changes to the hive.

NT's user account information includes:

- User Account Information
- Username
- Password (encrypted)
- User's full name
- Account description
- Groups to which user belongs
- Password settings
- Account disabled flag
- Location of logon script
- Rights

NT's password settings for each user in the User Manager include:

- User must change
- User cannot change
- A "never expire" flag

The aforementioned NT security policy specification considers some of the settings for user and system controls to be part of the security policy. They are managed on a system-wide basis with the User Manager's Policies menu. These parameters include the following groupings:

- Account policy
  ~Maximum password age
  ~Minimum password age
  ~Minimum password length
  ~Password uniqueness
  ~Account lockout
- User Rights policy
  ~Rights for groups
- Audit policy
  ~Logon/logoff
  ~File and object access
  ~Use of user rights
  ~User and group management
  ~Security policy changes
  ~System shutdown and restart
  ~Process tracking

Table 16.6 shows a comparison between the password management capabilities of each of these three operating systems. By far, OpenVMS is the most flexible in this arena. It allows most password-related parameters to be adjusted on a per-user basis. A few notes will illustrate some details.

To help protect against password grabbers, OpenVMS and NT offer what is commonly referred to as a "trusted path" in their mix of security features at the C2 level. Digital UNIX currently offers a trusted path only at the B level. With this scheme, the operating system is configured to recognize a special, pre-defined user key press. This special character ensures that the operating system gives the user a new process context and the real login program. This facility is provided so that users don't end up typing their password into another user's program that is merely pretending to be the legitimate login program.

Important differences are underscored by noting that OpenVMS requires an ACSII Break character to activate the trusted path for a hardwired ter-

TABLE 16.6 Password Attributes Compared

Password attribute	OpenVMS	Digital UNIX	NT
Maximum and minimum password age	X		X
Minimum password length	X		X
Password algorithm selection	X[1]		
Facility for additional authentication	X	X	X
Secondary password	X		X[2]
System and dial-up password	X[3]		RAS[4]
Maximum password lifetime	X	X	X
Minimum password length	X	X	X
Generated passwords	X	X	
Password history	X	X	X[5]
Password checking/filtering	X		X
Password never expires	X	X	X
Force password change at next logon	X		X
User cannot change password	X		X

[1]NT only allows its default logon sequence to be replaced. However, Digital UNIX and NT do not offer the granularity of a replaceable password-encryption algorithm.
[2]NT allows secondary passwords to be added by modifying the logon sequence.
[3]OpenVMS offers a system-wide password for all terminals that are enabled with it. On a terminal line that is enabled for this password, the operating system only offers a 1 character prompt for it—usually a Control-G (bell).
[4]NT's dial-in security is designed to work with its Remote Access Service (RAS)
[5]NT's password history mechanism is known as Password Uniqueness.

minal, if that terminal line is configured to use the OpenVMS Secure Server. All characters can be seen as measurable electrical conditions of a serial line, a typical character is a series of pulses. The ASCII Break is different in that it is defined as 10-character time's worth of holding an interface's data line at a specific level. OpenVMS's Secure Server interprets this steady electrical condition of the terminal line as a signal to give that line a new process context. In OpenVMS, the ACSII Break is permanently defined as the Secure Server's trusted path attention sequence. This makes the OpenVMS Secure Server unusable for any communications device that uses the Break key for its own purposes. On the other hand, NT defines the CONTROL-ALT-DELETE character for its trusted path activation sequence, and it can be changed. In either case, this trusted path is only good for the local keyboard. Network logins are a bit of a different breed for all three operating systems.

Table 16.7 offers a summary of the logon features of each of the three operating systems.

TABLE 16.7 Logon Control Feature Summary

Logon control	OpenVMS	Digital UNIX	NT
Valid username and password required	X	X	X
User login authorization check	X	X	X
Allowed log-in classes	X[1]		
Allowed log-in time periods	X		
Expire account	X		
Disable account	X	X	X
Restricted work times	X	X	
Primary/secondary work time restrictions	X		
Logfail limit	X[2]		X[3]
Break-in evasion–intrusion detection	X[4]		
Trusted path	X		X
Logon script	X	X	X
Shell choice	X	X	

[1]OpenVMS has a rich set of pre-defined logon source restrictions. Digital UNIX and NT can implement this by modifying the login sequence.

[2]OpenVMS has system-wide controls over how many logfails are allowed in what period of time and what the system does in response.

[3]NT has a system-wide facility called account lockout that counts logfails and disables logins on an account after a pre-set number of logfails.

[4]OpenVMS have system-wide controls that determine how the system behaves during log-fails, and it can hide from a heuristic password guessing attack even if the correct password is eventually given in a pre-determined length of time.

When a user on an OpenVMS or Digital UNIX system types a carriage return on his hardwired terminal, its device driver (which is waiting for that character) dispatches control to the assigned login program. Network log-ins are handled in a similar way, although each network idiom has its own way of doing things.

In NT, the Win32 Subsystem handles all keyboard and mouse I/O. Versions 3.1 and 3.5 of NT identify the workstation object (physical screen, keyboard, and mouse) as WinSta0. When Winlogon initializes as part of NT's startup, it registers the CTL+ALT+DEL Secure Attention Sequence (SAS) with the system to ensure that no other process has hooked that sequence. When the SAS is received, Winlogin creates three desktops (one for itself, one for the user, and one for the NT screen saver). Winlogon then sets the user's context to the appropriate one (usually, its own), and transfers control to the GINA DLL (mentioned above). Here are the six steps involved in a logon:

1. The user's username is sent to the Local Security Authority (LSA).

2. The LSA selects an authentication package.

3. The authentication package checks the username against those in the user accounts database.

4. If the account is validated, SAM (user account database owner) returns the user's SID and any associated Global Group Ids.

5. The authentication package outfits the logon session with the SID and an access token.

6. Win32 creates a process, outfits it with the access token's data, and presents the Program Manager Menu to the user.

The details of this process, as well as what happens in the case of logfails, is well documented. Figure 16.9 offers a highly stylized view of how NT handles logins, with local and network login identification and authentication paths emphasized.

It's important to note that each of the three operating systems handles its identification and authentication in a manner that can be trusted to enforce the security policy that is being used.

Intrusion Detection

OpenVMS has a built-in, sophisticated intrusion detection system that deals with logfails. This intrusion detection system tracks:

- Intrusion class, (node, username, terminal)
- Intrusion type (suspect, intruder)
- Number of logfails
- Expiration of tracking

The intrusion detection system is configured by system-wide parameters for:

- Password time-out
- Login retry limit
- Login retry timeout
- Logfail limit before activation
- Time before logfails are identified as an intrusion(s)
- Inclusion of terminal class
- Length of random evasive action time limit multiplier
- Lockout for affected accounts

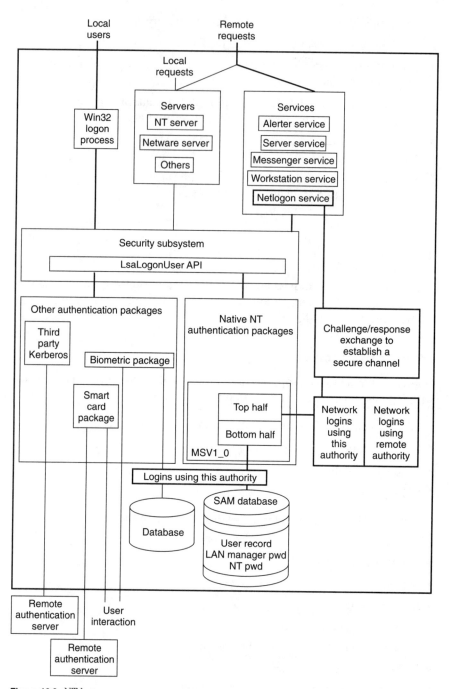

Figure 16.9 NT logons.

More sophisticated software that detects and reports intruders for networks, OpenVMS, and Digital UNIX is currently available from DEC and third parties. Such software is expected for NT soon.

Authorization and Access Control

OpenVMS, Digital UNIX, and NT all outfit their subjects (e.g., processes and thread contexts) and their objects (e.g., files) with the information their reference monitors use to make access control decisions. Compliments of its object-based design, NT offers a complex and ornate structure. Compliments of its design and history, OpenVMS offers the most complex and ornate capabilities. Compliments of its UNIX heritage, Digital UNIX offers the least complete capabilities. However, all three operating systems have similar capabilities.

Let's begin with some details of each operating system's authorization and access control information; then we'll present an overview of how each system uses it.

Groups

Like UNIX group members, NT users can belong to many different groups. However, there is no exact correspondence between groups in NT and groups in OpenVMS and Digital UNIX.

OpenVMS users can belong only to one User Identification Codes (UIC) group. The OpenVMS user grouping mechanism is spread between UIC and Rights Identifiers. Because UICs are historical remnants, rights identifiers are used for OpenVMS user groupings.

NT's group information includes:

- Group name
- Group description
- Group members
- Group rights

Windows NT 3.5—Guidelines for Security, Audit, and Control (see bibliography) defines groups as a collection of resource permissions and rights that can be assigned to users. It further classifies NT as having three kinds of user accounts:

1. **User Accounts**   These are Local or domain-wide user accounts.
2. **Local Groups**   These are groups of user accounts and/or global groups local to an individual system.

3. **Global Groups** These are domain-wide groupings that can be used in their own domain, servers, and workstations of the domain, and those domains that trust the domain where the group is defined.

NT global groups include:

- **Domain Administrators** Intended to allow all Administrators in a domain to belong to one group.
- **Domain Users** Intended to allow all users in a domain to belong to one group.

NT Advanced Server built-in local groups are:

- **Administrators** Loosely analogous to the concept of OpenVMS SYSTEM group (defined by the MAXSYSGROUP SYSGEN parameter) or the UNIX Admin group. This is NT's most powerful group; accordingly, its actions are auditable. If the system is in a domain, the domain's administrator is a member of this group but can be removed from it.
- **Server Operators** Designed for server managers. This group has many of the Administrator group's capabilities, except for security management.
- **Account Operators** User and group management capabilities.
- **Print Operators** Printer control operations.
- **Backup Operators** Backup and restore operations.
- **Replicator** Supports directory replication functions.
- **Users** This group is for normal tasks. New users automatically belong to this group.
- **Guests** This group is for one-time, restricted logins. NT's built-in guest account is a member of the guests group.

Like the NT Advanced Server, NT Workstations have the following built-in local groups:

- Administrators
- Backup Operators
- Users
- Replicators

In addition, NT Workstations have a Power Users group that can set the clock, share directories on the network, initialize/share/manage printers, create common groups, and add or remove users from the Power Users, Users, and Guests groups.

NT also has several Special groups which are created by NT for special purposes. NT's special groups are:

- Everyone. NT's Everyone identity that is not a group, but acts like one. The Everyone identity automatically and always identifies all users and user groups on all systems on the network. File permissions and rights can be assigned to Everyone. NT's Everyone identity provides a capability similar to the OpenVMS World and UNIX *Other* access control groupings.
- Interactive. Local computer users.
- Network. Network users.
- System. The operating system.
- Create Owner. Membership in this group transfers permissions to users who create subdirectories, files, and print jobs. This is done to ensure that users can't consume resources that they don't control. Consider that a denial of service attack could inadvertently take place at the hands of a user who could create files and not delete them. For instance, it is common for system administrators to allow users to create temporary files in a temporary, scratch directory that they don't own. This NT mechanism is similar to:

  ~This is the so-called gratuitous ACE that OpenVMS adds to the ACL of a file that a user creates in a directory that the user doesn't own. That is, OpenVMS itself recognizes the possibility of a denial of service attack and explicitly inserts Control permission for the file's creator into the file's ACL.

  ~This is the so-called sticky bit in UNIX file permissions; it controls what permissions users have for files created in directories that they don't own. The traditional use of this aspect of the UNIX sticky bit is to facilitate the control of user's ability to put files in a shared area.

NT groups can have rights, but the group member's user profile may not show them because they are associated with a group to which the user belongs. As a result of these capabilities, an NT user may end up having access to system resources because the user is a member of a group that has access to that resource, even though the user has no directly authorized access. This extrapolates into a general problem for most operating systems, and it's a liability that should not be overlooked. In and of itself, this is a compelling reason to invest in security assessment tools and specialized ACL analysis and reporting tools for all three operating systems. Such tools are the only way to completely determine and report user access capabilities.

Figure 16.10 shows how OpenVMS UIC member and group numbers work.

In UNIX, files are good examples of its objects. Three-digit octal values, called *permissions*, control access to files in UNIX. Files can have one owner UID and one owner GID.

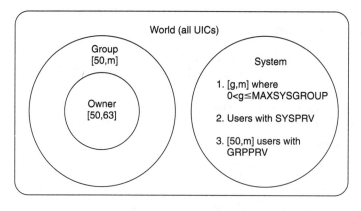

```
$ dir salary.dat/security
  Directory MK$USER: [PER]
  SALARY.DAT;1   [TSMITH] (RWE, RWED, RE,)
$
```

Figure 16.10 Open VMS UICs

Object Protection

In all three operating systems, objects are protected by permissions of one sort or another, and both files and their directories must be properly protected.

Each object has an owner under the discretionary access controls of the C2 version of OpenVMS, and its owner can set its protections. Ownership of objects is controlled by UIC, not by account name. In the B1 version of OpenVMS, this discretionary ability is subordinate to the mandatory controls that enforce the security policy. Discretionary controls are usually used in conjunction with mandatory controls, to allow such systems to be operated with enough flexibility to make them useful. By themselves, mandatory controls are not flexible.

The different terminology used by each operating system complicates a comparison. Table 16.8 presents a view of how each operating system's terminology classifies object protections, to help clarify information in the preceding identification and authentication section.

As mentioned earlier, OpenVMS Identifier-based Object Protections are based on User Identification Codes (UICs) that will probably always be used, for historical compatibility reasons. The reference monitor uses UICs in conjunction with ACLs to make access control decisions. UICs are two-part octal numbers—one for the user's group and one for the user's group membership number. Preferably, each user has a unique UIC. Table 16.9 shows how object access controls compare.

The leading dash (-) (Table Note #2) may be d, c, b, s, or dash (-). Here is how they are interpreted:

d directory
c Character device—hg
b Block device—disk or tap
s Socket
- File
l Link

As you can see, UNIX has no explicit delete permission. The ability to delete a file simply requires wx permissions on its directory, regardless of the file's permissions or owner.

Combinations of UNIX directory permissions are treated as follows:

wx Delete file, rename file, create new file.

x Search permission on directories. This is similar to the OpenVMS E (execute) protection. Files can be accessed for execution, but not read or listed.

r Read file names from directory.

rx Provide full/long listing.

The last character in a file protection display can be a "t." This is the so-called sticky bit. When set on directories, this indicates that files may only be renamed, deleted by the owner of the file, the owner of the directory, or the superuser.

Each NT object type can have up to 16 specific access types. NT's file and directory access permissions are a subset of these access types specific to

TABLE 16.8 Object Protections

	Term	Meaning
OpenVMS	Rights identifier	Alphanumeric string that identifies a user or group of users. There are five types: environmental, facility, general, resource, UIC.
	Privileges	Method of protecting system functions
Digital UNIX	Permissions	Read, write, execute file access permissions.
	Privileges	Method of protecting system functions
NT	Rights	System-wide access controls
	Permissions	Specific object access controls
	Privileges	User rights that implement policy specifications to protect system functions

TABLE 16.9 Object Access Control Comparison

Control aspect	OpenVMS	Digital UNIX	NT
Control basis	UICs ACLs	UIDs ACLs[7]	Only ACLs
User view	RWED + Control[1]	- [2]rwx - + Three triplets of: Read Write eXecute[3]	RWXD + Full control[4] Change Read No access Access not specified[5] Full control Other: Read Write Execute Delete Change permission Take ownership
Types	Read Write Execute Delete Control	Read, Write eXecute	Full control Change RWXD or RWX Read Write eXecute Delete List No access
Categories	System Owner Group World[6] Rights	User Group Others[6] Rights[7]	Groups Rights

The "+" indicates that the following notes explain additional things that users may see as representations of file permissions.

[1]Control access allows a user to control a resource he or she doesn't own. It shows up in user's views of OpenVMS ACLs. The UIC mask that is displayed only contains RWED. There are four groups of these codes—one for each category of access. One of the letters (for example, R, W, E, or D) appears for each access category.

[2]UNIX file permissions normally appear in lowercase and are preceded by a file type (for example, "d" for directory). There is an "rwx" triplet for each access type (for example, read, write, execute).

[3]The "x" in the "rwx" may appear as an "s" in the first two triplets and a "t" in the third triplet. "s" denotes increased privileges of SUID or SGID. "t" is the so-called "sticky bit" that denotes the aforementioned special treatment for directories.

[4]These permissions are shown in the File Manager's File Permissions menu.

[5]These permissions are shown in the Special File Access menu of the File Manager.

[6]OpenVMS "World," UNIX "Other," and NT's "Everyone" identities are similar.

[7]Digital UNIX is expected to have ACLs in the next major release.

the file system. File and directory permissions divide into two groups: standard permissions and special access permissions. Standard permissions can be thought of as predefined combinations of special access permissions. Standard permissions are broad permissions for files and directories. Special access permissions are narrowly defined permissions that can be set for selected files.

Special permissions are similar to OpenVMS protections and Digital UNIX permissions. Table 16.10 compares the meaning of NT permissions for files and directories.

NT's permissions are divided into two groups: standard permissions and special access permissions. Standard permissions are actually combinations of special access permissions. Special permissions are similar to OpenVMS protections and Digital UNIX permissions. Table 16.10 compares the meaning of NT permissions for files and directories. Tables 16.11 and 16.12 show how standard and special access permissions map together for files and directories.

NT directory permissions propagate to their subdirectories and files. Directory permissions are useful for controlling group access rather than having to worry about individual file protections.

Access Control Lists

The traditional use for Access Control Lists (ACLs) supports the fundamental security concepts of:

- Achieve separation of duties.
- Authorize access.
- Avoid concentration of power.
- Avoid captive, privileged accounts.

TABLE 16.10 NT Permissions

Permission	Files	Directories
Read	Read,Copy,View	List contents
Write	Change contents	Add files
Execute	Run program or script	Traverse to get access
Delete	Delete or move	Delete or move subdirectory
Change permission	Change protection	Change protection
Take ownership	Take ownership	Take ownership

TABLE 16.11 NT File Permissions

Standard permissions	Special permissions					
	Read	Write	Execute	Delete	Change permission	Take ownership
No access						
Read	X		X			
Change	X	X	X	X		
Full control	X	X	X	X	X	X

TABLE 16.12 NT Directory Permissions

Standard permissions	Special permissions					
	Read	Write	Execute	Delete	Change permission	Take ownership
No access						
List	X		X			
Read	X		X			
Add		X	X			
Add+Read	X	X	X			
Change	X	X	X	X		
Full control	X	X	X	X	X	X

Generally, object access through ACLs is specified by a list of identifiers that allows access by each identifier holder the access he is authorized. An access control list may be attached to any object controlled by the reference monitor, and is made up of individual Access Control Entries (ACEs).

Because Digital UNIX is not expected to have ACLs in the next major release, all three operating systems are expected to offer similar functions. However, as always, the devil is in the details.

One key consideration which is revealing itself is compatibility with developing standards for access control, such as OSF's DCE. In the case of most OSF-compliant UNIX derivatives, such as Digital UNIX, DCE access control compatibility is emerging as a requirement. So far, it is not clear where NT and OpenVMS stand on this critical issue.

Access Control Entries

An ACL's ACEs (pronounced as "aces") are what the reference monitor actually uses to control object access, by specifying the type of access granted to the identifier's holder. Usually, this is in the form of combinations of read, write, execute, and delete permission to the controlled object.

In preparation for a discussion of the details, Table 16.13 highlights the differences between the contents of NT and OpenVMS ACEs. Subsequent discussions will amplify these differences.

In addition to these differences, ACEs can be customized with the following attributes. These attributes allow identifier holders to:

Dynamic   Add and remove an identifier from their contexts.

Resource   Charge disk quote to an identifier if the identifier has been allocated a disk quota.

Subsystem   Create and maintain protected subsystems.

No Access   Make the access rights of the identifier null and void.

Holder Hidden   Prevent nonprivileged users from getting a list of identifier holders.

Name Hidden   Prevent unauthorized users from directly translating identifiers. Such translations are normally done by protected system code.

Finally, as mentioned above, NT has two kinds of ACLs: discretionary and system. As you might expect, ACE's system ACLs contain the additional options necessary for system functions such as security audit generation. Because there are considerable details left in this area for you to explore, let's take a look at a few ACL examples.

The example below shows the OpenVMS commands that a user can issue to create the ACEs in an ACL, for a file called salary.dat. These com-

TABLE 16.13 ACEs

	ACE access permissions	Effect
NT		
	Change permission	Change file and directory permissions
	Take ownership	Allows users to become file and directory owners
OpenVMS		
	Control	Grants owner access
	Security_alarm	Generates security alarms
	Audit	Generates audit trail entries
	Access success	Records successful accesses
	Access failure	Records failed accesses
	Use of privilege	Records use of privileges to gain access

mands are followed by an example of how the completed ACL looks to the user.

```
$set security/acl salary.dat/acl=(identifier=adminstration,access=read+write)
$set security/acl salary.dat/acl=(identifier=clerk, access=read)
$set security/protection=(world) salary.dat
$dir salary.dat/security

Directory MK$USER:[PER]

SALARY.DAT;1    [TSMITH]     (RWE,RWE,RE,)

    (IDENTIFIER=CLERK,ACCESS=READ)
    (IDENTIFIER=ADMINISTRATION,ACCESS=READ+WRITE)

$
```

As a result of the commands given here, users with the CLERK identifier have read access, while users with CLERK & ADMINISTRATION identifiers have read (not read and write) access. This is because the OpenVMS reference monitor stops its search of the file's ACL when it finds the first match between the identifier holder's context and the identifiers in the ACL's ACEs.

Confusion occurs unless ACEs with broadest access are placed first in the list. That is, OpenVMS requires that the ACEs be ordered to reflect the policy being implemented. Figure 16.11 illustrates a bad example of an NT ACL.

Omitting pictures of the File Manager File Permissions menus that could be used to add access controls, Figure 16.11 presents an example of a problematic NT ACL. The reason this example is problematic is twofold. First, if this ACE ordering were used where SJONES was in the ACCOUNTING group, SJONES would have write access rather than being restricted to read. In addition, members of both the ACCOUNTING and EVERYONE groups get write access. Second, the only way that this ACE ordering could be affected is by a custom application that explicitly added it. This behavior is explained by the fact that NT searches an ACL until the requested access

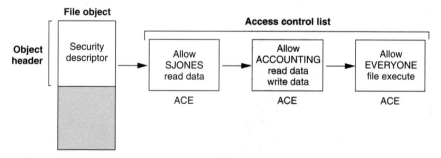

Figure 16.11 A bad NT ACL example

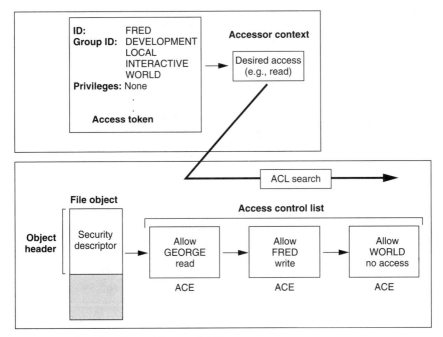

Figure 16.12 Security tokens, objects, and ACLs

is found. In OpenVMS, the ACL is searched until an identifier match is found, and then the ACE's access permissions are applied.

The Permissions Editor that NT utilities use reorders the ACEs, such that the most restrictive ACEs are placed in the ACL first. The lack of native NT tools to inspect the contents of ACLs has spawned some commercial products, such as Somar Software's Somar DumpAcl program to dump the permissions (ACLs) for the file system, registry, shares, and printers.

Figure 16.12 presents a more complete view of how NT handles its ACLs. The accessing contexts security token user ID, Group ID(s) , and privileges are combined with the desired access as a basis for the ACL search.

NT illustrates the complexity of the evaluation of ACLs:

- If the caller provides an ACL upon object creation, the security system applies it.

- If the caller does not provide an ACL upon object creation and the object has a name, the security system looks at the ACL on the object's directory. Some directory ACEs can be marked inherit, which cause the security system to clone them.

- If caller does not provide an ACL upon object creation and the object does not have a name, the security system redefines the default ACE from the accessor's access token and applies it to the object.

TABLE 16.14 OpenVMS Privileges and Privilege Groups

Class	Privileges
None	None
Normal	NETMBX, TMPMBX
Group	GROUP, GRPPRV
Devour	ACNT, ALLSPOOL, BUGCHK, EXQUOTA, GRPNAM, PRMCEB, PRMGBL, PRMMBX, SHMEM
System	AUDIT, ALTPRI, MOUNT, READALL, OPER, PSWARM, SECURITY, SHARE, SYSLCK, WORLD
Objects	DIAGNOSE, IMPORT, MOUNT, READALL, SYSGBL, VOLPRO
All	BYPASS, CMEXEC, CMKRNL, DETACH, DOWNGRADE, LOG_IO, PFNMAP, PHY_IO, SETPRV, SHARE, SYSNAM, SYSPRV, UPGRADE

Because OpenVMS does not have security tokens, the reference monitor uses data structures in the control region of each processor's system memory (its so-called P1 address space) to store UIC and right identifiers.

Privileges

OpenVMS, Digital UNIX, and NT all have the concept of privileges to allow selective access to their system functions. In all cases except the BSD security mechanism, which has very little granularity, an effort is made to allow extremely selective access.

VMS has the most privilege granularity. Table 16.14 lists the privileges and privilege groups of OpenVMS.

Of note are the Upgrade and Downgrade privileges. These are only visible and used in the SEVMS B level TCSEC derivatives the way that information is moved between classification levels by the security administrator.

Privilege control in the BSD mechanism of Digital UNIX is much less granular. It effectively has only four different privilege levels:

- None.
- Normal users.
- SUID and SGID (Files permission masks that allow the kernel to change the effective UID or GID of a process to that of a file's owner).
- The ability to become the Super User (root).

File permission bits on files are manipulated by the chmod command, and users become root (UID 0) with the SU command, change file to SUID.

The following commands set file permission bits to SUID and SGID respectively:

```
#chmod 4777 /u/bob/sh
#chmod 2777 /u/bob/sh
```

As explained earlier, the set user-id bit is indicated by a letter s (or uppercase S) in place of the user or group x (for execute) in long directory listings. Such a listing looks like:

```
#ls -l
-rwsr-sr-x 1 root sys 161864 Apr 18 12:59 /bin/sh
```

The su command can be restricted to active logins, and common practice is to force users to use it so that privileged operations can be audited. Above you see the use of the SU program. A user must know the root password to effect the switch to Super User. The code below illustrates this change from a user perspective, and Figure 16.13 shows how the user's effective UID changes.

```
host1> su
Password:
#
```

Figure 16.13 illustrates what happens when a user executes a SUID or SGID program. When a UNIX user executes the passwd command, the SUID permission bit allows the kernel to change the user's effective ID to that of root, so the passwd file protections can be overridden to change the user's password.

The user's real UID stays the same while his effective UID changes to root, because the passwd program has the SUID bit set and is owned by root.

As pointed out in the Chapter 14, file permissions are problematic for SUID and SGID files. Consider the following commands:

```
# chown root sh
# chmod 4755 sh
```

User action	Command prompt	Change password	Command prompt
Program	/bin/sh	/bin/passwd	/bin/sh
Effective user	sam	sam	sam
Real user	sam	root	sam

Figure 16.13 Effective user ID changes

If a user can execute these commands, the net result is a file that is owned by root, and with SUID and execute permissions for everyone. If this program is a general-purpose shell, or has a bug which allows shell access, unprivileged users can execute commands as root.

In OpenVMS, programs can be granted privileges when they are made memory resident with the Install utility. The UNIX SUID and SGID capability is similar. When an NT program is registered in the registry, privileges can be assigned to it and it can be made memory resident.

Unlike VMS, NT has a small number of privileges. However, unlike as with VMS, users do not access them directly from command lines. NT uses privileges to control access to services and objects more carefully than with the normal discretionary access controls. In NT, privileges are Locally Unique Identifiers with an associated identifying character string. The string name is meaningful across NT systems, but its local representation may differ from system to system. Each privilege has specific user rights and manipulation functions associated with it. Table 16.15 shows a few examples of NT's privileges, their user rights, their descriptions, and the policy they implement.

One key difference between the three operating systems is how privileges are granted:

- In NT, privileges are granted to programs, not users.

- In OpenVMS and Digital UNIX, privileges can be granted to either programs or users.

- NT groups user rights into groups that reflect the traditional reasons mentioned previously (e.g., separation of duties access authorization, avoiding concentration of power, and avoiding captive accounts). Rights can be assigned to groups, and privileges are normally assigned privileges or rights by placing a user within a built-in group. However, you can use the User Rights Policy dialogue box of User Manager to add or delete rights, provided you are logged-in as the Administrative user. The NT Guest group has no privileges, and there are additional advanced rights,

TABLE 16.15 NT Privileges and User Rights

Privilege name	User right	Description	Policy implemented
SE_TCB	SeTCBPrivilege	Identifies a context as part of the TCB	Act as part of the operating system
SE_AUDIT	SeAuditPrivilege	Required to generate audit entries	Generate audits
SE_DEBUG	SeDebugPrivilege	Required to debug a process context	Debug programs

TABLE 16.16 NT Groups and Their Rights

	Groups			
User right	Users	Power users	Backup operators	Administrators
Log on locally	X	X	X	X
Access from network		X		X
Take ownership				X
Manage security				X
Change system time		X		X
Shut down system	X	X	X	X
Remote shutdown		X		X
Backup			X	X
Restore			X	X

including those that concern security, such as Bypass Traverse Checking and the ability to logon as a service.

Table 16.16 show NT groups and their associated rights.

The only way to get these rights is to be assigned to a group. Table 16.17 shows the abilities of NT's built-in groups. The only way to give a user built-in abilities is to place the user in a group that has the desired built-in abilities. Users can belong to more than one group.

Finally, we present brief, stylized views of how each of the three operating systems' reference monitors actually use all this information to make access checks. Determining which users can access a particular file, and in what ways, can be quite challenging and usually requires specialized, automated tools.

In the usual case, Mandatory Access Control checks are done before Discretionary Access Control checks, to ensure that the security policy can be enforced.

Figure 16.14 shows a gross oversimplification of how OpenVMS does object access checks. The complete flow chart uses several pages of the OpenVMS Security Manual.

Of special note is the way OpenVMS handles privileges. Notice that this check is the last one. Because privileges such as BYPASS, SYSPRV, and GRPPRV can override access controls, they must be accommodated.

Figure 16.15 shows the access control flow in the BSD security mechanism of Digital UNIX.

If the user's effective UID matches the file's UID, the user owns the file. If the user belongs to a group or has an effective GID that matches the file's

TABLE 16.17 NT Built-In Abilities

	Groups			
	Users	Power users	Backup operators	Administrators
Manage accounts		X[1]		X
Manage local groups	X[2]	X[3]		X
Assign rights				X
Lock workstation		X		X
Override lock				X
Format disk				X
Create common groups		X		X
Local profiles		X	X	X
Manage shared directories		X		X
Manage shared printers		X		X

[1]A power user can create user accounts, but can modify only those accounts he or she creates.
[2]Users can create local groups, but can only modify the local groups he or she creates.
[3]A power user can create local groups and modify any groups he or she creates, as well as modify the Power Users, Users, and Guests local groups, but not the Administrators and Backup Operators local groups.

GID, his access will be treated according to the file's group permission bits.

Unlike OpenVMS, under the Digital UNIX BSD security mechanism, file permissions can be set so that everyone but the owner can access the file. While this is an unbalanced permission mask, the owner can change file access permission bits just as in OpenVMS. Figure 16.16 shows NT's access control flow.

NT's rights are used for access checks. As explained earlier, Take Ownership allows a user to assume the ownership of an object. By default, Bypass Traverse Checking is assigned to everyone. This allows users to traverse through any directory tree to access files, even if they do not have access to those directories. This capability is important so users can do backups and restores.

Object reuse

Object reuse is ensuring that physical storage (memory or disk space), released prior to its reuse, is cleared of any remnant of the previous use. All three operating systems implement TCSEC requirements for object reuse:

- **Memory protection** Protects the address spaces of users and the system itself from one another.

- **Memory reinitialization before reuse**   Virtual process address spaces that are zeroed upon process creation.

- **Protection against file scavenging**   Disk blocks that contain data from a previous use are not accessible to their current user. As an example, both OpenVMS and NT implement high water marking that prevents users from reading past the point that they have written into a file. In addition, OpenVMS has a capability called *erase on delete* that allows users to specifically write an erasure pattern over disk blocks when a file is deleted.

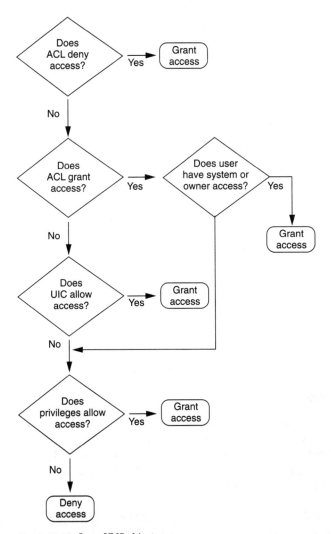

Figure 16.14 Open VMS object access

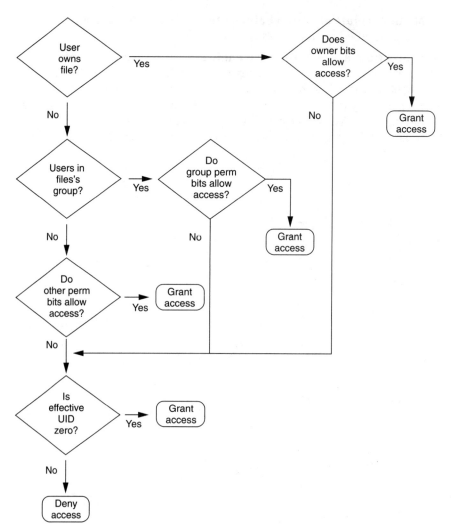

Figure 16.15 Digital UNIX object access for its BSD security mechanism

Networks and Network Security

OpenVMS, Digital UNIX, and NT are all quite feature-rich in the networking arena. Because the crux of secure client/server, distributed, and enterprise computing is found in the details of how their interconnectivity works, volumes have been, are being, and will be written about them. Accordingly, my comments are limited to a brief discussion of:

- The network capabilities of these three operating systems.
- The security-related aspects of networking and internetworking them.

The best place to start is with the problem at hand.

Interconnecting systems and networks securely

Each component of a distributed system is surrounded by a security perimeter that is defined and enforced by the security policy that defines it. From a technical perspective there are two parts to the problem of implementing distributed systems securely:

1. Defining and implementing security perimeters and security policies for:
   - Users
   - Applications
   - Data
   - Systems
   - Network security domains
   - Networks
   - Internetworks

2. Mapping security policies across security perimeters.

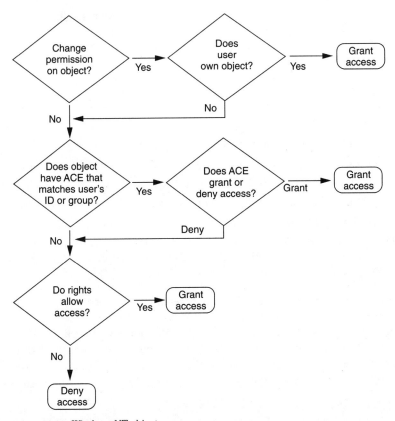

Figure 16.16 Windows NT object access

By themselves, these technical considerations can't stand alone. They exist in a real world of political abstractions that mirror how the technology is used:

- Organizations
- Intraorganizational communications (e.g., departments and workgroups)
- Interorganizational communications (e.g., suppliers, customers, and research partnerships)

Any given assembly of distributed computing components is a mix of these technical and political interactions. Moreover, at the most detailed levels, each assembly is unique from organization to organization. Figure 16.17 uses the concept of secure channels (first presented in Chapter 14) to illustrate this concept.[7]

Each distributed computing component's security perimeter is defined by rules that implement it. Referring to the section on reference monitors as you consider Figure 16.18's view of internetworked systems will give you a feel for how this works in an internetwork.

As we explore it, keep in mind that the security-related job of internetworking includes:

- Ensuring correspondence between real and phantom subjects of the various reference monitors involved. The challenge is to keep security policy on each interconnected system consistent.
- Making sure that each system manages object protection correctly.
- Ensuring that the remote subject's authorization on an originating system is mapped properly to the originating system's access controls.
- Ensuring that the phantom subject is authorized on the remote system.
- Ensuring that the phantom subject corresponds to the real subject on the source system. This requires a proxy, access control string, or default access mechanism on the remote system. If this information is being sent in the clear, a protected means of communication is needed.

Even the slightest look at the details reveals considerable complexity. From a security point of view, success in distributed computing security boils down to matching the capabilities of each shared network protocol and facility. This requires a detailed analysis of each, starting with the kind of network support that each system in the interconnected networks provide. Figure 16.19 illustrates how the connections between the components

---

[7]Morrie Gasser, Building A Secure Computer System, Van Nostrand Reinhold, NY, NY, 1988.

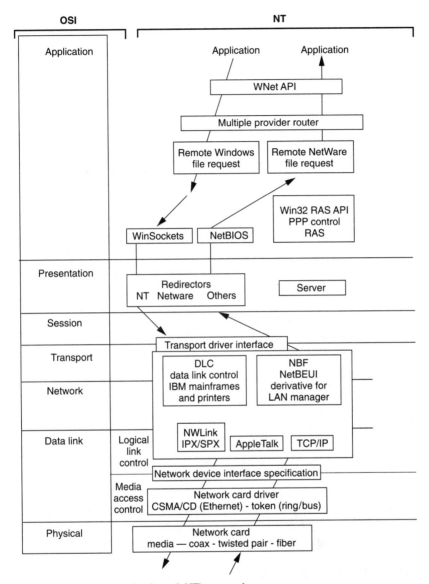

Figure 16.17 Example paths through NT's protocols

of the interconnected networks hide the capabilities of remote systems and networks.

A Note about Network Domains

We can define a network domain as a collection of users, applications, systems, and network components that are inside one security perimeter. We

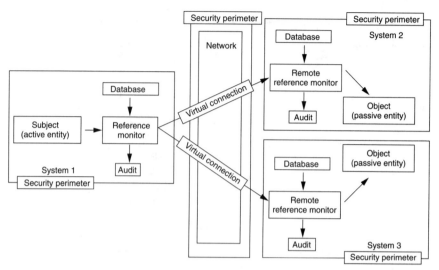

Figure 16.18 The reference monitor in a network

can call these *partitions* to emphasize that they are segmented from other domains by the security policy's implementation. However, between Open-VMS, Digital UNIX, and NT, there are two network domain idioms at work:

- OpenVMS and Digital UNIX
  ~Name/network address-based partitioning
  ~Security-based partitioning
- NT
  ~Security-based partitioning
  -Name/network address-based partitioning

This is a bit of an oversimplification, but it serves to illustrate that the idea of network domains has a slightly different meaning in the NT world. NT's concept of using network domains to implement a network trust model is built into the design of its security model. OpenVMS and Digital UNIX currently add the network domain concept to the basic operating system capabilities, because their designs have not historically incorporated it. Good examples of this fine point can be found in the weak security associated with traditional DECnet and TCP/IP networking and the OpenVMS Clusters.

Traditional DECnet and TCP/IP implementations for OpenVMS and Digital UNIX do not offer strong security services between network security partitions, and all the nodes in an OpenVMS Cluster are, by definition, in the same security partition. Currently, OpenVMS and Digital UNIX require

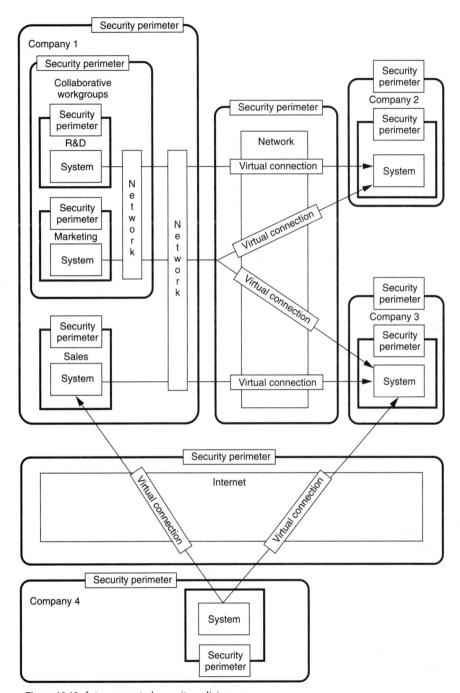

Figure 16.19 Interconnected security policies

additional products to partition their networks. Examples of these products include:

- DCE. The Secure European System for Applications in a Multivendor Environment (SESAME) (discussed in Chapter 14)
- Firewalls
- Gateways

For instance, DEC offers a product called the DECnet Security Gate to add security partitions to a DECnet network and a plethora of vendors offer firewalls for TCP/IP networks.

A note of caution is in order here. NT's security model can be broken as easily as any other model, by sloppy implementations that ignore the requirements of a security policy. Because NT's security domain model is transport protocol-independent, it is easily extended across a TCP/IP network. However, this does not imply that the security policy which surrounds an NT system can be maintained across a general connection to a TCP/IP network, such as the Internet. Connecting an NT-based network to another network requires some form of isolation. Solutions for this security domain interoperability problem include:

- Microsoft's Remote Access Server (RAS)
- Existing NT authenticated Remote Procedure Calls (RPCs) (which are not currently interoperable with those of DCE)
- Additional products that offer network security partitioning with security services
- NT Network Domains. Recall the earlier discussion of NT user accounts that divides the NT world into two groups:
  - ~**Global** Accounts on workstations and servers that are not domain controllers. These accounts are authenticated by the primary or backup domain controllers for their own domain.
  - ~**Local** Accounts made available only by local or remote login using the local system's database. They cannot be authenticated through domain trust relationships.

In the NT world, a domain is a group of servers that share the common security policy (including identification, authentication, authorization, and access control) maintained on the domain controller and its backups. A domain can be configured to trust other domains with the User Manager for Domains. The User Manager for Domains creates an interdomain trust account in the trusting domain's SAM database. The Netlogin service of the trusting domain "discovers" the trusted domain on the network and makes the accounts and resources of both domains available to each other, once the trusting domain's trust account is authenticated by the trusted domain's domain controller. A detailed discussion of domain trust relationships is beyond the scope of this chapter. However, several important topics need to be mentioned.

Resource discovery

The discovery mechanism described above joins the NT Browser as an interesting parts of NT's network architecture The NT Browser allows users to determine what domains and systems are available to them across a LAN or WAN network. Every NT server in a domain is a Browser, and one is designated as the domain's Master Browser. When a system is stated in an NT network, it announces itself to the Master Browser with decreasing frequency until its periodicity becomes twelve minutes. Browsers vote to determine which one will become a domain's Master Browser, and the Master Browsers augment their list of domains and systems with the ones that are registered in WINS. Underneath all this is an NT API that has calls such as NetServerEnum.

DECnet and traditional TCP/IP implementations have network node discovery mechanisms that make new nodes available to their networks as well. The difference between OpenVMS, Digital UNIX, and NT in this respect is that NT has refined the concept into a built-in mechanism that gives users an automatic, point-and-click way to access remote resources, which is built into the operating system. An important point is that the trust relationships between network security partitions determine which systems and network domains are visible in OpenVMS, Digital UNIX, and NT. When a resource is made available to the network, it may become available to anyone who has access to that network. Accordingly, a network security partition's security policy must be implemented by appropriate controls, security management, and administrative procedures.

The cultural nightmare

Consider that each operating system has unique aspects of its file system and the way that data is accessed, especially the way remote data is handled. All three can make the file systems on remote systems seem to be local, by providing a local client that interacts with a remote server that actually handles the interface to a remote file system. An example of this client/server-based file serving, common to all three operating systems, is the TCP/IP Network File System (NFS). Next, refer to the Object Access Control comparison. Imagine what it means to map them all together. To complete this nightmare, consider that the philosophy and culture of each operating system needs to be considered. Table 16.18 presents a highly subjective view of this, which emphasizes security management.

TABLE 16.18 Historic Security Predisposition

Historical and cultural predisposition	OpenVMS	Digital UNIX	Windows	NT
General security features	Rich, basic features	Very basic features	Few features	Rich, basic features
Native network security features	Few basic features	Few basic features	Very few features	Rich, basic features
Packaging	Prepackaged, extensible command line utilities, GUI	Prepackaged, extensible command line utilities, GUI	Prepackaged point and click	Prepackaged point and click
Documentation	Detailed internals	Detailed internals	Few details	Few details[2]
Programming	Good basic tools	Very good, very basic tools	Few basic tools	Rich API[2]
Operations and management	Good basic tools and utilities, GUI	Good basic tools and utilities, GUII	Point and click GUI	Point and click GUI
Usage style	Rich command line, GUI	Rich command line, GUI	DOS command line, point and click GUI	Limited command line, point and click GUI
Networking style	Multi-protocol, LAN, WAN, Glue it all together[3]	Multi-protocol, LAN, WAN, Glue it all together[3]	Limited LAN	Multi-protocol, LAN -> WAN
Client/server, distributed, and enterprise-wide computing	Powerful desktop, provides back-end support[4]	Powerful desktop, provides back-end support[4]	Basic desktop, needs back-end support	Native client/server design, powerful desktop, provides back-end support[5]

[1]The fact that ACLs are not expected until the next major version is telling. However, the fact that Digital UNIX ACLs are expected to be DCE compliant when they show up is evidence of a basic design that can support most anything that is needed.

[2]NT's most basic security features are completely hidden with its APIs.

[3]OpenVMS and Digital UNIX have traditionally supported very large systems as interconnectivity hubs.

[4]OpenVMS and Digital UNIX have traditionally supported very large systems as the glue that holds infrastructures together.

[5]While NT's long-term performance in this arena is unknown, it is clear that Microsoft intends to support enterprise-wide computing by using large numbers of interconnected servers.

Perhaps the most stunning part of NT's presence as a contender for client/server dominance is its combination of built-in security and the point-and-click world of Windows. Because OpenVMS and Digital UNIX have excellent basic designs, the tension between the three boils down to a race between the point-and-click idiom and how open each can become. A friend recently hired a consultant to make some simple changes in a UNIX-based system in a TCP/IP network. After an hour, the consultant was still not finished with the seemingly simple task of changing all the files required to effect some simple IP address changes.

At the same time, NT's point-and-click idiom tends to obscure the lower level details required to ensure secure operation. To make even a casual comparison between the security-related distributed computing capabilities of OpenVMS, Digital UNIX, and NT requires us to move deeper into the details of how things work inside. Let's start with a quick overview of OpenVMS, Digital UNIX, and NT networking capabilities.

Networking Capabilities

Digital UNIX networking capabilities can be traced through its UNIX lineage. Networking has been central to UNIX for most of its history, starting with TCP/IP. OpenVMS matched DEC's considerable network prowess with DECnet early in its life, and came to include TCP/IP in the 1980s.[8] Both DEC's UNIX and OpenVMS networking capabilities have continued to grow under the influence of the pressure for internetwork connectivity and client/server applications. Both OpenVMS and Digital UNIX have significant experience in being the "back room" that keeps many enterprise-wide computing efforts running. The OpenVMS and Digital UNIX TCSEC B level trusted system offerings (SEOpenVMS and MLS+) have trusted networking capabilities, based on the developing standards that are rooted in RFC 1108.

Between their native networking capabilities, DEC-layered products, third party products, and freeware that surround them, Digital UNIX and OpenVMS can support most any enterprise-wide computing efforts. Microsoft is constantly enhancing NT's networking capabilities amid a plethora of third-party products. While NT will certainly come to support most any enterprise-wide computing effort, it is not clear that its capabilities will ever equal or surpass the old guard's experience. As pointed out in the earlier discussion of open systems, experience shows that the accessibility of basic documentation and tools, together with the basic flexibility of an operating system's features, forms a basis for building and maintaining a secure infrastructure. While it is clear that Microsoft intends to give NT a fighting

---

[8]TGV, Inc., 101 Cooper St, Santa Cruz, CA, 95060, (408) 461-8633. Their www pages can be found at http://www.tgv.com/.

chance in enterprise computing, it is not clear if Microsoft will easily duplicate the experience of OpenVMS and Digital UNIX is actually making it all
work.

Since OpenVMS, Digital UNIX, and NT can all be used to solve most any
network problem to varying degrees, let us focus on comparing the security
aspects of network capabilities and leave the considerable job of exploring
the complete networking capabilities of each to you. Sorting all this out will
require considerable effort on your part. But at the same time, dismissing
any of these systems without a detailed study of their capabilities and your
needs will shortchange you.

Security feature deployment

Typically, each operating system vendor implements the security mechanisms required by its customers as they are required. Organizations often
complain to their operating system vendors that they don't have enough
built-in security to implement secure enterprise-wide solutions. However, it
can be shown that security was simply not an important consideration in
most nonmilitary organizations, until recently. As a result, OpenVMS,
Digital UNIX, and NT all have different biases in their security-related support for distributed applications. All three have been adding security features as quickly as the market can absorb them.

As the oldest among the three, OpenVMS and Digital UNIX are often
thought of as the slowest to make security services for distributed applications available, especially when compared to NT's built-in support. However, dismissing OpenVMS and Digital UNIX would be an oversight. While
they currently lack the homogeneity of NT built-in distributed applications
security support, OpenVMS and Digital UNIX have traditionally offered
support for secure distributed applications and they are moving forward
quite aggressively. Consider OpenVMS. DEC offers SEOpenVMS (the TC-
SEC level B rated version of VMS) and a SERDB (the TCSEC level B rated
version of DEC's Relational database). Both of these solutions have existed
for quite some time.

If I stopped here, I would run the risk of giving you the idea that implementing a trusted, secure, distributed system is as easy as buying
SEOpenVMS and RDB. Because DEC does not supply trusted networking
technology, that is not the case. In order to securely distribute the trust that
you can place in SEOpenVMS and SERDB, you must use a trusted network—one that provides the aforementioned secure channels between
components that can be trusted. Due to the expense and complexity, being
serious about this has led most organizations to use existing operating system and network security features over untrusted, public network bandwidth.

Network support

All of this begins with the basic capabilities of the network connectivity that each system supports. Table 16.19 presents a view of the networking capabilities of OpenVMS, Digital UNIX, and NT.

Because OpenVMS, Digital UNIX, and NT all offer a different selection of native networking capabilities, it's difficult to compare them, but each of the three operating systems has the native capabilities to implement and support most any networking solution. While only one connectivity solution might be

TABLE 16.19 Native Network Capabilities

Network support	OpenVMS	Digital UNIX	NT
Native network	DECnet	TCP/IP	NT services
Remote access	A[1]	A[1]	RAS
Microsoft networks			
Windows for Workgroups			Native
LAN Manager	A[1]	A[1]	Native
NT services	A[1]	A[1]	Native
Novell (NetWare)	A[1]	A[1]	Native
DEC (DECnet)	Native	A[1]	Native, A[2]
TCP/IP			
Standard UNIX	A[3]	Native	A[4] Native
Sun ONC	A[5], partial	A[5]	A[5] Partial
Trusted TCP/IP		MLS+[6]	*[7]
IBM networks			
SNA	A[8]	A[8]	Native
OS/2	A[1]	A[1]	Native
Apple (Mac)	A[1]	A[1]	Native
Sun (ONC)			

"A" represents features that are available in Additional products that are available from both operating system vendors and third parties. For instance, in DEC parlance, an optional product is called a *layered product*.

[1] DEC's offering for Windows, NetWare, OS/2, and Apple is called Pathworks.

[2] DEC supplies DECnet for DOS and NT offers compatibility with DECnet for use with DEC's Pathworks.

[3] DEC's TCP/IP services are called DEC TCP/IP Services for OpenVMS and many others are available, including TGV's Multinet.

[4] Besides Microsoft's native stack, third parties such as TGV supply TCP/IP for Windows.

[5] Digital UNIX supports Sun's Network File System V2, PCNFSd, Lock Manager, Status Monitor, NFSportmon, Network Information Service (NIS), automount, and user level RPC. OpenVMS and NT support a subset of these services.

[6] The B1 Digital UNIX implements the work of the TSIG in MLS+.

[7] Microsoft advertises the fact that NT is being evaluated under the so-called TCSEC Red Book. While the Red Book has fallen into disrepute, it seems possible that Microsoft could succeed in getting NT evaluated under its criteria.

[8] DEC supplies a variety of IBM interconnect solutions for OpenVMS and Digital UNIX.

best for any given networking problem, many others will usually work. For instance, DECnet is a reasonable solution for interconnecting OpenVMS, Digital UNIX, and NT, and we could use it as a basis for comparison.

However, DECnet is not a complete interconnectivity solution for all three operating systems, and a complete DECnet implementation is not native to all three operating systems. Accordingly, we are required to drop down into the mire of individual protocol implementation comparisons to find something that will work. Let's start with TCP/IP, because it is today's most popular interconnectivity option.

Network Protocol Support

Because many of the features you need are not available as native components, we'll have to diverge from native capabilities to make any headway in our comparison. Table 16.20 offers an overview of how Digital UNIX and NT support various, standard TCP/IP-based network facilities. I've used the combination of Digital UNIX and NT TCP/IP features as a baseline for this comparison, because reasonably complete TCP/IP implementations are native to both systems. Requests For Comment (RFCs) are the Internet community's standards, and they make a reasonable place to start.

Note that there are many gaps for both systems. Of course, these are only germane if you need a particular feature that is missing.

Adding OpenVMS to this chart is problematic for two reasons. First, running TCP/IP on OpenVMS requires the addition of DEC's TCP/IP Services for OpenVMS, or a third-party product such as TGV's Multinet. Second, each of these vendors document the capabilities of their TCP/IP implementations differently. Tables 16.21 and 16.22 summarize the features of those products as their vendors currently list them.

Finally, it is important to note that network protocol and service standards are quite volatile. While this standards-based comparison serves the purposes of this chapter's introductory treatment, it is not complete, definitive, or stable. To emphasize this, Table 16.23 shows a stylized history of the Point-to-Point protocol specifications.

Even a cursory discussion of the considerable security-related details found in the three preceding tables is beyond the scope of this chapter, which further illustrates the volatility of the protocol standards that vendors face. While this level of detail seems to be of interest only to vendor implementers, users will find the details of each protocol's security (or lack thereof) in these standards. As stated earlier, the success of your security-related internetworking efforts will depend on how deeply you explore these details, as well as your security architecture, policy, implementation, deployment, operation, and management. However, we can summarize from a security point of view.

TABLE 16.20 RFC Support

Standards and conventions	Digital UNIX	NT
RFCs		
678 Standard File Formats	X	
768 UDP—User Datagram Protocol	X	X
783 TFTP—Trivial File Transfer Protocol		X
791 IPInternet Protocol	X	X
792 ICMP—Internet Control Message Protocol	X	X
793 TCP—Transmission Control Protocol	X	X
821 SMTP—Simple Mail Transfer Protocol	X	
822 MAIL—Format of Electronic Mail Messages	X	
826 ARP—Address Resolution Protocol	X	X
854 TELNET—Telnet Protocol	X	X
862 ECHO—Echo Protocol		X
863 DISCARD—Discard Protocol		X
864 CHARGEN—Character Generator Protocol		X
865 QUOTE—Quote of the Day Protocol		X
867 DAYTIME—Daytime Protocol		X
868 TIME—Time Protocol	X	
893 Trailer Encapsulations	X	
894 IP-E—Internet Protocol on Ethernet Networks	X	X
903 RARP—Reverse Address Resolution Protocol	X	
904 EGP—Exterior Gateway Protocol	X	
919 Broadcast Datagram over IP	X	X
922 IP Broadcast Datagrams with Subnets	X	X
950 IP Subnet Extension	X	
951 Bootp	X	
954 RPC—NICNAME/WHOIS	X	
959 FTP—File Transfer Protocol	X	X
1001, 1002 NetBios Service Protocols		X
1014 XDR—External Data Representation	X	
1034, 1035 DOMAIN—Domain[R] Name System	X	X
1042 IP—Internet Protocol on IEEE 802	X	X
1049 Content—Type Field for Internet Messages	X	
1050 RPC—Sun[R] Remote Procedure Calls	X	
1055 SLIP—Serial Line Internet Protocol	X	X
1057 Portmapper	X	
1058 RIP—Routing Information Protocol	X	
1084 BOOTP—BOOTP Protocol	X	
1094 Sun Network File System Protocol NFS	X	
1112 Host Extensions for IP Multicast	X	X

TABLE 16.20 RFC Support (Continued)

Standards and conventions	Digital UNIX	NT
1116 Telnet Line Mode Option	X	
1119 NTP—Network Time Protocol	X	
1122 Hosts Communication Layers	X	X
1123 Applications and Support	X	X
1134 PPP—Point to Point Protocol		X
1144 CSLIP—TCP/IP Header Compression	X	X
1155 SMI—Structure of Management Information	X	
1156 MIB—Management Information Base	X	
1157 SNMP—Simple Network Management Protocol	X	X
1179 LPD—Line Printer Daemon Protocol		X
1188 IP—Transmission of IP over FDDI	X	X
1191 Path MTU Discovery		X
1201 IP over ARCNET		X
1212 Concise MIB	X	
1213 MIB-II—Management Information Base II	X	
1225 POP3—Post Office Protocol, Rev. 3	X	
1231 IEEE 802.5 Token Ring MIB	X	X
1282 BSD rlogin	X	
1285 FDDI Management Information Base	X	
1288 FINGER—(Finger Protocol)	X	
1323 TCP Extensions for High Performance	X	
1332 IPCP—PPP Internet Control Processor		X
1334 PPP Authentication Protocols		X
1340 Assigned Numbers	X	
1350 TFTP—Trivial File Transfer Protocol	X	
1483 Multiprotocol Encapsulation over ATM AAL5	X	
1533 DHCP Options and BOOTP Vendor Extensions		X
1534 Interoperation Between DHCP and BOOTP		X
1541 DHCP—Dynamic Host Configuration Protocol		X
1542 Clarifications and Extensions for the Bootstrap	X	
1547 PPP—Requirements for Point to Point Protocol		X
1548 PPP—Point to Point Protocol		X
1549 PPP—HDLC Framing	X	
1552 IPXCP—Internetwork Packet Exchange	X	
1553 IPX Header Compression		X
1570 LCP—Link Control Protocol Extensions		X

BSD UNIX Standard Conventions

4.3 BSD inetd	X	

TABLE 16.20 RFC Support (Continued)

Standards and conventions	Digital UNIX	NT
4.3 BSD lpd	X	
4.3 BSD netstato	X	
4.3 BSD ping	X	
4.3 BSD rcp	X	
4.3 BSD rexecd	X	
4.3 BSD rlogin	X	
4.3 BSD rmt	X	
4.3 BSD rsh	X	
4.3 BSD rmt	X	
4.3 BSD sendmail V5.65 with IDA enhancements	X	
4.3 BSD syslog	X	
General UNIX and TCP/IP conventions		
uucp Basic Networking Utilities (HoneyDanBer)	X	
X/Open Transport Interface (XTI)	X	
Sun Open Network Computing (ONC) 4.2	X	
New rdist command packaged as optional nrdisk	X	
NFS—Network File System V3 Protocol Specification	X	

Microsoft Corporation Digital Equipment Corp.

Table 16.24 offers a summary of the network security capabilities available in the three operating systems. As you look through it, a cautionary note is in order. Because the notes on these specifics could go on for pages, I've presented only a few comments.

Using Distributed Security

Beyond this point, exploring the security-related details is every bit as dicey as the previous discussion of general security features. Referring to Chapter 14's discussion of network security, distributed computing, and enterprise-wide security, and the resources section of this chapter, will help put all this into context. To give you some pointers, I've divided the balance of this network security discussion into sections:

- **Distributed application support** Support for client/server, distributed computing, and enterprise-wide computing all require support for the needs of distributed applications.

- **Homogeneous networks** In the simplest and most straightforward cases, like operating systems are connected with protocol stacks that are common to each system.

TABLE 16.21 TGV Multinet Features

BASE FEATURES	NFS Client
Supports VAX/VMS V5.0 or later	NFS over TCP or UDP
Supports OpenVMS AXP V1.0 or later	File locking
SMP support	ACL support
VMSINSTAL	VMS-to-VMS NFS support
ACL support	NetWare File Services
License Mgmt. Facility (LMF)	RCP
On-line VMS HELP	
Bookreader manuals	*PRINT SERVICES*
CD-ROM Distribution	LPD, LPR
Cluster Load balancing	Printing to Terminal Servers
Cluster Failover alias	PCNFS remote printing
	NetWare Print Services
LOGIN/TERMINAL SERVICES	
TELNET	*MAIL SERVICES*
TN3270	SMTP client/server
DECwindows support	VMS Mail Interface
X Windows Transport Gateway	ALL-IN-1 Mail interface
X Display Manager	Mail aliases and mailing lists
RLOGIN	SMTP-DECnet Gateway
NetWare Terminal Services	POP2 and POP3
FILE SERVICES	*DECnet SERVICES*
FTP client/server	DECnet Applications directly over TCP/IP
Uses LOGINOUT for validation	IP-over-DECnet tunneling
Retain record attributes between VMS systems	DECnet-over-IP tunneling
FTP Server sessions logged	
NFS Server	*SECURITY SERVICES*
NFS over TCP or UDP	Token-based user authentication
ACL support	
RPC/NFS Lock Manager	*KERBEROS (V4)*
RPC/NFS Status Monitor	Kerberos Ticket Server
PCNFSD V2.0	KTELNET
PCNFS remote printing	KLOGIN
RPC BootParams	KSH
NFS SERVER support for booting diskless	KCP
SUN, ULTRIX and OSF/1	KADMIN
	KINIT
	KDESTROY
ISO 9660 CD-ROM support	KLIST
Cluster Failover support	KPASSWD

UNIX "R" COMMANDS
RLOGIN, RSHELL, REXEC
RMT (Remote MagTape)
RCD (Remote Compact Disc Services)
RCP

DISTRIBUTED NAME/TIME SERVICES
BIND 4.9
NSLOOKUP
NTP

NETWORK MANAGEMENT
SNMP Agent
SET, GET, TRAP
SNMP Management capabilities
SET, SHOW, MIB II support
PING
TRACEROUTE
TCPDUMP
SYSLOG
CHECK
TCPVIEW
X11DEBUG (X WindowsDebug)
Display protocol statistics
Display device statistics

REMOTE BOOTING SERVICES
BOOTP Server
TFTP server/client
NFS Server support for booting diskless
    SUN, ULTRIX and OSF/1

*APPLICATIONS PROGRAMMING
    INTERFACE*
Socket library (4.3 BSD)
VAX C Socket Library
MultiNet/SRI $QIO interface
EXOS $QIO interface
UCX $QIO interface
ONC/RPC interface
DECrpc support
DCE for OpenVMS support

*BACKUP/SOFTWARE DISTRIBUTION
    SERVICES*
RMT (Remote MagTape backup & restore)
RCD (Remote Compact Disc access)

*REMOTE PROCEDURE CALL (RPC)
    SERVICES*
XDR/RPC Programming library
RPC Portmapper
RWALL
RUSERS
RPC/NFS Lock Manager
RPC/NFS Status Monitor

*TCP/IP NETWORK/TRANSPORT
    SERVICES*
IP (RFC 791)
TCP (RFC 793)
UDP (RFC 768)
ICMP (RFC 792)
ARP (RFC 1191)
RARP (RFC 903)
MULTICAST (RFC 1112)
Path MTU Discovery (RFC 1191)
Router Discovery (RFC 1256)

GATEWAY ROUTING PROTOCOLS
GATED V2.1
EGP (RFC 911)
BGP (RFC 1163)
RIP (RFC 1058)
HELLO

*IPX/SPX NETWORK/TRANSPORT
    SERVICES*
IPX/SPX support
IPX-over-IP (RFC 1234)

*DEC TCP/IP SERVICES for OpenVMS
    COMPATIBILITY*
DECWindows
PATHWORKS
DECrpc
PolyCenter/NetView (DEC MCC)
TeamLinks

TABLE 16.21 TGV Multinet Features (Continued)

TeamLinks	*SUPPORTED NETWORK DEVICES*
VAX C Socket Library	DEC Shared Ethernet
POSIX	DEC Shared FDDI
ADDITIONAL NETWORK SERVICES	DEC Shared Token Ring
TALK (old 4.2 BSD)	VCI (Virtual Communication Interface)
TALK (new 4.3 BSD)	SLIP (Serial Line IP)
FINGER	CSLIP (Compressed SLIP)
WHOIS	PPP (Point to Point Protocol)
	IP over X.25 via VAX PSI
	IP over DECnet

- **Heterogeneous networks** The most common case of the recent past has been the interconnection of a limited number of different operating systems with protocol stacks common to each system.

- **Interconnected networks** Today's most common case is the rampant internetworking of heterogeneous networks.

Distributed Applications Support

Protocols and networking capabilities are important, but typically, applications only want to get the job done. Accordingly, OpenVMS, Digital UNIX, and NT all supply APIs that can be used to access the network services needed to implement distributed applications.

All three operating systems support a variety of applications that use interprocess communication mechanisms to implement distributed computing and the client/server paradigm. A classic example of this is a contemporary database. It is quite common to find client applications on small desktop systems that serve as query generator/reporters for large database servers found elsewhere on a network. In general, an application-level standard API, such as Structured Query Language (SQL), is used to implement their functions remotely. An example is Microsoft's SQL Server. Table 16.25 shows some of the ways that Microsoft's SQL Server is supported by NT's interprocess communication mechanisms.

Applications-level APIs, such as SQL, can implement their own security or rely on those of the operating system on which they run. The fast-paced move to distributed computing and the lack of available security has left most distributed applications to develop their own security, if they even had any at all. Sadly, many of these application-specific security mechanisms are poorly designed and leave their applications insecure. Recognizing this, the industry has put an extraordinary amount of work into the development of security for distributed computing, such as that which is discussed in Chapter 14.

TABLE 16.22   DEC TCP/IP Services for Open VMS VAX Features

SLIP/CSLIP

NETWORK TIME PROTOCOL (NTP)

4.3 BERKELEY SOFTWARE DISTRIBUTION COMMUNICATIONS
Transmission Control Protocol (TCP)
Internet Protocol (IP)
Internet Control Message Protocol (ICMP)
Address Resolution Protocol (ARP)
User Datagram Protocol (UDP)
Routing Information Protocol (RIP)

AUXILIARY SERVER (INETD)
Provides security features
Offers event logging

BIND SERVER

REMOTE BOOTING
BOOTP
TFTP

SIMPLE NETWORK MANAGEMENT PROTOCOL (SNMP)
MIB II

SECURITY AND NETWORK ACCESS CONTROL
System managers use network security features to control the accessibility to OpenVMS VAX
systems from remote Internet hosts.

APPLICATION PROGRAMMING INTERFACES
C socket programming interface
QIO programming interface
SRI QIO interface

SUN RPC

FILE TRANSFER PROTOCOL (FTP)
TELNET
TELNET 3270
TELNET

BERKELEY REMOTE COMMANDS
rlogin
rsh
rexec

TABLE 16.22   DEC TCP/IP Services for Open VMS VAX Features (Continued)

REMOTE PRINTING

LPD protocol

TELNET Print Symbiont to print files on remote systems.

SIMPLE MAIL TRANSFER PROTOCOL (SMTP)

NETWORK FILE SYSTEM (NFS)

Automount

PC-NFS Server

Tested for interoperability with the following systems:

   OpenVMS VAX and OpenVMS AXP

   Sun Microsystems SunOS

   Hewlett-Packard[R] HP[R]-UX

   IBM[R] AIX[R]

   Apple[R] A/UX[R]

   Santa Cruz Operations SCO[TM] UNIX

   DEC UNIX, DEC OSF/ULTRIX

INTERFACES

Ethernet

FDDI

TURBO-channel systems to ANSI FDDI local area networks

XMI systems to both Ethernet and IEEE 802.3 local area networks

TABLE 16.23   Selected History of the Point-to-Point Protocol

RFC	Date	Comment
1134	11/01/1989	(Obsoleted by RFC1171)
1171	07/24/1990	(Obsoletes RFC1134) (Obsoleted by RFC1331)
1331	05/26/1992	(Obsoletes RFC1171) (Obsoleted by RFC1548)
1548	02/09/1993	(Obsoletes RFC1331) (Obsoleted by RFC1661) (Updated by RFC1570)
1570	01/11/1994	(Updates RFC1548)
1661	07/21/1994	(Obsoletes RFC1548) (STD 51)
1764	03/01/1995	New
1763	03/01/1995	New
1762	03/01/1995	(Obsoletes RFC1376)
1717	11/21/1994	New
1663	07/21/1994	New
1662	07/21/1994	(Obsoletes RFC1549) (STD 51)
1661	07/21/1994	(Obsoletes RFC1548) (STD 51)

TABLE 16.24 Network Security Feature Summary

Network security	OpenVMS	Digital UNIX	NT
Authentication			
Users	A	A	A, Native
Generalized capabilities	A	A	A, Native
RPC	A	A	A, Native[1]
Confidentiality and integrity	A	A	Native
Authorization/Access control	A[2]	DCE[3]	Native
Packet-level control			
Packet filtering	A, Partial	CMU/BPF	A, Partial
Packet access controls	A, Partial	Screened	A, Partial
Authenticated RPC			
DCE	A, Partial	A, Partial	A, Partial
Kerberos authenticated RPC	A	A	Native[1]
ACLs		A[2]	A, Native
Time	A	A	A
Remote Access	A, Partial	A, Partial	A, RAS

"A" represents features that are available in additional products that are available from both operating system vendors and third parties. For instance, in DEC parlance, an optional product is called a *layered product*.

[1]Currently limited to Microsoft security services. The next release of NT (Cairo) is expected to offer native support for DCE Kerberos.

[2]Digital UNIX is expected to have DCE-compliant ACLs in its next major release.

TABLE 16.25 Microsoft SQL Server Protocol Support

Interface	Protocol	Clients
Named pipes		
	NetBEUI—TCP/IP	LAN Manager
		Windows for WorkGroups
		NT
	NWLink	NT
Windows sockets		
	TCP/IP	UNIX
		Mac
		Various PC TCP/IP clients
	NWLink	NetWare 3.x
		OS/2
Vines sockets	Vines IP	Banyan Vines
		NT

Operating system vendors know that successful, enterprise-wide computing relies on robust security standards that are widely implemented. DEC and Microsoft offer a variety of security standard implementations in each of their operating systems. Both OpenVMS and Digital UNIX have rich, complete mechanisms that support distributed applications. NT's capabilities only appear to be more complete because they are free from the baggage that OpenVMS and Digital UNIX have to drag around.

NT was designed to be networked, whereas OpenVMS and Digital UNIX acquired their capabilities over the evolution of distributed computing. NT provides distributed application support in the form of several interprocess communication (IPC) mechanisms:

- **RPC: Remote Procedure Call**   An API that calls procedures through a mechanism that allows the procedure to be anywhere on the network.

- **NetBIOS: Network Basic I/O System**   A DLL that provides a session-level interface for applications.

- **Windows Sockets**   A BSD UNIX-based IPC that provides the endpoints of a bi-directional TCP/IP connection.

- **Named Pipes**   A peer-to-peer, file system-based IPC. This IPC uses the OS/2 API.

- **Mailslots**   A connectionless IPC that is a subset of the OS/2 LAN Manager.

One important point remains. Few organizations have the luxury of using one vendor for their infrastructure, and there are an enormous number of details associated with each type of interconnectivity to consider, even where a protocol stack that is common is used to interconnect several different operating systems.

Besides differences in the way the protocol stacks themselves are implemented, each different operating system's reference monitor is implemented differently. As an example, Figure 16.20 shows how applications use NT's IPCs to effect communications between applications.

Understanding how an operating system supports the implementation of a security policy requires scrutiny of this low-level detail. Specifying a security policy is usually as simple as an administrator's point-and-click interface. However, the subtleties and complexities of the underlying mechanisms must be understood and properly applied to actually implement the policy.

Audit

OpenVMS, Digital UNIX, and NT all have complete security auditing and resource use accounting capabilities. Although accounting is not often considered a security feature, resource use records are often useful in tracking security problems.

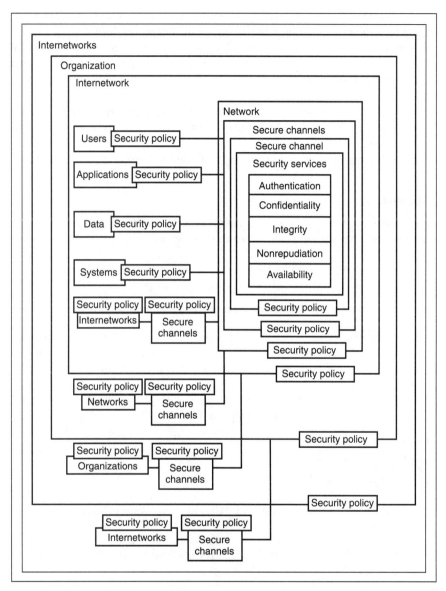

Figure 16.20 How applications use IPCs to communicate.

All three operating system's security audit trails contain:

- Log-in events
- Break-in detection
- Object access
- Use of privilege

The previously discussed differences between the break-in detection capabilities serve as examples of the differences that you'll find between the three systems. Because OpenVMS has been deployed longer than Digital UNIX or NT, it has the richest set of capabilities. However, all three systems can do the security audit job quite well, especially when additional products are added.

None of the three provide the application level monitoring generally necessary for Fraud detection, because user sessions need to be monitored to gather that information.

Here is a quick look at some aspects of each system's native capabilities.

OpenVMS

OpenVMS has two types of security auditing: security alarms and security audits. Security auditing is enabled in three ways:

1. The SET AUDIT command.
2. Specifying auditing parameters in an ACL's ACE.
3. Modifying a user's authorization record to include the audit flag.

Security Alarms can be directed to terminals that are enabled to receive them and audit entries can be written to the operator's log file or a binary file. OpenVMS auditable events include the following event classes:

- ACL: Access to any object protected by a Security Audit ACE.
- Audit: Any use of the SET AUDIT command.
- Authorization.
- Break-in: Break-in evasion.
- Logfailure: Login failures.

ACLs can contain audit or alarm ACEs and the system can report a wide range of activity:

- Privileged and nonprivileged access requests to all objects in a class.
- Audit or alarm ACEs.
- All changes to the authorization database's files.
- Logical links made via interprocess communications, DecWindows, DECnet Phase IV, or the SYSMAN utility.
- Protected object creation, deletion, and deaccess.
- Use of identifier as privileges.
- Use of the INSTALL utility.

- Logfailures.
- Logins.
- Mounts.
- Modifications to the network configuration databases.
- Use of privilege.
- Use of process control services.
- Use of the SYSGEN utility.
- System time changes.

Application and system programmers can use OpenVMS system services to generate audits, check access permissions, and check privilege levels. The ANALYZE/AUDIT command has many options that can be used to view and analyze audit messages.

Digital UNIX

To emphasize the anemic auditing capabilities of the past, the following represents a list of the traditional UNIX logs and tools in a DECnet environment:

- **wtmp**   All logins, logouts and shutdowns—use the last command to view.
- **daemon.log**   Messages generated by the system.
- **kern.log**   Messages generated by the kernel.
- **lpr.log**   Messages generated by the print spooling system.
- **mail.log**   Messages from the mail system.
- **user.log**   Messages generated by user processes.
- **auth.log**   Failed logins and system shutdowns.
- **syslog.log**   DECnet file transfers.

Typical audited events include:

- Local login and logout.
- ftp logins.
- External logins and logouts (rlogin and telnet).
- External logins and logouts (login and set host).
- Failed logins.
- Failed attempts to become super user.
- Reboots and crashes.

- rsh and rcp file transfer requests.
- DECnet file transfer requests.

Version 1.2 of Digital UNIX had the following audit features:

- **/user/adm/sulog** Records attempts to login as superuser (root)—can be displayed using *grep* command.
- **/user/adm/acct** Records each execution of a command, who executed it, and how long it took display via `lastcomm` command.
- **/user/adm/wtmp** Records login and logout time for each user—displayed using `who` and `last` commands.
- **/user/adm/lastlog** Records the most recent login time for each user login.

In Digital UNIX, if you do not use the `auditmask` command to tailor the list of audited events, then the events in the /etc/sec/audit_events file are audited. These are the so-called "trusted events":

- System calls
- Trusted events (e.g., logins)
- Site-defined events

A "trusted event" is associated with a security protection mechanism, but they do not always correspond to system calls. Other "trusted events" that relate to auditing and authentication activity include:

- audit_daemon_exit
- audit_log_change
- audit_log_create
- audit_log_overwrite
- audit_reboot
- audit_setup
- audit_start
- audit_stop
- audit_suspend
- audit_xmit_fail
- Site defined events

Digital UNIX includes the following audit files:

- **/var/audit/auditlog.nnn**   Default log file for the audit subsystem if audit_setup is used for automatic setup.

- **/user/adm/auditlog.nnn**   Default log file for audit subsystem if auditd is used for auto setup.

- **/etc/sec/event_aliases**   Set of aliases to represent the events to be audited.

- **/etc/sec/auditd_clients**   List of remote hosts that can send remote audit data to the local log.

- **/etc/sec/audit_events**   List of events for which audit is generated.

  System calls, trusted application events

- **/etc/sec/site_events**   List of site-defined events for which audit data is generated.

- **/etc/sec/auditd_cons**   Default log file for console audit messages.

- **/etc/sec/auditd_loc**   A list of alternate paths and hosts for audit logs.

  Digital UNIX auditing tools include:

- **audit_setup**   Establishes audit environment.

- **auditmask**   Selects events in logs and displays system-wide and user by user.

- **audgen**   Generates a log record from command lines.

- **auditd**   Activates auditing daemon and administers audit data storage.

- **audit_tool**   Selectively extracts information from the audit log.

NT

Windows NT auditing setup includes the following menus:

- Event Viewer, Log Settings dialogue box.
  ~Set maximum size of security log.
  ~Set action to take when full.

- User Manager, Audit Policy dialogue box.
  ~Specify events to audit.
  ~Audit event success, failure or both.

- File Manager, Security Auditing dialogue box.
  ~Specify directories and files to audit.
  ~Specify types of access to audit.
  ~Audit access success, failure or both.

NT audit records are sent to NT's security log file. When the disk fills up, there are several options:

- Have system halt.
- Wrap (overwrite oldest records).
- Overwrite records older than x days.

NT audit capabilities are similar to those of OpenVMS and they include:

- **User and group management** User or group was added, deleted, or changed.
- **Security policy changes** Change was made to the User Rights or Audit policy.
- **Restart, shutdown and system** System was shut down or rebooted, or an event occurred which affects system security or the Security Log file.
- **Process tracking** Details on process activities, such as program activation, some forms of handle duplication, indirect object accesses, and process exit.
- **Object Access**
- **Logon and logoff**
- **File and object access**
- **Use of user rights**

The NT Event Viewer is used to query the security log. It can view events by selections based on:

- Events which succeeded or failed
- Event type
- User
- System
- Time period

Conclusion

All the trusted system material that we discussed means that NT has been subjected to a formal evaluation and certification process to ensure that certain key security features are present in its design. A subtlety in all this is the testing that takes place to ensure that an operating system's design is actually implemented correctly under the criteria that are being used to evaluate it. While a formal attempt is made to test each implementation, the evaluation process does not become rigorous until a formal, mathematically verifiable model is used to build the operating system in the first place. This is only provided for in categories of evaluation criteria that (history has shown) far exceed the costs and operational difficulty that the commercial sector will tolerate. Currently, the whole evaluation criteria is being overhauled in the U.S. Only time will tell what all of it means.

One historical note will bring us to a stunning realization about NT's possibilities. While there are examples of operating systems that meet the highest levels of the dominant evaluation criteria, only a few have tried to market such a system to the commercial sector. Multics and a failed DEC effort stand out. Because the failure of Multics is well documented elsewhere, I'll touch on the DEC story as a prelude to my conclusions.

In the 1980s, DEC actually had such a system up, running, and ready to be marketed. But DEC had to make a hardheaded business decision to kill the project because it could not find any commercial customers for the system. The only likely customer was the Government, and the potential sales volume could not justify the project's continuation. Even worse, the careers of many of the industry's leading security engineers were derailed. Now, consider that this failed DEC effort was based on a model that met the requirements of the highest levels of the dominant evaluation criteria, using a virtual machine model. This operating system design model includes a core of basic hardware and software services that can support any operating system, application, or network that you might want to put on top of it. This design is not new, and all three of the operating systems we have discussed have this core in place to varying degrees.

However, Microsoft is actually shipping a commercially viable, inexpensive, easy to use product that has all the ingredients needed to actually succeed in making trusted systems ubiquitous. By all appearances, Bill Gates and the Microsoft team seem to have done it again. In the meantime, the combination of NT's design, implementation, presence in the market, and its potential sales volume are likely to challenge most every argument that has ever been made against the use of serious security.

The realization that traditional add-on security for the MS-DOS and Windows world is still needed in some cases will be even more disturbing. Moreover, the fact that NT must coexist with the traditional models of distributed systems security that are already in play is not a trivial matter. For instance, while Microsoft is promising interoperability with DCE security, a sound risk-assumption strategy that relies on it won't be able to live on hopes and dreams. While there is every expectation that NT security will come to interoperate with the likes of DCE, it's not there yet. The hope is that, between Microsoft's commitment to interoperability and the enormous market potential for add-on security products, there will be enough critical mass to spark the kind of development efforts that even the smallest vendors will have to support.

Select Bibliography

Cowart Robert. 1995. *Windows NT Unleashed*, Second edition. Indianapolis: Sams Publishing.

Custer, Helen. 1993. *Inside Windows NT*. Redmond, WA: Microsoft Press.

Eckel, George. 1993. *Inside Windows 95*. Carmel, IN: New Riders Publishing.

Feldman, Len. 1993. *Windows NT—The Next Generation*. SAMs Publishing, Carmel, IN: Sams Publishing.

Gasser, Morrie. 1988. *Building a Secure Computer System*. New York: Van Nostrand Reinhold.

Gasser, Morrie. *Security in Distributed Systems*, Recent Developments in Telecommunications. North-Holland: Elsevier Science Publishers.

Russell, Deborah and G.T. Gangemi. 1991. *Computer Security Basics*. Sebastapol, CA: O'Reilly & Associates.

Security Tools for Your DEC Shop, "Views On VAX." December, 1990.

Steinhardt, Ken. August 1994. *Positioning OpenVMS in an Open Client/Server World*. Available from http://www.dec.com/.

Microsoft Windows NT Resource Kit For Windows NT Workstation and Windows NT Server Version 3.5. 1995. Redmond, WA: Microsoft Press.

Windows NT 3.5—Guidelines for Security, Audit, and Control. 1994. Redmond, WA: Microsoft Press

NT Books with Security Information in Them

Groves, James. 1993. *Windows NT Answer Book*. Redmond, WA: Microsoft Press.

Minasi, Mark, Christina Anderson, and Elizabeth Creegan. 1995. *Mastering Windows NT Server 3.5*. Alemeda, CA: Sybex.

Ruley, John. 1994. *Networking Windows NT*. New York: John Wiley and Sons.

The Larger Body of OpenVMS, Digital UNIX, and NT Information

Between the book and magazine shelves of your local stores you'll find more material than you can probably afford. Of course, the details of each operating system's products can be obtained from their vendors in the form of books and manuals. DEC is located in Maynard, MA and Microsoft is located in Belluevue, WA. A call to information in area codes 508 and 206 will yield their main numbers. A call to 1-800-555-1212 will yield their 800 numbers.

Security Policy Series—UNIX Standards and Guidelines—An Overview of UNIX Security and RAXCO, Inc. This is a free, 70-page introduction explaining how to implement the platform specifics of a security policy on

UNIX systems. Available from Axent Technology/RAXCO, Inc., 371 East 800 South, Orem, UT 84058. (801) 224-5306. Fax, (801) 225-7684.

Multi-Platform, Enterprise Security Management. This is a paper on the future of enterprise-wide computing security. www pages can be found at http://www.axent.com/. From Axent Technology.

Charles, Ernest, Donna Diodati, and Walter Mozdzierz. *Information Technology Security & Business Continuity,* "Trusted Systems: Applying The Theory in a Commercial Environment." Aetna Life & Casualty, Mail Stop C14N, 151 Farmington Ave., Hartford, Connecticut 06156. This paper was presented at a computer security conference in 1993.

OpenVMS, Digital UNIX, and NT User Groups

By far, the most important resource you can have is your local NT user group. You can generally find one by contacting the local Microsoft and/or DEC sales offices.

DEC's user group is DECUS. It has chapters all over the world and sponsors many events, including two symposia per year in the U.S. and an active, online user community called DECUServe. They can be found at 334 South St., SHR3-1/T25, Shrewsbury, MA 01545-4195. 1-800-DECUS55. Internet mail: information@decus.org.

OpenVMS, Digital UNIX, and NT Conferences

Many conferences address security issues. These include professional security organizations and the user's groups of vendors that are closely allied with Microsoft, such as DEC.

The Computer Security Institute is a membership-based, security organization that conducts three security conferences each year, which include NT information. They are available at 600 Harrison St., San Francisco, CA 94107. 415-905-2626.

OpenVMS, Digital UNIX, and NT Internet Resources

Today's Internet connectivity is providing access to a huge array of detailed information on these operating systems. I suggest that you start with a www search service such as the one found at http://www.webcrawler.com/. Begin with searches based on simple strings, like WINDOWS NT, OSF DCE, or NETWORK SECURITY. You'll quickly find yourself buried in more information than you can handle. One recommendation is to seek out the www pages of user groups for further pointers after you have exhausted the resources that can be found at http://www..dec.com/ and http://www.microsoft.com/. One excellent pointer is http://www.hardware.com/ where you'll find a list of vendors and pointers to all manner of other resources, such as user groups.

Attribution

This work is based on a longstanding *Comparison of NT, Digital UNIX, and OpenVMS Security Features* conference presentation that Axent Technology's Robert Clyde and Ray Kaplan have delivered all over the world. Robert also contributed his original derivative paper on the topic.

17

Securing MVS

Patricia A. P. Fisher and Juan Carlos Jourde

In the end it will not matter to us whether we fought with flails or reeds. It will matter to us greatly on what side we fought.

G. K. CHESTERTON

The Multiple Virtual Storage (MVS) operating system is used on a wide variety of IBM-compatible mainframe computers. In today's terminology, it can be viewed as a very large server offering heavy-duty processing capabilities for its client operations. It is a workhorse operating system that supports the production environment for many organizations' large-database, computer-processing needs. The MVS product has been available for almost twenty years. Partly because of its longevity (and many enhancements), and also because users have increasingly pushed IBM and other vendors to develop more rigorous security capabilities, several products have become available over its lifetime that assist in better securing the MVS environment. In addition to these add-ons, IBM has publicly committed itself to making MVS more secure. What users need to understand, however, is that, in addition to the security of MVS itself, they must also pay close attention to the data which reside under MVS.

MVS and add-on products need to be able to protect the:

- Instructions the MVS operating system itself utilizes to direct it regarding what functions to perform, and in what order.

- Data that users of the MVS system have supplied, and which perform business application functions.

Protection must be provided by setting barriers against an ability to reach those data, either through deliberate, unauthorized attempts or unintentional error. Only by doing so can users consistently depend on the results of computer activities.

The data to be protected may reside either in storage (equivalent to the RAM memory used by microprocessors) or in external devices, such as disk drives or tapes. By effectively shielding the MVS operating system itself, access to all the data, wherever it resides, can be protected.

MVS Operating Methodology

To begin to understand how to adequately secure MVS, it helps also to comprehend how the mainframe hardware and MVS work together. At the hardware level the computer only executes very specific instructions, such as:

- Initiating an I/O operation to/from a user-specified location in a specific device.

- Reading (Fetch) or Modifying (Store) data in a specific storage location.

- Performing arithmetic operations accessing data from specified storage locations.

- Comparing data and doing something based on the results of the comparison.

In addition to these, a variety of other instructions might be performed. Operating systems such as MVS tell the attached hardware where a variety of things are; that is, printers, programs, and data. Operating systems are methods of organizing the circuits and other internal components of the hardware in a consistent way to permit programs written by programmers to execute specific instructions in order to perform multiple functions. An example of such a program is to access a particular piece of data, do something with it, and when done, put it somewhere. However, to be able to control user program operation in this environment, MVS needs to have the ability to maintain control over:

1. All input/output operations performed by the user program.
2. Storage locations the user program might access.

System architecture is designed to provide the necessary hardware functions to enable MVS to maintain those controls.

MVS Hardware Controls

MVS utilizes a series of both hardware and software controls. These include dual-state system and privileged instructions, storage protection, and address space control. Each of these provides a necessary component upon which the protection of MVS relies.

Dual-state system and privileged instructions

Since the introduction of the IBM System/370, computers have been built with two-state architectures that limit and control instructions that a program can execute. These two states are *supervisor* and *problem program*. The difference between them is that supervisor state permits a program to execute all instructions. Problem program state, on the other hand, allows a program to execute only those instructions that are related to application programs and do not require unique capabilities of the hardware. Supervisor instructions used to perform vital functions, such as load control storage, store into controlled storage, update the timer, set a storage key, diagnose, and switch state from supervisor to problem program state, should be done only by a privileged few. The term used to designate these types of instructions is "privileged." This means that they only can be executed by a program running under supervisor, or "authorized" state.

However, additional functions are needed by many users, and these can only be initiated from supervisor state. To be able to begin processing in such an authorized state, such as when input/output (I/O) functions are needed, the user program issues a supervisor call (SVC) or program call (PC) instruction. At the moment this happens the program state is changed to supervisor, the storage control registers are changed according to what is required by the program functions, and the specified routine begins executing. When this system routine terminates, it should change the control state back again to problem program state, and should reset the storage control registers to nonprivileged access. Whether this happens or not depends on how well-secured (and managed) the MVS operating system is.

Storage protection

There are several types of central storage protection designed into the architecture of these computers: multiple storage key protection, low address protection, page protection, address space protection, and segment protection. In addition to these techniques, a Dynamic Address Translation Mechanism prevents those users running in one address location from accessing any storage data from other users. Each of these is explained in more detail below.

Multiple storage key protection. In an MVS system, each 4 KB (4096 bytes) block of real storage is called one page. Each page has a hidden byte associated with it, called the *storage protection key* (SPK). The first four bits of the SPK contain a value that is compared against the storage protection

TABLE 17.1 Storage Protection Key Values

Key	Used by
0	MVS system control program; control blocks and code
1	JES2 and JES3
2	IBM's Virtual Storage Personal Computing (VSPC) subsystem
3	(reserved)
4	(reserved)
5	Data management for input/output
6	TCAM and VTAM services routines
7	Database/data communications subsystem; e.g., IMS
8-F	All batch jobs, TSO sessions, and virtual storage user programs
9	Used by CICS and specific hardware modifications
A-F	Application programs

key of the running program for every request for a main storage operation involving that block of storage. Table 17.1 contains values commonly used by the SPK.

The SPK also contains a special bit, called the *fetch protection bit*, which is used to determine whether a task will be allowed to read the contents of those storage locations. If the access is a read request, the key values do not need to match unless the fetch protection bit is on. The only exception to this is if a task is running under key 0 (this is known as the *Master Storage Key*). If this is the case, the hardware honors all requests for tasks running in key 0 segment protection. When executing with a key of zero, a program can store and fetch any data or code within storage that can be addressed.

Low address protection. Low address protection (LAP) protects the 512 bytes of real storage from damage. Low addresses are critical for hardware controls such as timer interrupts, Supervisor Call management, program checks, machine checks, and input/output interrupts.

For additional MVS reliability it is important to provide more protection to this critical data. The architecture was changed by IBM for this purpose, to require an additional control register operation before allowing alteration of the first 512 bytes of central storage. This means that Key 0 can still modify low storage, but two steps are required to ensure that such an alteration was truly intended.

Page protection. This protection is in addition to that provided by the storage protection keys. Its focus is on protecting MVS from itself, not from application programs. This capability assists in preventing accidental or intentional alteration of central storage pages, by marking them (each page) as "read only." It enforces the re-entrant characteristic of a program that might be wholly contained in one page of memory, to enable sharing by more than one task at a time. It therefore provides substantial savings of central storage. One page is the unit of control of virtual storage for the hardware. A storage protection key is associated with one page, and users' address spaces are assigned individual pages of virtual storage.

Address space control. Address space control provided by the dynamic address translation (DAT) table is the primary feature of virtual operating systems, and a hardware capability that allows for virtual storage support. DAT is a feature that uses dynamic address translation tables to isolate storage used by different users. An example of this is where TSOUSER1 cannot access virtual storage reserved for TSOUSER2, because TSOUSER1 has not been specifically permitted to address it.

Each process runs in a separate address space, with virtual storage mapped using different address translation tables. Those tables are used to translate any user-specified (logical) storage address to a real storage location. Thus, each user program runs as if it had its own continuous segment of virtual storage to use. Common storage areas (MVS-related areas used by all address spaces) have the same translation for all address spaces.

These tables are used to ensure that one program in one address space does not access the data or code of a program in another address space. The Dual Address Space (DAS) facility allows the operating system to establish an environment in which a single program can have access to two or more virtual storage address spaces at one time. This feature is not intended for general user programs and requires the use of privileged instructions to enable it.

DAS is intended for use in MVS operations and MVS extensions (APF authorized programs) such as IMS. Within IMS, a user program processing IMS TRX executes in a different address space than the IMS control region performing the database I/O. Before DAS availability, the storage areas used by IMS to maintain data had to be shared between application programs, and the control region needed to be maintained in common storage. With the advent of DAS, IMS set up areas to be shared by the two. IMS routines running in the address space that is processing the user program use DAS to access virtual storage areas belonging to the IMS control region.

Segment protection. Virtual storage can be partitioned into segments (64 KB in systems running MVS/SP, and 1 MB in MVS/XA and MVS/ESA). If a program has not previously obtained storage from the segment (through GETMAIN), or if the segment is not included as part of the common area, the area of virtual storage that is shared by all address spaces, then the entire segment is unavailable to the program.

Segments can also be marked "read only" to prevent the modification of areas.

Software Controls

The second area of focus in understanding how to secure MVS comes under the heading of software controls. The user who programs for MVS also needs to know how MVS itself is organized. The programmer then can utilize program commands to take advantage of that organizational methodology. Imagine if programmers had to assume that the computer was an empty box, and that every time a program was written, all the base level operating routines also had to be composed before execution. This would take enormous amounts of time, even assuming that each programmer could learn how the hardware worked.

By providing the MVS operating system as a core element, all programmers are given a standard format from which to organize their programs, and so to provide functions all operating in a somewhat organized fashion instead of in potential conflict. Thus, the user program that issues a GET instruction understands what that means without having to tell the hardware how to execute the GET, and expects that the desired data will be accessed unless some other instruction takes precedence and prevents or changes the instruction. In the simplest of environments the instruction will access the data and not care whether it can access that data—it simply does it. Obviously, you require some manner of control. Information might be confidential. Its originator might not want it changed or deleted. Thus, by understanding how MVS operates and what mechanisms are provided to better secure it, the MVS programmer can invoke those controls and better protect the MVS environment.

MVS system integrity

To be able to provide adequate levels of controls an operating system must have system integrity. For our purposes, system integrity simply can be defined as the ability to enforce system controls in any circumstance. IBM defined MVS integrity, in a programming statement issued in 1981, as the inability of any program *not authorized by a mechanism under user control* (emphasis added) to:

1. Circumvent or disable store or fetch protection.
2. Access an operating system password-protected or RACF-protected resource.
3. Get control in an authorized state (i.e., in a supervisor state) with a protection key of less than eight, or by being APF-authorized.

MVS accomplishes this by using dynamic address translation, multiple storage protection keys, low storage protection, and read-only protection for certain parts of the operating system storage areas. Supervisor State is reserved for the sole use of MVS and APF-authorized programs.

Input/output management

MVS provides access control for devices and datasets by reserving input/output (I/O) operations for itself. I/O operations are privileged instructions, and user programs are not authorized to directly issue them. A user program must call MVS I/O management routines to perform any I/O operation. These I/O routines require application programs to open a dataset, process it with an available access method, and close it when processing is complete. The primary control over accessing data is provided by use of the open process done when a user accesses a data set, providing a data set name, a volume serial, and a device type.

During the open process, MVS does verification to ensure the user is allowed access to the named data set. If access is allowed, a control block, called a data extent block (DEB), is constructed within protected storage. The user must specify this DEB to perform the actual I/O on the dataset. To determine whether access should be allowed, open processing performs validity checking based on the device containing the data set. If access control software (e.g., CA-ACF2, RACF, CA-TOP SECRET) has been installed, open processing calls this control software using system routines known as *system authorization facilities* to determine if the user is entitled to access the data set being opened.

System authorization facility (SAF)

The glue that holds the MVS system together from a security point of view is the system authorization facility (SAF). SAF establishes default security, provides security functions when a security package is not active, and performs propagation and token services. Token services are used to tie a process to its entry point in the system. For example, a computer program (a job) is initiated through network job entry (NJE). This job internally submits another job via TSO batch, and the third job issues an operator command to start a system task that might submit another job . . . and so on. Token services provide for the identification of the NJE entry point for the process.

SAF works in conjunction with MVS resource managers, which are software components in charge of specific functions. Examples of these resource managers include:

- DADSM for data set access authority.
- DFHSMS for data set allocation authority.
- CICS for CICS sign-on and transaction authorization.
- JES for identification and verification.

These contain the responsibility and functionality to call SAF for a decision on whether to permit a user to have access to the system. Once either a positive or negative decision is made, the product, subsystem or component requesting that the resource access be checked must enforce that decision. Neither SAF nor an installed security package has this enforcing capability: SAF simply returns the decision to the caller—the resource manager is the handler. Based on a specific user request, the resource manager formulates its own request that it passes to SAF. Depending on the specific type, SAF either responds directly or passes it on to the security package. In either case, the resource manager, after considering the SAF response, sends the user a response.

SAF functions can be broken down into three main categories. These consist of the following:

- **Early initialization**   For SAF to perform properly, it must be available for early verification for system use, because one of its first tasks is to research and validate whether the user should have access.

- **Token support**   SAF creates and maintains tokens, including default tokens and undefined user tokens, to enable the holder to associate a security environment with both active and nonactive units of work, such as a TSO user or a batch job. These tokens provide a means by which all work, including input and output, can be identified as it flows around the system until the job is purged.

- **Propagation**   SAF ensures that security-related information for the unit of work is correctly propagated. SAF also performs early verification and authorization of security-related information, such as USERID, PASSWORD, and SECLABEL. The advantage of this is that SAF and the security package can perform propagation and early verification in a single pass as opposed to a separate pass for each. This resides in SAF because it must be available even when the specific security package is not.

SAF concepts are enabled by a set of software routines contained within an MVS router. This MVS router is a system service that provides your installation with centralized control over system security processing. The system service provides a focal point and a common system interface for all products providing resource control. Resource managing components and subsystems call the MVS router as part of certain decision-making functions in their processing, such as access control checking and authorization-related checking. This single SAF interface encourages the use of common control functions across products and across systems. The MVS router provides an optional installation exit that is invoked whether or not a security package is installed and active on the system. The router exit acts as an installation-written security processing (or routing) routine.

MVS Control Areas

There are four major areas to consider regarding MVS security and identification of critical resources:

- Ability to modify MVS itself.
- Access to sensitive data.
- Ability to introduce Trojan horses.
- Access to critical business data.

Ability to modify MVS itself

If someone could modify MVS it is possible that system controls could be disabled, including those established by the use of external security packages such as CA-ACF2, RACF, or CA-TOP SECRET. A user with UPDATE or higher level access (more capabilities) to APF-authorized libraries, LINK-LIST libraries, LPA libraries, system nucleus (SYS1.NUCLEUS), or the MVS system parameter library (SYS1.PARMLIB), might use system functions to disable security package controls. Therefore, update access to those libraries should be carefully controlled. Review of the control points for those datasets should be conducted at least weekly to ensure that these remain in place.

Access to sensitive system data

Sensitive system data, such as user ID passwords, might be obtained from a variety of sources, including the JES SPOOL, SYSTEM DUMP, TRACE, and PAGING datasets. Another kind of sensitive system data is information related to security implementation. This includes parameter libraries such as SYS1.PARMLIB or the dataset that contains the JES2 initialization deck (HASPPARM), product installation libraries that might contain information about product security options, and features that are implemented and which might disclose potential flaws. Some examples of these types of information are:

- OMEGAMON installation libraries that might contain the JCL supplied with the product passwords to access different security levels of functions.
- CA-1 tape library installation libraries that could be used to review CA-1 implementation and establish that the foreign capabilities of CA-1 (EX PDT=98000) were not enforced on the particular installation. This could permit use without generating violations on the system audit reports.

Ability to introduce Trojan horses

If users have the ability to update a dataset that holds executable code, they also have the ability to modify the code and obtain unauthorized access.

Such modification is known as inserting a *Trojan horse*. An example of this in the CA-ACF2 environment might occur when a person can modify something that will be used by a CA-ACF2 administrator with security privileges. The modified code then might issue internally an ACF2 command to grant security privileges to that person without the administrator's even being aware that anything different has occurred. It is very difficult to completely control this possibility, unless update access to all datasets on the system are carefully controlled.

In an MVS system there are many executable datasets that should be protected against Trojan horses. However, it is not always evident what kind of datasets qualify as executable code in addition to those specific to MVS or TSO. Instead, it often depends on the particular software that is installed in the system. Table 17.2 contains a list of some of the most common ones that should be carefully protected and regularly monitored.

Access to critical business data

This area is very specific to each enterprise, but usually will at least include some human resources information (where privacy is an important consideration). Particular attention should be paid to copies of production data generated either by testing or end user access to production data. For example, users who have access to payroll information, and using query products, such as Focus, might generate unprotected work or report files under their user IDs, which could contain payroll information. Therefore, while payroll data using the standard naming conventions might be protected, authorized users who copy the data might leave it in some other named dataset, totally unprotected. Payroll data found in user dataset JSMITH might not be protected. SJONES might be a user in another department and might have universal access of READ for JSMITH datasets, thereby circumventing intended controls. Another area that should be carefully controlled

TABLE 17.2 Datasets Requiring Special Protection

Executables	Executable program libraries (load modules), such as SYS1.LINKLIB, SYS1.COBLIB, and CICS.V1R1M1.LOADLIB
Libraries	CLIST and REXX libraries.
Datasets	ISPF PROFILE datasets (the definition of program function keys PF1 to PF24 can be modified to execute unauthorized commands).
Menus	ISPF Panel libraries (menu panels can execute system commands).
Tables	ISPF Tables datasets (application commands are defined in these libraries).
JCL	Any library that contains JCL such as user and system procedure libraries, production and testing JCL libraries and ISPF JCL skeletons datasets (where JCL can be modified by adding steps to perform unauthorized functions).

is access to datasets used by software packages that manage reports, such as Sysout Archival & Retrieval System (SAR) or report distribution systems.

MVS Vulnerability Concerns

To adequately secure MVS, technical personnel must understand where the most significant vulnerabilities within MVS lay. With this knowledge they will be able to prioritize site problems or concerns and turn their attention to areas in which the greatest security problems reside. In addition to knowing what to secure, it is equally important to understand the possible ramifications of not securing these areas adequately in terms of loss of control, potential damage, and fraud possibilities. The following represent critical areas that are important to the security and integrity of MVS itself and to which the greatest level of attention should be given. By understanding these and how to protect against problems occurring in these areas, much of the MVS operating system environment will be improved and better secured.

APF authorized libraries

APF authorization is a mechanism supplied by MVS to allow an installation to intentionally designate programs that should be allowed to use sensitive system functions. A sensitive system function is the ability to modify MVS information in protected main storage. By using this capability, a program can bypass system controls, thus circumventing security measures in place. For example, a program loaded from an APF-authorized library might request storage protection key zero, and then modify MVS system control blocks to disable system security calls and any potential audit trail. The list of APF-authorized libraries is specified in SYS1.PARMLIB members IEAAPFnn, selected at IPL time. (MVS/ESA Release 4.3 supports the dynamic modification of this list, using the CSVAPF facility, which eliminates the need for IPL to add APF-authorized libraries but which also, because the list of APF libraries is dynamic, makes it more difficult to validate that they are protected.)

APF usage is controlled by requiring that these programs reside in a library identified as APF-authorized to MVS. Therefore, only users who are authorized to update an APF-authorized library might obtain unrestricted access to MVS controlled resources. By restricting update access to only a select few individuals, APF usage can also be better monitored centrally.

LINKLIST libraries

The MVS LINKLIST is a list of libraries containing programs that are intended to be made available to MVS, without having to specify the name of the library itself. These libraries contain programs that are usually executed by MVS processes. Examples are system utilities, compilers, and sort functions. By default, MVS considers any library in the LINKLIST to be APF-authorized. The LINKLIST is specified in SYS1.PARMLIB members LNKLSTnn and is activated at IPL time. As in the case of APF-authorized libraries, because the LINKLIST is APF-authorized, system integrity potentially can be circumvented. Malicious modification of a program residing in a LINKLIST library can be used to exploit another user's authority. Therefore, it is important to adequately secure the LINKLIST by preventing the capability to update to anyone without a direct need to do so.

Link pack area libraries

The MVS Link Pack Area (LPA) is a virtual storage area that contains a copy of the programs residing in the LPA libraries at the last LPA refresh time. Its use is similar to the LINKLIST libraries, but this particular structure is utilized because it vastly improves performance. Programs in the LPA are also considered APF-authorized by MVS. The LPA libraries are specified in SYS1.PARMLIB members LPALSTnn, and are used when the parameter CLPA is specified at IPL time. By doing this, the LPA libraries are copied (loaded) to both virtual storage and the page datasets. For subsequent IPLs, without specifying CLPA, MVS uses the data from the page datasets to support the LPA in virtual storage and no longer needs to access the libraries. This creates an additional auditability problem if auditors simply review the libraries to validate that only installation authorized programs are there.

An example of how this could be misused would occur when a malicious user or system programmer with access to LPA libraries included an unauthorized program there, and before an IPL with CLPA, and after the LPA is loaded, deleted the program from the library. The program would appear to be available for usage from the LPA, but the library would show nothing. A temporary override to the LPA contents could then be made by using the SYS1.PARMLIB member IEALPAnn. Programs loaded using IEALPAnn are active only for the duration of the IPL and do not require the CLPA option to be active. Thus, a hole in the security envelope would exist that could easily escape detection.

A major concern is that malicious modification of a program residing in the MVS LPA can be used to exploit another user's authority. Therefore, the ability to update the LPA libraries must be carefully controlled.

Restricted utilities

Restricted utilities are programs authorized by the installation to bypass system controls. They are needed for both system maintenance and debugging purposes. As the name implies, their use should be carefully restricted to only those personnel requiring each restricted utility's functionality to complete authorized work. Examples of restricted utilities include:

- Functions used to make direct writes to control information on disk. An example of this is IBM's service aid SUPERZAP. By using SUPERZAP in a malicious way, a person could change the name of a critical system dataset and perform unauthorized changes under a different dataset name, and possibly evade detection.

- In-house developed disk-backup programs or authorization exits for utilities that allow dumping and/or restoring of information for backup purposes, thereby bypassing the installed security software.

- A copy of a general-purpose utility, like IDCAMS, running with bypass password protection using the MVS Program Properties Table, signifying the assignor's desire to have all security bypassed (this is known as a back door).

A restricted utility is a program that lacks required controls. Although it is a poorly designed program from a controls point of view, it is one needing to bypass security in order to solve potential problems that would not otherwise be resolved. In theory, a secure and auditable environment should not have any restricted utilities. However, this is not practical where the need often exists for system programmers to solve technical problems.

Depending on the specific utility program functions involved, modification of protected control blocks in main storage or DASD might result because restricted utilities usually are granted the authority to bypass system access controls. Restricted utilities should be monitored closely on a regular basis and careful controls placed on who can execute these functions.

Program properties table

The Program Properties Table (PPT) is an internal table used by MVS to grant special properties (attributes) to selected programs (by program name) to enhance system performance. Program Properties Table attributes are controlled by MVS by maintaining the PPT itself in protected main storage and by requiring that all PPT defined programs be APF-authorized to execute with the special attribute. IBM supplies a base PPT with recommended properties for specific system programs. The base PPT can be modified at IPL time by using the SYS1.PARMLIB member SCHEDnn.

PPT security itself is a major concern, because some of its attributes have the ability to bypass all security package calls for dataset access authority. An example of this is the "bypass password protection" attribute. "System key" is another PPT attribute that needs special consideration. By granting a program this attribute, the security enhancing supplemental APF requirement of being link edited with authorization code (AC) '1' can be removed for the specific program being run.

Insufficient protection for dataset manipulation is a third PPT concern. An example of this is a utility used to copy tapes, and that runs with the bypass label protection attribute even when the utility validates user access to the dataset by internal calls to the security package. By manipulating any control statement dataset or report dataset allocation, this methodology could be used to bypass system security. Users seeking to better protect PPT-granted privileges should restrict very severely the ability to execute PPT functions to grant special attributes.

System nucleus

The MVS nucleus is named SYS1.NUCLEUS and resides in the system residence device. SYS1.NUCLEUS contains the modules that initialize and define the system as a result of the system generation process. Basic MVS routines that run in supervisor state reside in the MVS nucleus. Therefore, it is important not to permit update capability to anyone except those who explicitly need it.

System PARMLIB

The system parameter library contains critical initialization parameters, such as the list of APF-authorized libraries, local modifications to the PPT, and the list of LINKLIST libraries. It is named SYS1.PARMLIB and is accessed at IPL time to define these initialization parameters. When users modify SYS1.PARMLIB after an IPL, they can include nonauthorized libraries in the list of APF-authorized libraries. Because the list of APF-authorized libraries maintained in the IEAAPFnn member is obtained from the PARMLIB at IPL time and incorporated in the IPL, anyone who can update the system parameter library, can also have the capability to bypass system security. Therefore, the ability to update SYS1.PARMLIB should be severely limited to a select few.

Security databases

These are the datasets where security packages such as CA-ACF2, RACF, or CA-TOP SECRET maintain their information. For CA-TOP SECRET and CA-ACF2, start procedures specify the names of the datasets. In RACF, these datasets are defined at RACF implementation time. Users with update access to the security database might change how they are defined directly in the security database and obtain system privileges. The result of this could be the potential bypass of all security. Even the use of read access can be employed to review system protection surrounding sensitive system data. By looking for potential mistakes in the way the security has been set up, methods for exploitation might be found. Thus, nonauthorized individuals should be prevented from even reading the security database datasets.

System Management Facility (SMF) datasets

The System Management Facility (SMF) is a group of MVS modules and data center exits that collect data about the MVS system, jobs, and TSO sessions, and then write this data to system files as a permanent record of the transactions in the system. SMF datasets are used by security packages to maintain audit trails of dataset access requests (both authorized and unauthorized). Additionally, MVS itself might capture records of user activity that can be used for auditability purposes. These include what programs were executed, what datasets were processed, or what devices where allocated. The SMF datasets are named SYS1.MANx and are cataloged in the system catalog.

SMF data is important because it can be used as a permanent record of user activities. Both user violations (attempts to access protected resources while lacking proper authority) and authorized accesses are collected. One of the key elements in maintaining a secure system is timely and effective action taken to stop unauthorized activity. Individuals seeking to exploit system security might use the information in the SYS1.MANx datasets to verify whether their unsuccessful attempts to access protected datasets are being recorded. When SMF data is utilized to audit activity, and site staff uncovers unexplained actions, it is then possible to intercede by revoking the user ID. On the other hand, by being able to review the information maintained on these datasets, a potential intruder could stop activities that might be detected and might try different ways to penetrate system security without discovery. Thus, it is important to eliminate the ability to read SMF data.

Even where read access is allowed, however, it is critical to prevent users from updating SMF datasets, and so prevent them from erasing records of activity in the system. Such erasure could enable unauthorized individuals to continue exploring MVS until a way through the security envelope was found.

System catalogs

The system catalog is the central repository for the name of the dataset, the volume in which it resides, and the unit attributes of the volume. MVS supports both master and user catalogs, with the master catalog having pointers defined that direct some datasets to particular user catalogs. The system catalog is specified at system generation time and is pointed to by the MVS nucleus. It might have aliases defined to associate groups of datasets with specific user catalogs.

For newer MVS releases, there are two types of authority required to modify the catalog, based on the related dataset name authority or the catalog authority. Users who can delete the dataset also can uncatalog (modify the catalog) the dataset. In the RACF environment, when someone can control access to the catalog, they also can uncatalog the dataset even when they have no access to the dataset. You ought to protect MVS from inadvertent or intentional modification of information in the system catalogs (which could result in an incorrect dataset being made available for processing), by enabling modification of system catalog related data only when granted dataset related authority.

System supervisor call (SVC) and program call (PC) routines

System supervisor call (SVCs) and program call (PC) routines are types of MVS code invoked using the special hardware instructions SVC and PC. These two instructions provide mechanisms to enable a program to change machine status from nonauthorized mode to authorized. An SVC routine starts processing in supervisor state under the master storage protection key zero. A PC routine might start execution under supervisor or problem program state with any protection key which was specified when it was established.

A total of 256 SVC routines are possible, which are resident in virtual storage, and are either included in the MVS nucleus or reside in the Link Pack area. Using naming conventions and parameters specified in the parameter library, the system builds an SVC table that is used to access them (the SVCs). To these original SVCs, PC routines have now been added in newer releases of MVS. PC routines can be established by any program running in authorized state, when the authorized program specifies their operating characteristics. Unlimited numbers of PC programs are possible to support similar objectives as the SVCs, depending on the installation's needs.

There are several risks to the overall integrity of MVS associated with SVCs and PCs. The most common problem found in SVC-type routines is in the authorization SVCs. IBM designed them to permit programs' running without APF-authorization to become APF-authorized, and to run in supervisor state or under a system storage protection key, such as when issuing commands directly to read or write to any dataset on the system outside the limits of MVS or security package control, or when changing MVS control blocks.

Where they exist, they should validate that the program using them is the intended one and that no other program running concurrently in the same address space might use the authority granted by them. One method is to validate that the program was loaded from an APF-authorized library and that it is named as expected. Additionally, it is critical to verify that no other programs already loaded in the address space can take advantage of the authorization setting. (This is a difficult task and requires thorough knowledge of MVS internals.)

In order to maintain MVS integrity, the restrictions that MVS permits over the ability to obtain APF-authorization must be maintained. For example, if a program began without APF-authorization, it shouldn't be able to obtain APF-authorization. A properly designed authorization SVC should ensure that the program requiring authorization is the intended one. It should do this through a validation process. However, it is quite common to find authorization routines that perform little or no validation at all before granting authorized status.

Another potential problem occurs when storage areas specified by the calling program are not properly validated. Through this weakness, it is possible for a program to obtain access to protected storage areas. To prevent this, the SVC code itself has to validate that the calling program could access any storage that it is specifying. A basic example of how this works is as follows:

- A user program invokes SVC to read data, specifies some parameters to tell the SVC i) what to read; and, ii) where to put the data.

- The SVC starts execution in supervisor state and storage protection key 0 (enabling access of all areas of virtual storage). This starts the I/O activity and writes the data to the user-specified location. (If the user program did not have the authority to update the specific storage area originally, then a problem exists.)

In this environment, a user program might specify the storage area where RACF information is maintained for its session, and by reading a modified version of those control blocks might change them, perhaps changing the user ID that is running or changing the user attributes, such as RACF SPECIAL or RACF OPERATIONS.

SVC and PC routines should be viewed as MVS modifications requiring the same kind of validation and control that MVS routines require.

DUMP datasets

Dump datasets are used to copy the contents of main memory for problem analysis after an abend or at specified breakpoints. When a system task terminates abnormally, MVS writes a copy of the whole virtual storage address space into the dump dataset. Dump datasets follow the naming convention SYS1.DUMPnn (where nn is an installation-defined number), and are used by the DUMPSRV system service that is responsible for the dump process. Data that become available as the result of a dump often reveal a wealth of unexpected information. The dumped data might provide read access to fetch protected areas of virtual storage, or copies of the contents of other users' address spaces. It also is possible to find user IDs and passwords in clear text, especially when the dump includes storage areas used by teleprocessing monitors such as CICS, IMS/DC, or session managers such as TPX or TELEVIEW.

To adequately protect MVS, no one outside a narrow list of people whose job it is to review dump datasets for problem determination should be allowed to read dump datasets.

Trace datasets

Your organization can use trace datasets to accumulate and hold information gathered by different MVS components, or to add-on debugging products. They contain information for determining and diagnosing problems occurring during system operation. This trace information might include a dump of portions of virtual storage, as well as the contents of general registers. The most common trace product is the Generalized Trace Facility (GTF). You can tailor it to record very specific system and user program events for the purpose of finding logic or hardware problems. Once a GTF address space is started, and GTF is instructed to monitor certain events, it activates routines (hooks) which exist in predefined places in the MVS system and waits for events tracing, which is done either internally (in buffers located in virtual storage) or externally (to DASD or tape) by trapping information from the user program address space. Additional trace-related activity can be generated by database managers, such as IMS, to evaluate problems.

GTF trace is started using a procedure typically named GTF, and the trace dataset is usually named SYS1.TRACE (although both are customizable, resulting in name changes if the site wishes). Some installations customize both the procedure and trace datasets, but the name will usually suggest the specific trace product; for example, SYS1.GTFTRAC, SYS1.GTF, or SYSTEM.TRACE.VTAM. Depending on the specific type of trace started, very sensitive system information might be written to the trace datasets. For example, a VTAM trace begun to review network-related problems might include User Ids and passwords in clear text should users log on to the system during the trace period. Another example, although somewhat more rare, is that it is possible to start a trace of the RACINIT SVC by specifying that, when SVC number xxx (RACINIT) is issued, a dump of "n" bytes (some number) from the storage location pointed to by R1 (the dump parameter used by the RACINIT SVC) should be done. This will provide the RACF logon parameters.

If this is done, all LOGON activity will be captured and written to the trace datasets. To prevent such problems from occurring, no one should be allowed to read TRACE datasets without careful management of who is given this permission.

Procedure libraries

Procedure libraries are used to maintain sets of Job Control Language (JCL) to efficiently perform routine production tasks. They are used to schedule batch jobs to compile and link programs, perform system maintenance, and initiate production jobs such as payroll or accounting runs. A set of default procedure libraries is included within the JES startup procedures themselves, to enable sites to immediately have a skeleton structure available with which to begin processing work.

Recent releases of MVS now allow the user to specify what procedure library to use in the JOB stream. Users who can update procedure libraries can also add steps to that library. By permitting this, authorized users could unintentionally execute something that previously was placed by someone into the procedure library code. This, also, is known as inserting a Trojan horse. A particularly harmful example of this would be to modify a procedure used by a security administrator by adding one step to the execution of TSO in BATCH. System privileges could be granted to the potential intruder, which could result in the circumvention of system controls.

There is an additional concern even with permitting read access to procedure libraries. Such a capability provides a great deal of information that could then be used to penetrate the system's security controls. For example, should attackers want to find an unprotected procedure library, they could browse the JES2 procedure library to find the default list of procedure libraries in the system. This could then be used to try to update each one until the update was successful. If any could be updated, the attacker could introduce a Trojan horse by modifying a procedure that is used by authorized users. An example of this would be to add one TSO batch step to a procedure used by the security administrator, and issue a command to grant SPECIAL authority to the perpetrator.

Software installation libraries

Software developers provide installation libraries with sample JCL needed to install and customize their products. Site system programming staff make the required modifications for the particular installation and submits jobs to install the specific product. Software installation libraries can be found by reviewing the volumes used by system programming. The associated library name very often suggests its usage. The name typically will have some name aspect related to the product being installed, or will have characteristic names such as JCLINST, INSTALL, or INSTJCL included within the name. Even permitting read access to these libraries provides too much information about how the particular software package was installed, and/or what type of security is in place. As well, read access provides an opportunity to find errors in the implementation that can then be exploited.

Some products use product passwords to grant access to restricted functions. These are single passwords that are shipped with all copies of the product for the install process. This installation password often is hardcoded in the JCL. Therefore, anyone with an ability to read and thus browse the library could discover the password. This should be strictly prevented by eliminating read access to everyone except where explicitly needed.

System Spool Datasets

System Spool Datasets are datasets wherein JES maintains reports and copies of input streams, as well as internal JES control blocks. Clear text user IDs and password information related to batch jobs submitted with this information, and included in the job card, can usually be found in an internal JES2 control block maintained in the spool named JCT. These datasets are defined in the JES initialization stream and are most often named SYS1.HASPACE.

User IDs and passwords in clear text can be discovered by using utilities to read the spool dataset to find business reports that have been produced and that remain in the system spool dataset. Therefore, carefully controlling the ability to read system spool datasets also controls the ability to gather sensitive system data and confidential business data.

System commands

System commands are used by operators and system programmers to control system operation. They are needed to initiate system service address spaces, start and stop jobs being processed in the system, and change operating characteristics. A most powerful command is the START command used to initiate system service tasks. Security packages such as CA-ACF2, RACF, or CA-TOP SECRET associate a user ID with jobs initiated using the START command. System commands can be executed directly on the operations consoles authorized to do so. Or, they can be received from the network, imbedded in the JOB stream, or issued internally by software packages such as spool management tools, TSO, and performance and debugging related tools.

Often the user IDs associated with these are very powerful IDs and have the ability to issue system commands. Unless carefully controlled, these commands easily can be used to disrupt system operation. For example, a cancel operator command for the VTAM control address space will stop all network activity and stop system operations. Similarly, commands to purge jobs in the spool, either scheduled jobs to be run or reports from jobs that have already run, can be very disrupting. The START command allows the issuer the ability to run jobs using user IDs intended for maintenance purposes. A typical and worrisome scenario might be where a procedure called JOB or RDR exists that allows operators to submit their own jobs using a maintenance user ID.

Unless you carefully control the ability to execute system commands, someone could use the start command to initiate the JOB or RDR procedure to begin their jobs, and could also use maintenance user IDs to bypass access controls restrictions.

Residual information

Residual information has two areas that must be controlled. These are in-storage residual information and auxiliary storage residual information. The in-storage residual information area includes MVS private address space implementation, which allows only data utilized by programs running in the user's own address space to be accessed as residual information, minimizing the possibility of obtaining unauthorized access to information as residual data. This means that TSOUSER1 cannot read any in-storage residual data created by TSOUSER2. Before real storage that was used by TSOUSER2 is assigned to TSOUSER1, the system will clear the area.

Although this appears to be secure, one possibility for problems would exist where a program is authorized to access a full segment of a database but to show the user only selected fields. After the program execution is finished, the remainder fields of the database segment could be unprotected, and data could be seen by unauthorized individuals. An example of this is contained in Table 17.3.

The second area to protect is Auxiliary Storage Residual Information. When a dataset is deleted, only the pointers to the data are removed from the volume table of contents (VTOC) of the disk where it resides. The data itself still remains exactly as it was until cleanup activities are undertaken. In tape datasets, not even the label information is discarded. By allocating a new dataset in the same location, the potential exists that the whole dataset (or confidential segments) could be recovered by an unintended user. Even though it is difficult to recover a complete dataset, it does happen and the risk should be controlled. Security packages such as RACF or CA-TOP SE-CRET provide functions to totally overwrite datasets when they are deleted from the system, and these should always be used.

TABLE 17.3 Searching for Residual Data

The master personnel database includes the phone number for each employee in addition to restricted data such as compensation. A program is developed to allow users to obtain the employees' phone numbers. This program reads the personnel database and displays the employee name and phone number. All users are allowed access to the personnel database only if they are executing the intended phone display program.

When the phone display program finishes execution, database information remains in storage as residual data in the storage areas used by the program to read the data and the management buffers. A search in virtual storage for a specific name could be used to decode the database segment.

Privileged user IDs

Privileged user IDs are users that have any level of system privilege available to them. The most common cases are user IDs that are granted security package privileges. However, additional system privileges do exist (such as those that provide the ability to issue operator commands, to access critical system datasets, to access restricted utilities, or to access debugging tools) that should be controlled. Most authorizations are controlled by the security software; however, specific authorizations for individual software packages are also often employed. Privileged user IDs are the most likely target of a penetration attempt and should be stringently protected. All executable code used by privileged user IDs should be controlled for update capability, and all security rules for this group of users should be strictly enforced, especially password rules. Any violations pointing to attempts to guess this group's passwords should be carefully and thoroughly investigated.

JCL libraries

JCL libraries are used to maintain job streams to start batch jobs. They are maintained by each user ID for each owner's specific jobs, and also are used to hold production JCL. These are datasets with dataset organization (DSORG) partitioned (PO), and usually have a logical record length of eighty (80) characters. The names typically used suggest their usage, with examples such as JCL, JOBS, DATA, CNTL in the dataset name. JCL libraries need to be protected against potential risks similar to those of Procedure Libraries.

CLIST/REXX libraries

CLIST and REXX libraries are repositories that maintain REXX and CLIST code often used to support TSO users. A TSO logon procedure specifies what libraries can be used as CLIST/REXX libraries by allocating them under file names such as SYSPROC, SYSUPROC, and SYSEXEC. Additionally, software packages, such as ISPF, allow users to specify dynamically libraries to be searched for command procedures. CLIST and REXX commands can be used to issue any TSO command to exploit someone else's authority. Additionally, risks can become high because it is a simple process to edit the command procedure and add unauthorized commands. Update access should be restricted, and careful and consistent change control procedures should be enforced to prevent such occurrences.

ISPF datasets

ISPF is a dialog manager widely used in the MVS/TSO environment. It provides multiple facilities to develop dialogs through different ISPF libraries. The ISPF dialog manager also allows the user to create and manage panels (screens) and is basically a dialog (menus, data panels, and execute programs as requested by its users). ISPF uses different types of libraries for its operation, examples of which are:

- **ISPF PROFILE datasets** The definition of the program function keys (PF1 to PF24) are maintained in this dataset. By modifying them it is possible to spoof users to execute unintended commands, through misapplication of the directives associated with specific keys.

- **ISPF Panel libraries** The panel definition language allows for the execution of system commands.

- **ISPF Skeleton libraries** These are models used to generate JCL, which by adding steps could result in unauthorized commands being executed.

- **ISPF Tables datasets** Application commands are defined in these libraries. Changes here could result in the definition of application commands being changed to execute unauthorized code. Additionally, MVS risks are magnified because this requires only an editor to introduce unwanted modifications.

Dump/restore protection

In some cases, critical system or user datasets residing on direct access devices are adequately protected. However, for backup/restore purposes, a full copy of disk volumes is usually written to tape without the same stringent controls. Problems can be avoided by reviewing backup procedures and treating their handling as confidential information, if applicable.

Source/macro/include libraries

Libraries in which source code is maintained, or in which commonly used code such as record definitions is maintained, used when compiling source programs, are also areas where MVS controls can be weakened. The compile procedures will point to the applicable source and include libraries. Weak control over source/macro/include libraries could result in a Trojan horse's being introduced, by permitting the modification of the source libraries and waiting until a standard compilation is made by authorized personnel.

Other Executable Datasets

Any other dataset or library holding information that could be used to generate system commands should also be adequately protected against inadvertent or intentional compromise. The specifics of protecting MVS from the myriad problems each of these packages bring with them depends on the specifics of the software packages installed on the system. An example of this is SCRIPT/370, which allows commands to be included in the document to be formatted.

This capability could be used to introduce a Trojan horse by including TSO commands, or even security package commands. When the document is processed by an authorized user ID the commands could be executed, thereby granting the intruder unintended authorities. Each of these should be treated with the security measures which the product vendors indicate are warranted.

Utility control statement libraries

Utility control statement libraries are datasets used to maintain utility program control cards, such as sort statements, REPRO statements, and so forth. They often are used for production runs. When executing a utility such as IDCAMS (VSAM utility) or SORT, the file named SYSIN will point to a specific member in a utility control statement library. Using dynamic allocation, it is possible to make nonauthorized copies of data simply by using utility control statements.

An example of this might be an IDCAMS utility executed to generate a backup copy of a dataset at the end of a batch production run. The statement could read something like this:

```
REPRO IFILE(MASTER) OFILE(BACKUP)
```

An unauthorized user might include the following code to obtain copies of confidential datasets, using the authority of the individual who submitted the job:

```
REPRO IFILE(MASTER) OFILE(BACKUP)
REPRO IFILE(MASTER)
OUTDATASET('Hacker.Master')
REPRO INDA('PAY.MASTER')
OUTDATASET('HACKER.PAYROLL')
```

This is very simple to accomplish. Thus, it is equally important to ensure that nonauthorized users are not permitted to update, and thereby change, utility control statement libraries.

Other database access paths

There are a variety of other ways around MVS security. These include:

- **Dataset level access** Database products such as IMS, IDMS, and DB2 provide their own security code, or interfaces to the security package, to permit access to data. The data itself is maintained in MVS datasets and access is performed under the authority of the database manager address space. Users do not need any access to those datasets to process the transactions. Occasionally, by mistake, users are granted access to the datasets, enabling them to initiate update commands outside of application controls.

- **Inter-region communication type of access** It is possible for a BATCH job to access databases, using memory-to-memory access with the database manager. One common case in which this happens is during the backup process, where a batch job will be scheduled to make a full copy of specific databases. Often the access path used to accomplish this is not controlled and any user is able to submit batch jobs to access the database, thereby avoiding the intended security controls.

Debugging tools/performance monitors

Debugging tools and performance monitors are software packages intended for system programming staff use. These tools often allow the user to issue internal system commands, access memory, and even modify protected storage. These programs obtain their privileges by running with APF-authorization, or by incorporating SVC routines into the system. A most critical feature of these products is their ability to modify protected virtual storage. By modifying MVS control blocks, it is possible to disable security and accountability mechanisms. Access to debugging tools or performance monitors should be controlled on a need-to-use basis.

JES initialization parameters

The Job Entry Subsystem (JES) is initialized using a set of control statements known as the *JES initialization parameters*. The initialization has controls included in it, such as the authorization for commands to be executed when issued from different interfaces, as well as permission to either honor the Bypass Label Processing requirement for magnetic tapes or not to honor it. JES initialization parameters are specified in a dataset that is included in the JES startup procedure. By modifying the JES initialization deck, a user might nullify intended controls. For example, JES can be instructed to accept all commands included in the job stream, and then these commands also could be exploited. Read access to these data should be controlled, because users do not need this access. Then, if any security related problems are found there, an analysis of the initialization deck might help disclose the error.

User Attribute Dataset (UADS)

The User Attribute Dataset (UADS) is used by native TSO to maintain TSO users' passwords and authorizations. The UADS dataset functions have been replaced by security packages such as RACF. Even though the UADS capability still can be used by staff, this should not be the case. All UADS functions should be performed by a security package. If the UADS dataset is being used to define TSO users, the associated user passwords will be maintained in it in clear text. Additionally, any user capable of modifying the dataset might grant additional TSO privileges to his user IDs.

Summary

MVS, as an operating system, provides a good foundation for information integrity. However, MVS by itself does not provide an efficient access control mechanism with which to maintain a secure environment. With the implementation of add-on security packages, such as CA-ACF2, RACF, or CA-TOP SECRET, to provide needed access controls, MVS can be made more secure. However, this is not the total answer. Much of the final result of how well MVS is secured depends not only on installing an access control package but also in:

- Implementing MVS properly
- Integrating it adequately into a permanent test program for both MVS and the business data also residing under it.

Thorough security implementation requires that the enterprise make decisions regarding what its protection needs are (i.e., the risk if exposure occurs versus the cost to secure) and then carefully carries out this strategy with the mechanisms available.

Access authorities should be granted only to those who have a business need to know, rather than on a more global basis. Table 17.4 summarizes access rights for key MVS datasets.

TABLE 17.4 Access Levels for Key MVS Components

MVS component	Risk	Controlled access level
APF authorized libraries	System integrity compromise	UPDATE
LINKLIST libraries	System integrity	UPDATE
LPA libraries	System integrity	UPDATE
Restricted utilities	System control bypass	Execute
Program properties table	System control bypass	Execute
System nucleus	System integrity compromise	UPDATE
System PARMLIB	System modification	UPDATE
Security databases	System access bypass	READ

TABLE 17.4 Access Levels for Key MVS Components (Continued)

MVS component	Risk	Controlled access level
SMF datasets		READ
System catalogs		Control
SVCs, PCs	System integrity	Internal code
SYS1.DUMPnn	Sensitive system data or confidential business data exposed	READ
TRACE datasets	Sensitive system information exposed	READ
Procedure libraries	Trojan horse—inserting unauthorized code	UPDATE
Software installation libraries	Understanding of controls in place	READ
System spool datasets	Sensitive system information, confidential business data	READ
System commands	Trojan horses, system integrity	Execute
Residual information	Confidential business data	N/A
Privileged UserIDs	Penetration target	N/A
JCL libraries	Trojan horses	UPDATE
CLIST, REXX libraries	Trojan horses	UPDATE
ISPF datasets	Trojan horses	UPDATE
Dump/restore protection	Sensitive business information	READ
Source/macro/include libraries	Trojan horses	UPDATE
Other executable datasets	Trojan horses	UPDATE
Utility control statement libraries	Trojan horses	UPDATE
Other database access paths		
Debugging tools/ performance monitors	System integrity	Execute
JES initialization parameters	System integrity	UPDATE
UADS dataset		READ

In a dynamic environment such as MVS, it is very difficult to maintain a current evaluation of all system resources and identify the risks associated with access to each one. A better approach is to evaluate potential risks when access to the specific resource is required. The main considerations regarding MVS security and access controls include the following.

MVS modifications

Ensure that only authorized MVS modifications are made to MVS, using access controls and appropriate change control mechanisms. Also ensure that authorized system modifications do not introduce exposures to system integrity. All user modifications to MVS, such as APF authorized programs and user SVCs, should be reviewed for integrity following the same criteria as for MVS code.

Access to sensitive system data

Ensure that only authorized personnel have access to system-related passwords and any source of information about security implementation. By reviewing security implementation information, a potential intruder might discover a security deficiency and exploit it.

Ability to introduce Trojan horses

Ensure that appropriate controls exist over the modification of all executable code. It is critical to understand that, in this area, it does not matter if the code is important or not. What is critical is the authority of the person who uses the code, for this can determine what else the user can do.

Access to critical business data

The two main reasons why MVS needs to be secure are to:

- Ensure that someone has not interfered and made the system unavailable.
- Maintain the ability to process user applications and data while maintaining their integrity.

The former is important because, without system availability, work cannot get done. The latter is even more important, because employees must be able to depend on the results of their processing to answer questions and supply needed information. To continually ensure this outcome, MVS security is essential.

This is not the final step, however. The MVS operating system resides in a highly complex and dynamic environment. Because of the many changes that occur on a regular basis, and the difficulty in tracing all that those changes might affect, regular monitoring of MVS controls is a must. The enterprise cannot implement MVS and other software while continuing to assume that controls that once existed, still do. This simply is not the case. Thus, to ensure the security of MVS, a program of monitoring and review must be put in place. This combination of thorough implementation, coupled with ongoing attention, will assist the enterprise in achieving a properly secured MVS environment throughout the operating system's life.

Select Bibliography

IBM. March 1991. *MVS/ESA Planning Security. First Edition.* (GC28-1604-0).

Johnson, Robert H. 1989. *MVS: Concepts and Facilities.* New York: McGraw-Hill.

Soper, Keith R. 1986. *MVS Top-To-Bottom: An Analysis of MVS and Its Impact on Audit and Security.* Volume 1, Number 1. Framingham, MA: MIS Training Institute.

18

Using RACF to Control MVS-Based Servers

Darren M. Jones and Peter P.C.H. Kingston

Only those defenses are good, certain and
durable, which depend on yourself alone and
your ability.   NICCOLO MACHIAVELLI

Access control in the MVS environment cannot be managed effectively without the installation of external security software, such as Computer Associates' Access Control Facility 2 (CA-ACF2) or Top Secret (CA-Top Secret), or IBM's Resource Access Control Facility (RACF). These products, as "external security managers" to MVS, control the functions users might perform on MVS systems, by defining users, groupings of users, resources to be protected, and access rules protecting those resources.

Prudent implementation of an external security manager can provide many security benefits, foremost being an established framework for control. RACF also provides an approach for managing access to information resources, with capabilities for protecting the resources as desired.

RACF provides security authorization checking, which supports a mainframe installation in the control of resource access. RACF identifies and verifies user access to the system, verifies that the user might perform a requested action, provides logging and reporting facilities, and provides additional support for user and process interactions with MVS subsystems. RACF monitors and controls access to a variety of MVS resources, including application programs, specific DASD datasets, tape volumes, and system transactions.

The challenge is to mold the highly host-centric controls in RACF to reflect the network-centric security requirements of client/server systems.

Identifying the User

The basis for all RACF activities is determining whether a user gains access to an information resource. The first security issue, then, is the definition of potential users of the system to RACF. The system must be able to identify these people as authorized users of the system, or as intruders.

RACF identifies authorized users by user identification codes (user IDs), and their attempts to sign on to the system are authenticated by passwords. User IDs and encrypted passwords are stored in the RACF database, which is typically kept in datasets following a SYS1.RACF* naming standard. An elemental step in providing security is, then, to secure this dataset from unauthorized change or corruption.

For a user to access an RACF-protected system, the user must be identified to RACF. This identification is made when the user enters the user ID, which RACF compares with all of the user IDs present in the RACF database.

Defining User and Group Profiles

All user IDs on the RACF-controlled system have a defined user profile, which is a defined schematic of that user's definition to RACF. This definition includes the user ID's authorities, attributes, and restrictions. However, managing resource access rules on a user-ID-by-user-ID basis can become quite unwieldy. RACF provides the ability to organize users with similar access requirements into groups. Users can belong to a multiple number of groups, with the idea being that each group represents some representation of the user's access needs. For instance, I might belong to three groups: CORPAUD, because I am employed by Corporate Audit, FINANCE, because I also need access to some corporate financial resources, and AUTHORS because I need access to word processing and typesetting datasets to publish reports and articles on client/server security.

This multiplicity of group connections can allow for a very granular and well-managed approach to security. For example, the person sitting in the office next to mine might belong only to the FINANCE RACF group. Group profiles allow users to be connected with access to information based on functional requirements.

Protecting Information Resources

It is not enough for a security mechanism to allow a legitimate user to enter the system and complete all authorization checking at that point. There must exist some control over the activities a user might perform while in the system. The next key function of RACF, then, is to protect information resources. This protection involves two major steps: defining the class, or type, of information resource to be protected, and defining resource profiles that specify which users should access the resource. When a user attempts to access a resource, the RACF database is checked to verify that user's authority to do so.

A resource profile contains the resource name, the access list of user and group profiles authorized to access the resource, and the default level of access allowed to the resource. When a user attempts to access a resource, RACF refers to the user and group profiles in effect for that user, then compares these profiles with the access list contained in the related resource profile. If the user's access is not defined in the resource profile's access list, the resource profile's default access level (called the universal access authority, or UACC) manages access.

Resources with similar protection requirements can be grouped together into one profile. For instance, all datasets with a dataset name COR-PAUD.FINANCIAL.V94xxxx can be protected by a dataset profile of COR-PAUD.FINANCIAL.V*.

RACF can grant different categories of access to resources profiles:

- **NONE**   The user or group has no access to the resource.
- **READ**   The user or group can browse, copy, and read the resource.
- **UPDATE**   The user or group can change the contents of the resource.
- **ALTER**   The user or group can change the contents of the resource and can also delete it.

These levels of access can be granted to either users or groups. Although assigning resource access on a user ID level might provide for some excellent granularity, it's far more efficient to manage access on a group profile basis. This approach also promotes taking a functional view of security, which helps maintain consistency of resource profiles as users' responsibilities change. Of course, the security administrator must actively manage the connection of user IDs with group profiles.

There is a great deal of granularity involved in defining information resources to RACF. Thus far, I have referred to resources as if they were only datasets or data files. However, different types of resources can be classified in RACF according to the types of resources they are. For instance, DATASETS is an RACF class representing online MVS datasets to RACF. Other resource classes are available, to represent other types of system resources. Following are the classes that are referred to in this chapter, and the types of resources they protect:

- AIMS defines IMS group names.
- APPCLU verifies the identity of partner logical units during VTAM sessions.

- APPCTP controls use of APPC transaction programs.
- APPL controls access to applications.
- DATASET controls access to datasets.
- PTKTDATA defines all profiles that contain RACF PassTicket information.
- TIMS also defines IMS transactions.

In client/server systems, the user request typically comes to RACF through an application or subsystem. The user doesn't directly enter a command to access the resource, but such a request is embedded in the client/server system's processing logic. This process is briefly outlined in Figure 18.1. In step 1, the user issues a request to access a resource. This request is routed to RACF in step 2, which refers to an access control resource profile assigned to protect the resource, to determine whether the access request will be granted. In step 3, the user is notified of whether the access request will be fulfilled (actually, this step only occurs when access has been denied). Step 4 depicts subsequent user requests to access the same resource, which are routed by the application in step 5 to the actual resource.

Privileged Authorities on RACF

Privileged users are RACF users who have powerful system access authorities. To establish a good framework of control, these powerful system users must be limited to a reasonable number who have their activities closely monitored.

The most powerful of the privileged user attributes is the SPECIAL attribute. Users with the SPECIAL attribute can issue all RACF commands, and thus can gain complete control over all user, group, and resource profiles on the system. In planning for RACF security, the plan must ensure that system-wide SPECIAL attributes are limited to those security analysts responsible for performing high-level, system-wide procedures.

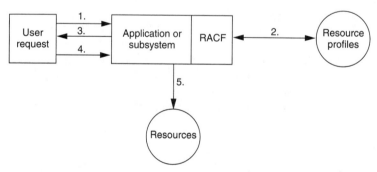

Figure 18.1 How RACF protects information resource profiles

The OPERATIONS authority permits the user to have full authorization to RACF-protected system resources, such as datasets. So, although a user with OPERATIONS cannot define user and resource profiles as a SPECIAL user can, this user can nonetheless gain full access to corporate data. As a result, OPERATIONS is an attribute that also must be limited, in this case to personnel responsible for supporting the operations of MVS itself.

RACF Mandatory Access Control

With the advent of the U.S. Department of Defense's Trusted Computer System guidelines, the idea of Mandatory Access Controls (MAC) has become an issue in systems that are required to support a B1 level of operating system security. In RACF version 1.9, MAC became an optional feature for the installation to implement.

Before the benefits of MAC can be truly understood, the familiarity with the concept of security labeling is necessary. In RACF, security labels can be given to all users to determine whether the user successfully accesses RACF objects, such as data files, transactions, or application menus. Every security label consists of two parts. The first part is a category, which in our example is represented by a letter (that is, from X to Z). These categories are used to separate resources and users on the basis of their job functions. Only those categories to which a subject or object has been assigned are part of its label.

Suppose for example, there are a series of resources relating to MVS's key system functions (for example, Authorized Program libraries or SYS1. PARMLIB) that must be limited to specific individuals. These resources have been assigned a category of Z. However, because all users that have been assigned category Z might not require access to all resources under the aegis of Z, assigning just categories to resources would not suffice to manage access.

This problem leads to the second part of the security label: the level. Levels are hierarchical in nature and indicate the degree of sensitivity assigned to the resource. Let's suppose, in our example, that levels are represented numerically, with 0 representing public access (that is, accessible by all users) and 4 representing the most restricted level of access (that is, top secret). Accordingly, users also will be assigned security levels, numbering from 0 through 4.

Level and category information are carried in the security label for each user and menu option. The security label is built for the resource when it is defined to RACF, such as when the resource is created. Security labels for users and groups are assigned to the related RACF user and group profiles.

The security label is important because is sets the maximum level and complete set of categories to be used for the session. When a user attempts to access a resource, RACF examines the security labels of both the user and the resource. Before access is granted, label dominance must be determined. Label dominance occurs when the authorization of one label exceeds the authorization of another label. Users are allowed access to the resource when they have label dominance over that resource, or have a label that matches that resource. For instance, a user with a level of 4 in the Z category can access any resource with a Z security label equal to or less than 4. Access to resources with a Z security label equal to 5 will not be permitted, as the resource's security label has dominance over the user's security label. This process is depicted in Figure 18.2.

RACF's security labeling approach to managing access requests makes it much easier to share data between users with a need to know that is based on job responsibilities. In this way, only users with a need for access are assigned access to a resource. However, there is a complexity in managing the access needs of thousands of active users with a dozen or so categories, each extending across many thousands of resources. Due to this complexity, RACF security specialists need to review the options available and the user and group profiles assigned access to them.

This is the point at which the phrase *Mandatory Access Control* (MAC) becomes much more understandable. As security labels assign level and category information for each user, group, and resource profile, we now have the opportunity to restrict what is done with a resource by a user that has access to it. Recall that in the definition of user and group access to resource profiles, the access level of READ means that any user with READ could make a copy of the resource.

While not by definition a problem, this copying capability has ended up being a major headache for security planners. A user with access to a sensitive or confidential resource could copy it to another, less-secured location. What this effectively means is that the carefully defined resource security rule is circumvented. With MAC, however, the security level assigned by the security label cannot be compromised. If a user has access to a level 4

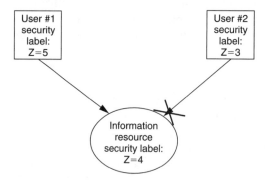

Figure 18.2 Security label processing

dataset, this user cannot copy that dataset to any location that does not have level 4 security.

As mentioned above, the maintenance of MAC and security labeling requires a great deal of ongoing planning, management, and monitoring. First made available in RACF 1.9, MAC requires considerable up-front analysis and effort to convert to it properly.

Client/Server Connections with MVS Subsystems

The discussion so far has centered on RACF's role in protecting resources on an MVS mainframe, as though there were no subsystems or application front ends to protect as well. Clearly, the use of RACF in protecting MVS-based systems entails far more than managing the direct access of users and groups to MVS resources. In client/server applications that use MVS, it is difficult to imagine the application functioning without some interaction with a subsystem.

MVS subsystems offer unique security challenges. Each MVS subsystem has its own way of representing data, its own method of interfacing with the user, and often its own approach to managing security.

Managing controls over these subsystems can be a very complex undertaking. Variances in how products like Database 2 (DB2), Customer Information Control System (CICS), and the Information Management System (IMS) can be installed add to this complexity. On the user side, data communications subsystems are by far the predominant method used to allow end-user interaction with the mainframe. Subsystems provide for menu-driven IMS and CICS applications; hence their popularity in managing mainframe application data. More important for this discussion, client/server interactions with MVS make extensive use of subsystems.

It has become apparent that managing security within subsystems is not the most effective way of achieving control. With security decision making fragmented among subsystems, security measures applied by different subsystems might not be consistent, particularly when the subsystems are managed by different personnel. Security measures might even work at cross-purposes, especially when compensating administrative controls are not in place. A basic principle that should be applied to subsystems is that security decisions should be made by RACF, not by the subsystem. This way, security management is focused at a central point of authentication. Authorization, therefore, is greatly simplified and can be made more cost-effective.

Controlling VTAM—Connecting the Subsystems

The first line of defense in a computer network is to control who can connect to the system, and in what way. In IBM mainframe networks, these controls are managed by the Virtual Telecommunications Access Method (VTAM), which identifies network nodes and the method they are using to connect to MVS. These methods also are called sessions, and each session is identified to VTAM by an application identifier (APPLID) (for a full discussion of VTAM, see Chapter 10). For instance, an IMS development session might have a VTAM APPLID of IMSDV1. To initiate the session, the user types IMSDV1 at the VTAM screen. Without strong subsystem controls, the VTAM screen can be breached by whoever knows the related APPLID. VTAM operates by managing one application per terminal at a time.

VTAM was originally designed as an unsecured application, as a communications front door to the mainframe. As a result, VTAM itself should be protected from unauthorized changes, by limiting access to SYS1.VTAMLST and similar datasets (for example, SYS1.VTAMLIB). VTAMLST defines all of the VTAM nodes to the network. These nodes include MVS subsystems, such as CICS, as well as terminals. The SAF (System Authorization Facility) interface of VTAMAPPL can be used to control the connection of sessions to VTAM, and to prevent unauthorized sessions from being initiated.

Often, the management of VTAM sessions is controlled using session managers. Some session manager products include SuperSession from Candle, VMAN from Computer Associates, and TPX from Legent Corp. Session managers are VTAM applications and allow a physical terminal to establish several SNA conversations at one time. Although several sessions might be active, VTAM still manages the conversations as though there is only one session taking place. Session managers allow the security administration to apply controls by linking the user ID or terminal to only those VTAM sessions the user or terminal is authorized to use.

In running a session manager, there are some security needs to be addressed. First, there must be a supported exit interface to an external security manager. Second, the session manager must be able to respond to all return codes provided to it by the security manager. In keeping with our goal of managing security at a central authorization and authentication point, the session manager product should be capable of operating with its own application security turned disabled. Finally, it must allow the pass through of user ID and password to applications connected by the session manager.

Where SAF becomes involved, control is managed by the RACROUTE security macro. RACROUTE specifications can be used to form the basis for validating a user, managing password and system access, and checking a user's authority to access a resource. As a result, SAF interfaces are often desirable features in subsystems and session managers. RACF handles authentication with a RACROUTE TYPE=VERIFY.

To issue a RACROUTE VERIFY the application must either be APF-authorized, be in system key, or be in a supervisor state. The security product, not the session manager, should control the applications a user can select. The session manager merely should present the available selections. In

RACF, the session manager validates resources by issuing a RACROUTE TYPE=EXTRACT call for the SESSION segment, which is used in conjunction with the APPCLU class to support VTAM.

Controlling VTAM, then, is the necessary first step in controlling subsystems. Controlling VTAM consists of limiting access to key VTAM libraries and managing changes to VTAM via strong quality assurance processes.

Managing Data with IMS

The Information Management System (IMS) is a hierarchical database manager and controls a great deal of information kept on corporate legacy systems. The most common way IMS information is accessed is through IMS transactions. These transactions are defined for specific purposes and have access to information only within the limits of that function. IMS transactions cannot be manipulated by the person requesting the function to operate outside those limits.

For this reason, IMS transactions are used to manage access to other database manager information (e.g., DB2) as well. The most important concept in the IMS architecture is transaction authorization; that is, controlling who can access what functions.

The IMS Security Maintenance Utility (SMU) provides security checking internal to IMS transactions (in addition to the external security provided by RACF control over activation of the transactions). However, use of the SMU entails a lack of individual accountability. This is because SMU provides terminal-based security, rather than security based on individual user identifiers.

Further, SMU assigns passwords to IMS resources such as transactions, commands, and terminals. Because so many passwords need to be known, circumstances arise in which it is difficult to keep all passwords secure. Finally, all SMU passwords are stored by IMS in clear text! As a result, security can be more consistently applied if the IMS Security Maintenance Utility is not in use. Rather, effective use of the external security manager and IMS exits is more desirable.

IMS can use external security checking for sign-on and transaction authorization checking. This checking is enforced by the SECLVL parameters of TRANAUTH and SIGNON in the IMS SECUPRD0 macro. Access to IMS control regions is restricted by the APPLICATION class for IMS in SAF. This process checks application names and access lists to the IMS control region's application identifier during sign-on, and gives permission to access resources. This process uses the external security manager to control access to program specification blocks and transaction names. In RACF, IMS transaction classes are defined to control the activities of IMS programs; for example, AIMS for IMS group names and TIMS for IMS transactions.

External security products interact with IMS to control sign-on and sign-off processing, transaction authorization, and resource access authorization functions. RACF/IMS interfaces for applications also need to be controlled. These interfaces can define what each application can reference or change.

The first cornerstone of IMS security is user sign-on. When IMS users are forced to sign-on, they are identified at the terminal. Every external security product provides for the ability for sign-on transaction security in an IMS online environment. Only RACF, version 2.0, and CA-Top Secret provide security for IMS commands.

The next cornerstone is transaction security. In client/server systems that access mainframe data, IMS transactions can be used to receive client/server calls from outside of MVS, and to perform the data access request on behalf of the client/server call. The benefit in this approach is that the IMS transaction has already been encoded to access specific data in a particular way. As long as only particular client/server calls can activate the IMS transaction, then existing IMS and RACF controls can be used for security.

RACF provides IMS transaction security by defining protected transactions as profiles within the TIMS class. RACF user and group profiles can then be granted access to specific IMS transactions through these transaction profiles. For IMS transactions that service client/server calls, it is recommended that the default security for each transaction be set to NONE. Note that the type of access users and groups have to the data cannot be segregated within the IMS transaction profile. Users and groups can only be given access to execute the transaction or be prevented from executing it. Decisions about READ or UPDATE access to data are made within the transaction programming logic. That is, whether I have READ or UPDATE access to data depends on how the transaction I use is defined. For example, PAYREAD might be defined as an IMS transaction that gives its user READ access to certain payroll information. If I issue a client/server request that uses PAYREAD to access information, I cannot manipulate PAYREAD to do anything else but read payroll information.

In client/server systems, a common approach is to link remote procedure calls from clients with IMS transactions on servers. This approach has the benefit of requiring application developers to simply call the remote procedure call and, by extension, the IMS transaction, without having to know how the transaction operates.

This approach is also beneficial from a control perspective, as client requests can be packaged into well-defined and RACF-controlled IMS transactions.

Managing Access with CICS

The Customer Information Control System (CICS) subsystem also presents a set of security issues that require exploration. CICS manages user and terminal communications by defining and managing access to specific transactions. These transactions control and manage the user's access to data. Just as in IMS, these transactions are defined for specific purposes and have access to information only within the limits of that function. CICS transactions cannot be manipulated by the user to operate outside those limits. CICS transactions also are used to manage access to database manager information (e.g., DB2 tables).

CICS transactions are often packaged together into CICS regions. These regions are VTAM sessions that the user must activate (hence they are defined to SYS1.VTAMLST) before sign-on. For example, to sign-on to a payroll application kept in a distinct CICS region, the user would have to type in CICSPAY at the VTAM screen to allocate the CICSPAY session. CICS provides a sign-on screen to challenge for the userid and password before access to CICS and the application is actually granted. As a result, difficulties in managing security between CICS and the external security manager might arise when close attention is not paid to the operating parameters in all CICS regions.

For instance, the CICS System Initialization Table (called DFHSIT by CICS) defines the parameters to be invoked at system startup. These parameters' calls to the external security product might be overridden at system startup by the PARM statement in the CICS startup PROC.

The Sign-On Table (DFHSNT) defines the default user access parameters and whether users will be controlled by RACF. DFHSNT defines default access (TYPE=DEFAULT) and the default relationship a user will have with RACF (EXTSEC=YES). This table can be used to override external security calls to RACF individually by user or globally by default when EXTSEC=NO.

The definition of default access can be significant when many programs are executed by a single transaction. An application's access control could be based on a strategy to place security only where needed, leaving less critical or sensitive programs unprotected. This leads to the existence of unsecured inquiry and menus, along with secured update screens. This access strategy complicates the administration of access because similar controls exist within both RACF and CICS.

The Resource Definition Online dataset (also known as DFHCSD—the CSD table) defines CICS region, and groups of transactions, programs, and data accessed by programs for the CICS region. Most important, the CSD table defines whether a transaction will interface with RACF by an entry in the TRANSEC parameter. TRANSEC=NO means there will be no call placed to RACF or CICS security. TRANSEC=YES means CICS security will be used. TRANSEC=EXTSEC means a call to RACF will be made. To ensure an overall objective of consistent and complete security management, TRANSEC= EXTSEC should be used as an installation's default for all CICS regions.

Programs not defined to RACF might be permitted to execute on the basis of no security or native CICS security. Release 4 of CICS enables the ALWAYS CALL option for all CICS transactions, in effect forcing RACF to control CICS transactions. Therefore all CICS programs, by virtue of the

ALWAYS CALL option, will be required to be defined to RACF. In this way, controls are improved and the need for managing specialized application security disappears.

As with IMS, client/server systems can link remote procedure calls from clients with CICS transactions on MVS servers. This approach is beneficial from a control perspective, as client requests are packaged into well-defined and RACF-controlled CICS transactions.

Managing Relational Data with DB2

IBM's Database 2 (DB2) is a relational database management system for the MVS environment (although versions exist for OS/2 and AS/400). In relational systems, data is represented by a number of related columns and rows. All accesses to the data are performed using one comprehensive language, SQL (Structured Query Language). Using SQL, you can manipulate and modify rows and columns within the table.

The userid used to connect to DB2 from IMS, CICS, or TSO is known to DB2 as the primary authorization id (authid). DB2 exits that execute when a user initially connects to DB2 accept this primary user ID and can assign additional secondary authids. When DB2 performs security checking against a resource, these primary and secondary IDs are checked to see whether at least one of them permits the user to access the resource.

The authids that will be used for DB2 security are established during connection or sign-on processing by the exits mentioned before. The processing that takes place with these exits depends on the environment from which the DB2 request is coming.

Connection processing is driven as a region attempts to establish the connection with DB2. In handling a connection request, DB2: Y issues a SAF call to determine if the userid associated with the connecting region is known to the external security system. If not, the DB2 connection is terminated. Y passes the userid to the connection exit (named DSN3@ATH). This exit examines the environment and can permit or deny access to DB2. The exit can also specify values for the primary and secondary authids and the SQLID.

Sign-on processing is driven in multiuser environments such as IMS and CICS when a user makes a DB2 request. The userid is passed to both exit routines (DSN3@ATH and another called DSN3@SGN). The exits examine the environment and permit or deny access to DB2, and also specify values for the primary and secondary authids.

DB2 requests that come from TSO, JES2 batch jobs, started tasks, and DB2 utilities can only go through connection processing. DB2 requests that come from CICS recovery coordination tasks and IMS tasks can go through both sign-on and connection processing. DB2 requests that come from IMS tasks or CICS transactions can only go through sign-on processing.

For IMS tasks, if the request is associated with a terminal user, the user ID is passed on to DB2 as the DB2 requester. If the request is associated with a terminal but no one is signed on, the IMS logical terminal name (LTERM) is used.

For CICS transactions, connections are defined by the use of access paths between CICS and the DB2 resources. The threads within the connection establish the communication path between the subsystems and DB2. Where access is gained through CICS, there are seven possible authids that could be assigned:

1. The signed-on userid.
2. The CICS operator ID.
3. The RACF group ID.
4. The CICS terminal ID.
5. The CICS transaction code.
6. The VTAM application name for the CICS subsystem.
7. The value supplied by the CICS systems Resource Control Table.

One way of managing DB2 security is to define DB2 as a RACF resource. Where TSO connections take place, the primary authid can be set to the TSO user ID, while the queue of secondary authids can be built through passing the RACF groups through the DB2 exits. For IMS connections, a transaction can initiate a generic authid, as RACF controls can be applied to the individual IMS transactions themselves.

Under CICS, the approach is a little different. The default primary authid is the CICS sign-on ID, where the CICS Resource Control Table specifies AUTH=USERID. AUTH=USERID forces the user to access CICS via the sign-on transaction (CSSN). Therefore, all CICS transactions requiring sign-on and authentication with RACF will require a valid user ID. As a result, the default primary authid in DB2 always will be a valid CICS user ID for CICS connections.

Subsystem Controls with RACF

Irrespective of which subsystems are being used, RACF controls always should be applied in a way that ensures that the external security product operates as a single identification and authorization mechanism. It also is important, when session managers are used to control how subsystems are presented to end users, that the session manager's controls not be used as a substitute for RACF security. Use of external security requires careful fine tuning of subsystem exits and interfaces, as these exits and interfaces are the links between the subsystem and external security.

Managing MVS security in a consistent manner, across mainframes and across subsystems, is an important responsibility that requires a great deal of active management. The mainframe operating environment is one that is very dynamic—in the last year we have seen major upgrades to CICS and IMS alone—and every change in the way a subsystem processes information can affect the controls security practitioners are responsible for.

Controlling APPC

Application Program to Program Communication (APPC) is an IBM application subsystem for distributed processing. APPC uses the Logical Unit 6.2 protocol (LU 6.2) for communications. APPC works quite well in client/server systems, as it manages network connections as conversations. In this conversational mode of operating, the client issues an ALLOCATE request to establish a session with the application server. Once the session is established, the client issues a SEND command, and the server issues a RECEIVE. This interaction of SEND and RECEIVE commands between clients and the server is called APPC conversation mode.

A key benefit of APPC is that it allows for (almost) seamless communications between DB2, DB2/2, and Sybase databases. The client machine can embed an SQL INSERT command, for example, into an LU 6.2 packet, and can SEND this command to the server database as depicted in Figure 18.3. No translation of the data communications packet needs to take place. If the client is APPC-conversant, then the client request is formatted into the LU 6.2 data communications protocol, and routed to the APPC-conversant server. The MVS subsystems mentioned above, CICS, DB2, and IMS, are all conversant with APPC, as are nonmainframe operating platforms such as AS/400.

APPC can be used to facilitate RACF's authentication services. When APPC receives a request to allocate an APPC transaction program, it uses RACF to verify the userid and password associated with that transaction. The verification includes checking the user's authority to use both the partner LU and the LU to which the transaction request was routed. RACF uses the APPL class to control the attach request. To authenticate APPC connections, passwords are passed on to RACF on the MVS side when the session is established, and RACF verifies passwords received through APPC requests.

In the IMS world, for instance, we already have discussed protecting requests at the transaction level. This is even critical with APPC/MVS seeing that all data access goes through RACF (for example, file open, DB2 access). Unfortunately, the APPC/IMS message regions will allow the requester to access all regions in IMS. This means that an APPC connection to native IMS will allow the user to access all IMS regions. Therefore, it's critical to ensure that inbound APPC/IMS requests are linked to a specific IMS transaction, so that the controls applied by RACF transaction-level security cannot be circumvented.

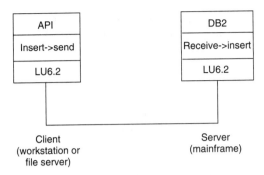

Figure 18.3 APPC conversation management

When the requestor system is communicating through APPC with MVS instead of IMS, RACF verifies that the userid has access to the datasets being accessed within MVS. This verification takes place because the address space that the TP runs in acts under the authenticated RACF user ID's authority.

It is also necessary to protect the execution of APPC transaction programs. The security administrator can define profiles to the APPCTP class to protect APPC applications in which the outbound transaction program issues an allocate request for an inbound transaction program on MVS.

As with all RACF resources, a resource list that contains only those users who need access to the transaction program profile must be defined. It is important to be aware that UACC settings for each profile in the APPCTP class determines what the public level of access to the TP will be. Unless there are compelling reasons to do otherwise, it is a good idea to give every profile in the APPCTP class a UACC of NONE.

Controlling How Sessions Bind to the Server

In a client/server application that uses APPC and RACF, there is a need to control how client and server logical units connect (or bind) with each other. Otherwise, there is a possibility of unknown or unauthorized clients connecting with the server, or of unauthorized clients masquerading as legitimate ones (that is, client spoofing).

To understand how logical unit binding can be controlled, an understanding of how the VTAM subsystem manages the binding of sessions is necessary. For more background, the reader should review Chapter 10 of this book. With release 3.2 and later of the CICS subsystem, or release 3.3 and later of VTAM, LU bind control is provided by defining which LU type 6.2 logical units can establish sessions with each other. The network ID and the LU identifiers for each member of the VTAM LU 6.2 pair are needed to allow RACF to control the sessions. The goal should be to have every LU 6.2 pair in the entire client/server network defined to RACF in this way. Not only is control provided over which LUs might connect to the network, but control is also provided over which LUs may bind with which LUs, and in which way. Using RACF for LU controls allows for a network-centric view of controls over the client/server network.

For each LU 6.2 pair, two profiles in the APPCLU class must be created in RACF. Each profile must identify that NETID is the network ID, which is specified on the VTAM start option NETID (this is in the ATCSTRxx member of SYS1.VTAMLST). Each profile also must identify the LU names of the partners. In all cases, the first LU name specified is the local LU name, and the second LU name is the partner LU name. It is advisable to set the UACC of each APPCLU profile to NONE.

Generic characters for the NETIDs and LUIDs should not be specified in the APPCLU profiles, as otherwise there is a possibility of LUs binding with each other in unanticipated ways. When these profiles are created, specifying values for the SESSION segment provides much of the function of the profiles. To use the protection defined in the profiles, the APPCLU profiles on every system must be defined.

Using the RACF Secured Signon Function

Client/server installations typically include workstations and client machines that connect with MVS from outside the VTAM-managed computer network. For this reason, the RACF Secured Signon function was developed to leverage RACF's security capabilities and provide enhanced security across a client/server network. The Secured Signon function provides a PassTicket, which allows workstations and client machines to communicate with a host without using an RACF password.

By using Secured Signon, you can reduce the complexities in managing authentication schemes across all clients in an APPC client/server network.

This PassTicket removes the need to send RACF passwords across the network and allows for the moving of user authentication from RACF to another product or function. The end users of an application can use the Pass-Ticket to authenticate their user IDs and log on to computer systems that contain RACF. What this approach effectively does is allow RACF to take even more of a network-centric view of the client/server network. The client from which the PassTicket is generated is a trusted client to RACF, once the PassTicket is authenticated by RACF.

The PassTicket is a one-time-only password that is generated by an application requestor. This alternative removes the need to send RACF passwords across the network in clear text. It makes it possible to move the authentication of a mainframe application user ID from RACF to another authorized function executing on the host system, or to a local area network (LAN).

Before the Secured Signon function can be used, the PTKTDATA class must be activated. This RACF class defines all profiles containing PassTicket information. For each application that users are allowed to access with the PassTicket, you must create a profile in the PTKTDATA class. This profile associates a secret Secured Signon application key with a particular application on a particular system.

Depending on the application, the Secured Signon function uses a specific method for determining profile names in the PTKTDATA class. PTKTDATA profile names for CICS, IMS, APPC, TSO, and MVS batch applications must be defined. For example, in a CICS, IMS, or APPC application, the profile must be defined to the PTKTDATA class using the standard naming conventions used to define these applications to the APPL class.

Secured Signon allows RACF to trust another platform to prove a user's identity. The other platform communicates with RACF by providing the PassTicket. NetSP uses Generic Security Service (GSS) API protocols, an emerging standard adopted by the Internet Engineering Task Force.

GSS API was developed by Digital Equipment Corporation and is expected to be adopted into Kerberos v5.3, and in the next release of the Open Systems Foundation's Distributed Computing Environment (OSF/DCE). When the client requests security services, the GSS API performs the authentication request by verifying the user with an authentication server (step 1). At the same time, the authentication server verifies that the requested application server exists on the client/server network (step 2). The results of the authentication request are communicated by the authentication server to the client application program. Once the authentication is performed, the client application communicates directly with the server (step 3). Note that GSS API does not perform authorization checking to determine whether the requesting user is authorized to access data on the server. Those functions are performed by the authorization management software on the application server; for instance, by RACF resource profiles.

When Secured Signon application keys are defined, RACF either masks or encrypts each key. If the system has a cryptographic product installed and available, Secured Signon application keys can be encrypted for added protection. To prevent unauthorized users from looking at or copying the Secured Signon application keys that are stored in the RACF database, the universal access authority (UACC) of the RACF database must be set to NONE.

The Secured Signon application keys can be encrypted only when all of the MVS systems generating or evaluating the PassTicket are running on MVS Version 3 or later, and have a common cryptographic architecture (CCA) cryptographic product installed. Using a cryptographic product ensures the maximum possible security for the Secured Signon application keys. RACF uses the functions of the cryptographic product to ensure that the encrypted keys do not exist in clear-text form within system main stor-

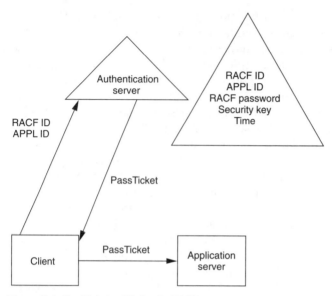

Figure 18.4 PassTicket validation in RACF

age for RACF processing, except when they are being defined. Therefore, when a system storage dump occurs, the keys are not exposed in the dump.

To validate a password or PassTicket (see Figure 18.4), RACF first determines whether the value in the password field is the RACF password for the userid (step 1). If the value is not the RACF password, then it must be a PassTicket. In step 2, RACF determines whether a Secured Signon application profile has been defined for the application in the PTKTDATA class. In step 3, RACF evaluates the value entered in the password field. The evaluation determines whether the value is a PassTicket consistent with this particular user ID, application, and time range. This evaluation also determines whether the PassTicket has been used previously on this computer system for this user ID, application, and time range. Finally, RACF determines whether the value is a valid PassTicket (step 4). If the PassTicket is valid, RACF gives the user access to the desired application. If the Secured Signon application key is encrypted, the cryptographic product must be active when RACF tries to authenticate the PassTicket.

A PassTicket is within the valid time range when the time of generation is within plus or minus ten minutes of the time of ticket evaluation. For this to work, the MVS system and the evaluating computer use clock values that are within that time range. RACF uses the value stored for coordinated universal time (formerly called Greenwich mean time) in the algorithms that process PassTickets.

One way to ensure the values are synchronized is to use the time value of the MVS clock and to set a similar value in each of the other systems with which RACF shares PassTicket information. Time processing is important, as if the value was used before, the user receives a message from the application indicating that the password is not valid.

Summary

The first step in any client/server security framework should be to identify the source and identity of the access request. In a client/server application involving the technical constructs discussed in this chapter (APPC, MVS, DB2, and RACF), inbound remote requests can be isolated and controlled by location with APPC's logical unit identification process. These connections, when they occur through a client-initiated process, can be made through a system process bundled into a remote procedure call. Remote procedure calls, as processes inbound to MVS, can also be isolated on a location-by-location basis. RACF's user verification process can then take over and fully identify and authenticate the user connection.

There then is a need to control the authorities and privileges that are granted to the users and manage the activities of connected users and workstations. RACF group profiles provide the opportunity to manage access requirements on a functional basis. Among the activities that can be controlled are the connected user's ability to execute only particular IMS and CICS transactions. These inbound connections can be packaged through remote procedure call wrappers that link directly with system transactions.

RACF group IDs can be linked with DB2 secondary authids for server databases to enable individual users to be grouped together in one or more security groups. When the user's SQL process is connected with DB2, the primary authid can be associated with one or more RACF groups, and the RACF group is corresponded with a DB2 secondary authid. Within DB2, the user is identified to DB2 via the secondary authid, and access is controlled accordingly.

In a network-centric world, the security goal is to achieve effective controls from end-to-end, client-to-server-to-client. Using RACF alone will not fully achieve this end-to-end security. Taking a proactive, network-centric view of client/server security requirements allows for RACF to be applied to achieve controls using a combination of software. A significant first step to achieving the security needed in a client/server system can be made by using the concepts and techniques introduced in this chapter, and described elsewhere in this book.

Securing ORACLE
Frank W. Lyons

Few enterprises of great labor or hazard
would be undertaken if we had not the power
of magnifying the advantages we expect from
them.   SAMUEL JOHNSON

Database management systems have been around for many years as repositories of data. During the last several years, the relational database management system has occupied the industry as it moves toward storing large
amounts of data in an easy-to-use form. With the advent of the client/server
architecture, the database management system has become a key component within the application system. In fact, the database management system is the heart of the client/server architecture.

The database management system allows for multiple users to access various data fields at the same time, to complete application transaction processing. The database management system protects the integrity of each
data field during updates, to ensure that only one transaction at a time affects the specific data field. Concurrent access is a key attribute of the database management system, in that it also allows many users to work on
different data fields at the same time. The database management system
maintains the necessary locks to protect the data until each concurrent
transaction is completed.

All of the application data and many of the application programs are
stored within the database management system. In addition, you will see
that the database allows for the physical distribution of the data across a

computer network. This capability allows the designer to physically move the application data, for performance or security reasons, without affecting the end user's interface.

The relational database management system provides for data integrity checks that can be enforced each time the application data is accessed, modified, or deleted. These integrity checks help to ensure that the application data is properly maintained as it relates to other data fields or entities.

The database management system is a complex software product that sets the tone for how the client/server application works within a complex networked environment.

What Is an ORACLE Database Management System?

ORACLE is a relational database management system (RDBMS). Oracle Corporation was one of the first companies to design a true relational design paradigm. Its popularity has allowed Oracle Corporation to develop many versions of its database, to run on different machines and under many operating environments. Along with its technical capabilities, the ORACLE database's portability has provided many companies the cornerstone to build sophisticated client/server applications.

The ORACLE database management system is a collection of data within a table definition. A table is nothing more than a two-dimensional structure similar to a spreadsheet. The table is defined with columns (fields) across the top of the table, and rows (records) down the side of the table. The table can have many columns or fields, and the number of rows depends on how many records the table holds at any given time.

An application can be made up of many tables that are related to each other for transaction processing. All the application tables are part of the makeup of a logical structure called a database. The database is composed of tables, views, indexes, clusters, sequences, and stored procedures. Each of these will be defined as we examine the specifics of how they work. Right now it is important to note that the payroll application stores its data in an ORACLE database that might be called Payroll. After the database is named or defined to ORACLE, the various logical structures are described to the newly created database to complete the definition.

The database also has a physical structure. Each of the logical structures are grouped, according to use, into logical storage units called *tablespaces*. These tablespaces are then mapped to one or more physical files. The complete database definition is called a *schema* definition.

A key component of the ORACLE database management system is the data dictionary. The data dictionary of an ORACLE database is a set of system-owned tables and views that are used to list all the entities defined to the database management system. What this means is that each user, table, or column is defined in the data dictionary. In this way the ORACLE database management system can real-time authenticate who is authorized to access application data. Every time an administrator creates a new database or table, the ORACLE database management system automatically updates the proper data dictionary table. These data dictionary tables will be important to you when you are reviewing the integrity and control aspects of a system.

It all boils down to two levels of activity against the application database. A transaction submitted by the user in either a *dynamic* or *static* form is processed against the database if the user is authorized to perform the activity.

Static activity comes in the form of a program or a procedure. Static programs or procedures are compiled processes that are designed to perform a certain activity within the application database.

Dynamic activity comes in the form of a Query. This query is usually in Structured Query Language (SQL). These requests are submitted and resolved dynamically by the database management system. The required user authority to run these transaction types will be discussed in later sections.

Structured Query Language is divided into three major parts. The first is called Data Definition Language (DDL) and includes CREATE, ALTER, and DROP statements for creating objects such as tables. To use these commands you must have been granted a certain level of authority within the database. The second is called Data Manipulation Language (DML) and includes INSERT, DELETE, UPDATE, and SELECT. Again, the user who submits these commands must have the proper authority to affect the database. Finally, the Data Control Language (DCL) includes GRANT and REVOKE to allow users to perform activities within the database.

Database Initialization

For a database to start and be available for system use requires three steps: start an instance, mount the database, and open the database.

Start an instance

An instance is an allocation of the appropriate system processes and memory buffers for database processing.

Before an instance is actually created, the ORACLE database management system reads a parameter file (that is, INIT.ORA), which determines how the instance will be initialized. To see the current parameter settings issue the following command:

```
SQL*DBA> SHOW PARAMETERS BLOCK
```

This file includes several security and control parameters that affect the overall integrity of transaction processing. These key parameters are as follows:

AUDIT_TRAIL	Enables or disables the audit trail. It is disabled by default.
B_DOMAIN	Allows for the unique identification of database names.
FIXED_DATE	Should be set to null.
IFILE	Names of other parameter files that might affect system integrity.
MTS_LISTENER_PORT	Sets up listen process for specific network activity.
OS_AUTHENT_PREFIX	Sets the prefix to identify operating system authentication (default = OPS$).
OS_ROLES	Set to true, allows the operating system to identify each username's roles.

Mount the database

Mounting a database is the process of associating a database with a previously started instance.

Open the database

Opening a mounted database is the process of making the database available for normal database operations. Any valid user can connect to the database and access its information once it has been opened. In most cases, the database administrator opens the database so it is available for general system use.

Starting and stopping the database are powerful administrative functions and are protected by the ORACLE database management system by connecting to the database as INTERNAL. INTERNAL is an operating system privilege. Only the database administrators should have the capability to connect to a database using INTERNAL. Connection as INTERNAL allows the user unlimited access to the database. The INTERNAL keyword should be protected by the OSOPER and OSDBA roles. Roles are the easiest way to delineate the capability within the ORACLE database management system. Roles are defined in more detail in the section on database security.

The ORACLE owner requires DBA privileges in order to create, start up, shut down, and connect internal to the database. Making this account a member of the DBA group within the operating system (UNIX) automatically gives it these privileges. When you access a tool like SQL*DBA, it looks for the group membership of your account. If it is the DBA group, then it grants you access to the system privileged functions.

Database Administration

The database administration function is an individual or group responsible for setting up, installing, and administrating the ORACLE RDBMS. This administration function is given special privileges to operate on the database. In fact, these administrators have full access rights to system and application data. For this reason, the right to be a database administrator should be highly restricted. Anyone with database administration privileges can enroll users, create roles, grant out access rights, and create databases with all the logical structural components. All database administrators should be separated from the day-to-day operations of programming and security administration.

To perform many of the administrative duties, the database administrator must be able to execute operating system commands. So you need to review the operating system accounts to determine who has been given this capability. In addition, the SQL*DBA program requires that the administrator's operating system account be given the capability to execute SQL*DBA commands. Access to the database administrator's operating system account, and to these commands, should be tightly controlled.

Within the ORACLE RDBMS, specifically within the data dictionary, an administrator can be identified by a pre-defined role named DBA. Anyone granted privileges to the DBA role has all database system privileges. For this reason, only authorized administrators should be granted the rights to this role.

During the installation process for ORACLE, two user accounts are automatically created and granted DBA role:

- username SYS, password CHANGE_ON_INSTALL
- username SYSTEM, password MANAGER

The SYS account owns all the database tables and views for the data dictionary. To protect the integrity of the data dictionary tables, the password for the SYS account should be changed.

The SYSTEM account is automatically enrolled with all system privileges for any new database that is created. Because of its critical nature, the password for the SYSTEM account also should be changed immediately after the ORACLE RDBMS is installed.

If the ORACLE database system is re-installed, then these user IDs will be reset to their original state and will have to be changed again.

For the database administrator to perform his job responsibilities, certain database utilities are provided for his use. One in particular is the SQL*DBA utility mentioned earlier. Another is the SQL*Loader that is used to load data from standard operating system files. The Import/Export utility allows the administrator to move existing data from one ORACLE database to another. It has been our experience that some of these utilities might store the administrator's password in clear text. These utilities are placed in operating system directories and should be restricted to the database administrator. But if the directories in which these utilities are stored are not properly protected, then special operating system commands could be used to search and find password strings. To prevent any exposure, all passwords for any level of privileges, including administrator's rights, should be stored only in a one-way encrypted fashion.

Database security

ORACLE is a comprehensive database management system that has many system and application objects. Each of these objects needs to be accessed in some manner by different users. In order to allow authorized users the ability to perform their work without compromising the integrity of the system, ORACLE RDBMS has a discretionary access control system. With the discretionary access control system, users can be assigned privileges to objects. A privilege is a permission to access a named object in a prescribed manner.

The first step in the security process is to create a user. Users can be created using either the Create User dialog box of SQL*DBA, or the SQL command CREATE USER. A typical example of an ORACLE RDBMS authentication process would be as follows:

```
CREATE USER frank
IDENTIFIED BY hop-scot
DEFAULT TABLESPACE p_data
TEMPORARY TABLESPACE t_data
QUOTA 250M ON sys_test
QUOTA 800M ON p_data
PROFILE manager;
```

If you were interested in authenticating this user through the operating system, the CREATE USER statement would be set to:

```
CREATE USER OPS$frank
IDENTIFIED EXTERNALLY;
```

OPS$ is the prefix set in the OS_AUTHENT_PREFIX parameter. If the OS_AUTHENT_PREFIX parameter is different, then the prefix would have to be set to match this parameter.

Authentication of a user to the database can be accomplished either by the operating system or by the associated ORACLE database, as indicated above. A review of the authentication process would be required to ensure that proper integrity checks are performed. These checks or characteristics include password construction rules, password aging, and violation attempts reporting.

To create a user, the creator must have CREATE USER system privilege. Normally, this person would be the database or security administrator. Any of the security settings can be altered by the administrator. The actual users can change their own passwords but are restricted from changing their security domain.

User profiles

The second step in the security process is the user profile. User profiles are used to restrict resource limits. These profiles assign values for the use of tablespaces and space usage quotas and CPU time. Each user can be assigned only one profile at any given time. Profiles can be assigned only to users, and not to roles. If a user is not assigned a profile, then the system DEFAULT profile is used to set the user's limits. The DEFAULT profile is set up initially as UNLIMITED.

The data dictionary has a complete listing of all users and their associated profiles. This includes the following data dictionary views:

ALL_USERS	Information about all users of the database: username and user_id created.
USER_USERS	Information about the current user: username, user_id, default_tablespace, temporary_tablespace created.
DBA_USERS	Information about all users of the database: username, user_id, password (encrypted), default_tablespace, temporary _tablespace created, profile.
USER_TS_QUOTAS	Tablespace quotas for the user: tablespace_ name, bytes, max_bytes, blocks, max_ blocks.
DBA_TS_QUOTAS	Tablespace quotas for all users: tablespace_ name, username, bytes, max_bytes, blocks, max_blocks.
USER_RESOURCE_LIMITS	Displays the resource limits for the current user: resource_name, limit.
DBA_PROFILES	Profiles assigned to each user: profile, resource_name, limit.
RESOURCE_COST	Cost for each resource: resource_name, unit_cost.

Establishment of privileges

The third step in the security process is the establishment of privileges. A privilege is a right to execute a particular type of SQL statement, or access to another user's object. Privileges can be granted to a user explicitly. Privileges also can be granted to roles acting like a named group for privileges. For example, the privileges to select and update the PAY table can be granted to the role named PAYROLL, which in turn can be granted to Anne and Frank. The assignment of privileges to roles is an easier way to manage access rights.

There are two categories of privileges. These are the system and object privileges. System privileges usually are assigned only to security and database administrators. There are many system privileges, and each one allows the user to perform selective activity on a particular object. The key system privileges that require review are who has the following:

ALTER DATABASE	Allows grantee to alter the database.
GRANT ANY PRIVILEGE	Allows grantee to grant any system privilege.
CREATE PROFILE	Allows grantee to create profiles (Review ALTER and DROP too).
CREATE ROLE	Allows grantee to create roles (Review ALTER and DROP too).
RESTRICTED SESSION	Allows grantee to connect after the database is started using STARTUP.
RESTRICT	The special OSOPER and OSDBA roles contain this privilege.
CREATE SNAPSHOT	Allows grantee to create snapshots of data.
ALTER SYSTEM	Allows grantee to issue ALTER SYSTEM statements.
CREATE USER	Allows grantee to create users.
ALTER USER	Allows grantee to alter other users.

The granting of system privileges to users or roles can be accomplished by using the SQL*DBA dialog box Grant System Privileges/Roles or Revoke System Privileges/Roles, or the SQL commands of GRANT and REVOKE. Only users granted a system privilege with the WITH ADMIN OPTION, or a user with GRANT ANY PRIVILEGE system privilege, can grant or revoke a system privilege to or from other users or roles of the database.

Establishment of roles

The fourth step in the security process is the establishment of roles. Roles are named groups of related privileges that are granted to users or other roles. Roles allow for easier security administration. They also allow for the change in the role privileges and all the security domains of all users granted the role are automatically changed by reference. Roles allow for selective enabling or disabling of capabilities. Passwords can be incorporated to verify the use of a role by an application or a user.

An application role is used to define the privileges necessary to run an application. A user role is used to group users that have common privilege requirements.

A role can have a system or object level of privileges granted to it. It can be granted to other roles. Any user can be granted a role, and the role can be enabled or disabled. A user's security domain does not include any role that is not enabled. Any user with GRANT ANY ROLE system privilege can grant or revoke any role to or from other users or roles of the database. Any user granted a role with the WITH ADMIN OPTION can grant or revoke the role to or from other users or roles of the database.

Within a database, each role or name must be unique, and a username and a role cannot be the same.

Predefined roles are automatically defined for ORACLE databases. These roles are special but can be modified by an authorized administrator. Following are the predefined roles:

CONNECT	The privileges are alter session, create cluster, create database link, create sequence, create synonym, create table, create view.
RESOURCE	The privileges are create cluster, create procedures, create sequence, create table, create trigger.
DBA	The privileges are all system privileges with admin option.
EXP_FULL_DATABASE	The privileges are select any table, backup any table, insert, delete, and update on sys .incvid, sys.incfil, and sys.incexp.
IMP_FULL_DATABASE	The privileges are become user.

The data dictionary has a listing of all the system privileges and roles. These tables include the following:

- DBA_ROLES
- DBA_ROLE_PRIVS
- DBA_SYS_PRIVS
- ROLE_ROLE_PRIVS
- ROLE_SYS_PRIVS
- ROLE_TAB_PRIVS
- SESSION_PRIVS
- SESSION_ROLES

Each user database has a user called PUBLIC. The PUBLIC user has access to any resources granted to this user. Any user that can connect to the database can use the PUBLIC privileges. A review of the privileges granted would ensure that only authorized and required access has been granted to this special user.

Application Security

The user of a database application must first sign-on to the database, either through the operating system or directly into the database management system. Once the user gets onto the system an application level password might be required. This level of password would be part of the application design. Once the user is properly authenticated to the application, work can begin.

There are two primary ways that a user can access data for an application. The first is direct access to the database tables. This access level allows the user to issue direct SQL statements (dynamic requests) such as select, insert, delete, and update. In order for a user to use these commands, the user must have been granted table level access for each command. Another way that the user could be granted this level of access is when the table has been granted to the PUBLIC user. If a table has been granted to PUBLIC, then any command by any user can be used against the table. Obviously, PUBLIC definitions are a major exposure in today's client/server world. This is because many client programs, such as Access, Paradox, PowerBuilder, and SQL/PLUS, are available on client platforms that would allow a user to submit a dynamic request.

The second and preferred way to access the application is to allow the user to EXECUTE a stored procedure. Stored procedures are like programs, in that they are compiled and stored in executable form in the data dictionary. A user can be granted EXECUTE authority to the stored procedures, which allows the user to run the procedure to affect the application data. This places a high reliance on the ability of the procedure to only perform authorized activity.

Procedures also are preferred due to their increased performance characteristics. Procedures are stored in the data dictionary on the file server close to the data. This architecture allows the procedure to use CPU speed versus network speed to perform the activity. Compare this with a dynamic SQL that is issued from the client across the network. With dynamic SQL queries, the work is split between the client and the server. For dynamic queries against large databases, the performance of the system might be affected. At a minimum, the performance and the resulting service level might fluctuate greatly, depending on how many queries the users are running. For this reason and for security and control, it is preferable not to allow users direct access to the database tables. Some companies allow direct access for SQL selects. This eliminates the direct update risk but does not eliminate the performance issue that might occur.

So, if you look at the process of how to establish a user within a client/server environment running ORACLE as the database management system, the following must occur.

User authentication

First the user must be properly authenticated. This, as described before, would be completed by submitting a userid and password from the client to the server. This authentication could be completed at the operating system level or at the database management system level. This authentication has a major weakness today, in that the user ID and password might travel across the network in clear text. Certain operating systems have eliminated this exposure by going to a challenge and response system. A challenge and response system allows the user to submit his user ID and password with a one-time ticket mechanism. The system incorporates the user's password into a one-time key that is resolved by the server. This eliminates the ability to capture the clear text, or even the encrypted version of the password, and replay it to sign-on as that specific user. Some systems that provide for the challenge and response are the Novell operating system, IBM LAN Server, and Microsoft Windows NT (see Chapters 13, 14, and 17). At the database level, ORACLE and Sybase's System 10 have options that allow the administrator to set up a challenge and response authentication.

Whether the user is authenticated through the operating system or by the database management system, the user always has to be defined to the ORACLE database management system as a valid user. This is the only way that the ORACLE RDBMS can check the authorization level of the user as they access database objects.

Working with the application

Next, the user would start to work with his application. Most of the time the user would be sitting at a workstation using a Graphical User Interface (GUI) or an Object-Oriented User Interface (OOUI). When the user clicked on some activity, the front-end program would submit a dynamic SQL request or call a remote procedure stored in the data dictionary. The bottom line is that the user would be able to affect the application data. So, to validate the user authority we need to perform the following:

1. Obtain a schema definition of the database that is being reviewed. This represents all the tables for the database, their relationships to each other, and the columns (fields) that are in each table.

2. By reviewing the columns within each table, determine what columns are sensitive or critical.

3. Determine who has what access rights for each of the sensitive or critical columns. This would effectively be either a user, a stored procedure, or a role. Also, be sure that the tables have not been granted to Public.

4. If a user has direct table authority such as SQL select, update, delete, or insert, then this user could write a dynamic SQL command to directly affect the application's data. To understand the significance of this level of authority, it is important to remember that any client program today probably can issue SQL commands. This means that a user who is using an application's GUI, or OOUI, could have been granted direct authority into the database tables as part of the application design. The user in most cases would not even know that this level of authority had been granted to them. As long as the user goes through the GUI or OOUI front end, then all the application edits would be properly performed. But if the user wanted to buy and install his own front-end tool that generates dynamic SQL, he would be able to access the database tables without going through the application's front-end edits. So the bottom line is, try not to provide direct table authority for a user or a role. Force everyone to use stored procedures when accessing a database.

5. Review all roles that have access to the application's sensitive or critical data fields. Verify what users are granted the right to use the role(s). Determine that each user really needs the role privileges to perform his job. An application role is one that is granted all privileges necessary to run a given database application. A user role is one that is created for a group of database users with common privilege requirements.

6. Review all stored procedures that have access to the application's sensitive or critical data fields. Verify what users are granted execute authority to the procedure. Determine that each user needs the capability that the stored procedures provide. There only is one object privilege for procedures, including stand-alone procedures and functions, and packages. A user must have EXECUTE authority. Packages allow for the storage of multiple procedures and functions. Any procedure or function granted to PUBLIC can be used by any user with access to the system.

7. Obtain a listing of all of the profiles for the application users. Review the profiles to ensure that security standards are being met.

8. Obtain a listing of all the views for the application tables. Determine whether the user that has access to the view definition should have this level of access.

9. Obtain a listing of all the triggers for the application tables. Determine whether the triggers are properly constructed to help ensure the integrity of the application system.

Creating views

Views are security mechanisms to reduce the full access rights to a table. By creating a view of a table you ensure that only the pertinent columns can be displayed within the view, thereby restricting the user to those columns only. Views can restrict the columns that are displayed, and can use attributes such as loan amounts less than $25,000 as further restrictions on the column itself. By using views, you ensure that every column of every table, along with its attributes, can be restricted to authorized users only.

First the view is created by an administrator, and then the user is granted the privilege to use the view. To use the view, a user only needs to be granted access to the view. The user does not require any privileges for the base object (base table definition) that underlie the view.

Using triggers

Triggers are an ORACLE RDBMS implementation that allows a procedure to be executed when a table is affected by an SQL insert, update, or delete statement. Triggers are similar to stored procedures, but they are used to check referential integrity. For example, let's say that the application transaction is getting ready to delete a particular customer. The normal operation would be to just match the customer number and delete the entry and go on to the next transaction.

But what if the customer had orders in a database table, called ORDERS? In this case, if the system did not check to see whether the customer had orders, there would be an entry or record in the ORDERS table that would still be pointing to the deleted customer. For this and other reasons, triggers were invented. Triggers are bound directly to the table definition. This means that no command activity can bypass the trigger established for a particular table or column on a table. Triggers help to maintain referential integrity, but can also be used for edits, rules, and auditing.

Listing user privileges

To list the privileges or roles for a user, use the following data dictionary tables:

ALL_COL_PRIVS	Grants on columns for which the user or PUBLIC is the grantee.
ALL_TAB_PRIVS	Grants on objects for which the user or PUBLIC is the grantee.
USER_ROLE_PRIVS	Roles granted to the user.
ROLE_TAB_PRIVS	Information about table privileges granted to roles.
ROLE_ROLE_PRIVS	Information about roles granted to other roles.

| **USER_COL_PRIVS** | Grants on columns for which the user is the owner, grantor, or grantee. |
| **COLUMN_PRIVILEGES** | Grants on columns for which the user is the grantor, grantee, or owner, or PUBLIC is the grantee. |

Application IDs

Recent application security designs have changed the techniques for user authentication to the database. In some of these applications, the user must first sign-on to an application server to verify his rights to use the LAN and the application in question. This application server might be a Novell server which ensures that the user ID and password do not go across the network in clear text.

Once the ID and password are authenticated, the application server downloads some application objects to the workstation. These objects present the user with another sign-on screen for the application. This sign-on session goes to the database server, which might be running under UNIX. Again, the sign-on must not send the clear text user ID or password across the network. The database server has some application modules that store the user's authentication and authority levels inside the database for this user or session.

Next, the database disconnects the user's session with his individual user ID and connects the user to the database with an application ID. This application ID could be one ID for all users, or various IDs could be set up for each user within a role or a group. At this point, the user's workstation is on-line to the database application with this application ID.

The application ID is password-protected in the database and cannot be signed onto directly by any user. In this way, the application user has no direct rights into the database system at all. No table level access, no procedure access, and yet he can perform his application transactions as long as they are authenticated through the application server.

This approach eliminates the dynamic SQL problem altogether. Of course, some organizations just might want to provide read (SELECT) authority to their users. Using this approach, the update-type functions could be run though the application server and the read functions could be allowed under the user's actual userid and password. The only problem now is, what do you let the user read (VIEWS), and will his dynamic queries adversely affect system performance?

Distributed Database Security

Prior to this section, we have been talking about an application that has all of its data on one machine. However, in the real world the actual application data might be on several different machines. All these machines might be running ORACLE, or in some cases the data might be on an IBM mainframe using a DB2-type relational database. In any event, the complexity of the application grows as you distribute the data physically through the network.

First let's look at our task, and that is to secure the application data from unauthorized access. To accomplish this goal, you already have reviewed the controls surrounding the authentication and authorization of a user's access to data. But this did not take into account that the application data might be physically distributed. So the first step, in any review, is to diagram the physical application. Remember that you needed the logical application diagram to understand the tables and columns within a table. Well, now you need the physical diagram to determine the physical location of this logical diagram. Be careful during this process, because what you are trying to obtain is the location of the primary data tables. That is, you are not interested in any replication or downloaded copy of the database at this time. You only want to certify that the master copy, if you will, is properly protected. Later you will deal with replication of data.

Once the physical nature of the application is known, you must also obtain the following information about the physical environment.

- Is the machine physically secured?
- What operating system does the application run under?
- Who are the administrators for the operating environment?
- What database management system is being used by these environments?
- Who has database administration within these environments?
- What is the authentication process for a user to sign on to these environments? In this case, the database management system might handle the authentication with Remote Procedure Calls (RPCs). This is the database's way of accessing information remote to a primary machine. Or, the database management system could use SQL to obtain the information. To accomplish these tasks, the ORACLE RDBMS uses an object type called database links. We will discuss links shortly.
- What access rights do users (all types of users) have to the application tables?

Now, how do you obtain this information and determine that the physical map provided to you really represents the location of all the primary data? Well, in order to accomplish this task, you need to understand two distributed components. One is ORACLE's SQL*Net and the other is database links.

SQL*Net is ORACLE's remote data access software. It is based on the ORACLE Transparent Network Substrate (TNS) technology for both client/server and server/server communications across any type of network.

Within this environment, SQL*Net is responsible for enabling communications between the cooperating partners during a distributed transaction. During the initial connection, the name of the remote database must be specified by the application or user. After that, the application requests are the same as if the data were on the local computer, even if it is remote across the network. SQL*Net provides the following functions:

- **Network transparency** The location of the data is invisible to the end user.

- **Protocol independence** An application running SQL*Net can run any protocol (network formatting rules).

- **Media/topology independence** SQL*Net allows the network protocol to use any means of network transmission, such as Ethernet, Token Ring, or FDDI.

- **Heterogeneous networking** From the IBM mainframe to the desktop, SQL*Net allows for communication in a typical organization with many different machines and operating environments.

- **Location transparency** With SQL*Net, remote objects such as tables look as if they reside locally.

To use the distributed database functionality, a database link must be created. Database links serve as logical names for each remote database you want to access. Each link is defined in the data dictionary as either a private or public link. Private links are known only to the user who defined them. Public links can be used by all users. To view each of these links, query the data dictionary's user_db_links for privately defined links, and the dba_db _links table for the publicly defined links.

Once the link is established, the server must be configured to listen for activity. A TNS Listener process is established by defining a proper configuration in files such as LISTENER.ORA and TNSNAMES.ORA. This listener process listens for any activity from users, applications, or other servers. The listener process in the LISTENER.ORA file looks like:

```
LISTENER_ORLANDO1 =
(PROTOCOL = TCP)
(HOST = orlando1)
(PORT = 1621)
```

This listener has a TCP/IP protocol connection with a name of LISTENER_ORLANDO1 and a listening port of 1621. If you wanted to list the active processes under UNIX, then you would run the following command.

```
$ps -ef |grep ora
```

There are a number of ways to connect or initiate a connection with an ORACLE database server: from the command line, logging on to a tool, using a 3generation language (3GL), or using special commands.

Command line

You can use the command line as follows.

```
tool username/password@database_name
```

The tool could be SQL*DBA, SQL*Plus, etc. Username specifies the user on the ORACLE server. Password specifies the user password. If the password is not entered on the command line, it will be prompted for after the command is entered. Commands to connect should not be in files that could be obtained by unauthorized individuals, when the password is stored with the command. Database_name specifies the database name entered in the TNSNAMES.ORA file.

ORACLE, in order to provide examples of how to connect to the database, might have left a user called SCOTT and a password called TIGER on the server. Be sure to remove this user and any authorities this user may have on the server.

Logon screen for a tool

This would be a normal logon screen for a tool.

3GL programs

This type of connection could allow an application to store the username and password within a program, as a variable. Be sure that this type of connection does not compromise the password security of the system by letting someone have access to this variable.

Special commands

These commands are entered through one of the software tools. It looks like an operating system command, except that it is entered in response to the tool's prompt instead of the operating system prompt.

Once you know where the physical data resides and are comfortable with the level of security and control with the primary application data, you can turn your attention to the aspect of replication and downloads of critical or sensitive data.

Data replication

Replication of data is an application design objective to save on processing time, network cost, or improve reliability. Dynamic updates to data that is replicated is a complex issue that requires careful consideration. Partly because of the integrity issues that could be involved, we recommend either not to allow for replication of dynamic data or to allow for only one update master with many replications.

Static data is less of an issue, as it can be replicated without the real-time need to update. The only real issue is that you must maintain the same level of security and control for the replicated site as you do for the primary site, and you need a procedure for properly distributing any updates to the static data in a secured manner.

ORACLE has a feature that allows for the table snapshots, or replication. Snapshots can be created to replicate some of the database information to a remote machine. This information could be used for Executive Information Systems (EIS), for Decision Support Systems (DSS), or for end-user computing.

ORACLE improvements in the area of replication include multiple master tables that can be defined n-ways, with full synchronization of tables at multiple sites. All master copies can be updated and any changes can be broadcasted across the network to other copies.

Snapshots improvements can be established to dynamically refresh both the master and the copy when changes have occurred. This is done through a logging mechanism that updates the master and then refreshes the snapshot. All of the conflicts for the updates would be resolved by the master.

Replication can be completed for any ORACLE object, including tables, stored procedures, and packages. Database links offer one way used to establish the replication process. Another is to use the database triggers for replication of certain data records. You need to identify all the replication that is defined to the application and ensure that it has the integrity and control required by the sensitivity of the data.

Downloading of data, by either using a File Transfer Protocol or a copy command, is a difficult issue today. The user, in order to use the power of the desktop, wants access to data that he can manipulate with PC tools. And he should have this right. If he understands the level of sensitivity, then he should be able to properly protect the data. However, certain aspects of computing do come into play.

First, security professionals need to develop software agents that identify the normal activity for a user, so that if they do download a file they can tell whether it is a normal activity. If it is not, then it is logged and can be investigated by a security professional. Second, you need to help the user when he is developing end-user computing reports or new derived data fields. New fields need to be captured and properly defined as a corporate resource when corporate decisions are to be made from the use of the data. Reports need to be reviewed by the user, by performing an integrity check that verifies the information before a critical decision is made based on it. If management is making a key decision on an end-user computing report, then management can ask for an independent verification of the integrity of the information.

Training for the users also is key, to ensure that they know how to use the software properly on their desktops. And, of course, policies, standards, and procedures should be written or automated to help the user in developing effective end-user computing systems and reports.

Database Backup and Recovery

The system administrators or database administrators are responsible for performing database backups. These backups are necessary to ensure that the integrity of the system is maintained if a crisis occurs. Backups should include all the database's data files, redo log files, and control files. Redo files are ORACLE journal files used to recover the application data, both in real time and after the fact. The control files are needed to ensure that the proper parameters are established for the environment.

Backups can be accomplished several different ways, but typically a full backup is completed once a week, with partial backups or incremental backups daily. If you have a full backup copy of the database weekly, then the redo logs could be used to roll forward to reach a sync point in processing in the event of a crisis.

All backup files should be rotated offsite with a copy on-site in a physically secured location. The running of the backups should be restricted to authorized individuals or groups. Running backups usually requires full database privileges, and when not properly controlled could affect the overall integrity and control of the database system.

The use of the Import/Export utilities to move data in or out of the ORACLE database is a common practice. However, make sure that these utilities do not have the database administrator's password stored with an Import/Export utility file.

Recovery procedures should be periodically tested to ensure that the backup procedures work properly.

Database Auditing

Database auditing is a hot topic from everyone's perspective. The security and audit professionals want to audit critical and sensitive data accesses. The database administrator usually looks at auditing as a necessary evil but a performance drain. The system administrator for the operating environment usually does not have the time to review the audit or violation reports, let alone review the activity of the system in detail. And the user usually performs auditing only as a matter of compliance. Yet when a problem occurs, these audit reports are wanted by everyone.

So let's talk about what needs to be audited, and where. The first rule is that auditing should always occur at the location of the data. That is, if it is on one platform or if it is replication of different platforms, then all auditing should occur on the platform on which the data resides. Specifically, it should occur at the data field level in the database. This means using the auditing features of ORACLE, or using triggers to establish the criteria for auditing.

ORACLE has an extensive audit capability.

- **Statement Auditing** This includes the auditing of SQL statements such as GRANTs. For this type of auditing a security administrator could be set up to add all users and to grant and revoke privileges. Because the DBA staff also can add users and grant and revoke privileges, the integrity of the separation of duties could be compromised. To ensure that the separation is procedurally maintained, auditing of all grants and revokes should be established.

  The weakness in this approach is that the DBA group could turn off auditing so that some SQL grants and revokes would be missed. To compensate for this exposure, a hardcopy console log, or a write-once read-many (WORM) drive, could be used to ensure that all commands are recorded, including the starting and stopping of auditing.

- **Privilege Auditing** This allows for the auditing of the use of special privileges such as DBA privileges, such things as creating tables, or the privilege of selecting any table.

- **Object Auditing** This is usually the application level auditing in which you record the actual changes to the data. For example, all changes to the payroll table could be audited.

These audit features allow for a comprehensive picture of the changes to the application. However, as mentioned before, auditing creates a lot of overhead in ORACLE, and you might be fighting with database administration on security versus performance issues. And unless you can convince management of the sensitivity of the data, robust auditing probably will not take place within your environment when system performance is adversely affected. Unless, of course, you design auditing into the application process.

Auditing is a business process and should be designed as a business object to be called when sensitive or critical data is being changed. In this way, any new application does not have to setup its own audit process, but could define, to the audit process, the fields that need to be tracked based on type of activity. This type of activity will become more prevalent as smart object agents are further deployed within the network and inside the database management systems.

Until then you need a strategy. So as a minimum, you need to audit the following:

- All log-ons and log-offs.
- All new users or changes to user group relationships.
- All system privilege changes or additions by user.
- All grants and revokes.
- All updates to sensitive or critical data. (This could be completed by the database, by a trigger, by a stored procedure, by an audit business object, or by the application itself.) I personally do not like the auditing to take place in the application, because there are so many ways to go around the application with today's tools.

Summary

ORACLE is a powerful database management system which, when properly used, can protect the integrity and control of your application data. However, several application vendors have set up their applications to rely on menu-level types of security. Menu-level security means that the vendor uses front-end menus that set up the user's authority. A user must be authorized to the application and then must belong to a certain group. This all looks fine on the surface, but underneath the application is a powerful database controlling access to the application tables.

In setting up the application this way, the vendor does not warn the user that an operating system such as UNIX needs protection, because it controls access to the application files, or that the database management system could be used to change any application data. Instead, the vendor installs the database with all the application tables defined to a user called PUBLIC, which allows for complete and unlimited access by anyone authorized to go around the application menu security system. Authorization in this case means that a user can signon to the server on which the application is running. If the user in question can submit a dynamic SQL request, then your security and control is cooked, because this request would be evaluated by the database management system and not the application's menu system. And because the database was defined to PUBLIC, the user could perform any SQL statement he wanted, including UPDATE.

In today's world there are probably not less than two hundred products that will allow you to submit a dynamic SQL. These include Access, Paradox, PowerBuilder, SQL/Windows, and not to mention ORACLE's own SQL* PLUS and other associated products.

ORACLE does have a trusted version of their database that provides additional security and control features. Also, ORACLE is committed to the Open Software Foundation's Distributed Computing Environment (DCE). DCE provides additional integrity, security, and control features within a distributed environment.

With the advent of faster networks and faster personal computers, the database world will evolve, and ORACLE seems likely to be one of the leaders during the evolution.

20

Securing Client/Server Transaction Processing
Geoff Sharman and Scott McDermott

*I usually get my stuff from people who promised
somebody else that they would keep it a secret.*
                    WALTER WINCHELL

What Is the Next Challenge for Client/Server Computing?

By "client/server," we mean a style of computing in which a desktop client
system makes requests across a network to one or more shared server systems. These servers provide services that cannot be offered at the desktop
easily or economically. This technology is now routinely used at the departmental level to augment the disk storage and printing facilities available to
end users, and to increase extent to provide information access for decision
support activities. However, client/server is only just now starting to be deployed for line-of-business, enterprise-wide production applications. Customers seeking to develop client/server applications for line-of-business
functions face some significant challenges.

These challenges arise from the fact that production systems must be deployed across the enterprise, which may be geographically dispersed, and
must be robust enough to meet the service level criteria needed both for
successful business operations and to deal with a changing business environment. These criteria have long been applied to the mainframe systems
which run the world's business, but are still poorly understood in relation to
the new client/server technologies.

To rise to these challenges, client/server systems must be able to deal with several new problems:

- Scaling to large servers and large, heterogeneous networks
- Delivering service reliably for long periods of time
- Providing high integrity; that is, not losing business data or messages and not allowing them to become corrupted
- Allowing users to exploit resources such as applications, data, and devices, no matter where they may be in the network
- Allowing the applications to be reconfigured across the network to deal with changing patterns of usage

In the first stages of client/server, most customer requirements were adequately met by network operating systems (sometimes known as NOS or as LAN servers) such as Novell NetWare and by server-oriented databases such as Sybase. The industry is now becoming aware that a new technology—known as a Transaction Processing (TP) monitor—is needed to meet the requirements posed by the next stage of client/server.

TP monitors have been used for over two decades in mainframe and traditional midrange systems but have not been well-known outside these environments. However, in the last few years, transaction monitors have started to appear on systems such as UNIX and OS/2 and are now experiencing 150 percent annual growth in these environments.

What Is a TP Monitor?

The basic function of a TP monitor is to allow the connection of large numbers of end users to an application server, which runs shared-line business applications and which, in turn, can access shared corporate data. TP monitors perform much more efficiently than operating systems and database managers; they multiplex large numbers of end-user requests across a small number of application servers continually recycled between these users, rather than giving each user his or her own permanent allocation of resources. This works well because most user requests are for short sequences of processing on small amounts of data, and because most end users are (from a system perspective) idle most of the time. Allocating an operating system process and a database connection permanently to an end user is extremely wasteful and leads to systems that bottleneck quite rapidly with just 50 active users. By contrast, TP monitors can support thousands of users and maintain acceptable performance.

TP monitors also provide a range of other functions that make it easy to write lines of business applications. These include services (known as resource managers) for managing files, queues, terminals, communications, timers, and events, plus a transaction management service (also known as a transaction coordinator or sync point manager) for ensuring that all the system activities associated with a business transaction are completed as an atomic unit.

As an example of a business transaction, a customer might purchase an airline ticket and pay for it with his credit card. When the airline's computer system captures this transaction, it's important to both parties that the actions of issuing the ticket and debiting the card are performed as a unit. The airline does not want to issue the ticket until it is paid for, and the customer does not want to pay unless she actually receives the ticket.

To ensure this takes place, the transaction management service provides a mechanism that allows the system to determine whether both the ticket issuing module and the card debiting module can complete their tasks before the transaction is allowed to proceed.

And, in the event that the transaction is started but for some reason is not completed (perhaps due to a system failure), the transaction management service will initiate recovery processing that will restore everything to the state that it was in prior to the transaction. In other words, the transaction will be completed in its entirety or not at all.

In a real system, where many thousands of users may be performing many hundreds of transactions concurrently, we also need to ensure that a given transaction will have the same outcome, no matter what else is happening at that time, that the execution of one transaction does not affect the execution of others, and that the results of each transaction are preserved for subsequent use regardless of system failures along the way. Collectively these characteristics are referred to as the following ACID properties of a transaction system:

Atomic	Transaction runs as a unit
Consistent	Transaction always has the same effect
Isolated	Transactions runs as if nothing else were happening
Durable	Results of transaction are preserved

In the subsequent sections of this chapter, we examine CICS as a prime example of a commercial transaction processing monitor.

An Overview of CICS

In 1995, CICS actually is a family of products that provides TP monitor capabilities across a wide range of operating systems and hardware platforms, including OS/2, Windows NT, UNIX, AS/400 and IBM S/390 mainframes. It provides the infrastructure needed to allow a business to run its transaction processing applications across all the systems and communication paths that collectively make up the enterprise network. CICS has evolved over many years to become the most pervasive and successful TP monitor available today, and it continues to evolve:

- Supporting an increasing number of IBM and non-IBM platforms
- Supporting new networking options such as TCP/IP
- Providing new services such as transactional messaging
- Providing enhanced features for installation and configuration
- Providing superior performance for high workloads
- Providing an advanced integrated approach to the operational management of large transaction processing networks

CICS provides a very rich and comprehensive set of services. The following list highlights some important features:

- Transaction management: Facilities are provided that allow applications to control the disposition of transactions (commit/abort processing). CICS provides transparent support for starting transactions.
- Extensive data management support for both databases and flat files: Databases are supported through integration interfaces, depending on the platform. File control provides access/update of fixed and variable length record structured files. File organizations can be sequential, relative record, or indexed with multiple indexes.
- Terminal and screen handling: CICS applications can access a variety of terminals. Screen mapping services, provided by CICS Basic Mapping Services, provide a method of building forms management into CICS applications, and additional tools facilitate the development of such applications. Graphical interfaces can be used on platforms where they are available.
- Queue management: Extensive queuing facilities are provided. These facilities provide scratchpad support, asynchronous communications between applications, transaction batching, general data storage, and many other capabilities that offer flexibility in application construction.
- Interval control: This allows application-related events to be triggered by some interval or time of day—an essential part of any real-time system.
- Abnormal and exception situation handling: Extensive support is provided for applications to handle abnormal and exception situations in a consistent high-level way. This includes support for application recovery and restart, and also orderly termination with diagnostics.
- Storage management: Functions allow applications to manage storage for their own use. CICS tracks storage allocation to ensure against leakage (leakage being storage that the system loses track of, leading to a system crash).

- Serialization: An enqueue/dequeue function enables serialization of applications that need to share application-related topics.

- Logging/journaling: Functions that provide reliable storage and retrieval of information by the system for use during application or system start and recovery.

- Work area management: CICS manages various transaction- or application-related work areas for applications, automatically providing and freeing them as transactions start and finish, or maintaining them across transactions.

- Distributed applications: Extensive support is provided for constructing distributed applications.

- Recovery and restart: CICS has facilities that allow the recovery and restart of applications, the system, and its resources. These do not require any application involvement; however, application-specific processing can optionally be included as part of the recovery/start processing.

- Application development tools: Many tools support the development of applications, including 4GLs, screen design aids, debug facilities, and various utilities for data management, as well as the standard programming languages such as COBOL, PL/I and C++.

- System management: Extensive management facilities including the definition and management of system and application resources, security at varying levels of granularity (user access to the system, resources and communication links), workload management, diagnostic and serviceability aids, and operator controls.

- Trace facilities: These help with the problem determination on both applications and the system.

Access to many of these services, described above, is through a high level Application Programming Interface (API). This API allows application development in a consistent style, independent from the programming language used and the functionality of the underlying operating system.

CICS transactions can be distributed transparently across multiple interconnected systems. CICS has peer-to-peer and Remote Procedure Call (RPC) communication facilities, similar to those available in UNIX systems. The following Inter-System Communication (ISC) mechanisms provide extensive flexibility in constructing applications:

- Distributed Program Link (DPL): Allows functions to be distributed in a call/return fashion. This RPC mechanism offers a powerful, yet simple means for distributing transactions in client/server style.

- Distributed Transaction Processing (DTP): Allows application functions to be distributed across remotely connected systems in a peer-to-peer fashion, and also to construct client/server applications.

- Transaction Routing (TR): Allows transactions that are entered on one system to be routed and executed on another system—transparent to the user who enters the transaction.

- Function Shipping (FS): Allows certain CICS API calls to be transparently executed on a remote system.

- Asynchronous Transaction Processing (ATP): Allows an application to issue another transaction that will be executed asynchronously.

For the AIX environment, these mechanisms run over SNA and TCP/IP networking protocols, with a gateway facility between the SNA and TCP/IP networks.

Several of these capabilities can also be used from the CICS Clients. These are lightweight implementations of the CICS Intersystem Communication function that can run on DOS, Windows, OS/2, Macintosh, and UNIX, allowing the connection of terminal and desktop systems into CICS systems wherever they may be in a network.

CICS and Security

CICS uses several techniques to help users with security issues: authentication, transaction authorization, and resource authorization.

Authentication

Each user is required to authenticate himself/herself to CICS before executing transactions. This means identifying who the user is and proving that he or she is who they say they are. The most usual method is by signing on with a user ID (something that identifies the user) and a secret password known only to the user (which confirms that the user is who they say they are). Any other method of achieving these functions can be used: for example, a fingerprint might be used in place of a password as confirmation of the user's identity.

Increasingly, the authentication process used by CICS is integrated with that used by the underlying operating system or software environment. For example, in MVS/ESA, the CICS User ID is integrated with RACF; in OS/400, the CICS User ID is integrated with the OS/400 logon process; in AIX, the CICS User ID is integrated with DCE logon process. This means that the user need only log on once and will be authenticated to CICS as well as to the underlying operating system.

In client/server systems, users must authenticate themselves to each of the systems within a network where they need to access in order to run transactions or access data. Traditionally, this was achieved by a separate logon process for each system, leading to administrative problems with management of multiple user IDs and passwords. DCE, for example, provides an elegant solution to this problem, allowing the user to log on once to an entire network of systems. The user is authenticated to his/her local system by the DCE Security Server, which then issues an encrypted "ticket" when the user needs to access another system. The receiving system can verify that the ticket is valid (that the user is authentic) by referring to the DCE security server.

Transaction authorization

CICS users are not allowed to access resources (such as data) directly. Instead, they are authorized to run application programs known as transactions—for example, an order entry or an insurance claim. By defining what transactions each user is allowed to run, a company can exercise tight control over who may view information, who may change it, and exactly what changes may be performed.

As a second step, each transaction is authorized to access specific resources it needs, such as data records, queued messages, and even other programs. So, for example, an order entry might be authorized to access product inventory and price data, but might not be authorized to access customer sales data, regardless of which user runs this transaction. Normally, these authorization mechanisms use the facilities provided by an underlying security manager, such as RACF (see Chapter 19), which will allow all security administration to be performed in one place. This security mechanism provides a finer control—and less administrative overhead—than the authorization mechanisms provided by database systems. Database systems typically define but do not control how a data item can be changed. Defining each user's access to each data item also creates a combinatorial problem in that very large numbers of such links must be created and managed.

The essence of the CICS transaction processing approach is that the user can only run transactions that represent well-defined business processes and that normally include appropriate validation checks to ensure that a correct business action is performed. It's also possible to separate groups of users so that (for example) no one user can access all of the sales data or that no one user can access both salary and personnel details of employees.

Resource authorization

CICS itself is authorized to access major resources such as databases, message queues, and communication links. CICS establishes connections to each of the resources needed in the transactional environment and ensures that each of these connections is correctly identified and authorized. It maintains these connections to ensure that applications are run in a secure environment. Once again, CICS uses the facilities of the underlying operating system to achieve this operation.

What Does a Transaction Processing Monitor Offer the UNIX World?

AIX/6000 Version 3.2 onwards is IBM's POSIX- and XPG3-compliant version of UNIX on the RISC System/6000. It provides foundation services for TP (such as process, storage, and file management), and aspects of systems management, such as Systems Management Interface Tool (SMIT) and System Resources Controller (SRC). Its most significant features for TP, however, include the elimination of "panic" system terminations, which are characteristics of UNIX and result in major reliability, serviceability, and availability problems. There are many features of AIX/6000 Version 3.2 beyond the scope of this article, which eliminate some classic UNIX shortcomings for TP and so provide a good foundation for IBM's CICS implementation on RISC System/6000 (namely, CICS/6000).

CICS/6000 has a modular open architecture that uses AIX components. Where relevant, the components in the layers are based upon current and emerging industry standards (such as POSIX services interfaces and X/Open distributed transaction processing interfaces) and existing industry standard technologies such as elements of the Open Software Foundation's (OSF's) Distributed Computing Environment (DCE). IBM used these rather than building alternatives into CICS/6000. There are two benefits to this approach: CICS fits naturally into any open systems platform and also provides a high degree of integrity and longevity to the design. This allows easy evolution of the product as new technologies and standards emerge.

The CICS/6000 TP monitor builds on the lower level DCE distributed services layer, and on the Encina transaction processing components supplied by Transarc Corporation. These provide transactional communications services, a transactional file system, and the base transaction management service. CICS also exploits SNA and TCP/IP communication services. It allows the attachment of popular UNIX database management systems, such as DB2, Oracle, Sybase, and Informix. And it allows the use of transactional messaging services, such as IBM's MQSeries. Overall, CICS role is to integrate these components, enabling and complementing their function to provide the familiar, consistent CICS application environment across the entire CICS family of products.

Because CICS/6000 is a natural extension to the AIX environment, CICS/6000 applications can access AIX facilities directly, such as when using Motif for building graphical front ends or using AIX print services.

What Does a UNIX Transaction Processing Monitor Offer Database Users?

CICS/6000—together with the CICS family of products—allows the integration of enterprise, departmental, and personal data within an organization. Data may be placed and processing may be accomplished at the most appropriate place within that organization. Placement can vary as the needs of the organization vary.

CICS/6000 allows database users to make even more effective use of their data by allowing integration with CICS, IMS, and DB2 mainframe data, in addition to data from other UNIX RDBMS vendors. Furthermore, CICS/6000 presents the opportunity for a wealth of existing CICS applications to be brought to a UNIX database environment. Relational databases, such as DB2, can provide access to local databases through the Structured Query Language (SQL) API. The level of remote data support will vary depending on the database product. Database access and updates are bound into the transaction through the X/Open XA interface.

The combination of CICS Clients with CICS Intersystem Communication allows customers to build entire enterprise networks, utilizing database elements as they may exist in the network. For example, a desktop application can access data on a remote system using CICS Distributed Program Link to send access requests to a server application that issues the database calls. These requests may be routed to a server running on UNIX and accessing any UNIX database, or they may be routed onward to a host system running CICS and DB2. There is no need for any database-specific gateway products and each CICS server can access a different vendor's database system. CICS/6000 ensures that the actions against these remote databases are bound into the transaction commitment processing.

CICS/6000 coordinates this commitment processing regardless of how many databases are involved or where they are actually located, thus ensuring complete data integrity.

Summary

The need for transactional control is only starting to be recognized by the PC community. As the popularity of client/server computing grows, so does the expectations and the complexity of the computer networks that link clients and servers. As companies start to run their business-critical applications on these complex client/server networks, the need to secure and manage the data and transactions between applications will be paramount. TP monitors such as CICS will play a vital role in ensuring security in the client/server world and beyond.

Securing Lotus Notes

Peter T. Davis

*It is more than probable that the average man
could, with no injury to his health, increase
his efficiency fifty percent.*   WALTER SCOTT

A groupware product, Lotus Notes, reportedly has sold over a million licenses to roughly 2000 companies, while its revenues have soared from $21 million in 1991 to approximately $90 million in 1993. Also, you saw that IBM bought Lotus Development to get their hands on Notes. You are probably thinking that's nice, but what is groupware? And what is Lotus Notes? Well, in this chapter, you will learn about groupware and Lotus Notes, and how to secure it. But first, let's turn our attention to groupware.

Defining Groupware

As mentioned in Chapter 1, *groupware* is an emerging technology that is here to stay. The Workgroup Technologies market research firm predicts the groupware market will grow from $430 million in 1993 to almost $3 billion by 1996. That's not counting the sizable cottage industry developing around Notes—databases, templates, macros, etc. The rapid growth is occurring because groupware can transform a company, by changing the way people communicate with each other and, as a result, changing the business processes.

For example, groupware can automate a customer's claim and make an insurance company more responsive. Regrettably, groupware probably is a term that is as misused as client/server. As a term it is unquestionably the most "blurred" of the client/server software categories. More than 200 products label themselves groupware. Wouldn't you, after seeing the sales projections for groupware!

Having said that, let's try to define it. At heart, groupware is software that supports the management—the creation, storage, flow, and tracking—of nonstructured information in direct support of collaborative group activity. Other terms are used as synonyms for groupware, such as "collaborative computing," "computer-supported cooperative working," and "workgroup computing." Groupware is the easiest to remember. Just think: software, hardware, wetware, and groupware.

Essentially, client/server groupware is five basic technologies for representing complex processes centering around collaborative human activities. Unfortunately, as yet no single groupware product incorporates all of these basic technologies:

- Conferencing
- Electronic mail
- Multimedia document management
- Scheduling
- Workflow

Unlike other client/server technologies, groupware is not a downsized mainframe technology. It's a genuinely new form of computing that sprang from networking. Groupware provides an excellent example of how client/server technology can be used to extend the technology into uncharted waters. Or, as Thorstein Veblen once said, "Invention is the mother of necessity." Groupware is a technology that will make feasible possibilities that people have not yet dreamed, once it is available.

The Benefits of Groupware

Groupware allows direct contributors, wherever their physical locations, to work together on projects using local or wide area networks. Several authors have seized upon this concept and predicted the growth of "virtual corporations" formed by independent people collaborating on particular projects. Groupware can help manage the project through its various phases, and can allow the contributors to exchange ideas and coordinate their work.

Within "real corporations," groupware will allow departments to develop their own applications. Anyone who can create a simple spreadsheet can learn how to create a Lotus Notes application; few programming skills are required. The ability for departments to develop and create their own client/server applications is leading to phenomenal returns on investment. Lotus boasts that experience (backed by an independent study of seventeen Notes customers) shows the initial Notes investment is recoverable within three months. The groupware phenomenon, like spreadsheets or Macintosh Hypercards, is self-fueling. The difference is that groupware is a self-fueling client/server application, for it is networked and interpersonal.

Groupware, Databases, and TP Monitors

Now that you understand groupware is involved with the management of information and its activities, you most likely are musing about what makes groupware different from database managers and TP Monitors. They do fill distinct and separate niches.

Relational databases deal with highly structured data accessed using structured query language (SQL). They are excellent for managing applications requiring high concurrency controls, including locking and isolation features that are needed for immediate updates. So, they are ideal for mission-critical systems, because they provide strong integrity and availability features. They also provide excellent ad hoc query facilities.

In contrast, groupware deals with highly unstructured data, including text, image, graphics, faxes, mail, and bulletin boards. Groupware provides the tools to capture this data at the point of entry and organize it in a nebulous thing called a "document." You can think of a document as a container of diverse types of information. The document is to a workgroup what a table is to an SQL database; that is, the basic unit of management. Groupware helps end users create document databases. It can move these documents as electronic mail and database replicas. And it provides everything you need to query, manage, and navigate through document databases. Hence, documents are the currency of groupware.

SQL databases are great for providing access to structured data that's organized in table formats, but when it comes to multimedia and nonstructured data, they're almost useless. Groupware document management fills this niche very well.

TP Monitors deal with the management of transaction processes across client/server networks. But, when it comes to document stores, TP Monitors can complement groupware software very well. The TP Monitor treats the document store like any other resource manager. If it supports a two-phase commit, then the TP Monitor will gladly coordinate a distributed transaction that includes the document store. However, TP Monitors and groupware compete in the area of workflow. Groupware workflow is a much more developed technology than the TP Monitor long-lived transaction (but it's less protected).

The current workflow model—and groupware in general—is not transaction-oriented in the true sense. Groupware is good at reflecting the changing states of information over time, but it does not do very well when it comes to reflecting the current state of the data in real time (that is, consistency is lacking). For example, groupware (and workflow) does not use two-phase commits to synchronize distributed changes across resource managers. It would be nice if TP Monitors and groupware combined efforts to infuse workflow with atomicity, consistency, isolation, and durability.

Now that you understand groupware basics, you can apply them to Notes.

Defining Lotus Notes

Lotus Notes is now in its third release (with four available January 22, 1996) and is inarguably the best known and most widely used client/server groupware product in the industry. It holds a special place in the development of groupware products. It's been by far the best noticed and most successful example of its type. Even though Notes has been in the field for more than four years and has sold more than a million copies, it still remains a mystery to the vast majority of PC users. It's even a mystery to its competitors. At times, it's been labeled derisively as a graphical bulletin board, turbocharged e-mail, or an unstructured database management system. In reality, Notes is a multifaceted, client/server groupware product. Notes provides three key features of interest to security, audit, and control professionals— change management, security, and efficiency.

Change Management

A Notes document gives you a convenient way of reading and modifying information. Over time, many people will make changes to documents. At our insurance agency, for example, homeowner policies get added and canceled or premium rates might increase. Because they're centralized, easily accessed, and systematically revised through replication, Notes documents remain more current and accurate than a paper document can. This is important, because individuals and groups of individuals share the information. Different people use a document database to make decisions. Inaccurate information could hurt an organization and result in bad decisions. Notes gives you and your workgroup the means to keep your organization's information up-to-date.

Information Security

Notes requires that every user be assigned an access level. For example, an insurance adjuster would have access to claim records that an account agent would not; account agents would have access only to their clients' records. Because information is sensitive, Notes enables an organization to build security mechanisms into a database.

An organization needs to protect a database's design from unauthorized modification, in addition to protecting the data stored within. The database designer needs to make sure that only certain people can see certain information. The designer also might want to control the operations that each user can perform within a particular database. For each database, the Notes' administrator assigns users access levels specifying who can design and manage the database, and who can read, modify, and add documents to it. You'll learn more about the different user access levels and the Access Control List (ACL) feature later in this chapter.

Worker Efficiency

Notes promotes the efficient flow of information in a group. Lotus Notes was a groupware pioneer in developing software that enables a group of people in an organization to use the same information but in different ways, depending on their specific needs.

Lotus Notes allows groups of users to interact and share information that can be of a highly unstructured nature. As you can see in Figure 21.1, Notes

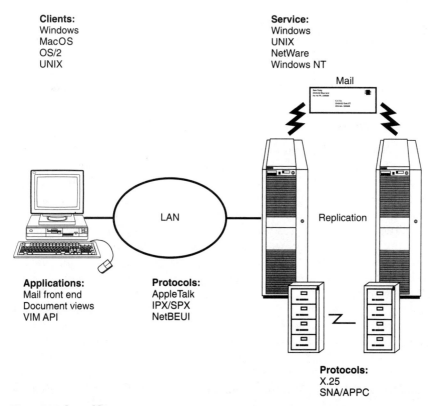

Figure 21.1 Lotus Notes

provides a client/server application development and run-time environment that provides the following functions:

- A document database server stores and manages multiuser client access to semi- or unstructured data, including text, images, audio, and video.
- An e-mail server manages multiuser client mail access.
- A backbone server-to-server infrastructure supports both mail routing and database replication. The replication mechanism synchronizes copies of the same database, which can reside on multiple servers or clients.
- A graphical client environment presents views of the document databases and provides an electronic mail front end. Users can navigate through the databases and their document contents. Views are stored queries that act as filters for the information in the databases. The e-mail front cnd, for example, is just a specialized view of a mail database. Views can help an organization implement its confidentiality policies. Notes can attach private or public graphics-based forms to the various databases used for data entry.

Distributed services include electronic signatures, security and access control lists, database administration services, system management, and a global naming service. Application development tools include a forms generator, tools and templates for creating databases, a primitive scripting language consisting of formulas, macros, and an open application program interface.

Notes Openness

All Notes communications—client-to-server and server-to-server—are accomplished via a proprietary remote procedure call (RPC). Notes supports client/server drivers for NetBEUI, TCP/IP, IPX/SPX, and AppleTalk stacks. Optionally, APPC and X.25 drivers are available for server-to-server communications. These should cover the major enterprise networking protocols.

On the client side, Notes provides access to many client/server applications, including those for Windows, OS/2, and MacOS. Notes includes an interprocess communication (IPC) feature that provides some integration and interoperability among applications. For the largest number of users (those who run Windows), Notes provides an IPC in the form of Object Linking and Embedding (OLE). OLE, a Microsoft standard, itself is a set of programming interfaces that initially work only among Windows applications, but can offer other features, including data exchange over a network.

As a server application, Notes can tap the expanding power of platforms such as NetWare. In this role, Notes is being set up as a set of NetWare Loadable Modules (NLMs) to run on a server. This will give Notes access to the NetWare Global Messaging system for links with external mail systems.

As you can see from Figure 21.1, the key to Notes' success is that it relies on open platforms and the client/server model. This makes it easier for both users and third-party developers to build links with other applications. Significantly, the push for Notes extends outward from users from their PCs, instead of downward from host-centric systems.

The Multimedia Document Database

The foundation of the Notes architecture is a database engine for semi-structured and unstructured information. The model of the database is more akin to computer conferencing than Online Transaction Processing (OLTP). The Notes database was designed as a vehicle for gathering and disseminating all types of information; it was not meant to be a database of record reflecting the real-time state of your business. If you need this, then a relational DBMS would better suit your needs. In this respect, Notes is more like an Information Warehouse or repository, except that the data tends to be formless. Notes is more interested in adding and capturing real-time information than in providing consistent access to shared data for updates.

The primary commodity in a Notes system is a semi-structured, multimedia document that can contain a variety of data types, including text, voice, image (or BLOBs), and video. A Notes system organizes, stores, replicates, and provides shared access to these documents. Related collections of Notes documents are stored in a database, which are indexable and retrievable using any of the documents' properties or the actual contents of the documents. Notes supports full-text indexing and searching. You can search, with Boolean, wildcard and text search criteria, or by date and numeric operator ($>$, $<$, $<>$, $>=$, and $<=$), and you can retrieve text across more than one database.

A Notes document consists of a set of fields, also known as properties; each has a name, type, and value. For example, a Notes document can be tagged with properties such as client, region, and subject. The regions can contain any number of BLOB-like attachments (or embedded files). Embedded files are managed and organized as part of a Notes document.

Notes stores an entire database in a single file. A Notes application typically consists of many databases organized by topic. Again, the Notes concept of a database is more akin to conferencing (data is organized, or threaded, by topic) rather than relational DBMSs (in which all data is organized in a single database consisting of multiple tables).

Notes Database Replication

A most impressive feature of Lotus Notes is a process known as *database replication*. Basically, replication is a procedure that updates and distributes copies of the same Notes database, known as replicas, which are stored on different servers.

Suppose there are two copies of an insurance policy database, one on a claims adjuster's notebook computer and the other back at the company's headquarters, used by an assistant. Yesterday the copies were identical, but today the claims adjuster investigated a car involved in an accident. The adjuster subsequently wrote up a report and added it to the copy of the database on a notebook computer. Meanwhile, back at company head-quarters, the assistant responded to a telephone call from the distraught policyholder and recorded the status of the call in the copy of the database on the workstation.

The two copies of the database now don't match each other, because the adjuster and the assistant made changes to their copies. Both copies now must be resynchronized through replication, to make them identical again. Notes can handle this task automatically when the claims adjuster returns to the office. The claims adjuster replicates the copy of the database on the notebook computer with the insurance company's database.

Replication is a powerful tool, because it enables you to place copies of the same database on different networks, located in different locations or even different time zones, to capture changes and become identical over time. The servers connect to each other at scheduled intervals, and the databases replicate changes to documents, access control lists, and the de-sign elements in forms and views.

The Mechanics of Replication

Over time, replication makes all copies of a database essentially identical, which means they don't become exact copies instantly. The process is an ongoing one. When a user makes changes in one copy of a database, repli-cation ensures that those changes are added to all copies, as long as the replication options are set correctly. However, because many people might use copies of the same database and might update their individual copies daily (think back to the adjuster and the assistant), making all of them iden-tical at the same time is unlikely and impractical.

Replication takes time and requires specific Notes server resources. If you are developing a database for a multiserver environment and you want to have the database replicated, determine the replication schedule that makes the most sense for the system topology and the database's use.

You can set up replication between servers or between a workstation and a server for dial-up users. Like information warehouses, Notes allows you to replicate databases across servers and clients. Unlike the information ware-houses, Notes has no notion of a master database—it uses replicas. The replicator is responsible for bi-directionally adding, deleting, or updating documents among all replicas of the database. Notes uses replication as a means to disseminate (or broadcast) information across geographically dis-tributed locations.

Handling Frequent Document Updates

There are two types of replication you can consider for handling periodic document updates: server-to-server replication and workstation-to-server replication (that is, dial-up). Server-to-server replication occurs during scheduled server replication, or when the Notes Administrator manually forces replication. Replication for a local database on a workstation occurs when you perform a data exchange using the replication command.

Dial-up (workstation-to-server) replication is handy when you use Notes on a LAN workstation, as well as remotely on a notebook computer. You can create a complete or partial database replica on your computer before leaving your office, save it to a floppy disk, and then copy it to your laptop or remote workstation once you are offsite or on the road.

Scheduling Regular Replication

Replication is typically scheduled every few hours of a workday for Notes databases with time-sensitive information. This can be critical for organizations whose databases are accessed and modified by many people. For databases that aren't modified frequently, or where the information isn't critical, replication can be conducted once a day. When a database is replicated over telephone lines between remote sites, replication might be scheduled once or twice a week, during the evening hours, to take advantage of lower long distance rates.

Normally, the Notes Administrator is the person responsible for setting up and scheduling replication of databases. If users work offsite or on the road and they use Dial-up Notes, the Notes Administrator should establish the best time to replicate.

Monitoring Database Replication

If you're a Dial-up Notes user who is using Notes offsite, replication keeps your workstation copy of a database current with the database on the server. However, the process isn't foolproof and isn't without its problems, especially when you're using telephone lines. You always should monitor the process once databases begin replicating, to make sure they continue to replicate as you want them to. If a problem or conflict should occur, such as the sudden interruption of a telephone call (especially when you have Call Waiting) that results in stopping replication, Notes will notify you.

The Notes replicator supports both full and partial replication, and has a tunable level of consistency based on the desired frequency of replication. Notes time stamps all new and modified (edited or updated) documents that are known to have replicas. Unattended servers can dial each other up, compare notes, and swap changes at times previously configured by an administrator. You also can store replicas on client workstations and initiate swaps from there.

In addition, Notes Release 3 introduced background replication, which allows Notes laptop clients to continue working in Notes while replication takes place in the background. Laptop users will find replication very helpful when they go on the road. They can copy a Notes database, work on it, and then swap changes with the server when they next make a connection. Selective replication limits the sections in documents that get replicated. You can choose not to replicate binary attachments to save on local disk space. You also can limit the size of each document to be replicated (for example, the first 100 characters). Or you can choose to only replicate unread messages from your boss.

Handling Concurrent Updates

Prior to Notes Release 3, when two users simultaneously updated a server-based document, the first save was accepted and the next user attempting to save was notified that it was overwriting someone else's changes. The decision of whether or not to overwrite the data was left to the user (not a very comforting thought if your organization relies on the integrity of the data).

Notes Release 3 introduced a versioning capability that lets an edited document become a response to the original document, or the last updated version can become the main document with all previous versions displayed as responses. Versioning does not guarantee that the last version is the most accurate, and it cannot merge changes into a single copy of the data.

So even Notes Release 3 is not a suitable technology for OLTP database applications or applications that require high concurrency controls involving immediate updates. This loosely synchronized style of information update is adequate for most conferencing applications, but it is a far cry from the synchronous two-phase commit updates used in OLTP applications. However, versioning eliminates the loss of data through concurrent updates or through replication. It's quite adequate for its intended use: document-centric groupware applications, an area that OLTP doesn't even touch.

Building Notes Applications

A database designer typically creates a new Notes database by using one of the Lotus-provided templates and customizing it. A database is simply a new file; it can be given an identifying icon, a title, help panels, and a policy document that explains what it's all about. Forms are used to enter information or view information in a database. To create a form, you can start with one of the pre-existing forms and modify one using the graphical editor. Forms provide data entry fields, text fields, and graphic areas in which pictures or other sources of multimedia data can be pasted (or attached). Lotus provides a scripting language (similar to Lotus 1-2-3 spreadsheet formulas) that allows you to associate commands with specific events and actions. The forms you create are associated with the database. You can designate them as *public*, which means they're available to all client applications that have access to the database, or you can make them *private*, which means only the creator can use them. Later on, we'll look at this in more depth.

Views are stored queries that display the contents of a database or document. They're used for navigation and for the securing and filtering of information—examples are display documents less than one month old "by region" or "by agent." The view will display the list of documents in a tabular or outline fashion. Any database has one or more views that the designer creates for easy access to information. Users also can create private views to provide a listing or access criteria that the database designer didn't anticipate.

On the client side, a user has a workspace (a notebook-like visual, similar to At Ease for the Macintosh) that organizes databases by topics. A notebook consists of six color-coded workpages; each has a folder-like tab that identifies a category into which you want to organize your databases. Each workpage can contain from zero to hundreds of databases. Each database is represented by an icon and a title. You must associate a new database to a workpage. Release 3 lets you open multiple databases and gives each its own window. However, you still cannot join documents from different databases into a single view. But you can create hypertext links from any document in any database to any other database.

The process of creating a new Notes client/server application and tailoring forms and views can take less than an hour. If you can use Visual Basic, Visual C++, or Hypercard, then you can use the advanced features of Lotus Notes. For you, the Notes scripting language—or formula macro language—provides about 200 functions to control almost everything, from field input validation to database queries and document routing. Release 3 provides periodic macros that can be used to launch macros at a specific time interval, or as a result of a particular action or condition—for example, when a document is deleted. This is the Notes equivalent of a trigger.

Using Notes Electronic Mail

From a client workstation's perspective, e-mail is just another Notes database that contains a collection of mail documents. The procedures used to read incoming mail, sort through mail, or create a mail document are the same ones for creating and reading documents in any Notes database. You simply use forms and views tailored to your mail documents. Of course, a difference is that the mail documents you create will be sent to somebody else's mailbox. Notes provides visual indicators to let you know when you have incoming mail. You then open the database and read it.

The Notes e-mail server is open. If you don't like the Notes mail front end, you can create your own. Or, you can simply use a program interface to mail-enable your applications, using the Notes server as a back end. cc:Mail clients can use the Notes mail server.

The Notes Mail Server

So what kind of services does a Notes Mail server provide? It provides mail backbone functions with the following features:

- **Routing optimization** You can optimize your outbound messages by priority and dynamic adaptive route selection, based on link costs.

- **Separate router threads** All server-to-server communications are handled by separate transfer threads. Threads allow multiple concurrent transfers to occur on different backbone routes. In addition, threads prevent large mail messages from delaying other server tasks.

- **Delivery failure notification** The server can notify the senders when delivery isn't possible (including the reasons).

- **X.500 namespace support** Notes Release 3 supports X.500-compliant hierarchical naming as its native means of identifying users within the system. This makes it straightforward for Notes directories to interoperate at the naming level with other X.500-compliant systems. It avoids naming-conflict headaches.

- **Mail gateways and directory services** Notes provides e-mail gateways to the most popular e-mail networks, including X.400, SMTP, MHS, cc:Mail, PROFS, VinesMail, FAX, and VAXmail.

- **Electronic signatures** Notes uses the RSA public key cryptography for all aspects of Notes security, including encryption. If you sign a message, it takes Notes a few seconds longer to send it because it must generate an RSA electronic signature. You will learn more about signing and encrypting mail later in the chapter.

The Notes mail engine can serve both Notes and cc:Mail front ends. Notes provides a true client/server e-mail architecture. The clients and servers communicate via an RPC.

Access Privileges

Using a Notes database isn't difficult. If you have the appropriate access level, you can select one or more databases to add to your workspace. Every Notes database has an access control list (ACL) specifying those users, user groups, and servers that can access the database, and what tasks each can perform. Both of the ACL's elements—access levels and access roles—are set by the database designer or manager. You can check the settings for any database you want to open.

If your name is not listed in the database's ACL, either explicitly or as a member of a group, your access level is the default access level, which is No access.

Notes offers seven access levels. The access levels, from highest to lowest, are:

1. **Manager**   Can perform almost any operation—reading, writing, or modifying—on documents, forms, views, and the database icon. A manager also can record or stop recording user activity, modify the ACL and replication settings, and delete the database. However, a manager can be prevented from deleting documents. A database always has at least one manager, who might or might not be the person who created the database.

2. **Designer**   Can perform the same operations as a manager, except for modifying the ACL, User Activity, Replication, or other settings, and deleting the database. Should you desire, you can prevent Designers from deleting documents.

3. **Editor**   Can read, write, and modify all documents in a database, but cannot modify forms, views, or the ACL. You can prevent Editors from deleting documents.

4. **Author**   Can read existing documents and create new ones, but can only modify the documents the author created. You can prevent Authors from deleting or creating documents.

5. **Reader**   Can read documents but cannot add new ones or modify existing ones.

6. **Depositor**   Can add new documents but cannot read existing ones. Use this level for mail databases as well as for databases such as ballot boxes or suggestion boxes, because it lets users compose their own documents but not read anyone else's document. You also might use Depositor for data entry personnel entering new policies in, for example, an insurance company.

7. **No access**   Cannot open database or mail documents.

Unlike other systems and applications, the symbol for your access level appears at the right end of the status bar when you open a database. You'll need to ask your database manager or Notes Administrator to change your access level if you want to use a database in a different way than your current access level allows.

If you use Notes mail, you also can discover the names of the managers of a database. If you don't use Notes mail, you can discover the names of the database managers in the Database Catalog, a Notes database that should be available on a Notes server in your organization.

Protecting Access to Databases

Each Notes database contains an access control list (ACL) that you can see in the Database Access Control List dialog box. The ACL details who can open the database and what they can do with the information. If users have the appropriate access level, they can access the particular database. If not, access is denied. Both ACL elements (i.e., access levels and access roles) are set by either the database author, the designer, or the manager. The database manager usually should create and maintain the access control list.

In addition to designating access levels, Notes protects your work and the work of other users on shared databases in a variety of other ways.

- User IDs can be protected with passwords.
- Users are granted or denied access to Notes servers through the certificates stored in their user IDs.
- Information can be encrypted so that only specific users can decrypt it.
- If you're using Notes with a modem, you can use a secure modem channel by selecting Encrypt Network Data in the Port Setup dialog box.

User IDs and Passwords

A user ID is a file that uniquely identifies a Notes user. Every Notes user, person or server, must have a unique user ID. The terms user ID, ID, and ID file are used interchangeably in Notes. The contents of a user ID are either assigned by a certifier when the ID is created or added later.

The following information can be assigned:

- The name of the ID owner, which can be changed later by the owner or certifier.
- The Notes license number, which comes with the software.
- A certificate, which allows access to servers that trust the certifier.
- A public key, which is used to encrypt documents sent to the owner.
- A private key, which is used to decrypt documents sent to the owner.
- An optional password to prevent unauthorized access to Notes servers using the ID, which is added by the owner.
- Additional certificates to allow access to additional servers, which are added by certifiers.

When you try to open a database on a server, the server looks at your ID to see if you have any certificates in common. When you do, access is allowed; when you don't, access is denied. This checking process is called authentication.

You also need an ID to sign Notes mail memos. When you sign a Notes mail memo and send it, all of your certificate(s) are attached to the memo. The recipient's workstation checks these against its own certificates.

If you receive a signed memo and you don't have a certificate in common with the sender, Notes displays a message saying that it cannot assure the authenticity of the memo. If you know that you and the sender have a certificate in common, the memo might have been tampered with en route.

Users also can change their user names, copy their public key to the Clipboard (if they have a distinguished name they can copy their certified public key), and find out the name of the certifier who created the user ID.

Changing User Names

You can change the user name associated with your user ID file. You might change your user name for any number of reasons: maybe you took over an existing user ID, or maybe you just got married and changed your last name, or maybe you've decided you'd rather use your nickname.

The Notes Administrator updates the Person document and Group documents in the public Name & Address Book to reflect a name change. The Notes Administrator, and various database managers, also might need to change the access control list for any databases used that listed names individually. This includes changing the Notes Mail database. If the Administrator doesn't have the necessary access to change the ACL, he or she would contact the database managers.

If you're not a Notes Mail user, changing the user name removes all the certificates from the ID, so after you change the name you'll need to acquire new certificates before you can use any shared databases.

Switching to a Different User ID

You can share a workstation with another Notes user (who has a different user ID) by telling Notes that one of you is leaving and the other is beginning Notes. You both can keep your IDs on floppy disks or on the workstation's hard disk. Be sure to password-protect your IDs. After you use the command to select the ID you want to use, Notes prompts you for a password when that ID file is password-protected.

When two or more people use Notes on the same PC or Macintosh workstation, each installs Notes separately, storing the Notes program files in the same directory, but storing data files in his or her own data directory. This provides each user with his or her own copy of the desktop file, which lets each user see a different set of database icons in the Notes Workspace. In Windows, each user also must have his or her own copy of the notes initialization (NOTES.INI) file; other copies, such as the one usually stored in the Windows directory, must be removed.

Each user, after switching to his or her ID, can change to his or her personal data directory.

Keeping the User ID Secure

Keeping a user ID electronically secure means:

- Keeping an ID physically secure.
- Password-protecting it.
- Logging off servers when leaving the office.

You can keep a user ID on a floppy disk, a hard disk, or a file server. The most secure option is to keep it on a floppy disk, which you store in a safe place when you aren't using it (perhaps in a locked drawer). Just make a backup copy of your ID file on a floppy disk, using your operating system's file copy procedure. Store the backup in a secure place.

If you change your mind about where to keep your ID, you can tell Notes where your ID is located during setup, right after installation. You can change your mind later, though. If you originally told Notes that your ID is stored on the hard disk, you can later copy it to a floppy disk and delete the file from the hard disk (use Windows to copy and delete the file). When Notes asks for the location of your ID file the next time you access a Notes server, type in its new location.

When you keep your user ID on a floppy disk, you must insert the disk whenever you access a server, sign mail, or read encrypted mail. Most people just leave it in their floppy drive while they use Notes. If you remove the floppy from the drive, you cannot access Notes servers.

You should log off your password when you leave your workstation, to prevent an unauthorized person from accessing your organization's databases using your user ID (posing as you). This is especially important if you work in a cubicle or you don't lock your office when you step out. In the Enter Password dialog box, you can set automatic logoff to occur after any number of minutes that you specify. Otherwise, you can press F5 to log off, thus clearing your password and forcing the next person (which might be you or someone else) to enter a password in order to access the server.

Setting Your Password

As mentioned above, you can protect your user ID by setting a password that controls access from your Workspace to databases on Notes servers.

You also can change your existing password. However, this password doesn't protect databases stored locally (on your hard disk), which includes all replicas you might have made. Once you set a password, you must enter it when you access a Notes server for the first time after launching Notes. However, you can change your password after it's been set, unless your Notes Administrator specified that you cannot change it when you were registered as a new Notes user.

For your protection, the entry isn't displayed on your screen. It's safest to use at least eight characters; the maximum number of characters you can use is thirty-one. However, your Notes Administrator might have set a minimum password length when your ID was created.

Notes passwords are case-sensitive. For example, Notes considers ClientServer, clientServer, Clientserver, and clientserver to be different passwords. Notes won't accept a password unless it matches the original exactly.

Password Controls

As mentioned, you set password protection to force you to enter your current password every time you want to access databases from your Workspace, or databases on Notes servers. The Notes Administrator can decide whether users are required to use a password when the ID was created.

Users can change the password that controls access from their Workspace to databases on Notes servers. During the password entry procedure, you also can have Notes automatically logoff (prevent access to servers from your workspace) after a number of minutes of inactivity (a quiescent period, of say, 10 minutes) that you specify. This is a useful security precaution when users forget to logoff when leaving their desks.

Examining Your User ID Certificates

A certificate is an electronic stamp attached to your user ID by a Notes certifier. The certifier is usually the Notes Administrator. Certificates allow you access to specific Notes servers.

When the Notes Administrator registers a Notes user, the user ID should include the certificate(s) required to access the servers the user needs for the job. As you make wider use of Notes, your job changes, or your organization adds servers, you might need access to other servers. If you're denied access to them because you're not certified, ask the proper certifier for the certificate you need.

You can see information about the certificates that are attached to your user ID. The information provided about your certificates includes:

- The names of each certificate on your ID.
- The date and time each one was created, and the date and time they expire.
- The ID number and name of the certifier.

Users can review the certificates that they already have. They also can delete a certificate by selecting it and clicking on Delete.

Sending and Receiving Certificates

You might send an ID file to a certifier and receive it back for several reasons. Generally, you send an ID file to get certificates you didn't already have. But you also might send an ID file to request cross certificates, to request a new username, or to get a new public key.

The certifier's name might be a person, such as PTDAVIS, or an organizational unit, such as Administration.

User Logoff

User Logoff protects a user ID from unauthorized entry into databases stored on Notes servers. However, when you leave your office and workstation unlocked, anyone can use your local databases.

If you have a password for your user ID, you must type it into the Password dialog box the first time you open a database on a Notes server. When you leave your workstation unattended you can choose User Logoff. When you return to Notes and try to access a Notes server, you must re-enter your password again. In the Enter Password dialog box, you can set up automatic logoff after any number of minutes that you specify.

If your user ID isn't password-protected and if your user ID is on your hard disk, User Logoff has no real effect. Although it seems to log you out, as soon as anyone attempts to access a shared database, Notes looks for the user ID, finds it on your hard disk, sees that no password is set, and permits database access.

If your user ID is on a floppy disk and someone enters your office and can find your ID floppy, they can insert it into your floppy drive and access shared databases.

Encrypting Documents

Notes provides document security by letting you encrypt fields in documents. Encryption means encoding or scrambling data so that only those who have the secret encryption key(s) can read your documents; otherwise it is unintelligible. There are some differences between encrypting document fields and encrypting Notes mail memos.

Encrypting a document means applying a secret encryption key to one or more fields, and then sending the key to users you choose. Users who don't have this key can still read any unencrypted fields in an encrypted document.

A document cannot be encrypted unless its form has one or more fields defined as encryptable by the database designer. If you have a color monitor, and you're composing a document, you can recognize encryptable fields by their red field brackets. To encrypt an encryptable field, use an existing encryption key of your own or create a new encryption key.

All encryptable fields in a document will be encrypted using the key(s) you select. You cannot select a different key for each encryptable field in a single document.

Any user who has the key(s) to a document can read all the encrypted fields in that document. Be careful not to give out a key to one field and forget that you're providing access to some other field you want to keep secret.

A database designer can encrypt all documents created with a specific form. There are two ways to do this: by adding encryption keys to the form, or by adding keywords that refer to encryption keys. Add encryption keys when you, as the database designer, want to decide what key(s) will be used with a form. Add keywords that refer to encryption keys when you want users to choose the key(s) they want from a set of keys that you provide. However, you must send the appropriate encryption key(s) to any user whom you want to read encrypted documents.

Notes will ask you whether you want to let the recipients send the key to other users. When you select Yes, the recipients can distribute the key; otherwise they can only use it themselves. Your decision depends on the nature of the documents encrypted with this key, and your relationship with the recipients.

Encrypting incoming mail

You can prevent any unauthorized access to your mail when it reaches your mail server, either by administrative access to your mail database or by unauthorized access to the server. Only you can read your encrypted incoming mail. Either the Administrator sets a default for all incoming mail to be encrypted, by using `MailEncryptIncoming=1` in the NOTES.INI file that's located on the server, or each user can elect to encrypt his own incoming mail by setting the option in the person entry on the server's Name & Address (N&A) Book.

Encrypting outgoing mail

You also can encrypt outgoing mail to ensure that nobody except your recipients can read your memos while in transit, when stored in intermediate mail boxes, or on arrival in the recipient's mail file. A user can decide whether to

- Encrypt (or not encrypt) each document when sent.
- Encrypt all documents by default when sent.
- Sign every document when sent.

When you want to send a person encrypted information, or someone wants to send you encrypted information, Notes gets the recipient's public key from the N&A Book. When you encrypt a document, Notes scrambles the information using the recipient's public key, so that it can be decoded only by the recipient. If the recipient doesn't have a public key listed, then you cannot send encrypted mail. A user's public key is a 600-character string of pseudo-random letters and numbers assigned to each new Notes user. The system stores a public key on the Person record in the organization's Name & Address Book.

The Notes administrator can set the encryption option for all users, which takes precedence over the settings of individual users.

Encrypting incoming and saved mail

You can ensure that your saved copies of mail memos are always encrypted whether or not you send them to others encrypted. Encrypting saved mail effectively prevents anyone from reading your mail on the server; even the server administrator or others with access to the server.

In order to encrypt mail, Notes creates a unique public and private key for each user. If someone sends you encrypted mail, Notes uses your public key to encrypt the message, making it unreadable to any user except the recipient. When it delivers the message, Notes uses your private key to decrypt (or decode) the message for you.

Because your public key must be available to anyone wanting to send you encrypted mail, the Notes Administrator must put your public key in the public N&A Book (the special database that lists users, user groups, servers, and server connections) when you're registered as a Notes user. However, to maintain security, your private key is stored in your user ID where only you can access it. This means that any user who has access to your public key can send you encrypted mail, but only you can decrypt that mail. If your public key is ever lost or corrupted in the Name & Address Book, you must send a new copy to your Notes Administrator.

Selecting an encryption key

You can select encryption keys to apply to an open document or a form. In addition, you must select an encryption key to remove it from a document.

If you add an encryption key to a form, then all documents composed with that form are automatically encrypted with the selected key.

You also can select encryption keys to apply to documents in a view, or remove a current encryption key from a document. An encryption key can provide extra security for draft documents you're working on in Notes Mail. For example, some users share a mail file with a co-worker or assistant. When you do this, your associate has the public key to your mail file, but you can still apply an encryption key to a draft in process to prevent your associate from having access to it.

Because you'll be sharing valuable documents with other people in your workgroup, you'll need to give them the encryption keys you've used. They must have the keys stored on their workstations or they won't be able to access the documents.

As a precaution, you can specify a password for an encryption key when you export it. Although you can export an encryption key without password-protecting it, doing so undermines the security obtained by using an encryption key and sharing it with a limited number of users. It is highly recommended that you specify a password of at least eight characters, to protect the exported key.

Dial-Up Security

You can use Dial-up Notes to work locally because you can make local replicas and then work on these replicas. You also can send and receive Notes mail by working in a local replica of your mail database, and then exchanging documents with your mail database on the server.

When you set up the New Remote Connection, you can set the time of day and day of week that access is allowed.

When setting up the port for your modem, you also can set the maximum time your workstation maintains a connection to a Notes server before it terminates the connection. This option will disconnect the workstation from the server when the workstation isn't transmitting or receiving data beyond the specified time. When someone specifies a different hang-up time for the server's modem, the shorter time period takes precedence.

In addition, the hang-up when idle option only will work when the value you set is less than the value set for the mail polling interval when at mail setup. Optionally, you can select to log modem control strings and responses in the workstation's Notes log, to determine or monitor communication problems.

The Lotus Notes Programming Interface

Notes also provides a programming interface, which developers can use to store and retrieve Notes documents. It also gives you broad access to many of the features of the Notes user interface. The interface allows you to:

- Create or delete databases.
- Read, write, and modify any document or any field in the document.
- Create and use database views.
- Control database access with access control lists.
- Monitor server performance.
- Register new workstations and servers.
- Write custom tasks that you can add to the Notes server software, and specify the schedule under which the custom task executes.
- Create, read, and run Notes macros using the programming interface.
- Perform full-text searches using a search-engine.
- Issue calls to restrict what documents get exchanged during replication.
- Obtain the list of names and address books in use locally or on a server.
- Issue mail gateway calls.
- Because you can store these queries for future use, you will want to ensure they are adequately protected from unauthorized change.

Summary

Notes is an excellent example of a fast-growing area of client/server applications. Because of its functionality and ease-of-use, the product excites workers who are creating collaborative client/server applications. These applications allow the employees to manage unstructured data. So in many ways, Lotus Notes might leverage client/server computing and do for it what Lotus 1-2-3 did for personal computing.

From an empowerment viewpoint, this is exciting; however, from a control viewpoint it is frightening. Notes databases have a tendency to proliferate like tribbles. Without proper policies for security, database replication, telecommuting, and remote access, your organization is courting disaster.

Notes is highly recommended for certain classes of applications. It is a very good fit for applications that collect multimedia information, perform very few updates, and need to be integrated with e-mail. But Notes is not very good at handling applications that deal with structured data, are query intensive, and require multiuser updates with high levels of integrity. Notes does not do very well with transactions, which are best handled by TP Monitors, Information Warehouses, transactional MOMs, and SQL and Object databases.

Select Bibliography

Baker, Richard H. 1993. *Networking the Enterprise*. New York: McGraw-Hill.

Brown, Kevin, Kenyon Brown and Kyle Brown. 1995. *Mastering Lotus Notes*. San Francisco: Sybex Inc.

Celko, Joe. September 1992. *An Introduction to Concurrency Control*. DBMS, p. 70.

Orfali, Robert, Dan Harkey and Jeri Edwards. 1994. *Essential Client/Server Survival Guide*. New York: Van Nostrand Reinhold.

Glossary

access list A catalogue of users, programs, or processes and the specifications of access categories whereto each is assigned.

ACF/VTAM Advanced Communications Facility/Virtual Telecommunications Access Method.

application gateway A type of firewall system that only allows information to flow between networks across application layer protocols. These systems might provide access control on the basis of information contained in application level protocol messages.

application protocol layer The layer of the protocol stack that performs high level services, usually directly to network users. Examples include e-mail, file transfer, and remote terminal emulation. The application layer is the highest layer in a network protocol stack.

APPN Implementers' Workshop (AIW) The group of APPN implementers and users that define future changes to APPN.

atomicity A property of a transaction, where a transaction is an indivisible unit of work.

authenticate (1) To confirm that the object is what it purports to be. To verify the identity of a person (or other agent external to the protection system) making a request. (2) To identify or verify the eligibility of a station, originator, or individual to access specific categories of information.

authorize To grant the necessary and sufficient permissions for the intended purpose.

CA-ACF2 (Computer Associates Access Control Facility 2) A logical access control software package produced by Computer Associates for securing mainframes.

CA-Top Secret (Computer Associates Top Secret) A logical access control software package produced by Computer Associates for securing mainframes.

client/server A network system design in which a processor or computer designated as a server (file server, database server, etc.) provides services to other client processors or computers.

Common Programming Interface Communications (CPI-C) The portable, standard interface to APPC and OSI-TP.

Computer Emergency Response Team (CERT) An organization established to track and report on serious failures occurring to computer systems. CERT's primary focus is on security problems, including those encountered by hosts connected to the Internet.

confidentiality The security objective to protect information from being revealed to unauthorized people.

consistency After a transaction executes, it must leave the system in a correct state or it must abort—this is consistency. If the transaction cannot achieve a stable state, then it must return the system to its original or initial state.

control point A special logical unit that manages APPN control flows.

conversation A logical connection between two transaction programs. A conversation uses a session.

CPI-C Implementers' Workshop (CIW) The group of CPI-C implementers and users that define future changes to CPI-C.

cryptography The transforming of plain text into coded form (encryption), or coded form into plain text (decryption).

database (1) A collection of information organized in a form that can be readily manipulated and sorted by a computer user; (2) short for database management system.

database management system A software system for organizing, storing, retrieving, analyzing and modifying information in a database.

database server A database server is the "back-end" processor that manages the database and fulfills database requests in a client/server database system.

decryption Translate a message that has been encoded using an encryption procedure, so that the message is returned to its original, readable form.

denial of service The computer security threat associated with unauthorized actions that prevent authorized users from using computer services, or that cause a computer system to crash.

device interface protocol layer The layer of the protocol stack that interacts with specific networks attached to the host computer. The device interface layer might, for example, provide an Ethernet, serial line, or token ring interface. This is the lowest layer in the protocol stack.

digital signature A facility that computes a distinctive hash value across a block of data and associates it with a secret key value assigned to a particular individual or entity. A separate computation can verify that the digital signature is associated with that data and individual without using the secret key value, so this computation can be performed by third parties to reliably associate the information with the identity.

disclosure The computer security threat associated with the revelation of information that is not supposed to be revealed.

durability   A transaction's effects are permanent after a commit.

eavesdropping   Unauthorized interception of data transmissions.

encryption   Translate a message from its original, readable form into an encoded form that protects its contents from disclosure.

file server   A computer that provides network stations with controlled access to shareable resources.

file transfer protocol (FTP)   A very old Internet protocol used to interactively search for files on a server, and to transfer files between the server and client.

firewall   A device that connects a sensitive network to a public network such as the Internet, and that provides security protections against attacks on the sensitive network from the public network.

hacker   A computer enthusiast; also, one who seeks to gain unauthorized access to computer systems.

identification   The process that enables recognition of users or resources as identical with those previously described to a system, generally by using unique, machine-readable names.

integrity   Freedom from errors.

Internet Protocol (IP)   The protocol that provides connectivity across all networks connected in an internetwork.

internet protocol layer   The layer of the protocol stack that provides connectivity across multiple networks. This layer runs the IP protocol.

IP address   A logical address for a host connected to a network. Hosts might have more than one IP address if they are connected to more than one network. Each IP address has two parts, the logical network address contained in the high bits, and the logical host address on that network contained in the low bits.

isolation   A transaction's behavior cannot affect another transaction that is processing concurrently.

Kerberos   A third-party authentication service originating from MIT.

key-encrypting-key   An encryption key used to encrypt other encryption keys.

local area network (LAN)   A communications system using directly connected computers, printers, and hard disks allowing shared access to all resources on the network.

logical unit   The APPC/APPN entity that provides communications services to applications.

masquerade   The security threat of network messages that allege to be from one source when, in fact, they are from a different one. An example would be a forged e-mail message claiming to be from one person when, in fact, it was produced by someone else.

message-oriented middleware (MOM)   A protocol, from the MOM Consortium, that allows general-purpose messages to be exchanged in a client/server system, using messages queues.

mode   The characteristic that determines the capabilities of a session.

modification   The security threat associated with unauthorized changes being made to messages as they traverse a network.

network node   A node in an APPN network that supplies topology, routing, and transport services.

nonrepudiation   A service requirement that combines the contents of a message with the identity of the author with enough reliability that the author cannot deny authorship.

persistent verification   A form of APPC security in which the user's password is only sent once.

port number   A numeric value in Internet packets that identifies the application layer software responsible for processing a packet. Standard application protocols have preassigned numbers, often called "well known ports."

protocol   A set of characters at the beginning and end of a message that enables two computers to communicate with each other.

protocol layer   A protocol software element consisting of one or more components or services that are largely interchangeable. Interfaces between layers tend to be fixed while the behavior of a particular layer depends on the particular protocol it provides.

RACF (Resource Access Control Facility)   A logical access control software package produced by IBM for securing mainframes.

risk analysis   An analysis of system assets and vulnerabilities to establish extent of possible loss from certain events based on estimated probabilities of the occurrence of those events.

security   Protection of all those resources that the client uses to complete its mission.

server   A network device that provides services to client stations. Servers include file servers, disk servers, and print servers.

session   A logical connection between two logical units.

Simple Mail Transport Protocol (SMTP)   The standard protocol for interchanging e-mail messages between Internet hosts.

SNA (Systems Network Architecture)   The architecture produced by IBM for managing its network components.

sniff   View packets and their data on a network.

structured query language (SQL)   A set-oriented language for manipulating, defining, and controlling data in a database.

TCP/IP   A widely used acronym that refers to either the transport layer protocols in the Internet protocol family or, occasionally, to the entire protocol family.

Telnet   The Internet's application layer terminal emulation protocol.

transaction program   Any program that uses APPC services.

Transmission Control Protocol (TCP) The standard protocol in the Internet protocol suite that provides a reliable connection-oriented protocol between Internet hosts. Most traditional Internet services (for example, FTP, Telnet, e-mail) use TCP.

transport protocol layer The protocol layer that provides the interface between the Internet layer and the Application layer. The Transport layer provides either a datagram delivery protocol (User Datagram Protocol, or UDP) or a reliable connection-oriented protocol (TCP) depending on application requirements.

Trojan horse A program, purporting to do useful work, which instead conceals instructions to breach security whenever the software is invoked.

TSO (Time Sharing Option) A subsystem commonly used to provide systems staff with editing capabilities.

two-phase commit A synchronous replication technique used to synchronize updates on different machines, so that they either all fail or all complete. In other words, an update to multiple databases will occur only when all locations can be updated successfully at the same time.

wetware Homo sapiens gray matter.

Contributors

The Coordinating Editor/Author

During twenty years in information systems, **Peter T. Davis** worked in data processing in large-scale installations in the financial and government sectors, where he was involved in the development and implementation of applications and specification of requirements. Most recently, he worked as director of information systems audit for the office of the provincial auditor (Ontario). In addition, Peter was a principal in an international public accounting firm's information systems audit practice, and has acted as the Canadian representative for a U.S. company specializing in the manufacturing and integration of communications products. Peter is now principal of Peter Davis & Associates, a training and consulting firm specializing in the security, audit, and control of information systems.

Peter is an internationally known speaker on security and audit, frequently speaking at local user meetings and international conferences sponsored by professional organizations and industry groups. In addition, he has had numerous articles published on security and audit. He has authored or co-authored *Complete LAN Security and Control, Teach Yourself NetWare in 14 Days*, and *Wireless Local Area Networks: Technology, Issues, and Strategies.*

Peter is a member of the international committee formed to develop Generally Accepted System Security Principles (GSSP). Also, he was an advisory council (1994–1995) member for the Computer Security Institute.

Peter Davis received his Bachelor of Commerce (B. Comm) degree from Carleton University. He also is a Certified Management Accountant (CMA), Certified Information Systems Auditor (CISA), Certified Systems Professional (CSP), Certified Data Processor (CDP), Certified Information Systems Security Professional (CISSP), Certified Computing Professional (CCP), and Certified Novell Administrator (CNA).

He currently lives in Toronto, Ontario, with his wife and daughter. Besides coordinating this client/server project, Peter Davis also wrote Chapters 1, 2, 3 and 21.

Other Contributors

Robert Clyde (Chapter 14) is vice-president of security technology at Axent Technologies. His experience in information security derives from an extensive management and technical background in consulting, systems and application programming, systems management, and security product development. Mr. Clyde is a frequent speaker at the CSI, ISSA, ISACA, and other conferences. Mr. Clyde is the original author of numerous software products that aid in the prevention, detection, and investigation of information security problems. He has twenty years of experience in information security and holds a patent for one of his software inventions. Robert Clyde is available on the Internet at robcly@axent.com and http://www.axent.com.

Geoff Cooke (Chapter 15) is with the Advanced Technology Group of Oracle Corporation, where he assists organizations as they design, change, and adapt their information infrastructures to new business realities. He is the author of the *Information Controls Implementation Methodology*, the standard method used by Oracle Services to assist organizations as they determine and implement appropriate information controls. Mr. Cooke has had a number of engagements with Fortune 500 organizations, both domestic and international, assisting them in producing policies and procedures to reduce the risk their information systems pose to their ongoing operations. His clients have been from many industrial sectors, including financial services, petrochemicals, pharmaceuticals, and government. He has spoken at many national and international symposia, and has been published in a wide range of journals and magazines.

Richard L. Daugherty (Chapter 9) is currently IBM's lead architect for CPI-C and APPC. He joined the CPI-C/APPC architecture group in Research Triangle Park, North Carolina, in 1992. Mr. Daughterty did the CPI-C and APPC architecture for both Password Substitution and Usage of Distributed Authentication services. Mr. Daughterty has both a B.A. from Western Kentucky University and an M.S. from Marist College. He also has represented IBM in various external bodies, including GUIDE, the OSF Security SIG, and the POSIX Distributed Security Study Group.

Patricia A. P. Fisher (Chapter 17) is president of JANUS Associates, Inc., a leading information security and contingency planning service and software firm. Ms. Fisher has over twenty years of information systems and security experience. She was formerly with IBM and had responsibility for information security for IBM's Latin American sites, as well as for direction of an IBM corporate headquarters data processing center. Ms. Fisher has assisted business and government organizations throughout the world on security and contingency needs. She lives in Stamford, Connecticut, with her husband and one son.

Gary Hunt (Chapter 13) is a senior programmer in the LAN systems area of the IBM Personal Software Products Division in Austin, Texas. He has worked on the LAN server since its inception in 1987, and is currently the lead designer for the LAN server product, both current and future. Mr. Hunt has worked on all LAN server releases in various roles, including managing a programming department during the development of the 1.2, 1.3, and 2.0 releases. Mr. Hunt has also been extensively involved in supporting OS/2 technical conferences and industry users' groups such as SHARE, COMMON, and GUIDE, presenting a wide variety of LAN server topics. He joined IBM in 1975 and holds a B.S. and an M.S. in electrical engineering from the University of Texas in Austin.

Cheri A. Jacoby (Chapter 5) is a senior manager with Price Waterhouse LLP, responsible for the computer information systems audit function in the Pittsburgh, Cleveland, and Detroit offices. Ms. Jacoby's experience ranges across a broad spectrum of computer auditing functions, including data security, operations, applications, and microcomputer systems reviews. Ms. Jacoby is responsible for ensuring the consistency and quality of the firm's approach to auditing computerized information systems and to business continuity planning. Ms. Jacoby was previously on the ISSA board of directors, serving as director of education. She is a frequent speaker on information security topics.

Darren M. Jones (Chapters 7 and 18) is an information systems auditor with The Mutual Group, a large financial institution located in Waterloo, Ontario. In addition to conducting reviews of data communications, MVS, ACF2, RACF, and LANs, Mr. Jones has most recently contributed to the development of a key client server application at Mutual. In six years of systems auditing, Mr. Jones has also worked for IBM Canada, the Ministry of Revenue, and the Ontario provincial auditor's office. Mr. Jones has a B.A. in math from the University of Waterloo and is currently pursuing a degree in arts/philosophy. He also has the Certified Management Accountant designation. Mr. Jones has been a speaker on client/server controls, IBM LAN Server security, RACF security, and MVS exits and interfaces. Additionally, he has published articles on DB2 security, client/server database security, and MVS subsystems controls.

Juan Carlos Jourde (Chapter 17) is a leading MVS and VM operating systems technical expert who regularly conducts penetration tests and analyzes operating system or technical application controls. He concentrates his testing primarily on RACF, TOP SECRET, CICS, IMS, IDMS, PROFS, TSO, SQL, and DB2. In addition, Juan Carlos designs and programs security software solutions for JANUS software and their clients. Prior to joining JANUS, Juan Carlos worked sixteen years for IBM, where he assumed constantly increasing responsibilities in systems operations, production control, and application development using a wide range of software. He has had responsibilities for technical guidance for Information Asset Security and has performed MVS system penetration testing across the United States, Latin America, and Canada. Currently, he lives in Tampa, Florida.

Ray Kaplan (Chapters 14 and 16) has been actively involved with system and network security as a consultant for over half of his more than twenty years in the industry. His clients have included the world's largest financial institution, the smallest commodities broker, and a wide variety of organizations, including multinational and Fortune 100 companies from all segments of the economy, as well as public institutions all over the world. He is also a very prolific lecturer, instructor, and writer who consults, lectures, and teaches technical system and network-related topics worldwide. Ray Kaplan is available on the Internet at ray@rayk.com and at www page http://www.rayk.com/rayk.

Peter P. C. H. Kingston (Chapter 18) is president of The Kingston Group, which specializes in finding innovative solutions to unique problems. His primary focus is on assistance to corporate management on such topics as information handling, strategic and tactical planning, and analysis of information systems, computer systems management, security, EDP audit, and business continuity planning. In his successful career at IBM and Art Benjamin Associates he was responsible for the completion of many large and complex timeline-oriented, security-related projects. Mr. Kingston has more than thirty years of experience in data processing.

Barry Lewis (Chapter 10) is a partner in the firm Cerberus Information Security Consulting Inc. Cerberus specializes in the delivery of security solutions for a variety of organizations. Barry has been actively involved in computer security for more than fourteen years and is a Certified Information Systems Security Professional (CISSP). He has been an active participant within the security community, holding various positions on local user groups, including president of ISSA Toronto and director, International Information Systems Security Certification Consortium (IISSCC). Mr. Lewis has written numerous articles on telecommunications, electronic authorization, dial-up security, and other topics for publications such as *Computer Security Institute, Infocanada Magazine*, and *Journal of Systems Management*, as well as publishers such as Auerbach Publications. In addition, Mr. Lewis is an award-winning international speaker and has lectured on various information security issues for the Computer Associates Enterprise-Wide Security & Audit Conference, CSI, the EDPAA, ISSA, and many local user groups.

Frank Lyons (Chapters 6 and 19) is president of Entellus Technology Group, a consulting firm specializing in developing, managing, securing, and auditing large and small networked information systems. A recognized leader in the field, he has been involved in data security and database technology for nearly twenty years. As EDP audit manager for Blue Shield and

Sun Banks, Mr. Lyons designed a functional approach to EDP auditing which he later used as manager of advanced technology for the Institute of Internal Auditors. He has been with Cullinet Database Systems and a partner in the Plagman Group, where he developed database auditing and data security seminars.

Scott McDermott (Chapter 20) is an employee of IBM Corporation.

William H. Murray (Foreword) is information system security consultant to Deloitte & Touche. He has more than thirty-five years of experience in data processing and more than twenty years in security. During more than twenty-five years with IBM, his management responsibilities included development of access-control programs, advising IBM customers on security, and the articulation of the security product plan. In 1987, he received the Fitzgerald Memorial Award for leadership in data security. In 1989, he received the Joseph J. Wasserman Award for contributions to security, audit, and control. Mr. Murray holds a B.S. in business administration from Louisiana State University.

Geoff Sharman (Chapter 20) is an employee of IBM Corporation.

Denise A. Silon (Chapter 5) is a senior consultant with Price Waterhouse LLP and has served several Fortune 500 companies in the Great Lakes region of the U.S. with computer information systems audits and consulting. Ms. Silon's experience covers a wide spectrum of CIS technology, including analyses of data security practices for a multitude of processing platforms, and audits of financial application software and system development projects. Ms. Silon is currently a member of the Information Systems Audit and Control Association.

Larry A. Simon (Chapter 4) is a Partner in Ernst & Young's Toronto Information Technology practice and leads the firm's Navigator Systems Series systems development methodology group. Mr. Simon was also a director of Ernst & Young's CASE Technologies, a leading computer-assisted software engineering technology vendor. Mr. Simon has been with Ernst & Young since 1983 and has focused primarily on helping client companies improve their applications systems development functions. He also has assisted a number of clients in planning and managing the implementation of a variety of information systems. Prior to joining Ernst & Young, Mr. Simon's information technology experience included employment with Garmaise & Associates, Bell Canada, and the Ontario Ministry of the Environment. He has fifteen years of business and IT experience and is also a member of Ernst & Young's Computer and Electronics Industry Group. Larry holds a B.A. in mathematics from Waterloo, holds an M.B.A. from the University of Toronto, and is a Certified Management Consultant.

Dr. Rick Smith (Chapter 8) is principal systems engineer for Secure Computing Corporation, associated with the Sidewinder firewall system and the SNS Mail Guard program. He also has served as task group co-chair on the Secure Data Network System (SDNS) program for the U.S. government.

Dr. Smith's background also includes research and development work in fault tolerance, wide area networks, and artificial intelligence. He has published works in network security, industrial robotics, and computer history.

John Tannahill (Chapters 11 and 12) is an independent information security consultant based in Toronto, Canada. He has detailed knowledge of the major operating environments commonly encountered, especially IBM's MVS & VM operating systems, and the major associated security software packages. John is a member of the Institute of Chartered Accountants of Scotland, the Computer Security Institute, and NaSPA. He can be reached at the Internet address: `70641.3502@compuserve.com`.

Index